# The Book of Common Prayer

and Administration of the Sacraments
and Other Rites
and Ceremonies of the Church

Together with The Psalter or Psalms of David

*According to the use of*
The Episcopal Church

 CHURCH

*Church Publishing Incorporated, New York*

**Certificate**

I certify that this edition of The Book of Common Prayer
has been compared with a certified copy of the Standard Book,
as the Canon directs, and that it conforms thereto.

Charles Mortimer Guilbert
*Custodian of the Standard Book of Common Prayer*
September, 1979

# Table of Contents

# The Ratification of
# The Book of Common Prayer (1789)

By the Bishops, the Clergy, and the Laity of the Protestant Episcopal
Church in the United States of America, in Convention, this Sixteenth
Day of October, in the Year of Our Lord One Thousand Seven Hundred
and Eighty-Nine.

This Convention having, in their present session, set forth *A Book of
Common Prayer, and Administration of the Sacraments, and other Rites
and Ceremonies of the Church,* do hereby establish the said Book: And
they declare it to be the Liturgy of this Church: And require that it be
received as such by all the members of the same: And this Book shall be in
use from and after the First Day of October, in the Year of our Lord one
thousand seven hundred and ninety.

# Preface

It is a most invaluable part of that blessed "liberty wherewith Christ hath made us free," that in his worship different forms and usages may without offence be allowed, provided the substance of the Faith be kept entire; and that, in every Church, what cannot be clearly determined to belong to Doctrine must be referred to Discipline; and therefore, by common consent and authority, may be altered, abridged, enlarged, amended, or otherwise disposed of, as may seem most convenient for the edification of the people, "according to the various exigency of times and occasions."

The Church of England, to which the Protestant Episcopal Church in these States is indebted, under God, for her first foundation and a long continuance of nursing care and protection, hath, in the Preface of her Book of Common Prayer, laid it down as a rule, that "The particular Forms of Divine Worship, and the Rites and Ceremonies appointed to be used therein, being things in their own nature indifferent, and alterable, and so acknowledged; it is but reasonable that upon weighty and important considerations, according to the various exigency of times and occasions, such changes and alterations should be made therein, as to those that are in place of Authority should, from time to time, seem either necessary or expedient."

The same Church hath not only in her Preface, but likewise in her Articles and Homilies, declared the necessity and expediency of occasional alterations and amendments in her Forms of Public Worship; and we find accordingly, that, seeking to keep the happy mean between too much stiffness in refusing, and too much easiness in admitting variations in things once advisedly established, she hath, in the reign of several Princes, since the first compiling of her Liturgy in the time of Edward the Sixth, upon just and weighty considerations her thereunto moving, yielded to make such alterations in some particulars, as in their respective times were thought convenient; yet so as that the main body and essential parts of the same (as well in the chiefest materials, as in the frame and order thereof) have still been continued firm and unshaken.

Her general aim in these different reviews and alterations hath been, as she further declares in her said Preface, to do that which, according to her best understanding, might most tend to the preservation of peace and unity in the Church; the procuring of reverence, and the exciting of piety and devotion in the worship of God; and, finally, the cutting off occasion, from them that seek occasion, of cavil or quarrel against her Liturgy. And although, according to her judgment, there be not any thing in it contrary to the Word of God, or to sound doctrine, or which a godly man may not with a good conscience use and submit unto, or which is not fairly defensible, if allowed such just and favourable construction as in common equity ought to be allowed to all human writings; yet upon the principles already laid down, it cannot but be supposed that further alterations would in time be found expedient. Accordingly, a Commission for a review was issued in the year 1689: but this great and good work miscarried at that time; and the Civil Authority has not since thought proper to revive it by any new Commission.

But when in the course of Divine Providence, these American States became independent with respect to civil government, their ecclesiastical independence was necessarily included; and the different religious denominations of Christians in these States were left at full and equal liberty to model and organize their respective Churches, and forms of worship, and discipline, in such manner as they might judge most convenient for their future prosperity; consistently with the constitution and laws of their country.

The attention of this Church was in the first place drawn to those alterations in the Liturgy which became necessary in the prayers for our Civil Rulers, in consequence of the Revolution. And the principal care herein was to make them conformable to what ought to be the proper end of all such prayers, namely, that "Rulers may have grace, wisdom, and understanding to execute justice, and to maintain truth;" and that the people "may lead quiet and peaceable lives, in all godliness and honesty."

But while these alterations were in review before the Convention, they could not but, with gratitude to God, embrace the happy occasion which was offered to them (uninfluenced and unrestrained by any worldly authority whatsoever) to take a further review of the Public Service, and to establish such other alterations and amendments therein as might be deemed expedient.

It seems unnecessary to enumerate all the different alterations and amendments. They will appear, and it is to be hoped, the reasons of them also, upon a comparison of this with the Book of Common Prayer of the Church of England. In which it will also appear that this Church is far from intending to depart from the Church of England in any essential point of doctrine, discipline, or worship; or further than local circumstances require.

And now, this important work being brought to a conclusion, it is hoped the whole will be received and examined by every true member of our Church, and every sincere Christian, with a meek, candid, and charitable frame of mind; without prejudice or prepossessions; seriously considering what Christianity is, and what the truths of the Gospel are; and earnestly beseeching Almighty God to accompany with his blessing every endeavour for promulgating them to mankind in the clearest, plainest, most affecting and majestic manner, for the sake of Jesus Christ, our blessed Lord and Saviour.

*Philadelphia, October, 1789.*

# Concerning the Service
# of the Church

The Holy Eucharist, the principal act of Christian worship on the Lord's Day and other major Feasts, and Daily Morning and Evening Prayer, as set forth in this Book, are the regular services appointed for public worship in this Church.

In addition to these services and the other rites contained in this Book, other forms set forth by authority within this Church may be used. Also, subject to the direction of the bishop, special devotions taken from this Book, or from Holy Scripture, may be used when the needs of the congregation so require.

For special days of fasting or thanksgiving, appointed by civil or Church authority, and for other special occasions for which no service or prayer has been provided in this Book, the bishop may set forth such forms as are fitting to the occasion.

In all services, the entire Christian assembly participates in such a way that the members of each order within the Church, lay persons, bishops, priests, and deacons, fulfill the functions proper to their respective orders, as set forth in the rubrical directions for each service.

The leader of worship in a Christian assembly is normally a bishop or priest. Deacons by virtue of their order do not exercise a presiding function; but, like lay persons, may officiate at the Liturgy of the Word, whether in the form provided in the Daily Offices, or (when a bishop or priest is not present) in the form appointed at the Eucharist. Under exceptional circumstances, when the services of a priest cannot be obtained, the bishop may, at discretion, authorize a deacon to preside at other rites also, subject to the limitations described in the directions for each service.

In any of the Proper Liturgies for Special Days, and in other services contained in this Book celebrated in the context of a Rite One service, the contemporary idiom may be conformed to traditional language.

Hymns referred to in the rubrics of this Book are to be understood as those authorized by this Church. The words of anthems are to be from Holy Scripture, or from this Book, or from texts congruent with them.

On occasion, and as appropriate, instrumental music may be substituted for a hymn or anthem.

Where rubrics indicate that a part of a service is to be"said," it must be understood to include"or sung,"and *vice versa*.

When it is desired to use music composed for them, previously authorized liturgical texts may be used in place of the corresponding texts in this Book.

Scriptural citations in this Book, except for the Psalms, follow the numeration of the Revised Standard Version of the Bible.

# The Calendar
# of the Church Year

The Church Year consists of two cycles of feasts and holy days: one is dependent upon the movable date of the Sunday of the Resurrection or Easter Day; the other, upon the fixed date of December 25, the Feast of our Lord's Nativity or Christmas Day.

Easter Day is always the first Sunday after the full moon that falls on or after March 21. It cannot occur before March 22 or after April 25.

The sequence of all Sundays of the Church Year depends upon the date of Easter Day. But the Sundays of Advent are always the four Sundays before Christmas Day, whether it occurs on a Sunday or a weekday. The date of Easter also determines the beginning of Lent on Ash Wednesday, and the feast of the Ascension on a Thursday forty days after Easter Day.

## 1. Principal Feasts

The Principal Feasts observed in this Church are the following:

Easter Day                     All Saints' Day, *November 1*
Ascension Day                  Christmas Day, *December 25*
The Day of Pentecost           The Epiphany, *January 6*
Trinity Sunday

These feasts take precedence of any other day or observance. All Saints' Day may always be observed on the Sunday following November 1, in addition to its observance on the fixed date.

## 2. Sundays

All Sundays of the year are feasts of our Lord Jesus Christ. In addition to the dated days listed above, only the following feasts, appointed on fixed days, take precedence of a Sunday:

The Holy Name
The Presentation
The Transfiguration

The feast of the Dedication of a Church, and the feast of its patron or title, may be observed on, or be transferred to, a Sunday, except in the seasons of Advent, Lent, and Easter.

All other Feasts of our Lord, and all other Major Feasts appointed on fixed days in the Calendar, when they occur on a Sunday, are normally transferred to the first convenient open day within the week. When desired, however, the Collect, Preface, and one or more of the Lessons appointed for the Feast may be substituted for those of the Sunday, but not from the Last Sunday after Pentecost through the First Sunday after the Epiphany, or from the Last Sunday after the Epiphany through Trinity Sunday.

With the express permission of the bishop, and for urgent and sufficient reason, some other special occasion may be observed on a Sunday.

## 3. Holy Days

The following Holy Days are regularly observed throughout the year. Unless otherwise ordered in the preceding rules concerning Sundays, they have precedence over all other days of commemoration or of special observance:

*Other Feasts of our Lord*

| | |
|---|---|
| The Holy Name | Saint John the Baptist |
| The Presentation | The Transfiguration |
| The Annunciation | Holy Cross Day |
| The Visitation | |

*Other Major Feasts*

| | |
|---|---|
| All feasts of Apostles | Saint Mary the Virgin |
| All feasts of Evangelists | Saint Michael and All Angels |
| Saint Stephen | Saint James of Jerusalem |
| The Holy Innocents | Independence Day |
| Saint Joseph | Thanksgiving Day |
| Saint Mary Magdalene | |

*Fasts*

| | |
|---|---|
| Ash Wednesday | Good Friday |

Feasts appointed on fixed days in the Calendar are not observed on the days of Holy Week or of Easter Week. Major Feasts falling in these weeks are transferred to the week following the Second Sunday of Easter, in the order of their occurrence.

Feasts appointed on fixed days in the Calendar do not take precedence of Ash Wednesday.

Feasts of our Lord and other Major Feasts appointed on fixed days, which fall upon or are transferred to a weekday, may be observed on any open day within the week. This provision does not apply to Christmas Day, the Epiphany, and All Saints' Day.

## 4. Days of Special Devotion

The following days are observed by special acts of discipline and self-denial:

Ash Wednesday and the other weekdays of Lent and of Holy Week, except the feast of the Annunciation.

Good Friday and all other Fridays of the year, in commemoration of the Lord's crucifixion, except for Fridays in the Christmas and Easter seasons, and any Feasts of our Lord which occur on a Friday.

## 5. Days of Optional Observance

Subject to the rules of precedence governing Principal Feasts, Sundays, and Holy Days, the following may be observed with the Collects, Psalms, and Lessons duly authorized by this Church:

Commemorations listed in the Calendar
Other Commemorations, using the Common of Saints
The Ember Days, traditionally observed on the Wednesdays, Fridays, and Saturdays after the First Sunday in Lent, the Day of Pentecost, Holy Cross Day, and December 13
The Rogation Days, traditionally observed on Monday, Tuesday, and Wednesday before Ascension Day
Various Occasions

Provided, that there is no celebration of the Eucharist for any such occasion on Ash Wednesday, Maundy Thursday, Good Friday, and Holy Saturday; and provided further, that none of the Propers appointed for Various Occasions is used as a substitute for, or as an addition to, the Proper appointed for the Principal Feasts.

# January

| | | |
|---|---|---|
| 1 | A | **The Holy Name of Our Lord Jesus Christ** |
| 2 | b | |
| 3 | c | |
| 4 | d | |
| 5 | e | |
| 6 | f | **The Epiphany of Our Lord Jesus Christ** |
| 7 | g | |
| 8 | A | |
| 9 | b | Julia Chester Emery, 1922 |
| 10 | c | William Laud, Archbishop of Canterbury, 1645 |
| 11 | d | |
| 12 | e | Aelred, Abbot of Rievaulx, 1167 |
| 13 | f | Hilary, Bishop of Poitiers, 367 |
| 14 | g | |
| 15 | A | |
| 16 | b | |
| 17 | c | Antony, Abbot in Egypt, 356 |
| 18 | d | **The Confession of Saint Peter the Apostle** |
| 19 | e | Wulfstan, Bishop of Worcester, 1095 |
| 20 | f | Fabian, Bishop and Martyr of Rome, 250 |
| 21 | g | Agnes, Martyr at Rome, 304 |
| 22 | A | Vincent, Deacon of Saragossa, and Martyr, 304 |
| 23 | b | Phillips Brooks, Bishop of Massachusetts, 1893 |
| 24 | c | |
| 25 | d | **The Conversion of Saint Paul the Apostle** |
| 26 | e | Timothy and Titus, Companions of Saint Paul |
| 27 | f | John Chrysostom, Bishop of Constantinople, 407 |
| 28 | g | Thomas Aquinas, Priest and Friar, 1274 |
| 29 | A | |
| 30 | b | |
| 31 | c | |

# February

# March

| | | |
|---|---|---|
| 1 | d | David, Bishop of Menevia, Wales, c. 544 |
| 2 | e | Chad, Bishop of Lichfield, 672 |
| 3 | f | John and Charles Wesley, Priests, 1791, 1788 |
| 4 | g | |
| 5 | A | |
| 6 | b | |
| 7 | c | Perpetua and her Companions, Martyrs at Carthage, 202 |
| 8 | d | |
| 9 | e | Gregory, Bishop of Nyssa, c. 394 |
| 10 | f | |
| 11 | g | |
| 12 | A | Gregory the Great, Bishop of Rome, 604 |
| 13 | b | |
| 14 | c | |
| 15 | d | |
| 16 | e | |
| 17 | f | Patrick, Bishop and Missionary of Ireland, 461 |
| 18 | g | Cyril, Bishop of Jerusalem, 386 |
| 19 | A | **Saint Joseph** |
| 20 | b | Cuthbert, Bishop of Lindisfarne, 687 |
| 21 | c | Thomas Ken, Bishop of Bath and Wells, 1711 |

| 14 | 22 | d | James De Koven, Priest, 1879 |
|---|---|---|---|
| 3 | 23 | e | Gregory the Illuminator, Bishop and Missionary of Armenia, c. 332 |
| | 24 | f | |
| 11 | 25 | g | **The Annunciation of Our Lord Jesus Christ to the Blessed Virgin Mary** |
| | 26 | A | |
| 19 | 27 | b | Charles Henry Brent, Bishop of the Philippines, and of Western New York, 1929 |
| 8 | 28 | c | |
| | 29 | d | John Keble, Priest, 1866 |
| 16 | 30 | e | |
| 5 | 31 | f | John Donne, Priest, 1631 |

# April

| | | | |
|---|---|---|---|
| | 1 | g | Frederick Denison Maurice, Priest, 1872 |
| 13 | 2 | A | James Lloyd Breck, Priest, 1876 |
| 2 | 3 | b | Richard, Bishop of Chichester, 1253 |
| | 4 | c | Martin Luther King, Jr., Civil Rights Leader, 1968 |
| 10 | 5 | d | |
| | 6 | e | |
| 18 | 7 | f | |
| 7 | 8 | g | William Augustus Muhlenberg, Priest, 1877 |
| | 9 | A | Dietrich Bonhoeffer, 1945 |
| 15 | 10 | b | William Law, Priest, 1761 |
| 4 | 11 | c | George Augustus Selwyn, Bishop of New Zealand, and of Lichfield, 1878 |
| | 12 | d | |
| 12 | 13 | e | |
| | 14 | f | |
| | 15 | g | |
| 9 | 16 | A | |
| 17 | 17 | b | |
| 6 | 18 | c | |
| | 19 | d | Alphege, Archbishop of Canterbury, and Martyr, 1012 |
| | 20 | e | |
| | 21 | f | Anselm, Archbishop of Canterbury, 1109 |
| | 22 | g | |
| | 23 | A | |
| | 24 | b | |
| | 25 | c | **Saint Mark the Evangelist** |
| | 26 | d | |
| | 27 | e | |
| | 28 | f | |
| | 29 | g | Catherine of Siena, 1380 |
| | 30 | A | |

# May

| | | |
|---|---|---|
| 1 | b | **Saint Philip and Saint James, Apostles** |
| 2 | c | Athanasius, Bishop of Alexandria, 373 |
| 3 | d | |
| 4 | e | Monnica, Mother of Augustine of Hippo, 387 |
| 5 | f | |
| 6 | g | |
| 7 | A | |
| 8 | b | Dame Julian of Norwich, c. 1417 |
| 9 | c | Gregory of Nazianzus, Bishop of Constantinople, 389 |
| 10 | d | |
| 11 | e | |
| 12 | f | |
| 13 | g | |
| 14 | A | |
| 15 | b | |
| 16 | c | |
| 17 | d | |
| 18 | e | |
| 19 | f | Dunstan, Archbishop of Canterbury, 988 |
| 20 | g | Alcuin, Deacon, and Abbot of Tours, 804 |
| 21 | A | |
| 22 | b | |
| 23 | c | |
| 24 | d | Jackson Kemper, First Missionary Bishop in the United States, 1870 |
| 25 | e | Bede, the Venerable, Priest, and Monk of Jarrow, 735 |
| 26 | f | Augustine, First Archbishop of Canterbury, 605 |
| 27 | g | |
| 28 | A | |
| 29 | b | |
| 30 | c | |
| 31 | d | **The Visitation of the Blessed Virgin Mary** |

*The First Book of Common Prayer, 1549, is appropriately
observed on a weekday following the Day of Pentecost.*

# June

# July

| | | |
|---|---|---|
| 1 | g | |
| 2 | A | |
| 3 | b | |
| 4 | c | **Independence Day** |
| 5 | d | |
| 6 | e | |
| 7 | f | |
| 8 | g | |
| 9 | A | |
| 10 | b | |
| 11 | c | Benedict of Nursia, Abbot of Monte Cassino, c. 540 |
| 12 | d | |
| 13 | e | |
| 14 | f | |
| 15 | g | |
| 16 | A | |
| 17 | b | William White, Bishop of Pennsylvania, 1836 |
| 18 | c | |
| 19 | d | Macrina, 379 |
| 20 | e | Elizabeth Cady Stanton, Amelia Bloomer, Sojouner Truth, and Harriett Ross Tubman |
| 21 | f | |
| 22 | g | **Saint Mary Magdalene** |
| 23 | A | |
| 24 | b | Thomas a Kempis, Priest, 1471 |
| 25 | c | **Saint James the Apostle** |
| 26 | d | The Parents of the Blessed Virgin Mary |
| 27 | e | William Reed Huntington, Priest, 1909 |
| 28 | f | |
| 29 | g | Mary and Martha of Bethany |
| 30 | A | William Wilberforce, 1833 |
| 31 | b | Ignatius of Loyola, 1556 |

## August

| | | |
|---|---|---|
| 1 | c | Joseph of Arimathaea |
| 2 | d | |
| 3 | e | |
| 4 | f | |
| 5 | g | |
| 6 | A | **The Transfiguration of Our Lord Jesus Christ** |
| 7 | b | John Mason Neale, Priest, 1866 |
| 8 | c | Dominic, Priest and Friar, 1221 |
| 9 | d | |
| 10 | e | Laurence, Deacon, and Martyr at Rome, 258 |
| 11 | f | Clare, Abbess at Assisi, 1253 |
| 12 | g | |
| 13 | A | Jeremy Taylor, Bishop of Down, Connor, and Dromore, 1667 |
| 14 | b | Jonathan Myrick Daniels |
| 15 | c | **Saint Mary the Virgin, Mother of Our Lord Jesus Christ** |
| 16 | d | |
| 17 | e | |
| 18 | f | William Porcher DuBose, Priest, 1918 |
| 19 | g | |
| 20 | A | Bernard, Abbot of Clairvaux, 1153 |
| 21 | b | |
| 22 | c | |
| 23 | d | |
| 24 | e | **Saint Bartholomew the Apostle** |
| 25 | f | Louis, King of France, 1270 |
| 26 | g | |
| 27 | A | Thomas Gallaudet, 1902 and Henry Winter Syle, 1890 |
| 28 | b | Augustine, Bishop of Hippo, 430 |
| 29 | c | |
| 30 | d | |
| 31 | e | Aidan, Bishop of Lindisfarne, 651 |

## September

| | | |
|---|---|---|
| 1 | f | David Pendleton Oakerhater, Deacon and Missionary, 1931 |
| 2 | g | The Martyrs of New Guinea, 1942 |
| 3 | A | |
| 4 | b | Paul Jones, 1941 |
| 5 | c | |
| 6 | d | |
| 7 | e | |
| 8 | f | |
| 9 | g | Constance, Nun, and her Companions, 1878 |
| 10 | A | Alexander Crummell, 1898 |
| 11 | b | |
| 12 | c | John Henry Hobart, Bishop of New York, 1830 |
| 13 | d | Cyprian, Bishop and Martyr of Carthage, 258 |
| 14 | e | **Holy Cross Day** |
| 15 | f | |
| 16 | g | Ninian, Bishop in Galloway, c. 430 |
| 17 | A | Hildegard, 1179 |
| 18 | b | Edward Bouverie Pusey, Priest, 1882 |
| 19 | c | Theodore of Tarsus, Archbishop of Canterbury, 690 |
| 20 | d | John Coleridge Patteson, Bishop of Melanesia, and his Companions, Martyrs, 1871 |
| 21 | e | **Saint Matthew, Apostle and Evangelist** |
| 22 | f | |
| 23 | g | |
| 24 | A | |
| 25 | b | Sergius, Abbot of Holy Trinity, Moscow, 1392 |
| 26 | c | Lancelot Andrewes, Bishop of Winchester, 1626 |
| 27 | d | |
| 28 | e | |
| 29 | f | **Saint Michael and All Angels** |
| 30 | g | Jerome, Priest, and Monk of Bethlehem, 420 |

# October

| | | |
|---|---|---|
| 1 | A | Remigius, Bishop of Rheims, c. 530 |
| 2 | b | |
| 3 | c | |
| 4 | d | Francis of Assisi, Friar, 1226 |
| 5 | e | |
| 6 | f | William Tyndale, Priest, 1536 |
| 7 | g | |
| 8 | A | |
| 9 | b | Robert Grosseteste, Bishop of Lincoln, 1253 |
| 10 | c | |
| 11 | d | |
| 12 | e | |
| 13 | f | |
| 14 | g | Samuel Isaac Joseph Schereschewsky, Bishop of Shanghai, 1906 |
| 15 | A | Teresa of Avila, Nun, 1582 |
| 16 | b | Hugh Latimer and Nicholas Ridley, Bishops, 1555 and Thomas Cranmer, Archbishop of Canterbury, 1556 |
| 17 | c | Ignatius, Bishop of Antioch, and Martyr, c. 115 |
| 18 | d | **Saint Luke the Evangelist** |
| 19 | e | Henry Martyn, Priest, and Missionary to India and Persia, 1812 |
| 20 | f | |
| 21 | g | |
| 22 | A | |
| 23 | b | **Saint James of Jerusalem, Brother of Our Lord Jesus Christ, and Martyr, c. 62** |
| 24 | c | |
| 25 | d | |
| 26 | e | Alfred the Great, King of the West Saxons, 899 |
| 27 | f | |
| 28 | g | **Saint Simon and Saint Jude, Apostles** |
| 29 | A | James Hannington, Bishop of Eastern Equatorial Africa, and his Companions, Martyrs, 1885 |
| 30 | b | |
| 31 | c | |

# November

| | | |
|---|---|---|
| 1 | d | **All Saints** |
| 2 | e | Commemoration of All Faithful Departed |
| 3 | f | Richard Hooker, Priest, 1600 |
| 4 | g | |
| 5 | A | |
| 6 | b | |
| 7 | c | Willibrord, Archbishop of Utrecht, Missionary to Frisia, 739 |
| 8 | d | |
| 9 | e | |
| 10 | f | Leo the Great, Bishop of Rome, 461 |
| 11 | g | Martin, Bishop of Tours, 397 |
| 12 | A | Charles Simeon, Priest, 1836 |
| 13 | b | |
| 14 | c | Consecration of Samuel Seabury, First American Bishop, 1784 |
| 15 | d | |
| 16 | e | Margaret, Queen of Scotland, 1093 |
| 17 | f | Hugh, Bishop of Lincoln, 1200 |
| 18 | g | Hilda, Abbess of Whitby, 680 |
| 19 | A | Elizabeth, Princess of Hungary, 1231 |
| 20 | b | Edmund, King of East Anglia, 870 |
| 21 | c | |
| 22 | d | |
| 23 | e | Clement, Bishop of Rome, c. 100 |
| 24 | f | |
| 25 | g | James Otis Sargent Huntington, Priest and Monk, 1935 |
| 26 | A | |
| 27 | b | |
| 28 | c | Kamehameha and Emma, King and Queen of Hawaii, 1864, 1885 |
| 29 | d | |
| 30 | e | **Saint Andrew the Apostle** |

# December

| | | |
|---|---|---|
| 1 | f | Nicholas Ferrar, Deacon, 1637 |
| 2 | g | Channing Moore Williams, Missionary Bishop in China and Japan, 1910 |
| 3 | A | |
| 4 | b | John of Damascus, Priest, c. 760 |
| 5 | c | Clement of Alexandria, Priest, c. 210 |
| 6 | d | Nicholas, Bishop of Myra, c. 342 |
| 7 | e | Ambrose, Bishop of Milan, 397 |
| 8 | f | |
| 9 | g | |
| 10 | A | |
| 11 | b | |
| 12 | c | |
| 13 | d | |
| 14 | e | |
| 15 | f | |
| 16 | g | |
| 17 | A | |
| 18 | b | |
| 19 | c | |
| 20 | d | |
| 21 | e | Saint Thomas the Apostle |
| 22 | f | |
| 23 | g | |
| 24 | A | |
| 25 | b | The Nativity of Our Lord Jesus Christ |
| 26 | c | Saint Stephen, Deacon and Martyr |
| 27 | d | Saint John, Apostle and Evangelist |
| 28 | e | The Holy Innocents |
| 29 | f | Thomas Becket, 1170 |
| 30 | g | |
| 31 | A | |

**The Titles of the Seasons**
**Sundays and Major Holy Days**
**observed in this Church throughout the Year**

*Advent Season*

The First Sunday of Advent
The Second Sunday of Advent
The Third Sunday of Advent
The Fourth Sunday of Advent

*Christmas Season*

The Nativity of Our Lord Jesus Christ: Christmas Day, *December 25*
The First Sunday after Christmas Day
The Holy Name of Our Lord Jesus Christ, *January 1*
The Second Sunday after Christmas Day

*Epiphany Season*

The Epiphany, or the Manifestation of Christ to the Gentiles, *January 6*
The First Sunday after the Epiphany: The Baptism of Our Lord
    Jesus Christ
The Second Sunday through the Eighth Sunday after the Epiphany
The Last Sunday after the Epiphany

*Lenten Season*

The First Day of Lent, or Ash Wednesday
The First Sunday in Lent
The Second Sunday in Lent
The Third Sunday in Lent
The Fourth Sunday in Lent
The Fifth Sunday in Lent

*Holy Week*

The Sunday of the Passion: Palm Sunday
Monday in Holy Week

Tuesday in Holy Week
Wednesday in Holy Week
Maundy Thursday
Good Friday
Holy Saturday

*Easter Season*

Easter Eve
The Sunday of the Resurrection, or Easter Day
Monday in Easter Week
Tuesday in Easter Week
Wednesday in Easter Week
Thursday in Easter Week
Friday in Easter Week
Saturday in Easter Week
The Second Sunday of Easter
The Third Sunday of Easter
The Fourth Sunday of Easter
The Fifth Sunday of Easter
The Sixth Sunday of Easter
Ascension Day
The Seventh Sunday of Easter: The Sunday after Ascension Day
The Day of Pentecost: Whitsunday

*The Season After Pentecost*

The First Sunday after Pentecost: Trinity Sunday
The Second Sunday through the Twenty-Seventh Sunday after Pentecost
The Last Sunday after Pentecost

*Holy Days*

Saint Andrew the Apostle, *November 30*
Saint Thomas the Apostle, *December 21*
Saint Stephen, Deacon and Martyr, *December 26*
Saint John, Apostle and Evangelist, *December 27*
The Holy Innocents, *December 28*
The Confession of Saint Peter the Apostle, *January 18*

The Conversion of Saint Paul the Apostle, *January 25*
The Presentation of Our Lord Jesus Christ in the Temple,
    also called the Purification of Saint Mary the Virgin, *February 2*
Saint Matthias the Apostle, *February 24*
Saint Joseph, *March 19*
The Annunciation of Our Lord Jesus Christ
    to the Blessed Virgin Mary, *March 25*
Saint Mark the Evangelist, *April 25*
Saint Philip and Saint James, Apostles, *May 1*
The Visitation of the Blessed Virgin Mary, *May 31*
Saint Barnabas the Apostle, *June 11*
The Nativity of Saint John the Baptist, *June 24*
Saint Peter and Saint Paul, Apostles, *June 29*
Saint Mary Magdalene, *July 22*
Saint James the Apostle, *July 25*
The Transfiguration of Our Lord Jesus Christ, *August 6*
Saint Mary the Virgin, Mother of Our Lord Jesus Christ, *August 15*
Saint Bartholomew the Apostle, *August 24*
Holy Cross Day, *September 14*
Saint Matthew, Apostle and Evangelist, *September 21*
Saint Michael and All Angels, *September 29*
Saint Luke the Evangelist, *October 18*
Saint James of Jerusalem, Brother of Our Lord Jesus Christ,
    and Martyr, *October 23*
Saint Simon and Saint Jude, Apostles, *October 28*
All Saints' Day, *November 1*

*National Days*

Independence Day, *July 4*
Thanksgiving Day

# The Daily Office

# Concerning the Service

In the Daily Office, the term "Officiant" is used to denote the person, clerical or lay, who leads the Office.

It is appropriate that other persons be assigned to read the Lessons, and to lead other parts of the service not assigned to the officiant. The bishop, when present, appropriately concludes the Office with a blessing.

At celebrations of the Holy Eucharist, the Order for Morning or Evening Prayer may be used in place of all that precedes the Offertory.

Additional Directions are on page 141.

# Daily Morning Prayer:
# Rite One

*The Officiant begins the service with one or more of these sentences of Scripture, or with the versicle "O Lord, open thou our lips" on page 42.*

*Advent*

Watch ye, for ye know not when the master of the house cometh, at even, or at midnight, or at the cock-crowing, or in the morning; lest coming suddenly he find you sleeping. *Mark 13:35, 36*

Prepare ye the way of the Lord, make straight in the desert a highway for our God.    *Isaiah 40:3*

The glory of the Lord shall be revealed, and all flesh shall see it together.    *Isaiah 40:5*

*Christmas*

Behold, I bring you good tidings of great joy, which shall be to all people. For unto you is born this day in the city of David a Savior, which is Christ the Lord.    *Luke 2:10, 11*

Behold, the tabernacle of God is with men, and he will dwell with them, and they shall be his people, and God himself shall be with them, and be their God.    *Revelation 21:3*

*Epiphany*

The Gentiles shall come to thy light, and kings to the brightness of thy rising.    *Isaiah 60:3*

I will give thee for a light to the Gentiles, that thou mayest be my salvation unto the end of the earth.    *Isaiah 49:6b*

From the rising of the sun even unto the going down of the same my Name shall be great among the Gentiles, and in every place incense shall be offered unto my Name, and a pure offering: for my Name shall be great among the heathen, saith the Lord of hosts.    *Malachi 1:11*

*Lent*

If we say that we have no sin, we deceive ourselves, and the truth is not in us; but if we confess our sins, God is faithful and just to forgive us our sins, and to cleanse us from all unrighteousness.    *1 John 1:8, 9*

Rend your heart, and not your garments, and turn unto the Lord your God; for he is gracious and merciful, slow to anger and of great kindness, and repenteth him of the evil.
*Joel 2:13*

I will arise and go to my father, and will say unto him, "Father, I have sinned against heaven, and before thee, and am no more worthy to be called thy son."    *Luke 15:18, 19*

To the Lord our God belong mercies and forgivenesses, though we have rebelled against him; neither have we obeyed the voice of the Lord our God, to walk in his laws which he set before us.    *Daniel 9:9, 10*

Jesus said, "Whosoever will come after me, let him deny himself, and take up his cross, and follow me."    *Mark 8:34*

## Holy Week

All we like sheep have gone astray; we have turned every one to his own way; and the Lord hath laid on him the iniquity of us all.    *Isaiah 53:6*

Is it nothing to you, all ye that pass by? Behold and see if there be any sorrow like unto my sorrow which is done unto me, wherewith the Lord hath afflicted me.    *Lamentations 1:12*

## Easter Season, including Ascension Day and the Day of Pentecost

Alleluia! Christ is risen.
*The Lord is risen indeed. Alleluia!*

This is the day which the Lord hath made; we will rejoice and be glad in it.    *Psalm 118:24*

Thanks be to God, which giveth us the victory through our Lord Jesus Christ.    *1 Corinthians 15:57*

If ye then be risen with Christ, seek those things which are above, where Christ sitteth on the right hand of God.
*Colossians 3:1*

Christ is not entered into the holy places made with hands, which are the figures of the true; but into heaven itself, now to appear in the presence of God for us.    *Hebrews 9:24*

Ye shall receive power, after that the Holy Ghost is come upon you; and ye shall be witnesses unto me both in Jerusalem, and in all Judaea, and in Samaria, and unto the uttermost part of the earth.    *Acts 1:8*

## Trinity Sunday

Holy, holy, holy, Lord God Almighty, which was, and is, and is to come.    *Revelation 4:8*

## All Saints and other Major Saints' Days

We give thanks unto the Father, which hath made us meet to be partakers of the inheritance of the saints in light.
*Colossians 1:12*

Ye are no more strangers and foreigners, but fellow-citizens with the saints and of the household of God. *Ephesians 2:19*

Their sound is gone out into all lands; and their words into the ends of the world. *Psalm 19:4*

## Occasions of Thanksgiving

O give thanks unto the Lord, and call upon his Name; tell the people what things he hath done. *Psalm 105:1*

## At any Time

Grace be unto you, and peace, from God our Father, and from the Lord Jesus Christ. *Philippians 1:2*

I was glad when they said unto me, "We will go into the house of the Lord." *Psalm 122:1*

Let the words of my mouth, and the meditation of my heart, be alway acceptable in thy sight, O Lord, my strength and my redeemer. *Psalm 19:14*

O send out thy light and thy truth, that they may lead me, and bring me unto thy holy hill, and to thy dwelling.
*Psalm 43:3*

The Lord is in his holy temple; let all the earth keep silence before him. *Habakkuk 2:20*

The hour cometh, and now is, when the true worshipers shall worship the Father in spirit and in truth; for the Father seeketh such to worship him. *John 4:23*

Thus saith the high and lofty One that inhabiteth eternity,

whose name is Holy," I dwell in the high and holy place, with him also that is of a contrite and humble spirit, to revive the spirit of the humble, and to revive the heart of the contrite ones."    *Isaiah 57:15*

*The following Confession of Sin may then be said; or the Office may continue at once with "O Lord, open thou our lips."*

## Confession of Sin

*The Officiant says to the people*

Dearly beloved, we have come together in the presence of Almighty God our heavenly Father, to render thanks for the great benefits that we have received at his hands, to set forth his most worthy praise, to hear his holy Word, and to ask, for ourselves and on behalf of others, those things that are necessary for our life and our salvation. And so that we may prepare ourselves in heart and mind to worship him, let us kneel in silence, and with penitent and obedient hearts confess our sins, that we may obtain forgiveness by his infinite goodness and mercy.

*or this*

Let us humbly confess our sins unto Almighty God.

*Silence may be kept.*

*Officiant and People together, all kneeling*

Almighty and most merciful Father,
we have erred and strayed from thy ways like lost sheep,
we have followed too much the devices and desires of our
    own hearts,
we have offended against thy holy laws,
we have left undone those things which we ought to
    have done,

and we have done those things which we ought not to
    have done.
But thou, O Lord, have mercy upon us,
spare thou those who confess their faults,
restore thou those who are penitent,
according to thy promises declared unto mankind
in Christ Jesus our Lord;
and grant, O most merciful Father, for his sake,
that we may hereafter live a godly, righteous, and sober life,
to the glory of thy holy Name. Amen.

*The Priest alone stands and says*

The Almighty and merciful Lord grant you absolution and
remission of all your sins, true repentance, amendment of
life, and the grace and consolation of his Holy Spirit. *Amen.*

*A deacon or lay person using the preceding form remains kneeling, and
substitutes "us" for "you" and "our" for "your."*


# The Invitatory and Psalter

*All stand*

Officiant    O Lord, open thou our lips.
People       And our mouth shall show forth thy praise.

*Officiant and People*

Glory to the Father, and to the Son, and to the Holy Spirit: as
it was in the beginning, is now, and will be for ever. Amen.

*Except in Lent,*    Alleluia    *may be added.*

*Then follows one of the Invitatory Psalms, Venite or Jubilate.*

*One of the following Antiphons may be sung or said with the Invitatory Psalm*

*In Advent*

Our King and Savior draweth nigh: O come, let us adore him.

*On the Twelve Days of Christmas*

Alleluia. Unto us a child is born: O come, let us adore him. Alleluia.

*From the Epiphany through the Baptism of Christ, and on the Feasts of the Transfiguration and Holy Cross*

The Lord hath manifested forth his glory: O come, let us adore him.

*In Lent*

The Lord is full of compassion and mercy: O come, let us adore him.

*From Easter Day until the Ascension*

Alleluia. The Lord is risen indeed: O come, let us adore him. Alleluia.

*From Ascension Day until the Day of Pentecost*

Alleluia. Christ the Lord ascendeth into heaven: O come, let us adore him. Alleluia.

*On the Day of Pentecost*

Alleluia. The Spirit of the Lord filleth the world: O come, let us adore him. Alleluia.

*On Trinity Sunday*

Father, Son, and Holy Ghost, one God: O come, let us adore him.

*On other Sundays and Weekdays*

The earth is the Lord's for he made it: O come, let us
adore him.

*or this*

Worship the Lord in the beauty of holiness: O come, let us
adore him.

*or this*

The mercy of the Lord is everlasting: O come, let us adore him.

*The Alleluias in the following Antiphons are used only in Easter Season.*

*On Feasts of the Incarnation*

[Alleluia.] The Word was made flesh and dwelt among us:
O come, let us adore him. [Alleluia.]

*On All Saints and other Major Saints' Days*

[Alleluia.] The Lord is glorious in his saints: O come, let us
adore him. [Alleluia.]


**Venite**   *Psalm 95:1-7; 96:9, 13*

O come, let us sing unto the Lord; *
    let us heartily rejoice in the strength of our salvation.
Let us come before his presence with thanksgiving, *
    and show ourselves glad in him with psalms.

For the Lord is a great God, *
    and a great King above all gods.
In his hand are all the corners of the earth, *
    and the strength of the hills is his also.
The sea is his and he made it, *
    and his hands prepared the dry land.

O come, let us worship and fall down *
    and kneel before the Lord our Maker.
For he is the Lord our God, *
    and we are the people of his pasture
    and the sheep of his hand.

O worship the Lord in the beauty of holiness; *
    let the whole earth stand in awe of him.
For he cometh, for he cometh to judge the earth, *
    and with righteousness to judge the world
    and the peoples with his truth.

*or Psalm 95, page 146.*


**Jubilate**   *Psalm 100*

O be joyful in the Lord all ye lands; *
    serve the Lord with gladness
    and come before his presence with a song.

Be ye sure that the Lord he is God;
it is he that hath made us and not we ourselves;*
    we are his people and the sheep of his pasture.

O go your way into his gates with thanksgiving
and into his courts with praise; *
    be thankful unto him and speak good of his Name.

For the Lord is gracious;
his mercy is everlasting; *
    and his truth endureth from generation to generation.

*In Easter Week, in place of an Invitatory Psalm, the following is sung or said. It may also be used daily until the Day of Pentecost.*

**Christ our Passover**   *Pascha nostrum*

*1 Corinthians 5:7-8; Romans 6:9-11; 1 Corinthians 15:20-22*

Alleluia.
Christ our Passover is sacrificed for us, *
    therefore let us keep the feast,
Not with old leaven,
neither with the leaven of malice and wickedness, *
    but with the unleavened bread of sincerity and truth. Alleluia.

Christ being raised from the dead dieth no more; *
    death hath no more dominion over him.
For in that he died, he died unto sin once; *
    but in that he liveth, he liveth unto God.
Likewise reckon ye also yourselves to be dead indeed unto sin, *
    but alive unto God through Jesus Christ our Lord. Alleluia.

Christ is risen from the dead, *
    and become the first fruits of them that slept.
For since by man came death, *
    by man came also the resurrection of the dead.
For as in Adam all die, *
    even so in Christ shall all be made alive. Alleluia.


*Then follows*

**The Psalm or Psalms Appointed**

*At the end of the Psalms is sung or said*

Glory to the Father, and to the Son, and to the Holy Spirit: *
    as it was in the beginning, is now, and will be for ever. Amen

# The Lessons

*One or two Lessons, as appointed, are read, the Reader first saying*

A Reading (Lesson) from _____.

*A citation giving chapter and verse may be added.*

*After each Lesson the Reader may say*

       The Word of the Lord.
*Answer*    Thanks be to God.

*Or the Reader may say*   Here endeth the Lesson (Reading).

*Silence may be kept after each Reading. One of the following Canticles,
or one of those on pages 85-95 (Canticles 8-21), is sung or said after
each Reading. If three Lessons are used, the Lesson from the Gospel is
read after the second Canticle.*

## 1  A Song of Creation   *Benedicite, omnia opera Domini*
*Song of the Three Young Men, 35-65*

*This Canticle may be shortened by omitting section II or III*

### I   Invocation

O all ye works of the Lord, bless ye the Lord; *
   praise him and magnify him for ever.
O ye angels of the Lord, bless ye the Lord; *
   praise him and magnify him for ever.

### II   The Cosmic Order

O ye heavens, bless ye the Lord; *
   O ye waters that be above the firmament, bless ye the Lord;
O all ye powers of the Lord, bless ye the Lord; *
   praise him and magnify him for ever.

O ye sun and moon, bless ye the Lord; *
    O ye stars of heaven, bless ye the Lord;
O ye showers and dew, bless ye the Lord; *
    praise him and magnify him for ever.

O ye winds of God, bless ye the Lord; *
    O ye fire and heat, bless ye the Lord;
O ye winter and summer, bless ye the Lord; *
    praise him and magnify him for ever.

O ye dews and frosts, bless ye the Lord; *
    O ye frost and cold, bless ye the Lord;
O ye ice and snow, bless ye the Lord; *
    praise him and magnify him for ever.

O ye nights and days, bless ye the Lord; *
    O ye light and darkness, bless ye the Lord;
O ye lightnings and clouds, bless ye the Lord; *
    praise him and magnify him for ever.

*III   The Earth and its Creatures*

O let the earth bless the Lord; *
    O ye mountains and hills, bless ye the Lord;
O all ye green things upon the earth, bless ye the Lord; *
    praise him and magnify him for ever.

O ye wells, bless ye the Lord; *
    O ye seas and floods, bless ye the Lord;
O ye whales and all that move in the waters, bless ye the Lord;
    praise him and magnify him for ever.

O all ye fowls of the air, bless ye the Lord; *
    O all ye beasts and cattle, bless ye the Lord;
O ye children of men, bless ye the Lord; *
    praise him and magnify him for ever.

## IV  The People of God

O ye people of God, bless ye the Lord; *
    O ye priests of the Lord, bless ye the Lord;
O ye servants of the Lord, bless ye the Lord; *
    praise him and magnify him for ever.

O ye spirits and souls of the righteous, bless ye the Lord; *
    O ye holy and humble men of heart, bless ye the Lord.
Let us bless the Father, the Son, and the Holy Spirit; *
    praise him and magnify him for ever.

## 2  A Song of Praise  *Benedictus es, Domine*

*Song of the Three Young Men, 29-34*

Blessed art thou, O Lord God of our fathers; *
    praised and exalted above all for ever.
Blessed art thou for the Name of thy Majesty; *
    praised and exalted above all for ever.
Blessed art thou in the temple of thy holiness; *
    praised and exalted above all for ever.
Blessed art thou that beholdest the depths,
and dwellest between the Cherubim; *
    praised and exalted above all for ever.
Blessed art thou on the glorious throne of thy kingdom; *
    praised and exalted above all for ever.
Blessed art thou in the firmament of heaven; *
    praised and exalted above all for ever.
Blessed art thou, O Father, Son, and Holy Spirit; *
    praised and exalted above all for ever.

## 3  The Song of Mary  *Magnificat*

*Luke 1:46-55*

My soul doth magnify the Lord, *
    and my spirit hath rejoiced in God my Savior.
For he hath regarded *
    the lowliness of his handmaiden.
For behold from henceforth *
    all generations shall call me blessed.
For he that is mighty hath magnified me, *
    and holy is his Name.
And his mercy is on them that fear him *
    throughout all generations.
He hath showed strength with his arm; *
    he hath scattered the proud in the imagination of their hearts.
He hath put down the mighty from their seat, *
    and hath exalted the humble and meek.
He hath filled the hungry with good things, *
    and the rich he hath sent empty away.
He remembering his mercy hath holpen his servant Israel, *
    as he promised to our forefathers,
    Abraham and his seed for ever.

Glory to the Father, and to the Son, and to the Holy Spirit: *
    as it was in the beginning, is now, and will be for ever. Amen.

## 4  The Song of Zechariah  *Benedictus Dominus Deus*

*Luke 1:68-79*

Blessed be the Lord God of Israel, *
    for he hath visited and redeemed his people;
And hath raised up a mighty salvation for us *
    in the house of his servant David,
As he spake by the mouth of his holy prophets,*
    which have been since the world began:

That we should be saved from our enemies, *
   and from the hand of all that hate us;
To perform the mercy promised to our forefathers, *
   and to remember his holy covenant;
To perform the oath which he sware to our forefather Abraham, *
   that he would give us,
That we being delivered out of the hand of our enemies *
   might serve him without fear,
In holiness and righteousness before him, *
   all the days of our life.

And thou, child, shalt be called the prophet of the Highest, *
   for thou shalt go before the face of the Lord
                  to prepare his ways;
To give knowledge of salvation unto his people *
   for the remission of their sins,
Through the tender mercy of our God, *
   whereby the dayspring from on high hath visited us;
To give light to them that sit in darkness
and in the shadow of death, *
   and to guide our feet into the way of peace.

Glory to the Father, and to the Son, and to the Holy Spirit: *
   as it was in the beginning, is now, and will be for ever. Amen.


5   **The Song of Simeon**   *Nunc dimittis*
   *Luke 2:29-32*


Lord, now lettest thou thy servant depart in peace, *
   according to thy word;
For mine eyes have seen thy salvation, *
   which thou hast prepared before the face of all people,
To be a light to lighten the Gentiles, *
   and to be the glory of thy people Israel.

Glory to the Father, and to the Son, and to the Holy Spirit: *
    as it was in the beginning, is now, and will be for ever. Amen.

## 6    Glory be to God    *Gloria in excelsis*

Glory be to God on high,
    and on earth peace, good will towards men.

We praise thee, we bless thee,
    we worship thee,
    we glorify thee,
    we give thanks to thee for thy great glory,
O Lord God, heavenly King, God the Father Almighty.

O Lord, the only-begotten Son, Jesus Christ;
O Lord God, Lamb of God, Son of the Father,
    that takest away the sins of the world,
    have mercy upon us.
Thou that takest away the sins of the world,
    receive our prayer.
Thou that sittest at the right hand of God the Father,
    have mercy upon us.

For thou only art holy,
thou only art the Lord,
thou only, O Christ,
    with the Holy Ghost,
    art most high in the glory of God the Father. Amen.

## 7    We Praise Thee    *Te Deum laudamus*

We praise thee, O God; we acknowledge thee to be the Lord.
All the earth doth worship thee, the Father everlasting.
To thee all Angels cry aloud,
    the Heavens and all the Powers therein.
To thee Cherubim and Seraphim continually do cry:

Holy, holy, holy, Lord God of Sabaoth;
   Heaven and earth are full of the majesty of thy glory.
The glorious company of the apostles praise thee.
The goodly fellowship of the prophets praise thee.
The noble army of martyrs praise thee.
The holy Church throughout all the world
                    doth acknowledge thee,
   the Father, of an infinite majesty,
   thine adorable, true, and only Son,
   also the Holy Ghost the Comforter.

Thou art the King of glory, O Christ.
Thou art the everlasting Son of the Father.
When thou tookest upon thee to deliver man,
thou didst humble thyself to be born of a Virgin.
When thou hadst overcome the sharpness of death,
thou didst open the kingdom of heaven to all believers.
Thou sittest at the right hand of God, in the glory of the Father.
We believe that thou shalt come to be our judge.
   We therefore pray thee, help thy servants,
   whom thou hast redeemed with thy precious blood.
   Make them to be numbered with thy saints,
   in glory everlasting.

## The Apostles' Creed

*Officiant and People together, all standing*

I believe in God, the Father almighty,
   maker of heaven and earth;
And in Jesus Christ his only Son our Lord;
   who was conceived by the Holy Ghost,
   born of the Virgin Mary,
   suffered under Pontius Pilate,
   was crucified, dead, and buried.
   He descended into hell.

The third day he rose again from the dead.
He ascended into heaven,
and sitteth on the right hand of God the Father almighty.
From thence he shall come to judge the quick and the dead.
I believe in the Holy Ghost,
the holy catholic Church,
the communion of saints,
the forgiveness of sins,
the resurrection of the body,
and the life everlasting. Amen.

*The text of the Creed on page 96 may be used instead.*

# The Prayers

*The people stand or kneel*

*Officiant*   The Lord be with you.
*People*   And with thy spirit.
*Officiant*   Let us pray.

*Officiant and People*

Our Father, who art in heaven,
hallowed be thy Name,
thy kingdom come,
thy will be done,
on earth as it is in heaven.
Give us this day our daily bread.
And forgive us our trespasses,
as we forgive those who trespass against us.
And lead us not into temptation,
but deliver us from evil.
For thine is the kingdom, and the power, and the glory,
for ever and ever. Amen.

*Then follows one of these sets of Suffrages*

### A

V. O Lord, show thy mercy upon us;
R. And grant us thy salvation.
V. Endue thy ministers with righteousness;
R. And make thy chosen people joyful.
V. Give peace, O Lord, in all the world;
R. For only in thee can we live in safety.
V. Lord, keep this nation under thy care;
R. And guide us in the way of justice and truth.
V. Let thy way be known upon earth;
R. Thy saving health among all nations.
V. Let not the needy, O Lord, be forgotten;
R. Nor the hope of the poor be taken away.
V. Create in us clean hearts, O God;
R. And sustain us with thy Holy Spirit.

### B

V. O Lord, save thy people, and bless thine heritage;
R. Govern them and lift them up for ever.
V. Day by day we magnify thee;
R. And we worship thy Name ever, world without end.
V. Vouchsafe, O Lord, to keep us this day without sin;
R. O Lord, have mercy upon us, have mercy upon us.
V. O Lord, let thy mercy be upon us;
R. As our trust is in thee.
V. O Lord, in thee have I trusted;
R. Let me never be confounded.

*The Officiant then says one or more of the following Collects*

*The Collect of the Day*

*A Collect for Sundays*

O God, who makest us glad with the weekly remembrance of the glorious resurrection of thy Son our Lord: Grant us this day such blessing through our worship of thee, that the days to come may be spent in thy favor; through the same Jesus Christ our Lord. *Amen.*

*A Collect for Fridays*

Almighty God, whose most dear Son went not up to joy but first he suffered pain, and entered not into glory before he was crucified: Mercifully grant that we, walking in the way of the cross, may find it none other than the way of life and peace; through the same thy Son Jesus Christ our Lord. *Amen.*

*A Collect for Saturdays*

Almighty God, who after the creation of the world didst rest from all thy works and sanctify a day of rest for all thy creatures: Grant that we, putting away all earthly anxieties, may be duly prepared for the service of thy sanctuary, and that our rest here upon earth may be a preparation for the eternal rest promised to thy people in heaven; through Jesus Christ our Lord. *Amen.*

*A Collect for the Renewal of Life*

O God, the King eternal, who dividest the day from the night and turnest the shadow of death into the morning: Drive far from us all wrong desires, incline our hearts to keep thy law, and guide our feet into the way of peace; that, having done thy will with cheerfulness while it was day, we may, when the night cometh, rejoice to give thee thanks; through Jesus Christ our Lord. *Amen.*

## A Collect for Peace

O God, who art the author of peace and lover of concord, in knowledge of whom standeth our eternal life, whose service is perfect freedom: Defend us, thy humble servants, in all assaults of our enemies; that we, surely trusting in thy defense, may not fear the power of any adversaries; through the might of Jesus Christ our Lord. *Amen.*

## A Collect for Grace

O Lord, our heavenly Father, almighty and everlasting God, who hast safely brought us to the beginning of this day: Defend us in the same with thy mighty power; and grant that this day we fall into no sin, neither run into any kind of danger; but that we, being ordered by thy governance, may do always what is righteous in thy sight; through Jesus Christ our Lord. *Amen.*

## A Collect for Guidance

O heavenly Father, in whom we live and move and have our being: We humbly pray thee so to guide and govern us by thy Holy Spirit, that in all the cares and occupations of our life we may not forget thee, but may remember that we are ever walking in thy sight; through Jesus Christ our Lord. *Amen.*

*Then, unless the Eucharist or a form of general intercession is to follow, one of these prayers for mission is added*

Almighty and everlasting God, by whose Spirit the whole body of thy faithful people is governed and sanctified: Receive our supplications and prayers which we offer before thee for all members of thy holy Church, that in their vocation and ministry they may truly and godly serve thee; through our Lord and Savior Jesus Christ. *Amen.*

*or the following*

O God, who hast made of one blood all the peoples of the earth, and didst send thy blessed Son to preach peace to those who are far off and to those who are near: Grant that people everywhere may seek after thee and find thee; bring the nations into thy fold; pour out thy Spirit upon all flesh; and hasten the coming of thy kingdom; through the same thy Son Jesus Christ our Lord. *Amen.*

*or this*

Lord Jesus Christ, who didst stretch out thine arms of love on the hard wood of the cross that everyone might come within the reach of thy saving embrace: So clothe us in thy Spirit that we, reaching forth our hands in love, may bring those who do not know thee to the knowledge and love of thee; for the honor of thy Name. *Amen.*

*Here may be sung a hymn or anthem.*

*Authorized intercessions and thanksgivings may follow.*

*Before the close of the Office one or both of the following may be used*

## The General Thanksgiving

*Officiant and People*

Almighty God, Father of all mercies,
we thine unworthy servants
do give thee most humble and hearty thanks
for all thy goodness and loving-kindness
to us and to all men.
We bless thee for our creation, preservation,
and all the blessings of this life;
but above all for thine inestimable love
in the redemption of the world by our Lord Jesus Christ,
for the means of grace, and for the hope of glory.

And, we beseech thee,
give us that due sense of all thy mercies,
that our hearts may be unfeignedly thankful;
and that we show forth thy praise,
not only with our lips, but in our lives,
by giving up our selves to thy service,
and by walking before thee
in holiness and righteousness all our days;
through Jesus Christ our Lord,
to whom, with thee and the Holy Ghost,
be all honor and glory, world without end. Amen.

*A Prayer of St. Chrysostom*

Almighty God, who hast given us grace at this time with one
accord to make our common supplication unto thee, and
hast promised through thy well-beloved Son that when two
or three are gathered together in his Name thou wilt be in the
midst of them: Fulfill now, O Lord, the desires and petitions
of thy servants as may be best for us; granting us in this
world knowledge of thy truth, and in the world to come life
everlasting. *Amen.*

*Then may be said*

Let us bless the Lord.
*Thanks be to God.*

*From Easter Day through the Day of Pentecost "Alleluia, alleluia" may
be added to the preceding versicle and response.*

*The Officiant may then conclude with one of the following*

The grace of our Lord Jesus Christ, and the love of God, and
the fellowship of the Holy Ghost, be with us all evermore.
*Amen.*   2 Corinthians 13:14

May the God of hope fill us with all joy and peace in
believing through the power of the Holy Spirit. *Amen.*
Romans 15:13

Glory to God whose power, working in us, can do infinitely
more than we can ask or imagine: Glory to him from
generation to generation in the Church, and in Christ Jesus
for ever and ever. *Amen.*    Ephesians 3:20, 21

# Daily Evening Prayer: Rite One

*The Officiant begins the service with one or more of the following sentences of Scripture, or of those on pages 37-40;*

*or with the Service of Light on pages 109-112, and continuing with the appointed Psalmody;*

*or with the versicle "O God, make speed to save us" on page 63.*

Let my prayer be set forth in thy sight as the incense, and let the lifting up of my hands be an evening sacrifice.
*Psalm 141:2*

Grace be unto you, and peace, from God our Father, and from the Lord Jesus Christ.     *Philippians 1:2*

O worship the Lord in the beauty of holiness; let the whole earth stand in awe of him.     *Psalm 96:9*

Thine is the day, O God, thine also the night; thou hast established the moon and the sun. Thou hast fixed all the boundaries of the earth; thou hast made summer and winter.
*Psalm 74:15, 16*

I will bless the Lord who giveth me counsel; my heart teacheth me, night after night. I have set the Lord always before me; because he is at my right hand, I shall not fall.
*Psalm 16:7, 8*

Seek him that made the Pleiades and Orion, that turneth deep darkness into the morning, and darkeneth the day into night; that calleth for the waters of the sea, and poureth them out upon the face of the earth: The Lord is his Name.    *Amos 5:8*

If I say, "Surely the darkness will cover me, and the light around me turn to night," darkness is not dark to thee, O Lord; the night is as bright as the day; darkness and light to thee are both alike.    *Psalm 139:10, 11*

Jesus said, "I am the light of the world; he that followeth me shall not walk in darkness, but shall have the light of life." *John 8:12*

*The following Confession of Sin may then be said; or the Office may continue at once with "O God, make speed to save us."*

### Confession of Sin

*The Officiant says to the people*

Dear friends in Christ, here in the presence of Almighty God, let us kneel in silence, and with penitent and obedient hearts confess our sins, so that we may obtain forgiveness by his infinite goodness and mercy.

*or this*

Let us humbly confess our sins unto Almighty God.

*Silence may be kept.*

*Officiant and People together, all kneeling*

Almighty and most merciful Father,
we have erred and strayed from thy ways like lost sheep,
we have followed too much the devices and desires of our
    own hearts,

we have offended against thy holy laws,
we have left undone those things which we ought to
     have done,
and we have done those things which we ought not to
     have done.
But thou, O Lord, have mercy upon us,
spare thou those who confess their faults,
restore thou those who are penitent,
according to thy promises declared unto mankind
in Christ Jesus our Lord;
and grant, O most merciful Father, for his sake,
that we may hereafter live a godly, righteous, and sober life,
to the glory of thy holy Name. Amen.

*The Priest alone stands and says*

The Almighty and merciful Lord grant you absolution and
remission of all your sins, true repentance, amendment of
life, and the grace and consolation of his Holy Spirit. *Amen.*

*A deacon or lay person using the preceding form remains kneeling, and
substitutes "us" for "you" and "our" for "your."*


# The Invitatory and Psalter

*All stand*

Officiant    O God, make speed to save us.
People      O Lord, make haste to help us.

*Officiant and People*

Glory to the Father, and to the Son, and to the Holy Spirit: as
it was in the beginning, is now, and will be for ever. Amen.

*Except in Lent,* Alleluia *may be added.*

*The following, or some other suitable hymn, or an Invitatory Psalm, may be sung or said*

## O Gracious Light   *Phos hilaron*

O gracious Light,
pure brightness of the everliving Father in heaven,
O Jesus Christ, holy and blessed!

Now as we come to the setting of the sun,
and our eyes behold the vesper light,
we sing thy praises, O God: Father, Son, and Holy Spirit.

Thou art worthy at all times to be praised by happy voices,
O Son of God, O Giver of life,
and to be glorified through all the worlds.

*Then follows*

## The Psalm or Psalms Appointed

*At the end of the Psalms is sung or said*

Glory to the Father, and to the Son, and to the Holy Spirit: *
    as it was in the beginning, is now, and will be for ever. Amen

# The Lessons

*One or two Lessons, as appointed, are read, the Reader first saying*

A Reading (Lesson) from _____.

*A citation giving chapter and verse may be added.*

*After each Lesson the Reader may say*

> The Word of the Lord.
*Answer*  Thanks be to God.

*Or the Reader may say*  Here endeth the Lesson (Reading).

*Silence may be kept after each Reading. One of the following Canticles, or one of those on pages 47-52, or 85-95, is sung or said after each Reading. If three Lessons are used, the Lesson from the Gospel is read after the second Canticle.*

## The Song of Mary    *Magnificat*
*Luke 1:46-55*

My soul doth magnify the Lord, *
  and my spirit hath rejoiced in God my Savior.
For he hath regarded *
  the lowliness of his handmaiden.
For behold from henceforth *
  all generations shall call me blessed.
For he that is mighty hath magnified me, *
  and holy is his Name.
And his mercy is on them that fear him *
  throughout all generations.
He hath showed strength with his arm; *
  he hath scattered the proud in the imagination of their hearts.
He hath put down the mighty from their seat, *
  and hath exalted the humble and meek.
He hath filled the hungry with good things, *
  and the rich he hath sent empty away.
He remembering his mercy hath holpen his servant Israel, *
  as he promised to our forefathers,
  Abraham and his seed for ever.

Glory to the Father, and to the Son, and to the Holy Spirit: *
  as it was in the beginning, is now, and will be for ever. Amen.

**The Song of Simeon**   *Nunc dimittis*

*Luke 2:29-32*

Lord, now lettest thou thy servant depart in peace, *
    according to thy word;
For mine eyes have seen thy salvation, *
    which thou hast prepared before the face of all people,
To be a light to lighten the Gentiles, *
    and to be the glory of thy people Israel.

Glory to the Father, and to the Son, and to the Holy Spirit: *
    as it was in the beginning, is now, and will be for ever. Amen.

**The Apostles' Creed**

*Officiant and People together, all standing*

I believe in God, the Father almighty,
    maker of heaven and earth;
And in Jesus Christ his only Son our Lord;
    who was conceived by the Holy Ghost,
    born of the Virgin Mary,
    suffered under Pontius Pilate,
    was crucified, dead, and buried.
    He descended into hell.
    The third day he rose again from the dead.
    He ascended into heaven,
    and sitteth on the right hand of God the Father almighty.
    From thence he shall come to judge the quick and the dead.
I believe in the Holy Ghost,
    the holy catholic Church,
    the communion of saints,
    the forgiveness of sins,
    the resurrection of the body,
    and the life everlasting. Amen.

*The text of the Creed on page 120 may be used instead.*

# The Prayers

*The people stand or kneel*

| | |
|---|---|
| *Officiant* | The Lord be with you. |
| *People* | And with thy spirit. |
| *Officiant* | Let us pray. |

*Officiant and People*

Our Father, who art in heaven,
    hallowed be thy Name,
    thy kingdom come,
    thy will be done,
        on earth as it is in heaven.
Give us this day our daily bread.
And forgive us our trespasses,
    as we forgive those who trespass against us.
And lead us not into temptation,
    but deliver us from evil.
For thine is the kingdom, and the power, and the glory,
    for ever and ever. Amen.

*Then follows one of these sets of Suffrages*

### A

V. O Lord, show thy mercy upon us;
R. And grant us thy salvation.
V. Endue thy ministers with righteousness;
R. And make thy chosen people joyful.
V. Give peace, O Lord, in all the world;
R. For only in thee can we live in safety.
V. Lord, keep this nation under thy care;
R. And guide us in the way of justice and truth.

V.   Let thy way be known upon earth;
R.   Thy saving health among all nations.
V.   Let not the needy, O Lord, be forgotten;
R.   Nor the hope of the poor be taken away.
V.   Create in us clean hearts, O God;
R.   And sustain us with thy Holy Spirit.

## B

That this evening may be holy, good, and peaceful,
*We entreat thee, O Lord.*

That thy holy angels may lead us in paths of peace and
goodwill,
*We entreat thee, O Lord.*

That we may be pardoned and forgiven for our sins
and offenses,
*We entreat thee, O Lord.*

That there may be peace to thy Church and to the whole
world,
*We entreat thee, O Lord.*

That we may depart this life in thy faith and fear, and
not be condemned before the great judgment seat
of Christ,
*We entreat thee, O Lord.*

That we may be bound together by thy Holy Spirit in
the communion of [ _____ and] all thy saints,
entrusting one another and all our life to Christ,
*We entreat thee, O Lord.*

*The Officiant then says one or more of the following Collects*

*The Collect of the Day*

## A Collect for Sundays

Lord God, whose Son our Savior Jesus Christ triumphed
over the powers of death and prepared for us our place in the
new Jerusalem: Grant that we, who have this day given
thanks for his resurrection, may praise thee in that City of
which he is the light; and where he liveth and reigneth for ever
and ever. *Amen.*

## A Collect for Fridays

O Lord Jesus Christ, who by thy death didst take away the
sting of death: Grant unto us thy servants so to follow in
faith where thou hast led the way, that we may at length fall
asleep peacefully in thee, and awake up after thy likeness; for
thy tender mercies' sake. *Amen.*

## A Collect for Saturdays

O God, the source of eternal light: Shed forth thine unending
day upon us who watch for thee, that our lips may praise thee,
our lives may bless thee, and our worship on the morrow may
give thee glory; through Jesus Christ our Lord. *Amen.*

## A Collect for Peace

O God, from whom all holy desires, all good counsels, and
all just works do proceed: Give unto thy servants that peace
which the world cannot give, that our hearts may be set to
obey thy commandments, and also that by thee, we, being
defended from the fear of all enemies, may pass our time in
rest and quietness; through the merits of Jesus Christ our
Savior. *Amen.*

## A Collect for Aid against Perils

Lighten our darkness, we beseech thee, O Lord; and by thy
great mercy defend us from all perils and dangers of this
night; for the love of thy only Son, our Savior Jesus Christ.
*Amen.*

## A Collect for Protection

O God, who art the life of all who live, the light of the faithful,
the strength of those who labor, and the repose of the dead:
We thank thee for the timely blessings of the day, and humbly
beseech thy merciful protection all the night. Bring us, we
pray thee, in safety to the morning hours; through him who
died for us and rose again, thy Son our Savior Jesus Christ.
*Amen.*

## A Collect for the Presence of Christ

Lord Jesus, stay with us, for evening is at hand and the day
is past; be our companion in the way, kindle our hearts, and
awaken hope, that we may know thee as thou art revealed in
Scripture and the breaking of bread. Grant this for the sake
of thy love. *Amen.*

*Then, unless the Eucharist or a form of general intercession is to follow,
one of these prayers for mission is added*

O God and Father of all, whom the whole heavens adore:
Let the whole earth also worship thee, all nations obey thee,
all tongues confess and bless thee, and men and women everywhere love thee and serve thee in peace; through Jesus Christ
our Lord. *Amen.*

*or the following*

Keep watch, dear Lord, with those who work, or watch, or weep this night, and give thine angels charge over those who sleep. Tend the sick, Lord Christ; give rest to the weary, bless the dying, soothe the suffering, pity the afflicted, shield the joyous; and all for thy love's sake. *Amen.*

*or this*

O God, who dost manifest in thy servants the signs of thy presence: Send forth upon us the Spirit of love, that in companionship with one another thine abounding grace may increase among us; through Jesus Christ our Lord. *Amen.*

*Here may be sung a hymn or anthem.*

*Authorized intercessions and thanksgivings may follow.*

*Before the close of the Office one or both of the following may be used*

## The General Thanksgiving

*Officiant and People*

Almighty God, Father of all mercies,
we thine unworthy servants
do give thee most humble and hearty thanks
for all thy goodness and loving-kindness
to us and to all men.
We bless thee for our creation, preservation,
and all the blessings of this life;
but above all for thine inestimable love
in the redemption of the world by our Lord Jesus Christ,
for the means of grace, and for the hope of glory.
And, we beseech thee,
give us that due sense of all thy mercies,
that our hearts may be unfeignedly thankful;

and that we show forth thy praise,
not only with our lips, but in our lives,
by giving up our selves to thy service,
and by walking before thee
in holiness and righteousness all our days;
through Jesus Christ our Lord,
to whom, with thee and the Holy Ghost,
be all honor and glory, world without end. Amen.

*A Prayer of St. Chrysostom*

Almighty God, who hast given us grace at this time with one
accord to make our common supplication unto thee, and
hast promised through thy well-beloved Son that when two
or three are gathered together in his Name thou wilt be in the
midst of them: Fulfill now, O Lord, the desires and petitions
of thy servants as may be best for us; granting us in this
world knowledge of thy truth, and in the world to come life
everlasting. *Amen.*

*Then may be said*

Let us bless the Lord.
*Thanks be to God.*

*From Easter Day through the Day of Pentecost "Alleluia, alleluia" may
be added to the preceding versicle and response.*

*The Officiant may then conclude with one of the following*

The grace of our Lord Jesus Christ, and the love of God, and
the fellowship of the Holy Ghost, be with us all evermore.
*Amen.*    2 *Corinthians* 13:14

May the God of hope fill us with all joy and peace in believing through the power of the Holy Spirit. *Amen.*
Romans 15:13

Glory to God whose power, working in us, can do infinitely more than we can ask or imagine: Glory to him from generation to generation in the Church, and in Christ Jesus for ever and ever. *Amen.*     Ephesians 3:20, 21

# Concerning the Service

In the Daily Office, the term "Officiant" is used to denote the person, clerical or lay, who leads the Office.

It is appropriate that other persons be assigned to read the Lessons, and to lead other parts of the service not assigned to the officiant. The bishop, when present, appropriately concludes the Office with a blessing.

At celebrations of the Holy Eucharist, the Order for Morning or Evening Prayer may be used in place of all that precedes the Offertory.

Additional Directions are on page 141.

# Daily Morning Prayer:
# Rite Two

*The Officiant begins the service with one or more of these sentences of Scripture, or with the versicle "Lord, open our lips" on page 80.*

### Advent

Watch, for you do not know when the master of the house will come, in the evening, or at midnight, or at cockcrow, or in the morning, lest he come suddenly and find you asleep. *Mark 13:35, 36*

In the wilderness prepare the way of the Lord, make straight in the desert a highway for our God. *Isaiah 40:3*

The glory of the Lord shall be revealed, and all flesh shall see it together. *Isaiah 40:5*

### Christmas

Behold, I bring you good news of a great joy which will come to all the people; for to you is born this day in the city of David, a Savior, who is Christ the Lord. *Luke 2:10, 11*

Behold, the dwelling of God is with mankind. He will dwell with them, and they shall be his people, and God himself will be with them, and be their God. *Revelation 21:3*

*Epiphany*

Nations shall come to your light, and kings to the brightness of your rising.   *Isaiah 60:3*

I will give you as a light to the nations, that my salvation may reach to the end of the earth.   *Isaiah 49:6b*

From the rising of the sun to its setting my Name shall be great among the nations, and in every place incense shall be offered to my Name, and a pure offering; for my Name shall be great among the nations, says the Lord of hosts.   *Malachi 1:11*

*Lent*

If we say we have no sin, we deceive ourselves, and the truth is not in us, but if we confess our sins, God, who is faithful and just, will forgive our sins and cleanse us from all unrighteousness.   *1 John 1:8, 9*

Rend your hearts and not your garments. Return to the Lord your God, for he is gracious and merciful, slow to anger and abounding in steadfast love, and repents of evil.   *Joel 2:13*

I will arise and go to my father, and I will say to him, "Father, I have sinned against heaven and before you; I am no longer worthy to be called your son."   *Luke 15:18, 19*

To the Lord our God belong mercy and forgiveness, because we have rebelled against him and have not obeyed the voice of the Lord our God by following his laws which he set before us.   *Daniel 9:9, 10*

Jesus said, "If anyone would come after me, let him deny himself and take up his cross and follow me."   *Mark 8:34*

*Holy Week*

All we like sheep have gone astray; we have turned every one to his own way; and the Lord has laid on him the iniquity of us all.    *Isaiah 53:6*

Is it nothing to you, all you who pass by? Look and see if there is any sorrow like my sorrow which was brought upon me, whom the Lord has afflicted.    *Lamentations 1:12*

*Easter Season, including Ascension Day*
*and the Day of Pentecost*

Alleluia! Christ is risen.
*The Lord is risen indeed. Alleluia!*

On this day the Lord has acted; we will rejoice and be glad in it.    *Psalm 118:24*

Thanks be to God, who gives us the victory through our Lord Jesus Christ.    *1 Corinthians 15:57*

If then you have been raised with Christ, seek the things that are above, where Christ is, seated at the right hand of God.
*Colossians 3:1*

Christ has entered, not into a sanctuary made with hands, a copy of the true one, but into heaven itself, now to appear in the presence of God on our behalf.    *Hebrews 9:24*

You shall receive power when the Holy Spirit has come upon you; and you shall be my witnesses in Jerusalem, and in all Judea, and Samaria, and to the ends of the earth.    *Acts 1:8*

*Trinity Sunday*

Holy, holy, holy is the Lord God Almighty, who was, and is, and is to come!    *Revelation 4:8*

*All Saints and other Major Saints' Days*

We give thanks to the Father, who has made us worthy to share in the inheritance of the saints in light.    *Colossians 1:12*

You are no longer strangers and sojourners, but fellow citizens with the saints and members of the household of God.   *Ephesians 2:19*

Their sound has gone out into all lands, and their message to the ends of the world.   *Psalm 19:4*

*Occasions of Thanksgiving*

Give thanks to the Lord, and call upon his Name; make known his deeds among the peoples.   *Psalm 105:1*

*At any Time*

Grace to you and peace from God our Father and the Lord Jesus Christ.   *Philippians 1:2*

I was glad when they said to me, "Let us go to the house of the Lord."   *Psalm 122:1*

Let the words of my mouth and the meditation of my heart be acceptable in your sight, O Lord, my strength and my redeemer.   *Psalm 19:14*

Send out your light and your truth, that they may lead me, and bring me to your holy hill and to your dwelling.
*Psalm 43:3*

The Lord is in his holy temple; let all the earth keep silence before him.   *Habakkuk 2:20*

The hour is coming, and now is, when the true worshipers will worship the Father in spirit and truth, for such the Father seeks to worship him.   *John 4:23*

Thus says the high and lofty One who inhabits eternity, whose name is Holy, " I dwell in the high and holy place and also with the one who has a contrite and humble spirit, to revive the spirit of the humble and to revive the heart of the contrite."   *Isaiah 57:15*

*The following Confession of Sin may then be said; or the Office may continue at once with "Lord, open our lips."*

## Confession of Sin

*The Officiant says to the people*

Dearly beloved, we have come together in the presence of Almighty God our heavenly Father, to set forth his praise, to hear his holy Word, and to ask, for ourselves and on behalf of others, those things that are necessary for our life and our salvation. And so that we may prepare ourselves in heart and mind to worship him, let us kneel in silence, and with penitent and obedient hearts confess our sins, that we may obtain forgiveness by his infinite goodness and mercy.

*or this*

Let us confess our sins against God and our neighbor.

*Silence may be kept.*

*Officiant and People together, all kneeling*

Most merciful God,
we confess that we have sinned against you
in thought, word, and deed,
by what we have done,
and by what we have left undone.
We have not loved you with our whole heart;
we have not loved our neighbors as ourselves.
We are truly sorry and we humbly repent.
For the sake of your Son Jesus Christ,
have mercy on us and forgive us;
that we may delight in your will,
and walk in your ways,
to the glory of your Name. Amen.

*The Priest alone stands and says*

Almighty God have mercy on you, forgive you all your sins through our Lord Jesus Christ, strengthen you in all goodness, and by the power of the Holy Spirit keep you in eternal life. *Amen.*

*A deacon or lay person using the preceding form remains kneeling, and substitutes "us" for "you" and "our" for "your."*

# The Invitatory and Psalter

*All stand*

Officiant Lord, open our lips.
People And our mouth shall proclaim your praise.

*Officiant and People*

Glory to the Father, and to the Son, and to the Holy Spirit: as it was in the beginning, is now, and will be for ever. Amen.

*Except in Lent, add* Alleluia.

*Then follows one of the Invitatory Psalms, Venite or Jubilate.*

*One of the following Antiphons may be sung or said with the Invitatory Psalm*

*In Advent*

Our King and Savior now draws near: Come let us adore him.

*On the Twelve Days of Christmas*

Alleluia. To us a child is born: Come let us adore him. Alleluia.

*From the Epiphany through the Baptism of Christ, and on the Feasts of the Transfiguration and Holy Cross*

The Lord has shown forth his glory: Come let us adore him.

*In Lent*

The Lord is full of compassion and mercy: Come let us adore him.

*From Easter Day until the Ascension*

Alleluia. The Lord is risen indeed: Come let us adore him. Alleluia.

*From Ascension Day until the Day of Pentecost*

Alleluia. Christ the Lord has ascended into heaven: Come let us adore him. Alleluia.

*On the Day of Pentecost*

Alleluia. The Spirit of the Lord renews the face of the earth: Come let us adore him. Alleluia.

*On Trinity Sunday*

Father, Son, and Holy Spirit, one God: Come let us adore him.

*On other Sundays and weekdays*

The earth is the Lord's for he made it: Come let us adore him.

*or this*

Worship the Lord in the beauty of holiness: Come let us adore him.

*or this*

The mercy of the Lord is everlasting: Come let us adore him.

*The Alleluias in the following Antiphons are used only in Easter Season.*

*On Feasts of the Incarnation*

[Alleluia.] The Word was made flesh and dwelt among us:
Come let us adore him. [Alleluia.]

*On All Saints and other Major Saints' Days*

[Alleluia.] The Lord is glorious in his saints: Come let us
adore him. [Alleluia.]

**Venite**   *Psalm 95:1-7*

Come, let us sing to the Lord; *
    let us shout for joy to the Rock of our salvation.
Let us come before his presence with thanksgiving *
    and raise a loud shout to him with psalms.

For the Lord is a great God, *
    and a great King above all gods.
In his hand are the caverns of the earth, *
    and the heights of the hills are his also.
The sea is his, for he made it, *
    and his hands have molded the dry land.

Come, let us bow down, and bend the knee, *
    and kneel before the Lord our Maker.
For he is our God,
and we are the people of his pasture and the sheep of his hand.
    Oh, that today you would hearken to his voice!

*or Psalm 95, page 724.*

**Jubilate**   *Psalm 100*

Be joyful in the Lord, all you lands; *
    serve the Lord with gladness
    and come before his presence with a song.

Know this: The Lord himself is God; *
    he himself has made us, and we are his;
    we are his people and the sheep of his pasture.

Enter his gates with thanksgiving;
go into his courts with praise; *
    give thanks to him and call upon his Name.

For the Lord is good;
his mercy is everlasting; *
    and his faithfulness endures from age to age.

*In Easter Week, in place of an Invitatory Psalm, the following is sung or said. It may also be used daily until the Day of Pentecost.*

**Christ our Passover**   *Pascha nostrum*

*1 Corinthians 5:7-8; Romans 6:9-11; 1 Corinthians 15:20-22*

Alleluia.
Christ our Passover has been sacrificed for us; *
    therefore let us keep the feast,
Not with the old leaven, the leaven of malice and evil, *
    but with the unleavened bread of sincerity and truth. Alleluia.

Christ being raised from the dead will never die again; *
    death no longer has dominion over him.
The death that he died, he died to sin, once for all; *
    but the life he lives, he lives to God.
So also consider yourselves dead to sin, *
    and alive to God in Jesus Christ our Lord. Alleluia.

Christ has been raised from the dead, *
    the first fruits of those who have fallen asleep.
For since by a man came death, *
    by a man has come also the resurrection of the dead.
For as in Adam all die, *
    so also in Christ shall all be made alive. Alleluia.

*Then follows*

## The Psalm or Psalms Appointed

*At the end of the Psalms is sung or said*

Glory to the Father, and to the Son, and to the Holy Spirit: *
    as it was in the beginning, is now, and will be for ever. Amen

# The Lessons

*One or two Lessons, as appointed, are read, the Reader first saying*

A Reading (Lesson) from _____.

*A citation giving chapter and verse may be added.*

*After each Lesson the Reader may say*

      The Word of the Lord.
*Answer*    Thanks be to God.

*Or the Reader may say*   Here ends the Lesson (Reading).

*Silence may be kept after each Reading. One of the following Canticles,
or one of those on pages 47-52 (Canticles 1-7), is sung or said after
each Reading. If three Lessons are used, the Lesson from the Gospel is
read after the second Canticle.*

# 8 The Song of Moses *Cantemus Domino*

*Exodus 15:1-6, 11-13, 17-18*

*Especially suitable for use in Easter Season*

I will sing to the Lord, for he is lofty and uplifted; *
   the horse and its rider has he hurled into the sea.
The Lord is my strength and my refuge; *
   the Lord has become my Savior.
This is my God and I will praise him, *
   the God of my people and I will exalt him.
The Lord is a mighty warrior; *
   Yahweh is his Name.
The chariots of Pharaoh and his army has he hurled into the sea; *
   the finest of those who bear armor have been
                    drowned in the Red Sea.
The fathomless deep has overwhelmed them; *
   they sank into the depths like a stone.
Your right hand, O Lord, is glorious in might; *
   your right hand, O Lord, has overthrown the enemy.
Who can be compared with you, O Lord, among the gods? *
   who is like you, glorious in holiness,
   awesome in renown, and worker of wonders?
You stretched forth your right hand; *
   the earth swallowed them up.
With your constant love you led the people you redeemed; *
   with your might you brought them in safety to
                    your holy dwelling.
You will bring them in and plant them *
   on the mount of your possession,
The resting-place you have made for yourself, O Lord, *
   the sanctuary, O Lord, that your hand has established.
The Lord shall reign *
   for ever and for ever.

Glory to the Father, and to the Son, and to the Holy Spirit: *
   as it was in the beginning, is now, and will be for ever. Amen.

## 9 The First Song of Isaiah  *Ecce, Deus*
### Isaiah 12:2-6

Surely, it is God who saves me; *
  I will trust in him and not be afraid.
For the Lord is my stronghold and my sure defense, *
  and he will be my Savior.
Therefore you shall draw water with rejoicing *
  from the springs of salvation.
And on that day you shall say, *
  Give thanks to the Lord and call upon his Name;
Make his deeds known among the peoples; *
  see that they remember that his Name is exalted.
Sing the praises of the Lord, for he has done great things, *
  and this is known in all the world.
Cry aloud, inhabitants of Zion, ring out your joy, *
  for the great one in the midst of you is the Holy One of Israel.

Glory to the Father, and to the Son, and to the Holy Spirit: *
  as it was in the beginning, is now, and will be for ever. Amen

## 10 The Second Song of Isaiah  *Quærite Dominum*
### Isaiah 55:6-11

Seek the Lord while he wills to be found; *
  call upon him when he draws near.
Let the wicked forsake their ways *
  and the evil ones their thoughts;
And let them turn to the Lord, and he will have compassion, *
  and to our God, for he will richly pardon.
For my thoughts are not your thoughts, *
  nor your ways my ways, says the Lord.
For as the heavens are higher than the earth, *
  so are my ways higher than your ways,
  and my thoughts than your thoughts.

For as rain and snow fall from the heavens *
  and return not again, but water the earth,
Bringing forth life and giving growth, *
  seed for sowing and bread for eating,
So is my word that goes forth from my mouth; *
  it will not return to me empty;
But it will accomplish that which I have purposed, *
  and prosper in that for which I sent it.

Glory to the Father, and to the Son, and to the Holy Spirit: *
  as it was in the beginning, is now, and will be for ever. Amen.


## 11  The Third Song of Isaiah  *Surge, illuminare*
  *Isaiah 60:1-3, 11a, 14c, 18-19*

Arise, shine, for your light has come, *
  and the glory of the Lord has dawned upon you.
For behold, darkness covers the land; *
  deep gloom enshrouds the peoples.
But over you the Lord will rise, *
  and his glory will appear upon you.
Nations will stream to your light, *
  and kings to the brightness of your dawning.
Your gates will always be open; *
  by day or night they will never be shut.
They will call you, The City of the Lord, *
  The Zion of the Holy One of Israel.
Violence will no more be heard in your land, *
  ruin or destruction within your borders.
You will call your walls, Salvation, *
  and all your portals, Praise.
The sun will no more be your light by day; *
  by night you will not need the brightness of the moon.

The Lord will be your everlasting light, *
    and your God will be your glory.

Glory to the Father, and to the Son, and to the Holy Spirit: *
    as it was in the beginning, is now, and will be for ever. Ame

## 12 A Song of Creation *Benedicite, omnia opera Domini*
### Song of the Three Young Men, 35-65

*One or more sections of this Canticle may be used. Whatever the
selection, it begins with the Invocation and concludes with the Doxology.*

### Invocation

Glorify the Lord, all you works of the Lord, *
    praise him and highly exalt him for ever.
In the firmament of his power, glorify the Lord, *
    praise him and highly exalt him for ever.

### I   The Cosmic Order

Glorify the Lord, you angels and all powers of the Lord, *
    O heavens and all waters above the heavens.
Sun and moon and stars of the sky, glorify the Lord, *
    praise him and highly exalt him for ever.

Glorify the Lord, every shower of rain and fall of dew, *
    all winds and fire and heat.
Winter and summer, glorify the Lord, *
    praise him and highly exalt him for ever.

Glorify the Lord, O chill and cold, *
    drops of dew and flakes of snow.
Frost and cold, ice and sleet, glorify the Lord, *
    praise him and highly exalt him for ever.

Glorify the Lord, O nights and days, *
   O shining light and enfolding dark.
Storm clouds and thunderbolts, glorify the Lord, *
   praise him and highly exalt him for ever.

## II   *The Earth and its Creatures*

Let the earth glorify the Lord, *
   praise him and highly exalt him for ever.
Glorify the Lord, O mountains and hills,
and all that grows upon the earth, *
   praise him and highly exalt him for ever.

Glorify the Lord, O springs of water, seas, and streams, *
   O whales and all that move in the waters.
All birds of the air, glorify the Lord, *
   praise him and highly exalt him for ever.

Glorify the Lord, O beasts of the wild, *
   and all you flocks and herds.
O men and women everywhere, glorify the Lord, *
   praise him and highly exalt him for ever.

## III   *The People of God*

Let the people of God glorify the Lord, *
   praise him and highly exalt him for ever.
Glorify the Lord, O priests and servants of the Lord, *
   praise him and highly exalt him for ever.

Glorify the Lord, O spirits and souls of the righteous, *
   praise him and highly exalt him for ever.
You that are holy and humble of heart, glorify the Lord, *
   praise him and highly exalt him for ever.

*Doxology*

Let us glorify the Lord: Father, Son, and Holy Spirit; *
    praise him and highly exalt him for ever.
In the firmament of his power, glorify the Lord, *
    praise him and highly exalt him for ever.


## 13   A Song of Praise   *Benedictus es, Domine*
    *Song of the Three Young Men, 29-34*

Glory to you, Lord God of our fathers; *
    you are worthy of praise; glory to you.
Glory to you for the radiance of your holy Name; *
    we will praise you and highly exalt you for ever.

Glory to you in the splendor of your temple; *
    on the throne of your majesty, glory to you.
Glory to you, seated between the Cherubim; *
    we will praise you and highly exalt you for ever.

Glory to you, beholding the depths; *
    in the high vault of heaven, glory to you.
Glory to you, Father, Son, and Holy Spirit; *
    we will praise you and highly exalt you for ever.


## 14   A Song of Penitence   *Kyrie Pantokrator*
    *Prayer of Manasseh, 1-2, 4, 6-7, 11-15*

*Especially suitable in Lent, and on other penitential occasions*

O Lord and Ruler of the hosts of heaven, *
    God of Abraham, Isaac, and Jacob,
    and of all their righteous offspring:
You made the heavens and the earth, *
    with all their vast array.

All things quake with fear at your presence; *
    they tremble because of your power.
But your merciful promise is beyond all measure; *
    it surpasses all that our minds can fathom.
O Lord, you are full of compassion, *
    long-suffering, and abounding in mercy.
You hold back your hand; *
    you do not punish as we deserve.
In your great goodness, Lord,
you have promised forgiveness to sinners, *
    that they may repent of their sin and be saved.
And now, O Lord, I bend the knee of my heart, *
    and make my appeal, sure of your gracious goodness.
I have sinned, O Lord, I have sinned, *
    and I know my wickedness only too well.
Therefore I make this prayer to you: *
    Forgive me, Lord, forgive me.
Do not let me perish in my sin, *
    nor condemn me to the depths of the earth.
For you, O Lord, are the God of those who repent, *
    and in me you will show forth your goodness.
Unworthy as I am, you will save me,
in accordance with your great mercy, *
    and I will praise you without ceasing all the days of my life.
For all the powers of heaven sing your praises, *
    and yours is the glory to ages of ages. Amen.

15   The Song of Mary   *Magnificat*

   *Luke 1:46-55*

My soul proclaims the greatness of the Lord,
my spirit rejoices in God my Savior; *
    for he has looked with favor on his lowly servant.

From this day all generations will call me blessed: *
    the Almighty has done great things for me,
    and holy is his Name.
He has mercy on those who fear him *
    in every generation.
He has shown the strength of his arm, *
    he has scattered the proud in their conceit.
He has cast down the mighty from their thrones, *
    and has lifted up the lowly.
He has filled the hungry with good things, *
    and the rich he has sent away empty.
He has come to the help of his servant Israel, *
    for he has remembered his promise of mercy,
The promise he made to our fathers, *
    to Abraham and his children for ever.

Glory to the Father, and to the Son, and to the Holy Spirit: *
    as it was in the beginning, is now, and will be for ever. Amen

## 16  The Song of Zechariah  *Benedictus Dominus Deus*
    *Luke 1:68-79*

Blessed be the Lord, the God of Israel; *
    he has come to his people and set them free.
He has raised up for us a mighty savior, *
    born of the house of his servant David.
Through his holy prophets he promised of old,
    that he would save us from our enemies, *
    from the hands of all who hate us.
He promised to show mercy to our fathers *
    and to remember his holy covenant.
This was the oath he swore to our father Abraham, *
    to set us free from the hands of our enemies,
Free to worship him without fear, *
    holy and righteous in his sight
    all the days of our life.

You, my child, shall be called the prophet of the Most High, *
   for you will go before the Lord to prepare his way,
To give his people knowledge of salvation *
   by the forgiveness of their sins.
In the tender compassion of our God *
   the dawn from on high shall break upon us,
To shine on those who dwell in darkness and the
                    shadow of death, *
   and to guide our feet into the way of peace.

Glory to the Father, and to the Son, and to the Holy Spirit: *
   as it was in the beginning, is now, and will be for ever. Amen.

## 17  The Song of Simeon  *Nunc dimittis*
    *Luke 2:29-32*

Lord, you now have set your servant free *
   to go in peace as you have promised;
For these eyes of mine have seen the Savior, *
   whom you have prepared for all the world to see:
A Light to enlighten the nations, *
   and the glory of your people Israel.

Glory to the Father, and to the Son, and to the Holy Spirit: *
   as it was in the beginning, is now, and will be for ever. Amen.

## 18  A Song to the Lamb  *Dignus es*
    *Revelation 4:11; 5:9-10, 13*

Splendor and honor and kingly power *
   are yours by right, O Lord our God,
For you created everything that is, *
   and by your will they were created and have their being;

And yours by right, O Lamb that was slain, *
　　for with your blood you have redeemed for God,
From every family, language, people, and nation, *
　　a kingdom of priests to serve our God.

And so, to him who sits upon the throne, *
　　and to Christ the Lamb,
Be worship and praise, dominion and splendor, *
　　for ever and for evermore.

## 19　The Song of the Redeemed　*Magna et mirabilia*

*Revelation 15:3-4*

O ruler of the universe, Lord God,
great deeds are they that you have done, *
　　surpassing human understanding.
Your ways are ways of righteousness and truth, *
　　O King of all the ages.

Who can fail to do you homage, Lord,
and sing the praises of your Name? *
　　for you only are the Holy One.
All nations will draw near and fall down before you, *
　　because your just and holy works have been revealed.

Glory to the Father, and to the Son, and to the Holy Spirit: *
　　as it was in the beginning, is now, and will be for ever. Amen

## 20　Glory to God　*Gloria in excelsis*

Glory to God in the highest,
　　and peace to his people on earth.

Lord God, heavenly King,
almighty God and Father,

we worship you, we give you thanks,
    we praise you for your glory.

Lord Jesus Christ, only Son of the Father,
Lord God, Lamb of God,
you take away the sin of the world
    have mercy on us;
you are seated at the right hand of the Father:
    receive our prayer.

For you alone are the Holy One,
you alone are the Lord,
you alone are the Most High,
    Jesus Christ,
    with the Holy Spirit,
    in the glory of God the Father. Amen.


## 21  You are God  *Te Deum laudamus*

You are God: we praise you;
You are the Lord: we acclaim you;
You are the eternal Father:
All creation worships you.
To you all angels, all the powers of heaven,
Cherubim and Seraphim, sing in endless praise:
    Holy, holy, holy Lord, God of power and might,
    heaven and earth are full of your glory.
The glorious company of apostles praise you.
The noble fellowship of prophets praise you.
The white-robed army of martyrs praise you.
Throughout the world the holy Church acclaims you;
    Father, of majesty unbounded,
    your true and only Son, worthy of all worship,
    and the Holy Spirit, advocate and guide.

You, Christ, are the king of glory,
the eternal Son of the Father.
When you became man to set us free
you did not shun the Virgin's womb.
You overcame the sting of death
and opened the kingdom of heaven to all believers.
You are seated at God's right hand in glory.
We believe that you will come and be our judge.
    Come then, Lord, and help your people,
    bought with the price of your own blood,
    and bring us with your saints
    to glory everlasting.


## The Apostles' Creed

*Officiant and People together, all standing*

I believe in God, the Father almighty,
    creator of heaven and earth.
I believe in Jesus Christ, his only Son, our Lord.
    He was conceived by the power of the Holy Spirit
        and born of the Virgin Mary.
    He suffered under Pontius Pilate,
        was crucified, died, and was buried.
    He descended to the dead.
    On the third day he rose again.
    He ascended into heaven,
        and is seated at the right hand of the Father.
    He will come again to judge the living and the dead.
I believe in the Holy Spirit,
    the holy catholic Church,
    the communion of saints,
    the forgiveness of sins,
    the resurrection of the body,
    and the life everlasting. Amen.

# The Prayers

*The people stand or kneel*

| | |
|---|---|
| *Officiant* | The Lord be with you. |
| *People* | And also with you. |
| *Officiant* | Let us pray. |

*Officiant and People*

Our Father, who art in heaven,
    hallowed be thy Name,
    thy kingdom come,
    thy will be done,
        on earth as it is in heaven.
Give us this day our daily bread.
And forgive us our trespasses,
    as we forgive those
        who trespass against us.
And lead us not into temptation,
    but deliver us from evil.
For thine is the kingdom,
    and the power, and the glory,
    for ever and ever. Amen.

Our Father in heaven,
    hallowed be your Name,
    your kingdom come,
    your will be done,
        on earth as in heaven.
Give us today our daily bread.
Forgive us our sins
    as we forgive those
        who sin against us.
Save us from the time of trial,
    and deliver us from evil.
For the kingdom, the power,
    and the glory are yours,
    now and for ever. Amen.

*Then follows one of these sets of Suffrages*

### A

V.    Show us your mercy, O Lord;
R.    And grant us your salvation.
V.    Clothe your ministers with righteousness;
R.    Let your people sing with joy.
V.    Give peace, O Lord, in all the world;
R.    For only in you can we live in safety.

| V. | Lord, keep this nation under your care; |
|---|---|
| R. | And guide us in the way of justice and truth. |
| V. | Let your way be known upon earth; |
| R. | Your saving health among all nations. |
| V. | Let not the needy, O Lord, be forgotten; |
| R. | Nor the hope of the poor be taken away. |
| V. | Create in us clean hearts, O God; |
| R. | And sustain us with your Holy Spirit. |

### B

| V. | Save your people, Lord, and bless your inheritance; |
|---|---|
| R. | Govern and uphold them, now and always. |
| V. | Day by day we bless you; |
| R. | We praise your Name for ever. |
| V. | Lord, keep us from all sin today; |
| R. | Have mercy on us, Lord, have mercy. |
| V. | Lord, show us your love and mercy; |
| R. | For we put our trust in you. |
| V. | In you, Lord, is our hope; |
| R. | And we shall never hope in vain. |

*The Officiant then says one or more of the following Collects*

*The Collect of the Day*

*A Collect for Sundays*

O God, you make us glad with the weekly remembrance of the glorious resurrection of your Son our Lord: Give us this day such blessing through our worship of you, that the week to come may be spent in your favor; through Jesus Christ our Lord. *Amen.*

## A Collect for Fridays

Almighty God, whose most dear Son went not up to joy but first he suffered pain, and entered not into glory before he was crucified: Mercifully grant that we, walking in the way of the cross, may find it none other than the way of life and peace; through Jesus Christ your Son our Lord. *Amen.*

## A Collect for Saturdays

Almighty God, who after the creation of the world rested from all your works and sanctified a day of rest for all your creatures: Grant that we, putting away all earthly anxieties, may be duly prepared for the service of your sanctuary, and that our rest here upon earth may be a preparation for the eternal rest promised to your people in heaven; through Jesus Christ our Lord. *Amen.*

## A Collect for the Renewal of Life

O God, the King eternal, whose light divides the day from the night and turns the shadow of death into the morning: Drive far from us all wrong desires, incline our hearts to keep your law, and guide our feet into the way of peace; that, having done your will with cheerfulness during the day, we may, when night comes, rejoice to give you thanks; through Jesus Christ our Lord. *Amen.*

## A Collect for Peace

O God, the author of peace and lover of concord, to know you is eternal life and to serve you is perfect freedom: Defend us, your humble servants, in all assaults of our enemies; that we, surely trusting in your defense, may not fear the power of any adversaries; through the might of Jesus Christ our Lord. *Amen.*

### A Collect for Grace

Lord God, almighty and everlasting Father, you have
brought us in safety to this new day: Preserve us with your
mighty power, that we may not fall into sin, nor be overcome
by adversity; and in all we do, direct us to the fulfilling of
your purpose; through Jesus Christ our Lord. *Amen.*

### A Collect for Guidance

Heavenly Father, in you we live and move and have our
being: We humbly pray you so to guide and govern us by
your Holy Spirit, that in all the cares and occupations of our
life we may not forget you, but may remember that we are
ever walking in your sight; through Jesus Christ our Lord.
*Amen.*

*Then, unless the Eucharist or a form of general intercession is to follow,
one of these prayers for mission is added*

Almighty and everlasting God, by whose Spirit the whole
body of your faithful people is governed and sanctified:
Receive our supplications and prayers which we offer before
you for all members of your holy Church, that in their
vocation and ministry they may truly and devoutly serve you;
through our Lord and Savior Jesus Christ. *Amen.*

*or this*

O God, you have made of one blood all the peoples of the
earth, and sent your blessed Son to preach peace to those
who are far off and to those who are near: Grant that people
everywhere may seek after you and find you; bring the
nations into your fold; pour out your Spirit upon all flesh;
and hasten the coming of your kingdom; through Jesus
Christ our Lord. *Amen.*

*or the following*

Lord Jesus Christ, you stretched out your arms of love on
the hard wood of the cross that everyone might come within
the reach of your saving embrace: So clothe us in your Spirit
that we, reaching forth our hands in love, may bring those
who do not know you to the knowledge and love of you; for
the honor of your Name. *Amen.*

*Here may be sung a hymn or anthem.*

*Authorized intercessions and thanksgivings may follow.*

*Before the close of the Office one or both of the following may be used*

## The General Thanksgiving

*Officiant and People*

Almighty God, Father of all mercies,
we your unworthy servants give you humble thanks
for all your goodness and loving-kindness
to us and to all whom you have made.
We bless you for our creation, preservation,
and all the blessings of this life;
but above all for your immeasurable love
in the redemption of the world by our Lord Jesus Christ;
for the means of grace, and for the hope of glory.
And, we pray, give us such an awareness of your mercies,
that with truly thankful hearts we may show forth your praise,
not only with our lips, but in our lives,
by giving up our selves to your service,
and by walking before you
in holiness and righteousness all our days;
through Jesus Christ our Lord,
to whom, with you and the Holy Spirit,
be honor and glory throughout all ages. Amen.

## A Prayer of St. Chrysostom

Almighty God, you have given us grace at this time with one accord to make our common supplication to you; and you have promised through your well-beloved Son that when two or three are gathered together in his Name you will be in the midst of them: Fulfill now, O Lord, our desires and petitions as may be best for us; granting us in this world knowledge of your truth, and in the age to come life everlasting. *Amen.*

*Then may be said*

Let us bless the Lord.
*Thanks be to God.*

*From Easter Day through the Day of Pentecost "Alleluia, alleluia" may be added to the preceding versicle and response.*

*The Officiant may then conclude with one of the following*

The grace of our Lord Jesus Christ, and the love of God, and the fellowship of the Holy Spirit, be with us all evermore. *Amen.*     *2 Corinthians 13:14*

May the God of hope fill us with all joy and peace in believing through the power of the Holy Spirit. *Amen.* *Romans 15:13*

Glory to God whose power, working in us, can do infinitely more than we can ask or imagine: Glory to him from generation to generation in the Church, and in Christ Jesus for ever and ever. *Amen.*     *Ephesians 3:20, 21*

# An Order of Service for Noonday

*Officiant*   O God, make speed to save us.
*People*   O Lord, make haste to help us.

*Officiant and People*

Glory to the Father, and to the Son, and to the Holy Spirit: as it was in the beginning, is now, and will be for ever. Amen.

*Except in Lent, add*   Alleluia.

*A suitable hymn may be sung.*

*One or more of the following Psalms is sung or said. Other suitable selections include Psalms 19, 67, one or more sections of Psalm 119, or a selection from Psalms 120 through 133.*

**Psalm 119**   *Lucerna pedibus meis*

105   Your word is a lantern to my feet *
      and a light upon my path.

106   I have sworn and am determined *
      to keep your righteous judgments.

107    I am deeply troubled; *
        preserve my life, O LORD, according to your word.

108    Accept, O LORD, the willing tribute of my lips, *
        and teach me your judgments.

109    My life is always in my hand, *
        yet I do not forget your law.

110    The wicked have set a trap for me, *
        but I have not strayed from your commandments.

111    Your decrees are my inheritance for ever; *
        truly, they are the joy of my heart.

112    I have applied my heart to fulfill your statutes *
        for ever and to the end.

## Psalm 121   *Levavi oculos*

1    I lift up my eyes to the hills; *
        from where is my help to come?

2    My help comes from the LORD, *
        the maker of heaven and earth.

3    He will not let your foot be moved *
        and he who watches over you will not fall asleep.

4    Behold, he who keeps watch over Israel *
        shall neither slumber nor sleep;

5    The LORD himself watches over you; *
        the LORD is your shade at your right hand,

6    So that the sun shall not strike you by day, *
        nor the moon by night.

7    The LORD shall preserve you from all evil; *
        it is he who shall keep you safe.

8   The LORD shall watch over your going out and
                                your coming in, *
      from this time forth for evermore.

**Psalm 126**   *In convertendo*

1   When the LORD restored the fortunes of Zion, *
      then were we like those who dream.

2   Then was our mouth filled with laughter, *
      and our tongue with shouts of joy.

3   Then they said among the nations, *
      "The LORD has done great things for them."

4   The LORD has done great things for us, *
      and we are glad indeed.

5   Restore our fortunes, O LORD, *
      like the watercourses of the Negev.

6   Those who sowed with tears *
      will reap with songs of joy.

7   Those who go out weeping, carrying the seed, *
      will come again with joy, shouldering their sheaves.

*At the end of the Psalms is sung or said*

Glory to the Father, and to the Son, and to the Holy Spirit: *
      as it was in the beginning, is now, and will be for ever. Amen.

*One of the following, or some other suitable passage of Scripture, is read*

The love of God has been poured into our hearts through the
Holy Spirit that has been given to us.   *Romans 5:5*

*People*      Thanks be to God.

*or the following*

If anyone is in Christ he is a new creation; the old has passed away, behold the new has come. All this is from God, who through Christ reconciled us to himself and gave us the ministry of reconciliation. *2 Corinthians 5:17-18*

*People*    Thanks be to God.

*or this*

From the rising of the sun to its setting my Name shall be great among the nations, and in every place incense shall be offered to my Name, and a pure offering; for my Name shall be great among the nations, says the Lord of Hosts. *Malachi 1:11*

*People*    Thanks be to God.

*A meditation, silent or spoken, may follow.*

*The Officiant then begins the Prayers*

Lord, have mercy.
*Christ, have mercy.*
Lord, have mercy.

*Officiant and People*

| | |
|---|---|
| Our Father, who art in heaven,<br>    hallowed be thy Name,<br>    thy kingdom come,<br>    thy will be done,<br>        on earth as it is in heaven.<br>Give us this day our daily bread.<br>And forgive us our trespasses,<br>    as we forgive those<br>        who trespass against us.<br>And lead us not into temptation,<br>    but deliver us from evil. | Our Father in heaven,<br>    hallowed be your Name,<br>    your kingdom come,<br>    your will be done,<br>        on earth as in heaven.<br>Give us today our daily bread.<br>Forgive us our sins<br>    as we forgive those<br>        who sin against us.<br>Save us from the time of trial,<br>    and deliver us from evil. |

| Officiant | Lord, hear our prayer; |
|-----------|------------------------|
| People | And let our cry come to you. |
| Officiant | Let us pray. |

*The Officiant then says one of the following Collects. If desired, the Collect of the Day may be used.*

Heavenly Father, send your Holy Spirit into our hearts, to direct and rule us according to your will, to comfort us in all our afflictions, to defend us from all error, and to lead us into all truth; through Jesus Christ our Lord. *Amen.*

Blessed Savior, at this hour you hung upon the cross, stretching out your loving arms: Grant that all the peoples of the earth may look to you and be saved; for your tender mercies' sake. *Amen.*

Almighty Savior, who at noonday called your servant Saint Paul to be an apostle to the Gentiles: We pray you to illumine the world with the radiance of your glory, that all nations may come and worship you; for you live and reign for ever and ever. *Amen.*

Lord Jesus Christ, you said to your apostles, "Peace I give to you; my own peace I leave with you:" Regard not our sins, but the faith of your Church, and give to us the peace and unity of that heavenly City, where with the Father and the Holy Spirit you live and reign, now and for ever. *Amen.*

*Free intercessions may be offered.*

*The service concludes as follows*

| Officiant | Let us bless the Lord. |
|-----------|------------------------|
| People | Thanks be to God. |

# Concerning the Service

This Order provides a form of evening service or vespers for use on suitable occasions in the late afternoon or evening. It may be used as a complete rite in place of Evening Prayer, or as the introduction to Evening Prayer or some other service, or as the prelude to an evening meal or other activity. It is appropriate also for use in private houses.

Any part or parts of this service may be led by lay persons. A priest or deacon, when presiding, should read the Prayer for Light, and the Blessing or Dismissal at the end. The bishop, when present, should give the Blessing.

This order is not appropriate for use on Monday, Tuesday, or Wednesday in Holy Week, or on Good Friday. Easter Eve has its own form for the Lighting of the Paschal Candle.

For the Short Lesson at the beginning of the service, any one of the following is also appropriate, especially for the seasons suggested:

Isaiah 60:19-20 (Advent)        Revelation 21:10, 22-24 (Easter)
Luke 12:35-37 (Advent)          Psalm 36:5-9 (Ascension)
John 1:1-5 (Christmas)          Joel 2:28-30 (Whitsunday)
Isaiah 60:1-3 (Epiphany)        Colossians 1:9, 11-14 (Saints' Days)
1 John 1:5-7 (Lent)             1 Peter 2:9 (Saints' Days)
John 12:35-36a (Lent)           Revelation 22:1, 4-5 (Saints' Days)

Any of the prayers in contemporary language may be adapted to traditional language by changing the pronouns and the corresponding verbs.

Additional Directions are on page 142.

# An Order of Worship
# for the Evening

*The church is dark, or partially so, when the service is to begin.*

*All stand, and the Officiant greets the people with these words*

> Light and peace, in Jesus Christ our Lord.

*People*    Thanks be to God.

*In place of the above, from Easter Day through the Day of Pentecost*

*Officiant*    Alleluia. Christ is risen.
*People*    The Lord is risen indeed. Alleluia.

*In Lent and on other penitential occasions*

*Officiant*    Bless the Lord who forgives all our sins.
*People*    His mercy endures for ever.

*One of the following, or some other Short Lesson of Scripture appropriate to the occasion or to the season, may then be read*

Jesus said,"You are the light of the world. A city built on a hill cannot be hid. No one lights a lamp to put it under a bucket, but on a lamp-stand where it gives light for everyone in the house. And you, like the lamp, must shed light among your fellow men, so that they may see the good you do, and give glory to your Father in heaven."    *Matthew 5:14-16*

It is not ourselves that we proclaim; we proclaim Christ
Jesus as Lord, and ourselves as your servants, for Jesus' sake.
For the same God who said, "Out of darkness let light shine,"
has caused his light to shine within us, to give the light of
revelation — the revelation of the glory of God in the face of
Jesus Christ.    *2 Corinthians 4:5-6*

If I say, "Surely the darkness will cover me, and the light
around me turn to night," darkness is not dark to you, O
Lord; the night is as bright as the day; darkness and light to
you are both alike.    *Psalm 139:10-11*

*The Officiant then says the Prayer for Light, using any one of the*
*following or some other suitable prayer, first saying*

Let us pray.

Almighty God, we give you thanks for surrounding us, as
daylight fades, with the brightness of the vesper light; and we
implore you of your great mercy that, as you enfold us with
the radiance of this light, so you would shine into our hearts
the brightness of your Holy Spirit; through Jesus Christ our
Lord. *Amen.*

Grant us, Lord, the lamp of charity which never fails, that it
may burn in us and shed its light on those around us, and
that by its brightness we may have a vision of that holy City,
where dwells the true and never-failing Light, Jesus Christ
our Lord. *Amen.*

O Lord God Almighty, as you have taught us to call the
evening, the morning, and the noonday one day; and have
made the sun to know its going down: Dispel the darkness of
our hearts, that by your brightness we may know you to be
the true God and eternal light, living and reigning for ever
and ever. *Amen.*

Lighten our darkness, we beseech thee, O Lord; and by thy great mercy defend us from all perils and dangers of this night; for the love of thy only Son, our Savior, Jesus Christ. *Amen.*

## Advent

Collect for the First Sunday of Advent

## Christmas, Epiphany, and other Feasts of the Incarnation

Collect for the First Sunday after Christmas

## Lent and other times of penitence

Almighty and most merciful God, kindle within us the fire of love, that by its cleansing flame we may be purged of all our sins and made worthy to worship you in spirit and in truth; through Jesus Christ our Lord. *Amen.*

## Easter Season

Eternal God, who led your ancient people into freedom by a pillar of cloud by day and a pillar of fire by night: Grant that we who walk in the light of your presence may rejoice in the liberty of the children of God; through Jesus Christ our Lord. *Amen.*

## Festivals of Saints

Lord Christ, your saints have been the lights of the world in every generation: Grant that we who follow in their footsteps may be made worthy to enter with them into that heavenly country where you live and reign for ever and ever. *Amen.*

*The candles at the Altar are now lighted, as are other candles and lamps as may be convenient.*

*During the candle-lighting, an appropriate anthem or psalm may be sung, or silence kept.*

*The following hymn, or a metrical version of it, or some other hymn, is then sung*

## O Gracious Light   *Phos hilaron*

O gracious Light,
pure brightness of the everliving Father in heaven,
O Jesus Christ, holy and blessed!

Now as we come to the setting of the sun,
and our eyes behold the vesper light,
we sing your praises, O God: Father, Son, and Holy Spirit.

You are worthy at all times to be praised by happy voices,
O Son of God, O Giver of life,
and to be glorified through all the worlds.

*The service may then continue in any of the following ways:*

*With Evening Prayer, beginning with the Psalms; or with some other Office or Devotion;*

*With the celebration of the Holy Eucharist, beginning with the Salutation and Collect of the Day;*

*Or, it may be followed by a meal or other activity, in which case Phos hilaron may be followed by the Lord's Prayer and a grace or blessing;*

*Or, it may continue as a complete evening Office with the following elements:*

**Selection from the Psalter.** Silence, or a suitable Collect, or both, may follow the Psalmody.

**Bible Reading.** A sermon or homily, a passage from Christian literature, or a brief silence, may follow the Reading.

**Canticle.** The Magnificat or other canticle, or some other hymn of praise.

**Prayers.** A litany, or other suitable devotions, including the Lord's Prayer.

**Blessing or Dismissal,** or both. The Peace may then be exchanged.

*On feasts or other days of special significance, the Collect of the Day, or one proper to the season, may precede the Blessing or Dismissal. On other days, either of the following, or one of the Collects from Evening Prayer or from Compline, may be so used.*

Blessed are you, O Lord, the God of our fathers, creator of the changes of day and night, giving rest to the weary, renewing the strength of those who are spent, bestowing upon us occasions of song in the evening. As you have protected us in the day that is past, so be with us in the coming night; keep us from every sin, every evil, and every fear; for you are our light and salvation, and the strength of our life. To you be glory for endless ages. *Amen.*

Almighty, everlasting God, let our prayer in your sight be as incense, the lifting up of our hands as the evening sacrifice. Give us grace to behold you, present in your Word and Sacraments, and to recognize you in the lives of those around us. Stir up in us the flame of that love which burned in the heart of your Son as he bore his passion, and let it burn in us to eternal life and to the ages of ages. *Amen.*

*A bishop or priest may use the following or some other blessing or grace*

The Lord bless you and keep you. *Amen.*
The Lord make his face to shine upon you
 and be gracious to you. *Amen.*
The Lord lift up his countenance upon you
 and give you peace. *Amen.*

*A deacon or lay person using the preceding blessing substitutes "us"
for "you."*

*A Dismissal may be used (adding "Alleluia, alleluia" in Easter Season)*

*The People respond*

Thanks be to God.

*In Easter Season the People respond*

Thanks be to God. Alleluia, alleluia.

# Daily Evening Prayer:
# Rite Two

*The Officiant begins the service with one or more of the following sentences of Scripture, or of those on pages 75-78;*

*or with the Service of Light on pages 109-112, and continuing with the appointed Psalmody;*

*or with the versicle "O God, make speed to save us" on page 117*

Let my prayer be set forth in your sight as incense, the lifting up of my hands as the evening sacrifice.   *Psalm 141:2*

Grace to you and peace from God our Father and from the Lord Jesus Christ.   *Philippians 1:2*

Worship the Lord in the beauty of holiness; let the whole earth tremble before him.   *Psalm 96:9*

Yours is the day, O God, yours also the night; you established the moon and the sun. You fixed all the boundaries of the earth; you made both summer and winter.   *Psalm 74:15,16*

I will bless the Lord who gives me counsel; my heart teaches me, night after night. I have set the Lord always before me; because he is at my right hand, I shall not fall.   *Psalm 16:7,8*

Seek him who made the Pleiades and Orion, and turns deep darkness into the morning, and darkens the day into night; who calls for the waters of the sea and pours them out upon the surface of the earth: The Lord is his name.   *Amos 5:8*

If I say, "Surely the darkness will cover me, and the light around me turn to night," darkness is not dark to you, O Lord; the night is as bright as the day; darkness and light to you are both alike. *Psalm 139:10, 11*

Jesus said, "I am the light of the world; whoever follows me will not walk in darkness, but will have the light of life." *John 8:12*

*The following Confession of Sin may then be said; or the Office may continue at once with "O God, make speed to save us."*

## Confession of Sin

*The Officiant says to the people*

Dear friends in Christ, here in the presence of Almighty God, let us kneel in silence, and with penitent and obedient hearts confess our sins, so that we may obtain forgiveness by his infinite goodness and mercy.

*or this*

Let us confess our sins against God and our neighbor.

*Silence may be kept.*

*Officiant and People together, all kneeling*

Most merciful God,
we confess that we have sinned against you
in thought, word, and deed,
by what we have done,
and by what we have left undone.
We have not loved you with our whole heart;
we have not loved our neighbors as ourselves.
We are truly sorry and we humbly repent.

For the sake of your Son Jesus Christ,
have mercy on us and forgive us;
that we may delight in your will,
and walk in your ways,
to the glory of your Name. Amen.

*The Priest alone stands and says*

Almighty God have mercy on you, forgive you all your
sins through our Lord Jesus Christ, strengthen you in all
goodness, and by the power of the Holy Spirit keep you in
eternal life. *Amen.*

*A deacon or lay person using the preceding form remains kneeling, and
substitutes "us" for "you" and "our" for "your."*


# The Invitatory and Psalter

*All stand*

Officiant   O God, make speed to save us.
People      O Lord, make haste to help us.

*Officiant and People*

Glory to the Father, and to the Son, and to the Holy Spirit: as
it was in the beginning, is now, and will be for ever. Amen.

*Except in Lent, add*   Alleluia.

*The following, or some other suitable hymn, or an Invitatory Psalm, may
be sung or said*

**O Gracious Light**  *Phos hilaron*

O gracious Light,
pure brightness of the everliving Father in heaven,
O Jesus Christ, holy and blessed!

Now as we come to the setting of the sun,
and our eyes behold the vesper light,
we sing your praises, O God: Father, Son, and Holy Spirit.

You are worthy at all times to be praised by happy voices,
O Son of God, O Giver of life,
and to be glorified through all the worlds.

*Then follows*

**The Psalm or Psalms Appointed**

*At the end of the Psalms is sung or said*

Glory to the Father, and to the Son, and to the Holy Spirit: *
    as it was in the beginning, is now, and will be for ever. Amen.

# The Lessons

*One or two Lessons, as appointed, are read, the Reader first saying*

A Reading (Lesson) from _____.

*A citation giving chapter and verse may be added.*

*After each Lesson the Reader may say*

> The Word of the Lord.
*Answer*   Thanks be to God.

*Or the Reader may say*   Here ends the Lesson (Reading).

*Silence may be kept after each Reading. One of the following Canticles, or one of those on pages 47-52, or 85-95, is sung or said after each Reading. If three Lessons are used, the Lesson from the Gospel is read after the second Canticle.*

## The Song of Mary   *Magnificat*

*Luke 1:46-55*

My soul proclaims the greatness of the Lord,
my spirit rejoices in God my Savior; *
      for he has looked with favor on his lowly servant.
From this day all generations will call me blessed: *
      the Almighty has done great things for me,
      and holy is his Name.
He has mercy on those who fear him *
      in every generation.
He has shown the strength of his arm, *
      he has scattered the proud in their conceit.
He has cast down the mighty from their thrones, *
      and has lifted up the lowly.
He has filled the hungry with good things, *
      and the rich he has sent away empty.
He has come to the help of his servant Israel, *
      for he has remembered his promise of mercy,
The promise he made to our fathers, *
      to Abraham and his children for ever.

Glory to the Father, and to the Son, and to the Holy Spirit: *
      as it was in the beginning, is now, and will be for ever. Amen.

**The Song of Simeon**  *Nunc dimittis*

*Luke 2:29-32*

Lord, you now have set your servant free *
   to go in peace as you have promised;
For these eyes of mine have seen the Savior, *
   whom you have prepared for all the world to see:
A Light to enlighten the nations, *
   and the glory of your people Israel.

Glory to the Father, and to the Son, and to the Holy Spirit: *
   as it was in the beginning, is now, and will be for ever. Amen

**The Apostles' Creed**

*Officiant and People together, all standing*

I believe in God, the Father almighty,
   creator of heaven and earth.
I believe in Jesus Christ, his only Son, our Lord.
   He was conceived by the power of the Holy Spirit
     and born of the Virgin Mary.
   He suffered under Pontius Pilate,
     was crucified, died, and was buried.
   He descended to the dead.
   On the third day he rose again.
   He ascended into heaven,
     and is seated at the right hand of the Father.
   He will come again to judge the living and the dead.
I believe in the Holy Spirit,
   the holy catholic Church,
   the communion of saints,
   the forgiveness of sins,
   the resurrection of the body,
   and the life everlasting. Amen.

# The Prayers

*The people stand or kneel*

Officiant   The Lord be with you.
People      And also with you.
Officiant   Let us pray.

*Officiant and People*

| | |
|---|---|
| Our Father, who art in heaven,<br>  hallowed be thy Name,<br>  thy kingdom come,<br>  thy will be done,<br>    on earth as it is in heaven.<br>Give us this day our daily bread.<br>And forgive us our trespasses,<br>  as we forgive those<br>    who trespass against us.<br>And lead us not into temptation,<br>  but deliver us from evil.<br>For thine is the kingdom,<br>  and the power, and the glory,<br>  for ever and ever. Amen. | Our Father in heaven,<br>  hallowed be your Name,<br>  your kingdom come,<br>  your will be done,<br>    on earth as in heaven.<br>Give us today our daily bread.<br>Forgive us our sins<br>  as we forgive those<br>    who sin against us.<br>Save us from the time of trial,<br>  and deliver us from evil.<br>For the kingdom, the power,<br>  and the glory are yours,<br>  now and for ever. Amen. |

*Then follows one of these sets of Suffrages*

## A

V.   Show us your mercy, O Lord;
R.   And grant us your salvation.
V.   Clothe your ministers with righteousness;
R.   Let your people sing with joy.
V.   Give peace, O Lord, in all the world;
R.   For only in you can we live in safety.

| V. | Lord, keep this nation under your care; |
|----|----------------------------------------|
| R. | And guide us in the way of justice and truth. |
| V. | Let your way be known upon earth; |
| R. | Your saving health among all nations. |
| V. | Let not the needy, O Lord, be forgotten; |
| R. | Nor the hope of the poor be taken away. |
| V. | Create in us clean hearts, O God; |
| R. | And sustain us with your Holy Spirit. |

### B

That this evening may be holy, good, and peaceful,
*We entreat you, O Lord.*

That your holy angels may lead us in paths of peace and
goodwill,
*We entreat you, O Lord.*

That we may be pardoned and forgiven for our sins
and offenses,
*We entreat you, O Lord.*

That there may be peace to your Church and to the whole
world,
*We entreat you, O Lord.*

That we may depart this life in your faith and fear,
and not be condemned before the great judgment seat
of Christ,
*We entreat you, O Lord.*

That we may be bound together by your Holy Spirit in
the communion of [ _____ and] all your saints,
entrusting one another and all our life to Christ,
*We entreat you, O Lord.*

*The Officiant then says one or more of the following Collects*

*The Collect of the Day*

*A Collect for Sundays*

Lord God, whose Son our Savior Jesus Christ triumphed over the powers of death and prepared for us our place in the new Jerusalem: Grant that we, who have this day given thanks for his resurrection, may praise you in that City of which he is the light, and where he lives and reigns for ever and ever. *Amen.*

*A Collect for Fridays*

Lord Jesus Christ, by your death you took away the sting of death: Grant to us your servants so to follow in faith where you have led the way, that we may at length fall asleep peacefully in you and wake up in your likeness; for your tender mercies' sake. *Amen.*

*A Collect for Saturdays*

O God, the source of eternal light: Shed forth your unending day upon us who watch for you, that our lips may praise you, our lives may bless you, and our worship on the morrow give you glory; through Jesus Christ our Lord. *Amen.*

*A Collect for Peace*

Most holy God, the source of all good desires, all right judgments, and all just works: Give to us, your servants, that peace which the world cannot give, so that our minds may be fixed on the doing of your will, and that we, being delivered from the fear of all enemies, may live in peace and quietness; through the mercies of Christ Jesus our Savior. *Amen.*

*A Collect for Aid against Perils*

Be our light in the darkness, O Lord, and in your great mercy defend us from all perils and dangers of this night; for the love of your only Son, our Savior Jesus Christ. *Amen.*

*A Collect for Protection*

O God, the life of all who live, the light of the faithful, the
strength of those who labor, and the repose of the dead: We
thank you for the blessings of the day that is past, and
humbly ask for your protection through the coming night.
Bring us in safety to the morning hours; through him who
died and rose again for us, your Son our Savior Jesus Christ.
*Amen.*

*A Collect for the Presence of Christ*

Lord Jesus, stay with us, for evening is at hand and the day
is past; be our companion in the way, kindle our hearts, and
awaken hope, that we may know you as you are revealed in
Scripture and the breaking of bread. Grant this for the sake
of your love. *Amen.*

*Then, unless the Eucharist or a form of general intercession is to follow,
one of these prayers for mission is added*

O God and Father of all, whom the whole heavens adore:
Let the whole earth also worship you, all nations obey you,
all tongues confess and bless you, and men and women
everywhere love you and serve you in peace; through Jesus
Christ our Lord. *Amen.*

*or this*

Keep watch, dear Lord, with those who work, or watch, or
weep this night, and give your angels charge over those who
sleep. Tend the sick, Lord Christ; give rest to the weary, bless
the dying, soothe the suffering, pity the afflicted, shield the
joyous; and all for your love's sake. *Amen.*

*or the following*

O God, you manifest in your servants the signs of your
presence: Send forth upon us the Spirit of love, that in
companionship with one another your abounding grace may
increase among us; through Jesus Christ our Lord. *Amen.*

*Here may be sung a hymn or anthem.*

*Authorized intercessions and thanksgivings may follow.*

*Before the close of the Office one or both of the following may be used*

## The General Thanksgiving

*Officiant and People*

Almighty God, Father of all mercies,
we your unworthy servants give you humble thanks
for all your goodness and loving-kindness
to us and to all whom you have made.
We bless you for our creation, preservation,
and all the blessings of this life;
but above all for your immeasurable love
in the redemption of the world by our Lord Jesus Christ;
for the means of grace, and for the hope of glory.
And, we pray, give us such an awareness of your mercies,
that with truly thankful hearts we may show forth your praise,
not only with our lips, but in our lives,
by giving up our selves to your service,
and by walking before you
in holiness and righteousness all our days;
through Jesus Christ our Lord,
to whom, with you and the Holy Spirit,
be honor and glory throughout all ages. Amen.

## A Prayer of St. Chrysostom

Almighty God, you have given us grace at this time with one
accord to make our common supplication to you; and you
have promised through your well-beloved Son that when two
or three are gathered together in his Name you will be in the
midst of them: Fulfill now, O Lord, our desires and petitions
as may be best for us; granting us in this world knowledge of
your truth, and in the age to come life everlasting. *Amen.*

*Then may be said*

Let us bless the Lord.
*Thanks be to God.*

*From Easter Day through the Day of Pentecost "Alleluia, alleluia" may
be added to the preceding versicle and response.*

*The Officiant may then conclude with one of the following*

The grace of our Lord Jesus Christ, and the love of God, and
the fellowship of the Holy Spirit, be with us all evermore.
*Amen.*    *2 Corinthians 13:14*

May the God of hope fill us with all joy and peace in
believing through the power of the Holy Spirit. *Amen.*
*Romans 15:13*

Glory to God whose power, working in us, can do infinitely
more than we can ask or imagine: Glory to him from
generation to generation in the Church, and in Christ Jesus
for ever and ever. *Amen.*    *Ephesians 3:20,21*

# An Order for Compline

The Officiant begins

The Lord Almighty grant us a peaceful night and a perfect
end. *Amen.*

Officiant    Our help is in the Name of the Lord;
People       The maker of heaven and earth.

*The Officiant may then say*

Let us confess our sins to God.

*Silence may be kept.*

*Officiant and People*

Almighty God, our heavenly Father:
We have sinned against you,
through our own fault,
in thought, and word, and deed,
and in what we have left undone.
For the sake of your Son our Lord Jesus Christ,
forgive us all our offenses;
and grant that we may serve you
in newness of life,
to the glory of your Name. Amen.

*Officiant*

May the Almighty God grant us forgiveness of all our sins, and the grace and comfort of the Holy Spirit. *Amen.*

*The Officiant then says*

O God, make speed to save us.
*People*  O Lord, make haste to help us.

*Officiant and People*

Glory to the Father, and to the Son, and to the Holy Spirit: it was in the beginning, is now, and will be for ever. Amen.

*Except in Lent, add*  Alleluia.

*One or more of the following Psalms are sung or said. Other suitable selections may be substituted.*

## Psalm 4  *Cum invocarem*

1  Answer me when I call, O God, defender of my cause; *
     you set me free when I am hard-pressed;
     have mercy on me and hear my prayer.

2  "You mortals, how long will you dishonor my glory? *
     how long will you worship dumb idols
     and run after false gods?"

3  Know that the LORD does wonders for the faithful; *
     when I call upon the LORD, he will hear me.

4  Tremble, then, and do not sin; *
     speak to your heart in silence upon your bed.

5  Offer the appointed sacrifices *
     and put your trust in the LORD.

6 Many are saying,
   "Oh, that we might see better times!" *
      Lift up the light of your countenance upon us, O LORD.

7 You have put gladness in my heart, *
      more than when grain and wine and oil increase.

8 I lie down in peace; at once I fall asleep; *
      for only you, LORD, make me dwell in safety.


**Psalm 31** *In te, Domine, speravi*

1 In you, O LORD, have I taken refuge;
   let me never be put to shame: *
      deliver me in your righteousness.

2 Incline your ear to me; *
      make haste to deliver me.

3 Be my strong rock, a castle to keep me safe,
   for you are my crag and my stronghold; *
      for the sake of your Name, lead me and guide me.

4 Take me out of the net that they have secretly set for me, *
      for you are my tower of strength.

5 Into your hands I commend my spirit, *
      for you have redeemed me,
      O LORD, O God of truth.


**Psalm 91** *Qui habitat*

1 He who dwells in the shelter of the Most High *
      abides under the shadow of the Almighty.

2 He shall say to the LORD ,
   "You are my refuge and my stronghold, *
      my God in whom I put my trust."

3 He shall deliver you from the snare of the hunter *
    and from the deadly pestilence.

4 He shall cover you with his pinions,
    and you shall find refuge under his wings; *
      his faithfulness shall be a shield and buckler.

5 You shall not be afraid of any terror by night, *
    nor of the arrow that flies by day;

6 Of the plague that stalks in the darkness, *
    nor of the sickness that lays waste at mid-day.

7 A thousand shall fall at your side
    and ten thousand at your right hand, *
      but it shall not come near you.

8 Your eyes have only to behold *
    to see the reward of the wicked.

9 Because you have made the LORD your refuge, *
    and the Most High your habitation,

10 There shall no evil happen to you, *
    neither shall any plague come near your dwelling.

11 For he shall give his angels charge over you, *
    to keep you in all your ways.

12 They shall bear you in their hands, *
    lest you dash your foot against a stone.

13 You shall tread upon the lion and adder; *
    you shall trample the young lion and the serpent
      under your feet.

14 Because he is bound to me in love,
    therefore will I deliver him; *
      I will protect him, because he knows my Name.

He shall call upon me, and I will answer him; *
  I am with him in trouble;
  I will rescue him and bring him to honor.

With long life will I satisfy him, *
  and show him my salvation.


**Psalm 134**  *Ecce nunc*

Behold now, bless the LORD, all you servants of the LORD, *
  you that stand by night in the house of the LORD.

Lift up your hands in the holy place and bless the LORD; *
  the LORD who made heaven and earth bless you out of Zion.

*At the end of the Psalms is sung or said*

Glory to the Father, and to the Son, and to the Holy Spirit: *
  as it was in the beginning, is now, and will be for ever. Amen.

*One of the following, or some other suitable passage of Scripture, is read*

Lord, you are in the midst of us, and we are called by your
Name: Do not forsake us, O Lord our God.  *Jeremiah 14:9, 22*

*People*     Thanks be to God.

*or this*

Come to me, all who labor and are heavy-laden, and I will
give you rest. Take my yoke upon you, and learn from me;
for I am gentle and lowly in heart, and you will find rest for
your souls. For my yoke is easy, and my burden is light.
*Matthew 11:28-30*

*People*     Thanks be to God.

*or the following*

May the God of peace, who brought again from the dead our Lord Jesus, the great shepherd of the sheep, by the blood of the eternal covenant, equip you with everything good that yo may do his will, working in you that which is pleasing in his sight; through Jesus Christ, to whom be glory for ever and ever.  *Hebrews 13:20-21*

*People*    Thanks be to God.

*or this*

Be sober, be watchful. Your adversary the devil prowls around like a roaring lion, seeking someone to devour. Resist him, firm in your faith.   *1 Peter 5:8-9a*

*People*    Thanks be to God.

*A hymn suitable for the evening may be sung.*


*Then follows*

V.    Into your hands, O Lord, I commend my spirit;
R.    For you have redeemed me, O Lord, O God of truth.
V.    Keep us, O Lord, as the apple of your eye;
R.    Hide us under the shadow of your wings.

Lord, have mercy.
*Christ, have mercy.*
Lord, have mercy.

*Officiant and People*

| | |
|---|---|
| Our Father, who art in heaven,<br>    hallowed be thy Name,<br>    thy kingdom come,<br>    thy will be done,<br>        on earth as it is in heaven. | Our Father in heaven,<br>    hallowed be your Name,<br>    your kingdom come,<br>    your will be done,<br>        on earth as in heaven. |

Give us this day our daily bread.
And forgive us our trespasses,
   as we forgive those
     who trespass against us.
And lead us not into temptation,
   but deliver us from evil.

Give us today our daily bread.
Forgive us our sins
   as we forgive those
     who sin against us.
Save us from the time of trial,
   and deliver us from evil.

*Officiant*   Lord, hear our prayer;
*People*     And let our cry come to you.
*Officiant*   Let us pray.

*The Officiant then says one of the following Collects*

Be our light in the darkness, O Lord, and in your great mercy
defend us from all perils and dangers of this night; for the
love of your only Son, our Savior Jesus Christ. *Amen.*

Be present, O merciful God, and protect us through the hours
of this night, so that we who are wearied by the changes and
chances of this life may rest in your eternal changelessness;
through Jesus Christ our Lord. *Amen.*

Look down, O Lord, from your heavenly throne, and
illumine this night with your celestial brightness; that by
night as by day your people may glorify your holy Name;
through Jesus Christ our Lord. *Amen.*

Visit this place, O Lord, and drive far from it all snares of the
enemy; let your holy angels dwell with us to preserve us in
peace; and let your blessing be upon us always; through Jesus
Christ our Lord. *Amen.*

## A Collect for Saturdays

We give you thanks, O God, for revealing your Son Jesus
Christ to us by the light of his resurrection: Grant that as we
sing your glory at the close of this day, our joy may abound
in the morning as we celebrate the Paschal mystery; through
Jesus Christ our Lord. *Amen.*

*One of the following prayers may be added*

Keep watch, dear Lord, with those who work, or watch, or
weep this night, and give your angels charge over those who
sleep. Tend the sick, Lord Christ; give rest to the weary, bless
the dying, soothe the suffering, pity the afflicted, shield the
joyous; and all for your love's sake. *Amen.*

*or this*

O God, your unfailing providence sustains the world we live
in and the life we live: Watch over those, both night and day,
who work while others sleep, and grant that we may never
forget that our common life depends upon each other's toil;
through Jesus Christ our Lord. *Amen.*

*Silence may be kept, and free intercessions and thanksgivings may be
offered.*

*The service concludes with the Song of Simeon with this Antiphon, which
is sung or said by all*

Guide us waking, O Lord, and guard us sleeping; that awake
we may watch with Christ, and asleep we may rest in peace.

*In Easter Season, add*    Alleluia, alleluia, alleluia.

Lord, you now have set your servant free *
    to go in peace as you have promised;

For these eyes of mine have seen the Savior, *
    whom you have prepared for all the world to see:

A Light to enlighten the nations, *
    and the glory of your people Israel.

Glory to the Father, and to the Son, and to the Holy Spirit: *
    as it was in the beginning, is now, and will be for ever. Amen.

*All repeat the Antiphon*

Guide us waking, O Lord, and guard us sleeping; that awake
we may watch with Christ, and asleep we may rest in peace.

*In Easter Season, add*    Alleluia, alleluia, alleluia.

*Officiant*   Let us bless the Lord.
*People*      Thanks be to God.

*The Officiant concludes*

The almighty and merciful Lord, Father, Son, and Holy Spirit,
bless us and keep us. *Amen.*

# Daily Devotions for Individuals and Families

These devotions follow the basic structure of the Daily Office of the Church.

When more than one person is present, the Reading and the Collect should be read by one person, and the other parts said in unison, or in some other convenient manner. (For suggestions about reading the Psalms, see page 582.)

For convenience, appropriate Psalms, Readings, and Collects are provided in each service. When desired, however, the Collect of the Day, or any of the Collects appointed in the Daily Offices, may be used instead.

The Psalms and Readings may be replaced by those appointed in

a) the Lectionary for Sundays, Holy Days, the Common of Saints, and Various Occasions, page 888

b) the Daily Office Lectionary, page 934

c) some other manual of devotion which provides daily selections for the Church Year.

## In the Morning

*From Psalm 51*

Open my lips, O Lord, *
   and my mouth shall proclaim your praise.
Create in me a clean heart, O God, *
   and renew a right spirit within me.
Cast me not away from your presence *
   and take not your holy Spirit from me.
Give me the joy of your saving help again *
   and sustain me with your bountiful Spirit.
Glory to the Father, and to the Son, and to the Holy Spirit: *
   as it was in the beginning, is now, and will be for ever. Amen.

*A Reading*

Blessed be the God and Father of our Lord Jesus Christ!
By his great mercy we have been born anew to a living hope
through the resurrection of Jesus Christ from the dead.
   *Peter 1:3*

*A period of silence may follow.*

*A hymn or canticle may be used; the Apostles' Creed may be said.*

*Prayers may be offered for ourselves and others.*

*The Lord's Prayer*

*The Collect*

Lord God, almighty and everlasting Father, you have brought
us in safety to this new day: Preserve us with your mighty
power, that we may not fall into sin, nor be overcome by
adversity; and in all we do, direct us to the fulfilling of your
purpose; through Jesus Christ our Lord. *Amen.*

**At Noon**

*From Psalm 113*

Give praise, you servants of the LORD; *
    praise the Name of the LORD.
Let the Name of the LORD be blessed, *
    from this time forth for evermore.
From the rising of the sun to its going down *
    let the Name of the LORD be praised.
The LORD is high above all nations, *
    and his glory above the heavens.

*A Reading*

O God, you will keep in perfect peace those whose minds are
fixed on you; for in returning and rest we shall be saved; in
quietness and trust shall be our strength.   *Isaiah 26:3; 30:15*

*Prayers may be offered for ourselves and others.*

*The Lord's Prayer*

*The Collect*

Blessed Savior, at this hour you hung upon the cross,
stretching out your loving arms: Grant that all the peoples of
the earth may look to you and be saved; for your mercies'
sake. *Amen.*

*or this*

Lord Jesus Christ, you said to your apostles, "Peace I give to
you; my own peace I leave with you:" Regard not our sins,
but the faith of your Church, and give to us the peace and
unity of that heavenly City, where with the Father and the
Holy Spirit you live and reign, now and for ever. *Amen.*

# In the Early Evening

*This devotion may be used before or after the evening meal.*

*The Order of Worship for the Evening, page 109, may be used instead.*

O gracious Light,
pure brightness of the everliving Father in heaven,
O Jesus Christ, holy and blessed!

Now as we come to the setting of the sun,
and our eyes behold the vesper light,
we sing your praises O God: Father, Son, and Holy Spirit.

You are worthy at all times to be praised by happy voices,
O Son of God, O Giver of life,
and to be glorified through all the worlds.

## A Reading

It is not ourselves that we proclaim; we proclaim Christ
Jesus as Lord, and ourselves as your servants, for Jesus' sake.
For the same God who said, "Out of darkness let light
shine," has caused his light to shine within us, to give the
light of revelation—the revelation of the glory of God in the
face of Jesus Christ.   *2 Corinthians 4:5-6*

*Prayers may be offered for ourselves and others.*

## The Lord's Prayer

## The Collect

Lord Jesus, stay with us, for evening is at hand and the day is
past; be our companion in the way, kindle our hearts, and
awaken hope, that we may know you as you are revealed in
Scripture and the breaking of bread. Grant this for the sake
of your love. *Amen.*

## At the Close of Day

*Psalm 134*

Behold now, bless the LORD, all you servants of the LORD, *
    you that stand by night in the house of the LORD.
Lift up your hands in the holy place and bless the LORD; *
    the LORD who made heaven and earth bless you out of Zion

*A Reading*

Lord, you are in the midst of us and we are called by your
Name: Do not forsake us, O Lord our God.   *Jeremiah 14:9,22*

*The following may be said*

Lord, you now have set your servant free *
    to go in peace as you have promised;
For these eyes of mine have seen the Savior, *
    whom you have prepared for all the world to see:
A Light to enlighten the nations, *
    and the glory of your people Israel.

*Prayers for ourselves and others may follow. It is appropriate that
prayers of thanksgiving for the blessings of the day, and penitence for our
sins, be included.*

*The Lord's Prayer*

*The Collect*

Visit this place, O Lord, and drive far from it all snares of the
enemy; let your holy angels dwell with us to preserve us in
peace; and let your blessing be upon us always; through Jesus
Christ our Lord. *Amen.*

The almighty and merciful Lord, Father, Son, and Holy Spirit
bless us and keep us. *Amen.*

# Additional Directions

## Morning and Evening Prayer

Any of the opening sentences of Scripture, including those listed for
specific seasons or days, may be used at any time according to the
discretion of the officiant.

The proper antiphons on pages 43-44 and 80-82 may be used as refrains
with either of the Invitatory Psalms.

Antiphons drawn from the Psalms themselves, or from the opening
sentences given in the Offices, or from other passages of Scripture may be
used with the Psalms and biblical Canticles.

Gloria Patri is always sung or said at the conclusion of the entire portion
of the Psalter; and may be used after the Invitatory Psalm or the Canticle
"Christ our Passover," after each Psalm, and after each section of Psalm 119.

The Gloria printed at the conclusion of certain Canticles may be omitted
when desired.

The following pointing of the Gloria may be used:

Glory to the Father, and to the Son, *
    and to the Holy Spirit:

As it was in the beginning, is now, *
    and will be for ever. Amen.

In Rite One services of Morning Prayer and Evening Prayer, the following
form of the Gloria may be used:

Glory be to the Father, and to the Son, *
    and to the Holy Ghost:

As it was in the beginning, is now, and ever shall be, *
    world without end. Amen.

Metrical versions of the Invitatory Psalms, and of the Canticles after the
Readings, may be used.

In special circumstances, in place of a Canticle, a hymn may be sung.

The Apostles' Creed is omitted from the Office when the Eucharist with its own Creed is to follow. It may also be omitted at one of the Offices on weekdays.

The Lord's Prayer may be omitted from the Office when the Litany or the Eucharist is to follow immediately.

In the Intercessions and Thanksgivings, opportunity may be given for the members of the congregation to express intentions or objects of prayer and thanksgiving, either at the bidding, or in the course of the prayer; and opportunity may be given for silent prayer.

A sermon may be preached after the Office; or, within the Office, after the Readings or at the time of the hymn or anthem after the Collects.

On occasion, at the discretion of the Minister, a reading from non-biblical Christian literature may follow the biblical Readings.

An offering may be received and presented at the Office.


## When there is a Communion

When Morning or Evening Prayer is used as the Liturgy of the Word at the Eucharist, the Nicene Creed may take the place of the Apostles' Creed, and the officiant may pass at once from the salutation "The Lord be with you," and its response, to the Collect of the Day. A Lesson from the Gospel is always included.

The Intercessions on such occasions are to conform to the directions on page 383.

The service then continues with the [Peace and] Offertory.


## Order of Worship for the Evening

Before this service, there should be as little artificial light as possible in the church. A musical prelude or processional is not appropriate.

When the ministers enter, one or two lighted candles may be carried before them, and used to provide light for reading the opening Short Lesson and the Prayer for Light. From Easter Day through the Day of Pentecost, the Paschal Candle, if used, should be burning in its customary place before the people assemble; the officiant then goes to a place close by it to begin the service by its light.

The Short Lessons may be read from any version of the Scriptures authorized for public worship in this Church, and should be read without announcement or conclusion. When one or more Scripture Lessons are to be read later in the service, the Short Lesson may be omitted.

For the lighting of the candles at the Altar and elsewhere, in Easter Season the flame may be taken from the Paschal Candle. At other times, the candle or candles carried in at the beginning of the service may be placed on or near the Altar, and other candles may be lighted from them. During Advent, the lighting of an Advent Wreath may take place after the Prayer for Light. On special occasions, lighted candles may be distributed to members of the congregation.

When this service is used in private houses, candles may be lighted at the dining table, or at some other convenient place.

If incense is to be used, it is appropriate after the candles have been lighted and while the hymn Phos hilaron is being sung.

When this service continues as a complete Office, Psalms and Lessons from the Office Lectionary or the Proper of the Day, or ones suitable to the season or the occasion, may be used. Psalms generally appropriate to the evening include: 8, 23, 27, 36, 84, 93, 113, 114, 117, 121, 134, 139, 141, 143. When desired, more than one Lesson may be read, with silence or singing between them.

If an additional hymn is desired, it may be sung immediately before the Blessing or Dismissal.

When a meal is to follow, a blessing over food may serve as the conclusion of this form of service.

## Suggested Canticles at Morning Prayer

|  | After the Old Testament Reading | After the New Testament Reading |
|---|---|---|
| **Sun.** | 4. or 16. Benedictus Dominus | 7. or 21. Te Deum laudamus |
|  | *Advent:* | *Advent and Lent:* |
|  | 11. Surge, illuminare | 4. or 16. Benedictus Domini |
|  | *Lent:* | |
|  | 14. Kyrie Pantokrator | |
|  | *Easter:* | |
|  | 8. Cantemus Domino | |
| **Mon.** | 9. Ecce, Deus | 19. Magna et mirabilia |
| **Tue.** | 2. or 13. Benedictus es | 18. Dignus es |
| **Wed.** | 11. Surge, illuminare | 4. or 16. Benedictus Domini |
|  | *Lent:* | |
|  | 14. Kyrie Pantokrator | |
| **Thu.** | 8. Cantemus Domino | 6. or 20. Gloria in excelsis |
|  | | *Advent and Lent:* |
|  | | 19. Magna et mirabilia |
| **Fri.** | 10. Quærite Dominum | 18. Dignus es |
|  | *Lent:* | |
|  | 14. Kyrie Pantokrator | |
| **Sat.** | 1. or 12. Benedicite | 19. Magna et mirabilia |

*On Feasts of our Lord and other Major Feasts*

4. or 16. Benedictus Dominus   7. or 21. Te Deum laudamus

## Suggested Canticles at Evening Prayer

|  | *After the Old Testament Reading* | *After the New Testament Reading* |
|---|---|---|
| **Sun.** | Magnificat | Nunc dimittis* |
| **Mon.** | 8. Cantemus Domino<br>*Lent:*<br>14. Kyrie Pantokrator | Nunc dimittis |
| **Tue.** | 10. Quærite Dominum | Magnificat |
| **Wed.** | 1. or 12. Benedicite | Nunc dimittis |
| **Thu.** | 11. Surge, illuminare | Magnificat |
| **Fri.** | 2. or 13. Benedictus es | Nunc dimittis |
| **Sat.** | 9. Ecce, Deus | Magnificat |

*On Feasts of our Lord and other Major Feasts*

|  | Magnificat | Nunc dimittis* |
|---|---|---|

*If only one Reading is used, the suggested Canticle is the Magnificat.*

## Psalm 95: Traditional     *Venite, exultemus*

O come, let us sing unto the Lord; *
  let us heartily rejoice in the strength of our salvation.
Let us come before his presence with thanksgiving, *
  and show ourselves glad in him with psalms.

For the Lord is a great God, *
  and a great King above all gods.
In his hand are all the corners of the earth, *
  and the strength of the hills is his also.
The sea is his and he made it, *
  and his hands prepared the dry land.

O come, let us worship and fall down *
  and kneel before the Lord our Maker.
For he is the Lord our God, *
  and we are the people of his pasture
  and the sheep of his hand.

Today if ye will hear his voice, harden not your hearts*
  as in the provocation,
  and as in the day of temptation in the wilderness;
When your fathers tempted me, *
  proved me, and saw my works.

Forty years long was I grieved with this generation, and said, *
  It is a people that do err in their hearts,
  for they have not known my ways;
Unto whom I sware in my wrath, *
  that they should not enter into my rest.

# The Great Litany

# The Great Litany

*To be said or sung, kneeling, standing, or in procession; before the Eucharist or after the Collects of Morning or Evening Prayer; or separately; especially in Lent and on Rogation days.*

O God the Father, Creator of heaven and earth,
*Have mercy upon us.*

O God the Son, Redeemer of the world,
*Have mercy upon us.*

O God the Holy Ghost, Sanctifier of the faithful,
*Have mercy upon us.*

O holy, blessed, and glorious Trinity, one God,
*Have mercy upon us.*

Remember not, Lord Christ, our offenses, nor the offenses of our forefathers; neither reward us according to our sins. Spare us, good Lord, spare thy people, whom thou hast redeemed with thy most precious blood, and by thy mercy preserve us for ever.
*Spare us, good Lord.*

From all evil and wickedness; from sin; from the crafts and assaults of the devil; and from everlasting damnation,
*Good Lord, deliver us.*

From all blindness of heart; from pride, vainglory, and hypocrisy; from envy, hatred, and malice; and from all want of charity,
*Good Lord, deliver us.*

From all inordinate and sinful affections; and from all the deceits of the world, the flesh, and the devil,
*Good Lord, deliver us.*

From all false doctrine, heresy, and schism; from hardness of heart, and contempt of thy Word and commandment,
*Good Lord, deliver us.*

From lightning and tempest; from earthquake, fire, and flood; from plague, pestilence, and famine,
*Good Lord, deliver us.*

From all oppression, conspiracy, and rebellion; from violence, battle, and murder; and from dying suddenly and unprepared,
*Good Lord, deliver us.*

By the mystery of thy holy Incarnation; by thy holy Nativity and submission to the Law; by thy Baptism, Fasting, and Temptation,
*Good Lord, deliver us.*

By thine Agony and Bloody Sweat; by thy Cross and Passion; by thy precious Death and Burial; by thy glorious Resurrection and Ascension; and by the Coming of the Holy Ghost,
*Good Lord, deliver us.*

In all time of our tribulation; in all time of our prosperity; in the hour of death, and in the day of judgment,
*Good Lord, deliver us.*

We sinners do beseech thee to hear us, O Lord God; and that it may please thee to rule and govern thy holy Church Universal in the right way,
*We beseech thee to hear us, good Lord.*

That it may please thee to illumine all bishops, priests, and deacons, with true knowledge and understanding of thy Word; and that both by their preaching and living, they may set it forth, and show it accordingly,
*We beseech thee to hear us, good Lord.*

That it may please thee to bless and keep all thy people,
*We beseech thee to hear us, good Lord.*

That it may please thee to send forth laborers into thy harvest, and to draw all mankind into thy kingdom,
*We beseech thee to hear us, good Lord.*

That it may please thee to give to all people increase of grace to hear and receive thy Word, and to bring forth the fruits of the Spirit,
*We beseech thee to hear us, good Lord.*

That it may please thee to bring into the way of truth all such as have erred, and are deceived,
*We beseech thee to hear us, good Lord.*

That it may please thee to give us a heart to love and fear thee, and diligently to live after thy commandments,
*We beseech thee to hear us, good Lord.*

That it may please thee so to rule the hearts of thy servants, the President of the United States (*or* of this nation), and all others in authority, that they may do justice, and love mercy, and walk in the ways of truth,
*We beseech thee to hear us, good Lord.*

That it may please thee to make wars to cease in all the world; to give to all nations unity, peace, and concord; and to bestow freedom upon all peoples,
*We beseech thee to hear us, good Lord.*

That it may please thee to show thy pity upon all prisoners and captives, the homeless and the hungry, and all who are desolate and oppressed,
*We beseech thee to hear us, good Lord.*

That it may please thee to give and preserve to our use the bountiful fruits of the earth, so that in due time all may enjoy them,
*We beseech thee to hear us, good Lord.*

That it may please thee to inspire us, in our several callings, to do the work which thou givest us to do with singleness of heart as thy servants, and for the common good,
*We beseech thee to hear us, good Lord.*

That it may please thee to preserve all who are in danger by reason of their labor or their travel,
*We beseech thee to hear us, good Lord.*

That it may please thee to preserve, and provide for, all women in childbirth, young children and orphans, the widowed, and all whose homes are broken or torn by strife,
*We beseech thee to hear us, good Lord.*

That it may please thee to visit the lonely; to strengthen all who suffer in mind, body, and spirit; and to comfort with thy presence those who are failing and infirm,
*We beseech thee to hear us, good Lord.*

That it may please thee to support, help, and comfort all who are in danger, necessity, and tribulation,
*We beseech thee to hear us, good Lord.*

That it may please thee to have mercy upon all mankind,
*We beseech thee to hear us, good Lord.*

That it may please thee to give us true repentance; to forgive us all our sins, negligences, and ignorances; and to endue us with the grace of thy Holy Spirit to amend our lives according to thy holy Word,
*We beseech thee to hear us, good Lord.*

That it may please thee to forgive our enemies, persecutors, and slanderers, and to turn their hearts,
*We beseech thee to hear us, good Lord.*

That it may please thee to strengthen such as do stand; to comfort and help the weak-hearted; to raise up those who fall; and finally to beat down Satan under our feet,
*We beseech thee to hear us, good Lord.*

That it may please thee to grant to all the faithful departed eternal life and peace,
*We beseech thee to hear us, good Lord.*

That it may please thee to grant that, in the fellowship of [_____ and] all the saints, we may attain to thy heavenly kingdom,
*We beseech thee to hear us, good Lord.*


Son of God, we beseech thee to hear us.
*Son of God, we beseech thee to hear us.*


O Lamb of God, that takest away the sins of the world,
*Have mercy upon us.*

O Lamb of God, that takest away the sins of the world,
*Have mercy upon us.*

O Lamb of God, that takest away the sins of the world,
*Grant us thy peace.*

O Christ, hear us.
*O Christ, hear us.*

Lord, have mercy upon us.                Kyrie eleison.
*Christ, have mercy upon us.*   *or*   *Christe eleison.*
Lord, have mercy upon us.                Kyrie eleison.

*When the Litany is sung or said immediately before the Eucharist, the
Litany concludes here, and the Eucharist begins with the Salutation and
the Collect of the Day.*

*On all other occasions, the Officiant and People say together*

Our Father, who art in heaven,
    hallowed be thy Name,
    thy kingdom come,
    thy will be done,
        on earth as it is in heaven.
Give us this day our daily bread.
And forgive us our trespasses,
    as we forgive those who trespass against us.
And lead us not into temptation,
    but deliver us from evil. Amen.

V.    O Lord, let thy mercy be showed upon us;
R.    As we do put our trust in thee.

*The Officiant concludes with the following or some other Collect*

Let us pray.

Almighty God, who hast promised to hear the petitions of
those who ask in thy Son's Name: We beseech thee mercifully
to incline thine ear to us who have now made our prayers
and supplications unto thee; and grant that those things
which we have asked faithfully according to thy will, may be
obtained effectually, to the relief of our necessity, and to the
setting forth of thy glory; through Jesus Christ our Lord.
Amen.

*The Officiant may add other Prayers, and end the Litany, saying*

The grace of our Lord Jesus Christ, and the love of God, and the fellowship of the Holy Ghost, be with us all evermore. *Amen.*


# The Supplication

*For use in the Litany in place of the Versicle and Collect which follows the Lord's Prayer; or at the end of Morning or Evening Prayer; or as a separate devotion; especially in times of war, or of national anxiety, or of disaster.*

O Lord, arise, help us;
*And deliver us for thy Name's sake.*

O God, we have heard with our ears, and our fathers have declared unto us, the noble works that thou didst in their days, and in the old time before them.

*O Lord, arise, help us;*
*and deliver us for thy Name's sake.*

Glory be to the Father, and to the Son, and to the Holy Ghost; as it was in the beginning, is now, and ever shall be, world without end. Amen.

*O Lord, arise, help us;*
*and deliver us for thy Name's sake.*

V.   From our enemies defend us, O Christ;
R.   Graciously behold our afflictions.
V.   With pity behold the sorrows of our hearts;
R.   Mercifully forgive the sins of thy people.

V.  Favorably with mercy hear our prayers;
R.  O Son of David, have mercy upon us.
V.  Both now and ever vouchsafe to hear us, O Christ;
R.  Graciously hear us, O Christ; graciously hear us, O Lord
    Christ.

*The Officiant concludes*

Let us pray.

We humbly beseech thee, O Father, mercifully to look upon
our infirmities; and, for the glory of thy Name, turn from us
all those evils that we most justly have deserved; and grant
that in all our troubles we may put our whole trust and
confidence in thy mercy, and evermore serve thee in holiness
and pureness of living, to thy honor and glory; through our
only Mediator and Advocate, Jesus Christ our Lord. *Amen.*

# The Collects
for the
Church Year

# Concerning the Proper
## of the Church Year

The Proper of the Church Year includes the appointed Collects; the Proper Prefaces, directions for which are to be found in the pages following; and the appointed Psalms and Lessons, which appear in tables beginning on page 889.

The Proper appointed for the Sunday is also used at celebrations of the Eucharist on the weekdays following, unless otherwise ordered for Holy Days and Various Occasions.

The Proper to be used on each of the Sundays after Pentecost (except for Trinity Sunday) is determined by the calendar date of that Sunday. Thus, in any year, the Proper for the Sunday after Trinity Sunday (the Second Sunday after Pentecost) is the numbered Proper (number 3 through number 8), the calendar date of which falls on that Sunday, or is closest to it, whether before or after. Thereafter, the Propers are used consecutively. For example, if the Sunday after Trinity Sunday is May 26, the sequence begins with Proper 3 (Propers 1 and 2 being used on the weekdays of Pentecost and Trinity weeks). If the Sunday after Trinity Sunday is June 13, the sequence begins with Proper 6 (Propers 1 through 3 being omitted that year, and Propers 4 and 5 being used in Pentecost and Trinity weeks). See also the Table on pages 884-885.

The Collect appointed for any Sunday or other Feast may be used at the evening service of the day before.

Directions concerning the Common of Saints and services for Various Occasions are on pages 195, 199, 246 and 251.

# Collects: Traditional

**First Sunday of Advent**

Almighty God, give us grace that we may cast away the works of darkness, and put upon us the armor of light, now in the time of this mortal life in which thy Son Jesus Christ came to visit us in great humility; that in the last day, when he shall come again in his glorious majesty to judge both the quick and the dead, we may rise to the life immortal; through him who liveth and reigneth with thee and the Holy Ghost, one God, now and for ever. *Amen.*

*Preface of Advent*

**Second Sunday of Advent**

Merciful God, who didst send thy messengers the prophets to preach repentance and prepare the way for our salvation: Give us grace to heed their warnings and forsake our sins, that we may greet with joy the coming of Jesus Christ our Redeemer; who liveth and reigneth with thee and the Holy Spirit, one God, now and for ever. *Amen.*

*Preface of Advent*

**Third Sunday of Advent**

Stir up thy power, O Lord, and with great might come
among us; and, because we are sorely hindered by our sins,
let thy bountiful grace and mercy speedily help and deliver
us; through Jesus Christ our Lord, to whom, with thee and
the Holy Ghost, be honor and glory, world without end.
*Amen.*

*Preface of Advent*

*Wednesday, Friday, and Saturday of this week are the traditional winter
Ember Days.*

**Fourth Sunday of Advent**

We beseech thee, Almighty God, to purify our consciences by
thy daily visitation, that when thy Son our Lord cometh he
may find in us a mansion prepared for himself; through the
same Jesus Christ our Lord, who liveth and reigneth with
thee, in the unity of the Holy Spirit, one God, now and for
ever. *Amen.*

*Preface of Advent*

**The Nativity of Our Lord: Christmas Day**   *December 25*

O God, who makest us glad with the yearly remembrance of
the birth of thy only Son Jesus Christ: Grant that as we
joyfully receive him for our Redeemer, so we may with sure
confidence behold him when he shall come to be our Judge;
who liveth and reigneth with thee and the Holy Ghost, one
God, world without end. *Amen.*

*or the following*

God, who hast caused this holy night to shine with the
umination of the true Light: Grant us, we beseech thee,
at as we have known the mystery of that Light upon earth,
may we also perfectly enjoy him in heaven; where with
ee and the Holy Spirit he liveth and reigneth, one God, in
ory everlasting. *Amen.*

*this*

lmighty God, who hast given us thy only-begotten Son to
ke our nature upon him and as at this time to be born of a
ure virgin: Grant that we, being regenerate and made thy
ildren by adoption and grace, may daily be renewed by thy
loly Spirit; through the same our Lord Jesus Christ, who
veth and reigneth with thee and the same Spirit ever, one
od, world without end. *Amen.*

*reface of the Incarnation*

*e Collect immediately preceding and any of the sets of Proper Lessons
r Christmas Day serve for any weekdays between Holy Innocents' Day
d the First Sunday after Christmas Day.*

## irst Sunday after Christmas Day

*his Sunday takes precedence over the three Holy Days which follow
hristmas Day. As necessary, the observance of one, two, or all three
 them, is postponed one day.*

lmighty God, who hast poured upon us the new light of
ine incarnate Word: Grant that the same light, enkindled in
ur hearts, may shine forth in our lives; through the same
sus Christ our Lord, who liveth and reigneth with thee, in
e unity of the Holy Spirit, one God, now and for ever.
*men.*

*reface of the Incarnation*

**The Holy Name**   *January 1*

Eternal Father, who didst give to thine incarnate Son the holy
name of Jesus to be the sign of our salvation: Plant in every
heart, we beseech thee, the love of him who is the Savior of
the world, even our Lord Jesus Christ; who liveth and
reigneth with thee and the Holy Spirit, one God, in glory
everlasting. *Amen.*

*Preface of the Incarnation*

**Second Sunday after Christmas Day**

O God, who didst wonderfully create, and yet more
wonderfully restore, the dignity of human nature: Grant
that we may share the divine life of him who humbled
himself to share our humanity, thy Son Jesus Christ; who
liveth and reigneth with thee, in the unity of the Holy Spirit,
one God, for ever and ever. *Amen.*

*Preface of the Incarnation*

**The Epiphany**   *January 6*

O God, who by the leading of a star didst manifest thy only-
begotten Son to the peoples of the earth: Lead us, who know
thee now by faith, to thy presence, where we may behold thy
glory face to face; through the same Jesus Christ our Lord,
who liveth and reigneth with thee and the Holy Spirit, one
God, now and for ever. *Amen.*

*Preface of the Epiphany*

*The preceding Collect, with the Psalm and Lessons for the Epiphany, or
those for the Second Sunday after Christmas Day, serves for weekdays
between the Epiphany and the following Sunday. The Preface of the
Epiphany is used.*

## First Sunday after the Epiphany: The Baptism of our Lord

Father in heaven, who at the baptism of Jesus in the River Jordan didst proclaim him thy beloved Son and anoint him with the Holy Spirit: Grant that all who are baptized into his Name may keep the covenant they have made, and boldly confess him as Lord and Savior; who with thee and the same Spirit liveth and reigneth, one God, in glory everlasting. *Amen.*

*Preface of the Epiphany*

## Second Sunday after the Epiphany

Almighty God, whose Son our Savior Jesus Christ is the light of the world: Grant that thy people, illumined by thy Word and Sacraments, may shine with the radiance of Christ's glory, that he may be known, worshiped, and obeyed to the ends of the earth; through the same Jesus Christ our Lord, who with thee and the Holy Spirit liveth and reigneth, one God, now and for ever. *Amen.*

*Preface of the Epiphany, or of the Lord's Day*

## Third Sunday after the Epiphany

Give us grace, O Lord, to answer readily the call of our Savior Jesus Christ and proclaim to all people the Good News of his salvation, that we and all the whole world may perceive the glory of his marvelous works; who liveth and reigneth with thee and the Holy Spirit, one God, for ever and ever. *Amen.*

*Preface of the Epiphany, or of the Lord's Day*

### Fourth Sunday after the Epiphany

Almighty and everlasting God, who dost govern all things in heaven and earth: Mercifully hear the supplications of thy people, and in our time grant us thy peace; through Jesus Christ our Lord, who liveth and reigneth with thee and the Holy Spirit, one God, for ever and ever. *Amen.*

*Preface of the Epiphany, or of the Lord's Day*

### Fifth Sunday after the Epiphany

Set us free, O God, from the bondage of our sins and give us, we beseech thee, the liberty of that abundant life which thou hast manifested to us in thy Son our Savior Jesus Christ; who liveth and reigneth with thee, in the unity of the Holy Spirit, one God, now and for ever. *Amen.*

*Preface of the Epiphany, or of the Lord's Day*

### Sixth Sunday after the Epiphany

O God, the strength of all those who put their trust in thee: Mercifully accept our prayers; and because, through the weakness of our mortal nature, we can do no good thing without thee, grant us the help of thy grace, that in keeping thy commandments we may please thee both in will and deed; through Jesus Christ our Lord, who liveth and reigneth with thee and the Holy Spirit, one God, for ever and ever. *Amen.*

*Preface of the Epiphany, or of the Lord's Day*

### Seventh Sunday after the Epiphany

O Lord, who hast taught us that all our doings without charity are nothing worth: Send thy Holy Ghost and pour to our hearts that most excellent gift of charity, the very bond of peace and of all virtues, without which whosoever liveth is counted dead before thee. Grant this for thine only Son Jesus Christ's sake, who liveth and reigneth with thee and the same Holy Ghost, one God, now and for ever. *Amen.*

*Preface of the Epiphany, or of the Lord's Day*

## Eighth Sunday after the Epiphany

O most loving Father, who willest us to give thanks for all things, to dread nothing but the loss of thee, and to cast all our care on thee who carest for us: Preserve us from faithless fears and worldly anxieties, and grant that no clouds of this mortal life may hide from us the light of that love which is immortal, and which thou hast manifested unto us in thy Son Jesus Christ our Lord; who liveth and reigneth with thee, in the unity of the Holy Spirit, one God, now and for ever. *Amen.*

*Preface of the Epiphany, or of the Lord's Day*

## Last Sunday after the Epiphany

*This Proper is always used on the Sunday before Ash Wednesday.*

O God, who before the passion of thy only-begotten Son didst reveal his glory upon the holy mount: Grant unto us that we, beholding by faith the light of his countenance, may be strengthened to bear our cross, and be changed into his likeness from glory to glory; through the same Jesus Christ our Lord, who liveth and reigneth with thee and the Holy Spirit, one God, for ever and ever. *Amen.*

*Preface of the Epiphany*

## Ash Wednesday

*The Proper Liturgy for this day is on page 264.*

Almighty and everlasting God, who hatest nothing that thou hast made and dost forgive the sins of all those who are penitent: Create and make in us new and contrite hearts, that we, worthily lamenting our sins and acknowledging our wretchedness, may obtain of thee, the God of all mercy, perfect remission and forgiveness; through Jesus Christ our Lord, who liveth and reigneth with thee and the Holy Spirit, one God, for ever and ever. *Amen.*

*Preface of Lent*

*This Collect, with the corresponding Psalm and Lessons, serves for the weekdays which follow, except as otherwise appointed.*

## First Sunday in Lent

Almighty God, whose blessed Son was led by the Spirit to be tempted of Satan: Make speed to help thy servants who are assaulted by manifold temptations; and, as thou knowest their several infirmities, let each one find thee mighty to save, through Jesus Christ thy Son our Lord, who liveth and reigneth with thee and the Holy Spirit, one God, now and for ever. *Amen.*

*Preface of Lent*

*Wednesday, Friday, and Saturday of this week are the traditional spring Ember Days.*

## Second Sunday in Lent

O God, whose glory it is always to have mercy: Be gracious to all who have gone astray from thy ways, and bring them again with penitent hearts and steadfast faith to embrace and hold fast the unchangeable truth of thy Word, Jesus Christ hy Son; who with thee and the Holy Spirit liveth and reigneth, one God, for ever and ever. *Amen.*

*Preface of Lent*

### Third Sunday in Lent

Almighty God, who seest that we have no power of ourselves to help ourselves: Keep us both outwardly in our bodies and inwardly in our souls, that we may be defended from all adversities which may happen to the body, and from all evil thoughts which may assault and hurt the soul; through Jesus Christ our Lord, who liveth and reigneth with thee and the Holy Spirit, one God, for ever and ever. *Amen.*

*Preface of Lent*

### Fourth Sunday in Lent

Gracious Father, whose blessed Son Jesus Christ came down from heaven to be the true bread which giveth life to the world: Evermore give us this bread, that he may live in us, and we in him; who liveth and reigneth with thee and the Holy Spirit, one God, now and for ever. *Amen.*

*Preface of Lent*

### Fifth Sunday in Lent

O Almighty God, who alone canst order the unruly wills and affections of sinful men: Grant unto thy people that they may love the thing which thou commandest, and desire that which thou dost promise; that so, among the sundry and manifold changes of the world, our hearts may surely there be fixed where true joys are to be found; through Jesus Christ our Lord, who liveth and reigneth with thee and the Holy Spirit, one God, now and for ever. *Amen.*

*Preface of Lent*

*Collects: Traditional* 167

### Sunday of the Passion: Palm Sunday

*The Proper Liturgy for this day is on page 270.*

Almighty and everlasting God, who, of thy tender love towards mankind, hast sent thy Son our Savior Jesus Christ to take upon him our flesh, and to suffer death upon the cross, that all mankind should follow the example of his great humility: Mercifully grant that we may both follow the example of his patience, and also be made partakers of his resurrection; through the same Jesus Christ our Lord, who liveth and reigneth with thee and the Holy Spirit, one God, for ever and ever. *Amen.*

*Preface of Holy Week*


### Monday in Holy Week

Almighty God, whose most dear Son went not up to joy but first he suffered pain, and entered not into glory before he was crucified: Mercifully grant that we, walking in the way of the cross, may find it none other than the way of life and peace; through the same thy Son Jesus Christ our Lord, who liveth and reigneth with thee and the Holy Spirit, one God, for ever and ever. *Amen.*

*Preface of Holy Week*


### Tuesday in Holy Week

O God, who by the passion of thy blessed Son didst make an instrument of shameful death to be unto us the means of life: Grant us so to glory in the cross of Christ, that we may gladly suffer shame and loss for the sake of thy Son our Savior Jesus Christ; who liveth and reigneth with thee and the Holy Spirit, one God, for ever and ever. *Amen.*

*Preface of Holy Week*

## Wednesday in Holy Week

O Lord God, whose blessed Son our Savior gave his back to
the smiters and hid not his face from shame: Grant us grace
to take joyfully the sufferings of the present time, in full
assurance of the glory that shall be revealed; through the same
thy Son Jesus Christ our Lord, who liveth and reigneth with
thee and the Holy Spirit, one God, for ever and ever. *Amen.*

*Preface of Holy Week*

## Maundy Thursday

*The Proper Liturgy for this day is on page 274.*

Almighty Father, whose dear Son, on the night before he
suffered, did institute the Sacrament of his Body and Blood:
Mercifully grant that we may thankfully receive the same in
remembrance of him who in these holy mysteries giveth us a
pledge of life eternal, the same thy Son Jesus Christ our Lord;
who now liveth and reigneth with thee and the Holy Spirit
ever, one God, world without end. *Amen.*

*Preface of Holy Week*

## Good Friday

*The Proper Liturgy for this day is on page 276.*

Almighty God, we beseech thee graciously to behold this thy
family, for which our Lord Jesus Christ was contented to be
betrayed, and given up into the hands of sinners, and to suffer
death upon the cross; who now liveth and reigneth with thee
and the Holy Ghost ever, one God, world without end. *Amen.*

## Holy Saturday

*The Proper Liturgy for this day is on page 283.*

O God, Creator of heaven and earth: Grant that, as the crucified body of thy dear Son was laid in the tomb and rested on this holy Sabbath, so we may await with him the coming of the third day, and rise with him to newness of life; who now liveth and reigneth with thee and the Holy Spirit, one God, for ever and ever. *Amen.*

## Easter Day

*The Liturgy of the Easter Vigil is on page 285.*

O God, who for our redemption didst give thine only-begotten Son to the death of the cross, and by his glorious resurrection hast delivered us from the power of our enemy: Grant us so to die daily to sin, that we may evermore live with him in the joy of his resurrection; through the same thy Son Christ our Lord, who liveth and reigneth with thee and the Holy Spirit, one God, now and for ever. *Amen.*

*or this*

O God, who didst make this most holy night to shine with the glory of the Lord's resurrection: Stir up in thy Church that Spirit of adoption which is given to us in Baptism, that we, being renewed both in body and mind, may worship thee in sincerity and truth; through the same Jesus Christ our Lord, who liveth and reigneth with thee in the unity of the same Spirit, one God, now and for ever. *Amen.*

*or this*

Almighty God, who through thine only-begotten Son Jesus Christ hast overcome death and opened unto us the gate of everlasting life: Grant that we, who celebrate with joy the day of the Lord's resurrection, may be raised from the death of sin by thy life-giving Spirit; through the same Jesus Christ our Lord, who liveth and reigneth with thee and the same Spirit ever, one God, world without end. *Amen.*

*Preface of Easter*

## Monday in Easter Week

Grant, we beseech thee, Almighty God, that we who celebrate with reverence the Paschal feast may be found worthy to attain to everlasting joys; through Jesus Christ our Lord, who liveth and reigneth with thee and the Holy Spirit, one God, now and for ever. *Amen.*

*Preface of Easter*

## Tuesday in Easter Week

O God, who by the glorious resurrection of thy Son Jesus Christ didst destroy death and bring life and immortality to light: Grant that we, who have been raised with him, may abide in his presence and rejoice in the hope of eternal glory; through the same Jesus Christ our Lord, to whom, with thee and the Holy Spirit, be dominion and praise for ever and ever. *Amen.*

*Preface of Easter*

## Wednesday in Easter Week

O God, whose blessed Son did manifest himself to his disciples in the breaking of bread: Open, we pray thee, the eyes of our faith, that we may behold him in all his redeeming work; through the same thy Son Jesus Christ our Lord, who liveth and reigneth with thee, in the unity of the Holy Spirit, one God, now and for ever. *Amen.*

*Preface of Easter*

### Thursday in Easter Week

Almighty and everlasting God, who in the Paschal mystery hast established the new covenant of reconciliation: Grant that all who have been reborn into the fellowship of Christ's Body may show forth in their lives what they profess by their faith; through the same Jesus Christ our Lord, who liveth and reigneth with thee and the Holy Spirit, one God, for ever and ever. *Amen.*

*Preface of Easter*

### Friday in Easter Week

Almighty Father, who hast given thine only Son to die for our sins and to rise again for our justification: Grant us so to put away the leaven of malice and wickedness, that we may always serve thee in pureness of living and truth; through the same thy Son Jesus Christ our Lord, who liveth and reigneth with thee and the Holy Spirit, one God, now and for ever. *Amen.*

*Preface of Easter*

### Saturday in Easter Week

We thank thee, heavenly Father, for that thou hast delivered us from the dominion of sin and death and hast brought us into the kingdom of thy Son; and we pray thee that, as by his death he hath recalled us to life, so by his love he may raise us to joys eternal; who liveth and reigneth with thee, in the unity of the Holy Spirit, one God, now and for ever. *Amen.*

*Preface of Easter*

### Second Sunday of Easter

Almighty and everlasting God, who in the Paschal mystery hast established the new covenant of reconciliation: Grant that all who have been reborn into the fellowship of Christ's

Body may show forth in their lives what they profess by their faith; through the same Jesus Christ our Lord, who liveth and reigneth with thee and the Holy Spirit, one God, for ever and ever. *Amen.*

*Preface of Easter*

### Third Sunday of Easter

O God, whose blessed Son did manifest himself to his disciples in the breaking of bread: Open, we pray thee, the eyes of our faith, that we may behold him in all his redeeming work; through the same thy Son Jesus Christ our Lord, who liveth and reigneth with thee, in the unity of the Holy Spirit, one God, now and for ever. *Amen.*

*Preface of Easter*

### Fourth Sunday of Easter

O God, whose Son Jesus is the good shepherd of thy people: Grant that when we hear his voice we may know him who calleth us each by name, and follow where he doth lead; who, with thee and the Holy Spirit, liveth and reigneth, one God, for ever and ever. *Amen.*

*Preface of Easter*

### Fifth Sunday of Easter

O Almighty God, whom truly to know is everlasting life: Grant us so perfectly to know thy Son Jesus Christ to be the way, the truth, and the life, that we may steadfastly follow his steps in the way that leadeth to eternal life; through the same thy Son Jesus Christ our Lord, who liveth and reigneth with thee, in the unity of the Holy Spirit, one God, for ever and ever. *Amen.*

*Preface of Easter*

**Sixth Sunday of Easter**

O God, who hast prepared for those who love thee such good things as pass man's understanding: Pour into our hearts such love toward thee, that we, loving thee in all things and above all things, may obtain thy promises, which exceed all that we can desire; through Jesus Christ our Lord, who liveth and reigneth with thee and the Holy Spirit, one God, for ever and ever. *Amen.*

*Preface of Easter*

*Monday, Tuesday, and Wednesday of this week are the traditional Rogation Days.*


**Ascension Day**

O Almighty God, whose blessed Son our Savior Jesus Christ ascended far above all heavens that he might fill all things: Mercifully give us faith to perceive that, according to his promise, he abideth with his Church on earth, even unto the end of the ages; through the same Jesus Christ our Lord, who liveth and reigneth with thee and the Holy Spirit, one God, in glory everlasting. *Amen.*

*or this*

Grant, we beseech thee, Almighty God, that like as we do believe thy only-begotten Son our Lord Jesus Christ to have ascended into the heavens, so we may also in heart and mind thither ascend, and with him continually dwell; who liveth and reigneth with thee and the Holy Ghost, one God, world without end. *Amen.*

*Preface of the Ascension*

*Either of the preceding Collects, with the proper Psalm and Lessons for Ascension Day, serves for the following weekdays, except as otherwise appointed.*

## Seventh Sunday of Easter: The Sunday after Ascension Day

O God, the King of glory, who hast exalted thine only Son
Jesus Christ with great triumph unto thy kingdom in heaven:
We beseech thee, leave us not comfortless, but send to us
thine Holy Ghost to comfort us, and exalt us unto the same
place whither our Savior Christ is gone before; who liveth
and reigneth with thee and the same Holy Ghost, one God,
world without end. *Amen.*

*Preface of the Ascension*

## The Day of Pentecost: Whitsunday

*When a Vigil of Pentecost is observed, it begins with the Service of Light,
page 109 (substituting, if desired, the Gloria in excelsis for the Phos
hilaron), and continues with the Salutation and Collect of the Day. Three
or more of the appointed Lessons are read before the Gospel, each
followed by a Psalm, Canticle, or hymn. Holy Baptism or Confirmation
(beginning with the Presentation of the Candidates), or the Renewal of
Baptismal Vows, page 292, follows the Sermon.*

Almighty God, who on this day didst open the way of eternal
life to every race and nation by the promised gift of thy Holy
Spirit: Shed abroad this gift throughout the world by the
preaching of the Gospel, that it may reach to the ends of the
earth; through Jesus Christ our Lord, who liveth and reigneth
with thee, in the unity of the same Spirit, one God, for ever
and ever. *Amen.*

*or this*

O God, who on this day didst teach the hearts of thy faithful
people by sending to them the light of thy Holy Spirit: Grant
us by the same Spirit to have a right judgment in all things, and
evermore to rejoice in his holy comfort; through the merits of
Christ Jesus our Savior, who liveth and reigneth with thee, in
the unity of the same Spirit, one God, world without end. *Amen.*

*Preface of Pentecost*

*On the weekdays which follow, the numbered Proper which corresponds most closely to the date of Pentecost in that year is used. See page 158.*

*Wednesday, Friday, and Saturday of this week are the traditional summer Ember Days.*

### First Sunday after Pentecost: Trinity Sunday

Almighty and everlasting God, who hast given unto us
thy servants grace, by the confession of a true faith, to
acknowledge the glory of the eternal Trinity, and in the power
of the Divine Majesty to worship the Unity: We beseech thee
that thou wouldest keep us steadfast in this faith and worship,
and bring us at last to see thee in thy one and eternal glory,
O Father; who with the Son and the Holy Spirit livest and
reignest, one God, for ever and ever. *Amen.*

*Preface of Trinity Sunday*

*On the weekdays which follow, the numbered Proper which corresponds most closely to the date of Trinity Sunday in that year is used.*

# The Season after Pentecost

*Directions for the use of the Propers which follow are on page 158.*

**Proper 1**   *Week of the Sunday closest to May 11*

Remember, O Lord, what thou hast wrought in us and not
what we deserve; and, as thou hast called us to thy service,
make us worthy of our calling; through Jesus Christ our

Lord, who liveth and reigneth with thee and the Holy Spirit, one God, now and for ever. *Amen.*

*No Proper Preface is used.*

**Proper 2**  *Week of the Sunday closest to May 18*

O Almighty and most merciful God, of thy bountiful goodness keep us, we beseech thee, from all things that may hurt us, that we, being ready both in body and soul, may with free hearts accomplish those things which belong to thy purpose; through Jesus Christ our Lord, who liveth and reigneth with thee and the Holy Spirit, one God, now and for ever. *Amen.*

*No Proper Preface is used.*

**Proper 3**  *The Sunday closest to May 25*

Grant, O Lord, we beseech thee, that the course of this world may be peaceably governed by thy providence, and that thy Church may joyfully serve thee in confidence and serenity; through Jesus Christ our Lord, who liveth and reigneth with thee and the Holy Spirit, one God, for ever and ever. *Amen.*

*Preface of the Lord's Day*

**Proper 4**  *The Sunday closest to June 1*

O God, whose never-failing providence ordereth all things both in heaven and earth: We humbly beseech thee to put away from us all hurtful things, and to give us those things which are profitable for us; through Jesus Christ our Lord, who liveth and reigneth with thee and the Holy Spirit, one God, for ever and ever. *Amen.*

*Preface of the Lord's Day*

**Proper 5**  *The Sunday closest to June 8*

O God, from whom all good doth come: Grant that by thy inspiration we may think those things that are right, and by thy merciful guiding may perform the same; through Jesus Christ our Lord, who liveth and reigneth with thee and the Holy Spirit, one God, for ever and ever. *Amen.*

*Preface of the Lord's Day*


**Proper 6**  *The Sunday closest to June 15*

Keep, O Lord, we beseech thee, thy household the Church in thy steadfast faith and love, that by the help of thy grace we may proclaim thy truth with boldness, and minister thy justice with compassion; for the sake of our Savior Jesus Christ, who liveth and reigneth with thee and the Holy Spirit, one God, now and for ever. *Amen.*

*Preface of the Lord's Day*


**Proper 7**  *The Sunday closest to June 22*

O Lord, we beseech thee, make us to have a perpetual fear and love of thy holy Name, for thou never failest to help and govern those whom thou hast set upon the sure foundation of thy loving-kindness; through Jesus Christ our Lord, who liveth and reigneth with thee and the Holy Spirit, one God, for ever and ever. *Amen.*

*Preface of the Lord's Day*


**Proper 8**  *The Sunday closest to June 29*

O Almighty God, who hast built thy Church upon the foundation of the apostles and prophets, Jesus Christ himself being the chief cornerstone: Grant us so to be joined together in unity of spirit by their doctrine, that we may be made an holy temple acceptable unto thee; through the same Jesus Christ our Lord, who liveth and reigneth with thee and the Holy Spirit, one God, for ever and ever. *Amen.*

*Preface of the Lord's Day*

## Proper 9  *The Sunday closest to July 6*

O God, who hast taught us to keep all thy commandments by loving thee and our neighbor: Grant us the grace of thy Holy Spirit, that we may be devoted to thee with our whole heart, and united to one another with pure affection; through Jesus Christ our Lord, who liveth and reigneth with thee and the same Spirit, one God, for ever and ever. *Amen.*

*Preface of the Lord's Day*

## Proper 10  *The Sunday closest to July 13*

O Lord, we beseech thee mercifully to receive the prayers of thy people who call upon thee, and grant that they may both perceive and know what things they ought to do, and also may have grace and power faithfully to fulfill the same; through Jesus Christ our Lord, who liveth and reigneth with thee and the Holy Spirit, one God, now and for ever. *Amen.*

*Preface of the Lord's Day*

## Proper 11  *The Sunday closest to July 20*

Almighty God, the fountain of all wisdom, who knowest our necessities before we ask and our ignorance in asking: Have compassion, we beseech thee, upon our infirmities, and those things which for our unworthiness we dare not, and for our blindness we cannot ask, mercifully give us for the worthiness of thy Son Jesus Christ our Lord; who liveth and reigneth with thee and the Holy Spirit, one God, now and for ever. *Amen.*

*Preface of the Lord's Day*

**Proper 12**   *The Sunday closest to July 27*

O God, the protector of all that trust in thee, without whom
nothing is strong, nothing is holy: Increase and multiply
upon us thy mercy, that, thou being our ruler and guide, we
may so pass through things temporal, that we finally lose not
the things eternal; through Jesus Christ our Lord, who liveth
and reigneth with thee and the Holy Spirit, one God, for ever
and ever. *Amen.*

*Preface of the Lord's Day*

**Proper 13**   *The Sunday closest to August 3*

O Lord, we beseech thee, let thy continual pity cleanse and
defend thy Church, and, because it cannot continue in safety
without thy succor, preserve it evermore by thy help and
goodness; through Jesus Christ our Lord, who liveth and
reigneth with thee and the Holy Spirit, one God, for ever and
ever. *Amen.*

*Preface of the Lord's Day*

**Proper 14**   *The Sunday closest to August 10*

Grant to us, Lord, we beseech thee, the spirit to think and do
always such things as are right, that we, who cannot exist
without thee, may by thee be enabled to live according to thy
will; through Jesus Christ our Lord, who liveth and reigneth
with thee and the Holy Spirit, one God, for ever and ever. *Am*

*Preface of the Lord's Day*

**Proper 15**   *The Sunday closest to August 17*

Almighty God, who hast given thy only Son to be unto us
both a sacrifice for sin and also an example of godly life:
Give us grace that we may always most thankfully receive
that his inestimable benefit, and also daily endeavor

urselves to follow the blessed steps of his most holy life;
through the same thy Son Jesus Christ our Lord, who
liveth and reigneth with thee and the Holy Spirit, one
God, now and for ever. *Amen.*

*Preface of the Lord's Day*

## Proper 16    *The Sunday closest to August 24*

Grant, we beseech thee, merciful God, that thy Church,
being gathered together in unity by thy Holy Spirit, may
manifest thy power among all peoples, to the glory of thy
Name; through Jesus Christ our Lord, who liveth and
reigneth with thee and the same Spirit, one God, world
without end. *Amen.*

*Preface of the Lord's Day*

## Proper 17    *The Sunday closest to August 31*

Lord of all power and might, who art the author and giver of
all good things: Graft in our hearts the love of thy Name,
increase in us true religion, nourish us with all goodness,
and bring forth in us the fruit of good works; through Jesus
Christ our Lord, who liveth and reigneth with thee and the
Holy Spirit, one God, for ever and ever. *Amen.*

*Preface of the Lord's Day*

## Proper 18    *The Sunday closest to September 7*

Grant us, O Lord, we pray thee, to trust in thee with all our
heart; seeing that, as thou dost alway resist the proud who
confide in their own strength, so thou dost not forsake those
who make their boast of thy mercy; through Jesus Christ our
Lord, who liveth and reigneth with thee and the Holy Spirit,
one God, now and for ever. *Amen.*

*Preface of the Lord's Day*

**Proper 19**   *The Sunday closest to September 14*

O God, forasmuch as without thee we are not able to please thee, mercifully grant that thy Holy Spirit may in all things direct and rule our hearts; through Jesus Christ our Lord, who with thee and the same Spirit liveth and reigneth, one God, now and for ever. *Amen.*

*Preface of the Lord's Day*

*The Wednesday, Friday, and Saturday after September 14 are the traditional autumnal Ember Days.*


**Proper 20**   *The Sunday closest to September 21*

Grant us, O Lord, not to mind earthly things, but to love things heavenly; and even now, while we are placed among things that are passing away, to cleave to those that shall abide; through Jesus Christ our Lord, who liveth and reigneth with thee and the Holy Spirit, one God, for ever and ever. *Amen.*

*Preface of the Lord's Day*


**Proper 21**   *The Sunday closest to September 28*

O God, who declarest thy almighty power chiefly in showing mercy and pity: Mercifully grant unto us such a measure of thy grace, that we, running to obtain thy promises, may be made partakers of thy heavenly treasure; through Jesus Christ our Lord, who liveth and reigneth with thee and the Holy Spirit, one God, for ever and ever. *Amen.*

*Preface of the Lord's Day*


**Proper 22**   *The Sunday closest to October 5*

Almighty and everlasting God, who art always more ready to hear than we to pray, and art wont to give more than either we desire or deserve: Pour down upon us the abundance of thy mercy, forgiving us those things whereof our conscience is afraid, and giving us those good things which we are not worthy to ask, but through the merits and mediation of Jesus Christ thy Son our Lord; who liveth and reigneth with thee and the Holy Spirit, one God, for ever and ever. *Amen.*

*Preface of the Lord's Day*

## Proper 23 *The Sunday closest to October 12*

Lord, we pray thee that thy grace may always precede and follow us, and make us continually to be given to all good works; through Jesus Christ our Lord, who liveth and reigneth with thee and the Holy Spirit, one God, now and for ever. *Amen.*

*Preface of the Lord's Day*

## Proper 24 *The Sunday closest to October 19*

Almighty and everlasting God, who in Christ hast revealed thy glory among the nations: Preserve the works of thy mercy, that thy Church throughout the world may persevere with steadfast faith in the confession of thy Name; through the same Jesus Christ our Lord, who liveth and reigneth with thee and the Holy Spirit, one God, for ever and ever. *Amen.*

*Preface of the Lord's Day*

## Proper 25 *The Sunday closest to October 26*

Almighty and everlasting God, give unto us the increase of faith, hope, and charity; and, that we may obtain that which thou dost promise, make us to love that which thou dost command; through Jesus Christ our Lord, who liveth and reigneth with thee and the Holy Spirit, one God, for ever and ever. *Amen.*

*Preface of the Lord's Day*

**Proper 26**   *The Sunday closest to November 2*

Almighty and merciful God, of whose only gift it cometh that
thy faithful people do unto thee true and laudable service:
Grant, we beseech thee, that we may run without stumbling
to obtain thy heavenly promises; through Jesus Christ our
Lord, who liveth and reigneth with thee and the Holy Spirit,
one God, now and for ever. *Amen.*

*Preface of the Lord's Day*


**Proper 27**   *The Sunday closest to November 9*

O God, whose blessed Son was manifested that he might
destroy the works of the devil and make us the children of
God and heirs of eternal life: Grant us, we beseech thee, that,
having this hope, we may purify ourselves even as he is pure;
that, when he shall appear again with power and great glory,
we may be made like unto him in his eternal and glorious
kingdom; where with thee, O Father, and thee, O Holy Ghost,
he liveth and reigneth ever, one God, world without end.
*Amen.*

*Preface of the Lord's Day*


**Proper 28**   *The Sunday closest to November 16*

Blessed Lord, who hast caused all holy Scriptures to be
written for our learning: Grant that we may in such wise
hear them, read, mark, learn, and inwardly digest them; that,
by patience and comfort of thy holy Word, we may embrace
and ever hold fast the blessed hope of everlasting life, which
thou hast given us in our Savior Jesus Christ; who liveth and
reigneth with thee and the Holy Spirit, one God, for ever and
ever. *Amen.*

*Preface of the Lord's Day*

**Proper 29**  *The Sunday closest to November 23*

Almighty and everlasting God, whose will it is to restore all
things in thy well-beloved Son, the King of kings and Lord of
lords: Mercifully grant that the peoples of the earth, divided
and enslaved by sin, may be freed and brought together
under his most gracious rule; who liveth and reigneth with
thee and the Holy Spirit, one God, now and for ever. *Amen.*

*Preface of the Lord's Day, or of Baptism*

# Holy Days

**Saint Andrew**  *November 30*

Almighty God, who didst give such grace to thine apostle
Andrew that he readily obeyed the call of thy Son Jesus
Christ, and brought his brother with him: Give unto us, who
are called by thy Word, grace to follow him without delay,
and to bring those near to us into his gracious presence; who
liveth and reigneth with thee and the Holy Spirit, one God,
now and for ever. *Amen.*

*Preface of Apostles*

**Saint Thomas**  *December 21*

Everliving God, who didst strengthen thine apostle Thomas
with sure and certain faith in thy Son's resurrection: Grant us
so perfectly and without doubt to believe in Jesus Christ, our
Lord and our God, that our faith may never be found wanting
in thy sight; through him who liveth and reigneth with thee
and the Holy Spirit, one God, now and for ever. *Amen.*

*Preface of Apostles*

### Saint Stephen  *December 26*

We give thee thanks, O Lord of glory, for the example of the
first martyr Stephen, who looked up to heaven and prayed
for his persecutors to thy Son Jesus Christ, who standeth at
thy right hand; where he liveth and reigneth with thee and
the Holy Spirit, one God, in glory everlasting. *Amen.*

*Preface of the Incarnation*

### Saint John  *December 27*

Shed upon thy Church, we beseech thee, O Lord, the
brightness of thy light; that we, being illumined by the
teaching of thine apostle and evangelist John, may so walk
in the light of thy truth, that we may at length attain to the
fullness of life everlasting; through Jesus Christ our Lord,
who liveth and reigneth with thee and the Holy Spirit, one
God, for ever and ever. *Amen.*

*Preface of the Incarnation*

### The Holy Innocents  *December 28*

We remember this day, O God, the slaughter of the holy
innocents of Bethlehem by the order of King Herod. Receive,
we beseech thee, into the arms of thy mercy all innocent
victims; and by thy great might frustrate the designs of evil
tyrants and establish thy rule of justice, love, and peace;
through Jesus Christ our Lord, who liveth and reigneth with
thee, in the unity of the Holy Spirit, one God, for ever and
ever. *Amen.*

*Preface of the Incarnation*

**Confession of Saint Peter**   *January 18*

Almighty Father, who didst inspire Simon Peter, first among
the apostles, to confess Jesus as Messiah and Son of the living
God: Keep thy Church steadfast upon the rock of this faith,
that in unity and peace we may proclaim the one truth and
follow the one Lord, our Savior Jesus Christ; who liveth and
reigneth with thee and the Holy Spirit, one God, now and for
ever. *Amen.*

*Preface of Apostles*

**Conversion of Saint Paul**   *January 25*

O God, who, by the preaching of thine apostle Paul, hast
caused the light of the Gospel to shine throughout the world:
Grant, we beseech thee, that we, having his wonderful
conversion in remembrance, may show forth our thankfulness
unto thee for the same by following the holy doctrine which
he taught; through Jesus Christ our Lord, who liveth and
reigneth with thee, in the unity of the Holy Spirit, one God,
now and for ever. *Amen.*

*Preface of Apostles*

**The Presentation**   *February 2*

Almighty and everliving God, we humbly beseech thee that,
as thy only-begotten Son was this day presented in the
temple, so we may be presented unto thee with pure and
clean hearts by the same thy Son Jesus Christ our Lord; who
liveth and reigneth with thee and the Holy Spirit, one God,
now and for ever. *Amen.*

*Preface of the Epiphany*

### Saint Matthias    *February 24*

O Almighty God, who into the place of Judas didst choose thy
faithful servant Matthias to be of the number of the Twelve:
Grant that thy Church, being delivered from false apostles,
may always be ordered and guided by faithful and true pastors;
through Jesus Christ our Lord, who liveth and reigneth with
thee, in the unity of the Holy Spirit, one God, now and for
ever. *Amen.*

*Preface of Apostles*

### Saint Joseph    *March 19*

O God, who from the family of thy servant David didst raise
up Joseph to be the guardian of thy incarnate Son and the
spouse of his virgin mother: Give us grace to imitate his
uprightness of life and his obedience to thy commands;
through the same thy Son Jesus Christ our Lord, who liveth
and reigneth with thee and the Holy Spirit, one God, for ever
and ever. *Amen.*

*Preface of the Epiphany*

### The Annunciation    *March 25*

We beseech thee, O Lord, pour thy grace into our hearts, that
we who have known the incarnation of thy Son Jesus Christ,
announced by an angel to the Virgin Mary, may by his cross
and passion be brought unto the glory of his resurrection;
who liveth and reigneth with thee, in the unity of the Holy
Spirit, one God, now and for ever. *Amen.*

*Preface of the Epiphany*

### Saint Mark    *April 25*

Almighty God, who by the hand of Mark the evangelist hast
given to thy Church the Gospel of Jesus Christ the Son of

God: We thank thee for this witness, and pray that we may
be firmly grounded in its truth; through the same Jesus Christ
our Lord, who liveth and reigneth with thee and the Holy
Spirit, one God, for ever and ever. *Amen.*

*Preface of All Saints*

## Saint Philip and Saint James   *May 1*

Almighty God, who didst give to thine apostles Philip and
James grace and strength to bear witness to the truth: Grant
that we, being mindful of their victory of faith, may glorify in
life and death the Name of our Lord Jesus Christ; who liveth
and reigneth with thee and the Holy Spirit, one God, now
and for ever. *Amen.*

*Preface of Apostles*

## The Visitation   *May 31*

Father in heaven, by whose grace the virgin mother of thy
incarnate Son was blessed in bearing him, but still more blessed
in keeping thy word: Grant us who honor the exaltation of her
lowliness to follow the example of her devotion to thy will;
through the same Jesus Christ our Lord, who liveth and reigneth
with thee and the Holy Spirit, one God, for ever and ever. *Amen.*

*Preface of the Epiphany*

## Saint Barnabas   *June 11*

Grant, O God, that we may follow the example of thy
faithful servant Barnabas, who, seeking not his own renown
but the well-being of thy Church, gave generously of his life
and substance for the relief of the poor and the spread of the
Gospel; through Jesus Christ our Lord, who liveth and
reigneth with thee and the Holy Spirit, one God, for ever and
ever. *Amen.*

*Preface of Apostles*

### The Nativity of Saint John the Baptist  *June 24*

Almighty God, by whose providence thy servant John the
Baptist was wonderfully born, and sent to prepare the way of
thy Son our Savior by preaching repentance: Make us so to
follow his doctrine and holy life, that we may truly repent
according to his preaching; and after his example constantly
speak the truth, boldly rebuke vice, and patiently suffer for
the truth's sake; through the same thy Son Jesus Christ our
Lord, who liveth and reigneth with thee and the Holy Spirit,
one God, for ever and ever. *Amen.*

*Preface of Advent*

### Saint Peter and Saint Paul  *June 29*

Almighty God, whose blessed apostles Peter and Paul
glorified thee by their martyrdom: Grant that thy Church,
instructed by their teaching and example, and knit together
in unity by thy Spirit, may ever stand firm upon the one
foundation, which is Jesus Christ our Lord; who liveth and
reigneth with thee, in the unity of the same Spirit, one God,
for ever and ever. *Amen.*

*Preface of Apostles*

### Independence Day  *July 4*

Lord God Almighty, in whose Name the founders of this
country won liberty for themselves and for us, and lit the
torch of freedom for nations then unborn: Grant, we beseech
thee, that we and all the people of this land may have grace
to maintain these liberties in righteousness and peace;
through Jesus Christ our Lord, who liveth and reigneth with
thee and the Holy Spirit, one God, for ever and ever. *Amen.*

*The Collect "For the Nation," page 207, may be used instead.*

*Preface of Trinity Sunday*

## Saint Mary Magdalene   *July 22*

Almighty God, whose blessed Son restored Mary Magdalene
to health of body and mind, and called her to be a witness of
his resurrection: Mercifully grant that by thy grace we may
be healed of all our infirmities and know thee in the power of
his endless life; who with thee and the Holy Spirit liveth and
reigneth, one God, now and for ever. *Amen.*

*Preface of All Saints*

## Saint James   *July 25*

O gracious God, we remember before thee this day thy
servant and apostle James, first among the Twelve to suffer
martyrdom for the Name of Jesus Christ; and we pray that
thou wilt pour out upon the leaders of thy Church that spirit
of self-denying service by which alone they may have true
authority among thy people; through the same Jesus Christ
our Lord, who liveth and reigneth with thee and the Holy
Spirit, one God, now and for ever. *Amen.*

*Preface of Apostles*

## The Transfiguration   *August 6*

O God, who on the holy mount didst reveal to chosen
witnesses thy well-beloved Son, wonderfully transfigured, in
raiment white and glistening: Mercifully grant that we, being
delivered from the disquietude of this world, may by faith
behold the King in his beauty; who with thee, O Father, and
thee, O Holy Ghost, liveth and reigneth, one God, world
without end. *Amen.*

*Preface of the Epiphany*

### Saint Mary the Virgin   *August 15*

O God, who hast taken to thyself the blessed Virgin Mary,
mother of thy incarnate Son: Grant that we, who have been
redeemed by his blood, may share with her the glory of thine
eternal kingdom; through the same thy Son Jesus Christ our
Lord, who liveth and reigneth with thee, in the unity of the
Holy Spirit, one God, now and for ever. *Amen.*

*Preface of the Incarnation*


### Saint Bartholomew   *August 24*

O Almighty and everlasting God, who didst give to thine
apostle Bartholomew grace truly to believe and to preach thy
Word: Grant, we beseech thee, unto thy Church to love what
he believed and to preach what he taught; through Jesus
Christ our Lord, who liveth and reigneth with thee and the
Holy Spirit, one God, for ever and ever. *Amen.*

*Preface of Apostles*


### Holy Cross Day   *September 14*

Almighty God, whose Son our Savior Jesus Christ was lifted
high upon the cross that he might draw the whole world unto
himself: Mercifully grant that we, who glory in the mystery
of our redemption, may have grace to take up our cross and
follow him; who liveth and reigneth with thee and the Holy
Spirit, one God, in glory everlasting. *Amen.*

*Preface of Holy Week*


### Saint Matthew   *September 21*

We thank thee, heavenly Father, for the witness of thine
apostle and evangelist Matthew to the Gospel of thy Son our
Savior; and we pray that, after his example, we may with

ready wills and hearts obey the calling of our Lord to follow him; through Jesus Christ our Lord, who liveth and reigneth with thee and the Holy Spirit, one God, now and for ever. *Amen*.

*Preface of Apostles*

## Saint Michael and All Angels  *September 29*

O everlasting God, who hast ordained and constituted the ministries of angels and men in a wonderful order: Mercifully grant that, as thy holy angels always serve and worship thee in heaven, so by thy appointment they may help and defend us on earth; through Jesus Christ our Lord, who liveth and reigneth with thee and the Holy Spirit, one God, for ever and ever. *Amen*.

*Preface of Trinity Sunday*

## Saint Luke  *October 18*

Almighty God, who didst inspire thy servant Luke the physician to set forth in the Gospel the love and healing power of thy Son: Graciously continue in thy Church the like love and power to heal, to the praise and glory of thy Name; through the same thy Son Jesus Christ our Lord, who liveth and reigneth with thee, in the unity of the Holy Spirit, one God, now and for ever. *Amen*.

*Preface of All Saints*

## Saint James of Jerusalem  *October 23*

Grant, we beseech thee, O God, that after the example of thy servant James the Just, brother of our Lord, thy Church may give itself continually to prayer and to the reconciliation of all who are at variance and enmity; through the same our Lord Jesus Christ, who liveth and reigneth with thee and the Holy Spirit, one God, now and for ever. *Amen*.

*Preface of All Saints*

### Saint Simon and Saint Jude   *October 28*

O God, we thank thee for the glorious company of the
apostles, and especially on this day for Simon and Jude; and
we pray that, as they were faithful and zealous in their
mission, so we may with ardent devotion make known the
love and mercy of our Lord and Savior Jesus Christ; who
liveth and reigneth with thee and the Holy Spirit, one God,
for ever and ever. *Amen.*

*Preface of Apostles*

### All Saints' Day   *November 1*

O Almighty God, who hast knit together thine elect in one
communion and fellowship in the mystical body of thy Son
Christ our Lord: Grant us grace so to follow thy blessed
saints in all virtuous and godly living, that we may come to
those ineffable joys which thou hast prepared for those who
unfeignedly love thee; through the same Jesus Christ our
Lord, who with thee and the Holy Spirit liveth and reigneth,
one God, in glory everlasting. *Amen.*

*Preface of All Saints*

### Thanksgiving Day

Almighty and gracious Father, we give thee thanks for the
fruits of the earth in their season and for the labors of those
who harvest them. Make us, we beseech thee, faithful steward
of thy great bounty, for the provision of our necessities and
the relief of all who are in need, to the glory of thy Name;
through Jesus Christ our Lord, who liveth and reigneth with
thee and the Holy Spirit, one God, now and for ever. *Amen.*

*For the Prayers of the People, the Litany of Thanksgiving on page 836
may be used.*

*Preface of Trinity Sunday*

# The Common of Saints

*The festival of a saint is observed in accordance with the rules of precedence set forth in the Calendar of the Church Year.*

*At the discretion of the Celebrant, and as appropriate, any of the following Collects, with one of the corresponding sets of Psalms and Lessons, may be used*

*a) at the commemoration of a saint listed in the Calendar for which no Proper is provided in this Book*

*b) at the patronal festival or commemoration of a saint not listed in the Calendar.*

## Of a Martyr

O Almighty God, who didst give to thy servant N. boldness to confess the Name of our Savior Jesus Christ before the rulers of this world, and courage to die for this faith: Grant that we may always be ready to give a reason for the hope that is in us, and to suffer gladly for the sake of the same our Lord Jesus Christ; who liveth and reigneth with thee and the Holy Spirit, one God, for ever and ever. *Amen.*

*or this*

O Almighty God, by whose grace and power thy holy martyr N. triumphed over suffering and was faithful even unto death: Grant us, who now remember *him* with thanksgiving, to be so faithful in our witness to thee in this world, that we may receive with *him* the crown of life; through Jesus Christ our Lord, who liveth and reigneth with thee and the Holy Spirit, one God, for ever and ever. *Amen.*

*or the following*

Almighty and everlasting God, who didst enkindle the flame of thy love in the heart of thy holy martyr N.: Grant to us, thy humble servants, a like faith and power of love, that we who rejoice in *her* triumph may profit by *her* example; through Jesus Christ our Lord, who liveth and reigneth with thee and the Holy Spirit, one God, for ever and ever. *Amen*.

*Preface of a Saint*

## Of a Missionary

Almighty and everlasting God, we thank thee for thy servant N., whom thou didst call to preach the Gospel to the people of _____ (*or* to the _____ people). Raise up, we beseech thee, in this and every land evangelists and heralds of thy kingdom, that thy Church may proclaim the unsearchable riches of our Savior Jesus Christ; who liveth and reigneth with thee and the Holy Spirit, one God, now and for ever. *Amen*.

*or this*

Almighty God, who willest to be glorified in thy saints, and didst raise up thy servant N. to be a light in the world: Shine, we pray thee, in our hearts, that we also in our generation may show forth thy praise, who hast called us out of darkness into thy marvelous light; through Jesus Christ our Lord, who liveth and reigneth with thee and the Holy Spirit, one God, now and for ever. *Amen*.

*Preface of Pentecost*

## Of a Pastor

O heavenly Father, Shepherd of thy people, we give thee thanks for thy servant N., who was faithful in the care and nurture of thy flock; and we pray that, following *his* example and the teaching of *his* holy life, we may by thy grace grow into the stature of the fullness of our Lord and Savior Jesus Christ; who liveth and reigneth with thee and the Holy Spirit, one God, for ever and ever. *Amen.*

*or this*

O God, our heavenly Father, who didst raise up thy faithful servant N. to be a [bishop and] pastor in thy Church and to feed thy flock: Give abundantly to all pastors the gifts of thy Holy Spirit, that they may minister in thy household as true servants of Christ and stewards of thy divine mysteries; through the same Jesus Christ our Lord, who liveth and reigneth with thee and the same Spirit, one God, for ever and ever. *Amen.*

*Preface of a Saint*

## Of a Theologian and Teacher

O God, who by thy Holy Spirit dost give to some the word of wisdom, to others the word of knowledge, and to others the word of faith: We praise thy Name for the gifts of grace manifested in thy servant N., and we pray that thy Church may never be destitute of such gifts; through Jesus Christ our Lord, who with thee and the same Spirit liveth and reigneth, one God, for ever and ever. *Amen.*

*or this*

O Almighty God, who didst give to thy servant N. special gifts of grace to understand and teach the truth as it is in Christ Jesus: Grant, we beseech thee, that by this teaching we may know thee, the one true God, and Jesus Christ whom thou hast sent; who liveth and reigneth with thee and the Holy Spirit, one God, for ever and ever. *Amen.*

*Preface of a Saint, or of Trinity Sunday*

## Of a Monastic

O God, whose blessed Son became poor that we through his
poverty might be rich: Deliver us, we pray thee, from an
inordinate love of this world, that, inspired by the devotion
of thy servant N., we may serve thee with singleness of heart,
and attain to the riches of the age to come; through the same
thy Son Jesus Christ our Lord, who liveth and reigneth with
thee, in the unity of the Holy Spirit, one God, now and for
ever. *Amen.*

*or this*

O God, by whose grace thy servant N., enkindled with the
fire of thy love, became a burning and a shining light in thy
Church: Grant that we also may be aflame with the spirit
of love and discipline, and may ever walk before thee as
children of light; through Jesus Christ our Lord, who with
thee, in the unity of the Holy Spirit, liveth and reigneth, one
God, now and for ever. *Amen.*

*Preface of a Saint*

## Of a Saint

O Almighty God, who hast compassed us about with so great
a cloud of witnesses: Grant that we, encouraged by the good
example of thy servant N., may persevere in running the race
that is set before us, until at length, through thy mercy, we may
with *him* attain to thine eternal joy; through Jesus Christ, the
author and perfecter of our faith, who liveth and reigneth
with thee and the Holy Spirit, one God, for ever and ever. *Am*

*or this*

O God, who hast brought us near to an innumerable
company of angels and to the spirits of just men made
perfect: Grant us during our earthly pilgrimage to abide in
their fellowship, and in our heavenly country to become

partakers of their joy; through Jesus Christ our Lord, who liveth and reigneth with thee and the Holy Spirit, one God, now and for ever. *Amen.*

*or this*

O Almighty God, who by thy Holy Spirit hast made us one with thy saints in heaven and on earth: Grant that in our earthly pilgrimage we may ever be supported by this fellowship of love and prayer, and may know ourselves to be surrounded by their witness to thy power and mercy. We ask this for the sake of Jesus Christ, in whom all our intercessions are acceptable through the Spirit, and who liveth and reigneth for ever and ever. *Amen.*

*Preface of a Saint*

# Various Occasions

*For optional use, when desired, subject to the rules set forth in the Calendar of the Church Year.*

## 1. Of the Holy Trinity

Almighty God, who hast revealed to thy Church thine eternal Being of glorious majesty and perfect love as one God in Trinity of Persons: Give us grace to continue steadfast in the confession of this faith, and constant in our worship of thee, Father, Son, and Holy Spirit; who livest and reignest, one God, now and for ever. *Amen.*

*Preface of Trinity Sunday*

## 2. Of the Holy Spirit

Almighty and most merciful God, grant, we beseech thee,
that by the indwelling of thy Holy Spirit we may be enlightened
and strengthened for thy service; through Jesus Christ our
Lord, who liveth and reigneth with thee, in the unity of the
same Spirit ever, one God, world without end. *Amen.*

*Preface of Pentecost*


## 3. Of the Holy Angels

O everlasting God, who hast ordained and constituted the
ministries of angels and men in a wonderful order: Mercifully
grant that, as thy holy angels always serve and worship thee in
heaven, so by thy appointment they may help and defend us
on earth; through Jesus Christ our Lord, who liveth and
reigneth with thee and the Holy Spirit, one God, for ever
and ever. *Amen.*

*Preface of Trinity Sunday*


## 4. Of the Incarnation

O God, who didst wonderfully create, and yet more
wonderfully restore, the dignity of human nature: Grant
that we may share the divine life of him who humbled
himself to share our humanity, thy Son Jesus Christ; who
liveth and reigneth with thee, in the unity of the Holy Spirit,
one God, for ever and ever. *Amen.*

*Preface of the Epiphany*

## 5. Of the Holy Eucharist

*Especially suitable for Thursdays*

God our Father, whose Son our Lord Jesus Christ in a
wonderful Sacrament hath left unto us a memorial of his
passion: Grant us so to venerate the sacred mysteries of his
Body and Blood, that we may ever perceive within ourselves
the fruit of his redemption; who liveth and reigneth with
thee and the Holy Spirit, one God, for ever and ever. *Amen*.

*Preface of the Epiphany*

## 6. Of the Holy Cross

*Especially suitable for Fridays*

Almighty God, whose beloved Son willingly endured the
agony and shame of the cross for our redemption: Give us
courage, we beseech thee, to take up our cross and follow
him; who liveth and reigneth with thee and the Holy Spirit,
one God, now and for ever. *Amen*.

*Preface of Holy Week*

## 7. For All Baptized Christians

*Especially suitable for Saturdays*

Grant, O Lord God, to all who have been baptized into the
death and resurrection of thy Son Jesus Christ, that, as we
have put away the old life of sin, so we may be renewed in
the spirit of our minds, and live in righteousness and true
holiness; through the same Jesus Christ our Lord, who liveth
and reigneth with thee, in the unity of the Holy Spirit, one
God, now and for ever. *Amen*.

*Preface of Baptism*

### 8. For the Departed

O eternal Lord God, who holdest all souls in life: Give, we
beseech thee, to thy whole Church in paradise and on earth
thy light and thy peace; and grant that we, following the
good examples of those who have served thee here and are
now at rest, may at the last enter with them into thine
unending joy; through Jesus Christ our Lord, who liveth and
reigneth with thee, in the unity of the Holy Spirit, one God,
now and for ever. *Amen.*

*or this*

Almighty God, we remember this day before thee thy faithful
servant *N.*; and we pray that, having opened to *him* the gates
of larger life, thou wilt receive *him* more and more into thy
joyful service, that, with all who have faithfully served thee in
the past, *he* may share in the eternal victory of Jesus Christ
our Lord; who liveth and reigneth with thee, in the unity of
the Holy Spirit, one God, for ever and ever. *Amen.*

*Any of the Collects appointed for use at the Burial of the Dead may be
used instead.*

*For the Prayers of the People, one of the forms appointed for the Burial
of the Dead may be used.*

### Preface of the Commemoration of the Dead

*The postcommunion prayer on page 482 may be used.*

### 9. Of the Reign of Christ

Almighty and everlasting God, whose will it is to restore all
things in thy well-beloved Son, the King of kings and Lord of

lords: Mercifully grant that the peoples of the earth, divided and enslaved by sin, may be freed and brought together under his most gracious rule; who liveth and reigneth with thee and the Holy Spirit, one God, now and for ever. *Amen*.

*Preface of the Ascension, or of Baptism*

## 10. At Baptism

Almighty God, who by our baptism into the death and resurrection of thy Son Jesus Christ dost turn us from the old life of sin: Grant that we, being reborn to new life in him, may live in righteousness and holiness all our days; through the same thy Son Jesus Christ our Lord, who liveth and reigneth with thee and the Holy Spirit, one God, now and for ever. *Amen*.

*Preface of Baptism*

## 11. At Confirmation

Grant, Almighty God, that we, who have been redeemed from the old life of sin by our baptism into the death and resurrection of thy Son Jesus Christ, may be renewed in thy Holy Spirit, and live in righteousness and true holiness; through the same Jesus Christ our Lord, who liveth and reigneth with thee and the same Spirit, one God, now and for ever. *Amen*.

*Preface of Baptism, or of Pentecost*

## 12. On the Anniversary of the Dedication of a Church

O Almighty God, to whose glory we celebrate the dedication of this house of prayer: We give thee thanks for the fellowship of those who have worshiped in this place; and we pray that all who seek thee here may find thee, and be filled with thy joy and peace; through Jesus Christ our Lord, who liveth and reigneth with thee, in the unity of the Holy Spirit, one God, now and for ever. *Amen.*

*The Litany of Thanksgiving for a Church, page 578, may be used for the Prayers of the People.*

*Preface of the Dedication of a Church*

## 13. For a Church Convention

Almighty and everlasting Father, who hast given the Holy Spirit to abide with us for ever: Bless, we beseech thee, with his grace and presence, the bishops and the other clergy and the laity here (*or now, or soon to be*) assembled in thy Name, that thy Church, being preserved in true faith and godly discipline, may fulfill all the mind of him who loved it and gave himself for it, thy Son Jesus Christ our Savior; who liveth and reigneth with thee, in the unity of the same Spirit, one God, now and for ever. *Amen.*

*Preface of Pentecost, or of the Season*

## 14. For the Unity of the Church

Almighty Father, whose blessed Son before his passion prayed for his disciples that they might be one, even as thou and he are one: Grant that thy Church, being bound together in love and obedience to thee, may be united in one body by the one Spirit, that the world may believe in him whom thou

didst send, the same thy Son Jesus Christ our Lord; who
liveth and reigneth with thee, in the unity of the same Spirit,
one God, now and for ever. *Amen*.

*Preface of Baptism, or of Trinity Sunday*

## 15. For the Ministry (Ember Days)

*For use on the traditional days or at other times*

### I. For those to be ordained

Almighty God, the giver of all good gifts, who of thy divine
providence hast appointed various orders in thy Church:
Give thy grace, we humbly beseech thee, to all who are [now]
called to any office and ministry for thy people; and so fill
them with the truth of thy doctrine and clothe them with
holiness of life, that they may faithfully serve before thee, to
the glory of thy great Name and for the benefit of thy holy
Church; through Jesus Christ our Lord, who liveth and
reigneth with thee, in the unity of the Holy Spirit, one God,
now and for ever. *Amen*.

*Preface of Apostles*

### II. For the choice of fit persons for the ministry

O God, who didst lead thy holy apostles to ordain ministers
in every place: Grant that thy Church, under the guidance of
the Holy Spirit, may choose suitable persons for the ministry
of Word and Sacrament, and may uphold them in their work
for the extension of thy kingdom; through him who is the
Shepherd and Bishop of our souls, Jesus Christ our Lord,
who liveth and reigneth with thee and the same Spirit, one
God, for ever and ever. *Amen*.

*Preface of the Season*

### III. For all Christians in their vocation

Almighty and everlasting God, by whose Spirit the whole body of thy faithful people is governed and sanctified: Receive our supplications and prayers, which we offer before thee for all members of thy holy Church, that in their vocation and ministry they may truly and godly serve thee; through our Lord and Savior Jesus Christ, who liveth and reigneth with thee, in the unity of the same Spirit, one God, now and for ever. *Amen.*

*Preface of Baptism, or of the Season*

### 16. For the Mission of the Church

O God, who hast made of one blood all the peoples of the earth, and didst send thy blessed Son to preach peace to those who are far off and to those who are near: Grant that people everywhere may seek after thee and find thee, bring the nations into thy fold, pour out thy Spirit upon all flesh, and hasten the coming of thy kingdom; through the same thy Son Jesus Christ our Lord, who liveth and reigneth with thee and the same Spirit, one God, now and for ever. *Amen.*

*or this*

O God of all the nations of the earth: Remember the multitudes who have been created in thine image but have not known the redeeming work of our Savior Jesus Christ; and grant that, by the prayers and labors of thy holy Church, they may be brought to know and worship thee as thou hast been revealed in thy Son; who liveth and reigneth with thee and the Holy Spirit, one God, for ever and ever. *Amen.*

*Preface of the Season, or of Pentecost*

## 17. For the Nation

Lord God Almighty, who hast made all peoples of the earth for thy glory, to serve thee in freedom and peace: Grant to the people of our country a zeal for justice and the strength of forbearance, that we may use our liberty in accordance with thy gracious will; through Jesus Christ our Lord, who liveth and reigneth with thee and the Holy Spirit, one God, for ever and ever. *Amen.*

*The Collect for Independence Day may be used instead.*

*Preface of Trinity Sunday*

## 18. For Peace

O Almighty God, kindle, we beseech thee, in every heart the true love of peace, and guide with thy wisdom those who take counsel for the nations of the earth, that in tranquillity thy dominion may increase till the earth is filled with the knowledge of thy love; through Jesus Christ our Lord, who liveth and reigneth with thee, in the unity of the Holy Spirit, one God, now and for ever. *Amen.*

*Preface of the Season*

## 19. For Rogation Days

*For use on the traditional days or at other times*

### I. For fruitful seasons

Almighty God, Lord of heaven and earth: We humbly pray that thy gracious providence may give and preserve to our use the harvests of the land and of the seas, and may prosper all who labor to gather them, that we, who constantly receive good things from thy hand, may always give thee thanks; through Jesus Christ our Lord, who liveth and reigneth with thee and the Holy Spirit, one God, for ever and ever. *Amen.*

*Preface of the Season*

## II. For commerce and industry

Almighty God, whose Son Jesus Christ in his earthly life
shared our toil and hallowed our labor: Be present with
thy people where they work; make those who carry on
the industries and commerce of this land responsive to thy
will; and give to us all a pride in what we do, and a just
return for our labor; through Jesus Christ our Lord, who
liveth and reigneth with thee, in the unity of the Holy Spirit,
one God, now and for ever. *Amen.*

*Preface of the Season*

## III. For stewardship of creation

O merciful Creator, whose hand is open wide to satisfy the
needs of every living creature: Make us, we beseech thee,
ever thankful for thy loving providence; and grant that we,
remembering the account that we must one day give, may be
faithful stewards of thy bounty; through Jesus Christ our
Lord, who with thee and the Holy Spirit liveth and reigneth,
one God, for ever and ever. *Amen.*

*Preface of the Season*

## 20. For the Sick

Heavenly Father, giver of life and health: Comfort and
relieve thy sick servants, and give thy power of healing to
those who minister to their needs, that those (*or N., or NN.*)
for whom our prayers are offered may be strengthened in
*their* weakness and have confidence in thy loving care;
through Jesus Christ our Lord, who liveth and reigneth with
thee and the Holy Spirit, one God, now and for ever. *Amen.*

*Preface of the Season*

*The postcommunion prayer on page 457 may be used.*

### 21. For Social Justice

Almighty God, who hast created us in thine own image:
Grant us grace fearlessly to contend against evil and to make
no peace with oppression; and, that we may reverently use
our freedom, help us to employ it in the maintenance of
justice in our communities and among the nations, to the
glory of thy holy Name; through Jesus Christ our Lord, who
liveth and reigneth with thee and the Holy Spirit, one God,
now and for ever. *Amen.*

*Preface of the Season*

### 22. For Social Service

O Lord our heavenly Father, whose blessed Son came not to
be ministered unto but to minister: Bless, we beseech thee, all
who, following in his steps, give themselves to the service of
others; that with wisdom, patience, and courage, they may
minister in his name to the suffering, the friendless, and the
needy; for the love of him who laid down his life for us, the
same thy Son our Savior Jesus Christ, who liveth and reigneth
with thee and the Holy Spirit, one God, for ever and ever.
*Amen.*

*Preface of the Season*

### 23. For Education

Almighty God, the fountain of all wisdom: Enlighten by thy
Holy Spirit those who teach and those who learn, that,
rejoicing in the knowledge of thy truth, they may worship
thee and serve thee from generation to generation; through
Jesus Christ our Lord, who liveth and reigneth with thee and
the same Spirit, one God, for ever and ever. *Amen.*

*Preface of the Season*

### 24. For Vocation in Daily Work

Almighty God our heavenly Father, who declarest thy glory and showest forth thy handiwork in the heavens and in the earth: Deliver us, we beseech thee, in our several occupations from the service of self alone, that we may do the work which thou givest us to do, in truth and beauty and for the common good; for the sake of him who came among us as one that serveth, thy Son Jesus Christ our Lord, who liveth and reigneth with thee and the Holy Spirit, one God, for ever and ever. *Amen.*

*Preface of the Season*

### 25. For Labor Day

Almighty God, who hast so linked our lives one with another that all we do affecteth, for good or ill, all other lives: So guide us in the work we do, that we may do it not for self alone, but for the common good; and, as we seek a proper return for our own labor, make us mindful of the rightful aspirations of other workers, and arouse our concern for those who are out of work; through Jesus Christ our Lord, who liveth and reigneth with thee and the Holy Spirit, one God, for ever and ever. *Amen.*

*Preface of the Season*

# Collects: Contemporary

## First Sunday of Advent

Almighty God, give us grace to cast away the works of darkness, and put on the armor of light, now in the time of this mortal life in which your Son Jesus Christ came to visit us in great humility; that in the last day, when he shall come again in his glorious majesty to judge both the living and the dead, we may rise to the life immortal; through him who lives and reigns with you and the Holy Spirit, one God, now and for ever. *Amen.*

*Preface of Advent*

## Second Sunday of Advent

Merciful God, who sent your messengers the prophets to preach repentance and prepare the way for our salvation: Give us grace to heed their warnings and forsake our sins, that we may greet with joy the coming of Jesus Christ our Redeemer; who lives and reigns with you and the Holy Spirit, one God, now and for ever. *Amen.*

*Preface of Advent*

### Third Sunday of Advent

Stir up your power, O Lord, and with great might come
among us; and, because we are sorely hindered by our sins,
let your bountiful grace and mercy speedily help and deliver
us; through Jesus Christ our Lord, to whom, with you and
the Holy Spirit, be honor and glory, now and for ever. *Amen.*

*Preface of Advent*

*Wednesday, Friday, and Saturday of this week are the traditional winter
Ember Days.*

### Fourth Sunday of Advent

Purify our conscience, Almighty God, by your daily visitation,
that your Son Jesus Christ, at his coming, may find in us a
mansion prepared for himself; who lives and reigns with you,
in the unity of the Holy Spirit, one God, now and for ever.
*Amen.*

*Preface of Advent*

### The Nativity of Our Lord: Christmas Day  *December 25*

O God, you make us glad by the yearly festival of the birth
of your only Son Jesus Christ: Grant that we, who joyfully
receive him as our Redeemer, may with sure confidence
behold him when he comes to be our Judge; who lives and
reigns with you and the Holy Spirit, one God, now and
for ever. *Amen.*

*or this*

O God, you have caused this holy night to shine with the
brightness of the true Light: Grant that we, who have known
the mystery of that Light on earth, may also enjoy him
perfectly in heaven; where with you and the Holy Spirit he
lives and reigns, one God, in glory everlasting. *Amen.*

*or this*

Almighty God, you have given your only-begotten Son to take our nature upon him, and to be born [this day] of a pure virgin: Grant that we, who have been born again and made your children by adoption and grace, may daily be renewed by your Holy Spirit; through our Lord Jesus Christ, to whom with you and the same Spirit be honor and glory, now and for ever. *Amen.*

*Preface of the Incarnation*

*The Collect immediately preceding and any of the sets of Proper Lessons for Christmas Day serve for any weekdays between Holy Innocents' Day and the First Sunday after Christmas Day.*

## First Sunday after Christmas Day

*This Sunday takes precedence over the three Holy Days which follow Christmas Day. As necessary, the observance of one, two, or all three of them, is postponed one day.*

Almighty God, you have poured upon us the new light of your incarnate Word: Grant that this light, enkindled in our hearts, may shine forth in our lives; through Jesus Christ our Lord, who lives and reigns with you, in the unity of the Holy Spirit, one God, now and for ever. *Amen.*

*Preface of the Incarnation*

## The Holy Name    *January 1*

Eternal Father, you gave to your incarnate Son the holy name of Jesus to be the sign of our salvation: Plant in every heart, we pray, the love of him who is the Savior of the world, our Lord Jesus Christ; who lives and reigns with you and the Holy Spirit, one God, in glory everlasting. *Amen.*

*Preface of the Incarnation*

*Collects: Contemporary*   213

### Second Sunday after Christmas Day

O God, who wonderfully created, and yet more wonderfully
restored, the dignity of human nature: Grant that we may
share the divine life of him who humbled himself to share
our humanity, your Son Jesus Christ; who lives and reigns
with you, in the unity of the Holy Spirit, one God, for ever
and ever. *Amen.*

*Preface of the Incarnation*


### The Epiphany   *January 6*

O God, by the leading of a star you manifested your only Son
to the peoples of the earth: Lead us, who know you now by
faith, to your presence, where we may see your glory face to
face; through Jesus Christ our Lord, who lives and reigns
with you and the Holy Spirit, one God, now and for ever.
*Amen.*

*Preface of the Epiphany*

*The preceding Collect, with the Psalm and Lessons for the Epiphany, or
those for the Second Sunday after Christmas, serves for weekdays
between the Epiphany and the following Sunday. The Preface of the
Epiphany is used.*


### First Sunday after the Epiphany: The Baptism of our Lord

Father in heaven, who at the baptism of Jesus in the River
Jordan proclaimed him your beloved Son and anointed him
with the Holy Spirit: Grant that all who are baptized into his
Name may keep the covenant they have made, and boldly
confess him as Lord and Savior; who with you and the Holy
Spirit lives and reigns, one God, in glory everlasting. *Amen.*

*Preface of the Epiphany*

## Second Sunday after the Epiphany

Almighty God, whose Son our Savior Jesus Christ is the light of the world: Grant that your people, illumined by your Word and Sacraments, may shine with the radiance of Christ's glory, that he may be known, worshiped, and obeyed to the ends of the earth; through Jesus Christ our Lord, who with you and the Holy Spirit lives and reigns, one God, now and for ever. *Amen.*

*Preface of the Epiphany, or of the Lord's Day*

## Third Sunday after the Epiphany

Give us grace, O Lord, to answer readily the call of our Savior Jesus Christ and proclaim to all people the Good News of his salvation, that we and the whole world may perceive the glory of his marvelous works; who lives and reigns with you and the Holy Spirit, one God, for ever and ever. *Amen.*

*Preface of the Epiphany, or of the Lord's Day*

## Fourth Sunday after the Epiphany

Almighty and everlasting God, you govern all things both in heaven and on earth: Mercifully hear the supplications of your people, and in our time grant us your peace; through Jesus Christ our Lord, who lives and reigns with you and the Holy Spirit, one God, for ever and ever. *Amen.*

*Preface of the Epiphany, or of the Lord's Day*

### Fifth Sunday after the Epiphany

Set us free, O God, from the bondage of our sins, and give us the liberty of that abundant life which you have made known to us in your Son our Savior Jesus Christ; who lives and reigns with you, in the unity of the Holy Spirit, one God, now and for ever. *Amen.*

*Preface of the Epiphany, or of the Lord's Day*

### Sixth Sunday after the Epiphany

O God, the strength of all who put their trust in you: Mercifully accept our prayers; and because in our weakness we can do nothing good without you, give us the help of your grace, that in keeping your commandments we may please you both in will and deed; through Jesus Christ our Lord, who lives and reigns with you and the Holy Spirit, one God, for ever and ever. *Amen.*

*Preface of the Epiphany, or of the Lord's Day*

### Seventh Sunday after the Epiphany

O Lord, you have taught us that without love whatever we do is worth nothing: Send your Holy Spirit and pour into our hearts your greatest gift, which is love, the true bond of peace and of all virtue, without which whoever lives is accounted dead before you. Grant this for the sake of your only Son Jesus Christ, who lives and reigns with you and the Holy Spirit, one God, now and for ever. *Amen.*

*Preface of the Epiphany, or of the Lord's Day*

### Eighth Sunday after the Epiphany

Most loving Father, whose will it is for us to give thanks for all things, to fear nothing but the loss of you, and to cast all our care on you who care for us: Preserve us from faithless fears and worldly anxieties, that no clouds of this mortal life may hide from us the light of that love which is immortal, and which you have manifested to us in your Son Jesus Christ our Lord; who lives and reigns with you, in the unity of the Holy Spirit, one God, now and for ever. *Amen.*

*Preface of the Epiphany, or of the Lord's Day*

## Last Sunday after the Epiphany

*This Proper is always used on the Sunday before Ash Wednesday*

O God, who before the passion of your only-begotten Son revealed his glory upon the holy mountain: Grant to us that we, beholding by faith the light of his countenance, may be strengthened to bear our cross, and be changed into his likeness from glory to glory; through Jesus Christ our Lord, who lives and reigns with you and the Holy Spirit, one God, for ever and ever. *Amen.*

*Preface of the Epiphany*

## Ash Wednesday

*The Proper Liturgy for this day is on page 264.*

Almighty and everlasting God, you hate nothing you have made and forgive the sins of all who are penitent: Create and make in us new and contrite hearts, that we, worthily lamenting our sins and acknowledging our wretchedness, may obtain of you, the God of all mercy, perfect remission and forgiveness; through Jesus Christ our Lord, who lives and reigns with you and the Holy Spirit, one God, for ever and ever. *Amen.*

*Preface of Lent*

*This Collect, with the corresponding Psalm and Lessons, also serves for the weekdays which follow, except as otherwise appointed.*

**First Sunday in Lent**

Almighty God, whose blessed Son was led by the Spirit to be tempted by Satan: Come quickly to help us who are assaulted by many temptations; and, as you know the weaknesses of each of us, let each one find you mighty to save; through Jesus Christ your Son our Lord, who lives and reigns with you and the Holy Spirit, one God, now and for ever. *Amen.*

*Preface of Lent*

*Wednesday, Friday, and Saturday of this week are the traditional spring Ember Days.*

**Second Sunday in Lent**

O God, whose glory it is always to have mercy: Be gracious to all who have gone astray from your ways, and bring them again with penitent hearts and steadfast faith to embrace and hold fast the unchangeable truth of your Word, Jesus Christ your Son; who with you and the Holy Spirit lives and reigns, one God, for ever and ever. *Amen.*

*Preface of Lent*

**Third Sunday in Lent**

Almighty God, you know that we have no power in ourselves to help ourselves: Keep us both outwardly in our bodies and inwardly in our souls, that we may be defended from all adversities which may happen to the body, and from all evil thoughts which may assault and hurt the soul; through Jesus Christ our Lord, who lives and reigns with you and the Holy Spirit, one God, for ever and ever. *Amen.*

*Preface of Lent*

### Fourth Sunday in Lent

Gracious Father, whose blessed Son Jesus Christ came down from heaven to be the true bread which gives life to the world: Evermore give us this bread, that he may live in us, and we in him; who lives and reigns with you and the Holy Spirit, one God, now and for ever. *Amen.*

*Preface of Lent*

### Fifth Sunday in Lent

Almighty God, you alone can bring into order the unruly wills and affections of sinners: Grant your people grace to love what you command and desire what you promise; that, among the swift and varied changes of the world, our hearts may surely there be fixed where true joys are to be found; through Jesus Christ our Lord, who lives and reigns with you and the Holy Spirit, one God, now and for ever. *Amen.*

*Preface of Lent*

### Sunday of the Passion: Palm Sunday

*The Proper Liturgy for this day is on page 270.*

Almighty and everliving God, in your tender love for the human race you sent your Son our Savior Jesus Christ to take upon him our nature, and to suffer death upon the cross, giving us the example of his great humility: Mercifully grant that we may walk in the way of his suffering, and also share in his resurrection; through Jesus Christ our Lord, who lives and reigns with you and the Holy Spirit, one God, for ever and ever. *Amen.*

*Preface of Holy Week*

## Monday in Holy Week

Almighty God, whose most dear Son went not up to joy but first he suffered pain, and entered not into glory before he was crucified: Mercifully grant that we, walking in the way of the cross, may find it none other than the way of life and peace; through Jesus Christ your Son our Lord, who lives and reigns with you and the Holy Spirit, one God, for ever and ever. *Amen.*

*Preface of Holy Week*

## Tuesday in Holy Week

O God, by the passion of your blessed Son you made an instrument of shameful death to be for us the means of life: Grant us so to glory in the cross of Christ, that we may gladly suffer shame and loss for the sake of your Son our Savior Jesus Christ; who lives and reigns with you and the Holy Spirit, one God, for ever and ever. *Amen.*

*Preface of Holy Week*

## Wednesday in Holy Week

Lord God, whose blessed Son our Savior gave his body to be whipped and his face to be spit upon: Give us grace to accept joyfully the sufferings of the present time, confident of the glory that shall be revealed; through Jesus Christ your Son our Lord, who lives and reigns with you and the Holy Spirit, one God, for ever and ever. *Amen.*

*Preface of Holy Week*

## Maundy Thursday

*The Proper Liturgy for this day is on page 274.*

Almighty Father, whose dear Son, on the night before he
suffered, instituted the Sacrament of his Body and Blood:
Mercifully grant that we may receive it thankfully in
remembrance of Jesus Christ our Lord, who in these holy
mysteries gives us a pledge of eternal life; and who now lives
and reigns with you and the Holy Spirit, one God, for ever
and ever. *Amen.*

*Preface of Holy Week*

## Good Friday

*The Proper Liturgy for this day is on page 276.*

Almighty God, we pray you graciously to behold this your
family, for whom our Lord Jesus Christ was willing to be
betrayed, and given into the hands of sinners, and to suffer
death upon the cross; who now lives and reigns with you and
the Holy Spirit, one God, for ever and ever. *Amen.*

## Holy Saturday

*The Proper Liturgy for this day is on page 283.*

O God, Creator of heaven and earth: Grant that, as the
crucified body of your dear Son was laid in the tomb and
rested on this holy Sabbath, so we may await with him the
coming of the third day, and rise with him to newness of life;
who now lives and reigns with you and the Holy Spirit, one
God, for ever and ever. *Amen.*

## Easter Day

*The Liturgy of the Easter Vigil is on page 285.*

O God, who for our redemption gave your only-begotten
Son to the death of the cross, and by his glorious resurrection
delivered us from the power of our enemy: Grant us so to die
daily to sin, that we may evermore live with him in the joy of
his resurrection; through Jesus Christ your Son our Lord,
who lives and reigns with you and the Holy Spirit, one God,
now and for ever. *Amen.*

*or this*

O God, who made this most holy night to shine with the
glory of the Lord's resurrection: Stir up in your Church that
Spirit of adoption which is given to us in Baptism, that we,
being renewed both in body and mind, may worship you in
sincerity and truth; through Jesus Christ our Lord, who lives
and reigns with you, in the unity of the Holy Spirit, one God,
now and for ever. *Amen.*

*or this*

Almighty God, who through your only-begotten Son Jesus
Christ overcame death and opened to us the gate of
everlasting life: Grant that we, who celebrate with joy the
day of the Lord's resurrection, may be raised from the death
of sin by your life-giving Spirit; through Jesus Christ our
Lord, who lives and reigns with you and the Holy Spirit, one
God, now and for ever. *Amen.*

*Preface of Easter*

## Monday in Easter Week

Grant, we pray, Almighty God, that we who celebrate with
awe the Paschal feast may be found worthy to attain to

everlasting joys; through Jesus Christ our Lord, who lives
and reigns with you and the Holy Spirit, one God, now and
for ever. *Amen.*

*Preface of Easter*

## Tuesday in Easter Week

O God, who by the glorious resurrection of your Son Jesus
Christ destroyed death and brought life and immortality to
light: Grant that we, who have been raised with him, may
abide in his presence and rejoice in the hope of eternal glory;
through Jesus Christ our Lord, to whom, with you and the
Holy Spirit, be dominion and praise for ever and ever. *Amen.*

*Preface of Easter*

## Wednesday in Easter Week

O God, whose blessed Son made himself known to his
disciples in the breaking of bread: Open the eyes of our faith,
that we may behold him in all his redeeming work; who lives
and reigns with you, in the unity of the Holy Spirit, one God,
now and for ever. *Amen.*

*Preface of Easter*

## Thursday in Easter Week

Almighty and everlasting God, who in the Paschal mystery
established the new covenant of reconciliation: Grant that all
who have been reborn into the fellowship of Christ's Body
may show forth in their lives what they profess by their faith;
through Jesus Christ our Lord, who lives and reigns with you
and the Holy Spirit, one God, for ever and ever. *Amen.*

*Preface of Easter*

**Friday in Easter Week**

Almighty Father, who gave your only Son to die for our sins and to rise for our justification: Give us grace so to put away the leaven of malice and wickedness, that we may always serve you in pureness of living and truth; through Jesus Christ your Son our Lord, who lives and reigns with you and the Holy Spirit, one God, now and for ever. *Amen.*

*Preface of Easter*

**Saturday in Easter Week**

We thank you, heavenly Father, that you have delivered us from the dominion of sin and death and brought us into the kingdom of your Son; and we pray that, as by his death he has recalled us to life, so by his love he may raise us to eternal joys; who lives and reigns with you, in the unity of the Holy Spirit, one God, now and for ever. *Amen.*

*Preface of Easter*

**Second Sunday of Easter**

Almighty and everlasting God, who in the Paschal mystery established the new covenant of reconciliation: Grant that all who have been reborn into the fellowship of Christ's Body may show forth in their lives what they profess by their faith; through Jesus Christ our Lord, who lives and reigns with you and the Holy Spirit, one God, for ever and ever. *Amen.*

*Preface of Easter*

**Third Sunday of Easter**

O God, whose blessed Son made himself known to his disciples in the breaking of bread: Open the eyes of our faith, that we may behold him in all his redeeming work; who lives and reigns with you, in the unity of the Holy Spirit, one God, now and for ever. *Amen.*

*Preface of Easter*

## Fourth Sunday of Easter

O God, whose Son Jesus is the good shepherd of your people: Grant that when we hear his voice we may know him who calls us each by name, and follow where he leads; who, with you and the Holy Spirit, lives and reigns, one God, for ever and ever. *Amen.*

*Preface of Easter*

## Fifth Sunday of Easter

Almighty God, whom truly to know is everlasting life: Grant us so perfectly to know your Son Jesus Christ to be the way, the truth, and the life, that we may steadfastly follow his steps in the way that leads to eternal life; through Jesus Christ your Son our Lord, who lives and reigns with you, in the unity of the Holy Spirit, one God, for ever and ever. *Amen.*

*Preface of Easter*

## Sixth Sunday of Easter

O God, you have prepared for those who love you such good things as surpass our understanding: Pour into our hearts such love towards you, that we, loving you in all things and above all things, may obtain your promises, which exceed all that we can desire; through Jesus Christ our Lord, who lives and reigns with you and the Holy Spirit, one God, for ever and ever. *Amen.*

*Preface of Easter*

*Monday, Tuesday, and Wednesday of this week are the traditional Rogation Days.*

## Ascension Day

Almighty God, whose blessed Son our Savior Jesus Christ ascended far above all heavens that he might fill all things: Mercifully give us faith to perceive that, according to his promise, he abides with his Church on earth, even to the end of the ages; through Jesus Christ our Lord, who lives and reigns with you and the Holy Spirit, one God, in glory everlasting. *Amen.*

*or this*

Grant, we pray, Almighty God, that as we believe your only-begotten Son our Lord Jesus Christ to have ascended into heaven, so we may also in heart and mind there ascend, and with him continually dwell; who lives and reigns with you and the Holy Spirit, one God, for ever and ever. *Amen.*

*Preface of the Ascension*

*Either of the preceding Collects, with the proper Psalm and Lessons for Ascension Day, serves for the following weekdays, except as otherwise appointed.*

## Seventh Sunday of Easter: The Sunday after Ascension Day

O God, the King of glory, you have exalted your only Son Jesus Christ with great triumph to your kingdom in heaven: Do not leave us comfortless, but send us your Holy Spirit to strengthen us, and exalt us to that place where our Savior Christ has gone before; who lives and reigns with you and the Holy Spirit, one God, in glory everlasting. *Amen.*

*Preface of the Ascension*

# The Day of Pentecost: Whitsunday

*When a Vigil of Pentecost is observed, it begins with the Service of Light, page 109 (substituting, if desired, the Gloria in excelsis for the Phos hilaron), and continues with the Salutation and Collect of the Day. Three or more of the appointed Lessons are read before the Gospel, each followed by a Psalm, Canticle, or hymn. Holy Baptism or Confirmation (beginning with the Presentation of the Candidates), or the Renewal of Baptismal Vows, page 292, follows the Sermon.*

Almighty God, on this day you opened the way of eternal life to every race and nation by the promised gift of your Holy Spirit: Shed abroad this gift throughout the world by the preaching of the Gospel, that it may reach to the ends of the earth; through Jesus Christ our Lord, who lives and reigns with you, in the unity of the Holy Spirit, one God, for ever and ever. *Amen.*

*or this*

O God, who on this day taught the hearts of your faithful people by sending to them the light of your Holy Spirit: Grant us by the same Spirit to have a right judgment in all things, and evermore to rejoice in his holy comfort; through Jesus Christ your Son our Lord, who lives and reigns with you, in the unity of the Holy Spirit, one God, for ever and ever. *Amen.*

*Preface of Pentecost*

*On the weekdays which follow, the numbered Proper which corresponds most closely to the date of Pentecost in that year is used. See page 158.*

*Wednesday, Friday, and Saturday of this week are the traditional summer Ember Days.*

**First Sunday after Pentecost: Trinity Sunday**

Almighty and everlasting God, you have given to us
your servants grace, by the confession of a true faith, to
acknowledge the glory of the eternal Trinity, and in the
power of your divine Majesty to worship the Unity: Keep
us steadfast in this faith and worship, and bring us at last to
see you in your one and eternal glory, O Father; who with
the Son and the Holy Spirit live and reign, one God, for ever
and ever. *Amen.*

*Preface of Trinity Sunday*

*On the weekdays which follow, the numbered Proper which corresponds
most closely to the date of Trinity Sunday in that year is used.*

# The Season after Pentecost

*Directions for the use of the Propers which follow are on page 158.*

**Proper 1**    *Week of the Sunday closest to May 11*

Remember, O Lord, what you have wrought in us and not
what we deserve; and, as you have called us to your service,
make us worthy of our calling; through Jesus Christ our Lord,
who lives and reigns with you and the Holy Spirit, one God,
now and for ever. *Amen.*

*No Proper Preface is used.*

**Proper 2**    *Week of the Sunday closest to May 18*

Almighty and merciful God, in your goodness keep us, we
pray, from all things that may hurt us, that we, being ready

both in mind and body, may accomplish with free hearts
those things which belong to your purpose; through Jesus
Christ our Lord, who lives and reigns with you and the Holy
Spirit, one God, now and for ever. *Amen.*

*No Proper Preface is used.*

**Proper 3**   *The Sunday closest to May 25*

Grant, O Lord, that the course of this world may be
peaceably governed by your providence; and that your
Church may joyfully serve you in confidence and serenity;
through Jesus Christ our Lord, who lives and reigns with you
and the Holy Spirit, one God, for ever and ever. *Amen.*

*Preface of the Lord's Day*

**Proper 4**   *The Sunday closest to June 1*

O God, your never-failing providence sets in order all things
both in heaven and earth: Put away from us, we entreat you,
all hurtful things, and give us those things which are profitable
for us; through Jesus Christ our Lord, who lives and reigns
with you and the Holy Spirit, one God, for ever and ever.
*Amen.*

*Preface of the Lord's Day*

**Proper 5**   *The Sunday closest to June 8*

O God, from whom all good proceeds: Grant that by your
inspiration we may think those things that are right, and by
your merciful guiding may do them; through Jesus Christ our
Lord, who lives and reigns with you and the Holy Spirit, one
God, for ever and ever. *Amen.*

*Preface of the Lord's Day*

**Proper 6** *The Sunday closest to June 15*

Keep, O Lord, your household the Church in your steadfast
faith and love, that through your grace we may proclaim
your truth with boldness, and minister your justice with
compassion; for the sake of our Savior Jesus Christ, who
lives and reigns with you and the Holy Spirit, one God, now
and for ever. *Amen.*

*Preface of the Lord's Day*

**Proper 7** *The Sunday closest to June 22*

O Lord, make us have perpetual love and reverence for your
holy Name, for you never fail to help and govern those whom
you have set upon the sure foundation of your loving-kindness;
through Jesus Christ our Lord, who lives and reigns with you
and the Holy Spirit, one God, for ever and ever. *Amen.*

*Preface of the Lord's Day*

**Proper 8** *The Sunday closest to June 29*

Almighty God, you have built your Church upon the
foundation of the apostles and prophets, Jesus Christ himself
being the chief cornerstone: Grant us so to be joined together
in unity of spirit by their teaching, that we may be made a
holy temple acceptable to you; through Jesus Christ our Lord,
who lives and reigns with you and the Holy Spirit, one God,
for ever and ever. *Amen.*

*Preface of the Lord's Day*

**Proper 9** *The Sunday closest to July 6*

O God, you have taught us to keep all your commandments
by loving you and our neighbor: Grant us the grace of your
Holy Spirit, that we may be devoted to you with our whole

heart, and united to one another with pure affection; through Jesus Christ our Lord, who lives and reigns with you and the Holy Spirit, one God, for ever and ever. *Amen.*

*Preface of the Lord's Day*

**Proper 10**    *The Sunday closest to July 13*

O Lord, mercifully receive the prayers of your people who call upon you, and grant that they may know and understand what things they ought to do, and also may have grace and power faithfully to accomplish them; through Jesus Christ our Lord, who lives and reigns with you and the Holy Spirit, one God, now and for ever. *Amen.*

*Preface of the Lord's Day*

**Proper 11**    *The Sunday closest to July 20*

Almighty God, the fountain of all wisdom, you know our necessities before we ask and our ignorance in asking: Have compassion on our weakness, and mercifully give us those things which for our unworthiness we dare not, and for our blindness we cannot ask; through the worthiness of your Son Jesus Christ our Lord, who lives and reigns with you and the Holy Spirit, one God, now and for ever. *Amen.*

*Preface of the Lord's Day*

**Proper 12**    *The Sunday closest to July 27*

O God, the protector of all who trust in you, without whom nothing is strong, nothing is holy: Increase and multiply upon us your mercy; that, with you as our ruler and guide, we may so pass through things temporal, that we lose not the things eternal; through Jesus Christ our Lord, who lives and reigns with you and the Holy Spirit, one God, for ever and ever. *Amen.*

*Preface of the Lord's Day*

**Proper 13**   *The Sunday closest to August 3*

Let your continual mercy, O Lord, cleanse and defend your Church; and, because it cannot continue in safety without your help, protect and govern it always by your goodness; through Jesus Christ our Lord, who lives and reigns with you and the Holy Spirit, one God, for ever and ever. *Amen.*

*Preface of the Lord's Day*

**Proper 14**   *The Sunday closest to August 10*

Grant to us, Lord, we pray, the spirit to think and do always those things that are right, that we, who cannot exist without you, may by you be enabled to live according to your will; through Jesus Christ our Lord, who lives and reigns with you and the Holy Spirit, one God, for ever and ever. *Amen.*

*Preface of the Lord's Day*

**Proper 15**   *The Sunday closest to August 17*

Almighty God, you have given your only Son to be for us a sacrifice for sin, and also an example of godly life: Give us grace to receive thankfully the fruits of his redeeming work, and to follow daily in the blessed steps of his most holy life; through Jesus Christ your Son our Lord, who lives and reigns with you and the Holy Spirit, one God, now and for ever. *Amen.*

*Preface of the Lord's Day*

**Proper 16**   *The Sunday closest to August 24*

Grant, O merciful God, that your Church, being gathered together in unity by your Holy Spirit, may show forth your power among all peoples, to the glory of your Name;

through Jesus Christ our Lord, who lives and reigns with you and the Holy Spirit, one God, for ever and ever. *Amen.*

*Preface of the Lord's Day*

**Proper 17**   *The Sunday closest to August 31*

Lord of all power and might, the author and giver of all good things: Graft in our hearts the love of your Name; increase in us true religion; nourish us with all goodness; and bring forth in us the fruit of good works; through Jesus Christ our Lord, who lives and reigns with you and the Holy Spirit, one God, for ever and ever. *Amen.*

*Preface of the Lord's Day*

**Proper 18**   *The Sunday closest to September 7*

Grant us, O Lord, to trust in you with all our hearts; for, as you always resist the proud who confide in their own strength, so you never forsake those who make their boast of your mercy; through Jesus Christ our Lord, who lives and reigns with you and the Holy Spirit, one God, now and for ever. *Amen.*

*Preface of the Lord's Day*

**Proper 19**   *The Sunday closest to September 14*

O God, because without you we are not able to please you, mercifully grant that your Holy Spirit may in all things direct and rule our hearts; through Jesus Christ our Lord, who lives and reigns with you and the Holy Spirit, one God, now and for ever. *Amen.*

*Preface of the Lord's Day*

*The Wednesday, Friday, and Saturday after September 14 are the traditional autumnal Ember Days.*

**Proper 20**   *The Sunday closest to September 21*

Grant us, Lord, not to be anxious about earthly things, but to love things heavenly; and even now, while we are placed among things that are passing away, to hold fast to those that shall endure; through Jesus Christ our Lord, who lives and reigns with you and the Holy Spirit, one God, for ever and ever. *Amen*

*Preface of the Lord's Day*

**Proper 21**   *The Sunday closest to September 28*

O God, you declare your almighty power chiefly in showing mercy and pity: Grant us the fullness of your grace, that we, running to obtain your promises, may become partakers of your heavenly treasure; through Jesus Christ our Lord, who lives and reigns with you and the Holy Spirit, one God, for ever and ever. *Amen.*

*Preface of the Lord's Day*

**Proper 22**   *The Sunday closest to October 5*

Almighty and everlasting God, you are always more ready to hear than we to pray, and to give more than we either desire or deserve: Pour upon us the abundance of your mercy, forgiving us those things of which our conscience is afraid, and giving us those good things for which we are not worthy to ask, except through the merits and mediation of Jesus Christ our Savior; who lives and reigns with you and the Holy Spirit, one God, for ever and ever. *Amen.*

*Preface of the Lord's Day*

**Proper 23**   *The Sunday closest to October 12*

Lord, we pray that your grace may always precede and follow us, that we may continually be given to good works;

through Jesus Christ our Lord, who lives and reigns with you and the Holy Spirit, one God, now and for ever. *Amen.*

*Preface of the Lord's Day*

**Proper 24**  *The Sunday closest to October 19*

Almighty and everlasting God, in Christ you have revealed your glory among the nations: Preserve the works of your mercy, that your Church throughout the world may persevere with steadfast faith in the confession of your Name; through Jesus Christ our Lord, who lives and reigns with you and the Holy Spirit, one God, for ever and ever. *Amen.*

*Preface of the Lord's Day*

**Proper 25**  *The Sunday closest to October 26*

Almighty and everlasting God, increase in us the gifts of faith, hope, and charity; and, that we may obtain what you promise, make us love what you command; through Jesus Christ our Lord, who lives and reigns with you and the Holy Spirit, one God, for ever and ever. *Amen.*

*Preface of the Lord's Day*

**Proper 26**  *The Sunday closest to November 2*

Almighty and merciful God, it is only by your gift that your faithful people offer you true and laudable service: Grant that we may run without stumbling to obtain your heavenly promises; through Jesus Christ our Lord, who lives and reigns with you and the Holy Spirit, one God, now and for ever. *Amen.*

*Preface of the Lord's Day*

**Proper 27**   *The Sunday closest to November 9*

O God, whose blessed Son came into the world that he might destroy the works of the devil and make us children of God and heirs of eternal life: Grant that, having this hope, we may purify ourselves as he is pure; that, when he comes again with power and great glory, we may be made like him in his eternal and glorious kingdom; where he lives and reigns with you and the Holy Spirit, one God, for ever and ever. *Amen.*

*Preface of the Lord's Day*

**Proper 28**   *The Sunday closest to November 16*

Blessed Lord, who caused all holy Scriptures to be written for our learning: Grant us so to hear them, read, mark, learn, and inwardly digest them, that we may embrace and ever hold fast the blessed hope of everlasting life, which you have given us in our Savior Jesus Christ; who lives and reigns with you and the Holy Spirit, one God, for ever and ever. *Amen.*

*Preface of the Lord's Day*

**Proper 29**   *The Sunday closest to November 23*

Almighty and everlasting God, whose will it is to restore all things in your well-beloved Son, the King of kings and Lord of lords: Mercifully grant that the peoples of the earth, divided and enslaved by sin, may be freed and brought together under his most gracious rule; who lives and reigns with you and the Holy Spirit, one God, now and for ever. *Amen.*

*Preface of the Lord's Day, or of Baptism*

# Holy Days

**Saint Andrew**   *November 30*

Almighty God, who gave such grace to your apostle Andrew
that he readily obeyed the call of your Son Jesus Christ, and
brought his brother with him: Give us, who are called by
your holy Word, grace to follow him without delay, and to
bring those near to us into his gracious presence; who lives
and reigns with you and the Holy Spirit, one God, now and
for ever. *Amen.*

*Preface of Apostles*

**Saint Thomas**   *December 21*

Everliving God, who strengthened your apostle Thomas with
firm and certain faith in your Son's resurrection: Grant us so
perfectly and without doubt to believe in Jesus Christ, our
Lord and our God, that our faith may never be found wanting
in your sight; through him who lives and reigns with you and
the Holy Spirit, one God, now and for ever. *Amen.*

*Preface of Apostles*

**Saint Stephen**   *December 26*

We give you thanks, O Lord of glory, for the example of the
first martyr Stephen, who looked up to heaven and prayed
for his persecutors to your Son Jesus Christ, who stands at
your right hand; where he lives and reigns with you and the
Holy Spirit, one God, in glory everlasting. *Amen.*

*Preface of the Incarnation*

### Saint John   *December 27*

Shed upon your Church, O Lord, the brightness of your light,
that we, being illumined by the teaching of your apostle and
evangelist John, may so walk in the light of your truth, that
at length we may attain to the fullness of eternal life; through
Jesus Christ our Lord, who lives and reigns with you and the
Holy Spirit, one God, for ever and ever. *Amen.*

*Preface of the Incarnation*

### The Holy Innocents   *December 28*

We remember today, O God, the slaughter of the holy
innocents of Bethlehem by King Herod. Receive, we pray,
into the arms of your mercy all innocent victims; and by your
great might frustrate the designs of evil tyrants and establish
your rule of justice, love, and peace; through Jesus Christ
our Lord, who lives and reigns with you, in the unity of the
Holy Spirit, one God, for ever and ever. *Amen.*

*Preface of the Incarnation*

### Confession of Saint Peter   *January 18*

Almighty Father, who inspired Simon Peter, first among the
apostles, to confess Jesus as Messiah and Son of the living God:
Keep your Church steadfast upon the rock of this faith, so that
in unity and peace we may proclaim the one truth and follow
the one Lord, our Savior Jesus Christ; who lives and reigns with
you and the Holy Spirit, one God, now and for ever. *Amen.*

*Preface of Apostles*

### Conversion of Saint Paul   *January 25*

O God, by the preaching of your apostle Paul you have
caused the light of the Gospel to shine throughout the world:

Grant, we pray, that we, having his wonderful conversion in remembrance, may show ourselves thankful to you by following his holy teaching; through Jesus Christ our Lord, who lives and reigns with you, in the unity of the Holy Spirit, one God, now and for ever. *Amen.*

*Preface of Apostles*

## The Presentation   *February 2*

Almighty and everliving God, we humbly pray that, as your only-begotten Son was this day presented in the temple, so we may be presented to you with pure and clean hearts by Jesus Christ our Lord; who lives and reigns with you and the Holy Spirit, one God, now and for ever. *Amen.*

*Preface of the Epiphany*

## Saint Matthias   *February 24*

Almighty God, who in the place of Judas chose your faithful servant Matthias to be numbered among the Twelve: Grant that your Church, being delivered from false apostles, may always be guided and governed by faithful and true pastors; through Jesus Christ our Lord, who lives and reigns with you, in the unity of the Holy Spirit, one God, now and for ever. *Amen.*

*Preface of Apostles*

## Saint Joseph   *March 19*

O God, who from the family of your servant David raised up Joseph to be the guardian of your incarnate Son and the spouse of his virgin mother: Give us grace to imitate his uprightness of life and his obedience to your commands; through Jesus Christ our Lord, who lives and reigns with you and the Holy Spirit, one God, for ever and ever. *Amen.*

*Preface of the Epiphany*

### The Annunciation   *March 25*

Pour your grace into our hearts, O Lord, that we who have
known the incarnation of your Son Jesus Christ, announced
by an angel to the Virgin Mary, may by his cross and passion
be brought to the glory of his resurrection; who lives and
reigns with you, in the unity of the Holy Spirit, one God, now
and for ever. *Amen.*

*Preface of the Epiphany*

### Saint Mark   *April 25*

Almighty God, by the hand of Mark the evangelist you have
given to your Church the Gospel of Jesus Christ the Son of
God: We thank you for this witness, and pray that we may be
firmly grounded in its truth; through Jesus Christ our Lord,
who lives and reigns with you and the Holy Spirit, one God,
for ever and ever. *Amen.*

*Preface of All Saints*

### Saint Philip and Saint James   *May 1*

Almighty God, who gave to your apostles Philip and James grace
and strength to bear witness to the truth: Grant that we, being
mindful of their victory of faith, may glorify in life and death the
Name of our Lord Jesus Christ; who lives and reigns with you
and the Holy Spirit, one God, now and for ever. *Amen.*

*Preface of Apostles*

### The Visitation   *May 31*

Father in heaven, by your grace the virgin mother of your
incarnate Son was blessed in bearing him, but still more
blessed in keeping your word: Grant us who honor the
exaltation of her lowliness to follow the example of her
devotion to your will; through Jesus Christ our Lord, who

lives and reigns with you and the Holy Spirit, one God, for ever and ever. *Amen*.

*Preface of the Epiphany*

**Saint Barnabas** *June 11*

Grant, O God, that we may follow the example of your faithful servant Barnabas, who, seeking not his own renown but the well-being of your Church, gave generously of his life and substance for the relief of the poor and the spread of the Gospel; through Jesus Christ our Lord, who lives and reigns with you and the Holy Spirit, one God, for ever and ever. *Amen*.

*Preface of Apostles*

**The Nativity of Saint John the Baptist** *June 24*

Almighty God, by whose providence your servant John the Baptist was wonderfully born, and sent to prepare the way of your Son our Savior by preaching repentance: Make us so to follow his teaching and holy life, that we may truly repent according to his preaching; and, following his example, constantly speak the truth, boldly rebuke vice, and patiently suffer for the truth's sake; through Jesus Christ your Son our Lord, who lives and reigns with you and the Holy Spirit, one God, for ever and ever. *Amen*.

*Preface of Advent*

**Saint Peter and Saint Paul** *June 29*

Almighty God, whose blessed apostles Peter and Paul glorified you by their martyrdom: Grant that your Church, instructed by their teaching and example, and knit together in unity by your Spirit, may ever stand firm upon the one foundation, which is Jesus Christ our Lord; who lives and reigns with you, in the unity of the Holy Spirit, one God, now and for ever. *Amen*.

*Preface of Apostles*

**Independence Day**   *July 4*

Lord God Almighty, in whose Name the founders of this
country won liberty for themselves and for us, and lit the
torch of freedom for nations then unborn: Grant that we and
all the people of this land may have grace to maintain our
liberties in righteousness and peace; through Jesus Christ our
Lord, who lives and reigns with you and the Holy Spirit, one
God, for ever and ever. *Amen.*

*The Collect "For the Nation," page 258, may be used instead.*

*Preface of Trinity Sunday*


**Saint Mary Magdalene**   *July 22*

Almighty God, whose blessed Son restored Mary Magdalene
to health of body and of mind, and called her to be a witness
of his resurrection: Mercifully grant that by your grace we
may be healed from all our infirmities and know you in the
power of his unending life; who with you and the Holy Spirit
lives and reigns, one God, now and for ever. *Amen.*

*Preface of All Saints*


**Saint James**   *July 25*

O gracious God, we remember before you today your servant
and apostle James, first among the Twelve to suffer martyrdom
for the Name of Jesus Christ; and we pray that you will pour
out upon the leaders of your Church that spirit of self-denying
service by which alone they may have true authority among
your people; through Jesus Christ our Lord, who lives and
reigns with you and the Holy Spirit, one God, now and for
ever. *Amen.*

*Preface of Apostles*

## The Transfiguration  *August 6*

O God, who on the holy mount revealed to chosen witnesses your well-beloved Son, wonderfully transfigured, in raiment white and glistening: Mercifully grant that we, being delivered from the disquietude of this world, may by faith behold the King in his beauty; who with you, O Father, and you, O Holy Spirit, lives and reigns, one God, for ever and ever. *Amen.*

*Preface of the Epiphany*

## Saint Mary the Virgin  *August 15*

O God, you have taken to yourself the blessed Virgin Mary, mother of your incarnate Son: Grant that we, who have been redeemed by his blood, may share with her the glory of your eternal kingdom; through Jesus Christ our Lord, who lives and reigns with you, in the unity of the Holy Spirit, one God, now and for ever. *Amen.*

*Preface of the Incarnation*

## Saint Bartholomew  *August 24*

Almighty and everlasting God, who gave to your apostle Bartholomew grace truly to believe and to preach your Word: Grant that your Church may love what he believed and preach what he taught; through Jesus Christ our Lord, who lives and reigns with you and the Holy Spirit, one God, for ever and ever. *Amen.*

*Preface of Apostles*

**Holy Cross Day**  *September 14*

Almighty God, whose Son our Savior Jesus Christ was lifted
high upon the cross that he might draw the whole world to
himself: Mercifully grant that we, who glory in the mystery
of our redemption, may have grace to take up our cross and
follow him; who lives and reigns with you and the Holy
Spirit, one God, in glory everlasting. *Amen.*

*Preface of Holy Week*

**Saint Matthew**  *September 21*

We thank you, heavenly Father, for the witness of your apostle
and evangelist Matthew to the Gospel of your Son our Savior;
and we pray that, after his example, we may with ready wills
and hearts obey the calling of our Lord to follow him;
through Jesus Christ our Lord, who lives and reigns with you
and the Holy Spirit, one God, now and for ever. *Amen.*

*Preface of Apostles*

**Saint Michael and All Angels**  *September 29*

Everlasting God, you have ordained and constituted in a
wonderful order the ministries of angels and mortals:
Mercifully grant that, as your holy angels always serve and
worship you in heaven, so by your appointment they may
help and defend us here on earth; through Jesus Christ our
Lord, who lives and reigns with you and the Holy Spirit, one
God, for ever and ever. *Amen.*

*Preface of Trinity Sunday*

**Saint Luke**  *October 18*

Almighty God, who inspired your servant Luke the physician
to set forth in the Gospel the love and healing power of your
Son: Graciously continue in your Church this love and power

to heal, to the praise and glory of your Name; through Jesus
Christ our Lord, who lives and reigns with you, in the unity
of the Holy Spirit, one God, now and for ever. *Amen.*

*Preface of All Saints*

## Saint James of Jerusalem   *October 23*

Grant, O God, that, following the example of your servant
James the Just, brother of our Lord, your Church may give
itself continually to prayer and to the reconciliation of all
who are at variance and enmity; through Jesus Christ our
Lord, who lives and reigns with you and the Holy Spirit, one
God, now and for ever. *Amen.*

*Preface of All Saints*

## Saint Simon and Saint Jude   *October 28*

O God, we thank you for the glorious company of the apostles,
and especially on this day for Simon and Jude; and we pray
that, as they were faithful and zealous in their mission, so we
may with ardent devotion make known the love and mercy of
our Lord and Savior Jesus Christ; who lives and reigns with
you and the Holy Spirit, one God, for ever and ever. *Amen.*

*Preface of Apostles*

## All Saints' Day   *November 1*

Almighty God, you have knit together your elect in one
communion and fellowship in the mystical body of your Son
Christ our Lord: Give us grace so to follow your blessed saints
in all virtuous and godly living, that we may come to those
ineffable joys that you have prepared for those who truly love
you; through Jesus Christ our Lord, who with you and the Holy
Spirit lives and reigns, one God, in glory everlasting. *Amen.*

*Preface of All Saints*

**Thanksgiving Day**

Almighty and gracious Father, we give you thanks for the fruits of the earth in their season and for the labors of those who harvest them. Make us, we pray, faithful stewards of your great bounty, for the provision of our necessities and the relief of all who are in need, to the glory of your Name; through Jesus Christ our Lord, who lives and reigns with you and the Holy Spirit, one God, now and for ever. *Amen.*

*For the Prayers of the People, the Litany of Thanksgiving on page 836 may be used.*

*Preface of Trinity Sunday*

# The Common of Saints

*The festival of a saint is observed in accordance with the rules of precedence set forth in the Calendar of the Church Year.*

*At the discretion of the Celebrant, and as appropriate, any of the following Collects, with one of the corresponding sets of Psalms and Lessons, may be used*

*a) at the commemoration of a saint listed in the Calendar for which no Proper is provided in this Book*

*b) at the patronal festival or commemoration of a saint not listed in the Calendar.*

**Of a Martyr**

Almighty God, who gave to your servant N. boldness to confess the Name of our Savior Jesus Christ before the rulers of this world, and courage to die for this faith: Grant that we may always be ready to give a reason for the hope that is in us, and to suffer gladly for the sake of our Lord Jesus Christ; who lives and reigns with you and the Holy Spirit, one God, for ever and ever. *Amen.*

*or this*

Almighty God, by whose grace and power your holy martyr N. triumphed over suffering and was faithful even to death: Grant us, who now remember *him* in thanksgiving, to be so faithful in our witness to you in this world, that we may receive with *him* the crown of life; through Jesus Christ our Lord, who lives and reigns with you and the Holy Spirit, one God, for ever and ever. *Amen.*

*or this*

Almighty and everlasting God, who kindled the flame of your love in the heart of your holy martyr N.: Grant to us, your humble servants, a like faith and power of love, that we who rejoice in *her* triumph may profit by *her* example; through Jesus Christ our Lord, who lives and reigns with you and the Holy Spirit, one God, for ever and ever. *Amen.*

*Preface of a Saint*

## Of a Missionary

Almighty and everlasting God, we thank you for your servant N., whom you called to preach the Gospel to the people of _____ *(or to the* _____ *people).* Raise up in this and every land evangelists and heralds of your kingdom, that your Church may proclaim the unsearchable riches of our Savior Jesus Christ; who lives and reigns with you and the Holy Spirit, one God, now and for ever. *Amen.*

*or the following*

Almighty God, whose will it is to be glorified in your saints, and who raised up your servant N. to be a light in the world: Shine, we pray, in our hearts, that we also in our generation may show forth your praise, who called us out of darkness into your marvelous light; through Jesus Christ our Lord, who lives and reigns with you and the Holy Spirit, one God, now and for ever. *Amen.*

*Preface of Pentecost*

## Of a Pastor

Heavenly Father, Shepherd of your people, we thank you for your servant N., who was faithful in the care and nurture of your flock; and we pray that, following *his* example and the teaching of *his* holy life, we may by your grace grow into the stature of the fullness of our Lord and Savior Jesus Christ; who lives and reigns with you and the Holy Spirit, one God, for ever and ever. *Amen.*

*or this*

O God, our heavenly Father, who raised up your faithful servant N., to be a [bishop and] pastor in your Church and feed your flock: Give abundantly to all pastors the gifts of your Holy Spirit, that they may minister in your household as true servants of Christ and stewards of your divine mysteries; through Jesus Christ our Lord, who lives and reigns with you and the Holy Spirit, one God, for ever and ever. *Amen.*

*Preface of a Saint*

## Of a Theologian and Teacher

O God, by your Holy Spirit you give to some the word of wisdom, to others the word of knowledge, and to others the word of faith: We praise your Name for the gifts of grace manifested in your servant N., and we pray that your Church may never be destitute of such gifts; through Jesus Christ our Lord, who with you and the Holy Spirit lives and reigns, one God, for ever and ever. *Amen.*

*or this*

Almighty God, you gave to your servant N. special gifts of grace to understand and teach the truth as it is in Christ Jesus: Grant that by this teaching we may know you, the one true God, and Jesus Christ whom you have sent; who lives and reigns with you and the Holy Spirit, one God, for ever and ever. *Amen.*

*Preface of a Saint, or of Trinity Sunday*

## Of a Monastic

O God, whose blessed Son became poor that we through his poverty might be rich: Deliver us from an inordinate love of this world, that we, inspired by the devotion of your servant N., may serve you with singleness of heart, and attain to the riches of the age to come; through Jesus Christ our Lord, who lives and reigns with you, in the unity of the Holy Spirit, one God, now and for ever. *Amen.*

*or this*

O God, by whose grace your servant N., kindled with the flame of your love, became a burning and a shining light in your Church: Grant that we also may be aflame with the spirit of love and discipline, and walk before you as children of light; through Jesus Christ our Lord, who lives and reigns with you, in the unity of the Holy Spirit, one God, now and for ever. *Amen.*

*Preface of a Saint*

## Of a Saint

Almighty God, you have surrounded us with a great cloud of witnesses: Grant that we, encouraged by the good example of your servant *N.*, may persevere in running the race that is set before us, until at last we may with *him* attain to your eternal joy; through Jesus Christ, the pioneer and perfecter of our faith, who lives and reigns with you and the Holy Spirit, one God, for ever and ever. *Amen.*

*or this*

O God, you have brought us near to an innumerable company of angels, and to the spirits of just men made perfect: Grant us during our earthly pilgrimage to abide in their fellowship, and in our heavenly country to become partakers of their joy; through Jesus Christ our Lord, who lives and reigns with you and the Holy Spirit, one God, now and for ever. *Amen.*

*or this*

Almighty God, by your Holy Spirit you have made us one with your saints in heaven and on earth: Grant that in our earthly pilgrimage we may always be supported by this fellowship of love and prayer, and know ourselves to be surrounded by their witness to your power and mercy. We ask this for the sake of Jesus Christ, in whom all our intercessions are acceptable through the Spirit, and who lives and reigns for ever and ever. *Amen.*

*Preface of a Saint*

# Various Occasions

*For optional use, when desired, subject to the rules set forth in the Calendar of the Church Year.*

## 1. Of the Holy Trinity

Almighty God, you have revealed to your Church your eternal Being of glorious majesty and perfect love as one God in Trinity of Persons: Give us grace to continue steadfast in the confession of this faith, and constant in our worship of you, Father, Son, and Holy Spirit; for you live and reign, one God, now and for ever. *Amen.*

*Preface of Trinity Sunday*

## 2. Of the Holy Spirit

Almighty and most merciful God, grant that by the indwelling of your Holy Spirit we may be enlightened and strengthened for your service; through Jesus Christ our Lord, who lives and reigns with you, in the unity of the Holy Spirit, one God, now and for ever. *Amen.*

*Preface of Pentecost*

## 3. Of the Holy Angels

Everlasting God, you have ordained and constituted in a wonderful order the ministries of angels and mortals: Mercifully grant that, as your holy angels always serve and worship you in heaven, so by your appointment they may help and defend us here on earth; through Jesus Christ our Lord, who lives and reigns with you and the Holy Spirit, one God, for ever and ever. *Amen.*

*Preface of Trinity Sunday*

### 4. Of the Incarnation

O God, who wonderfully created, and yet more wonderfully restored, the dignity of human nature: Grant that we may share the divine life of him who humbled himself to share our humanity, your Son Jesus Christ; who lives and reigns with you in the unity of the Holy Spirit, one God, for ever and ever. *Amen*

*Preface of the Epiphany*

### 5. Of the Holy Eucharist

*Especially suitable for Thursdays*

God our Father, whose Son our Lord Jesus Christ in a wonderful Sacrament has left us a memorial of his passion: Grant us so to venerate the sacred mysteries of his Body and Blood, that we may ever perceive within ourselves the fruit of his redemption; who lives and reigns with you and the Holy Spirit, one God, for ever and ever. *Amen*.

*Preface of the Epiphany*

### 6. Of the Holy Cross

*Especially suitable for Fridays*

Almighty God, whose beloved Son willingly endured the agony and shame of the cross for our redemption: Give us courage to take up our cross and follow him; who lives and reigns with you and the Holy Spirit, one God, now and for ever. *Amen*.

*Preface of Holy Week*

### 7. For all Baptized Christians

*Especially suitable for Saturdays*

Grant, Lord God, to all who have been baptized into the

death and resurrection of your Son Jesus Christ, that, as we
have put away the old life of sin, so we may be renewed in the
spirit of our minds, and live in righteousness and true holiness;
through Jesus Christ our Lord, who lives and reigns with you,
in the unity of the Holy Spirit, one God, now and for ever.
*Amen.*

*Preface of Baptism*

## 8. For the Departed

Eternal Lord God, you hold all souls in life: Give to your
whole Church in paradise and on earth your light and your
peace; and grant that we, following the good examples of
those who have served you here and are now at rest, may at
the last enter with them into your unending joy; through
Jesus Christ our Lord, who lives and reigns with you, in the
unity of the Holy Spirit, one God, now and for ever. *Amen.*

*or this*

Almighty God, we remember before you today your faithful
servant N.; and we pray that, having opened to *him* the gates
of larger life, you will receive *him* more and more into your
joyful service, that, with all who have faithfully served you in
the past, *he* may share in the eternal victory of Jesus Christ
our Lord; who lives and reigns with you, in the unity of the
Holy Spirit, one God, for ever and ever. *Amen.*

*Any of the Collects appointed for use at the Burial of the Dead may be
used instead.*

*For the Prayers of the People, one of the forms appointed for the
Burial of the Dead may be used.*

*Preface of the Commemoration of the Dead*

*The postcommunion prayer on page 498 may be used.*

### 9. Of the Reign of Christ

Almighty and everlasting God, whose will it is to restore all
things in your well-beloved Son, the King of kings and Lord
of lords: Mercifully grant that the peoples of the earth,
divided and enslaved by sin, may be freed and brought together
under his most gracious rule; who lives and reigns with you
and the Holy Spirit, one God, now and for ever. *Amen.*

*Preface of the Ascension, or of Baptism*

### 10. At Baptism

Almighty God, by our baptism into the death and resurrection
of your Son Jesus Christ, you turn us from the old life of sin:
Grant that we, being reborn to new life in him, may live in
righteousness and holiness all our days; through Jesus Christ
our Lord, who lives and reigns with you and the Holy Spirit,
one God, now and for ever. *Amen.*

*Preface of Baptism*

### 11. At Confirmation

Grant, Almighty God, that we, who have been redeemed
from the old life of sin by our baptism into the death and
resurrection of your Son Jesus Christ, may be renewed in
your Holy Spirit, and live in righteousness and true holiness;
through Jesus Christ our Lord, who lives and reigns with you
and the Holy Spirit, one God, now and for ever. *Amen.*

*Preface of Baptism, or of Pentecost*

### 12. On the Anniversary of the Dedication of a Church

Almighty God, to whose glory we celebrate the dedication of
this house of prayer: We give you thanks for the fellowship

of those who have worshiped in this place, and we pray that all who seek you here may find you, and be filled with your joy and peace; through Jesus Christ our Lord, who lives and reigns with you, in the unity of the Holy Spirit, one God, now and for ever. *Amen.*

*The Litany of Thanksgiving for a Church, page 578, may be used for the Prayers of the People.*

*Preface of the Dedication of a Church*

## 13. For a Church Convention

Almighty and everlasting Father, you have given the Holy Spirit to abide with us for ever: Bless, we pray, with his grace and presence, the bishops and the other clergy and the laity here (*or* now, *or* soon to be) assembled in your Name, that your Church, being preserved in true faith and godly discipline, may fulfill all the mind of him who loved it and gave himself for it, your Son Jesus Christ our Savior; who lives and reigns with you, in the unity of the Holy Spirit, one God, now and for ever. *Amen.*

*Preface of Pentecost, or of the Season*

## 14. For the Unity of the Church

Almighty Father, whose blessed Son before his passion prayed for his disciples that they might be one, as you and he are one: Grant that your Church, being bound together in love and obedience to you, may be united in one body by the one Spirit, that the world may believe in him whom you have sent, your Son Jesus Christ our Lord; who lives and reigns with you, in the unity of the Holy Spirit, one God, now and for ever. *Amen.*

*Preface of Baptism, or of Trinity Sunday*

## 15. For the Ministry (Ember Days)

*For use on the traditional days or at other times*

### I. For those to be ordained

Almighty God, the giver of all good gifts, in your divine providence you have appointed various orders in your Church: Give your grace, we humbly pray, to all who are [now] called to any office and ministry for your people; and so fill them with the truth of your doctrine and clothe them with holiness of life, that they may faithfully serve before you, to the glory of your great Name and for the benefit of your holy Church; through Jesus Christ our Lord, who lives and reigns with you, in the unity of the Holy Spirit, one God, now and for ever. *Amen.*

*Preface of Apostles*

### II. For the choice of fit persons for the ministry

O God, you led your holy apostles to ordain ministers in every place: Grant that your Church, under the guidance of the Holy Spirit, may choose suitable persons for the ministry of Word and Sacrament, and may uphold them in their work for the extension of your kingdom; through him who is the Shepherd and Bishop of our souls, Jesus Christ our Lord, who lives and reigns with you and the Holy Spirit, one God, for ever and ever. *Amen.*

*Preface of the Season*

### III. For all Christians in their vocation

Almighty and everlasting God, by whose Spirit the whole body of your faithful people is governed and sanctified: Receive our supplications and prayers, which we offer before you for all members of your holy Church, that in their vocation and ministry they may truly and devoutly serve you; through our Lord and Savior Jesus Christ, who lives and reigns with you, in the unity of the Holy Spirit, one God, now and for ever. *Amen.*

*Preface of Baptism, or of the Season*

## 16. For the Mission of the Church

O God, you have made of one blood all the peoples of the earth, and sent your blessed Son to preach peace to those who are far off and to those who are near: Grant that people everywhere may seek after you and find you, bring the nations into your fold, pour out your Spirit upon all flesh, and hasten the coming of your kingdom; through Jesus Christ our Lord, who lives and reigns with you and the Holy Spirit, one God, now and for ever. *Amen.*

*or this*

O God of all the nations of the earth: Remember the multitudes who have been created in your image but have not known the redeeming work of our Savior Jesus Christ; and grant that, by the prayers and labors of your holy Church, they may be brought to know and worship you as you have been revealed in your Son; who lives and reigns with you and the Holy Spirit, one God, for ever and ever. *Amen.*

*Preface of the Season, or of Pentecost*

### 17. For the Nation

Lord God Almighty, you have made all the peoples of the earth for your glory, to serve you in freedom and in peace: Give to the people of our country a zeal for justice and the strength of forbearance, that we may use our liberty in accordance with your gracious will; through Jesus Christ our Lord, who lives and reigns with you and the Holy Spirit, one God, for ever and ever. *Amen.*

*The Collect for Independence Day may be used instead.*

*Preface of Trinity Sunday*


### 18. For Peace

Almighty God, kindle, we pray, in every heart the true love of peace, and guide with your wisdom those who take counsel for the nations of the earth, that in tranquillity your dominion may increase until the earth is filled with the knowledge of you love; through Jesus Christ our Lord, who lives and reigns with you, in the unity of the Holy Spirit, one God, now and for ever. *Amen.*

*Preface of the Season*


### 19. For Rogation Days

*For use on the traditional days or at other times*

*I. For fruitful seasons*

Almighty God, Lord of heaven and earth: We humbly pray that your gracious providence may give and preserve to our use the harvests of the land and of the seas, and may prosper all who labor to gather them, that we, who are constantly receiving good things from your hand, may always give you

thanks; through Jesus Christ our Lord, who lives and reigns
with you and the Holy Spirit, one God, for ever and ever.
*Amen.*

*Preface of the Season*

## II. For commerce and industry

Almighty God, whose Son Jesus Christ in his earthly life
shared our toil and hallowed our labor: Be present with your
people where they work; make those who carry on the industries
and commerce of this land responsive to your will; and give
to us all a pride in what we do, and a just return for our labor;
through Jesus Christ our Lord, who lives and reigns with
you, in the unity of the Holy Spirit, one God, now and for
ever. *Amen.*

*Preface of the Season*

## III. For stewardship of creation

O merciful Creator, your hand is open wide to satisfy the
needs of every living creature: Make us always thankful for
your loving providence; and grant that we, remembering the
account that we must one day give, may be faithful stewards
of your good gifts; through Jesus Christ our Lord, who with
you and the Holy Spirit lives and reigns, one God, for ever
and ever. *Amen.*

*Preface of the Season*

### 20. For the Sick

Heavenly Father, giver of life and health: Comfort and relieve your sick servants, and give your power of healing to those who minister to their needs, that those *(or N., or NN.)* for whom our prayers are offered may be strengthened in *their* weakness and have confidence in your loving care; through Jesus Christ our Lord, who lives and reigns with you and the Holy Spirit, one God, now and for ever. *Amen.*

*Preface of the Season*

*The postcommunion prayer on page 457 may be used.*


### 21. For Social Justice

Almighty God, who created us in your own image: Grant us grace fearlessly to contend against evil and to make no peace with oppression; and, that we may reverently use our freedom help us to employ it in the maintenance of justice in our communities and among the nations, to the glory of your holy Name; through Jesus Christ our Lord, who lives and reigns with you and the Holy Spirit, one God, now and for ever. *Amen.*

*Preface of the Season*


### 22. For Social Service

Heavenly Father, whose blessed Son came not to be served but to serve: Bless all who, following in his steps, give themselves to the service of others; that with wisdom, patience, and courage, they may minister in his Name to the suffering, the friendless, and the needy; for the love of him who laid down his life for us, your Son our Savior Jesus Christ, who lives and reigns with you and the Holy Spirit, one God, for ever and ever. *Amen.*

*Preface of the Season*

### 23. For Education

Almighty God, the fountain of all wisdom: Enlighten by your Holy Spirit those who teach and those who learn, that, rejoicing in the knowledge of your truth, they may worship you and serve you from generation to generation; through Jesus Christ our Lord, who lives and reigns with you and the Holy Spirit, one God, for ever and ever. *Amen.*

*Preface of the Season*

### 24. For Vocation in Daily Work

Almighty God our heavenly Father, you declare your glory and show forth your handiwork in the heavens and in the earth: Deliver us in our various occupations from the service of self alone, that we may do the work you give us to do in truth and beauty and for the common good; for the sake of him who came among us as one who serves, your Son Jesus Christ our Lord, who lives and reigns with you and the Holy Spirit, one God, for ever and ever. *Amen.*

*Preface of the Season*

### 25. For Labor Day

Almighty God, you have so linked our lives one with another that all we do affects, for good or ill, all other lives: So guide us in the work we do, that we may do it not for self alone, but for the common good; and, as we seek a proper return for our own labor, make us mindful of the rightful aspirations of other workers, and arouse our concern for those who are out of work; through Jesus Christ our Lord, who lives and reigns with you and the Holy Spirit, one God, for ever and ever. *Amen.*

*Preface of the Season*

# Proper Liturgies
for Special Days

# Ash Wednesday

*On this day, the Celebrant begins the liturgy with the Salutation and the Collect of the Day.*

Let us pray.

Almighty and everlasting God, you hate nothing you have made and forgive the sins of all who are penitent: Create and make in us new and contrite hearts, that we, worthily lamenting our sins and acknowledging our wretchedness, may obtain of you, the God of all mercy, perfect remission and forgiveness; through Jesus Christ our Lord, who lives and reigns with you and the Holy Spirit, one God, for ever and ever. *Amen.*

*Old Testament*    Joel 2:1-2, 12-17,   *or* Isaiah 58:1-12
*Psalm*    103,   *or* 103:8-14
*Epistle*    2 Corinthians 5:20b—6:10
*Gospel*    Matthew 6:1-6, 16-21

*After the Sermon, all stand, and the Celebrant or Minister appointed invites the people to the observance of a holy Lent, saying*

Dear People of God: The first Christians observed with great devotion the days of our Lord's passion and resurrection, and it became the custom of the Church to prepare for them by a season of penitence and fasting. This season of Lent provided a time in which converts to the faith were prepared for Holy Baptism. It was also a time when those who, because of notorious sins, had been separated from the body of the faithful were reconciled by penitence and forgiveness, and restored to the fellowship of the Church. Thereby, the whole congregation was put in mind of the message of pardon and absolution set forth in the Gospel of our Savior, and of the need which all Christians continually have to renew their repentance and faith.

I invite you, therefore, in the name of the Church, to the observance of a holy Lent, by self-examination and repentance; by prayer, fasting, and self-denial; and by reading and meditating on God's holy Word. And, to make a right beginning of repentance, and as a mark of our mortal nature, let us now kneel before the Lord, our maker and redeemer.

*Silence is then kept for a time, all kneeling.*

*If ashes are to be imposed, the Celebrant says the following prayer*

Almighty God, you have created us out of the dust of the earth: Grant that these ashes may be to us a sign of our mortality and penitence, that we may remember that it is only by your gracious gift that we are given everlasting life; through Jesus Christ our Savior. *Amen.*

*The ashes are imposed with the following words*

Remember that you are dust, and to dust you shall return.

*The following Psalm is then sung or said*

## Psalm 51 *Miserere mei, Deus*

1 Have mercy on me, O God, according to your
            loving-kindness; *
   in your great compassion blot out my offenses.

2 Wash me through and through from my wickedness *
   and cleanse me from my sin.

3 For I know my transgressions, *
   and my sin is ever before me.

4 Against you only have I sinned *
   and done what is evil in your sight.

5 And so you are justified when you speak *
   and upright in your judgment.

6 Indeed, I have been wicked from my birth, *
   a sinner from my mother's womb.

7 For behold, you look for truth deep within me, *
   and will make me understand wisdom secretly.

8 Purge me from my sin, and I shall be pure; *
   wash me, and I shall be clean indeed.

9 Make me hear of joy and gladness, *
   that the body you have broken may rejoice.

10 Hide your face from my sins *
   and blot out all my iniquities.

11 Create in me a clean heart, O God, *
   and renew a right spirit within me.

12 Cast me not away from your presence *
   and take not your holy Spirit from me.

13 Give me the joy of your saving help again *
   and sustain me with your bountiful Spirit.

4   I shall teach your ways to the wicked, *
      and sinners shall return to you.

5   Deliver me from death, O God, *
      and my tongue shall sing of your righteousness,
      O God of my salvation.

6   Open my lips, O Lord, *
      and my mouth shall proclaim your praise.

7   Had you desired it, I would have offered sacrifice; *
      but you take no delight in burnt-offerings.

8   The sacrifice of God is a troubled spirit; *
      a broken and contrite heart, O God, you will not despise.


**Litany of Penitence**

*The Celebrant and People together, all kneeling*

Most holy and merciful Father:
We confess to you and to one another,
and to the whole communion of saints
in heaven and on earth,
that we have sinned by our own fault
in thought, word, and deed;
by what we have done, and by what we have left undone.

*The Celebrant continues*

We have not loved you with our whole heart, and mind, and
strength. We have not loved our neighbors as ourselves. We
have not forgiven others, as we have been forgiven.
*Have mercy on us, Lord.*

We have been deaf to your call to serve, as Christ served us.
We have not been true to the mind of Christ. We have grieved
your Holy Spirit.
*Have mercy on us, Lord.*

We confess to you, Lord, all our past unfaithfulness: the pride, hypocrisy, and impatience of our lives,
*We confess to you, Lord.*

Our self-indulgent appetites and ways, and our exploitation of other people,
*We confess to you, Lord.*

Our anger at our own frustration, and our envy of those more fortunate than ourselves,
*We confess to you, Lord.*

Our intemperate love of worldly goods and comforts, and our dishonesty in daily life and work,
*We confess to you, Lord.*

Our negligence in prayer and worship, and our failure to commend the faith that is in us,
*We confess to you, Lord.*

Accept our repentance, Lord, for the wrongs we have done: for our blindness to human need and suffering, and our indifference to injustice and cruelty,
*Accept our repentance, Lord.*

For all false judgments, for uncharitable thoughts toward our neighbors, and for our prejudice and contempt toward those who differ from us,
*Accept our repentance, Lord.*

For our waste and pollution of your creation, and our lack of concern for those who come after us,
*Accept our repentance, Lord.*

Restore us, good Lord, and let your anger depart from us;
*Favorably hear us, for your mercy is great.*

Accomplish in us the work of your salvation,
*That we may show forth your glory in the world.*

By the cross and passion of your Son our Lord,
*Bring us with all your saints to the joy of his resurrection.*

*The Bishop, if present, or the Priest, stands and, facing the people, says*

Almighty God, the Father of our Lord Jesus Christ, who desires not the death of sinners, but rather that they may turn from their wickedness and live, has given power and commandment to his ministers to declare and pronounce to his people, being penitent, the absolution and remission of their sins. He pardons and absolves all those who truly repent, and with sincere hearts believe his holy Gospel.

Therefore we beseech him to grant us true repentance and his Holy Spirit, that those things may please him which we do on this day, and that the rest of our life hereafter may be pure and holy, so that at the last we may come to his eternal joy; through Jesus Christ our Lord. *Amen.*

*A deacon or lay reader leading the service remains kneeling and substitutes the prayer for forgiveness appointed at Morning Prayer.*

*The Peace is then exchanged.*

*In the absence of a bishop or priest, all that precedes may be led by a deacon or lay reader.*

*The Litany of Penitence may be used at other times, and may be preceded by an appropriate invitation and a penitential psalm.*

*When Communion follows, the service continues with the Offertory.*

*Preface of Lent*

# The Sunday of the Passion: Palm Sunday

**The Liturgy of the Palms**

*When circumstances permit, the congregation may gather at a place apart from the church, so that all may go into the church in procession.*

*The branches of palm or of other trees or shrubs to be carried in the procession may be distributed to the people before the service, or after the prayer of blessing.*

*The following or some other suitable anthem is sung or said, the people standing*

Blessed is the King who comes in the name of the Lord.
*Peace in heaven and glory in the highest.*

*Celebrant*  Let us pray.

Assist us mercifully with your help, O Lord God of our salvation, that we may enter with joy upon the contemplatio of those mighty acts, whereby you have given us life and immortality; through Jesus Christ our Lord. *Amen.*

*Here a Deacon or other person appointed reads one of the following*

Year A    Matthew 21:1-11
Year B    Mark 11:1-11a
Year C    Luke 19:29-40

*The Celebrant then says the following blessing*

Celebrant    The Lord be with you.
People        And also with you.
Celebrant    Let us give thanks to the Lord our God.
People        It is right to give him thanks and praise.

It is right to praise you, Almighty God, for the acts of love by
which you have redeemed us through your Son Jesus Christ
our Lord. On this day he entered the holy city of Jerusalem in
triumph, and was proclaimed as King of kings by those who
spread their garments and branches of palm along his way.
Let these branches be for us signs of his victory, and grant that
we who bear them in his name may ever hail him as our King,
and follow him in the way that leads to eternal life; who lives
and reigns in glory with you and the Holy Spirit, now and
for ever. *Amen.*

*The following or some other suitable anthem may then be sung or said*

Blessed is he who comes in the name of the Lord.
*Hosanna in the highest.*

*The Procession*

Deacon    Let us go forth in peace.
People     In the name of Christ. Amen.

*During the procession, all hold branches in their hands, and appropriate
hymns, psalms, or anthems are sung, such as the hymn "All glory, laud,
and honor" and Psalm 118:19-29.*

*At a suitable place, the procession may halt while the following or some
other appropriate Collect is said*

Almighty God, whose most dear Son went not up to joy but first he suffered pain, and entered not into glory before he was crucified: Mercifully grant that we, walking in the way of the cross, may find it none other than the way of life and peace; through Jesus Christ our Lord. *Amen.*

*In the absence of a bishop or priest, the preceding service may be led by a deacon or lay reader.*

*At services on this day other than the principal celebration, suitable portions of the preceding may be used.*

## At the Eucharist

*When the Liturgy of the Palms immediately precedes the Eucharist, the celebration begins with the Salutation and Collect of the Day*

Let us pray.

Almighty and everliving God, in your tender love for the human race you sent your Son our Savior Jesus Christ to take upon him our nature, and to suffer death upon the cross, giving us the example of his great humility: Mercifully grant that we may walk in the way of his suffering, and also share in his resurrection; through Jesus Christ our Lord, who lives and reigns with you and the Holy Spirit, one God, for ever and ever. *Amen.*

*Old Testament*   Isaiah 45:21-25,   *or* Isaiah 52:13—53:12
*Psalm*   22:1-21,   *or* 22:1-11
*Epistle*   Philippians 2:5-11

*The Passion Gospel is announced in the following manner*

The Passion of our Lord Jesus Christ according to _____

*The customary responses before and after the Gospel are omitted.*

Year A   Matthew 26:36—27:54(55-66)   or 27:1-54(55-66)
Year B   Mark 14:32—15:39(40-47)   or 15:1-39(40-47)
Year C   Luke 22:39—23:49(50-56)   or 23:1-49(50-56)

The Passion Gospel may be read or chanted by lay persons. Specific roles
may be assigned to different persons, the congregation taking the part
of the crowd.

The congregation may be seated for the first part of the Passion. At the
verse which mentions the arrival at Golgotha (Matthew 27:33,
Mark 15:22, Luke 23:33) all stand.

When the Liturgy of the Palms has preceded, the Nicene Creed and the
Confession of Sin may be omitted at this service.

*Preface of Holy Week*

# Maundy Thursday

*The Eucharist begins in the usual manner, using the following Collect, Psalm, and Lessons*

Almighty Father, whose dear Son, on the night before he suffered, instituted the Sacrament of his Body and Blood: Mercifully grant that we may receive it thankfully in remembrance of Jesus Christ our Lord, who in these holy mysteries gives us a pledge of eternal life; and who now lives and reigns with you and the Holy Spirit, one God, for ever and ever. *Amen.*

*Old Testament*   Exodus 12:1-14a
*Psalm*   78:14-20, 23-25
*Epistle*   1 Corinthians 11:23-26(27-32)
*Gospel*   John 13:1-15,   *or* Luke 22:14-30

*When observed, the ceremony of the washing of feet appropriately follows the Gospel and homily.*

*During the ceremony, the following or other suitable anthems may be sung or said*

The Lord Jesus, after he had supped with his disciples and had washed their feet, said to them, "Do you know what I, your Lord and Master, have done to you? I have given you an example, that you should do as I have done."

*Peace is my last gift to you, my own peace I now leave with you; peace which the world cannot give, I give to you.*

I give you a new commandment: Love one another as I have loved you.

*Peace is my last gift to you, my own peace I now leave with you; peace which the world cannot give, I give to you.*

By this shall the world know that you are my disciples: That you have love for one another.

*The service continues with the Prayers of the People.*

*Where it is desired to administer Holy Communion from the reserved Sacrament on Good Friday, the Sacrament for that purpose is consecrated at this service.*

*Preface of Holy Week*

# Good Friday

*On this day the ministers enter in silence.*

*All then kneel for silent prayer, after which the Celebrant stands and begins the liturgy with the Collect of the Day.*

*Immediately before the Collect, the Celebrant may say*

> **Blessed be our God.**

*People*  For ever and ever. Amen.

Let us pray.

Almighty God, we pray you graciously to behold this your family, for whom our Lord Jesus Christ was willing to be betrayed, and given into the hands of sinners, and to suffer death upon the cross; who now lives and reigns with you and the Holy Spirit, one God, for ever and ever. *Amen.*

*Old Testament*   Isaiah 52:13—53:12,   *or* Genesis 22:1-18,
              *or* Wisdom 2:1, 12-24
*Psalm*   22:1-11(12-21),   *or* 40:1-14,   *or* 69:1-23
*Epistle*   Hebrews 10:1-25

*The Passion Gospel is announced in the following manner*

The Passion of our Lord Jesus Christ according to John.

*The customary responses before and after the Gospel are omitted.*

John 18:1—19:37   *or* 19:1-37

*The Passion Gospel may be read or chanted by lay persons. Specific roles may be assigned to different persons, the congregation taking the part of the crowd.*

*The congregation may be seated for the first part of the Passion. At the verse which mentions the arrival at Golgotha (John 19:17) all stand.*

*The Sermon follows.*

*A hymn may then be sung.*

## The Solemn Collects

*All standing, the Deacon, or other person appointed, says to the people*

Dear People of God: Our heavenly Father sent his Son into the world, not to condemn the world, but that the world through him might be saved; that all who believe in him might be delivered from the power of sin and death, and become heirs with him of everlasting life.

We pray, therefore, for people everywhere according to their needs.

*In the biddings which follow, the indented petitions may be adapted by addition or omission, as appropriate, at the discretion of the Celebrant. The people may be directed to stand or kneel.*

*The biddings may be read by a Deacon or other person appointed. The Celebrant says the Collects.*

Let us pray for the holy Catholic Church of Christ
throughout the world;

> For its unity in witness and service
> For all bishops and other ministers
>     and the people whom they serve
> For N., our Bishop, and all the people of this diocese
> For all Christians in this community
> For those about to be baptized (particularly _____ )

That God will confirm his Church in faith, increase it in love,
and preserve it in peace.

*Silence*

Almighty and everlasting God, by whose Spirit the whole
body of your faithful people is governed and sanctified:
Receive our supplications and prayers which we offer before
you for all members of your holy Church, that in their
vocation and ministry they may truly and devoutly serve you;
through our Lord and Savior Jesus Christ. *Amen.*

Let us pray for all nations and peoples of the earth, and for
those in authority among them;

> For N., the President of the United States
> For the Congress and the Supreme Court
> For the Members and Representatives of the United Nations
> For all who serve the common good

That by God's help they may seek justice and truth, and live
in peace and concord.

*Silence*

Almighty God, kindle, we pray, in every heart the true love of
peace, and guide with your wisdom those who take counsel for
the nations of the earth; that in tranquillity your dominion may

increase, until the earth is filled with the knowledge of your love; through Jesus Christ our Lord. *Amen*.

Let us pray for all who suffer and are afflicted in body or in mind;

For the hungry and the homeless, the destitute
    and the oppressed
For the sick, the wounded, and the crippled
For those in loneliness, fear, and anguish
For those who face temptation, doubt, and despair
For the sorrowful and bereaved
For prisoners and captives, and those in mortal danger

That God in his mercy will comfort and relieve them, and grant them the knowledge of his love, and stir up in us the will and patience to minister to their needs.

*Silence*

Gracious God, the comfort of all who sorrow, the strength of all who suffer: Let the cry of those in misery and need come to you, that they may find your mercy present with them in all their afflictions; and give us, we pray, the strength to serve them for the sake of him who suffered for us, your Son Jesus Christ our Lord. *Amen*.

Let us pray for all who have not received the Gospel of Christ;

For those who have never heard the word of salvation
For those who have lost their faith
For those hardened by sin or indifference
For the contemptuous and the scornful
For those who are enemies of the cross of Christ and
    persecutors of his disciples
For those who in the name of Christ have persecuted others

That God will open their hearts to the truth, and lead them to faith and obedience.

*Silence*

**Merciful God, Creator of all the peoples of the earth and lover of souls: Have compassion on all who do not know you as you are revealed in your Son Jesus Christ; let your Gospel be preached with grace and power to those who have not heard it; turn the hearts of those who resist it; and bring home to your fold those who have gone astray; that there may be one flock under one shepherd, Jesus Christ our Lord. *Amen.***

Let us commit ourselves to our God, and pray for the grace of a holy life, that, with all who have departed this world and have died in the peace of Christ, and those whose faith is known to God alone, we may be accounted worthy to enter into the fullness of the joy of our Lord, and receive the crown of life in the day of resurrection.

*Silence*

O God of unchangeable power and eternal light: Look favorably on your whole Church, that wonderful and sacred mystery; by the effectual working of your providence, carry out in tranquillity the plan of salvation; let the whole world see and know that things which were cast down are being raised up, and things which had grown old are being made new, and that all things are being brought to their perfection by him through whom all things were made, your Son Jesus Christ our Lord; who lives and reigns with you, in the unity of the Holy Spirit, one God, for ever and ever. *Amen.*

*The service may be concluded here with the singing of a hymn or anthem, the Lord's Prayer, and the final prayer on page 282.*

*If desired, a wooden cross may now be brought into the church and placed in the sight of the people.*

*Appropriate devotions may follow, which may include any or all of the following, or other suitable anthems. If the texts are recited rather than sung, the congregation reads the parts in italics.*

## Anthem 1

We glory in your cross, O Lord,
*and praise and glorify your holy resurrection;*
*for by virtue of your cross*
*joy has come to the whole world.*

May God be merciful to us and bless us,
show us the light of his countenance, and come to us.

*Let your ways be known upon earth,*
*your saving health among all nations.*

Let the peoples praise you, O God;
let all the peoples praise you.

*We glory in your cross, O Lord,*
*and praise and glorify your holy resurrection;*
*for by virtue of your cross*
*joy has come to the whole world.*

## Anthem 2

We adore you, O Christ, and we bless you,
*because by your holy cross you have redeemed the world.*

If we have died with him, we shall also live with him;
if we endure, we shall also reign with him.

*We adore you, O Christ, and we bless you,*
*because by your holy cross you have redeemed the world.*

## Anthem 3

O Savior of the world,
who by thy cross and precious blood hast redeemed us:
*Save us and help us, we humbly beseech thee, O Lord.*

*The hymn "Sing, my tongue, the glorious battle," or some other hymn*
*extolling the glory of the cross, is then sung.*

*The service may be concluded here with the Lord's Prayer and the final*
*prayer below.*

*In the absence of a bishop or priest, all that precedes may be led by a*
*deacon or lay reader.*

*In places where Holy Communion is to be administered from the*
*reserved Sacrament, the following order is observed*

A Confession of Sin
The Lord's Prayer
The Communion

*The service concludes with the following prayer. No blessing or dismissal*
*is added.*

Lord Jesus Christ, Son of the living God, we pray you to set
your passion, cross, and death between your judgment and
our souls, now and in the hour of our death. Give mercy and
grace to the living; pardon and rest to the dead; to your holy
Church peace and concord; and to us sinners everlasting life
and glory; for with the Father and the Holy Spirit you
live and reign, one God, now and for ever. *Amen.*

# Holy Saturday

*There is no celebration of the Eucharist on this day.*

*When there is a Liturgy of the Word, the Celebrant begins with the Collect of the Day*

O God, Creator of heaven and earth: Grant that, as the crucified body of your dear Son was laid in the tomb and rested on this holy Sabbath, so we may await with him the coming of the third day, and rise with him to newness of life; who now lives and reigns with you and the Holy Spirit, one God, for ever and ever. *Amen.*

*Old Testament*   Job 14:1-14
*Psalm*   130,   *or* 31:1-5
*Epistle*   1 Peter 4:1-8
*Gospel*   Matthew 27:57-66,   *or* John 19:38-42

*After the Gospel (and homily), in place of the Prayers of the People, the Anthem "In the midst of life" (page 484 or 492) is sung or said.*

*The service then concludes with the Lord's Prayer and the Grace.*

# Concerning the Vigil

The Great Vigil, when observed, is the first service of Easter Day. It is celebrated at a convenient time between sunset on Holy Saturday and sunrise on Easter Morning.

The service normally consists of four parts:
1. The Service of Light.
2. The Service of Lessons.
3. Christian Initiation, or the Renewal of Baptismal Vows.
4. The Holy Eucharist with the administration of Easter Communion.

It is customary for all the ordained ministers present, together with lay readers, singers, and other persons, to take active parts in the service.

The bishop, when present, is the chief celebrant, presides at Baptism and administers Confirmation, and normally preaches the sermon.

The priests who are present share among them the reading of the Collects which follow each Lesson, and assist at Baptism and the Eucharist. In the absence of a bishop, a priest presides at the service.

It is the prerogative of a deacon to carry the Paschal Candle to its place, and to chant the Exsultet. Deacons likewise assist at Baptism and the Eucharist according to their order.

Lay persons read the Lessons and the Epistle, and assist in other ways. A lay person may be assigned to chant the Exsultet. It is desirable that each Lesson be read by a different reader.

In the absence of a bishop or priest, a deacon or lay reader may lead the first two parts of the service, the Renewal of Baptismal Vows, and the Ministry of the Word of the Vigil Eucharist, concluding with the Prayers of the People, the Lord's Prayer, and the Dismissal.

A deacon may also, when the services of a priest cannot be obtained, and with the authorization of the bishop, officiate at public Baptism; and may administer Easter Communion from the Sacrament previously consecrated

When the Vigil is not celebrated, the Service of Light may take place at a convenient time before the Liturgy on Easter Day.

# The Great Vigil of Easter

## The Lighting of the Paschal Candle

*In the darkness, fire is kindled; after which the Celebrant may address the people in these or similar words*

Dear friends in Christ: On this most holy night, in which our Lord Jesus passed over from death to life, the Church invites her members, dispersed throughout the world, to gather in vigil and prayer. For this is the Passover of the Lord, in which, by hearing his Word and celebrating his Sacraments, we share in his victory over death.

*The Celebrant may say the following prayer*

Let us pray.

O God, through your Son you have bestowed upon your people the brightness of your light: Sanctify this new fire, and grant that in this Paschal feast we may so burn with heavenly desires, that with pure minds we may attain to the festival of everlasting light; through Jesus Christ our Lord. *Amen.*

*The Paschal Candle is then lighted from the newly kindled fire, and the Deacon (the Celebrant if there is no deacon) bearing the Candle, leads the procession to the chancel, pausing three times and singing or saying*

The light of Christ.
*People*   Thanks be to God.

*If candles have been distributed to members of the congregation, they are lighted from the Paschal Candle at this time. Other candles and lamps in the church, except for those at the Altar, may also be lighted.*

*The Paschal Candle is placed in its stand.*

*Then the Deacon, or other person appointed, standing near the Candle, sings or says the Exsultet, as follows (the indicated sections may be omitted)*

Rejoice now, heavenly hosts and choirs of angels,
and let your trumpets shout Salvation
for the victory of our mighty King.

Rejoice and sing now, all the round earth,
bright with a glorious splendor,
for darkness has been vanquished by our eternal King.

Rejoice and be glad now, Mother Church,
and let your holy courts, in radiant light,
resound with the praises of your people.

All you who stand near this marvelous and holy flame,
pray with me to God the Almighty
for the grace to sing the worthy praise of this great light;
through Jesus Christ his Son our Lord,
who lives and reigns with him,
in the unity of the Holy Spirit,
one God, for ever and ever. *Amen.*

|           | The Lord be with you. |
|-----------|------------------------|
| *Answer*  | And also with you. |
| *Deacon*  | Let us give thanks to the Lord our God. |
| *Answer*  | It is right to give him thanks and praise. |

*Deacon*

It is truly right and good, always and everywhere, with our

whole heart and mind and voice, to praise you, the invisible, almighty, and eternal God, and your only-begotten Son, Jesus Christ our Lord; for he is the true Paschal Lamb, who at the feast of the Passover paid for us the debt of Adam's sin, and by his blood delivered your faithful people.

This is the night, when you brought our fathers, the children of Israel, out of bondage in Egypt, and led them through the Red Sea on dry land.

This is the night, when all who believe in Christ are delivered from the gloom of sin, and are restored to grace and holiness of life.

This is the night, when Christ broke the bonds of death and hell, and rose victorious from the grave.

How wonderful and beyond our knowing, O God, is your mercy and loving-kindness to us, that to redeem a slave, you gave a Son.

How holy is this night, when wickedness is put to flight, and sin is washed away. It restores innocence to the fallen, and joy to those who mourn. It casts out pride and hatred, and brings peace and concord.

How blessed is this night, when earth and heaven are joined and man is reconciled to God.

Holy Father, accept our evening sacrifice, the offering of this candle in your honor. May it shine continually to drive away all darkness. May Christ, the Morning Star who knows no setting, find it ever burning—he who gives his light to all creation, and who lives and reigns for ever and ever. *Amen.*

*It is customary that the Paschal Candle burn at all services from Easter Day through the Day of Pentecost.*

# The Liturgy of the Word

*The Celebrant may introduce the Scripture readings in these or similar words*

Let us hear the record of God's saving deeds in history, how he saved his people in ages past; and let us pray that our God will bring each of us to the fullness of redemption.

*At least two of the following Lessons are read, of which one is always t Lesson from Exodus. After each Lesson, the Psalm or Canticle listed, o some other suitable psalm, canticle, or hymn may be sung. A period of silence may be kept; and the Collect provided, or some other suitable Collect, may be said.*

**The story of Creation**
Genesis 1:1—2:2

Psalm 33:1-11, *or* Psalm 36:5-10

Let us pray. *(Silence)*

O God, who wonderfully created, and yet more wonderfully restored, the dignity of human nature: Grant that we may share the divine life of him who humbled himself to share our humanity, your Son Jesus Christ our Lord. *Amen.*

**The Flood**
Genesis 7:1-5, 11-18; 8:6-18; 9:8-13

Psalm 46

Let us pray. *(Silence)*

Almighty God, you have placed in the skies the sign of your covenant with all living things: Grant that we, who are saved through water and the Spirit, may worthily offer to you our sacrifice of thanksgiving; through Jesus Christ our Lord. *Amen.*

### Abraham's sacrifice of Isaac
Genesis 22:1-18

Psalm 33:12-22, *or* Psalm 16

Let us pray.  *(Silence)*

God and Father of all believers, for the glory of your Name multiply, by the grace of the Paschal sacrament, the number of your children; that your Church may rejoice to see fulfilled your promise to our father Abraham; through Jesus Christ our Lord. *Amen.*

### Israel's deliverance at the Red Sea
Exodus 14:10—15:1

Canticle 8, *The Song of Moses*

Let us pray.  *(Silence)*

O God, whose wonderful deeds of old shine forth even to our own day, you once delivered by the power of your mighty arm your chosen people from slavery under Pharaoh, to be a sign for us of the salvation of all nations by the water of baptism: Grant that all the peoples of the earth may be numbered among the offspring of Abraham, and rejoice in the inheritance of Israel; through Jesus Christ our Lord. *Amen.*

**God's Presence in a renewed Israel**
Isaiah 4:2-6

Psalm 122

Let us pray. *(Silence)*

O God, you led your ancient people by a pillar of cloud by day
and a pillar of fire by night: Grant that we, who serve you
now on earth, may come to the joy of that heavenly Jerusalem
where all tears are wiped away and where your saints for ever
sing your praise; through Jesus Christ our Lord. *Amen.*


**Salvation offered freely to all**
Isaiah 55:1-11

Canticle 9, *The First Song of Isaiah,* or Psalm 42:1-7

Let us pray. *(Silence)*

O God, you have created all things by the power of your
Word, and you renew the earth by your Spirit: Give now the
water of life to those who thirst for you, that they may bring
forth abundant fruit in your glorious kingdom; through Jesus
Christ our Lord. *Amen.*


**A new heart and a new spirit**
Ezekiel 36:24-28

Psalm 42:1-7, *or* Canticle 9, *The First Song of Isaiah*

Let us pray. *(Silence)*

Almighty and everlasting God, who in the Paschal mystery
established the new covenant of reconciliation: Grant that all

who are reborn into the fellowship of Christ's Body may show forth in their lives what they profess by their faith; through Jesus Christ our Lord. *Amen.*

The valley of dry bones
Ezekiel 37:1-14

Psalm 30, *or* Psalm 143

Let us pray. *(Silence)*

Almighty God, by the Passover of your Son you have brought us out of sin into righteousness and out of death into life: Grant to those who are sealed by your Holy Spirit the will and the power to proclaim you to all the world; through Jesus Christ our Lord. *Amen.*

The gathering of God's people
Zephaniah 3:12-20

Psalm 98, *or* Psalm 126

Let us pray. *(Silence)*

O God of unchangeable power and eternal light: Look favorably on your whole Church, that wonderful and sacred mystery; by the effectual working of your providence, carry out in tranquillity the plan of salvation; let the whole world see and know that things which were cast down are being raised up, and things which had grown old are being made new, and that all things are being brought to their perfection by him through whom all things were made, your Son Jesus Christ our Lord. *Amen.*

*A homily may be preached after any of the preceding Readings.*

*Holy Baptism (beginning with the Presentation of the Candidates, page 301, and concluding with the reception of the newly baptized) may be administered here or after the Gospel. Confirmation may also be administered.*

*In the absence of candidates for Baptism or Confirmation, the Celebrant leads the people in the Renewal of Baptismal Vows, either here or after the Gospel.*

*The Celebrant may first address the people in these or similar words, all standing*

Through the Paschal mystery, dear friends, we are buried with Christ by Baptism into his death, and raised with him to newness of life. I call upon you, therefore, now that our Lenten observance is ended, to renew the solemn promises and vows of Holy Baptism, by which we once renounced Satan and all his works, and promised to serve God faithfully in his holy Catholic Church.

# The Renewal of Baptismal Vows

*Celebrant*  Do you reaffirm your renunciation of evil and renew your commitment to Jesus Christ?
*People*  I do.

*Celebrant*  Do you believe in God the Father?
*People*  I believe in God, the Father almighty,
      creator of heaven and earth.

| | |
|---|---|
| *Celebrant* | Do you believe in Jesus Christ, the Son of God? |
| *People* | I believe in Jesus Christ, his only Son, our Lord. |

He was conceived by the power of the Holy Spirit
  and born of the Virgin Mary.
He suffered under Pontius Pilate,
  was crucified, died, and was buried.
He descended to the dead.
On the third day he rose again.
He ascended into heaven,
  and is seated at the right hand of the Father.
He will come again to judge the living and the dead.

| | |
|---|---|
| *Celebrant* | Do you believe in God the Holy Spirit? |
| *People* | I believe in the Holy Spirit, |

the holy catholic Church,
the communion of saints,
the forgiveness of sins,
the resurrection of the body,
and the life everlasting.

| | |
|---|---|
| *Celebrant* | Will you continue in the apostles' teaching and fellowship, in the breaking of bread, and in the prayers? |
| *People* | I will, with God's help. |
| *Celebrant* | Will you persevere in resisting evil, and, whenever you fall into sin, repent and return to the Lord? |
| *People* | I will, with God's help. |
| *Celebrant* | Will you proclaim by word and example the Good News of God in Christ? |
| *People* | I will, with God's help. |
| *Celebrant* | Will you seek and serve Christ in all persons, loving your neighbor as yourself? |
| *People* | I will, with God's help. |

Celebrant  Will you strive for justice and peace among all people
           and respect the dignity of every human being?
People     I will, with God's help.

*The Celebrant concludes the Renewal of Vows as follows*

May Almighty God, the Father of our Lord Jesus Christ, who
has given us a new birth by water and the Holy Spirit, and
bestowed upon us the forgiveness of sins, keep us in eternal
life by his grace, in Christ Jesus our Lord. *Amen.*


# At the Eucharist

*The candles at the Altar may now be lighted from the Paschal Candle.*

*One of the following Canticles is then sung. Immediately before the
Canticle the Celebrant may say to the people*

           Alleluia. Christ is risen.
People     The Lord is risen indeed. Alleluia.


## The Canticles

Gloria in excelsis
Te Deum laudamus
Pascha nostrum

*The Celebrant then says*

           The Lord be with you.
People     And also with you.
Celebrant  Let us pray.

*The Celebrant says one of the following Collects*

Almighty God, who for our redemption gave your only-begotten Son to the death of the cross, and by his glorious resurrection delivered us from the power of our enemy: Grant us so to die daily to sin, that we may evermore live with him in the joy of his resurrection; through Jesus Christ your Son our Lord, who lives and reigns with you and the Holy Spirit, one God, now and for ever. *Amen.*

*or this*

O God, who made this most holy night to shine with the glory of the Lord's resurrection: Stir up in your Church that Spirit of adoption which is given to us in Baptism, that we, being renewed both in body and mind, may worship you in sincerity and truth; through Jesus Christ our Lord, who lives and reigns with you, in the unity of the Holy Spirit, one God, now and for ever. *Amen.*

*Epistle*   Romans 6:3-11

*Alleluia" may be sung and repeated.*

*Psalm 114, or some other suitable psalm or a hymn may be sung.*

*Gospel*   Matthew 28:1-10

*If a sermon or homily was not preached earlier, it follows here.*

*The Nicene Creed is not used at this service.*

*Holy Baptism, Confirmation, or the Renewal of Baptismal Vows may take place here.*

*The celebration continues with the Prayers of the People.*

*Preface of Easter*

# Holy Baptism

# Concerning the Service

Holy Baptism is full initiation by water and the Holy Spirit into Christ's Body the Church. The bond which God establishes in Baptism is indissoluble.

Holy Baptism is appropriately administered within the Eucharist as the chief service on a Sunday or other feast.

The bishop, when present, is the celebrant; and is expected to preach the Word and preside at Baptism and the Eucharist. At Baptism, the bishop officiates at the Presentation and Examination of the Candidates; says the Thanksgiving over the Water; [consecrates the Chrism;] reads the prayer, "Heavenly Father, we thank you that by water and the Holy Spirit;" and officiates at what follows.

In the absence of a bishop, a priest is the celebrant and presides at the service. If a priest uses Chrism in signing the newly baptized, it must have been previously consecrated by the bishop.

Each candidate for Holy Baptism is to be sponsored by one or more baptized persons.

Sponsors of adults and older children present their candidates and thereby signify their endorsement of the candidates and their intention to support them by prayer and example in their Christian life. Sponsors of infants, commonly called godparents, present their candidates, make promises in their own names, and also take vows on behalf of their candidates.

It is fitting that parents be included among the godparents of their own children. Parents and godparents are to be instructed in the meaning of Baptism, in their duties to help the new Christians grow in the knowledge and love of God, and in their responsibilities as members of his Church.

Additional Directions are on page 312.

# Holy Baptism

*hymn, psalm, or anthem may be sung.*

*The people standing, the Celebrant says*

Blessed be God: Father, Son, and Holy Spirit.

*People*    And blessed be his kingdom, now and for ever. Amen.

*In place of the above, from Easter Day through the Day of Pentecost*

*Celebrant*    Alleluia. Christ is risen.

*People*    The Lord is risen indeed. Alleluia.

*In Lent and on other penitential occasions*

*Celebrant*    Bless the Lord who forgives all our sins.

*People*    His mercy endures for ever.

*The Celebrant then continues*

There is one Body and one Spirit;

*People*    There is one hope in God's call to us;

*Celebrant*    One Lord, one Faith, one Baptism;

*People*    One God and Father of all.

*Celebrant*    The Lord be with you.

*People*    And also with you.

*Celebrant*    Let us pray.

## The Collect of the Day

*People*     Amen.

*At the principal service on a Sunday or other feast, the Collect and Lessons are properly those of the Day. On other occasions they are selected from "At Baptism." (See Additional Directions, page 312.)*


## The Lessons

*The people sit. One or two Lessons, as appointed, are read, the Reader first saying*

A Reading (Lesson) from ＿＿＿＿.

*A citation giving chapter and verse may be added.*

*After each Reading, the Reader may say*

The Word of the Lord.
*People*     Thanks be to God.

*or the Reader may say*     Here ends the Reading (Epistle).

*Silence may follow.*

*A Psalm, hymn, or anthem may follow each Reading.*

*Then, all standing, the Deacon or a Priest reads the Gospel, first saying*

The Holy Gospel of our Lord Jesus Christ according to ＿＿＿＿.
*People*     Glory to you, Lord Christ.

*After the Gospel, the Reader says*

The Gospel of the Lord.
*People*     Praise to you, Lord Christ.

# The Sermon

*Or the Sermon may be preached after the Peace.*

# Presentation and Examination of the Candidates

*The Celebrant says*

The Candidate(s) for Holy Baptism will now be presented.

## Adults and Older Children

*The candidates who are able to answer for themselves are presented individually by their Sponsors, as follows*

*Sponsor*   I present N. to receive the Sacrament of Baptism.

*The Celebrant asks each candidate when presented*

    Do you desire to be baptized?

*Candidate*  I do.

## Infants and Younger Children

*When the candidates unable to answer for themselves are presented individually by their Parents and Godparents, as follows*

*Parents and Godparents*

I present N. to receive the Sacrament of Baptism.

*When all have been presented the Celebrant asks the parents and godparents*

Will you be responsible for seeing that the child you present is brought up in the Christian faith and life?

*Parents and Godparents*

I will, with God's help.

*Celebrant*

Will you by your prayers and witness help this child to grow into the full stature of Christ?

*Parents and Godparents*

I will, with God's help.

*Then the Celebrant asks the following questions of the candidates who can speak for themselves, and of the parents and godparents who speak on behalf of the infants and younger children*

Question  Do you renounce Satan and all the spiritual forces of wickedness that rebel against God?
Answer   I renounce them.

Question  Do you renounce the evil powers of this world which corrupt and destroy the creatures of God?
Answer   I renounce them.

Question  Do you renounce all sinful desires that draw you from the love of God?
Answer   I renounce them.

Question  Do you turn to Jesus Christ and accept him as your Savior?
Answer   I do.

Question  Do you put your whole trust in his grace and love?
Answer   I do.

*Question*   Do you promise to follow and obey him as your
             Lord?
*Answer*     I do.

*When there are others to be presented, the Bishop says*

The other Candidate(s) will now be presented.

*Presenters*   I present *these persons* for Confirmation.

*or*           I present *these persons* to be received into this
               Communion.

*or*           I present *these persons* who *desire* to reaffirm *their*
               baptismal vows.

*The Bishop asks the candidates*

Do you reaffirm your renunciation of evil?

*Candidate*  I do.

*Bishop*

Do you renew your commitment to Jesus Christ?

*Candidate*

I do, and with God's grace I will follow him as my Savior
and Lord.

*After all have been presented, the Celebrant addresses the congregation,
saying*

Will you who witness these vows do all in your
power to support *these persons* in *their* life in Christ?

*People*     We will.

*The Celebrant then says these or similar words*

Let us join with *those* who *are* committing *themselves* to Christ
and renew our own baptismal covenant.

# The Baptismal Covenant

*Celebrant*  Do you believe in God the Father?
*People*  I believe in God, the Father almighty,
    creator of heaven and earth.

*Celebrant*  Do you believe in Jesus Christ, the Son of God?
*People*  I believe in Jesus Christ, his only Son, our Lord.
    He was conceived by the power of the Holy Spirit
        and born of the Virgin Mary.
    He suffered under Pontius Pilate,
        was crucified, died, and was buried.
    He descended to the dead.
    On the third day he rose again.
    He ascended into heaven,
        and is seated at the right hand of the Father.
    He will come again to judge the living and the dead

*Celebrant*  Do you believe in God the Holy Spirit?
*People*  I believe in the Holy Spirit,
    the holy catholic Church,
    the communion of saints,
    the forgiveness of sins,
    the resurrection of the body,
    and the life everlasting.

*Celebrant*  Will you continue in the apostles' teaching and
    fellowship, in the breaking of bread, and in the
    prayers?
*People*  I will, with God's help.

*Celebrant*  Will you persevere in resisting evil, and, whenever
    you fall into sin, repent and return to the Lord?
*People*  I will, with God's help.

| Celebrant | Will you proclaim by word and example the Good News of God in Christ? |
|---|---|
| People | I will, with God's help. |

| Celebrant | Will you seek and serve Christ in all persons, loving your neighbor as yourself? |
|---|---|
| People | I will, with God's help. |

| Celebrant | Will you strive for justice and peace among all people, and respect the dignity of every human being? |
|---|---|
| People | I will, with God's help. |

## Prayers for the Candidates

*The Celebrant then says to the congregation*

Let us now pray for *these persons* who *are* to receive the Sacrament of new birth[and for those (this person) who *have* renewed *their* commitment to Christ.]

*A Person appointed leads the following petitions*

| Leader | Deliver *them*, O Lord, from the way of sin and death. |
|---|---|
| People | Lord, hear our prayer. |

| Leader | Open *their hearts* to your grace and truth. |
|---|---|
| People | Lord, hear our prayer. |

| Leader | Fill *them* with your holy and life-giving Spirit. |
|---|---|
| People | Lord, hear our prayer. |

| Leader | Keep *them* in the faith and communion of your holy Church. |
|---|---|
| People | Lord, hear our prayer. |

| Leader | Teach *them* to love others in the power of the Spirit. |
|---|---|
| People | Lord, hear our prayer. |

| *Leader* | Send *them* into the world in witness to your love. |
| *People* | Lord, hear our prayer. |

| *Leader* | Bring *them* to the fullness of your peace and glory. |
| *People* | Lord, hear our prayer. |

*The Celebrant says*

Grant, O Lord, that all who are baptized into the death
of Jesus Christ your Son may live in the power of his
resurrection and look for him to come again in glory; who
lives and reigns now and for ever. *Amen.*


## Thanksgiving over the Water

*The Celebrant blesses the water, first saying*

|          | The Lord be with you. |
| *People* | And also with you. |

| *Celebrant* | Let us give thanks to the Lord our God. |
| *People* | It is right to give him thanks and praise. |

*Celebrant*

We thank you, Almighty God, for the gift of water.
Over it the Holy Spirit moved in the beginning of creation.
Through it you led the children of Israel out of their bondage
in Egypt into the land of promise. In it your Son Jesus
received the baptism of John and was anointed by the Holy
Spirit as the Messiah, the Christ, to lead us, through his death
and resurrection, from the bondage of sin into everlasting life.

We thank you, Father, for the water of Baptism. In it we are
buried with Christ in his death. By it we share in his
resurrection. Through it we are reborn by the Holy Spirit.
Therefore in joyful obedience to your Son, we bring into his

fellowship those who come to him in faith, baptizing them in the Name of the Father, and of the Son, and of the Holy Spirit.

*At the following words, the Celebrant touches the water*

Now sanctify this water, we pray you, by the power of your Holy Spirit, that those who here are cleansed from sin and born again may continue for ever in the risen life of Jesus Christ our Savior.

To him, to you, and to the Holy Spirit, be all honor and glory, now and for ever. *Amen.*

## Consecration of the Chrism

*The Bishop may then consecrate oil of Chrism, placing a hand on the vessel of oil, and saying*

Eternal Father, whose blessed Son was anointed by the Holy Spirit to be the Savior and servant of all, we pray you to consecrate this oil, that those who are sealed with it may share in the royal priesthood of Jesus Christ; who lives and reigns with you and the Holy Spirit, for ever and ever. *Amen.*

# The Baptism

*Each candidate is presented by name to the Celebrant, or to an assisting priest or deacon, who then immerses, or pours water upon, the candidate, saying*

N., I baptize you in the Name of the Father, and of the Son, and of the Holy Spirit. *Amen.*

*When this action has been completed for all candidates, the Bishop or Priest, at a place in full sight of the congregation, prays over them, saying*

Let us pray.

Heavenly Father, we thank you that by water and the Holy Spirit you have bestowed upon *these* your *servants* the forgiveness of sin, and have raised *them* to the new life of grace. Sustain *them,* O Lord, in your Holy Spirit. Give *them* an inquiring and discerning heart, the courage to will and to persevere, a spirit to know and to love you, and the gift of joy and wonder in all your works. *Amen.*

*Then the Bishop or Priest places a hand on the person's head, marking on the forehead the sign of the cross [using Chrism if desired] and saying to each one*

N.,you are sealed by the Holy Spirit in Baptism and marked as Christ's own for ever. *Amen.*

*Or this action may be done immediately after the administration of the water and before the preceding prayer.*

*When all have been baptized, the Celebrant says*

Let us welcome the newly baptized.

*Celebrant and People*

We receive you into the household of God. Confess the faith of Christ crucified, proclaim his resurrection, and share with us in his eternal priesthood.

*If Confirmation, Reception, or the Reaffirmation of Baptismal Vows is not to follow, the Peace is now exchanged*

*Celebrant*  The peace of the Lord be always with you.
*People*      And also with you.

## At Confirmation, Reception, or Reaffirmation

*The Bishop says to the congregation*

Let us now pray for *these persons* who *have* renewed
*their* commitment to Christ.

*Silence may be kept.*

*Then the Bishop says*

Almighty God, we thank you that by the death and
resurrection of your Son Jesus Christ you have overcome sin
and brought us to yourself, and that by the sealing of your
Holy Spirit you have bound us to your service. Renew in
*these* your *servants* the covenant you made with *them* at *their*
Baptism. Send *them* forth in the power of that Spirit to
perform the service you set before *them*; through Jesus Christ
your Son our Lord, who lives and reigns with you and the
Holy Spirit, one God, now and for ever. *Amen.*


## For Confirmation

*The Bishop lays hands upon each one and says*

Strengthen, O Lord, your servant N. with your Holy Spirit;
empower *him* for your service; and sustain *him* all the days
of *his* life. *Amen.*

*or this*

Defend, O Lord, your servant N. with your heavenly grace,
that *he* may continue yours for ever, and daily increase in
your Holy Spirit more and more, until *he* comes to your
everlasting kingdom. *Amen.*

## For Reception

N., we recognize you as a member of the one holy catholic and apostolic Church, and we receive you into the fellowship of this Communion. God, the Father, Son, and Holy Spirit, bless, preserve, and keep you. *Amen.*

## For Reaffirmation

N., may the Holy Spirit, who has begun a good work in you, direct and uphold you in the service of Christ and his kingdom. *Amen.*

*Then the Bishop says*

Almighty and everliving God, let your fatherly hand ever be over *these* your *servants*; let your Holy Spirit ever be with *them*; and so lead *them* in the knowledge and obedience of your Word, that *they* may serve you in this life, and dwell with you in the life to come; through Jesus Christ our Lord. *Amen.*

*The Peace is then exchanged*

| | |
|---|---|
| *Bishop* | The peace of the Lord be always with you. |
| *People* | And also with you. |

## At the Eucharist

*The service then continues with the Prayers of the People or the Offertory of the Eucharist, at which the Bishop, when present, should be the principal Celebrant.*

*Except on Principal Feasts, the Proper Preface of Baptism may be used.*

## Alternative Ending

*If there is no celebration of the Eucharist, the service continues with the Lord's Prayer*

Our Father, who art in heaven,
  hallowed be thy Name,
  thy kingdom come,
  thy will be done,
    on earth as it is in heaven.
Give us this day our daily bread.
And forgive us our trespasses,
  as we forgive those
    who trespass against us.
And lead us not into temptation,
  but deliver us from evil.
For thine is the kingdom,
  and the power, and the glory,
  for ever and ever. Amen.

Our Father in heaven,
  hallowed be your Name,
  your kingdom come,
  your will be done,
    on earth as in heaven.
Give us today our daily bread.
Forgive us our sins
  as we forgive those
    who sin against us.
Save us from the time of trial
  and deliver us from evil.
For the kingdom, the power,
  and the glory are yours,
  now and for ever. Amen.

*The Celebrant then says*

All praise and thanks to you, most merciful Father, for adopting us as your own children, for incorporating us into your holy Church, and for making us worthy to share in the inheritance of the saints in light; through Jesus Christ your Son our Lord, who lives and reigns with you and the Holy Spirit, one God, for ever and ever. *Amen.*

*Alms may be received and presented, and other prayers may be added, concluding with this prayer*

Almighty God, the Father of our Lord Jesus Christ, from whom every family in heaven and earth is named, grant you to be strengthened with might by his Holy Spirit, that, Christ dwelling in your hearts by faith, you may be filled with all the fullness of God. *Amen.*

# Additional Directions

Holy Baptism is especially appropriate at the Easter Vigil, on the Day of Pentecost, on All Saints' Day or the Sunday after All Saints' Day, and on the Feast of the Baptism of our Lord (the First Sunday after the Epiphany). It is recommended that, as far as possible, Baptisms be reserved for these occasions or when a bishop is present.

If on any one of the above-named days the ministry of a bishop or priest cannot be obtained, the bishop may specially authorize a deacon to preside. In that case, the deacon omits the prayer over the candidates, page 308, and the formula and action which follow.

These omitted portions of the rite may be administered on some subsequent occasion of public baptism at which a bishop or priest presides.

If on the four days listed above there are no candidates for Baptism, the Renewal of Baptismal Vows, page 292, may take the place of the Nicene Creed at the Eucharist.

If desired, the hymn Gloria in excelsis may be sung immediately after the opening versicles and before the salutation "The Lord be with you."

When a bishop is present, or on other occasions for sufficient reason, the Collect (page 203 or 254) and one or more of the Lessons provided for use at Baptism (page 928) may be substituted for the Proper of the Day.

Lay persons may act as readers, and it is appropriate for sponsors to be assigned this function. The petitions (page 305) may also be led by one of the sponsors.

The Nicene Creed is not used at this service.

If the Presentation of the Candidates does not take place at the font, then before or during the petitions (page 305), the ministers, candidates, and sponsors go to the font for the Thanksgiving over the Water.

If the movement to the font is a formal procession, a suitable psalm, such as Psalm 42, or a hymn or anthem, may be sung.

Where practicable, the font is to be filled with clean water immediately before the Thanksgiving over the Water.

At the Thanksgiving over the Water, and at the administration of Baptism, the celebrant, whenever possible, should face the people across the font, and the sponsors should be so grouped that the people may have a clear view of the action.

After the Baptism, a candle (which may be lighted from the Paschal Candle) may be given to each of the newly baptized or to a godparent.

It may be found desirable to return to the front of the church for the prayer, "Heavenly Father, we thank you that by water and the Holy Spirit," and the ceremonies that follow it. A suitable psalm, such as Psalm 23, or a hymn or anthem, may be sung during the procession.

The oblations of bread and wine at the baptismal Eucharist may be presented by the newly baptized or their godparents.


## Conditional Baptism

*If there is reasonable doubt that a person has been baptized with water, "In the Name of the Father, and of the Son, and of the Holy Spirit" (which are the essential parts of Baptism), the person is baptized in the usual manner, but this form of words is used*

If you are not already baptized, N., I baptize you in the Name of the Father, and of the Son, and of the Holy Spirit.


## Emergency Baptism

*In case of emergency, any baptized person may administer Baptism according to the following form.*

*Using the given name of the one to be baptized (if known), pour water on him or her, saying*

I baptize you in the Name of the Father, and of the Son, and of the Holy Spirit.

*The Lord's Prayer is then said.*

*Other prayers, such as the following, may be added*

Heavenly Father, we thank you that by water and the Holy
Spirit you have bestowed upon this your servant the
forgiveness of sin and have raised *him* to the new life of
grace. Strengthen *him*, O Lord, with your presence, enfold
*him* in the arms of your mercy, and keep *him* safe for ever.

*The person who administers emergency Baptism should inform the priest
of the appropriate parish, so that the fact can be properly registered.*

*If the baptized person recovers, the Baptism should be recognized
at a public celebration of the Sacrament with a bishop or priest
presiding, and the person baptized under emergency conditions,
together with the sponsors or godparents, taking part in everything
except the administration of the water.*

# The Holy Eucharist

The Liturgy for the
Proclamation of the Word of God and
Celebration of the Holy Communion

## An Exhortation

*This Exhortation may be used, in whole or in part, either during the
Liturgy or at other times. In the absence of a deacon or priest, this
Exhortation may be read by a lay person. The people stand or sit.*

Beloved in the Lord: Our Savior Christ, on the night before
he suffered, instituted the Sacrament of his Body and
Blood as a sign and pledge of his love, for the continual
remembrance of the sacrifice of his death, and for a spiritual
sharing in his risen life. For in these holy Mysteries we are
made one with Christ, and Christ with us; we are made one
body in him, and members one of another.

Having in mind, therefore, his great love for us, and in
obedience to his command, his Church renders to Almighty
God our heavenly Father never-ending thanks for the
creation of the world, for his continual providence over us,
for his love for all mankind, and for the redemption of the
world by our Savior Christ, who took upon himself our flesh,
and humbled himself even to death on the cross, that he
might make us the children of God by the power of the Holy
Spirit, and exalt us to everlasting life.

But if we are to share rightly in the celebration of those holy
Mysteries, and be nourished by that spiritual Food, we must
remember the dignity of that holy Sacrament. I therefore call
upon you to consider how Saint Paul exhorts all persons to
prepare themselves carefully before eating of that Bread and
drinking of that Cup.

For, as the benefit is great, if with penitent hearts and living
faith we receive the holy Sacrament, so is the danger great, if
we receive it improperly, not recognizing the Lord's Body.
Judge yourselves, therefore, lest you be judged by the Lord.

Examine your lives and conduct by the rule of God's commandments, that you may perceive wherein you have offended in what you have done or left undone, whether in thought, word, or deed. And acknowledge your sins before Almighty God, with full purpose of amendment of life, being ready to make restitution for all injuries and wrongs done by you to others; and also being ready to forgive those who have offended you, in order that you yourselves may be forgiven. And then, being reconciled with one another, come to the banquet of that most heavenly Food.

And if, in your preparation, you need help and counsel, then go and open your grief to a discreet and understanding priest, and confess your sins, that you may receive the benefit of absolution, and spiritual counsel and advice; to the removal of scruple and doubt, the assurance of pardon, and the strengthening of your faith.

To Christ our Lord who loves us, and washed us in his own blood, and made us a kingdom of priests to serve his God and Father, to him be glory in the Church evermore. Through him let us offer continually the sacrifice of praise, which is our bounden duty and service, and, with faith in him, come boldly before the throne of grace [and humbly confess our sins to Almighty God].

## The Decalogue: Traditional

God spake these words, and said:
I am the Lord thy God who brought thee out of the land of Egypt, out of the house of bondage. Thou shalt have none other gods but me.
*Lord, have mercy upon us,*
*and incline our hearts to keep this law.*

Thou shalt not make to thyself any graven image, nor the likeness of any thing that is in heaven above, or in the earth beneath, or in the water under the earth; thou shalt not bow down to them, nor worship them.
*Lord, have mercy upon us,*
*and incline our hearts to keep this law.*

Thou shalt not take the Name of the Lord thy God in vain.
*Lord, have mercy upon us,*
*and incline our hearts to keep this law.*

Remember that thou keep holy the Sabbath day.
*Lord, have mercy upon us,*
*and incline our hearts to keep this law.*

Honor thy father and thy mother.
*Lord, have mercy upon us,*
*and incline our hearts to keep this law.*

Thou shalt do no murder.
*Lord, have mercy upon us,*
*and incline our hearts to keep this law.*

Thou shalt not commit adultery.
*Lord, have mercy upon us,*
*and incline our hearts to keep this law.*

Thou shalt not steal.
*Lord, have mercy upon us,*
*and incline our hearts to keep this law.*

Thou shalt not bear false witness against thy neighbor.
*Lord, have mercy upon us,*
*and incline our hearts to keep this law.*

Thou shalt not covet.
*Lord, have mercy upon us,*
*and write all these thy laws in our hearts, we beseech thee.*

# A Penitential Order: Rite One

*For use at the beginning of the Liturgy, or as a separate service.*

*A hymn, psalm, or anthem may be sung.*

*The people standing, the Celebrant says*

Blessed be God: Father, Son, and Holy Spirit.
People    And blessed be his kingdom, now and for ever.
Amen.

*In place of the above, from Easter Day through the Day of Pentecost*

Celebrant    Alleluia. Christ is risen.
People    The Lord is risen indeed. Alleluia.

*In Lent and on other penitential occasions*

Celebrant    Bless the Lord who forgiveth all our sins.
People    His mercy endureth for ever.

*When used as a separate service, the Exhortation, page 316, may be read, or a homily preached.*

*The Decalogue, page 317, may be said, the people kneeling.*

*The Celebrant may read one of the following sentences*

Hear what our Lord Jesus Christ saith:
Thou shalt love the Lord thy God with all thy heart, and with all thy soul, and with all thy mind. This is the first and great commandment. And the second is like unto it: Thou shalt love thy neighbor as thyself. On these two commandments hang all the Law and the Prophets.    *Matthew 22:37-40*

If we say that we have no sin, we deceive ourselves, and the truth is not in us; but if we confess our sins, God is faithful and just to forgive us our sins, and to cleanse us from all unrighteousness.   *1 John 1:8, 9*

Seeing that we have a great high priest, that is passed into the heavens, Jesus the Son of God, let us come boldly unto the throne of grace, that we may obtain mercy, and find grace to help in time of need.   *Hebrews 4:14, 16*

*The Deacon or Celebrant then says*

Let us humbly confess our sins unto Almighty God.

*Silence may be kept.*

*Minister and People*

Most merciful God,
we confess that we have sinned against thee
in thought, word, and deed,
by what we have done,
and by what we have left undone.
We have not loved thee with our whole heart;
we have not loved our neighbors as ourselves.
We are truly sorry and we humbly repent.
For the sake of thy Son Jesus Christ,
have mercy on us and forgive us;
that we may delight in thy will,
and walk in thy ways,
to the glory of thy Name. Amen.

*or this*

Almighty and most merciful Father,
we have erred and strayed from thy ways like lost sheep,
we have followed too much the devices and desires of our
    own hearts,

we have offended against thy holy laws,
we have left undone those things which we ought to
   have done,
and we have done those things which we ought not to
   have done.
But thou, O Lord, have mercy upon us,
spare thou those who confess their faults,
restore thou those who are penitent,
according to thy promises declared unto mankind
in Christ Jesus our Lord;
and grant, O most merciful Father, for his sake,
that we may hereafter live a godly, righteous, and sober life,
to the glory of thy holy Name. Amen.

*The Bishop when present, or the Priest, stands and says*

The Almighty and merciful Lord grant you absolution and
remission of all your sins, true repentance, amendment of
life, and the grace and consolation of his Holy Spirit. *Amen.*

*A deacon or lay person using the preceding form substitutes "us" for
"you" and "our" for "your."*

*When this Order is used at the beginning of the Liturgy, the service
continues with the Kyrie eleison, the Trisagion, or the Gloria in excelsis.*

*When used separately, it concludes with suitable prayers, and the Grace
or a blessing.*

# Concerning the Celebration

It is the bishop's prerogative, when present, to be the principal celebrant at the Lord's Table, and to preach the Gospel.

At all celebrations of the Liturgy, it is fitting that the principal celebrant, whether bishop or priest, be assisted by other priests, and by deacons and lay persons.

It is appropriate that the other priests present stand with the celebrant at the Altar, and join in the consecration of the gifts, in breaking the Bread, and in distributing Communion.

A deacon should read the Gospel and may lead the Prayers of the People. Deacons should also serve at the Lord's Table, preparing and placing on it the offerings of bread and wine, and assisting in the ministration of the Sacrament to the people. In the absence of a deacon, these duties may be performed by an assisting priest.

Lay persons appointed by the celebrant should normally be assigned the reading of the Lessons which precede the Gospel, and may lead the Prayers of the People.

Morning or Evening Prayer may be used in place of all that precedes the Peace and the Offertory, provided that a lesson from the Gospel is always included, and that the intercessions conform to the directions given for the Prayers of the People.

Additional Directions are on page 406.

# The Holy Eucharist: Rite One

## The Word of God

*A hymn, psalm, or anthem may be sung.*

*The people standing, the Celebrant may say*

> Blessed be God: Father, Son, and Holy Spirit.
>
> *People*     And blessed be his kingdom, now and for ever.
> Amen.

*In place of the above, from Easter Day through the Day of Pentecost*

*Celebrant*     Alleluia. Christ is risen.
*People*     The Lord is risen indeed. Alleluia.

*In Lent and on other penitential occasions*

*Celebrant*     Bless the Lord who forgiveth all our sins.
*People*     His mercy endureth for ever.

*The Celebrant says*

Almighty God, unto whom all hearts are open, all desires known, and from whom no secrets are hid: Cleanse the thoughts of our hearts by the inspiration of thy Holy Spirit, that we may perfectly love thee, and worthily magnify thy holy Name; through Christ our Lord. *Amen.*

*Then the Ten Commandments (page 317) may be said, or the following*

Hear what our Lord Jesus Christ saith:
Thou shalt love the Lord thy God with all thy heart, and with
all thy soul, and with all thy mind. This is the first and great
commandment. And the second is like unto it: Thou shalt
love thy neighbor as thyself. On these two commandments
hang all the Law and the Prophets.

*Here is sung or said*

| | | |
|---|---|---|
| Lord, have mercy upon us. | | Kyrie eleison. |
| *Christ, have mercy upon us.* | *or* | *Christe eleison.* |
| Lord, have mercy upon us. | | Kyrie eleison. |

*or this*

Holy God,
Holy and Mighty,
Holy Immortal One,
*Have mercy upon us.*

*When appointed, the following hymn or some other song of praise is
sung or said, in addition to, or in place of, the preceding, all standing*

Glory be to God on high,
   and on earth peace, good will towards men.

We praise thee, we bless thee,
   we worship thee,
   we glorify thee,
   we give thanks to thee for thy great glory,
O Lord God, heavenly King, God the Father Almighty.

O Lord, the only-begotten Son, Jesus Christ;
O Lord God, Lamb of God, Son of the Father,
   that takest away the sins of the world,
   have mercy upon us.

Thou that takest away the sins of the world,
  receive our prayer.
Thou that sittest at the right hand of God the Father,
  have mercy upon us.

For thou only art holy;
thou only art the Lord;
thou only, O Christ,
  with the Holy Ghost,
  art most high in the glory of God the Father. Amen.


## The Collect of the Day

*The Celebrant says to the people*

        The Lord be with you.
*People*    And with thy spirit.
*Celebrant*  Let us pray.

*The Celebrant says the Collect.*

*People*    Amen.


## The Lessons

*The people sit. One or two Lessons, as appointed, are read, the Reader
first saying*

A Reading (Lesson) from _____.

*A citation giving chapter and verse may be added.*

*After each Reading, the Reader may say*

        The Word of the Lord.
*People*    Thanks be to God.

*or the Reader may say*    Here endeth the Reading (Epistle).

*Silence may follow.*

*A Psalm, hymn, or anthem may follow each Reading.*

*Then, all standing, the Deacon or a Priest reads the Gospel, first saying*

> The Holy Gospel of our Lord Jesus Christ
> according to _____.

*People*    Glory be to thee, O Lord.

*After the Gospel, the Reader says*

> The Gospel of the Lord.

*People*    Praise be to thee, O Christ.

## The Sermon

*On Sundays and other Major Feasts there follows, all standing*

## The Nicene Creed

We believe in one God,
   the Father, the Almighty,
   maker of heaven and earth,
   of all that is, seen and unseen.

We believe in one Lord, Jesus Christ,
   the only Son of God,
   eternally begotten of the Father,
   God from God, Light from Light,
   true God from true God,
   begotten, not made,
   of one Being with the Father.
   Through him all things were made.
   For us and for our salvation
      he came down from heaven:

by the power of the Holy Spirit
   he became incarnate from the Virgin Mary,
   and was made man.
For our sake he was crucified under Pontius Pilate;
   he suffered death and was buried.
   On the third day he rose again
     in accordance with the Scriptures;
   he ascended into heaven
     and is seated at the right hand of the Father.
He will come again in glory to judge the living and the dead,
   and his kingdom will have no end.

We believe in the Holy Spirit, the Lord, the giver of life,
   who proceeds from the Father and the Son.
   With the Father and the Son he is worshiped and glorified.
   He has spoken through the Prophets.
   We believe in one holy catholic and apostolic Church.
   We acknowledge one baptism for the forgiveness of sins.
   We look for the resurrection of the dead,
     and the life of the world to come. Amen.

*or this*

I believe in one God,
   the Father Almighty,
   maker of heaven and earth,
   and of all things visible and invisible;

And in one Lord Jesus Christ,
   the only-begotten Son of God,
   begotten of his Father before all worlds,
   God of God, Light of Light,
   very God of very God,
   begotten, not made,
   being of one substance with the Father;
   by whom all things were made;

who for us men and for our salvation
   came down from heaven,
and was incarnate by the Holy Ghost of the Virgin Mary,
   and was made man;
and was crucified also for us under Pontius Pilate;
he suffered and was buried;
and the third day he rose again according to the Scriptures,
and ascended into heaven,
and sitteth on the right hand of the Father;
and he shall come again, with glory,
   to judge both the quick and the dead;
whose kingdom shall have no end.

And I believe in the Holy Ghost the Lord, and Giver of Life,
   who proceedeth from the Father and the Son;
who with the Father and the Son together is worshiped
   and glorified;
who spake by the Prophets.
And I believe one holy Catholic and Apostolic Church;
I acknowledge one Baptism for the remission of sins;
and I look for the resurrection of the dead,
   and the life of the world to come. Amen.


## The Prayers of the People

*Intercession is offered according to the following form, or in accordance with the directions on page 383.*

*The Deacon or other person appointed says*

Let us pray for the whole state of Christ's Church and the world.

*After each paragraph of this prayer, the People may make an appropriate response, as directed.*

Almighty and everliving God, who in thy holy Word hast
taught us to make prayers, and supplications, and to give
thanks for all men: Receive these our prayers which we offer
unto thy divine Majesty, beseeching thee to inspire
continually the Universal Church with the spirit of truth,
unity, and concord; and grant that all those who do confess
thy holy Name may agree in the truth of thy holy Word, and
live in unity and godly love.

Give grace, O heavenly Father, to all bishops and other
ministers [especially _____], that they may, both by
their life and doctrine, set forth thy true and lively Word,
and rightly and duly administer thy holy Sacraments.

And to all thy people give thy heavenly grace, and especially
to this congregation here present; that, with meek heart and
due reverence, they may hear and receive thy holy Word,
truly serving thee in holiness and righteousness all the days
of their life.

We beseech thee also so to rule the hearts of those who bear
the authority of government in this and every land [especially
_____], that they may be led to wise decisions and right
actions for the welfare and peace of the world.

Open, O Lord, the eyes of all people to behold thy gracious
hand in all thy works, that, rejoicing in thy whole creation,
they may honor thee with their substance, and be faithful
stewards of thy bounty.

And we most humbly beseech thee, of thy goodness, O Lord,
to comfort and succor [_____ and] all those who, in this
transitory life, are in trouble, sorrow, need, sickness, or any
other adversity.

*Additional petitions and thanksgivings may be included here.*

And we also bless thy holy Name for all thy servants departed this life in thy faith and fear [especially _____], beseeching thee to grant them continual growth in thy love and service; and to grant us grace so to follow the good examples of [_____ and of] all thy saints, that with them we may be partakers of thy heavenly kingdom.

Grant these our prayers, O Father, for Jesus Christ's sake, our only Mediator and Advocate. *Amen.*

*If there is no celebration of the Communion, or if a priest is not available, the service is concluded as directed on page 406.*

## Confession of Sin

*A Confession of Sin is said here if it has not been said earlier. On occasion, the Confession may be omitted.*

*The Deacon or Celebrant says the following, or else the Exhortation on page 316*

Ye who do truly and earnestly repent you of your sins, and are in love and charity with your neighbors, and intend to lead a new life, following the commandments of God, and walking from henceforth in his holy ways: Draw near with faith, and make your humble confession to Almighty God, devoutly kneeling.

*or this*

Let us humbly confess our sins unto Almighty God.

*Silence may be kept.*

*Minister and People*

Almighty God,
Father of our Lord Jesus Christ,
maker of all things, judge of all men:
We acknowledge and bewail our manifold sins
      and wickedness,
which we from time to time most grievously have committed,
by thought, word, and deed, against thy divine Majesty,
provoking most justly thy wrath and indignation against us.
We do earnestly repent,
and are heartily sorry for these our misdoings;
the remembrance of them is grievous unto us,
the burden of them is intolerable.
Have mercy upon us,
have mercy upon us, most merciful Father;
for thy Son our Lord Jesus Christ's sake,
forgive us all that is past;
and grant that we may ever hereafter
serve and please thee in newness of life,
to the honor and glory of thy Name;
through Jesus Christ our Lord. Amen.

*or this*

Most merciful God,
we confess that we have sinned against thee
in thought, word, and deed,
by what we have done,
and by what we have left undone.
We have not loved thee with our whole heart;
we have not loved our neighbors as ourselves.
We are truly sorry and we humbly repent.
For the sake of thy Son Jesus Christ,
have mercy on us and forgive us;
that we may delight in thy will,
and walk in thy ways,
to the glory of thy Name. Amen.

*The Bishop when present, or the Priest, stands and says*

Almighty God, our heavenly Father, who of his great mercy
hath promised forgiveness of sins to all those who with
hearty repentance and true faith turn unto him, have mercy
upon you, pardon and deliver you from all your sins, confirm
and strengthen you in all goodness, and bring you to
everlasting life; through Jesus Christ our Lord. *Amen*.

*A Minister may then say one or more of the following sentences, first saying*

Hear the Word of God to all who truly turn to him.

Come unto me, all ye that travail and are heavy laden, and
I will refresh you. *Matthew 11:28*

God so loved the world, that he gave his only-begotten Son,
to the end that all that believe in him should not perish, but
have everlasting life. *John 3:16*

This is a true saying, and worthy of all men to be received,
that Christ Jesus came into the world to save sinners.
*1 Timothy 1:15*

If any man sin, we have an Advocate with the Father, Jesus
Christ the righteous; and he is the perfect offering for our
sins, and not for ours only, but for the sins of the whole
world. *1 John 2:1-2*

### The Peace

*All stand. The Celebrant says to the people*

      The peace of the Lord be always with you.
*People*     And with thy spirit.

*Then the Ministers and People may greet one another in the name of
the Lord.*

# The Holy Communion

*The Celebrant may begin the Offertory with one of the sentences on pages 343-344, or with some other sentence of Scripture.*

*During the Offertory, a hymn, psalm, or anthem may be sung.*

*Representatives of the congregation bring the people's offerings of bread and wine, and money or other gifts, to the deacon or celebrant. The people stand while the offerings are presented and placed on the Altar.*

## The Great Thanksgiving

*An alternative form will be found on page 340.*

### Eucharistic Prayer I

*The people remain standing. The Celebrant, whether bishop or priest, faces them and sings or says*

|  | The Lord be with you. |
|---|---|
| *People* | And with thy spirit. |
| *Celebrant* | Lift up your hearts. |
| *People* | We lift them up unto the Lord. |
| *Celebrant* | Let us give thanks unto our Lord God. |
| *People* | It is meet and right so to do. |

*Then, facing the Holy Table, the Celebrant proceeds*

It is very meet, right, and our bounden duty, that we should at all times, and in all places, give thanks unto thee, O Lord, holy Father, almighty, everlasting God.

*Here a Proper Preface is sung or said on all Sundays, and on other occasions as appointed.*

Therefore with Angels and Archangels, and with all the company of heaven, we laud and magnify thy glorious Name; evermore praising thee, and saying,

*Celebrant and People*

Holy, holy, holy, Lord God of Hosts:
Heaven and earth are full of thy glory.
Glory be to thee, O Lord Most High.

*Here may be added*

Blessed is he that cometh in the name of the Lord.
Hosanna in the highest.

*The people kneel or stand.*

*Then the Celebrant continues*

All glory be to thee, Almighty God, our heavenly Father, for that thou, of thy tender mercy, didst give thine only Son Jesus Christ to suffer death upon the cross for our redemption; who made there, by his one oblation of himself once offered, a full, perfect, and sufficient sacrifice, oblation, and satisfaction, for the sins of the whole world; and did institute, and in his holy Gospel command us to continue, a perpetual memory of that his precious death and sacrifice, until his coming again.

*At the following words concerning the bread, the Celebrant is to hold it, or lay a hand upon it; and at the words concerning the cup, to hold or place a hand upon the cup and any other vessel containing wine to be consecrated.*

For in the night in which he was betrayed, he took bread; and when he had given thanks, he brake it, and gave it to his disciples, saying, "Take, eat, this is my Body, which is given for you. Do this in remembrance of me."

Likewise, after supper, he took the cup; and when he had given thanks, he gave it to them, saying, "Drink ye all of this; for this is my Blood of the New Testament, which is shed for you, and for many, for the remission of sins. Do this, as oft as ye shall drink it, in remembrance of me."

Wherefore, O Lord and heavenly Father, according to the institution of thy dearly beloved Son our Savior Jesus Christ, we, thy humble servants, do celebrate and make here before thy divine Majesty, with these thy holy gifts, which we now offer unto thee, the memorial thy Son hath commanded us to make; having in remembrance his blessed passion and precious death, his mighty resurrection and glorious ascension; rendering unto thee most hearty thanks for the innumerable benefits procured unto us by the same.

And we most humbly beseech thee, O merciful Father, to hear us; and, of thy almighty goodness, vouchsafe to bless and sanctify, with thy Word and Holy Spirit, these thy gifts and creatures of bread and wine; that we, receiving them according to thy Son our Savior Jesus Christ's holy institution, in remembrance of his death and passion, may be partakers of his most blessed Body and Blood.

And we earnestly desire thy fatherly goodness mercifully to accept this our sacrifice of praise and thanksgiving; most humbly beseeching thee to grant that, by the merits and death of thy Son Jesus Christ, and through faith in his blood, we, and all thy whole Church, may obtain remission of our sins, and all other benefits of his passion.

And here we offer and present unto thee, O Lord, our selves, our souls and bodies, to be a reasonable, holy, and living sacrifice unto thee; humbly beseeching thee that we, and all others who shall be partakers of this Holy Communion, may worthily receive the most precious Body and Blood of thy Son Jesus Christ, be filled with thy grace and heavenly benediction, and made one body with him, that he may dwell in us, and we in him.

And although we are unworthy, through our manifold sins, to offer unto thee any sacrifice, yet we beseech thee to accept this our bounden duty and service, not weighing our merits, but pardoning our offenses, through Jesus Christ our Lord;

By whom, and with whom, in the unity of the Holy Ghost all honor and glory be unto thee, O Father Almighty, world without end. *AMEN.*

And now, as our Savior Christ hath taught us, we are bold to say,

*People and Celebrant*

Our Father, who art in heaven,
    hallowed be thy Name,
    thy kingdom come,
    thy will be done,
        on earth as it is in heaven.
Give us this day our daily bread.
And forgive us our trespasses,
    as we forgive those who trespass against us.
And lead us not into temptation,
    but deliver us from evil.
For thine is the kingdom, and the power, and the glory,
    for ever and ever. Amen.

## The Breaking of the Bread

*The Celebrant breaks the consecrated Bread.*

*A period of silence is kept.*

*Then may be sung or said*

[Alleluia.] Christ our Passover is sacrificed for us;
*Therefore let us keep the feast.* [*Alleluia.*]

*In Lent, Alleluia is omitted, and may be omitted at other times except during Easter Season.*

*The following or some other suitable anthem may be sung or said here*

O Lamb of God, that takest away the sins of the world,
have mercy upon us.
O Lamb of God, that takest away the sins of the world,
have mercy upon us.
O Lamb of God, that takest away the sins of the world,
grant us thy peace.

*The following prayer may be said. The People may join in saying this prayer*

We do not presume to come to this thy Table, O merciful
Lord, trusting in our own righteousness, but in thy manifold
and great mercies. We are not worthy so much as to gather
up the crumbs under thy Table. But thou art the same Lord
whose property is always to have mercy. Grant us therefore,
gracious Lord, so to eat the flesh of thy dear Son Jesus Christ,
and to drink his blood, that we may evermore dwell in him,
and he in us. *Amen.*

*Facing the people, the Celebrant may say the following Invitation*

The Gifts of God for the People of God.
*and may add*  Take them in remembrance that Christ died for
you, and feed on him in your hearts by faith,
with thanksgiving.

*The ministers receive the Sacrament in both kinds, and then immediately deliver it to the people.*

*The Bread and the Cup are given to the communicants with these words*

The Body of our Lord Jesus Christ, which was given for thee, preserve thy body and soul unto everlasting life. Take and eat this in remembrance that Christ died for thee, and feed on him in thy heart by faith, with thanksgiving.

The Blood of our Lord Jesus Christ, which was shed for thee, preserve thy body and soul unto everlasting life. Drink this in remembrance that Christ's Blood was shed for thee, and be thankful.

*or with these words*

The Body (Blood) of our Lord Jesus Christ keep you in everlasting life. [*Amen.*]

*or with these words*

The Body of Christ, the bread of heaven. [*Amen.*]
The Blood of Christ, the cup of salvation. [*Amen.*]

*During the ministration of Communion, hymns, psalms, or anthems may be sung.*

*When necessary, the Celebrant consecrates additional bread and wine, using the form on page 408.*

*After Communion, the Celebrant says*

Let us pray.

*The People may join in saying this prayer*

Almighty and everliving God, we most heartily thank thee
for that thou dost feed us, in these holy mysteries, with the
spiritual food of the most precious Body and Blood of thy
Son our Savior Jesus Christ; and dost assure us thereby of
thy favor and goodness towards us; and that we are very
members incorporate in the mystical body of thy Son, the
blessed company of all faithful people; and are also heirs,
through hope, of thy everlasting kingdom. And we humbly
beseech thee, O heavenly Father, so to assist us with thy
grace, that we may continue in that holy fellowship, and do
all such good works as thou hast prepared for us to walk in;
through Jesus Christ our Lord, to whom, with thee and the
Holy Ghost, be all honor and glory, world without end.
*Amen.*

*The Bishop when present, or the Priest, gives the blessing*

The peace of God, which passeth all understanding, keep
your hearts and minds in the knowledge and love of God,
and of his Son Jesus Christ our Lord; and the blessing of
God Almighty, the Father, the Son, and the Holy Ghost, be
amongst you, and remain with you always. *Amen.*

*or this*

The blessing of God Almighty, the Father, the Son, and the
Holy Spirit, be upon you and remain with you for ever. *Amen.*

*The Deacon, or the Celebrant, may dismiss the people with these words*

       Let us go forth in the name of Christ.
*People*     Thanks be to God.

*or the following*

| | |
|---|---|
| *Deacon* | Go in peace to love and serve the Lord. |
| *People* | Thanks be to God. |

*or this*

| | |
|---|---|
| *Deacon* | Let us go forth into the world, rejoicing in the power of the Spirit. |
| *People* | Thanks be to God. |

*or this*

| | |
|---|---|
| *Deacon* | Let us bless the Lord. |
| *People* | Thanks be to God. |

*From the Easter Vigil through the Day of Pentecost "Alleluia, alleluia" may be added to any of the dismissals.*

*The People respond*   Thanks be to God. Alleluia, alleluia.

# Alternative Form of the Great Thanksgiving

### Eucharistic Prayer II

*The people remain standing. The Celebrant, whether bishop or priest, faces them and sings or says*

| | |
|---|---|
| | The Lord be with you. |
| *People* | And with thy spirit. |
| *Celebrant* | Lift up your hearts. |
| *People* | We lift them up unto the Lord. |
| *Celebrant* | Let us give thanks unto our Lord God. |
| *People* | It is meet and right so to do. |

*Then, facing the Holy Table, the Celebrant proceeds*

It is very meet, right, and our bounden duty, that we should at all times, and in all places, give thanks unto thee, O Lord, holy Father, almighty, everlasting God.

*Here a Proper Preface is sung or said on all Sundays, and on other occasions as appointed.*

Therefore with Angels and Archangels, and with all the company of heaven, we laud and magnify thy glorious Name; evermore praising thee, and saying,

*Celebrant and People*

Holy, holy, holy, Lord God of Hosts:
Heaven and earth are full of thy glory.
Glory be to thee, O Lord Most High.

*Here may be added*

Blessed is he that cometh in the name of the Lord.
Hosanna in the highest.

*The people kneel or stand.*

*Then the Celebrant continues*

All glory be to thee, O Lord our God, for that thou didst create heaven and earth, and didst make us in thine own image; and, of thy tender mercy, didst give thine only Son Jesus Christ to take our nature upon him, and to suffer death upon the cross for our redemption. He made there a full and perfect sacrifice for the whole world; and did institute, and in his holy Gospel command us to continue, a perpetual memory of that his precious death and sacrifice, until his coming again.

*At the following words concerning the bread, the Celebrant is to hold it,*
*or lay a hand upon it; and at the words concerning the cup, to hold or*
*place a hand upon the cup and any other vessel containing wine to be*
*consecrated.*

For in the night in which he was betrayed, he took bread;
and when he had given thanks to thee, he broke it, and gave it
to his disciples, saying, "Take, eat, this is my Body, which is
given for you. Do this in remembrance of me."

Likewise, after supper, he took the cup; and when he had
given thanks, he gave it to them, saying, "Drink this, all of
you; for this is my Blood of the New Covenant, which is shed
for you, and for many, for the remission of sins. Do this, as
oft as ye shall drink it, in remembrance of me."

Wherefore, O Lord and heavenly Father, we thy people do
celebrate and make, with these thy holy gifts which we now
offer unto thee, the memorial thy Son hath commanded us to
make; having in remembrance his blessed passion and precious
death, his mighty resurrection and glorious ascension; and
looking for his coming again with power and great glory.

And we most humbly beseech thee, O merciful Father, to
hear us, and, with thy Word and Holy Spirit, to bless and
sanctify these gifts of bread and wine, that they may be unto
us the Body and Blood of thy dearly-beloved Son Jesus
Christ.

And we earnestly desire thy fatherly goodness to accept this
our sacrifice of praise and thanksgiving, whereby we offer
and present unto thee, O Lord, our selves, our souls and
bodies. Grant, we beseech thee, that all who partake of this
Holy Communion may worthily receive the most precious
Body and Blood of thy Son Jesus Christ, and be filled with
thy grace and heavenly benediction; and also that we and all
thy whole Church may be made one body with him, that he

may dwell in us, and we in him; through the same Jesus Christ our Lord;

By whom, and with whom, and in whom, in the unity of the Holy Ghost all honor and glory be unto thee, O Father Almighty, world without end. *AMEN.*

And now, as our Savior Christ hath taught us, we are bold to say,

*Continue with the Lord's Prayer, page 336.*


# Offertory Sentences

*One of the following, or some other appropriate sentence of Scripture, may be used*

Offer to God a sacrifice of thanksgiving, and make good thy vows unto the Most High.    *Psalm 50:14*

Ascribe to the Lord the honor due his Name; bring offerings and come into his courts.    *Psalm 96:8*

Walk in love, as Christ loved us and gave himself for us, an offering and sacrifice to God.    *Ephesians 5:2*

I beseech you, brethren, by the mercies of God, to present yourselves as a living sacrifice, holy and acceptable to God, which is your spiritual worship.    *Romans 12:1*

If thou bring thy gift to the altar, and there rememberest that thy brother hath aught against thee, leave there thy gift before the altar, and go thy way; first be reconciled to thy brother, and then come and offer thy gift.    *Matthew 5:23,24*

Through Christ let us continually offer to God the sacrifice of praise, that is, the fruit of lips that acknowledge his Name. But to do good and to distribute, forget not; for with such sacrifices God is well pleased.    *Hebrews 13:15,16*

Worthy art thou, O Lord our God, to receive glory and honor and power; for thou hast created all things, and by thy will they were created and have their being.    *Revelation 4:11*

Thine, O Lord, is the greatness, and the power, and the glory, and the victory, and the majesty. For all that is in the heaven and in the earth is thine. Thine is the kingdom, O Lord, and thou art exalted as head above all.    *1 Chronicles 29:11*

*or this bidding*

Let us with gladness present the offerings and oblations of our life and labor to the Lord.


# Proper Prefaces


**Preface of the Lord's Day**

*To be used on Sundays as appointed, but not on the succeeding weekdays*

*1. Of God the Father*

Creator of the light and source of life, who hast made us in thine image, and called us to new life in Jesus Christ our Lord.

*or the following*

## 2. Of God the Son

Through Jesus Christ our Lord; who on the first day of the
week overcame death and the grave, and by his glorious
resurrection opened to us the way of everlasting life.

*or this*

## 3. Of God the Holy Spirit

Who by water and the Holy Spirit hast made us a new people
in Jesus Christ our Lord, to show forth thy glory in all the
world.

## Prefaces for Seasons

*To be used on Sundays and weekdays alike, except as otherwise
appointed for Holy Days and Various Occasions*

### Advent

Because thou didst send thy beloved Son to redeem us from
sin and death, and to make us heirs in him of everlasting life;
that when he shall come again in power and great triumph to
judge the world, we may without shame or fear rejoice to
behold his appearing.

### Incarnation

Because thou didst give Jesus Christ, thine only Son, to be
born for us; who, by the mighty power of the Holy Ghost,
was made very Man of the substance of the Virgin Mary his
mother; that we might be delivered from the bondage of sin,
and receive power to become thy children.

*Epiphany*

Because in the mystery of the Word made flesh, thou hast caused a new light to shine in our hearts, to give the knowledge of thy glory in the face of thy Son Jesus Christ our Lord.

*Lent*

Through Jesus Christ our Lord; who was in every way tempted as we are, yet did not sin; by whose grace we are able to triumph over every evil, and to live no longer unto ourselves, but unto him who died for us and rose again.

*or this*

Who dost bid thy faithful people cleanse their hearts, and prepare with joy for the Paschal feast; that, fervent in prayer and in works of mercy, and renewed by thy Word and Sacraments, they may come to the fullness of grace which thou hast prepared for those who love thee.

*Holy Week*

Through Jesus Christ our Lord; who for our sins was lifted high upon the cross, that he might draw the whole world to himself; who by his suffering and death became the author of eternal salvation for all who put their trust in him.

*Easter*

But chiefly are we bound to praise thee for the glorious resurrection of thy Son Jesus Christ our Lord; for he is the very Paschal Lamb, who was sacrificed for us, and hath taken away the sin of the world; who by his death hath destroyed death, and by his rising to life again hath won for us everlasting life.

## Ascension

Through thy dearly beloved Son Jesus Christ our Lord; who after his glorious resurrection manifestly appeared to his disciples; and in their sight ascended into heaven, to prepare a place for us; that where he is, there we might also be, and reign with him in glory.

## Pentecost

Through Jesus Christ our Lord; according to whose true promise the Holy Ghost came down [on this day] from heaven, lighting upon the disciples, to teach them and to lead them into all truth; uniting peoples of many tongues in the confession of one faith, and giving to thy Church the power to serve thee as a royal priesthood, and to preach the Gospel to all nations.

## Prefaces for Other Occasions

### Trinity Sunday

For with thy co-eternal Son and Holy Spirit, thou art one God, one Lord, in Trinity of Persons and in Unity of Substance; and we celebrate the one and equal glory of thee, O Father, and of the Son, and of the Holy Spirit.

### All Saints

Who, in the multitude of thy saints, hast compassed us about with so great a cloud of witnesses, that we, rejoicing in their fellowship, may run with patience the race that is set before us; and, together with them, may receive the crown of glory that fadeth not away.

## A Saint

For the wonderful grace and virtue declared in all thy saints, who have been the chosen vessels of thy grace, and the lights of the world in their generations.

*or this*

Who in the obedience of thy saints hast given us an example of righteousness, and in their eternal joy a glorious pledge of the hope of our calling.

*or this*

Because thou art greatly glorified in the assembly of thy saints. All thy creatures praise thee, and thy faithful servants bless thee, confessing before the rulers of this world the great Name of thine only Son.

## Apostles and Ordinations

Through the great shepherd of thy flock, Jesus Christ our Lord; who after his resurrection sent forth his apostles to preach the Gospel and to teach all nations; and promised to be with them always, even unto the end of the ages.

## Dedication of a Church

Through Jesus Christ our great High Priest; in whom we are built up as living stones of a holy temple, that we might offer before thee a sacrifice of praise and prayer which is holy and pleasing in thy sight.

## Baptism

Because in Jesus Christ our Lord thou hast received us as thy sons and daughters, made us citizens of thy kingdom, and given us the Holy Spirit to guide us into all truth.

## Marriage

Because in the love of wife and husband, thou hast given us an image of the heavenly Jerusalem, adorned as a bride for her bridegroom, thy Son Jesus Christ our Lord; who loveth her and gave himself for her, that he might make the whole creation new.

## Commemoration of the Dead

Through Jesus Christ our Lord; who rose victorious from the dead, and doth comfort us with the blessed hope of everlasting life; for to thy faithful people, O Lord, life is changed, not ended; and when our mortal body doth lie in death, there is prepared for us a dwelling place eternal in the heavens.

**The Decalogue: Contemporary**

Hear the commandments of God to his people:
I am the Lord your God who brought you out of bondage.
You shall have no other gods but me.
*Amen. Lord have mercy.*

You shall not make for yourself any idol.
*Amen. Lord have mercy.*

You shall not invoke with malice the Name of the Lord your G
*Amen. Lord have mercy.*

Remember the Sabbath day and keep it holy.
*Amen. Lord have mercy.*

Honor your father and your mother.
*Amen. Lord have mercy.*

You shall not commit murder.
*Amen. Lord have mercy.*

You shall not commit adultery.
*Amen. Lord have mercy.*

You shall not steal.
*Amen. Lord have mercy.*

You shall not be a false witness.
*Amen. Lord have mercy.*

You shall not covet anything that belongs to your neighbor.
*Amen. Lord have mercy.*

# A Penitential Order: Rite Two

*For use at the beginning of the Liturgy, or as a separate service.*

*A hymn, psalm, or anthem may be sung.*

*The people standing, the Celebrant says*

Blessed be God: Father, Son, and Holy Spirit.
People    And blessed be his kingdom, now and for ever.
Amen.

*In place of the above, from Easter Day through the Day of Pentecost*

Celebrant    Alleluia. Christ is risen.
People    The Lord is risen indeed. Alleluia.

*In Lent and on other penitential occasions*

Celebrant    Bless the Lord who forgives all our sins.
People    His mercy endures for ever.

*When used as a separate service, the Exhortation, page 316, may be read, or a homily preached.*

*The Decalogue may be said, the people kneeling.*

*The Celebrant may read one of the following sentences*

Jesus said,"The first commandment is this: Hear, O Israel:
The Lord our God is the only Lord. Love the Lord your
God with all your heart, with all your soul, with all your
mind, and with all your strength. The second is this: Love
your neighbor as yourself. There is no other commandment
greater than these."    *Mark 12:29-31*

If we say that we have no sin, we deceive ourselves, and the truth is not in us. But if we confess our sins, God, who is faithful and just, will forgive our sins and cleanse us from all unrighteousness.     *1 John 1:8,9*

Since we have a great high priest who has passed through the heavens, Jesus, the Son of God, let us with confidence draw near to the throne of grace, that we may receive mercy and find grace to help in time of need.     *Hebrews 4:14,16*

*The Deacon or Celebrant then says*

Let us confess our sins against God and our neighbor.

*Silence may be kept.*

*Minister and People*

Most merciful God,
we confess that we have sinned against you
in thought, word, and deed,
by what we have done,
and by what we have left undone.
We have not loved you with our whole heart;
we have not loved our neighbors as ourselves.
We are truly sorry and we humbly repent.
For the sake of your Son Jesus Christ,
have mercy on us and forgive us;
that we may delight in your will,
and walk in your ways,
to the glory of your Name. Amen.

*The Bishop when present, or the Priest, stands and says*

Almighty God have mercy on you, forgive you all your sins
through our Lord Jesus Christ, strengthen you in all
goodness, and by the power of the Holy Spirit keep you
in eternal life. *Amen.*

*A deacon or lay person using the preceding form substitutes "us" for
"you" and "our" for "your."*

*When this Order is used at the beginning of the Liturgy, the service
continues with the Gloria in excelsis, the Kyrie eleison, or the Trisagion.*

*When used separately, it concludes with suitable prayers, and the Grace
or a blessing.*

# Concerning the Celebration

It is the bishop's prerogative, when present, to be the principal celebrant at the Lord's Table, and to preach the Gospel.

At all celebrations of the Liturgy, it is fitting that the principal celebrant, whether bishop or priest, be assisted by other priests, and by deacons and lay persons.

It is appropriate that the other priests present stand with the celebrant at the Altar, and join in the consecration of the gifts, in breaking the Bread, and in distributing Communion.

A deacon should read the Gospel and may lead the Prayers of the People. Deacons should also serve at the Lord's Table, preparing and placing on it the offerings of bread and wine, and assisting in the ministration of the Sacrament to the people. In the absence of a deacon, these duties may be performed by an assisting priest.

Lay persons appointed by the celebrant should normally be assigned the reading of the Lessons which precede the Gospel, and may lead the Prayers of the People.

Morning or Evening Prayer may be used in place of all that precedes the Peace and the Offertory, provided that a lesson from the Gospel is always included, and that the intercessions conform to the directions given for the Prayers of the People.

Additional Directions are on page 406.

# The Holy Eucharist: Rite Two

## The Word of God

*A hymn, psalm, or anthem may be sung.*

*The people standing, the Celebrant says*

> Blessed be God: Father, Son, and Holy Spirit.

*People*      And blessed be his kingdom, now and for ever.
Amen.

*In place of the above, from Easter Day through the Day of Pentecost*

*Celebrant*    Alleluia. Christ is risen.
*People*        The Lord is risen indeed. Alleluia.

*In Lent and on other penitential occasions*

*Celebrant*    Bless the Lord who forgives all our sins.
*People*        His mercy endures for ever.

*The Celebrant may say*

Almighty God, to you all hearts are open, all desires known,
and from you no secrets are hid: Cleanse the thoughts of our
hearts by the inspiration of your Holy Spirit, that we may
perfectly love you, and worthily magnify your holy Name;
through Christ our Lord. *Amen.*

*When appointed, the following hymn or some other song of praise is sung or said, all standing*

Glory to God in the highest,
and peace to his people on earth.

Lord God, heavenly King,
almighty God and Father,
we worship you, we give you thanks,
we praise you for your glory.

Lord Jesus Christ, only Son of the Father,
Lord God, Lamb of God,
you take away the sin of the world:
have mercy on us;
you are seated at the right hand of the Father:
receive our prayer.

For you alone are the Holy One,
you alone are the Lord,
you alone are the Most High,
Jesus Christ,
with the Holy Spirit,
in the glory of God the Father. Amen.

*On other occasions the following is used*

| | | |
|---|---|---|
| Lord, have mercy. | | Kyrie eleison. |
| *Christ, have mercy.* | *or* | *Christe eleison.* |
| Lord, have mercy. | | Kyrie eleison. |

*or this*

Holy God,
Holy and Mighty,
Holy Immortal One,
*Have mercy upon us.*

## The Collect of the Day

*The Celebrant says to the people*

        The Lord be with you.
People     And also with you.
Celebrant Let us pray.

*The Celebrant says the Collect.*

People     Amen.

## The Lessons

*The people sit. One or two Lessons, as appointed, are read,
the Reader first saying*

A Reading (Lesson) from _____.

*A citation giving chapter and verse may be added.*

*After each Reading, the Reader may say*

        The Word of the Lord.
People     Thanks be to God.

*or the Reader may say*   Here ends the Reading (Epistle).

*Silence may follow.*

*A Psalm, hymn, or anthem may follow each Reading.*

*Then, all standing, the Deacon or a Priest reads the Gospel, first saying*

        The Holy Gospel of our Lord Jesus Christ
        according to _____.
People     Glory to you, Lord Christ.

*After the Gospel, the Reader says*

The Gospel of the Lord.

*People*     Praise to you, Lord Christ.

## The Sermon

*On Sundays and other Major Feasts there follows, all standing*

## The Nicene Creed

We believe in one God,
  the Father, the Almighty,
  maker of heaven and earth,
  of all that is, seen and unseen.

We believe in one Lord, Jesus Christ,
  the only Son of God,
  eternally begotten of the Father,
  God from God, Light from Light,
  true God from true God,
  begotten, not made,
  of one Being with the Father.
  Through him all things were made.
  For us and for our salvation
    he came down from heaven:
  by the power of the Holy Spirit
    he became incarnate from the Virgin Mary,
    and was made man.
  For our sake he was crucified under Pontius Pilate;
    he suffered death and was buried.
    On the third day he rose again
      in accordance with the Scriptures;
    he ascended into heaven
      and is seated at the right hand of the Father.

He will come again in glory to judge the living and the dead,
     and his kingdom will have no end.

We believe in the Holy Spirit, the Lord, the giver of life,
     who proceeds from the Father and the Son.
     With the Father and the Son he is worshiped and glorified.
     He has spoken through the Prophets.
     We believe in one holy catholic and apostolic Church.
     We acknowledge one baptism for the forgiveness of sins.
     We look for the resurrection of the dead,
          and the life of the world to come. Amen.

## The Prayers of the People

*Prayer is offered with intercession for*

*The Universal Church, its members, and its mission*
*The Nation and all in authority*
*The welfare of the world*
*The concerns of the local community*
*Those who suffer and those in any trouble*
*The departed (with commemoration of a saint when appropriate)*

*See the forms beginning on page 383.*

*If there is no celebration of the Communion, or if a priest is not available,
the service is concluded as directed on page 406.*

## Confession of Sin

*A Confession of Sin is said here if it has not been said earlier. On
occasion, the Confession may be omitted.*

*One of the sentences from the Penitential Order on page 351 may be said.*

*The Deacon or Celebrant says*

Let us confess our sins against God and our neighbor.

*Silence may be kept.*

*Minister and People*

Most merciful God,
we confess that we have sinned against you
in thought, word, and deed,
by what we have done,
and by what we have left undone.
We have not loved you with our whole heart;
we have not loved our neighbors as ourselves.
We are truly sorry and we humbly repent.
For the sake of your Son Jesus Christ,
have mercy on us and forgive us;
that we may delight in your will,
and walk in your ways,
to the glory of your Name. Amen.

*The Bishop when present, or the Priest, stands and says*

Almighty God have mercy on you, forgive you all your sins
through our Lord Jesus Christ, strengthen you in all
goodness, and by the power of the Holy Spirit keep you in
eternal life. *Amen.*

## The Peace

*All stand. The Celebrant says to the people*

The peace of the Lord be always with you.
People    And also with you.

*Then the Ministers and People may greet one another in the
name of the Lord.*

# The Holy Communion

*The Celebrant may begin the Offertory with one of the sentences on page 376, or with some other sentence of Scripture.*

*During the Offertory, a hymn, psalm, or anthem may be sung.*

*Representatives of the congregation bring the people's offerings of bread and wine, and money or other gifts, to the deacon or celebrant. The people stand while the offerings are presented and placed on the Altar.*

## The Great Thanksgiving

*Alternative forms will be found on page 367 and following.*

### Eucharistic Prayer A

*The people remain standing. The Celebrant, whether bishop or priest, faces them and sings or says*

> The Lord be with you.
*People*    And also with you.
*Celebrant* Lift up your hearts.
*People*    We lift them to the Lord.
*Celebrant* Let us give thanks to the Lord our God.
*People*    It is right to give him thanks and praise.

*Then, facing the Holy Table, the Celebrant proceeds*

It is right, and a good and joyful thing, always and everywhere to give thanks to you, Father Almighty, Creator of heaven and earth.

*Here a Proper Preface is sung or said on all Sundays, and on other occasions as appointed.*

*Holy Eucharist II*    361

Therefore we praise you, joining our voices with Angels and Archangels and with all the company of heaven, who for ever sing this hymn to proclaim the glory of your Name:

*Celebrant and People*

Holy, holy, holy Lord, God of power and might,
heaven and earth are full of your glory.
Hosanna in the highest.
Blessed is he who comes in the name of the Lord.
Hosanna in the highest.

*The people stand or kneel.*

*Then the Celebrant continues*

Holy and gracious Father: In your infinite love you made us for yourself; and, when we had fallen into sin and become subject to evil and death, you, in your mercy, sent Jesus Christ, your only and eternal Son, to share our human nature, to live and die as one of us, to reconcile us to you, the God and Father of all.

He stretched out his arms upon the cross, and offered himself, in obedience to your will, a perfect sacrifice for the whole world.

*At the following words concerning the bread, the Celebrant is to hold it, or lay a hand upon it; and at the words concerning the cup, to hold or place a hand upon the cup and any other vessel containing wine to be consecrated.*

On the night he was handed over to suffering and death, our Lord Jesus Christ took bread; and when he had given thanks to you, he broke it, and gave it to his disciples, and said,"Take eat: This is my Body, which is given for you. Do this for the remembrance of me."

After supper he took the cup of wine; and when he had given thanks, he gave it to them, and said, "Drink this, all of you: This is my Blood of the new Covenant, which is shed for you and for many for the forgiveness of sins. Whenever you drink it, do this for the remembrance of me."

Therefore we proclaim the mystery of faith:

*Celebrant and People*

Christ has died.
Christ is risen.
Christ will come again.

*The Celebrant continues*

We celebrate the memorial of our redemption, O Father, in this sacrifice of praise and thanksgiving. Recalling his death, resurrection, and ascension, we offer you these gifts.

Sanctify them by your Holy Spirit to be for your people the Body and Blood of your Son, the holy food and drink of new and unending life in him. Sanctify us also that we may faithfully receive this holy Sacrament, and serve you in unity, constancy, and peace; and at the last day bring us with all your saints into the joy of your eternal kingdom.

All this we ask through your Son Jesus Christ. By him, and with him, and in him, in the unity of the Holy Spirit all honor and glory is yours, Almighty Father, now and for ever. *AMEN.*

| | |
|---|---|
| And now, as our Savior Christ has taught us, we are bold to say, | As our Savior Christ has taught us, we now pray, |

Our Father, who art in heaven,
   hallowed be thy Name,
   thy kingdom come,
   thy will be done,
     on earth as it is in heaven.
Give us this day our daily bread.
And forgive us our trespasses,
   as we forgive those
     who trespass against us.
And lead us not into temptation,
   but deliver us from evil.
For thine is the kingdom,
   and the power, and the glory,
   for ever and ever. Amen.

Our Father in heaven,
   hallowed be your Name,
   your kingdom come,
   your will be done,
     on earth as in heaven.
Give us today our daily bread.
Forgive us our sins
   as we forgive those
     who sin against us.
Save us from the time of trial,
   and deliver us from evil.
For the kingdom, the power,
   and the glory are yours,
   now and for ever. Amen.

## The Breaking of the Bread

*The Celebrant breaks the consecrated Bread.*

*A period of silence is kept.*

*Then may be sung or said*

[Alleluia.] Christ our Passover is sacrificed for us;
*Therefore let us keep the feast.* [*Alleluia.*]

*In Lent, Alleluia is omitted, and may be omitted at other times except
during Easter Season.*

*In place of, or in addition to, the preceding, some other suitable
anthem may be used.*

*Facing the people, the Celebrant says the following Invitation*

The Gifts of God for the People of God.

*and may add*  Take them in remembrance that Christ died for
you, and feed on him in your hearts by faith,
with thanksgiving.

*The ministers receive the Sacrament in both kinds, and then immediately
deliver it to the people.*

*The Bread and the Cup are given to the communicants with these words*

The Body (Blood) of our Lord Jesus Christ keep you in
everlasting life. [*Amen.*]

*or with these words*

The Body of Christ, the bread of heaven. [*Amen.*]
The Blood of Christ, the cup of salvation. [*Amen.*]

*During the ministration of Communion, hymns, psalms, or anthems may
be sung.*

*When necessary, the Celebrant consecrates additional bread and wine,
using the form on page 408.*

*After Communion, the Celebrant says*

Let us pray.

*Celebrant and People*

Eternal God, heavenly Father,
you have graciously accepted us as living members
of your Son our Savior Jesus Christ,
and you have fed us with spiritual food
in the Sacrament of his Body and Blood.
Send us now into the world in peace,
and grant us strength and courage
to love and serve you
with gladness and singleness of heart;
through Christ our Lord. Amen.

*or the following*

Almighty and everliving God,
we thank you for feeding us with the spiritual food
of the most precious Body and Blood
of your Son our Savior Jesus Christ;
and for assuring us in these holy mysteries
that we are living members of the Body of your Son,
and heirs of your eternal kingdom.
And now, Father, send us out
to do the work you have given us to do,
to love and serve you
as faithful witnesses of Christ our Lord.
To him, to you, and to the Holy Spirit,
be honor and glory, now and for ever. Amen.

*The Bishop when present, or the Priest, may bless the people.*

*The Deacon, or the Celebrant, dismisses them with these words*

|  | Let us go forth in the name of Christ. |
| *People* | Thanks be to God. |

*or this*

| *Deacon* | Go in peace to love and serve the Lord. |
| *People* | Thanks be to God. |

*or this*

| *Deacon* | Let us go forth into the world, |
|  | rejoicing in the power of the Spirit. |
| *People* | Thanks be to God. |

*or this*

| *Deacon* | Let us bless the Lord. |
| *People* | Thanks be to God. |

*From the Easter Vigil through the Day of Pentecost "Alleluia, alleluia" may be added to any of the dismissals.*

*The People respond*   Thanks be to God. Alleluia, alleluia.

# Alternative Forms
# of the Great Thanksgiving

## Eucharistic Prayer B

*The people remain standing. The Celebrant, whether bishop or priest,
faces them and sings or says*

|  |  |
|---|---|
|  | The Lord be with you. |
| *People* | And also with you. |
| *Celebrant* | Lift up your hearts. |
| *People* | We lift them to the Lord. |
| *Celebrant* | Let us give thanks to the Lord our God. |
| *People* | It is right to give him thanks and praise. |

*Then, facing the Holy Table, the Celebrant proceeds*

It is right, and a good and joyful thing, always and everywhere to give thanks to you, Father Almighty, Creator of
heaven and earth.

*Here a Proper Preface is sung or said on all Sundays, and on other
occasions as appointed.*

Therefore we praise you, joining our voices with Angels and
Archangels and with all the company of heaven, who for ever
sing this hymn to proclaim the glory of your Name:

*Celebrant and People*

Holy, holy, holy Lord, God of power and might,
heaven and earth are full of your glory.
   Hosanna in the highest.
Blessed is he who comes in the name of the Lord.
   Hosanna in the highest.

*The people stand or kneel.*

*Then the Celebrant continues*

We give thanks to you, O God, for the goodness and love
which you have made known to us in creation; in the calling
of Israel to be your people; in your Word spoken through the
prophets; and above all in the Word made flesh, Jesus, your
Son. For in these last days you sent him to be incarnate from
the Virgin Mary, to be the Savior and Redeemer of the world.
In him, you have delivered us from evil, and made us worthy
to stand before you. In him, you have brought us out of error
into truth, out of sin into righteousness, out of death into life.

*At the following words concerning the bread, the Celebrant is to hold it,
or lay a hand upon it; and at the words concerning the cup, to hold or
place a hand upon the cup and any other vessel containing wine to be
consecrated.*

On the night before he died for us, our Lord Jesus Christ took
bread; and when he had given thanks to you, he broke it, and
gave it to his disciples, and said,"Take, eat: This is my Body,
which is given for you. Do this for the remembrance of me."

After supper he took the cup of wine; and when he had given
thanks, he gave it to them, and said,"Drink this, all of you:
This is my Blood of the new Covenant, which is shed for you
and for many for the forgiveness of sins. Whenever you drink
it, do this for the remembrance of me."

Therefore, according to his command, O Father,

*Celebrant and People*

We remember his death,
We proclaim his resurrection,
We await his coming in glory;

*The Celebrant continues*

And we offer our sacrifice of praise and thanksgiving to you,
O Lord of all; presenting to you, from your creation, this
bread and this wine.

We pray you, gracious God, to send your Holy Spirit upon
these gifts that they may be the Sacrament of the Body of
Christ and his Blood of the new Covenant. Unite us to your
Son in his sacrifice, that we may be acceptable through him,
being sanctified by the Holy Spirit. In the fullness of time,
put all things in subjection under your Christ, and bring us to
that heavenly country where, with [_____ and] all your
saints, we may enter the everlasting heritage of your sons and
daughters; through Jesus Christ our Lord, the firstborn of all
creation, the head of the Church, and the author of our
salvation.

By him, and with him, and in him, in the unity of the Holy
Spirit all honor and glory is yours, Almighty Father, now and
for ever. *AMEN.*

| | |
|---|---|
| And now, as our Savior Christ has taught us, we are bold to say, | As our Savior Christ has taught us, we now pray, |

*Continue with the Lord's Prayer on page 364.*

## Eucharistic Prayer C

*In this prayer, the lines in italics are spoken by the People.*

*The Celebrant, whether bishop or priest, faces them and sings or says*

The Lord be with you.
*And also with you.*

Lift up your hearts.
*We lift them to the Lord.*

Let us give thanks to the Lord our God.
*It is right to give him thanks and praise.*

*Then, facing the Holy Table, the Celebrant proceeds*

God of all power, Ruler of the Universe, you are worthy of glory and praise.
*Glory to you for ever and ever.*

At your command all things came to be: the vast expanse of interstellar space, galaxies, suns, the planets in their courses, and this fragile earth, our island home.
*By your will they were created and have their being.*

From the primal elements you brought forth the human race, and blessed us with memory, reason, and skill. You made us the rulers of creation. But we turned against you, and betrayed your trust; and we turned against one another.
*Have mercy, Lord, for we are sinners in your sight.*

Again and again, you called us to return. Through prophets and sages you revealed your righteous Law. And in the fullness of time you sent your only Son, born of a woman, to fulfill your Law, to open for us the way of freedom and peace.
*By his blood, he reconciled us.*
*By his wounds, we are healed.*

And therefore we praise you, joining with the heavenly chorus, with prophets, apostles, and martyrs, and with all those in every generation who have looked to you in hope, to proclaim with them your glory, in their unending hymn:

*Celebrant and People*

Holy, holy, holy Lord, God of power and might,
heaven and earth are full of your glory.
    Hosanna in the highest.
Blessed is he who comes in the name of the Lord.
    Hosanna in the highest.

*The Celebrant continues*

And so, Father, we who have been redeemed by him, and
made a new people by water and the Spirit, now bring before
you these gifts. Sanctify them by your Holy Spirit to be the
Body and Blood of Jesus Christ our Lord.

*At the following words concerning the bread, the Celebrant is to hold it,
or lay a hand upon it; and at the words concerning the cup, to hold or
place a hand upon the cup and any other vessel containing wine to be
consecrated.*

On the night he was betrayed he took bread, said the
blessing, broke the bread, and gave it to his friends, and
said, "Take, eat: This is my Body, which is given for you. Do
this for the remembrance of me."

After supper, he took the cup of wine, gave thanks, and
said, "Drink this, all of you: This is my Blood of the new
Covenant, which is shed for you and for many for the
forgiveness of sins. Whenever you drink it, do this for the
remembrance of me."

Remembering now his work of redemption, and offering to
you this sacrifice of thanksgiving,
*We celebrate his death and resurrection,
as we await the day of his coming.*

Lord God of our Fathers; God of Abraham, Isaac, and
Jacob; God and Father of our Lord Jesus Christ: Open our
eyes to see your hand at work in the world about us. Deliver
us from the presumption of coming to this Table for solace
only, and not for strength; for pardon only, and not for
renewal. Let the grace of this Holy Communion make us one
body, one spirit in Christ, that we may worthily serve the
world in his name.
*Risen Lord, be known to us in the breaking of the Bread.*

Accept these prayers and praises, Father, through Jesus
Christ our great High Priest, to whom, with you and the
Holy Spirit, your Church gives honor, glory, and worship,
from generation to generation. *AMEN.*

| | |
|---|---|
| And now, as our Savior Christ has taught us, we are bold to say, | As our Savior Christ has taught us, we now pray, |

*Continue with the Lord's Prayer on page 364.*

### Eucharistic Prayer D

*The people remain standing. The Celebrant, whether bishop or priest,
faces them and sings or says*

> The Lord be with you.
*People*    And also with you.
*Celebrant* Lift up your hearts.
*People*    We lift them to the Lord.
*Celebrant* Let us give thanks to the Lord our God.
*People*    It is right to give him thanks and praise.

*Then, facing the Holy Table, the Celebrant proceeds*

It is truly right to glorify you, Father, and to give you thanks; for you alone are God, living and true, dwelling in light inaccessible from before time and for ever.

Fountain of life and source of all goodness, you made all things and fill them with your blessing; you created them to rejoice in the splendor of your radiance.

Countless throngs of angels stand before you to serve you night and day; and, beholding the glory of your presence, they offer you unceasing praise. Joining with them, and giving voice to every creature under heaven, we acclaim you, and glorify your Name, as we sing (say),

*Celebrant and People*

Holy, holy, holy Lord, God of power and might,
heaven and earth are full of your glory.
    Hosanna in the highest.
Blessed is he who comes in the name of the Lord.
    Hosanna in the highest.

*The people stand or kneel.*

*Then the Celebrant continues*

We acclaim you, holy Lord, glorious in power. Your mighty works reveal your wisdom and love. You formed us in your own image, giving the whole world into our care, so that, in obedience to you, our Creator, we might rule and serve all your creatures. When our disobedience took us far from you, you did not abandon us to the power of death. In your mercy you came to our help, so that in seeking you we might find you. Again and again you called us into covenant with you, and through the prophets you taught us to hope for salvation.

*Holy Eucharist II*   373

Father, you loved the world so much that in the fullness of time you sent your only Son to be our Savior. Incarnate by the Holy Spirit, born of the Virgin Mary, he lived as one of us, yet without sin. To the poor he proclaimed the good news of salvation; to prisoners, freedom; to the sorrowful, joy. To fulfill your purpose he gave himself up to death; and, rising from the grave, destroyed death, and made the whole creation new.

And, that we might live no longer for ourselves, but for him who died and rose for us, he sent the Holy Spirit, his own first gift for those who believe, to complete his work in the world, and to bring to fulfillment the sanctification of all.

*At the following words concerning the bread, the Celebrant is to hold it, or lay a hand upon it; and at the words concerning the cup, to hold or place a hand upon the cup and any other vessel containing wine to be consecrated.*

When the hour had come for him to be glorified by you, his heavenly Father, having loved his own who were in the world, he loved them to the end; at supper with them he took bread, and when he had given thanks to you, he broke it, and gave it to his disciples, and said, "Take, eat: This is my Body, which is given for you. Do this for the remembrance of me."

After supper he took the cup of wine; and when he had given thanks, he gave it to them, and said, "Drink this, all of you: This is my Blood of the new Covenant, which is shed for you and for many for the forgiveness of sins. Whenever you drink it, do this for the remembrance of me."

Father, we now celebrate this memorial of our redemption. Recalling Christ's death and his descent among the dead, proclaiming his resurrection and ascension to your right hand, awaiting his coming in glory; and offering to you, from the gifts you have given us, this bread and this cup, we praise you and we bless you.

*Celebrant and People*

We praise you, we bless you,
we give thanks to you,
and we pray to you, Lord our God.

*The Celebrant continues*

Lord, we pray that in your goodness and mercy your Holy
Spirit may descend upon us, and upon these gifts, sanctifying
them and showing them to be holy gifts for your holy people,
the bread of life and the cup of salvation, the Body and Blood
of your Son Jesus Christ.

Grant that all who share this bread and cup may become one
body and one spirit, a living sacrifice in Christ, to the praise
of your Name.

Remember, Lord, your one holy catholic and apostolic
Church, redeemed by the blood of your Christ. Reveal its
unity, guard its faith, and preserve it in peace.

[Remember (*NN.* and) all who minister in your Church.]
[Remember all your people, and those who seek your truth.]
[Remember _____.]
[Remember all who have died in the peace of Christ, and
those whose faith is known to you alone; bring them into
the place of eternal joy and light.]

And grant that we may find our inheritance with [the Blessed
Virgin Mary, with patriarchs, prophets, apostles, and martyrs,
(with_____) and] all the saints who have found favor
with you in ages past. We praise you in union with them
and give you glory through your Son Jesus Christ our Lord.

Through Christ, and with Christ, and in Christ, all honor and
glory are yours, Almighty God and Father, in the unity of the
Holy Spirit, for ever and ever. *AMEN.*

| And now, as our Savior Christ has taught us, we are bold to say, | As our Savior Christ has taught us, we now pray, |

*Continue with the Lord's Prayer on page 364.*

# Offertory Sentences

*One of the following, or some other appropriate sentence of Scripture, may be used*

Offer to God a sacrifice of thanksgiving, and make good your vows to the Most High.  *Psalm 50:14*

Ascribe to the Lord the honor due his Name; bring offerings and come into his courts.  *Psalm 96:8*

Walk in love, as Christ loved us and gave himself for us, an offering and sacrifice to God.  *Ephesians 5:2*

I appeal to you, brethren, by the mercies of God, to present yourselves as a living sacrifice, holy and acceptable to God, which is your spiritual worship.  *Romans 12:1*

If you are offering your gift at the altar, and there remember that your brother has something against you, leave your gift there before the altar and go; first be reconciled to your brother, and then come and offer your gift.  *Matthew 5:23, 24*

Through Christ let us continually offer to God the sacrifice of praise, that is, the fruit of lips that acknowledge his Name.

But do not neglect to do good and to share what you have,
for such sacrifices are pleasing to God.    *Hebrews 13:15,16*

O Lord our God, you are worthy to receive glory and honor
and power; because you have created all things, and by your
will they were created and have their being.    *Revelation 4:11*

Yours, O Lord, is the greatness, the power, the glory, the
victory, and the majesty. For everything in heaven and on
earth is yours. Yours, O Lord, is the kingdom, and you are
exalted as head over all.    *1 Chronicles 29:11*

*or this bidding*

Let us with gladness present the offerings and oblations of
our life and labor to the Lord.


# Proper Prefaces

## Preface of the Lord's Day

*To be used on Sundays as appointed, but not on the succeeding weekdays*

### 1. Of God the Father

For you are the source of light and life, you made us in your
image, and called us to new life in Jesus Christ our Lord.

*or this*

### 2. Of God the Son

Through Jesus Christ our Lord; who on the first day of the
week overcame death and the grave, and by his glorious
resurrection opened to us the way of everlasting life.

*or the following*

### 3. Of God the Holy Spirit

For by water and the Holy Spirit you have made us a new people in Jesus Christ our Lord, to show forth your glory in all the world.

## Prefaces for Seasons

*To be used on Sundays and weekdays alike, except as otherwise appointed for Holy Days and Various Occasions*

### Advent

Because you sent your beloved Son to redeem us from sin and death, and to make us heirs in him of everlasting life; that when he shall come again in power and great triumph to judge the world, we may without shame or fear rejoice to behold his appearing.

### Incarnation

Because you gave Jesus Christ, your only Son, to be born for us; who, by the mighty power of the Holy Spirit, was made perfect Man of the flesh of the Virgin Mary his mother; so that we might be delivered from the bondage of sin, and receive power to become your children.

### Epiphany

Because in the mystery of the Word made flesh, you have caused a new light to shine in our hearts, to give the knowledge of your glory in the face of your Son Jesus Christ our Lord.

Through Jesus Christ our Lord; who was tempted in every way as we are, yet did not sin. By his grace we are able to triumph over every evil, and to live no longer for ourselves alone, but for him who died for us and rose again.

*this*

You bid your faithful people cleanse their hearts, and prepare with joy for the Paschal feast; that, fervent in prayer and in works of mercy, and renewed by your Word and Sacraments, they may come to the fullness of grace which you have prepared for those who love you.

*Holy Week*

Through Jesus Christ our Lord. For our sins he was lifted high upon the cross, that he might draw the whole world to himself; and, by his suffering and death, he became the source of eternal salvation for all who put their trust in him.

*Easter*

But chiefly are we bound to praise you for the glorious resurrection of your Son Jesus Christ our Lord; for he is the true Paschal Lamb, who was sacrificed for us, and has taken away the sin of the world. By his death he has destroyed death, and by his rising to life again he has won for us everlasting life.

*Ascension*

Through your dearly beloved Son Jesus Christ our Lord. After his glorious resurrection he openly appeared to his disciples, and in their sight ascended into heaven, to prepare a place for us; that where he is, there we might also be, and reign with him in glory.

*Pentecost*

Through Jesus Christ our Lord. In fulfillment of his true promise, the Holy Spirit came down [on this day] from heaven, lighting upon the disciples, to teach them and to lead them into all truth; uniting peoples of many tongues in the confession of one faith, and giving to your Church the power to serve you as a royal priesthood, and to preach the Gospel to all nations.

## Prefaces for Other Occasions

*Trinity Sunday*

For with your co-eternal Son and Holy Spirit, you are one God, one Lord, in Trinity of Persons and in Unity of Being; and we celebrate the one and equal glory of you, O Father, and of the Son, and of the Holy Spirit.

*All Saints*

For in the multitude of your saints you have surrounded us with a great cloud of witnesses, that we might rejoice in their fellowship, and run with endurance the race that is set before us; and, together with them, receive the crown of glory that never fades away.

*A Saint*

For the wonderful grace and virtue declared in all your saints, who have been the chosen vessels of your grace, and the lights of the world in their generations.

*or this*

Because in the obedience of your saints you have given us an example of righteousness, and in their eternal joy a glorious pledge of the hope of our calling.

*r this*

because you are greatly glorified in the assembly of your
saints. All your creatures praise you, and your faithful
servants bless you, confessing before the rulers of this world
the great Name of your only Son.

*Apostles and Ordinations*

Through the great shepherd of your flock, Jesus Christ our
Lord; who after his resurrection sent forth his apostles to
preach the Gospel and to teach all nations; and promised to
be with them always, even to the end of the ages.

*Dedication of a Church*

Through Jesus Christ our great High Priest; in whom we are
built up as living stones of a holy temple, that we might offer
before you a sacrifice of praise and prayer which is holy and
pleasing in your sight.

*Baptism*

because in Jesus Christ our Lord you have received us as your
sons and daughters, made us citizens of your kingdom, and
given us the Holy Spirit to guide us into all truth.

*Marriage*

because in the love of wife and husband, you have given us
an image of the heavenly Jerusalem, adorned as a bride for
her bridegroom, your Son Jesus Christ our Lord; who loves
her and gave himself for her, that he might make the whole
creation new.

## Commemoration of the Dead

Through Jesus Christ our Lord; who rose victorious from the dead, and comforts us with the blessed hope of everlasting life. For to your faithful people, O Lord, life is changed, not ended; and when our mortal body lies in death, there is prepared for us a dwelling place eternal in the heavens.

# The Prayers of the People

Prayer is offered with intercession for

The Universal Church, its members, and its mission
The Nation and all in authority
The welfare of the world
The concerns of the local community
Those who suffer and those in any trouble
The departed (with commemoration of a saint when appropriate)

*Any of the forms which follow may be used.*

*Adaptations or insertions suitable to the occasion may be made.*

*Any of the forms may be conformed to the language of the Rite being used.*

*A bar in the margin indicates petitions which may be omitted.*

*The Celebrant may introduce the Prayers with a sentence of invitation related to the occasion, or the season, or the Proper of the Day.*

## Form I

*Deacon or other leader*

With all our heart and with all our mind, let us pray to the Lord, saying, "Lord, have mercy."

For the peace from above, for the loving-kindness of God, and for the salvation of our souls, let us pray to the Lord.
*Lord, have mercy.*

For the peace of the world, for the welfare of the holy Church of God, and for the unity of all peoples, let us pray to the Lord.
*Lord, have mercy.*

For our Bishop, and for all the clergy and people, let us pray to the Lord.
*Lord, have mercy.*

For our President, for the leaders of the nations, and for all in authority, let us pray to the Lord.
*Lord, have mercy.*

For this city (town, village, _____ ), for every city and community, and for those who live in them, let us pray to the Lord.
*Lord, have mercy.*

For seasonable weather, and for an abundance of the fruits of the earth, let us pray to the Lord.
*Lord, have mercy.*

For the good earth which God has given us, and for the wisdom and will to conserve it, let us pray to the Lord.
*Lord, have mercy.*

For those who travel on land, on water, or in the air [or through outer space], let us pray to the Lord.
*Lord, have mercy.*

For the aged and infirm, for the widowed and orphans, and for the sick and the suffering, let us pray to the Lord.
*Lord, have mercy.*

For _____ , let us pray to the Lord.
*Lord, have mercy.*

For the poor and the oppressed, for the unemployed and the destitute, for prisoners and captives, and for all who remember and care for them, let us pray to the Lord.
*Lord, have mercy.*

For all who have died in the hope of the resurrection, and for all the departed, let us pray to the Lord.
*Lord, have mercy.*

For deliverance from all danger, violence, oppression, and degradation, let us pray to the Lord.
*Lord, have mercy.*

For the absolution and remission of our sins and offenses, let us pray to the Lord.
*Lord, have mercy.*

That we may end our lives in faith and hope, without suffering and without reproach, let us pray to the Lord.
*Lord, have mercy.*

Defend us, deliver us, and in thy compassion protect us, O Lord, by thy grace.
*Lord, have mercy.*

In the communion of [_____ and of all the] saints, let us commend ourselves, and one another, and all our life, to Christ our God.
*To thee, O Lord our God.*

*Silence*

*The Celebrant adds a concluding Collect.*

## Form II

*In the course of the silence after each bidding, the People offer their own prayers, either silently or aloud.*

I ask your prayers for God's people throughout the world; for our Bishop(s) _____ ; for this gathering; and for all ministers and people.
Pray for the Church.

*Silence*

I ask your prayers for peace; for goodwill among nations;
and for the well-being of all people.
Pray for justice and peace.

*Silence*

I ask your prayers for the poor, the sick, the hungry, the
oppressed, and those in prison.
Pray for those in any need or trouble.

*Silence*

I ask your prayers for all who seek God, or a deeper
knowledge of him.
Pray that they may find and be found by him.

*Silence*

I ask your prayers for the departed [especially _____ ].
Pray for those who have died.

*Silence*

*Members of the congregation may ask the prayers or the thanksgivings of
those present*

I ask your prayers for _____ .

I ask your thanksgiving for _____ .

*Silence*

Praise God for those in every generation in whom Christ has
been honored [especially _____ whom we remember
today].
Pray that we may have grace to glorify Christ in our own day

*Silence*

*The Celebrant adds a concluding Collect.*

## Form III

*The Leader and People pray responsively*

Father, we pray for your holy Catholic Church;
*That we all may be one.*

Grant that every member of the Church may truly and
humbly serve you;
*That your Name may be glorified by all people.*

We pray for all bishops, priests, and deacons;
*That they may be faithful ministers of your Word and
Sacraments.*

We pray for all who govern and hold authority in the nations
of the world;
*That there may be justice and peace on the earth.*

Give us grace to do your will in all that we undertake;
*That our works may find favor in your sight.*

Have compassion on those who suffer from any grief or
trouble;
*That they may be delivered from their distress.*

Give to the departed eternal rest;
*Let light perpetual shine upon them.*

We praise you for your saints who have entered into joy;
*May we also come to share in your heavenly kingdom.*

Let us pray for our own needs and those of others.

*Silence*

*The People may add their own petitions.*

*The Celebrant adds a concluding Collect.*

**Form IV**

*Deacon or other leader*

Let us pray for the Church and for the world.

Grant, Almighty God, that all who confess your Name may
be united in your truth, live together in your love, and reveal
your glory in the world.

*Silence*

Lord, in your mercy
*Hear our prayer.*

Guide the people of this land, and of all the nations, in the
ways of justice and peace; that we may honor one another
and serve the common good.

*Silence*

Lord, in your mercy
*Hear our prayer.*

Give us all a reverence for the earth as your own creation,
that we may use its resources rightly in the service of others
and to your honor and glory.

*Silence*

Lord, in your mercy
*Hear our prayer.*

Bless all whose lives are closely linked with ours, and grant
that we may serve Christ in them, and love one another as he
loves us.

*Silence*

Lord, in your mercy
*Hear our prayer.*

Comfort and heal all those who suffer in body, mind, or
spirit; give them courage and hope in their troubles, and
bring them the joy of your salvation.

*Silence*

Lord, in your mercy
*Hear our prayer.*

We commend to your mercy all who have died, that your will
for them may be fulfilled; and we pray that we may share
with all your saints in your eternal kingdom.

*Silence*

Lord, in your mercy
*Hear our prayer.*

*The Celebrant adds a concluding Collect.*

# Form V

*Deacon or other leader*

In peace, let us pray to the Lord, saying,"Lord, have mercy"
(*or* "Kyrie eleison").

For the holy Church of God, that it may be filled with truth
and love, and be found without fault at the day of your
coming, we pray to you, O Lord.

*Here and after every petition the People respond*

Kyrie eleison.      *or*      Lord, have mercy.

For N. our Presiding Bishop, for N. (N.) our own Bishop(s), for all bishops and other ministers, and for all the holy people of God, we pray to you, O Lord.

For all who fear God and believe in you, Lord Christ, that our divisions may cease, and that all may be one as you and the Father are one, we pray to you, O Lord.

For the mission of the Church, that in faithful witness it may preach the Gospel to the ends of the earth, we pray to you, O Lord.

For those who do not yet believe, and for those who have lost their faith, that they may receive the light of the Gospel, we pray to you, O Lord.

For the peace of the world, that a spirit of respect and forbearance may grow among nations and peoples, we pray to you, O Lord.

For those in positions of public trust [especially _____ ], that they may serve justice, and promote the dignity and freedom of every person, we pray to you, O Lord.

For all who live and work in this community [especially _____ ], we pray to you, O Lord.

For a blessing upon all human labor, and for the right use of the riches of creation, that the world may be freed from poverty, famine, and disaster, we pray to you, O Lord.

For the poor, the persecuted, the sick, and all who suffer; for refugees, prisoners, and all who are in danger; that they may be relieved and protected, we pray to you, O Lord.

For this *congregation* [for those who are present, and for those who are absent], that we may be delivered from hardness of heart, and show forth your glory in all that we do, we pray to you, O Lord.

For our enemies and those who wish us harm; and for all whom we have injured or offended, we pray to you, O Lord.

For ourselves; for the forgiveness of our sins, and for the grace of the Holy Spirit to amend our lives, we pray to you, O Lord.

For all who have commended themselves to our prayers; for our families, friends, and neighbors; that being freed from anxiety, they may live in joy, peace, and health, we pray to you, O Lord.

For _____ , we pray to you, O Lord.

For all who have died in the communion of your Church, and those whose faith is known to you alone, that, with all the saints, they may have rest in that place where there is no pain or grief, but life eternal, we pray to you, O Lord.

Rejoicing in the fellowship of [the ever-blessed Virgin Mary, *blessed N.*) and] all the saints, let us commend ourselves, and one another, and all our life to Christ our God.
*To you, O Lord our God.*

*Silence*

*The Celebrant adds a concluding Collect, or the following Doxology*

For yours is the majesty, O Father, Son, and Holy Spirit; yours is the kingdom and the power and the glory, now and for ever. *Amen.*

## Form VI

*The Leader and People pray responsively*

In peace, we pray to you, Lord God.

*Silence*

For all people in their daily life and work;
*For our families, friends, and neighbors, and for those who are alone.*

For this community, the nation, and the world;
*For all who work for justice, freedom, and peace.*

For the just and proper use of your creation;
*For the victims of hunger, fear, injustice, and oppression.*

For all who are in danger, sorrow, or any kind of trouble;
*For those who minister to the sick, the friendless, and the needy.*

For the peace and unity of the Church of God;
*For all who proclaim the Gospel, and all who seek the Truth.*

For [N. our Presiding Bishop, and N. (N.) our Bishop(s); and for] all bishops and other ministers;
*For all who serve God in his Church.*

For the special needs and concerns of this congregation.

*Silence*

*The People may add their own petitions*

Hear us, Lord;
*For your mercy is great.*

We thank you, Lord, for all the blessings of this life.

*Silence*

*The People may add their own thanksgivings*

We will exalt you, O God our King;
*And praise your Name for ever and ever.*

We pray for all who have died, that they may have a place in
your eternal kingdom.

*Silence*

*The People may add their own petitions*

Lord, let your loving-kindness be upon them;
*Who put their trust in you.*

We pray to you also for the forgiveness of our sins.

*Silence may be kept.*

*Leader and People*

Have mercy upon us, most merciful Father;
in your compassion forgive us our sins,
known and unknown,
things done and left undone;
and so uphold us by your Spirit
that we may live and serve you in newness of life,
to the honor and glory of your Name;
through Jesus Christ our Lord. Amen.

*The Celebrant concludes with an absolution or a suitable Collect.*

# The Collect at the Prayers

For the concluding Collect, the Celebrant selects

(a)  a Collect appropriate to the season or occasion being celebrated;

(b)  a Collect expressive of some special need in the life of the local congregation;

(c)  a Collect for the mission of the Church;

(d)  a general Collect such as the following:

## 1

Lord, hear the prayers of *thy* people; and what we have asked faithfully, grant that we may obtain effectually, to the glory of *thy* Name; through Jesus Christ our Lord. *Amen.*

## 2

Heavenly Father, you have promised to hear what we ask in the Name of your Son: Accept and fulfill our petitions, we pray, not as we ask in our ignorance, nor as we deserve in our sinfulness, but as you know and love us in your Son Jesus Christ our Lord. *Amen.*

## 3

Almighty and eternal God, ruler of all things in heaven and earth: Mercifully accept the prayers of your people, and strengthen us to do your will; through Jesus Christ our Lord. *Amen.*

## 4

Almighty God, to whom our needs are known before we ask Help us to ask only what accords with your will; and those good things which we dare not, or in our blindness cannot ask, grant us for the sake of your Son Jesus Christ our Lord. *Amen.*

5

O Lord our God, accept the fervent prayers of your people; in the multitude of your mercies, look with compassion upon us and all who turn to you for help; for you are gracious, O lover of souls, and to you we give glory, Father, Son, and Holy Spirit, now and for ever. *Amen.*

6

Lord Jesus Christ, you said to your apostles, "Peace I give to you; my own peace I leave with you:" Regard not our sins, but the faith of your Church, and give to us the peace and unity of that heavenly City, where with the Father and the Holy Spirit you live and reign, now and for ever. *Amen.*

7

Hasten, O Father, the coming of *thy* kingdom; and grant that we *thy* servants, who now live by faith, may with joy behold *thy* Son at his coming in glorious majesty; even Jesus Christ, our only Mediator and Advocate. *Amen.*

8

Almighty God, by your Holy Spirit you have made us one with your saints in heaven and on earth: Grant that in our earthly pilgrimage we may always be supported by this fellowship of love and prayer, and know ourselves to be surrounded by their witness to your power and mercy. We ask this for the sake of Jesus Christ, in whom all our intercessions are acceptable through the Spirit, and who lives and reigns for ever and ever. *Amen.*

# Communion under Special Circumstances

*This form is intended for use with those who for reasonable cause cannot be present at a public celebration of the Eucharist.*

*When persons are unable to be present for extended periods, it is desirable that the priest arrange to celebrate the Eucharist with them from time to time on a regular basis, using either the Proper of the Day or one of those appointed for Various Occasions. If it is necessary to shorten the service, the priest may begin the celebration at the Offertory, but it is desirable that a passage from the Gospel first be read.*

*At other times, or when desired, such persons may be communicated from the reserved Sacrament, using the following form.*

*It is desirable that fellow parishioners, relatives, and friends be present, when possible, to communicate with them.*

*The Celebrant, whether priest or deacon, reads a passage of Scripture appropriate to the day or occasion, or else one of the following*

God so loved the world that he gave his only Son, that whoever believes in him should not perish, but have eternal life. *John 3:16*

Jesus said, "I am the bread of life; whoever comes to me shall not hunger, and whoever believes in me shall never thirst." *John 6:35*

Jesus said, "I am the living bread which came down from heaven; if anyone eats of this bread, he will live for ever; and the bread which I shall give for the life of the world is my flesh. For my flesh is food indeed, and my blood is drink indeed. Whoever eats my flesh and drinks my blood abides in me, and I in him." *John 6:51,55-56*

Jesus said, "Abide in me, as I in you. As the branch cannot bear fruit by itself, unless it abides in the vine, neither can you, unless you abide in me. I am the vine, you are the branches. By this my Father is glorified, that you bear much fruit, and so prove to be my disciples. As the Father has loved me, so have I loved you; abide in my love." *John 15:4-5a,8-9*

*After the Reading, the Celebrant may comment on it briefly.*

*Suitable prayers may be offered, concluding with the following or some other Collect*

Almighty Father, whose dear Son, on the night before he suffered, instituted the Sacrament of his Body and Blood: Mercifully grant that we may receive it thankfully in remembrance of Jesus Christ our Lord, who in these holy mysteries gives us a pledge of eternal life; and who lives and reigns for ever and ever. *Amen.*

*A Confession of Sin may follow. The following or some other form is used*

Most merciful God,
we confess that we have sinned against you
in thought, word, and deed,
by what we have done,
and by what we have left undone.
We have not loved you with our whole heart;
we have not loved our neighbors as ourselves.

We are truly sorry and we humbly repent.
For the sake of your Son Jesus Christ,
have mercy on us and forgive us;
that we may delight in your will,
and walk in your ways,
to the glory of your Name. Amen.

*The Priest alone says*

Almighty God have mercy on you, forgive you all your sins
through our Lord Jesus Christ, strengthen you in all
goodness, and by the power of the Holy Spirit keep you in
eternal life. *Amen.*

*A deacon using the preceding form substitutes "us" for "you" and "our"
for "your."*

*The Peace may then be exchanged.*

*The Lord's Prayer is said, the Celebrant first saying*

Let us pray in the words our Savior Christ has taught us.

| | |
|---|---|
| Our Father, who art in heaven,<br>   hallowed be thy Name,<br>   thy kingdom come,<br>   thy will be done,<br>     on earth as it is in heaven.<br>Give us this day our daily bread.<br>And forgive us our trespasses,<br>   as we forgive those<br>     who trespass against us.<br>And lead us not into temptation,<br>   but deliver us from evil.<br>For thine is the kingdom,<br>   and the power, and the glory,<br>   for ever and ever. Amen. | Our Father in heaven,<br>   hallowed be your Name,<br>   your kingdom come,<br>   your will be done,<br>     on earth as in heaven.<br>Give us today our daily bread.<br>Forgive us our sins<br>   as we forgive those<br>     who sin against us.<br>Save us from the time of trial,<br>   and deliver us from evil.<br>For the kingdom, the power,<br>   and the glory are yours,<br>   now and for ever. Amen. |

*The Celebrant may say the following Invitation*

The Gifts of God for the People of God.

*and may add*    Take them in remembrance that Christ died for
you, and feed on him in your hearts by faith,
with thanksgiving.

*The Sacrament is administered with the following or other words*

The Body (Blood) of our Lord Jesus Christ keep you in
everlasting life. [*Amen.*]

*One of the usual postcommunion prayers is then said, or the following*

Gracious Father, we give you praise and thanks for this Holy
Communion of the Body and Blood of your beloved Son
Jesus Christ, the pledge of our redemption; and we pray that
it may bring us forgiveness of our sins, strength in our
weakness, and everlasting salvation; through Jesus Christ
our Lord. *Amen.*

*The service concludes with a blessing or with a dismissal*

Let us bless the Lord.
*Thanks be to God.*

# An Order for Celebrating the Holy Eucharist

*This rite requires careful preparation by the Priest and other participants.*

*It is not intended for use at the principal Sunday or weekly celebration of the Holy Eucharist.*

## The People and Priest

### Gather in the Lord's Name

### Proclaim and Respond to the Word of God

The proclamation and response may include readings, song, talk, dance, instrumental music, other art forms, silence. A reading from the Gospel is always included.

### Pray for the World and the Church

## Exchange the Peace

Either here or elsewhere in the service, all greet one another in the name of the Lord.

## Prepare the Table

Some of those present prepare the table; the bread, the cup of wine, and other offerings, are placed upon it.

## Make Eucharist

The Great Thanksgiving is said by the Priest in the name of the gathering, using one of the eucharistic prayers provided.

The people respond—Amen!

## Break the Bread

## Share the Gifts of God

The Body and Blood of the Lord are shared in a reverent manner; after all have received, any of the Sacrament that remains is then consumed.

*When a common meal or Agapé is a part of the celebration, it follows here.*

# At the Great Thanksgiving

*In making Eucharist, the Celebrant uses one of the Eucharistic Prayers from Rite One or Rite Two, or one of the following forms*

## Form 1

| | |
|---|---|
| *Celebrant* | The Lord be with you. |
| *People* | And also with you. |
| *Celebrant* | Lift up your hearts. |
| *People* | We lift them to the Lord. |
| *Celebrant* | Let us give thanks to the Lord our God. |
| *People* | It is right to give him thanks and praise. |

*The Celebrant gives thanks to God the Father for his work in creation and his revelation of himself to his people;*

*Recalls before God, when appropriate, the particular occasion being celebrated;*

*Incorporates or adapts the Proper Preface of the Day, if desired.*

*If the Sanctus is to be included, it is introduced with these or similar words*

And so we join the saints and angels in proclaiming your glory, as we sing (say),

*Celebrant and People*

Holy, holy, holy Lord, God of power and might,
heaven and earth are full of your glory.
  Hosanna in the highest.
Blessed is he who comes in the name of the Lord.
  Hosanna in the highest.

*he Celebrant now praises God for the salvation of the world through
esus Christ our Lord.*

*he Prayer continues with these words*

And so, Father, we bring you these gifts. Sanctify them by
our Holy Spirit to be for your people the Body and Blood
f Jesus Christ our Lord.

*t the following words concerning the bread, the Celebrant is to hold it,
* lay a hand upon it; and at the words concerning the cup, to hold or
lace a hand upon the cup and any other vessel containing wine to be
onsecrated.*

On the night he was betrayed he took bread, said the
lessing, broke the bread, and gave it to his friends, and
aid, "Take, eat: This is my Body, which is given for you.
Do this for the remembrance of me."

After supper, he took the cup of wine, gave thanks, and
aid, "Drink this, all of you: This is my Blood of the new
Covenant, which is shed for you and for many for the
orgiveness of sins. Whenever you drink it, do this for the
emembrance of me."

Father, we now celebrate the memorial of your Son. By
means of this holy bread and cup, we show forth the sacrifice
f his death, and proclaim his resurrection, until he comes
gain.

Gather us by this Holy Communion into one body in your
on Jesus Christ. Make us a living sacrifice of praise.

By him, and with him, and in him, in the unity of the Holy
pirit all honor and glory is yours, Almighty Father, now and
or ever. *AMEN.*

## Form 2

| | |
|---|---|
| *Celebrant* | The grace of our Lord Jesus Christ and the love of God and the fellowship of the Holy Spirit be with you all. |
| *People* | And also with you. |
| *Celebrant* | Lift up your hearts. |
| *People* | We lift them to the Lord. |
| *Celebrant* | Let us give thanks to the Lord our God. |
| *People* | It is right to give him thanks and praise. |

*The Celebrant gives thanks to God the Father for his work in creation and his revelation of himself to his people;*

*Recalls before God, when appropriate, the particular occasion being celebrated;*

*Incorporates or adapts the Proper Preface of the Day, if desired.*

*If the Sanctus is to be included, it is introduced with these or similar words*

And so we join the saints and angels in proclaiming your glory, as we sing (say),

*Celebrant and People*

Holy, holy, holy Lord, God of power and might,
heaven and earth are full of your glory.
    Hosanna in the highest.
Blessed is he who comes in the name of the Lord.
    Hosanna in the highest.

*The Celebrant now praises God for the salvation of the world through Jesus Christ our Lord.*

*At the following words concerning the bread, the Celebrant is to hold it, or lay a hand upon it; and at the words concerning the cup, to hold or place a hand upon the cup and any other vessel containing wine to be consecrated.*

On the night he was handed over to suffering and death, our Lord Jesus Christ took bread; and when he had given thanks to you, he broke it, and gave it to his disciples, and said, "Take, eat: This is my Body, which is given for you. Do this for the remembrance of me."

After supper he took the cup of wine; and when he had given thanks, he gave it to them, and said, "Drink this, all of you: This is my Blood of the new Covenant, which is shed for you and for many for the forgiveness of sins. Whenever you drink it, do this for the remembrance of me."

Recalling now his suffering and death, and celebrating his resurrection and ascension, we await his coming in glory.

Accept, O Lord, our sacrifice of praise, this memorial of our redemption.

Send your Holy Spirit upon these gifts. Let them be for us the Body and Blood of your Son. And grant that we who eat this bread and drink this cup may be filled with your life and goodness.

*The Celebrant then prays that all may receive the benefits of Christ's work, and the renewal of the Holy Spirit.*

*The Prayer concludes with these or similar words*

All this we ask through your Son Jesus Christ. By him, and with him, and in him, in the unity of the Holy Spirit all honor and glory is yours, Almighty Father, now and for ever. *AMEN.*

# Additional Directions

The Holy Table is spread with a clean white cloth during the celebration.

When the Great Litany is sung or said immediately before the Eucharist, the Litany concludes with the Kyries, and the Eucharist begins with the Salutation and the Collect of the Day. The Prayers of the People following the Creed may be omitted.

When a psalm is used, it may be concluded with Gloria Patri. In Rite One services, the following form of the Gloria may be used:

Glory be to the Father, and to the Son, *
 and to the Holy Ghost:

As it was in the beginning, is now, and ever shall be, *
 world without end. Amen.

The Kyrie eleison (or "Lord, have mercy") may be sung or said in threefold, sixfold, or ninefold form. The Trisagion, "Holy God," may be sung or said three times, or antiphonally.

Gloria in excelsis, or the hymn used in place of it, is sung or said from Christmas Day through the Feast of the Epiphany; on Sundays from Easter Day through the Day of Pentecost, on all the days of Easter Week, and on Ascension Day; and at other times as desired; but it is not used on the Sundays or ordinary weekdays of Advent or Lent.

It is desirable that the Lessons be read from a lectern or pulpit, and that the Gospel be read from the same lectern, or from the pulpit, or from the midst of the congregation. It is desirable that the Lessons and Gospel be read from a book or books of appropriate size and dignity.

When a portion of the congregation is composed of persons whose native tongue is other than English, a reader appointed by the celebrant may read the Gospel in the language of the people, either in place of, or in addition to, the Gospel in English.

If there is no Communion, all that is appointed through the Prayers of the People may be said. (If it is desired to include a Confession of Sin, the ervice begins with the Penitential Order.) A hymn or anthem may then be sung, and the offerings of the people received. The service may then conclude with the Lord's Prayer; and with either the Grace or a blessing, or with the exchange of the Peace.

In the absence of a priest, all that is described above, except for the blessing, may be said by a deacon, or, if there is no deacon, by a lay reader.

The greeting, "The peace of the Lord be always with you," is addressed to the entire assembly. In the exchange between individuals which may follow, any appropriate words of greeting may be used. If preferred, the exchange of the Peace may take place at the time of the administration of the Sacrament (before or after the sentence of Invitation).

Necessary announcements may be made before the service, after the Creed, before the Offertory, or at the end of the service, as convenient.

It is the function of a deacon to make ready the Table for the celebration, preparing and placing upon it the bread and cup of wine. It is customary to add a little water to the wine. The deacon may be assisted by other ministers.

During the Great Thanksgiving, it is appropriate that there be only one chalice on the Altar, and, if need be, a flagon of wine from which additional chalices may be filled after the Breaking of the Bread.

The following anthem may be used at the Breaking of the Bread:

Lamb of God, you take away the sins of the world:
  have mercy on us.
Lamb of God, you take away the sins of the world:
  have mercy on us.
Lamb of God, you take away the sins of the world:
  grant us peace.

While the people are coming forward to receive Communion, the celebrant receives the Sacrament in both kinds. The bishops, priests, and deacons at the Holy Table then communicate, and after them the people.

Opportunity is always to be given to every communicant to receive the consecrated Bread and Wine separately. But the Sacrament may be received in both kinds simultaneously, in a manner approved by the bishop.

When the celebrant is assisted by a deacon or another priest, it is customary for the celebrant to administer the consecrated Bread and the assistant the Chalice. When several deacons or priests are present, some may administer the Bread and others the Wine. In the absence of sufficient deacons and priests, lay persons licensed by the bishop according to the canon may administer the Chalice.

If the consecrated Bread or Wine does not suffice for the number of communicants, the celebrant is to return to the Holy Table, and consecrate more of either or both, by saying

Hear us, O heavenly Father, and with thy (your) Word and Holy Spirit bless and sanctify this bread (wine) that it, also, may be the Sacrament of the precious Body (Blood) of thy (your) Son Jesus Christ our Lord, who took bread (the cup) and said, "This is my Body (Blood)." *Amen.*

or else the celebrant may consecrate more of both kinds, saying again the words of the Eucharistic Prayer, beginning with the words which follow the Sanctus, and ending with the Invocation (in the case of Eucharistic Prayer C, ending with the narrative of the Institution).

When the services of a priest cannot be obtained, the bishop may, at discretion, authorize a deacon to distribute Holy Communion to the congregation from the reserved Sacrament in the following manner:

1. After the Liturgy of the Word (and the receiving of the people's offering), the deacon reverently places the consecrated Sacrament on the Altar, during which time a communion hymn may be sung.

2. The Lord's Prayer is then said, the deacon first saying, "Let us pray in the words our Savior Christ hath (has) taught us."

3. And then, omitting the breaking of the Bread, the deacon proceeds with what follows in the liturgy as far as the end of the postcommunion prayer, and then dismisses the people.

If any of the consecrated Bread or Wine remain, apart from any which may be required for the Communion of the sick, or of others who for weighty cause could not be present at the celebration, or for the administration of Communion by a deacon to a congregation when no priest is available, the celebrant or deacon, and other communicants, reverently eat and drink it, either after the Communion of the people or after the Dismissal.

A hymn may be sung before or after the postcommunion prayer.

## Disciplinary Rubrics

If the priest knows that a person who is living a notoriously evil life intends to come to Communion, the priest shall speak to that person privately, and tell *him* that *he* may not come to the Holy Table until *he* has given clear proof of repentance and amendment of life.

The priest shall follow the same procedure with those who have done wrong to their neighbors and are a scandal to the other members of the congregation, not allowing such persons to receive Communion until they have made restitution for the wrong they have done, or have at least promised to do so.

When the priest sees that there is hatred between members of the congregation, *he* shall speak privately to each of them, telling them that they may not receive Communion until they have forgiven each other. And if the person or persons on one side truly forgive the others and desire and promise to make up for their faults, but those on the other side refuse to forgive, the priest shall allow those who are penitent to come to Communion, but not those who are stubborn.

In all such cases, the priest is required to notify the bishop, within fourteen days at the most, giving the reasons for refusing Communion.

# Pastoral Offices

# Concerning the Service

In the course of their Christian development, those baptized at an early age are expected, when they are ready and have been duly prepared, to make a mature public affirmation of their faith and commitment to the responsibilities of their Baptism and to receive the laying on of hands by the bishop.

Those baptized as adults, unless baptized with laying on of hands by a bishop, are also expected to make a public affirmation of their faith and commitment to the responsibilities of their Baptism in the presence of a bishop and to receive the laying on of hands.

When there is no Baptism, the rites of Confirmation, Reception, and the Reaffirmation of Baptismal Vows are administered in the following form

If desired, the hymn Gloria in excelsis may be sung immediately after the opening versicles and before the salutation "The Lord be with you."

The Nicene Creed is not used at this service.

It is appropriate that the oblations of bread and wine be presented by persons newly confirmed.

# Confirmation
## with forms for Reception and for the Reaffirmation of Baptismal Vows

*A hymn, psalm, or anthem may be sung.*

*The people standing, the Bishop says*

   Blessed be God: Father, Son, and Holy Spirit.
*People*  And blessed be his kingdom, now and for ever. Amen.

*In place of the above, from Easter Day through the Day of Pentecost*

   Alleluia. Christ is risen.
*People*  The Lord is risen indeed. Alleluia.

*In Lent and on other penitential occasions*

*Bishop* Bless the Lord who forgives all our sins.
*People* His mercy endures for ever.

*The Bishop then continues*

   There is one Body and one Spirit;
*People* There is one hope in God's call to us;
*Bishop* One Lord, one Faith, one Baptism;
*People* One God and Father of all.

*Bishop* The Lord be with you.
*People* And also with you.
*Bishop* Let us pray.

## The Collect of the Day

*People*    Amen.

*At the principal service on a Sunday or other feast, the Collect and Lessons are properly those of the Day. At the discretion of the bishop, however, the Collect (page 203 or 254) and one or more of the Lessons provided "At Confirmation" (page 929) may be substituted.*

## The Lessons

*The people sit. One or two Lessons, as appointed, are read, the Reader first saying*

A Reading (Lesson) from _____.

*A citation giving chapter and verse may be added.*

*After each Reading the Reader may say*

    The Word of the Lord.
*People*    Thanks be to God.

*or the Reader may say*    Here ends the Reading (Epistle).

*Silence may follow.*

*A Psalm, hymn, or anthem may follow each Reading.*

*Then, all standing, the Deacon or a Priest reads the Gospel, first saying*

    The Holy Gospel of our Lord Jesus Christ according to _____.
*People*    Glory to you, Lord Christ.

*After the Gospel, the Reader says*

> The Gospel of the Lord.

*People*    Praise to you, Lord Christ.

**The Sermon**

# Presentation and Examination of the Candidates

*The Bishop says*

The Candidate(s) will now be presented.

*Presenters*   I present *these persons* for Confirmation.

*or*        I present *these persons* to be received into this Communion.

*or*        I present *these persons* who *desire* to reaffirm *their* baptismal vows.

*The Bishop asks the candidates*

Do you reaffirm your renunciation of evil?

*Candidate*   I do.

*Bishop*

Do you renew your commitment to Jesus Christ?

*Candidate*

I do, and with God's grace I will follow him as my Savior and Lord.

Will you who witness these vows do all in your power to support *these persons* in *their* life in Christ?

*People*    We will.

*The Bishop then says these or similar words*

Let us join with *those* who *are* committing *themselves* to Christ and renew our own baptismal covenant.

# The Baptismal Covenant

*Bishop*    Do you believe in God the Father?
*People*    I believe in God, the Father almighty,
        creator of heaven and earth.

*Bishop*    Do you believe in Jesus Christ, the Son of God?
*People*    I believe in Jesus Christ, his only Son, our Lord.
        He was conceived by the power of the Holy Spirit
           and born of the Virgin Mary.
        He suffered under Pontius Pilate,
           was crucified, died, and was buried.
        He descended to the dead.
        On the third day he rose again.
        He ascended into heaven,
           and is seated at the right hand of the Father.
        He will come again to judge the living and the dead

*Bishop*    Do you believe in God the Holy Spirit?
*People*    I believe in the Holy Spirit,
        the holy catholic Church,
        the communion of saints,

the forgiveness of sins,
the resurrection of the body,
and the life everlasting.

| | |
|---|---|
| Bishop | Will you continue in the apostles' teaching and fellowship, in the breaking of bread, and in the prayers? |
| People | I will, with God's help. |
| Bishop | Will you persevere in resisting evil, and, whenever you fall into sin, repent and return to the Lord? |
| People | I will, with God's help. |
| Bishop | Will you proclaim by word and example the Good News of God in Christ? |
| People | I will, with God's help. |
| Bishop | Will you seek and serve Christ in all persons, loving your neighbor as yourself? |
| People | I will, with God's help. |
| Bishop | Will you strive for justice and peace among all people, and respect the dignity of every human being? |
| People | I will, with God's help. |

## Prayers for the Candidates

*The Bishop then says to the congregation*

Let us now pray for *these persons* who *have* renewed *their* commitment to Christ.

*The petitions on pages 305-306 may be used.*

*A period of silence follows.*

*Then the Bishop says*

Almighty God, we thank you that by the death and
resurrection of your Son Jesus Christ you have overcome sin
and brought us to yourself, and that by the sealing of your
Holy Spirit you have bound us to your service. Renew in
*these* your *servants* the covenant you made with *them* at *their*
Baptism. Send *them* forth in the power of that Spirit to
perform the service you set before *them*; through Jesus Christ
your Son our Lord, who lives and reigns with you and the
Holy Spirit, one God, now and for ever. *Amen.*

## For Confirmation

*The Bishop lays hands upon each one and says*

Strengthen, O Lord, your servant N. with your Holy Spirit;
empower *him* for your service; and sustain *him* all the days
of *his* life. *Amen.*

*or this*

Defend, O Lord, your servant N. with your heavenly grace,
that *he* may continue yours for ever, and daily increase in
your Holy Spirit more and more, until *he* comes to your
everlasting kingdom. *Amen.*

## For Reception

N., we recognize you as a member of the one holy catholic
and apostolic Church, and we receive you into the fellowship
of this Communion. God, the Father, Son, and Holy Spirit,
bless, preserve, and keep you. *Amen.*

### For Reaffirmation

N., may the Holy Spirit, who has begun a good work in you,
direct and uphold you in the service of Christ and his
kingdom. *Amen.*

*The Bishop concludes with this prayer*

Almighty and everliving God, let your fatherly hand ever be
over *these* your *servants*; let your Holy Spirit ever be with
*them*; and so lead *them* in the knowledge and obedience of
your Word, that *they* may serve you in this life, and dwell
with you in the life to come; through Jesus Christ our Lord.
*Amen.*

*The Peace is then exchanged*

Bishop     The peace of the Lord be always with you.
People     And also with you.

*The service then continues with the Prayers of the People or the Offertory
of the Eucharist, at which the Bishop should be the principal celebrant.*

*If there is no celebration of the Eucharist, the service continues with the
Lord's Prayer and such other devotions as the Bishop may direct.*

*The Bishop may consecrate oil of Chrism for use at Baptism, using the
prayer on page 307.*

# A Form of Commitment to Christian Service

*This form may be used when a person wishes to make or renew a commitment to the service of Christ in the world, either in general terms, or upon undertaking some special responsibility.*

*It is essential that the person seeking to make or renew a commitment prepare in advance, in consultation with the celebrant, the Act of Commitment, which may be in the form either of a statement of intention or of a series of questions and answers, but which should include a reaffirmation of baptismal promises.*

*Before the Offertory of the Eucharist, the person comes forward at the invitation of the celebrant, and, standing before the congregation, makes the Act of Commitment.*

*After this, the Celebrant says these or similar words*

May the Holy Spirit guide and strengthen you, that in this, and in all things, you may do God's will in the service of the kingdom of his Christ. *Amen.*

In the name of this congregation I commend you to this work, and pledge you our prayers, encouragement, and support.

*The Celebrant then says this or some other appropriate prayer*

Let us pray.

Almighty God, look with favor upon *this person* who *has*
*now* reaffirmed *his* commitment to follow Christ and to serve
in his name. Give *him* courage, patience, and vision; and
strengthen us all in our Christian vocation of witness to the
world, and of service to others; through Jesus Christ our
Lord. *Amen*.

*A prayer for the special work in which the person will be engaged may
be added.*

*The service then continues with the exchange of the Peace and the
Offertory.*

# Concerning the Service

Christian marriage is a solemn and public covenant between a man and a woman in the presence of God. In the Episcopal Church it is required that one, at least, of the parties must be a baptized Christian; that the ceremony be attested by at least two witnesses; and that the marriage conform to the laws of the State and the canons of this Church.

A priest or a bishop normally presides at the Celebration and Blessing of a Marriage, because such ministers alone have the function of pronouncing the nuptial blessing, and of celebrating the Holy Eucharist.

When both a bishop and a priest are present and officiating, the bishop should pronounce the blessing and preside at the Eucharist.

A deacon, or an assisting priest, may deliver the charge, ask for the Declaration of Consent, read the Gospel, and perform other assisting functions at the Eucharist.

Where it is permitted by civil law that deacons may perform marriages, and no priest or bishop is available, a deacon may use the service which follows, omitting the nuptial blessing which follows The Prayers.

It is desirable that the Lessons from the Old Testament and the Epistles be read by lay persons.

In the opening exhortation (at the symbol of N.N.), the full names of the persons to be married are declared. Subsequently, only their Christian names are used.

Additional Directions are on page 437.

# The Celebration and Blessing of a Marriage

*At the time appointed, the persons to be married, with their witnesses, assemble in the church or some other appropriate place.*

*During their entrance, a hymn, psalm, or anthem may be sung, or instrumental music may be played.*

*Then the Celebrant, facing the people and the persons to be married, with the woman to the right and the man to the left, addresses the congregation and says*

Dearly beloved: We have come together in the presence of God to witness and bless the joining together of this man and this woman in Holy Matrimony. The bond and covenant of marriage was established by God in creation, and our Lord Jesus Christ adorned this manner of life by his presence and first miracle at a wedding in Cana of Galilee. It signifies to us the mystery of the union between Christ and his Church, and Holy Scripture commends it to be honored among all people.

The union of husband and wife in heart, body, and mind is intended by God for their mutual joy; for the help and comfort given one another in prosperity and adversity; and, when it is God's will, for the procreation of children and their nurture in the knowledge and love of the Lord. Therefore marriage is not to be entered into unadvisedly or lightly, but reverently, deliberately, and in accordance with the purposes for which it was instituted by God.

Into this holy union *N.N.* and *N.N.* now come to be joined.
If any of you can show just cause why they may not lawfully be
married, speak now; or else for ever hold your peace.

*Then the Celebrant says to the persons to be married*

I require and charge you both, here in the presence of God,
that if either of you know any reason why you may not be
united in marriage lawfully, and in accordance with God's
Word, you do now confess it.


## The Declaration of Consent

*The Celebrant says to the woman*

N., will you have this man to be your husband; to live
together in the covenant of marriage? Will you love him,
comfort him, honor and keep him, in sickness and in health;
and, forsaking all others, be faithful to him as long as you
both shall live?

*The Woman answers*

I will.

*The Celebrant says to the man*

N., will you have this woman to be your wife; to live
together in the covenant of marriage? Will you love her,
comfort her, honor and keep her, in sickness and in health;
and, forsaking all others, be faithful to her as long as you
both shall live?

*The Man answers*

I will.

Will all of you witnessing these promises do all in your
power to uphold these two persons in their marriage?

*People*     We will.

*If there is to be a presentation or a giving in marriage,
it takes place at this time. See page 437.*

*A hymn, psalm, or anthem may follow.*

# The Ministry of the Word

*The Celebrant then says to the people*

> The Lord be with you.

*People*     And also with you.

Let us pray.

O gracious and everliving God, you have created us male and
female in your image: Look mercifully upon this man and this
woman who come to you seeking your blessing, and assist
them with your grace, that with true fidelity and steadfast love
they may honor and keep the promises and vows they make;
through Jesus Christ our Savior, who lives and reigns with
you in the unity of the Holy Spirit, one God, for ever and ever.
*Amen.*

*Then one or more of the following passages from Holy Scripture is read. If there is to be a Communion, a passage from the Gospel always concludes the Readings.*

Genesis 1:26-28 (Male and female he created them)
Genesis 2:4-9, 15-24 (A man cleaves to his wife and they become one flesh)
Song of Solomon 2:10-13; 8:6-7 (Many waters cannot quench love)
Tobit 8:5b-8 (*New English Bible*) (That she and I may grow old together)

1 Corinthians 13:1-13 (Love is patient and kind)
Ephesians 3:14-19 (The Father from whom every family is named)
Ephesians 5:1-2, 21-33 (Walk in love, as Christ loved us)
Colossians 3:12-17 (Love which binds everything together in harmony)
1 John 4:7-16 (Let us love one another for love is of God)

*Between the Readings, a Psalm, hymn, or anthem may be sung or said. Appropriate Psalms are 67, 127, and 128.*

*When a passage from the Gospel is to be read, all stand, and the Deacon or Minister appointed says*

> The Holy Gospel of our Lord Jesus Christ
> according to ——————.

*People*  Glory to you, Lord Christ.

Matthew 5:1-10 (The Beatitudes)
Matthew 5:13-16 (You are the light . . . Let your light so shine)
Matthew 7:21, 24-29 (Like a wise man who built his house upon the rock)
Mark 10:6-9, 13-16 (They are no longer two but one)
John 15:9-12 (Love one another as I have loved you)

*After the Gospel, the Reader says*

> The Gospel of the Lord.

*People*  Praise to you, Lord Christ.

*A homily or other response to the Readings may follow.*

# The Marriage

*The Man, facing the woman and taking her right hand in his, says*

In the Name of God, I, N., take you, N., to be my wife, to have and to hold from this day forward, for better for worse, for richer for poorer, in sickness and in health, to love and to cherish, until we are parted by death. This is my solemn vow.

*Then they loose their hands, and the Woman, still facing the man, takes his right hand in hers, and says*

In the Name of God, I, N., take you, N., to be my husband, to have and to hold from this day forward, for better for worse, for richer for poorer, in sickness and in health, to love and to cherish, until we are parted by death. This is my solemn vow.

*They loose their hands.*

*The Priest may ask God's blessing on a ring or rings as follows*

Bless, O Lord, *this ring* to be *a sign* of the vows by which this man and this woman have bound themselves to each other; through Jesus Christ our Lord. *Amen.*

*The giver places the ring on the ring-finger of the other's hand and says*

N., I give you this ring as a symbol of my vow, and with all that I am, and all that I have, I honor you, in the Name of the Father, and of the Son, and of the Holy Spirit (*or* in the Name of God).

*Then the Celebrant joins the right hands of husband and wife and says*

Now that N. and N. have given themselves to each other by
solemn vows, with the joining of hands and the giving and
receiving of *a ring*, I pronounce that they are husband
and wife, in the Name of the Father, and of the Son, and
of the Holy Spirit.

Those whom God has joined together let no one put asunder.

*People*   Amen.


## The Prayers

*All standing, the Celebrant says*

Let us pray together in the words our Savior taught us.

*People and Celebrant*

| | |
|---|---|
| Our Father, who art in heaven,<br>    hallowed be thy Name,<br>    thy kingdom come,<br>    thy will be done,<br>        on earth as it is in heaven.<br>Give us this day our daily bread.<br>And forgive us our trespasses,<br>    as we forgive those<br>        who trespass against us.<br>And lead us not into temptation,<br>    but deliver us from evil.<br>For thine is the kingdom,<br>    and the power, and the glory,<br>    for ever and ever. Amen. | Our Father in heaven,<br>    hallowed be your Name,<br>    your kingdom come,<br>    your will be done,<br>        on earth as in heaven.<br>Give us today our daily bread.<br>Forgive us our sins<br>    as we forgive those<br>        who sin against us.<br>Save us from the time of trial,<br>    and deliver us from evil.<br>For the kingdom, the power,<br>    and the glory are yours,<br>    now and for ever. Amen. |

*If Communion is to follow, the Lord's Prayer may be omitted here.*

*The Deacon or other person appointed reads the following prayers, to which the People respond, saying, Amen.*

*If there is not to be a Communion, one or more of the prayers may be omitted.*

Let us pray.

Eternal God, creator and preserver of all life, author of salvation, and giver of all grace: Look with favor upon the world you have made, and for which your Son gave his life, and especially upon this man and this woman whom you make one flesh in Holy Matrimony. *Amen.*

Give them wisdom and devotion in the ordering of their common life, that each may be to the other a strength in need, a counselor in perplexity, a comfort in sorrow, and a companion in joy. *Amen.*

Grant that their wills may be so knit together in your will, and their spirits in your Spirit, that they may grow in love and peace with you and one another all the days of their life. *Amen.*

Give them grace, when they hurt each other, to recognize and acknowledge their fault, and to seek each other's forgiveness and yours. *Amen.*

Make their life together a sign of Christ's love to this sinful and broken world, that unity may overcome estrangement, forgiveness heal guilt, and joy conquer despair. *Amen.*

Bestow on them, if it is your will, the gift and heritage of children, and the grace to bring them up to know you, to love you, and to serve you. *Amen.*

Give them such fulfillment of their mutual affection that they may reach out in love and concern for others. *Amen.*

Grant that all married persons who have witnessed these vows may find their lives strengthened and their loyalties confirmed. *Amen.*

Grant that the bonds of our common humanity, by which all your children are united one to another, and the living to the dead, may be so transformed by your grace, that your will may be done on earth as it is in heaven; where, O Father, with your Son and the Holy Spirit, you live and reign in perfect unity, now and for ever. *Amen.*

# The Blessing of the Marriage

*The people remain standing. The husband and wife kneel, and the Priest says one of the following prayers*

Most gracious God, we give you thanks for your tender love in sending Jesus Christ to come among us, to be born of a human mother, and to make the way of the cross to be the way of life. We thank you, also, for consecrating the union of man and woman in his Name. By the power of your Holy Spirit, pour out the abundance of your blessing upon this man and this woman. Defend them from every enemy. Lead them into all peace. Let their love for each other be a seal upon their hearts, a mantle about their shoulders, and a crown upon their foreheads. Bless them in their work and in their companionship; in their sleeping and in their waking; in their joys and in their sorrows; in their life and in their death. Finally, in your mercy, bring them to that table where your saints feast for ever in your heavenly home; through Jesus Christ our Lord, who with you and the Holy Spirit lives and reigns, one God, for ever and ever. *Amen.*

*or this*

O God, you have so consecrated the covenant of marriage
that in it is represented the spiritual unity between Christ
and his Church: Send therefore your blessing upon these your
servants, that they may so love, honor, and cherish each other
in faithfulness and patience, in wisdom and true godliness,
that their home may be a haven of blessing and peace;
through Jesus Christ our Lord, who lives and reigns with you
and the Holy Spirit, one God, now and for ever. *Amen.*

*The husband and wife still kneeling, the Priest adds this blessing*

God the Father, God the Son, God the Holy Spirit, bless,
preserve, and keep you; the Lord mercifully with his favor
look upon you, and fill you with all spiritual benediction and
grace; that you may faithfully live together in this life, and
in the age to come have life everlasting. *Amen.*

# The Peace

*The Celebrant may say to the people*

        The peace of the Lord be always with you.

*People*      And also with you.

*The newly married couple then greet each other, after which greetings
may be exchanged throughout the congregation.*

*When Communion is not to follow, the wedding party leaves the church.
A hymn, psalm, or anthem may be sung, or instrumental music may be
played.*

## At the Eucharist

*The liturgy continues with the Offertory, at which the newly married couple may present the offerings of bread and wine.*

### Preface of Marriage

*At the Communion, it is appropriate that the newly married couple receive Communion first, after the ministers.*

*In place of the usual postcommunion prayer, the following is said*

O God, the giver of all that is true and lovely and gracious: We give you thanks for binding us together in these holy mysteries of the Body and Blood of your Son Jesus Christ. Grant that by your Holy Spirit, N. and N., now joined in Holy Matrimony, may become one in heart and soul, live in fidelity and peace, and obtain those eternal joys prepared for all who love you; for the sake of Jesus Christ our Lord. *Amen.*

*As the wedding party leaves the church, a hymn, psalm, or anthem may be sung; or instrumental music may be played.*

# The Blessing
# of a Civil Marriage

*The Rite begins as prescribed for celebrations of the Holy Eucharist, using the Collect and Lessons appointed in the Marriage service.*

*After the Gospel (and homily), the husband and wife stand before the Celebrant, who addresses them in these or similar words*

N. and N., you have come here today to seek the blessing of God and of his Church upon your marriage. I require, therefore, that you promise, with the help of God, to fulfill the obligations which Christian Marriage demands.

*The Celebrant then addresses the husband, saying*

N., you have taken N. to be your wife. Do you promise to love her, comfort her, honor and keep her, in sickness and in health; and, forsaking all others, to be faithful to her as long as you both shall live?

*The Husband answers*    I do.

*The Celebrant then addresses the wife, saying*

N., you have taken N. to be your husband. Do you promise to love him, comfort him, honor and keep him, in sickness and in health; and, forsaking all others, to be faithful to him as long as you both shall live?

*The Wife answers*    I do.

Will you who have witnessed these promises do all in your power to uphold these two persons in their marriage?

*People*   We will.

*If a ring or rings are to be blessed, the wife extends her hand (and the husband extends his hand) toward the Priest, who says*

Bless, O Lord, *this ring* to be *a sign* of the vows by which this man and this woman have bound themselves to each other; through Jesus Christ our Lord. *Amen.*

*The Celebrant joins the right hands of the husband and wife and says*

Those whom God has joined together let no one put asunder.

*The Congregation responds*   Amen.

*The service continues with The Prayers on page 428.*

# An Order for Marriage

*If it is desired to celebrate a marriage otherwise than as provided on page 423 of this Book, this Order is used.*

*Normally, the celebrant is a priest or bishop. Where permitted by civil law, and when no priest or bishop is available, a deacon may function as celebrant, but does not pronounce a nuptial blessing.*

*The laws of the State and the canons of this Church having been complied with, the man and the woman, together with their witnesses, families, and friends assemble in the church or in some other convenient place.*

1. The teaching of the Church concerning Holy Matrimony, as it is declared in the formularies and canons of this Church, is briefly stated.

2. The intention of the man and the woman to enter the state of matrimony, and their free consent, is publicly ascertained.

3. One or more Readings, one of which is always from Holy Scripture, may precede the exchange of vows. If there is to be a Communion, a Reading from the Gospel is always included.

4. The vows of the man and woman are exchanged, using the following form

In the Name of God, I, *N.*, take you, *N.*, to be my
(wife) (husband), to have and to hold from this day forward,
for better for worse, for richer for poorer, in sickness and in
health, to love and to cherish, until we are parted by death.
This is my solemn vow.

*or this*

I, *N.*, take thee, *N.*, to my wedded (wife) (husband), to have
and to hold from this day forward, for better for worse, for
richer for poorer, in sickness and in health, to love and to
cherish, till death us do part, according to God's holy
ordinance; and thereto I (plight) (give) thee my troth.

5. The Celebrant declares the union of the man and woman as husband
and wife, in the Name of the Father, and of the Son, and of the Holy
Spirit.

6. Prayers are offered for the husband and wife, for their life together, for
the Christian community, and for the world.

7. A priest or bishop pronounces a solemn blessing upon the couple.

8. If there is no Communion, the service concludes with the Peace, the
husband and wife first greeting each other. The Peace may be exchanged
throughout the assembly.

9. If there is to be a Communion, the service continues with the Peace an
the Offertory. The Holy Eucharist may be celebrated either according to
Rite One or Rite Two in this Book, or according to the Order on page 401

# Additional Directions

*If Banns are to be published, the following form is used*

I publish the Banns of Marriage between N.N. of _____ and N.N. of _____. If any of you know just cause why they may not be joined together in Holy Matrimony, you are bidden to declare it. This is the first (*or* second, *or* third) time of asking.

The Celebration and Blessing of a Marriage may be used with any authorized liturgy for the Holy Eucharist. This service then replaces the Ministry of the Word, and the Eucharist begins with the Offertory.

After the Declaration of Consent, if there is to be a giving in marriage, or presentation, the Celebrant asks,

Who gives (presents) this woman to be married to this man?

*or the following*

Who presents this woman and this man to be married to each other?

To either question, the appropriate answer is, "I do." If more than one person responds, they do so together.

For the Ministry of the Word it is fitting that the man and woman to be married remain where they may conveniently hear the reading of Scripture. They may approach the Altar, either for the exchange of vows, or for the Blessing of the Marriage.

It is appropriate that all remain standing until the conclusion of the Collect. Seating may be provided for the wedding party, so that all may be seated for the Lessons and the homily.

The Apostles' Creed may be recited after the Lessons, or after the homily, if there is one.

When desired, some other suitable symbol of the vows may be used in place of the ring.

At the Offertory, it is desirable that the bread and wine be presented to the ministers by the newly married persons. They may then remain before the Lord's Table and receive Holy Communion before other members of the congregation.

# A Thanksgiving for the Birth
# or Adoption of a Child

As soon as convenient after the birth of a child, or after receiving a child
by adoption, the parents, with other members of the family, should come
to the church to be welcomed by the congregation and to give thanks to
Almighty God. It is desirable that this take place at a Sunday service. In
the Eucharist it may follow the Prayers of the People preceding the
Offertory. At Morning or Evening Prayer it may take place before the
close of the Office.

When desired, a briefer form of this service may be used, especially in the
hospital or at home; in which case the Celebrant may begin with the Act
of Thanksgiving, or with the prayer "O God, you have taught us." A
passage from Scripture may first be read. Either Luke 2:41-51, or Luke
18:15-17, is appropriate.

During the prayers, some parents may wish to express thanks in their
own words.

At the proper time, the Celebrant invites the parents and other members
of the family to present themselves before the Altar.

## For the Birth of a Child

*The Celebrant addresses the congregation in these or similar words*

Dear Friends: The birth of a child is a joyous and solemn occasion in the life of a family. It is also an occasion for rejoicing in the Christian community. I bid you, therefore, to join N. [and N.] in giving thanks to Almighty God our heavenly Father, the Lord of all life, for the gift of N. to be their son (daughter) [and with N. (and NN.), for a new brother (sister)]. Let us say together:

*The service continues with the Magnificat or one of the Psalms on pages 441-443.*

## For an Adoption

*The Celebrant addresses the congregation in these or similar words*

Dear Friends: It has pleased God our heavenly Father to answer the earnest prayers of N. [and N.], member(s) of this Christian family, for the gift of a child. I bid you join with *them* [and with N. (and NN.), who now *has* a new brother (sister)] in offering heartfelt thanks for the joyful and solemn responsibility which is *theirs* by the coming of N. to be a member of *their* family. But first, our friends wish us, here assembled, to witness the inauguration of this new relationship.

*The Celebrant asks the parent or parents*

       N. [and N.], do you take this child for your own?
*Parent(s)*  I do.

*Then if the child is old enough to answer, the Celebrant asks*

        N., do you take this woman as your mother?

*Child*    I do.

*Celebrant*  Do you take this man as your father?

*Child*    I do.

*Then the Celebrant, holding or taking the child by the hand, gives the child to the mother or father, saying*

As God has made us his children by adoption and grace, may you receive N. as your own son (daughter).

*Then one or both parents say these or similar words*

May God, the Father of all, bless our child N., and us who have given to *him* our family name, that we may live together in love and affection; through Jesus Christ our Lord. *Amen.*

*The Celebrant says*

Since it has pleased God to bestow upon N. [and N.] the gift of a child, let us now give thanks to him, and say together:

## Act of Thanksgiving

*The Song of Mary*

My soul proclaims the greatness of the Lord,
my spirit rejoices in God my Savior;*
    for he has looked with favor on his lowly servant.
From this day all generations will call me blessed:*
    the Almighty has done great things for me,
    and holy is his Name.
He has mercy on those who fear him*
    in every generation.

He has shown the strength of his arm, *
 he has scattered the proud in their conceit.
He has cast down the mighty from their thrones, *
 and has lifted up the lowly.
He has filled the hungry with good things, *
 and the rich he has sent away empty.
He has come to the help of his servant Israel, *
 for he has remembered his promise of mercy,
The promise he made to our fathers, *
 to Abraham and his children for ever.
Glory to the Father, and to the Son, and to the Holy Spirit: *
 as it was in the beginning, is now, and will be for ever. Am

*or this*

### Psalm 116

I love the LORD, because he has heard the voice of my
 supplication; *
  because he has inclined his ear to me whenever I called
   upon him.
Gracious is the LORD and righteous; *
 our God is full of compassion.
How shall I repay the LORD *
 for all the good things he has done for me?
I will lift up the cup of salvation *
 and call upon the Name of the LORD,
I will fulfill my vows to the LORD *
 in the presence of all his people,
In the courts of the LORD's house, *
 in the midst of you, O Jerusalem.
 Hallelujah!
Glory to the Father, and to the Son, and to the Holy Spirit: *
 as it was in the beginning, is now, and will be for ever. Am

*salm 23*

The LORD is my shepherd; *
  I shall not be in want.

He makes me lie down in green pastures*
  and leads me beside still waters.

He revives my soul*
  and guides me along right pathways for his Name's sake.

Though I walk through the valley of the shadow of death,
  I shall fear no evil;*
    for you are with me;
    your rod and your staff, they comfort me.

You spread a table before me in the presence of those
                          who trouble me;*
    you have anointed my head with oil,
    and my cup is running over.

Surely your goodness and mercy shall follow me all the
                          days of my life,*
    and I will dwell in the house of the LORD for ever.

Glory to the Father, and to the Son, and to the Holy Spirit:*
  as it was in the beginning, is now, and will be for ever. Amen.

*The Celebrant then says this prayer*

Let us pray.

O God, you have taught us through your blessed Son that
whoever receives a little child in the name of Christ receives
Christ himself: We give you thanks for the blessing you have
bestowed upon this family in giving them a child. Confirm
their joy by a lively sense of your presence with them, and
give them calm strength and patient wisdom as they seek to
bring this child to love all that is true and noble, just and
pure, lovable and gracious, excellent and admirable,
following the example of our Lord and Savior, Jesus Christ.
Amen.

## Prayers

*The Celebrant may add one or more of the following prayers*

### For a safe delivery

O gracious God, we give you humble and hearty thanks that
you have preserved through the pain and anxiety of childbirth your servant N., who desires now to offer you her praise
and thanksgivings. Grant, most merciful Father, that by your
help she may live faithfully according to your will in this life,
and finally partake of everlasting glory in the life to come;
through Jesus Christ our Lord. *Amen.*

### For the parents

Almighty God, giver of life and love, bless N. and N. Grant
them wisdom and devotion in the ordering of their common
life, that each may be to the other a strength in need, a
counselor in perplexity, a comfort in sorrow, and a companion
in joy. And so knit their wills together in your will and their
spirits in your Spirit, that they may live together in love and
peace all the days of their life; through Jesus Christ our Lord.
*Amen.*

### For a child not yet baptized

O eternal God, you have promised to be a father to a
thousand generations of those who love and fear you: Bless
this child and preserve *his* life; receive *him* and enable *him* to
receive you, that through the Sacrament of Baptism *he* may
become the child of God; through Jesus Christ our Lord.
*Amen.*

### For a child already baptized

Into your hands, O God, we place your child N. Support *him*
in *his* successes and in *his* failures, in *his* joys and in *his*

sorrows. As *he* grows in age, may *he* grow in grace, and in the knowledge of *his* Savior Jesus Christ. *Amen.*

*The Celebrant may then bless the family*

May God the Father, who by Baptism adopts us as his children, grant you grace. *Amen.*

May God the Son, who sanctified a home at Nazareth, fill you with love. *Amen.*

May God the Holy Spirit, who has made the Church one family, keep you in peace. *Amen.*

*The Peace may be exchanged.*

*The Minister of the Congregation is directed to instruct the people, from time to time, about the duty of Christian parents to make prudent provision for the well-being of their families, and of all persons to make wills, while they are in health, arranging for the disposal of their temporal goods, not neglecting, if they are able, to leave bequests for religious and charitable uses.*

# Concerning the Rite

The ministry of reconciliation, which has been committed by Christ to his Church, is exercised through the care each Christian has for others, through the common prayer of Christians assembled for public worship, and through the priesthood of the Church and its ministers declaring absolution.

The Reconciliation of a Penitent is available for all who desire it. It is not restricted to times of sickness. Confessions may be heard anytime and anywhere.

Two equivalent forms of service are provided here to meet the needs of penitents. The absolution in these services may be pronounced only by a bishop or priest. Another Christian may be asked to hear a confession, but it must be made clear to the penitent that absolution will not be pronounced; instead, a declaration of forgiveness is provided.

When a confession is heard in a church building, the confessor may sit inside the altar rails or in a place set aside to give greater privacy, and the penitent kneels nearby. If preferred, the confessor and penitent may sit face to face for a spiritual conference leading to absolution or a declaration of forgiveness.

When the penitent has confessed all serious sins troubling the conscience and has given evidence of due contrition, the priest gives such counsel and encouragement as are needed and pronounces absolution. Before giving absolution, the priest may assign to the penitent a psalm, prayer, or hymn to be said, or something to be done, as a sign of penitence and act of thanksgiving.

The content of a confession is not normally a matter of subsequent discussion. The secrecy of a confession is morally absolute for the confessor, and must under no circumstances be broken.

# The Reconciliation
# of a Penitent

## Form One

*The Penitent begins*

Bless me, for I have sinned.

*The Priest says*

The Lord be in your heart and upon your lips that you may
truly and humbly confess your sins: In the Name of the
Father, and of the Son, and of the Holy Spirit. *Amen.*

*Penitent*

I confess to Almighty God, to his Church, and to you, that
I have sinned by my own fault in thought, word, and deed, in
things done and left undone; especially _____. For these
and all other sins which I cannot now remember, I am truly
sorry. I pray God to have mercy on me. I firmly intend
amendment of life, and I humbly beg forgiveness of God and
his Church, and ask you for counsel, direction, and absolution.

*Here the Priest may offer counsel, direction, and comfort.*

*The Priest then pronounces this absolution*

Our Lord Jesus Christ, who has left power to his Church to absolve all sinners who truly repent and believe in him, of his great mercy forgive you all your offenses; and by his authority committed to me, I absolve you from all your sins: In the Name of the Father, and of the Son, and of the Holy Spirit. *Amen.*

*or this*

Our Lord Jesus Christ, who offered himself to be sacrificed for us to the Father, and who conferred power on his Church to forgive sins, absolve you through my ministry by the grace of the Holy Spirit, and restore you in the perfect peace of the Church. *Amen.*

*The Priest adds*

The Lord has put away all your sins.

*Penitent*    Thanks be to God.

*The Priest concludes*

Go (*or* abide) in peace, and pray for me, a sinner.


*Declaration of Forgiveness
to be used by a Deacon or Lay Person*

Our Lord Jesus Christ, who offered himself to be sacrificed for us to the Father, forgives your sins by the grace of the Holy Spirit. *Amen.*

## Form Two

*The Priest and Penitent begin as follows*

Have mercy on me, O God, according to your loving-kindness;
   in your great compassion blot out my offenses.
Wash me through and through from my wickedness,
   and cleanse me from my sin.
For I know my transgressions only too well,
   and my sin is ever before me.

Holy God, Holy and Mighty, Holy Immortal One,
   have mercy upon us.

*Penitent*   Pray for me, a sinner.

*Priest*

May God in his love enlighten your heart, that you may
remember in truth all your sins and his unfailing mercy.
*Amen.*

*The Priest may then say one or more of these or other appropriate verses
of Scripture, first saying*

Hear the Word of God to all who truly turn to him.

Come unto me, all ye that travail and are heavy laden, and I
will refresh you.   *Matthew 11:28*

God so loved the world, that he gave his only-begotten Son,
to the end that all that believe in him should not perish, but
have everlasting life.   *John 3:16*

This is a true saying, and worthy of all men to be received,
that Christ Jesus came into the world to save sinners.
*Timothy 1:15*

If any man sin, we have an Advocate with the Father, Jesus Christ the righteous; and he is the perfect offering for our sins, and not for ours only, but for the sins of the whole world.    *1 John 2:1-2*

*The Priest then continues*

Now, in the presence of Christ, and of me, his minister, confess your sins with a humble and obedient heart to Almighty God, our Creator and our Redeemer.

*The Penitent says*

Holy God, heavenly Father, you formed me from the dust in your image and likeness, and redeemed me from sin and death by the cross of your Son Jesus Christ. Through the water of baptism you clothed me with the shining garment of his righteousness, and established me among your children in your kingdom. But I have squandered the inheritance of your saints, and have wandered far in a land that is waste.

Especially, I confess to you and to the Church . . .

*Here the Penitent confesses particular sins.*

Therefore, O Lord, from these and all other sins I cannot now remember, I turn to you in sorrow and repentance. Receive me again into the arms of your mercy, and restore me to the blessed company of your faithful people; through him in whom you have redeemed the world, your Son our Savior Jesus Christ. Amen.

*The Priest may then offer words of comfort and counsel.*

*Priest*

Will you turn again to Christ as your Lord?

*Penitent*    I will.

*Priest*

Do you, then, forgive those who have sinned against you?

*Penitent*   I forgive them.

*Priest*

May Almighty God in mercy receive your confession of sorrow and of faith, strengthen you in all goodness, and by the power of the Holy Spirit keep you in eternal life. *Amen.*

*The Priest then lays a hand upon the penitent's head (or extends a hand over the penitent), saying one of the following*

Our Lord Jesus Christ, who offered himself to be sacrificed for us to the Father, and who conferred power on his Church to forgive sins, absolve you through my ministry by the grace of the Holy Spirit, and restore you in the perfect peace of the Church. *Amen.*

*or this*

Our Lord Jesus Christ, who has left power to his Church to absolve all sinners who truly repent and believe in him, of his great mercy forgive you all your offenses; and by his authority committed to me, I absolve you from all your sins: in the Name of the Father, and of the Son, and of the Holy Spirit. *Amen.*

*The Priest concludes*

Now there is rejoicing in heaven; for you were lost, and are found; you were dead, and are now alive in Christ Jesus our Lord. Go (*or* abide) in peace. The Lord has put away all your sins.

*Penitent*   Thanks be to God.

*Declaration of Forgiveness*
*to be used by a Deacon or Lay Person*

Our Lord Jesus Christ, who offered himself to be sacrificed for us to the Father, forgives your sins by the grace of the Holy Spirit. *Amen.*

# Ministration to the Sick

*In case of illness, the Minister of the Congregation is to be notified.*

*At the Ministration, one or more parts of the following service are used, as appropriate; but when two or more are used together, they are used in the order indicated. The Lord's Prayer is always included.*

*Part One of this service may always be led by a deacon or lay person.*

*When the Laying on of Hands or Anointing takes place at a public celebration of the Eucharist, it is desirable that it precede the distribution of Holy Communion, and it is recommended that it take place immediately before the exchange of the Peace.*

*The Celebrant begins the service with the following or some other greeting*

Peace be to this house (place), and to all who dwell in it.

## Part I.   Ministry of the Word

*One or more of the following or other passages of Scripture are read*

*General*

  Corinthians 1:3-5   (God comforts us in affliction)
 Psalm 91   (He will give his angels charge over you)
 Luke 17:11-19   (Your faith has made you well)

## Penitence

Hebrews 12:1-2 (Looking to Jesus, the perfecter of our faith)
Psalm 103 (He forgives all your sins)
Matthew 9:2-8 (Your sins are forgiven)

## When Anointing is to follow

James 5:14-16 (Is any among you sick?)
Psalm 23 (You have anointed my head with oil)
Mark 6:7, 12-13 (They anointed with oil many that were sick)

## When Communion is to follow

1 John 5:13-15 (That you may know that you have eternal life)
Psalm 145:14-22 (The eyes of all wait upon you, O Lord)
John 6:47-51 (I am the bread of life)

*After any Reading, the Celebrant may comment on it briefly.*

*Prayers may be offered according to the occasion.*

*The Priest may suggest the making of a special confession, if the sick person's conscience is troubled, and use the form for the Reconciliation of a Penitent.*

*Or else the following general confession may be said*

Most merciful God,
we confess that we have sinned against you
in thought, word, and deed,
by what we have done,
and by what we have left undone.
We have not loved you with our whole heart;
we have not loved our neighbors as ourselves.
We are truly sorry and we humbly repent.

For the sake of your Son Jesus Christ,
have mercy on us and forgive us;
that we may delight in your will,
and walk in your ways,
to the glory of your Name. Amen.

*The Priest alone says*

Almighty God have mercy on you, forgive you all your sins
through our Lord Jesus Christ, strengthen you in all goodness,
and by the power of the Holy Spirit keep you in eternal life.
*Amen.*

*A deacon or lay person using the preceding form substitutes "us" for
"you" and "our" for "your."*

## Part II.   Laying on of Hands and Anointing

*If oil for the Anointing of the Sick is to be blessed, the Priest says*

O Lord, holy Father, giver of health and salvation: Send your
Holy Spirit to sanctify this oil; that, as your holy apostles
anointed many that were sick and healed them, so may those
who in faith and repentance receive this holy unction be
made whole; through Jesus Christ our Lord, who lives and
reigns with you and the Holy Spirit, one God, for ever and
ever. *Amen.*

*The following anthem is said*

Savior of the world, by your cross and precious blood you
have redeemed us;
*Save us, and help us, we humbly beseech you, O Lord.*

*The Priest then lays hands upon the sick person, and says one of the
following*

N., I lay my hands upon you in the Name of the Father, and of the Son, and of the Holy Spirit, beseeching our Lord Jesus Christ to sustain you with his presence, to drive away all sickness of body and spirit, and to give you that victory of life and peace which will enable you to serve him both now and evermore. *Amen.*

*or this*

N., I lay my hands upon you in the Name of our Lord and Savior Jesus Christ, beseeching him to uphold you and fill you with his grace, that you may know the healing power of his love. *Amen.*

*If the person is to be anointed, the Priest dips a thumb in the holy oil, and makes the sign of the cross on the sick person's forehead, saying*

N., I anoint you with oil in the Name of the Father, and of the Son, and of the Holy Spirit. *Amen.*

*The Priest may add*

As you are outwardly anointed with this holy oil, so may our heavenly Father grant you the inward anointing of the Holy Spirit. Of his great mercy, may he forgive you your sins, release you from suffering, and restore you to wholeness and strength. May he deliver you from all evil, preserve you in all goodness, and bring you to everlasting life; through Jesus Christ our Lord. *Amen.*

*In cases of necessity, a deacon or lay person may perform the anointing, using oil blessed by a bishop or priest.*

*If Communion is not to follow, the Lord's Prayer is now said.*

*The Priest concludes*

The Almighty Lord, who is a strong tower to all who put their trust in him, to whom all things in heaven, on earth, and under

he earth bow and obey: Be now and evermore your defense,
and make you know and feel that the only Name under
heaven given for health and salvation is the Name of our Lord
Jesus Christ. *Amen.*

## Part III. Holy Communion

*If the Eucharist is to be celebrated, the Priest begins with the [Peace and]
Offertory.*

*If Communion is to be administered from the reserved Sacrament, the
form for Communion under Special Circumstances is used, beginning
with the [Peace and] Lord's Prayer on page 398.*

*If the sick person cannot receive either the consecrated Bread or the
Wine, it is suitable to administer the Sacrament in one kind only.*

*One of the usual postcommunion prayers is said, or the following*

Gracious Father, we give you praise and thanks for this Holy
Communion of the Body and Blood of your beloved Son
Jesus Christ, the pledge of our redemption; and we pray that
it may bring us forgiveness of our sins, strength in our
weakness, and everlasting salvation; through Jesus Christ
our Lord. *Amen.*

*The service concludes with a blessing or with a dismissal*

Let us bless the Lord.
*Thanks be to God.*

*If a person desires to receive the Sacrament, but, by reason of extreme
sickness or physical disability, is unable to eat and drink the Bread and
Wine, the Celebrant is to assure that person that all the benefits of
Communion are received, even though the Sacrament is not received
with the mouth.*

### Prayers for the Sick

*For a Sick Person*

O Father of mercies and God of all comfort, our only help in time of need: We humbly beseech thee to behold, visit, and relieve thy sick servant N. for whom our prayers are desired. Look upon *him* with the eyes of thy mercy; comfort *him* with a sense of thy goodness; preserve *him* from the temptations of the enemy; and give *him* patience under *his* affliction. In thy good time, restore *him* to health, and enable *him* to lead the residue of *his* life in thy fear, and to thy glory; and grant that finally *he* may dwell with thee in life everlasting; through Jesus Christ our Lord. *Amen.*

*For Recovery from Sickness*

O God, the strength of the weak and the comfort of sufferers Mercifully accept our prayers, and grant to your servant N. the help of your power, that *his* sickness may be turned into health, and our sorrow into joy; through Jesus Christ our Lord. *Amen.*

*or this*

O God of heavenly powers, by the might of your command you drive away from our bodies all sickness and all infirmity Be present in your goodness with your servant N., that *his* weakness may be banished and *his* strength restored; and th *his* health being renewed, *he* may bless your holy Name; through Jesus Christ our Lord. *Amen.*

*For a Sick Child*

Heavenly Father, watch with us over your child N., and gra that *he* may be restored to that perfect health which it is yours alone to give; through Jesus Christ our Lord. *Amen.*

*r this*

Lord Jesus Christ, Good Shepherd of the sheep, you gather the lambs in your arms and carry them in your bosom: We commend to your loving care this child N. Relieve *his* pain, guard *him* from all danger, restore to *him* your gifts of gladness and strength, and raise *him* up to a life of service to you. Hear us, we pray, for your dear Name's sake. *Amen.*

## Before an Operation

Almighty God our heavenly Father, graciously comfort your servant N. in *his* suffering, and bless the means made use of for *his* cure. Fill *his* heart with confidence that, though at times *he* may be afraid, *he* yet may put *his* trust in you; through Jesus Christ our Lord. *Amen.*

*r this*

Strengthen your servant N., O God, to do what *he* has to do and bear what *he* has to bear; that, accepting your healing gifts through the skill of surgeons and nurses, *he* may be restored to usefulness in your world with a thankful heart; through Jesus Christ our Lord. *Amen.*

## For Strength and Confidence

Heavenly Father, giver of life and health: Comfort and relieve your sick servant N., and give your power of healing to those who minister to *his* needs, that *he* may be strengthened in *his* weakness and have confidence in your loving care; through Jesus Christ our Lord. *Amen.*

### For the Sanctification of Illness

Sanctify, O Lord, the sickness of your servant N., that the sense of *his* weakness may add strength to *his* faith and seriousness to *his* repentance; and grant that *he* may live with you in everlasting life; through Jesus Christ our Lord. *Amen.*

### For Health of Body and Soul

May God the Father bless you, God the Son heal you, God the Holy Spirit give you strength. May God the holy and undivided Trinity guard your body, save your soul, and bring you safely to his heavenly country; where he lives and reigns for ever and ever. *Amen.*

### For Doctors and Nurses

Sanctify, O Lord, those whom you have called to the study and practice of the arts of healing, and to the prevention of disease and pain. Strengthen them by your life-giving Spirit, that by their ministries the health of the community may be promoted and your creation glorified; through Jesus Christ our Lord. *Amen.*

### Thanksgiving for a Beginning of Recovery

O Lord, your compassions never fail and your mercies are new every morning: We give you thanks for giving our brother (sister) N. both relief from pain and hope of health renewed. Continue in *him*, we pray, the good work you have begun; that *he*, daily increasing in bodily strength, and rejoicing in your goodness, may so order *his* life and conduct that *he* may always think and do those things that please you; through Jesus Christ our Lord. *Amen.*

## Prayers for use by a Sick Person

### For Trust in God

O God, the source of all health: So fill my heart with faith in your love, that with calm expectancy I may make room for your power to possess me, and gracefully accept your healing; through Jesus Christ our Lord. Amen.

### In Pain

Lord Jesus Christ, by your patience in suffering you hallowed earthly pain and gave us the example of obedience to your Father's will: Be near me in my time of weakness and pain; sustain me by your grace, that my strength and courage may not fail; heal me according to your will; and help me always to believe that what happens to me here is of little account if you hold me in eternal life, my Lord and my God. Amen.

### For Sleep

O heavenly Father, you give your children sleep for the refreshing of soul and body: Grant me this gift, I pray; keep me in that perfect peace which you have promised to those whose minds are fixed on you; and give me such a sense of your presence, that in the hours of silence I may enjoy the blessed assurance of your love; through Jesus Christ our Savior. Amen.

### In the Morning

This is another day, O Lord. I know not what it will bring forth, but make me ready, Lord, for whatever it may be. If I am to stand up, help me to stand bravely. If I am to sit still, help me to sit quietly. If I am to lie low, help me to do it patiently. And if I am to do nothing, let me do it gallantly. Make these words more than words, and give me the Spirit of Jesus. Amen.

# Ministration at the
# Time of Death

*When a person is near death, the Minister of the Congregation should be notified, in order that the ministrations of the Church may be provided.*

## A Prayer for a Person near Death

Almighty God, look on this your servant, lying in great weakness, and comfort *him* with the promise of life everlasting, given in the resurrection of your Son Jesus Christ our Lord. *Amen.*

## Litany at the Time of Death

*When possible, it is desirable that members of the family and friends come together to join in the Litany.*

God the Father,
*Have mercy on your servant.*

God the Son,
*Have mercy on your servant.*

God the Holy Spirit,
*Have mercy on your servant.*

Holy Trinity, one God,
*have mercy on your servant.*

From all evil, from all sin, from all tribulation,
*good Lord, deliver* him.

By your holy Incarnation, by your Cross and Passion, by
your precious Death and Burial,
*good Lord, deliver* him.

By your glorious Resurrection and Ascension, and by the
coming of the Holy Spirit,
*good Lord, deliver* him.

We sinners beseech you to hear us, Lord Christ: That it may
please you to deliver the soul of your servant from the power
of evil, and from eternal death,
*We beseech you to hear us, good Lord.*

That it may please you mercifully to pardon all *his* sins,
*We beseech you to hear us, good Lord.*

That it may please you to grant *him* a place of refreshment
and everlasting blessedness,
*We beseech you to hear us, good Lord.*

That it may please you to give *him* joy and gladness in your
kingdom, with your saints in light,
*We beseech you to hear us, good Lord.*

Jesus, Lamb of God:
*have mercy on* him.

Jesus, bearer of our sins:
*have mercy on* him.

Jesus, redeemer of the world:
*give* him *your peace.*

Lord, have mercy.
*Christ, have mercy.*
Lord, have mercy.

*Officiant and People*

Our Father, who art in heaven,
hallowed be thy Name,
thy kingdom come,
thy will be done,
on earth as it is in heaven.
Give us this day our daily bread.
And forgive us our trespasses,
as we forgive those
who trespass against us.
And lead us not into temptation,
but deliver us from evil.

Our Father in heaven,
hallowed be your Name,
your kingdom come,
your will be done,
on earth as in heaven.
Give us today our daily bread.
Forgive us our sins
as we forgive those
who sin against us.
Save us from the time of trial,
and deliver us from evil.

*The Officiant says this Collect*

Let us pray.

Deliver your servant, N., O Sovereign Lord Christ, from all
evil, and set *him* free from every bond; that *he* may rest with
all your saints in the eternal habitations; where with the
Father and the Holy Spirit you live and reign, one God, for
ever and ever. *Amen.*

## A Commendation at the Time of Death

Depart, O Christian soul, out of this world;
In the Name of God the Father Almighty who created yo
In the Name of Jesus Christ who redeemed you;
In the Name of the Holy Spirit who sanctifies you.
May your rest be this day in peace,
and your dwelling place in the Paradise of God.

## A Commendatory Prayer

Into your hands, O merciful Savior, we commend your servant N. Acknowledge, we humbly beseech you, a sheep of your own fold, a lamb of your own flock, a sinner of your own redeeming. Receive *him* into the arms of your mercy, into the blessed rest of everlasting peace, and into the glorious company of the saints in light. *Amen.*

May *his* soul and the souls of all the departed, through the mercy of God, rest in peace. *Amen.*

## Prayers for a Vigil

*It is appropriate that the family and friends come together for prayers prior to the funeral. Suitable Psalms, Lessons, and Collects (such as those in the Burial service) may be used. The Litany at the Time of Death may be said, or the following*

Dear Friends: It was our Lord Jesus himself who said, "Come to me, all you who labor and are burdened, and I will give you rest." Let us pray, then, for our brother (sister) N., that *he* may rest from *his* labors, and enter into the light of God's eternal sabbath rest.

Receive, O Lord, your servant, for *he* returns to you.
*Into your hands, O Lord,*
*we commend our brother (sister) N.*

Wash *him* in the holy font of everlasting life, and clothe *him* in *his* heavenly wedding garment.
*Into your hands, O Lord,*
*we commend our brother (sister) N.*

May *he* hear your words of invitation, "Come, you blessed of my Father."
*Into your hands, O Lord,*
*we commend our brother (sister) N.*

May *he* gaze upon you, Lord, face to face, and taste the blessedness of perfect rest.
*Into your hands, O Lord,*
*we commend our brother (sister) N.*

May angels surround *him*, and saints welcome *him* in peace.
*Into your hands, O Lord,*
*we commend our brother (sister) N.*

*The Officiant concludes*

Almighty God, our Father in heaven, before whom live all who die in the Lord: Receive our *brother N.* into the courts of your heavenly dwelling place. Let *his* heart and soul now ring out in joy to you, O Lord, the living God, and the God of those who live. This we ask through Christ our Lord. *Amen.*


## Reception of the Body

*The following form may be used at whatever time the body is brought to the church.*

*The Celebrant meets the body at the door of the church and says*

With faith in Jesus Christ, we receive the body of our brother (sister) N. for burial. Let us pray with confidence to God, the Giver of life, that he will raise *him* to perfection in the company of the saints.

*Silence may be kept; after which the Celebrant says*

Deliver your servant, N., O Sovereign Lord Christ, from all evil, and set *him* free from every bond; that *he* may rest with all your saints in the eternal habitations; where with the Father and the Holy Spirit you live and reign, one God, for ever and ever. *Amen.*

Let us also pray for all who mourn, that they may cast their care on God, and know the consolation of his love.

*Silence may be kept; after which the Celebrant says*

Almighty God, look with pity upon the sorrows of your servants for whom we pray. Remember them, Lord, in mercy; nourish them with patience; comfort them with a sense of your goodness; lift up your countenance upon them; and give them peace; through Jesus Christ our Lord. *Amen.*

*If the Burial service is not to follow immediately, the body is then brought into the church, during which time a suitable psalm or anthem may be sung or said. Appropriate devotions, such as those appointed for the Vigil on page 465, may follow.*

*When the order for the Burial of the Dead follows immediately, the service continues on page 469 or 491.*

*A member of the congregation bearing the lighted Paschal Candle may lead the procession into the church.*

# Concerning the Service

The death of a member of the Church should be reported as soon as possible to, and arrangements for the funeral should be made in consultation with, the Minister of the Congregation.

Baptized Christians are properly buried from the church. The service should be held at a time when the congregation has opportunity to be present.

The coffin is to be closed before the service, and it remains closed thereafter. It is appropriate that it be covered with a pall or other suitable covering.

If necessary, or if desired, all or part of the service of Committal may be said in the church. If preferred, the Committal service may take place before the service in the church. It may also be used prior to cremation.

A priest normally presides at the service. It is appropriate that the bishop, when present, preside at the Eucharist and pronounce the Commendation.

It is desirable that the Lesson from the Old Testament, and the Epistle, be read by lay persons.

When the services of a priest cannot be obtained, a deacon or lay reader may preside at the service.

At the burial of a child, the passages from Lamentations, 1 John, and John 6, together with Psalm 23, are recommended.

It is customary that the celebrant meet the body and go before it into the church or towards the grave.

The anthems at the beginning of the service are sung or said as the body is borne into the church, or during the entrance of the ministers, or by the celebrant standing in the accustomed place.

# The Burial of the Dead:
# Rite One

*All stand while one or more of the following anthems is sung or said.*

I am the resurrection and the life, saith the Lord;
he that believeth in me, though he were dead, yet shall he live;
and whosoever liveth and believeth in me shall never die.

I know that my Redeemer liveth,
and that he shall stand at the latter day upon the earth;
and though this body be destroyed, yet shall I see God;
whom I shall see for myself and mine eyes shall behold,
and not as a stranger.

For none of us liveth to himself,
and no man dieth to himself.
For if we live, we live unto the Lord;
and if we die, we die unto the Lord.
Whether we live, therefore, or die, we are the Lord's.

Blessed are the dead who die in the Lord;
even so saith the Spirit, for they rest from their labors.

*The Celebrant says one of the following Collects, first saying*

The Lord be with you.
People      And with thy spirit.
Celebrant   Let us pray.

## At the Burial of an Adult

O God, whose mercies cannot be numbered: Accept our prayers on behalf of thy servant *N.*, and grant *him* an entrance into the land of light and joy, in the fellowship of thy saints; through Jesus Christ thy Son our Lord, who liveth and reigneth with thee and the Holy Spirit, one God, now and for ever. *Amen.*

## At the Burial of a Child

O God, whose beloved Son did take little children into his arms and bless them: Give us grace, we beseech thee, to entrust this child *N.* to thy never-failing care and love, and bring us all to thy heavenly kingdom; through the same thy Son Jesus Christ our Lord, who liveth and reigneth with thee and the Holy Spirit, one God, now and for ever. *Amen.*

*The people sit.*

*One or more of the following passages from Holy Scripture is read. If there is to be a Communion, a passage from the Gospel always concludes the Readings.*

## From the Old Testament

Isaiah 25:6-9 (He will swallow up death in victory)
Isaiah 61:1-3 (To comfort all that mourn)
Lamentations 3:22-26, 31-33 (The Lord is good unto them
   that wait for him)
Wisdom 3:1-5, 9 (The souls of the righteous are in the hand of God)
Job 19:21-27a (I know that my Redeemer liveth)

*After the Old Testament Lesson, a suitable canticle or one of the following Psalms may be sung or said*

**Psalm 42**  *Quemadmodum*

Like as the hart desireth the water-brooks, *
   so longeth my soul after thee, O God.

My soul is athirst for God, yea, even for the living God; *
   when shall I come to appear before the presence of God?

My tears have been my meat day and night, *
   while they daily say unto me, Where is now thy God?

Now when I think thereupon, I pour out my heart by myself; *
   for I went with the multitude, and brought them forth into
         the house of God;

In the voice of praise and thanksgiving, *
   among such as keep holy-day.

Why art thou so full of heaviness, O my soul? *
   and why art thou so disquieted within me?

O put thy trust in God; *
   for I will yet thank him, which is the help of my
         countenance, and my God.

**Psalm 46**  *Deus noster refugium*

God is our hope and strength, *
   a very present help in trouble.

Therefore will we not fear, though the earth be moved, *
   and though the hills be carried into the midst of the sea;

Though the waters thereof rage and swell, *
   and though the mountains shake at the tempest of the same.

There is a river, the streams whereof make glad the city of God, *
   the holy place of the tabernacle of the Most Highest.

God is in the midst of her,
therefore shall she not be removed; *
   God shall help her, and that right early.

Be still then, and know that I am God; *
   I will be exalted among the nations,
   and I will be exalted in the earth.

The LORD of hosts is with us; *
   the God of Jacob is our refuge.


**Psalm 90**   *Domine, refugium*

LORD, thou hast been our refuge, *
   from one generation to another.

Before the mountains were brought forth,
or ever the earth and the world were made, *
   thou art God from everlasting, and world without end.

Thou turnest man to destruction; *
   again thou sayest, Come again, ye children of men.

For a thousand years in thy sight are but as yesterday
             when it is past, *
   and as a watch in the night.

As soon as thou scatterest them they are even as a sleep, *
   and fade away suddenly like the grass.

In the morning it is green, and groweth up; *
   but in the evening it is cut down, dried up, and withered.

For we consume away in thy displeasure, *
   and are afraid at thy wrathful indignation.

Thou hast set our misdeeds before thee,*
   and our secret sins in the light of thy countenance.

For when thou art angry all our days are gone; *
  we bring our years to an end, as it were a tale that is told.

The days of our age are threescore years and ten;
and though men be so strong that they come to fourscore years, *
    yet is their strength then but labor and sorrow,
    so soon passeth it away, and we are gone.

So teach us to number our days, *
    that we may apply our hearts unto wisdom.

Psalm 121   *Levavi oculos*

I will lift up mine eyes unto the hills; *
  from whence cometh my help?

My help cometh even from the LORD, *
  who hath made heaven and earth.

He will not suffer thy foot to be moved, *
  and he that keepeth thee will not sleep.

Behold, he that keepeth Israel *
  shall neither slumber nor sleep.

The LORD himself is thy keeper; *
  the LORD is thy defence upon thy right hand;

So that the sun shall not burn thee by day, *
  neither the moon by night.

The LORD shall preserve thee from all evil; *
  yea, it is even he that shall keep thy soul.

The LORD shall preserve thy going out, and thy coming in, *
  from this time forth for evermore.

**Psalm 130**   *De profundis*

Out of the deep have I called unto thee, O LORD; *
   Lord, hear my voice.

O let thine ears consider well *
   the voice of my complaint.

If thou, LORD, wilt be extreme to mark what is done amiss, *
   O Lord, who may abide it?

For there is mercy with thee, *
   therefore shalt thou be feared.

I look for the LORD; my soul doth wait for him; *
   in his word is my trust.

My soul fleeth unto the Lord before the morning watch; *
   I say, before the morning watch.

O Israel, trust in the LORD,
for with the LORD there is mercy, *
   and with him is plenteous redemption.

And he shall redeem Israel *
   from all his sins.


**Psalm 139**   *Domine, probasti*

O LORD, thou hast searched me out, and known me. *
   Thou knowest my down-sitting and mine up-rising;
   thou understandest my thoughts long before.

Thou art about my path, and about my bed, *
   and art acquainted with all my ways.

For lo, there is not a word in my tongue, *
   but thou, O LORD, knowest it altogether.

'hou hast beset me behind and before, *
  and laid thine hand upon me.

uch knowledge is too wonderful and excellent for me; *
  I cannot attain unto it.

Vhither shall I go then from thy Spirit? *
  or whither shall I go then from thy presence?

f I climb up into heaven, thou art there; *
  if I go down to hell, thou art there also.

f I take the wings of the morning, *
  and remain in the uttermost parts of the sea;

ven there also shall thy hand lead me, *
  and thy right hand shall hold me.

f I say, Peradventure the darkness shall cover me, *
  then shall my night be turned to day.

ea, the darkness is no darkness with thee,
ut the night is as clear as day; *
  the darkness and light to thee are both alike.

## rom the New Testament

omans 8:14-19, 34-35, 37-39 (The glory that shall be revealed)
Corinthians 15:20-26, 35-38, 42-44, 53-58 (Raised in incorruption)
Corinthians 4:16—5:9 (Things which are not seen are eternal)
John 3:1-2 (We shall be like him)
evelation 7:9-17 (God shall wipe away all tears)
evelation 21:2-7 (Behold, I make all things new)

*ter the New Testament Lesson, a suitable canticle or hymn, or one of
e following Psalms may be sung or said*

## Psalm 23  *Dominus regit me*

The LORD is my shepherd; *
   therefore can I lack nothing.

He shall feed me in a green pasture, *
   and lead me forth beside the waters of comfort.

He shall convert my soul, *
   and bring me forth in the paths of righteousness for his
         Name's sake.

Yea, though I walk through the valley of the shadow of death
I will fear no evil; *
   for thou art with me;
   thy rod and thy staff comfort me.

Thou shalt prepare a table before me in the presence of them
         that trouble me; *
   thou hast anointed my head with oil,
   and my cup shall be full.

Surely thy loving-kindness and mercy shall follow me all the
         days of my life; *
   and I will dwell in the house of the LORD for ever.


## Psalm 23  *King James Version*

The LORD is my shepherd; *
   I shall not want.

He maketh me to lie down in green pastures; *
   he leadeth me beside the still waters.

He restoreth my soul; *
   he leadeth me in the paths of righteousness for his
         Name's sake.

Yea, though I walk through the valley of the shadow of death,
I will fear no evil; *
    for thou art with me;
    thy rod and thy staff, they comfort me.

Thou preparest a table before me in the presence of
                    mine enemies; *
    thou anointest my head with oil;
    my cup runneth over.

Surely goodness and mercy shall follow me all the days
                    of my life, *
    and I will dwell in the house of the LORD for ever.


Psalm 27    *Dominus illuminatio*

The LORD is my light and my salvation;
whom then shall I fear? *
    the LORD is the strength of my life;
    of whom then shall I be afraid?

One thing have I desired of the LORD, which I will require, *
    even that I may dwell in the house of the LORD all the
                    days of my life,
    to behold the fair beauty of the LORD, and to visit his temple.

For in the time of trouble he shall hide me in his tabernacle; *
    yea, in the secret place of his dwelling shall he hide me,
    and set me up upon a rock of stone.

And now shall he lift up mine head *
    above mine enemies round about me.

Therefore will I offer in his dwelling an oblation with
                    great gladness; *
    I will sing and speak praises unto the LORD.

Hearken unto my voice, O LORD, when I cry unto thee; *
    have mercy upon me, and hear me.

My heart hath talked of thee, Seek ye my face. *
    Thy face, LORD, will I seek.

O hide not thou thy face from me, *
    nor cast thy servant away in displeasure.

I should utterly have fainted, *
    but that I believe verily to see the goodness of the LORD in
            the land of the living.

O tarry thou the LORD's leisure; *
    be strong, and he shall comfort thine heart;
    and put thou thy trust in the LORD.

## Psalm 106   *Confitemini Domino*

O give thanks unto the LORD, for he is gracious, *
    and his mercy endureth for ever.

Who can express the noble acts of the LORD, *
    or show forth all his praise?

Blessed are they that alway keep judgment, *
    and do righteousness.

Remember me, O LORD, according to the favor that thou
           bearest unto thy people; *
    O visit me with thy salvation;

That I may see the felicity of thy chosen, *
    and rejoice in the gladness of thy people,
    and give thanks with thine inheritance.

## Psalm 116   *Dilexi, quoniam*

My delight is in the LORD, *
    because he hath heard the voice of my prayer;

ecause he hath inclined his ear unto me, *
   therefore will I call upon him as long as I live.

he snares of death compassed me round about, *
   and the pains of hell gat hold upon me.

found trouble and heaviness;
en called I upon the Name of the LORD; *
   O LORD, I beseech thee, deliver my soul.

racious is the LORD, and righteous; *
   yea, our God is merciful.

he LORD preserveth the simple; *
   I was in misery, and he helped me.

rn again then unto thy rest, O my soul, *
   for the LORD hath rewarded thee.

nd why? thou hast delivered my soul from death, *
   mine eyes from tears, and my feet from falling.

will walk before the LORD *
   in the land of the living.

will pay my vows now in the presence of all his people; *
   right dear in the sight of the LORD is the death of his saints.

## he Gospel

*hen, all standing, the Deacon or Minister appointed reads the Gospel,
*st saying*

       The Holy Gospel of our Lord Jesus Christ
       according to John.

*ople*     Glory be to thee, O Lord.

John 5:24-27 (He that believeth hath everlasting life)
John 6:37-40 (All that the Father giveth me shall come to me)
John 10:11-16 (I am the good shepherd)
John 11:21-27 (I am the resurrection and the life)
John 14:1-6 (In my Father's house are many mansions)

*At the end of the Gospel, the Reader says*

> ### The Gospel of the Lord.
> *People*     Praise be to thee, O Christ.

*A homily may be preached, the people being seated.*

*The Apostles' Creed may be said, all standing.*

*If there is not to be a Communion, the Lord's Prayer is said here, and the service continues with the following prayer of intercession, or with one or more suitable prayers (see pages 487-489).*

*When there is a Communion, the following serves for the Prayers of the People.*

*The People respond to every petition with Amen.*

*The Deacon or other leader says*

In peace, let us pray to the Lord.

Almighty God, who hast knit together thine elect in one communion and fellowship, in the mystical body of thy Son Christ our Lord: Grant, we beseech thee, to thy whole Church in paradise and on earth, thy light and thy peace. *Amen.*

Grant that all who have been baptized into Christ's death and resurrection may die to sin and rise to newness of life, and that through the grave and gate of death we may pass with him to our joyful resurrection. *Amen.*

Grant to us who are still in our pilgrimage, and who walk as yet by faith, that thy Holy Spirit may lead us in holiness and righteousness all our days. *Amen.*

Grant to thy faithful people pardon and peace, that we may be cleansed from all our sins, and serve thee with a quiet mind. *Amen.*

Grant to all who mourn a sure confidence in thy fatherly care, that, casting all their grief on thee, they may know the consolation of thy love. *Amen.*

Give courage and faith to those who are bereaved, that they may have strength to meet the days ahead in the comfort of a reasonable and holy hope, in the joyful expectation of eternal life with those they love. *Amen.*

Help us, we pray, in the midst of things we cannot understand, to believe and trust in the communion of saints, the forgiveness of sins, and the resurrection to life everlasting. *Amen.*

Grant us grace to entrust N. to thy never-failing love; receive *him* into the arms of thy mercy, and remember *him* according to the favor which thou bearest unto thy people. *Amen.*

Grant that, increasing in knowledge and love of thee, *he* may go from strength to strength in the life of perfect service in thy heavenly kingdom. *Amen.*

Grant us, with all who have died in the hope of the resurrection, to have our consummation and bliss in thy eternal and everlasting glory, and, with [blessed N. and] all thy saints, to receive the crown of life which thou dost promise to all who share in the victory of thy Son Jesus Christ; who liveth and reigneth with thee and the Holy Spirit, one God, for ever and ever. *Amen.*

*When there is no Communion, the service continues with the Commendation, or with the Committal.*

## At the Eucharist

*The service continues with the Peace and the Offertory.*

### Preface of the Commemoration of the Dead

*In place of the usual postcommunion prayer, the following is said*

Almighty God, we thank thee that in thy great love thou hast fed us with the spiritual food and drink of the Body and Blood of thy Son Jesus Christ, and hast given unto us a foretaste of thy heavenly banquet. Grant that this Sacrament may be unto us a comfort in affliction, and a pledge of our inheritance in that kingdom where there is no death, neither sorrow nor crying, but the fullness of joy with all thy saints; through Jesus Christ our Savior. *Amen.*

*If the body is not present, the service continues with the [blessing and] dismissal.*

*Unless the Committal follows immediately in the church, the following Commendation is used.*

## The Commendation

*The Celebrant and other ministers take their places at the body.*

*This anthem, or some other suitable anthem, or a hymn, may be sung or said*

Give rest, O Christ, to thy servant(s) with thy saints,
*where sorrow and pain are no more,*
*neither sighing, but life everlasting.*

Thou only art immortal, the creator and maker of mankind; and we are mortal, formed of the earth, and unto earth shall we return. For so thou didst ordain when thou createdst me, saying, "Dust thou art, and unto dust shalt thou return." All

e go down to the dust; yet even at the grave we make
ır song: Alleluia, alleluia, alleluia.

*ive rest, O Christ, to thy servant(s) with thy saints,*
*here sorrow and pain are no more,*
*either sighing, but life everlasting.*

*he Celebrant, facing the body, says*

ıto thy hands, O merciful Savior, we commend thy servant
*'.* Acknowledge, we humbly beseech thee, a sheep of thine
wn fold, a lamb of thine own flock, a sinner of thine own
·deeming. Receive *him* into the arms of thy mercy, into the
lessed rest of everlasting peace, and into the glorious
ɔmpany of the saints in light. *Amen.*

*he Celebrant, or the Bishop if present, may then bless the people, and a*
*eacon or other Minister may dismiss them, saying*

et us go forth in the name of Christ.
*hanks be to God.*

*s the body is borne from the church, a hymn, or one or more of these*
*ithems may be sung or said*

hrist is risen from the dead, trampling down death by death,
nd giving life to those in the tomb.

he Sun of Righteousness is gloriously risen, giving light to
ɪose who sat in darkness and in the shadow of death.

he Lord will guide our feet into the way of peace, having
ıken away the sin of the world.

`hrist will open the kingdom of heaven to all who believe in
is Name, saying, Come, O blessed of my Father; inherit the
ingdom prepared for you.

Into paradise may the angels lead thee; and at thy coming
may the martyrs receive thee, and bring thee into the holy
city Jerusalem.

*or one of these Canticles*

The Song of Zechariah, *Benedictus*
The Song of Simeon, *Nunc dimittis*
Christ our Passover, *Pascha nostrum*

# The Committal

*The following anthem is sung or said*

In the midst of life we are in death;
of whom may we seek for succor,
but of thee, O Lord,
who for our sins art justly displeased?

Yet, O Lord God most holy, O Lord most mighty,
O holy and most merciful Savior,
deliver us not into the bitter pains of eternal death.

Thou knowest, Lord, the secrets of our hearts;
shut not thy merciful ears to our prayer;
but spare us, Lord most holy, O God most mighty,
O holy and merciful Savior,
thou most worthy Judge eternal.
Suffer us not, at our last hour,
through any pains of death, to fall from thee.

*or this*

All that the Father giveth me shall come to me;
and him that cometh to me I will in no wise cast out.

He that raised up Jesus from the dead
will also give life to our mortal bodies,
by his Spirit that dwelleth in us.

Wherefore my heart is glad, and my spirit rejoiceth;
my flesh also shall rest in hope.

Thou shalt show me the path of life;
in thy presence is the fullness of joy,
and at thy right hand there is pleasure for evermore.

*Then, while earth is cast upon the coffin, the Celebrant says these words*

In sure and certain hope of the resurrection to eternal life
through our Lord Jesus Christ, we commend to Almighty
God our *brother* N; and we commit *his* body to the ground;*
earth to earth, ashes to ashes, dust to dust. The Lord bless
*him* and keep *him*, the Lord make his face to shine upon *him*
and be gracious unto *him*, the Lord lift up his countenance
upon *him* and give *him* peace. *Amen.*

*Or the deep, or the elements, or its resting place.*

*The Celebrant says*

      The Lord be with you.
*People*    And with thy spirit.
*Celebrant*  Let us pray.

*Celebrant and People*

Our Father, who art in heaven,
  hallowed be thy Name,
  thy kingdom come,
  thy will be done,
    on earth as it is in heaven.
Give us this day our daily bread.

And forgive us our trespasses,
    as we forgive those who trespass against us.
And lead us not into temptation,
    but deliver us from evil.
For thine is the kingdom, and the power, and the glory,
    for ever and ever. Amen.

*Then the Celebrant may say*

O Almighty God, the God of the spirits of all flesh, who by a
voice from heaven didst proclaim, Blessed are the dead who
die in the Lord: Multiply, we beseech thee, to those who rest
in Jesus the manifold blessings of thy love, that the good
work which thou didst begin in them may be made perfect
unto the day of Jesus Christ. And of thy mercy, O heavenly
Father, grant that we, who now serve thee on earth, may at
last, together with them, be partakers of the inheritance of
the saints in light; for the sake of thy Son Jesus Christ our
Lord. *Amen.*

*In place of this prayer, or in addition to it, the Celebrant may use any of
the Additional Prayers.*

*Then may be said*

Rest eternal grant to *him*, O Lord:
*And let light perpetual shine upon* him.

May *his* soul, and the souls of all the departed,
through the mercy of God, rest in peace. *Amen.*

*The Celebrant dismisses the people with these words*

The God of peace, who brought again from the dead our
Lord Jesus Christ, the great Shepherd of the sheep, through

he blood of the everlasting covenant: Make you perfect in
every good work to do his will, working in you that which is
well pleasing in his sight; through Jesus Christ, to whom be
glory for ever and ever. *Amen.*

## The Consecration of a Grave

*If the grave is in a place that has not previously been set apart for
Christian burial, the Priest may use the following prayer, either before
the service of Committal or at some other convenient time*

O God, whose blessed Son was laid in a sepulcher in the
garden: Bless, we pray, this grave, and grant that *he* whose
body is (is to be) buried here may dwell with Christ in
paradise, and may come to thy heavenly kingdom; through
thy Son Jesus Christ our Lord. *Amen.*

## Additional Prayers

Almighty and everlasting God, we yield unto thee most high
praise and hearty thanks for the wonderful grace and virtue
declared in all thy saints, who have been the choice vessels
of thy grace, and the lights of the world in their several
generations; most humbly beseeching thee to give us grace so
to follow the example of their steadfastness in thy faith, and
obedience to thy holy commandments, that at the day of the
general resurrection, we, with all those who are of the
mystical body of thy Son, may be set on his right hand, and
hear that his most joyful voice: "Come, ye blessed of my
Father, inherit the kingdom prepared for you from the
foundation of the world." Grant this, O Father, for the sake
of the same thy Son Jesus Christ, our only Mediator and
Advocate. *Amen.*

Almighty God, with whom do live the spirits of those who depart hence in the Lord, and with whom the souls of the faithful, after they are delivered from the burden of the flesh, are in joy and felicity: We give thee hearty thanks for the good examples of all those thy servants, who, having finished their course in faith, do now rest from their labors. And we beseech thee that we, with all those who are departed in the true faith of thy holy Name, may have our perfect consummation and bliss, both in body and soul, in thy eternal and everlasting glory; through Jesus Christ our Lord. *Amen.*

Into thy hands, O Lord, we commend thy servant *N.*, our dear *brother*, as into the hands of a faithful Creator and most merciful Savior, beseeching thee that *he* may be precious in thy sight. Wash *him*, we pray thee, in the blood of that immaculate Lamb that was slain to take away the sins of the world; that, whatsoever defilements *he* may have contracted in the midst of this earthly life being purged and done away, *he* may be presented pure and without spot before thee; through the merits of Jesus Christ thine only Son our Lord. *Amen.*

Remember thy servant, O Lord, according to the favor which thou bearest unto thy people; and grant that, increasing in knowledge and love of thee, *he* may go from strength to strength in the life of perfect service in thy heavenly kingdom; through Jesus Christ our Lord. *Amen.*

Almighty God, our heavenly Father, in whose hands are the living and the dead: We give thee thanks for all thy servants who have laid down their lives in the service of our country. Grant to them thy mercy and the light of thy presence; and give us such a lively sense of thy righteous will, that the work which thou hast begun in them may be perfected; through Jesus Christ thy Son our Lord. *Amen.*

O God, whose days are without end, and whose mercies cannot be numbered: Make us, we beseech thee, deeply sensible of the shortness and uncertainty of life; and let thy Holy Spirit lead us in holiness and righteousness all our days; that, when we shall have served thee in our generation, we may be gathered unto our fathers, having the testimony of a good conscience; in the communion of the Catholic Church; in the confidence of a certain faith; in the comfort of a reasonable, religious, and holy hope; in favor with thee our God; and in perfect charity with the world. All which we ask through Jesus Christ our Lord. *Amen.*

O God, the King of saints, we praise and magnify thy holy Name for all thy servants who have finished their course in thy faith and fear; for the blessed Virgin Mary; for the holy patriarchs, prophets, apostles, and martyrs; and for all other thy righteous servants, known to us and unknown; and we beseech thee that, encouraged by their examples, aided by their prayers, and strengthened by their fellowship, we also may be partakers of the inheritance of the saints in light; through the merits of thy Son Jesus Christ our Lord. *Amen.*

O Lord Jesus Christ, Son of the living God, we pray thee to set thy passion, cross, and death, between thy judgment and our souls, now and in the hour of our death. Give mercy and grace to the living, pardon and rest to the dead, to thy holy Church peace and concord, and to us sinners everlasting life and glory; who with the Father and the Holy Spirit livest and reignest, one God, now and for ever. *Amen.*

Almighty God, Father of mercies and giver of all comfort: Deal graciously, we pray thee, with all those who mourn, that casting every care on thee, they may know the consolation of thy love; through Jesus Christ our Lord. *Amen.*

# Concerning the Service

The death of a member of the Church should be reported as soon as possible to, and arrangements for the funeral should be made in consultation with, the Minister of the Congregation.

Baptized Christians are properly buried from the church. The service should be held at a time when the congregation has opportunity to be present.

The coffin is to be closed before the service, and it remains closed thereafter It is appropriate that it be covered with a pall or other suitable covering.

If necessary, or if desired, all or part of the service of Committal may be said in the church. If preferred, the Committal service may take place before the service in the church. It may also be used prior to cremation.

A priest normally presides at the service. It is appropriate that the bishop, when present, preside at the Eucharist and pronounce the Commendation

It is desirable that the Lesson from the Old Testament, and the Epistle, be read by lay persons.

When the services of a priest cannot be obtained, a deacon or lay reader may preside at the service.

At the burial of a child, the passages from Lamentations, 1 John, and John 6, together with Psalm 23, are recommended.

It is customary that the celebrant meet the body and go before it into the church or towards the grave.

The anthems at the beginning of the service are sung or said as the body is borne into the church, or during the entrance of the ministers, or by the celebrant standing in the accustomed place.

# The Burial of the Dead:
# Rite Two

*All stand while one or more of the following anthems is sung or said.*
*A hymn, psalm, or some other suitable anthem may be sung instead.*

I am Resurrection and I am Life, says the Lord.
Whoever has faith in me shall have life,
even though he die.
And everyone who has life,
and has committed himself to me in faith,
shall not die for ever.

As for me, I know that my Redeemer lives
and that at the last he will stand upon the earth.
After my awaking, he will raise me up;
and in my body I shall see God.
I myself shall see, and my eyes behold him
who is my friend and not a stranger.

For none of us has life in himself,
and none becomes his own master when he dies.
For if we have life, we are alive in the Lord,
and if we die, we die in the Lord.
So, then, whether we live or die,
we are the Lord's possession.

Happy from now on
are those who die in the Lord!
So it is, says the Spirit,
for they rest from their labors.

*Or else this anthem*

In the midst of life we are in death;
from whom can we seek help?
From you alone, O Lord,
who by our sins are justly angered.

*Holy God, Holy and Mighty,*
*Holy and merciful Savior,*
*deliver us not into the bitterness of eternal death.*

Lord, you know the secrets of our hearts;
shut not your ears to our prayers,
but spare us, O Lord.

*Holy God, Holy and Mighty,*
*Holy and merciful Savior,*
*deliver us not into the bitterness of eternal death.*

O worthy and eternal Judge,
do not let the pains of death
turn us away from you at our last hour.

*Holy God, Holy and Mighty,*
*Holy and merciful Savior,*
*deliver us not into the bitterness of eternal death.*

*When all are in place, the Celebrant may address the congregation,*
*acknowledging briefly the purpose of their gathering, and bidding their*
*prayers for the deceased and the bereaved.*

*The Celebrant then says*

       The Lord be with you.
*People*    And also with you.
*Celebrant*  Let us pray.

*Silence may be kept; after which the Celebrant says one of the following Collects*

## At the Burial of an Adult

O God, who by the glorious resurrection of your Son Jesus Christ destroyed death, and brought life and immortality to light: Grant that your servant N., being raised with him, may know the strength of his presence, and rejoice in his eternal glory; who with you and the Holy Spirit lives and reigns, one God, for ever and ever. *Amen.*

*or this*

O God, whose mercies cannot be numbered: Accept our prayers on behalf of your servant N., and grant *him* an entrance into the land of light and joy, in the fellowship of your saints; through Jesus Christ our Lord, who lives and reigns with you and the Holy Spirit, one God, now and for ever. *Amen.*

*or this*

O God of grace and glory, we remember before you this day our brother (sister) N. We thank you for giving *him* to us, *his* family and friends, to know and to love as a companion on our earthly pilgrimage. In your boundless compassion, console us who mourn. Give us faith to see in death the gate of eternal life, so that in quiet confidence we may continue our course on earth, until, by your call, we are reunited with those who have gone before; through Jesus Christ our Lord. *Amen.*

## At the Burial of a Child

O God, whose beloved Son took children into his arms and blessed them: Give us grace to entrust N. to your never-failing care and love, and bring us all to your heavenly kingdom; through Jesus Christ our Lord, who lives and reigns with you and the Holy Spirit, one God, now and for ever. *Amen.*

*The Celebrant may add the following prayer*

Most merciful God, whose wisdom is beyond our understanding: Deal graciously with *NN.* in *their* grief. Surround *them* with your love, that *they* may not be overwhelmed by *their* loss, but have confidence in your goodness, and strength to meet the days to come; through Jesus Christ our Lord. *Amen.*

*The people sit.*

*One or more of the following passages from Holy Scripture is read. If there is to be a Communion, a passage from the Gospel always concludes the Readings.*

## The Liturgy of the Word

### From the Old Testament

Isaiah 25:6-9 (He will swallow up death for ever)
Isaiah 61:1-3 (To comfort those who mourn)
Lamentations 3:22-26, 31-33 (The Lord is good to those who wait for him)
Wisdom 3:1-5, 9 (The souls of the righteous are in the hands of God)
Job 19:21-27a (I know that my Redeemer lives)

*A suitable psalm, hymn, or canticle may follow. The following Psalms are appropriate: 42:1-7, 46, 90:1-12, 121, 130, 139:1-11.*

*From the New Testament*

Romans 8:14-19, 34-35, 37-39 (The glory that shall be revealed)
Corinthians 15:20-26, 35-38, 42-44, 53-58 (The imperishable body)
Corinthians 4:16—5:9 (Things that are unseen are eternal)
John 3:1-2 (We shall be like him)
Revelation 7:9-17 (God will wipe away every tear)
Revelation 21:2-7 (Behold, I make all things new)

*A suitable psalm, hymn, or canticle may follow. The following Psalms are appropriate: 23, 27, 106:1-5, 116.*

## The Gospel

*Then, all standing, the Deacon or Minister appointed reads the Gospel, first saying*

> The Holy Gospel of our Lord Jesus Christ
> according to John.

*People*   Glory to you, Lord Christ.

John 5:24-27 (He who believes has everlasting life)
John 6:37-40 (All that the Father gives me will come to me)
John 10:11-16 (I am the good shepherd)
John 11:21-27 (I am the resurrection and the life)
John 14:1-6 (In my Father's house are many rooms)

*At the end of the Gospel, the Reader says*

> The Gospel of the Lord.

*People*   Praise to you, Lord Christ.

*Here there may be a homily by the Celebrant, or a member of the family, or a friend.*

*The Apostles' Creed may then be said, all standing. The Celebrant may introduce the Creed with these or similar words*

In the assurance of eternal life given at Baptism, let us proclaim our faith and say,

*Celebrant and People*

I believe in God, the Father almighty,
  creator of heaven and earth.

I believe in Jesus Christ, his only Son, our Lord.
  He was conceived by the power of the Holy Spirit
    and born of the Virgin Mary.
  He suffered under Pontius Pilate,
    was crucified, died, and was buried.
  He descended to the dead.
  On the third day he rose again.
  He ascended into heaven,
    and is seated at the right hand of the Father.
  He will come again to judge the living and the dead.

I believe in the Holy Spirit,
  the holy catholic Church,
  the communion of saints,
  the forgiveness of sins,
  the resurrection of the body,
  and the life everlasting. Amen.

*If there is not to be a Communion, the Lord's Prayer is said here, and the service continues with the Prayers of the People, or with one or more suitable prayers (see pages 503-505).*

*When there is a Communion, the following form of the Prayers of the People is used, or else the form on page 465 or 480.*

For our brother (sister) N., let us pray to our Lord Jesus Christ who said, "I am Resurrection and I am Life."

Lord, you consoled Martha and Mary in their distress; draw near to us who mourn for N., and dry the tears of those who weep.
*Hear us, Lord.*

You wept at the grave of Lazarus, your friend; comfort us in our sorrow.
*Hear us, Lord.*

You raised the dead to life; give to our brother (sister) eternal life.
*Hear us, Lord.*

You promised paradise to the thief who repented; bring our brother (sister) to the joys of heaven.
*Hear us, Lord.*

Our brother (sister) was washed in Baptism and anointed with the Holy Spirit; give *him* fellowship with all your saints.
*Hear us, Lord.*

*He* was nourished with your Body and Blood; grant *him* a place at the table in your heavenly kingdom.
*Hear us, Lord.*

Comfort us in our sorrows at the death of our brother (sister); let our faith be our consolation, and eternal life our hope.

*Silence may be kept.*

*The Celebrant concludes with one of the following or some other prayer*

Lord Jesus Christ, we commend to you our brother (sister) N., who was reborn by water and the Spirit in Holy Baptism. Grant that *his* death may recall to us your victory over death, and be an occasion for us to renew our trust in your Father's love. Give us, we pray, the faith to follow where you have led the way; and where you live and reign with the Father and the Holy Spirit, to the ages of ages. *Amen.*

*or this*

Father of all, we pray to you for N., and for all those whom we love but see no longer. Grant to them eternal rest. Let light perpetual shine upon them. May *his* soul and the souls of all the departed, through the mercy of God, rest in peace. *Amen.*

*When there is no Communion, the service continues with the Commendation, or with the Committal.*

## At the Eucharist.

*The service continues with the Peace and the Offertory.*

*Preface of the Commemoration of the Dead*

*In place of the usual postcommunion prayer, the following is said*

Almighty God, we thank you that in your great love you have fed us with the spiritual food and drink of the Body and Blood of your Son Jesus Christ, and have given us a foretaste of your heavenly banquet. Grant that this Sacrament may be to us a comfort in affliction, and a pledge of our inheritance in that kingdom where there is no death, neither sorrow nor crying, but the fullness of joy with all your saints; through Jesus Christ our Savior. *Amen.*

*If the body is not present, the service continues with the [blessing and] dismissal.*

*Unless the Committal follows immediately in the church, the following Commendation is used.*

## The Commendation

*The Celebrant and other ministers take their places at the body.*

*This anthem, or some other suitable anthem, or a hymn, may be sung or said*

Give rest, O Christ, to your servant(s) with your saints,
*where sorrow and pain are no more,*
*neither sighing, but life everlasting.*

You only are immortal, the creator and maker of mankind;
and we are mortal, formed of the earth, and to earth shall we
return. For so did you ordain when you created me, saying,
"You are dust, and to dust you shall return." All of us go down
to the dust; yet even at the grave we make our song: Alleluia,
alleluia, alleluia.

Give rest, O Christ, to your servant(s) with your saints,
*where sorrow and pain are no more,*
*neither sighing, but life everlasting.*

*The Celebrant, facing the body, says*

Into your hands, O merciful Savior, we commend your
servant N. Acknowledge, we humbly beseech you, a sheep of
your own fold, a lamb of your own flock, a sinner of your
own redeeming. Receive *him* into the arms of your mercy,
into the blessed rest of everlasting peace, and into the
glorious company of the saints in light. *Amen.*

*The Celebrant, or the Bishop if present, may then bless the people, and a Deacon or other Minister may dismiss them, saying*

Let us go forth in the name of Christ.
*Thanks be to God.*

*As the body is borne from the church, a hymn, or one or more of these anthems may be sung or said*

Christ is risen from the dead, trampling down death by death, and giving life to those in the tomb.

The Sun of Righteousness is gloriously risen, giving light to those who sat in darkness and in the shadow of death.

The Lord will guide our feet into the way of peace, having taken away the sin of the world.

Christ will open the kingdom of heaven to all who believe in his Name, saying, Come, O blessed of my Father; inherit the kingdom prepared for you.

Into paradise may the angels lead you. At your coming may the martyrs receive you, and bring you into the holy city Jerusalem.

*or one of these Canticles,*

The Song of Zechariah, *Benedictus*
The Song of Simeon, *Nunc dimittis*
Christ our Passover, *Pascha nostrum*

# The Committal

*The following anthem or one of those on pages 491-492 is sung or said*

Everyone the Father gives to me will come to me;
I will never turn away anyone who believes in me.

He who raised Jesus Christ from the dead
will also give new life to our mortal bodies
through his indwelling Spirit.

My heart, therefore, is glad, and my spirit rejoices;
my body also shall rest in hope.

You will show me the path of life;
in your presence there is fullness of joy,
and in your right hand are pleasures for evermore.

*Then, while earth is cast upon the coffin, the Celebrant says these words*

In sure and certain hope of the resurrection to eternal life
through our Lord Jesus Christ, we commend to Almighty
God our *brother* N., and we commit *his* body to the ground;*
earth to earth, ashes to ashes, dust to dust. The Lord bless
*him* and keep *him*, the Lord make his face to shine upon *him*
and be gracious to *him*, the Lord lift up his countenance upon
*him* and give *him* peace. *Amen.*

*Or the deep, or the elements, or its resting place.*

*The Celebrant says*

|  | The Lord be with you. |
|---|---|
| *People* | And also with you. |
| *Celebrant* | Let us pray. |

| Our Father, who art in heaven, | Our Father in heaven, |
| hallowed be thy Name, | hallowed be your Name, |
| thy kingdom come, | your kingdom come, |
| thy will be done, | your will be done, |
| on earth as it is in heaven. | on earth as in heaven. |
| Give us this day our daily bread. | Give us today our daily bread. |
| And forgive us our trespasses, | Forgive us our sins |
| as we forgive those | as we forgive those |
| who trespass against us. | who sin against us. |
| And lead us not into temptation, | Save us from the time of trial, |
| but deliver us from evil. | and deliver us from evil. |
| For thine is the kingdom, | For the kingdom, the power, |
| and the power, and the glory, | and the glory are yours, |
| for ever and ever. Amen. | now and for ever. Amen. |

*Other prayers may be added.*

*Then may be said*

Rest eternal grant to *him*, O Lord;
*And let light perpetual shine upon* him.

May *his* soul, and the souls of all the departed,
through the mercy of God, rest in peace. *Amen.*

*The Celebrant dismisses the people with these words*

        Alleluia. Christ is risen.
*People*     The Lord is risen indeed. Alleluia.
*Celebrant*  Let us go forth in the name of Christ.
*People*     Thanks be to God.

*or with the following*

The God of peace, who brought again from the dead our Lord Jesus Christ, the great Shepherd of the sheep, through the blood of the everlasting covenant: Make you perfect in every good work to do his will, working in you that which is well-pleasing in his sight; through Jesus Christ, to whom be glory for ever and ever. *Amen.*

## The Consecration of a Grave

*If the grave is in a place that has not previously been set apart for Christian burial, the Priest may use the following prayer, either before the service of Committal or at some other convenient time*

O God, whose blessed Son was laid in a sepulcher in the garden: Bless, we pray, this grave, and grant that *he* whose body is (is to be) buried here may dwell with Christ in paradise, and may come to your heavenly kingdom; through your Son Jesus Christ our Lord. *Amen.*

Additional Prayers

Almighty God, with whom still live the spirits of those who die in the Lord, and with whom the souls of the faithful are in joy and felicity: We give you heartfelt thanks for the good examples of all your servants, who, having finished their course in faith, now find rest and refreshment. May we, with all who have died in the true faith of your holy Name, have perfect fulfillment and bliss in your eternal and everlasting glory; through Jesus Christ our Lord. *Amen.*

O God, whose days are without end, and whose mercies cannot be numbered: Make us, we pray, deeply aware of the shortness and uncertainty of human life; and let your Holy Spirit lead us in holiness and righteousness all our days; that, when we shall have served you in our generation, we may be gathered to our ancestors, having the testimony of a good conscience, in the communion of the Catholic Church, in the confidence of a certain faith, in the comfort of a religious and holy hope, in favor with you, our God, and in perfect charity with the world. All this we ask through Jesus Christ our Lord. *Amen.*

O God, the King of saints, we praise and glorify your holy Name for all your servants who have finished their course in your faith and fear: for the blessed Virgin Mary; for the holy patriarchs, prophets, apostles, and martyrs; and for all your other righteous servants, known to us and unknown; and we pray that, encouraged by their examples, aided by their prayers, and strengthened by their fellowship, we also may be partakers of the inheritance of the saints in light; through the merits of your Son Jesus Christ our Lord. *Amen.*

Lord Jesus Christ, by your death you took away the sting of death: Grant to us your servants so to follow in faith where you have led the way, that we may at length fall asleep peacefully in you and wake up in your likeness; for your tender mercies' sake. *Amen.*

Father of all, we pray to you for those we love, but see no longer: Grant them your peace; let light perpetual shine upon them; and, in your loving wisdom and almighty power, work in them the good purpose of your perfect will; through Jesus Christ our Lord. *Amen.*

Merciful God, Father of our Lord Jesus Christ who is the Resurrection and the Life: Raise us, we humbly pray, from the death of sin to the life of righteousness; that when we depart this life we may rest in him, and at the resurrection receive that blessing which your well-beloved Son shall then pronounce:"Come, you blessed of my Father, receive the kingdom prepared for you from the beginning of the world." Grant this, O merciful Father, through Jesus Christ, our Mediator and Redeemer. *Amen.*

Grant, O Lord, to all who are bereaved the spirit of faith and courage, that they may have strength to meet the days to come with steadfastness and patience; not sorrowing as those without hope, but in thankful remembrance of your great goodness, and in the joyful expectation of eternal life with those they love. And this we ask in the Name of Jesus Christ our Savior. *Amen.*

Almighty God, Father of mercies and giver of comfort: Deal graciously, we pray, with all who mourn; that, casting all their care on you, they may know the consolation of your love; through Jesus Christ our Lord. *Amen.*

# An Order for Burial

*When, for pastoral considerations, neither of the burial rites in this Book is deemed appropriate, the following form is used.*

1. The body is received. The celebrant may meet the body and conduct it into the church or chapel, or it may be in place before the congregation assembles.

2. Anthems from Holy Scripture or psalms may be sung or said, or a hymn may be sung.

3. Prayer may be offered for the bereaved.

4. One or more passages of Holy Scripture are read. Psalms, hymns, or anthems may follow the readings. If there is to be a Communion, the last Reading is from the Gospel.

5. A homily may follow the Readings, and the Apostles' Creed may be recited.

6. Prayer, including the Lord's Prayer, is offered for the deceased, for those who mourn, and for the Christian community, remembering the promises of God in Christ about eternal life.

7. The deceased is commended to God, and the body is committed to its resting place. The committal may take place either where the preceding service has been held, or at the graveside.

8. If there is a Communion, it precedes the commendation, and begins with the Peace and Offertory of the Eucharist. Any of the authorized eucharistic prayers may be used.

**Note:**

*The liturgy for the dead is an Easter liturgy. It finds all its meaning in the resurrection. Because Jesus was raised from the dead, we, too, shall be raised.*

*The liturgy, therefore, is characterized by joy, in the certainty that 'neither death, nor life, nor angels, nor principalities, nor things present, nor things to come, nor powers, nor height, nor depth, nor anything else in all creation, will be able to separate us from the love of God in Christ Jesus our Lord."*

*This joy, however, does not make human grief unchristian. The very love we have for each other in Christ brings deep sorrow when we are parted by death. Jesus himself wept at the grave of his friend. So, while we rejoice that one we love has entered into the nearer presence of our Lord, we sorrow in sympathy with those who mourn.*

# Episcopal Services

# Preface to the Ordination Rites

The Holy Scriptures and ancient Christian writers make it clear that from the apostles' time, there have been different ministries within the Church. In particular, since the time of the New Testament, three distinct orders of ordained ministers have been characteristic of Christ's holy catholic Church. First, there is the order of bishops who carry on the apostolic work of leading, supervising, and uniting the Church. Secondly, associated with them are the presbyters, or ordained elders, in subsequent times generally known as priests. Together with the bishops, they take part in the governance of the Church, in the carrying out of its missionary and pastoral work, and in the preaching of the Word of God and administering his holy Sacraments. Thirdly, there are deacons who assist bishops and priests in all of this work. It is also a special responsibility of deacons to minister in Christ's name to the poor, the sick, the suffering, and the helpless.

The persons who are chosen and recognized by the Church as being called by God to the ordained ministry are admitted to these sacred orders by solemn prayer and the laying on of episcopal hands. It has been, and is, the intention and purpose of this Church to maintain and continue these three orders; and for this purpose these services of ordination and consecration are appointed. No persons are allowed to exercise the offices of bishop, priest, or deacon in this Church unless they are so ordained, or have already received such ordination with the laying on of hands by bishops who are themselves duly qualified to confer Holy Orders.

It is also recognized and affirmed that the threefold ministry is not the exclusive property of this portion of Christ's catholic Church, but is a gift from God for the nurture of his people and the proclamation of his Gospel everywhere. Accordingly, the manner of ordaining in this Church is to be such as has been, and is, most generally recognized by Christian people as suitable for the conferring of the sacred orders of bishop, priest, and deacon.

# Concerning the
# Ordination of a Bishop

In accordance with ancient custom, it is desirable, if possible, that bishops be ordained on Sundays and other feasts of our Lord or on the feasts of apostles or evangelists.

When a bishop is to be ordained, the Presiding Bishop of the Church, or a bishop appointed by the Presiding Bishop, presides and serves as chief consecrator. At least two other bishops serve as co-consecrators. Representatives of the presbyterate, diaconate, and laity of the diocese for which the new bishop is to be consecrated, are assigned appropriate duties in the service.

From the beginning of the service until the Offertory, the chief consecrator presides from a chair placed close to the people, so that all may see and hear what is done. The other bishops, or a convenient number of them, sit to the right and left of the chief consecrator.

The bishop-elect is vested in a rochet or alb, without stole, tippet, or other vesture distinctive of ecclesiastical or academic rank or order.

When the bishop-elect is presented, *his* full name (designated by the symbol N.N.) is used. Thereafter, it is appropriate to refer to *him* only by the Christian name by which *he* wishes to be known.

At the Offertory, it is appropriate that the bread and wine be brought to the Altar by the family or friends of the newly ordained.

The family of the newly ordained may receive Communion before other members of the congregation. Opportunity is always given to the people to communicate.

Additional Directions are on page 552.

# The Ordination of a Bishop

*Hymns, psalms, and anthems may be sung during the entrance of the bishops and other ministers.*

*The people standing, the Bishop appointed says*

        Blessed be God: Father, Son, and Holy Spirit.
*People*     And blessed be his kingdom, now and for ever.
        Amen.

*In place of the above, from Easter Day through the Day of Pentecost*

*Bishop*    Alleluia. Christ is risen.
*People*    The Lord is risen indeed. Alleluia.

*In Lent and on other penitential occasions*

*Bishop*    Bless the Lord who forgives all our sins.
*People*    His mercy endures for ever.

*The Bishop then says*

Almighty God, to you all hearts are open, all desires known, and from you no secrets are hid: Cleanse the thoughts of our hearts by the inspiration of your Holy Spirit, that we may perfectly love you, and worthily magnify your holy Name; through Christ our Lord. *Amen.*

# The Presentation

*The bishops and people sit. Representatives of the diocese, both Priests and Lay Persons, standing before the Presiding Bishop, present the Bishop-elect, saying*

N., Bishop in the Church of God, the clergy and people of the Diocese of N., trusting in the guidance of the Holy Spirit, have chosen N.N. to be a bishop and chief pastor. We therefore ask you to lay your hands upon *him* and in the power of the Holy Spirit to consecrate *him* a bishop in the one, holy, catholic, and apostolic Church.

*The Presiding Bishop then directs that testimonials of the election be read.*

*When the reading of the testimonials is ended, the Presiding Bishop requires the following promise from the Bishop-elect*

In the Name of the Father, and of the Son, and of the Holy Spirit, I, N.N., chosen Bishop of the Church in N., solemnly declare that I do believe the Holy Scriptures of the Old and New Testaments to be the Word of God, and to contain all things necessary to salvation; and I do solemnly engage to conform to the doctrine, discipline, and worship of The Episcopal Church.

*The Bishop-elect then signs the above Declaration in the sight of all present. The witnesses add their signatures.*

*All stand.*

*The Presiding Bishop then says the following, or similar words, and asks the response of the people*

Brothers and sisters in Christ Jesus, you have heard testimony given that *N.N.* has been duly and lawfully elected to be a bishop of the Church of God to serve in the Diocese of *N.* You have been assured of *his* suitability and that the Church has approved *him* for this sacred responsibility. Nevertheless, if any of you know any reason why we should not proceed, let it now be made known.

*If no objection is made, the Presiding Bishop continues*

Is it your will that we ordain *N.* a bishop?

*The People respond in these or other words*

That is our will.

*Presiding Bishop*

Will you uphold *N.* as bishop?

*The People respond in these or other words*

We will.

*The Presiding Bishop then says*

The Scriptures tell us that our Savior Christ spent the whole night in prayer before he chose and sent forth his twelve apostles. Likewise, the apostles prayed before they appointed Matthias to be one of their number. Let us, therefore, follow their examples, and offer our prayers to Almighty God before we ordain *N.* for the work to which we trust the Holy Spirit has called *him.*

*kneel, and the Person appointed leads the Litany for Ordinations, or*
*one other approved litany. At the end of the litany, after the Kyries, the*
*Presiding Bishop stands and reads the Collect for the Day, or the*
*following Collect, or both, first saying*

The Lord be with you
*People* And also with you.

*Let us pray.*

God of unchangeable power and eternal light: Look
favorably on your whole Church, that wonderful and sacred
mystery; by the effectual working of your providence, carry
out in tranquillity the plan of salvation; let the whole world
see and know that things which were cast down are being
raised up, and things which had grown old are being made
new, and that all things are being brought to their perfection
by him through whom all things were made, your Son Jesus
Christ our Lord; who lives and reigns with you, in the unity
of the Holy Spirit, one God, for ever and ever. *Amen.*


# The Ministry of the Word

*Three Lessons are read. Lay persons read the Old Testament Lesson and*
*the Epistle.*

*The Readings are ordinarily selected from the following list and may be*
*lengthened if desired. On a Major Feast or on a Sunday, the Presiding*
*Bishop may select Readings from the Proper of the Day.*

*Old Testament*   Isaiah 61:1-8,   *or* Isaiah 42:1-9

*Psalm*   99,   *or* 40:1-14,   *or* 100

*Epistle*   Hebrews 5:1-10,   *or* 1 Timothy 3:1-7,   *or* 2 Corinthians 3:4-9

*The Reader first says*

A Reading (Lesson) from _____ .

*A citation giving chapter and verse may be added.*

*After each Reading, the Reader may say*

> The Word of the Lord.
>
> People    Thanks be to God.

*or the Reader may say*    Here ends the Reading (Epistle).

*Silence may follow.*

*A Psalm, canticle, or hymn follows each Reading.*

*Then, all standing, a Deacon or a Priest reads the Gospel, first saying*

> The Holy Gospel of our Lord Jesus Christ
> according to _____ .
>
> People    Glory to you, Lord Christ.

> John 20:19-23,   *or* John 17:1-9, 18-21,   *or* Luke 24:44-49a

*After the Gospel, the Reader says*

> The Gospel of the Lord.
>
> People    Praise to you, Lord Christ.

## The Sermon

*After the Sermon, the Congregation sings a hymn.*

# The Examination

*All now sit, except the bishop-elect, who stands facing the bishops. The Presiding Bishop addresses the bishop-elect*

My *brother*, the people have chosen you and have affirmed their trust in you by acclaiming your election. A bishop in God's holy Church is called to be one with the apostles in proclaiming Christ's resurrection and interpreting the Gospel, and to testify to Christ's sovereignty as Lord of lords and King of kings.

You are called to guard the faith, unity, and discipline of the Church; to celebrate and to provide for the administration of the sacraments of the New Covenant; to ordain priests and deacons and to join in ordaining bishops; and to be in all things a faithful pastor and wholesome example for the entire flock of Christ.

With your fellow bishops you will share in the leadership of the Church throughout the world. Your heritage is the faith of patriarchs, prophets, apostles, and martyrs, and those of every generation who have looked to God in hope. Your joy will be to follow him who came, not to be served, but to serve, and to give his life a ransom for many.

Are you persuaded that God has called you to the office of bishop?

*Answer*     I am so persuaded.

*The following questions are then addressed to the bishop-elect by one or more of the other bishops*

| | |
|---|---|
| *Bishop* | Will you accept this call and fulfill this trust in obedience to Christ? |
| *Answer* | I will obey Christ, and will serve in his name. |
| *Bishop* | Will you be faithful in prayer, and in the study of Holy Scripture, that you may have the mind of Christ? |
| *Answer* | I will, for he is my help. |
| *Bishop* | Will you boldly proclaim and interpret the Gospel of Christ, enlightening the minds and stirring up the conscience of your people? |
| *Answer* | I will, in the power of the Spirit. |
| *Bishop* | As a chief priest and pastor, will you encourage and support all baptized people in their gifts and ministries, nourish them from the riches of God's grace, pray for them without ceasing, and celebrate with them the sacraments of our redemption? |
| *Answer* | I will, in the name of Christ, the Shepherd and Bishop of our souls. |
| *Bishop* | Will you guard the faith, unity, and discipline of the Church? |
| *Answer* | I will, for the love of God. |
| *Bishop* | Will you share with your fellow bishops in the government of the whole Church; will you sustain your fellow presbyters and take counsel with them; will you guide and strengthen the deacons and all others who minister in the Church? |
| *Answer* | I will, by the grace given me. |
| *Bishop* | Will you be merciful to all, show compassion to the poor and strangers, and defend those who have no helper? |
| *Answer* | I will, for the sake of Christ Jesus. |

N., through these promises you have committed yourself to
God, to serve his Church in the office of bishop. We therefore
call upon you, chosen to be a guardian of the Church's faith,
to lead us in confessing that faith.

*Bishop-elect*

We believe in one God.

*Then all sing or say together*

We believe in one God,
  the Father, the Almighty,
  maker of heaven and earth,
  of all that is, seen and unseen.

We believe in one Lord, Jesus Christ,
  the only Son of God,
  eternally begotten of the Father,
  God from God, Light from Light,
  true God from true God,
  begotten, not made,
  of one Being with the Father.
  Through him all things were made.
  For us and for our salvation
    he came down from heaven:
  by the power of the Holy Spirit
    he became incarnate from the Virgin Mary,
    and was made man.
  For our sake he was crucified under Pontius Pilate;
    he suffered death and was buried.
    On the third day he rose again
      in accordance with the Scriptures;
    he ascended into heaven
      and is seated at the right hand of the Father.

He will come again in glory to judge the living and the dead,
    and his kingdom will have no end.

We believe in the Holy Spirit, the Lord, the giver of life,
    who proceeds from the Father and the Son.
With the Father and the Son he is worshiped and glorified.
He has spoken through the Prophets.
We believe in one holy catholic and apostolic Church.
We acknowledge one baptism for the forgiveness of sins.
We look for the resurrection of the dead,
    and the life of the world to come. Amen.

# The Consecration of the Bishop

*All continue to stand, except the bishop-elect, who kneels before the Presiding Bishop. The other bishops stand to the right and left of the Presiding Bishop.*

*The hymn, Veni Creator Spiritus, or the hymn, Veni Sancte Spiritus, is sung.*

*A period of silent prayer follows, the people still standing.*

*The Presiding Bishop then begins this Prayer of Consecration*

God and Father of our Lord Jesus Christ, Father of mercies and God of all comfort, dwelling on high but having regard for the lowly, knowing all things before they come to pass: We give you thanks that from the beginning you have gathered and prepared a people to be heirs of the covenant of Abraham, and have raised up prophets, kings, and priests, never leaving your temple untended. We praise you also that from the creation you have graciously accepted the ministry of those whom you have chosen.

*e Presiding Bishop and other Bishops now lay their hands upon the
ad of the bishop-elect, and say together*

erefore, Father, make N. a bishop in your Church. Pour
t upon *him* the power of your princely Spirit, whom you
stowed upon your beloved Son Jesus Christ, with whom he
dowed the apostles, and by whom your Church is built up in
ery place, to the glory and unceasing praise of your Name.

*e Presiding Bishop continues*

you, O Father, all hearts are open; fill, we pray, the heart
this your servant whom you have chosen to be a bishop in
ur Church, with such love of you and of all the people, that
may feed and tend the flock of Christ, and exercise
tled *him*, serving before you day and night in the ministry
reconciliation, declaring pardon in your Name, offering the
ly gifts, and wisely overseeing the life and work of the
urch. In all things may *he* present before you the acceptable
ering of a pure, and gentle, and holy life; through Jesus
rist your Son, to whom, with you and the Holy Spirit, be
nor and power and glory in the Church, now and for ever.

*e People in a loud voice respond* Amen.

*new bishop is now vested according to the order of bishops.*

*ible is presented with these words*

ceive the Holy Scriptures. Feed the flock of Christ
nmitted to your charge, guard and defend them in his
th, and be a faithful steward of his holy Word and
craments.

*r this other symbols of office may be given.*

*The Presiding Bishop presents to the people their new bishop.*

*The Clergy and People offer their acclamation and applause.*

## The Peace

*The new Bishop then says*

The peace of the Lord be always with you.

People　　And also with you.

*The Presiding Bishop and other Bishops greet the new bishop.*

*The People greet one another.*

*The new Bishop also greets other members of the clergy, family members, and the congregation.*

*The new Bishop, if the Bishop of the Diocese, may now be escorted to the episcopal chair.*


## At the Celebration of the Eucharist

*The liturgy continues with the Offertory.*

*Deacons prepare the Table.*

*Then the new Bishop goes to the Lord's Table as chief Celebrant and, joined by other bishops and presbyters, proceeds with the celebration of the Eucharist.*


## After Communion

*In place of the usual postcommunion prayer, one of the bishops leads the people in the following*

mighty Father, we thank you for feeding us with the holy
od of the Body and Blood of your Son, and for uniting us
rough him in the fellowship of your Holy Spirit. We thank
u for raising up among us faithful servants for the ministry
your Word and Sacraments. We pray that N. may be to us
effective example in word and action, in love and patience,
d in holiness of life. Grant that we, with *him,* may serve
u now, and always rejoice in your glory; through Jesus
rist your Son our Lord, who lives and reigns with you and
: Holy Spirit, one God, now and for ever. Amen.

*new Bishop blesses the people, first saying*

|  |  |
|---|---|
|  | Our help is in the Name of the Lord; |
| *ple* | The maker of heaven and earth. |
| *v Bishop* | Blessed be the Name of the Lord; |
| *ple* | From this time forth for evermore. |
| *v Bishop* | The blessing, mercy, and grace of God Almighty, the Father, the Son, and the Holy Spirit, be upon you, and remain with you for ever. *Amen.* |

*eacon dismisses the people*

|  |  |
|---|---|
|  | Let us go forth into the world, rejoicing in the power of the Spirit. |
| *le* | Thanks be to God. |

*ı Easter Day through the Day of Pentecost "Alleluia, alleluia," may
dded to the dismissal and to the response.*

# Concerning the Service

When a bishop is to confer Holy Orders, at least two presbyters must be present.

From the beginning of the service until the Offertory, the bishop presides from a chair placed close to the people, and facing them, so that all may see and hear what is done.

The ordinand is to be vested in surplice or alb, without stole, tippet, or other vesture distinctive of ecclesiastical or academic rank or order.

When the ordinand is presented, *his* full name (designated by the symbol *N.N.*) is used. Thereafter, it is appropriate to refer to *him* only by the Christian name by which *he* wishes to be known.

At the Offertory, it is appropriate that the bread and wine be brought to the Altar by the family and friends of the newly ordained.

At the Great Thanksgiving, the new priest and other priests stand at the Altar with the bishop, as associates and fellow ministers of the Sacrament, and communicate with the bishop.

The family of the newly ordained may receive Communion before other members of the congregation. Opportunity is always given to the people to communicate.

Additional Directions are on page 552.

# The Ordination of a Priest

*A hymn, psalm, or anthem may be sung.*

*The people standing, the Bishop says*

       Blessed be God: Father, Son, and Holy Spirit.
*People*    And blessed be his kingdom, now and for ever.
       Amen.

*In place of the above, from Easter Day through the Day of Pentecost*

*Bishop*    Alleluia. Christ is risen.
*People*    The Lord is risen indeed. Alleluia.

*In Lent and on other penitential occasions*

*Bishop*    Bless the Lord who forgives all our sins.
*People*    His mercy endures for ever.

*Bishop*

Almighty God, to you all hearts are open, all desires known, and from you no secrets are hid: Cleanse the thoughts of our hearts by the inspiration of your Holy Spirit, that we may perfectly love you, and worthily magnify your holy Name; through Christ our Lord. *Amen.*

# The Presentation

*The bishop and people sit. A Priest and a Lay Person, and additional presenters if desired, standing before the bishop, present the ordinand, saying*

N., Bishop in the Church of God, on behalf of the clergy and people of the Diocese of N., we present to you N.N. to be ordained a priest in Christ's holy catholic Church.

*Bishop*

Has *he* been selected in accordance with the canons of this Church? And do you believe *his* manner of life to be suitable to the exercise of this ministry?

*Presenters*

We certify to you that *he* has satisfied the requirements of the canons, and we believe *him* to be qualified for this order.

*The Bishop says to the ordinand*

Will you be loyal to the doctrine, discipline, and worship of Christ as this Church has received them? And will you, in accordance with the canons of this Church, obey your bishop and other ministers who may have authority over you and your work?

*Answer*

I am willing and ready to do so; and I solemnly declare that I do believe the Holy Scriptures of the Old and New Testaments to be the Word of God, and to contain all things necessary to salvation; and I do solemnly engage to conform to the doctrine, discipline, and worship of The Episcopal Church.

*The Ordinand then signs the above Declaration in the sight of all present.*

*All stand. The Bishop says to the people*

Dear friends in Christ, you know the importance of this ministry, and the weight of your responsibility in presenting N.N. for ordination to the sacred priesthood. Therefore if any of you know any impediment or crime because of which we should not proceed, come forward now, and make it known.

*If no objection is made, the Bishop continues*

Is it your will that N. be ordained a priest?

*The People respond in these or other words*

It is.

*Bishop*

Will you uphold *him* in this ministry?

*The People respond in these or other words*

We will.

*The Bishop then calls the people to prayer with these or similar words*

In peace let us pray to the Lord.

*All kneel, and the Person appointed leads the Litany for Ordinations, or some other approved litany. At the end of the litany, after the Kyries, the Bishop stands and reads the Collect for the Day, or the following Collect, or both, first saying*

       The Lord be with you.
*People*    And also with you.

Let us pray.

O God of unchangeable power and eternal light: Look favorably on your whole Church, that wonderful and sacred mystery; by the effectual working of your providence, carry out in tranquillity the plan of salvation; let the whole world see and know that things which were cast down are being raised up, and things which had grown old are being made new, and that all things are being brought to their perfection by him through whom all things were made, your Son Jesus Christ our Lord; who lives and reigns with you, in the unity of the Holy Spirit, one God, for ever and ever. *Amen.*

# The Ministry of the Word

*Three Lessons are read. Lay persons read the Old Testament Lesson and the Epistle.*

*The Readings are ordinarily selected from the following list and may be lengthened if desired. On a Major Feast, or on a Sunday, the Bishop may select Readings from the Proper of the Day.*

*Old Testament*    Isaiah 6:1-8,   *or* Numbers 11:16-17, 24-25
(omitting the final clause)

*Psalm*   43,   *or* 132:8-19

*Epistle*   1 Peter 5:1-4,*   *or* Ephesians 4:7, 11-16,   *or* Philippians 4:4-9

*It is to be noted that where the words elder, elders, and fellow elder, appear in translations of 1 Peter 5:1, the original Greek terms presbyter, presbyters, and fellow presbyter, are to be substituted.*

*The Reader first says*

A Reading (Lesson) from _____ .

*A citation giving chapter and verse may be added.*

*fter each Reading, the Reader may say*

The Word of the Lord.
*eople*      Thanks be to God.

*r the Reader may say*      Here ends the Reading (Epistle).

*lence may follow.*

*Psalm, canticle, or hymn follows each Reading.*

*hen, all standing, the Deacon or, if no deacon is present, a Priest reads*
*ie Gospel, first saying*

The Holy Gospel of our Lord Jesus Christ
according to _____.
*eople*      Glory to you, Lord Christ.

Matthew 9:35-38,   *or* John 10:11-18,   *or* John 6:35-38

*fter the Gospel, the Reader says*

The Gospel of the Lord.
*eople*      Praise to you, Lord Christ.


## he Sermon


*he Congregation then says or sings the Nicene Creed*

Ve believe in one God,
  the Father, the Almighty,
  maker of heaven and earth,
  of all that is, seen and unseen.

We believe in one Lord, Jesus Christ,
    the only Son of God,
    eternally begotten of the Father,
    God from God, Light from Light,
    true God from true God,
    begotten, not made,
    of one Being with the Father.
    Through him all things were made.
    For us and for our salvation
        he came down from heaven:
    by the power of the Holy Spirit
        he became incarnate from the Virgin Mary,
        and was made man.
    For our sake he was crucified under Pontius Pilate;
        he suffered death and was buried.
        On the third day he rose again
            in accordance with the Scriptures;
        he ascended into heaven
            and is seated at the right hand of the Father.
    He will come again in glory to judge the living and the dead,
        and his kingdom will have no end.

We believe in the Holy Spirit, the Lord, the giver of life,
    who proceeds from the Father and the Son.
    With the Father and the Son he is worshiped and glorified.
    He has spoken through the Prophets.
    We believe in one holy catholic and apostolic Church.
    We acknowledge one baptism for the forgiveness of sins.
    We look for the resurrection of the dead,
        and the life of the world to come. Amen.

# The Examination

*All are seated except the ordinand, who stands before the Bishop.*

*The Bishop addresses the ordinand as follows*

My *brother,* the Church is the family of God, the body of Christ, and the temple of the Holy Spirit. All baptized people are called to make Christ known as Savior and Lord, and to share in the renewing of his world. Now you are called to work as a pastor, priest, and teacher, together with your bishop and fellow presbyters, and to take your share in the councils of the Church.

As a priest, it will be your task to proclaim by word and deed the Gospel of Jesus Christ, and to fashion your life in accordance with its precepts. You are to love and serve the people among whom you work, caring alike for young and old, strong and weak, rich and poor. You are to preach, to declare God's forgiveness to penitent sinners, to pronounce God's blessing, to share in the administration of Holy Baptism and in the celebration of the mysteries of Christ's Body and Blood, and to perform the other ministrations entrusted to you.

In all that you do, you are to nourish Christ's people from the riches of his grace, and strengthen them to glorify God in this life and in the life to come.

My *brother,* do you believe that you are truly called by God and his Church to this priesthood?

| | |
|---|---|
| *Answer* | I believe I am so called. |
| *Bishop* | Do you now in the presence of the Church commit yourself to this trust and responsibility? |
| *Answer* | I do. |

| | |
|---|---|
| *Bishop* | Will you respect and be guided by the pastoral direction and leadership of your bishop? |
| *Answer* | I will. |
| *Bishop* | Will you be diligent in the reading and study of the Holy Scriptures, and in seeking the knowledge of such things as may make you a stronger and more able minister of Christ? |
| *Answer* | I will. |
| *Bishop* | Will you endeavor so to minister the Word of God and the sacraments of the New Covenant, that the reconciling love of Christ may be known and received? |
| *Answer* | I will. |
| *Bishop* | Will you undertake to be a faithful pastor to all whom you are called to serve, laboring together with them and with your fellow ministers to build up the family of God? |
| *Answer* | I will. |
| *Bishop* | Will you do your best to pattern your life [and that of your family, *or* household, *or* community] in accordance with the teachings of Christ, so that you may be a wholesome example to your people? |
| *Answer* | I will. |
| *Bishop* | Will you persevere in prayer, both in public and in private, asking God's grace, both for yourself and for others, offering all your labors to God, through the mediation of Jesus Christ, and in the sanctification of the Holy Spirit? |
| *Answer* | I will. |
| *Bishop* | May the Lord who has given you the will to do these things give you the grace and power to perform the. |
| *Answer* | Amen. |

# The Consecration of the Priest

*All now stand except the ordinand, who kneels facing the Bishop and the presbyters who stand to the right and left of the Bishop.*

*The hymn, Veni Creator Spiritus, or the hymn, Veni Sancte Spiritus, is sung.*

*A period of silent prayer follows, the people still standing.*

*The Bishop then says this Prayer of Consecration*

God and Father of all, we praise you for your infinite love in calling us to be a holy people in the kingdom of your Son Jesus our Lord, who is the image of your eternal and invisible glory, the firstborn among many brethren, and the head of the Church. We thank you that by his death he has overcome death, and, having ascended into heaven, has poured his gifts abundantly upon your people, making some apostles, some prophets, some evangelists, some pastors and teachers, to equip the saints for the work of ministry and the building up of his body.

*Here the Bishop lays hands upon the head of the ordinand, the priests who are present also laying on their hands. At the same time the Bishop prays*

Therefore, Father, through Jesus Christ your Son, give your Holy Spirit to N.; fill *him* with grace and power, and make *him* a priest in your Church.

*The Bishop then continues*

May *he* exalt you, O Lord, in the midst of your people; offer spiritual sacrifices acceptable to you; boldly proclaim the gospel of salvation; and rightly administer the sacraments of the New Covenant. Make *him* a faithful pastor, a patient teacher, and a wise councilor. Grant that in all things *he* may serve without reproach, so that your people may be strengthened and your Name glorified in all the world. All this we ask through Jesus Christ our Lord, who with you and the Holy Spirit lives and reigns, one God, for ever and ever.

*The People in a loud voice respond*     Amen.

*The new priest is now vested according to the order of priests.*

*The Bishop then gives a Bible to the newly ordained, saying*

Receive this Bible as a sign of the authority given you to preach the Word of God and to administer his holy Sacraments. Do not forget the trust committed to you as a priest of the Church of God.

*The Bishop greets the newly ordained.*


## The Peace

*The new Priest then says to the congregation*

　　　　The peace of the Lord be always with you.
People　　And also with you.

*The Presbyters present greet the newly ordained; who then greets family members and others, as may be convenient. The Clergy and People greet one another.*

## the Celebration of the Eucharist

*The liturgy continues with the Offertory. Deacons prepare the Table.*

*Standing at the Lord's Table, with the Bishop and other presbyters, the newly ordained Priest joins in the celebration of the Holy Eucharist and the Breaking of the Bread.*

## After Communion

*In place of the usual postcommunion prayer, the following is said*

Almighty Father, we thank you for feeding us with the holy food of the Body and Blood of your Son, and for uniting us through him in the fellowship of your Holy Spirit. We thank you for raising up among us faithful servants for the ministry of your Word and Sacraments. We pray that N. may be to us an effective example in word and action, in love and patience, and in holiness of life. Grant that we, with *him*, may serve you now, and always rejoice in your glory; through Jesus Christ your Son our Lord, who lives and reigns with you and the Holy Spirit, one God, now and for ever. *Amen.*

*The Bishop then asks the new priest to bless the people.*

*The new Priest says*

The blessing of God Almighty, the Father, the Son, and the Holy Spirit, be among you, and remain with you always. *Amen.*

*A Deacon, or a Priest if no deacon is present, dismisses the people.*

> Let us go forth into the world, rejoicing in the
> power of the Spirit.

*People*    Thanks be to God.

*From Easter Day through the Day of Pentecost "Alleluia, alleluia," may be added to the dismissal and to the response.*

# Concerning the Service

When a bishop is to confer Holy Orders, at least two presbyters must be present.

From the beginning of the service until the Offertory, the bishop preside from a chair placed close to the people, and facing them, so that all may see and hear what is done.

The ordinand is to be vested in a surplice or alb, without tippet or other vesture distinctive of ecclesiastical or academic rank or office.

When the ordinand is presented, *his* full name (designated by the symbo *N.N.*) is used. Thereafter, it is appropriate to refer to *him* only by the Christian name by which *he* wishes to be known.

At the Offertory, it is appropriate that the bread and wine be brought to the Altar by the family or friends of the newly ordained.

After receiving Holy Communion, the new deacon assists in the distribution of the Sacrament, ministering either the Bread or the Wine, or both.

The family of the newly ordained may receive Communion before other members of the congregation. Opportunity is always given to the people to communicate.

Additional Directions are on page 552.

# The Ordination of a Deacon

*A hymn, psalm, or anthem may be sung.*

*The people standing, the Bishop says*

      Blessed be God: Father, Son, and Holy Spirit.
People     And blessed be his kingdom, now and for ever. Amen.

*In place of the above, from Easter Day through the Day of Pentecost*

Bishop    Alleluia. Christ is risen.
People    The Lord is risen indeed. Alleluia.

*In Lent and on other penitential occasions*

Bishop    Bless the Lord who forgives all our sins.
People    His mercy endures for ever.

*Bishop*

Almighty God, to you all hearts are open, all desires known, and from you no secrets are hid: Cleanse the thoughts of our hearts by the inspiration of your Holy Spirit, that we may perfectly love you, and worthily magnify your holy Name; through Christ our Lord. *Amen.*

# The Presentation

*The bishop and people sit. A Priest and a Lay Person, and additional*
*presenters if desired, standing before the bishop, present the ordinand,*
*saying*

N., Bishop in the Church of God, on behalf of the clergy and
people of the Diocese of N., we present to you N.N. to be
ordained a deacon in Christ's holy catholic Church.

*Bishop*

Has *he* been selected in accordance with the canons of this
Church? And do you believe *his* manner of life to be suitable
to the exercise of this ministry?

*Presenters*

We certify to you that *he* has satisfied the requirements of the
canons, and we believe *him* qualified for this order.

*The Bishop says to the ordinand*

Will you be loyal to the doctrine, discipline, and worship of
Christ as this Church has received them? And will you, in
accordance with the canons of this Church, obey your bishop
and other ministers who may have authority over you and
your work?

*Answer*

I am willing and ready to do so; and I solemnly declare that I
do believe the Holy Scriptures of the Old and New Testaments
to be the Word of God, and to contain all things necessary to
salvation; and I do solemnly engage to conform to the doctrine,
discipline, and worship of The Episcopal Church.

*The Ordinand then signs the above Declaration in the sight of all present.*

*All stand. The Bishop says to the people*

Dear friends in Christ, you know the importance of this ministry, and the weight of your responsibility in presenting N.N. for ordination to the sacred order of deacons. Therefore if any of you know any impediment or crime because of which we should not proceed, come forward now and make it known.

*If no objection is made, the Bishop continues*

Is it your will that N. be ordained a deacon?

*The People respond in these or other words*

It is.

*Bishop*

Will you uphold *him* in this ministry?

*The People respond in these or other words*

We will.

*The Bishop then calls the people to prayer with these or similar words*

In peace let us pray to the Lord.

*All kneel, and the Person appointed leads the Litany for Ordinations, or some other approved litany. At the end of the litany, after the Kyries, the Bishop stands and reads the Collect for the Day, or the following Collect, or both, first saying*

|           | The Lord be with you. |
|-----------|------------------------|
| *People*  | And also with you.     |

Let us pray.

O God of unchangeable power and eternal light: Look favorably on your whole Church, that wonderful and sacred mystery; by the effectual working of your providence, carry out in tranquillity the plan of salvation; let the whole world see and know that things which were cast down are being raised up, and things which had grown old are being made new, and that all things are being brought to their perfection by him through whom all things were made, your Son Jesus Christ our Lord; who lives and reigns with you, in the unity of the Holy Spirit, one God, for ever and ever. *Amen.*

# The Ministry of the Word

*Three Lessons are read. Lay persons read the Old Testament Lesson and the Epistle.*

*The Readings are ordinarily selected from the following list and may be lengthened if desired. On a Major Feast, or on a Sunday, the Bishop may select Readings from the Proper of the Day.*

*Old Testament*   Jeremiah 1:4-9,   *or* Ecclesiasticus 39:1-8
*Psalm*   84,   *or* 119:33-40
*Epistle*   2 Corinthians 4:1-6,   *or* 1 Timothy 3:8-13,   *or* Acts 6:2-7

*The Reader first says*

A Reading (Lesson) from _____ .

*A citation giving chapter and verse may be added.*

*After each Reading, the Reader may say*

>The Word of the Lord.

People    Thanks be to God.

*or the Reader may say*    Here ends the Reading (Epistle).

*Silence may follow.*

*A Psalm, canticle, or hymn follows each Reading.*

*Then, all standing, the Deacon or, if no deacon is present, a Priest reads the Gospel, first saying*

>The Holy Gospel of our Lord Jesus Christ
>according to _____ .

People    Glory to you, Lord Christ.

>Luke 12:35-38,   *or* Luke 22:24-27

*After the Gospel, the Reader says*

>The Gospel of the Lord.

People    Praise to you, Lord Christ.

## The Sermon

*The Congregation then says or sings the Nicene Creed*

We believe in one God,
    the Father, the Almighty,
    maker of heaven and earth,
    of all that is, seen and unseen.

We believe in one Lord, Jesus Christ,
   the only Son of God,
   eternally begotten of the Father,
   God from God, Light from Light,
   true God from true God,
   begotten, not made,
   of one Being with the Father.
   Through him all things were made.
   For us and for our salvation
      he came down from heaven:
   by the power of the Holy Spirit
      he became incarnate from the Virgin Mary,
      and was made man.
   For our sake he was crucified under Pontius Pilate;
      he suffered death and was buried.
      On the third day he rose again
         in accordance with the Scriptures;
      he ascended into heaven
         and is seated at the right hand of the Father.
   He will come again in glory to judge the living and the dead,
      and his kingdom will have no end.

We believe in the Holy Spirit, the Lord, the giver of life,
   who proceeds from the Father and the Son.
   With the Father and the Son he is worshiped and glorified.
   He has spoken through the Prophets.
   We believe in one holy catholic and apostolic Church.
   We acknowledge one baptism for the forgiveness of sins.
   We look for the resurrection of the dead,
      and the life of the world to come. Amen.

# The Examination

*All are seated except the ordinand, who stands before the Bishop.*
*The Bishop addresses the ordinand as follows*

My *brother*, every Christian is called to follow Jesus Christ,
serving God the Father, through the power of the Holy Spirit.
God now calls you to a special ministry of servanthood
directly under your bishop. In the name of Jesus Christ, you
are to serve all people, particularly the poor, the weak, the
sick, and the lonely.

As a deacon in the Church, you are to study the Holy
Scriptures, to seek nourishment from them, and to model
your life upon them. You are to make Christ and his
redemptive love known, by your word and example, to those
among whom you live, and work, and worship. You are to
interpret to the Church the needs, concerns, and hopes of the
world. You are to assist the bishop and priests in public
worship and in the ministration of God's Word and
Sacraments, and you are to carry out other duties assigned to
you from time to time. At all times, your life and teaching are
to show Christ's people that in serving the helpless they are
serving Christ himself.

My *brother*, do you believe that you are truly called by God
and his Church to the life and work of a deacon?

Answer  I believe I am so called.

Bishop  Do you now in the presence of the Church commit
yourself to this trust and responsibility?

Answer  I do.

Bishop  Will you be guided by the pastoral direction and
leadership of your bishop?

Answer  I will.

| | |
|---|---|
| *Bishop* | Will you be faithful in prayer, and in the reading and study of the Holy Scriptures? |
| *Answer* | I will. |
| *Bishop* | Will you look for Christ in all others, being ready to help and serve those in need? |
| *Answer* | I will. |
| *Bishop* | Will you do your best to pattern your life [and that of your family, *or* household, *or* community] in accordance with the teachings of Christ, so that you may be a wholesome example to all people? |
| *Answer* | I will. |
| *Bishop* | Will you in all things seek not your glory but the glory of the Lord Christ? |
| *Answer* | I will. |
| *Bishop* | May the Lord by his grace uphold you in the service he lays upon you. |
| *Answer* | Amen. |

# The Consecration of the Deacon

*All now stand except the ordinand, who kneels facing the bishop.*

*The hymn, Veni Creator Spiritus, or the hymn, Veni Sancte Spiritus, is sung.*

*A period of silent prayer follows, the people still standing.*

*The Bishop then says this Prayer of Consecration*

O God, most merciful Father, we praise you for sending your Son Jesus Christ, who took on himself the form of a servant, and humbled himself, becoming obedient even to death on the cross. We praise you that you have highly exalted him, and made him Lord of all; and that, through him, we know that whoever would be great must be servant of all. We praise you for the many ministries in your Church, and for calling this your servant to the order of deacons.

*Here the Bishop lays hands upon the head of the ordinand, and prays*

Therefore, Father, through Jesus Christ your Son, give your Holy Spirit to N.; fill *him* with grace and power, and make *him* a deacon in your Church.

*The Bishop then continues*

Make *him*, O Lord, modest and humble, strong and constant, to observe the discipline of Christ. Let *his* life and teaching so reflect your commandments, that through *him* many may come to know you and love you. As your Son came not to be served but to serve, may this deacon share in Christ's service, and come to the unending glory of him who, with you and the Holy Spirit, lives and reigns, one God, for ever and ever.

*The People in a loud voice respond*   Amen.

*The new deacon is now vested according to the order of deacons.*

*The Bishop gives a Bible to the newly ordained, saying*

Receive this Bible as the sign of your authority to proclaim God's Word and to assist in the ministration of his holy sacraments.

## The Peace

*The Bishop then says to the congregation*

The peace of the Lord be always with you.

People     And also with you.

*The Bishop and the Clergy present now greet the newly ordained.*

*The new Deacon then exchanges greetings with family members and others, as may be convenient.*

*The Clergy and People greet one another.*

## At the Celebration of the Eucharist

*The liturgy continues with the Offertory.*

*The newly ordained Deacon prepares the bread, pours sufficient wine (and a little water) into the chalice, and places the vessels on the Lord's Table.*

*The Bishop goes to the Table and begins the Great Thanksgiving.*

## After Communion

*In place of the usual postcommunion prayer, the following is said*

Almighty Father, we thank you for feeding us with the holy food of the Body and Blood of your Son, and for uniting us through him in the fellowship of your Holy Spirit. We thank you for raising up among us faithful servants for the ministry

of your Word and Sacraments. We pray that *N.* may be to us
an effective example in word and action, in love and patience,
and in holiness of life. Grant that we, with *him,* may serve
you now, and always rejoice in your glory; through Jesus
Christ your Son our Lord, who lives and reigns with you and
the Holy Spirit, one God, now and for ever. *Amen.*

*The Bishop blesses the people, after which the new Deacon dismisses
them*

>Let us go forth into the world,
>    rejoicing in the power of the Spirit.
*People*    Thanks be to God.

*From Easter Day through the Day of Pentecost, "Alleluia, alleluia" may
be added to the dismissal and to the response.*

# The Litany for Ordinations

*For use at Ordinations as directed. On Ember Days or other occasions, if desired, this Litany may be used for the Prayers of the People at the Eucharist or the Daily Office, or it may be used separately.*

God the Father,
*Have mercy on us.*

God the Son,
*Have mercy on us.*

God the Holy Spirit,
*Have mercy on us.*

Holy Trinity, one God,
*Have mercy on us.*

We pray to you, Lord Christ.
*Lord, hear our prayer.*

For the holy Church of God, that it may be filled with truth and love, and be found without fault at the Day of your Coming,
we pray to you, O Lord.
*Lord, hear our prayer.*

For all members of your Church in their vocation and ministry, that they may serve you in a true and godly life,
we pray to you, O Lord.
*Lord, hear our prayer.*

For N., our Presiding Bishop, and for all bishops, priests, and deacons, that they may be filled with your love, may hunger for truth, and may thirst after righteousness,
we pray to you, O Lord.
*Lord, hear our prayer.*

For N., chosen bishop (priest, deacon) in your Church,
we pray to you, O Lord.
*Lord, hear our prayer.*

That *he* may faithfully fulfill the duties of this ministry, build
up your Church, and glorify your Name,
we pray to you, O Lord.
*Lord, hear our prayer.*

That by the indwelling of the Holy Spirit *he* may be sustained
and encouraged to persevere to the end,
we pray to you, O Lord.
*Lord, hear our prayer.*

For *his* family [the members of *his* household *or* community],
that they may be adorned with all Christian virtues,
we pray to you, O Lord.
*Lord, hear our prayer.*

For all who fear God and believe in you, Lord Christ, that
our divisions may cease and that all may be one as you
and the Father are one,
we pray to you, O Lord.
*Lord, hear our prayer.*

For the mission of the Church, that in faithful witness it may
preach the Gospel to the ends of the earth,
we pray to you, O Lord.
*Lord, hear our prayer.*

For those who do not yet believe, and for those who have lost
their faith, that they may receive the light of the Gospel,
we pray to you, O Lord.
*Lord, hear our prayer.*

For the peace of the world, that a spirit of respect and
forbearance may grow among nations and peoples,
we pray to you, O Lord.
*Lord, hear our prayer.*

For those in positions of public trust [especially _____],
that they may serve justice and promote the dignity and
freedom of every person,
we pray to you, O Lord.
*Lord, hear our prayer.*

For a blessing upon all human labor, and for the right use
of the riches of creation, that the world may be freed from
poverty, famine, and disaster,
we pray to you, O Lord.
*Lord, hear our prayer.*

For the poor, the persecuted, the sick, and all who suffer; for
refugees, prisoners, and all who are in danger; that they may
be relieved and protected,
we pray to you, O Lord.
*Lord, hear our prayer.*

For ourselves; for the forgiveness of our sins, and for the
grace of the Holy Spirit to amend our lives,
we pray to you, O Lord.
*Lord, hear our prayer.*

For all who have died in the communion of your Church, and
those whose faith is known to you alone, that, with all the
saints, they may have rest in that place where there is no pain
or grief, but life eternal,
we pray to you, O Lord.
*Lord, hear our prayer.*

Rejoicing in the fellowship of [the ever-blessed Virgin Mary,
(*blessed N.*) and] all the saints, let us commend ourselves,
and one another, and all our life to Christ our God.
*To you, O Lord our God.*

Lord, have mercy.
*Christ, have mercy.*
Lord, have mercy.

*At ordinations, the Bishop who is presiding stands and says*

The Lord be with you.
*People*    And also with you.
*Bishop*    Let us pray.

*The Bishop says the appointed Collect.*

*When this Litany is used on other occasions, the Officiant concludes with a suitable Collect.*

# Additional Directions

## At all Ordinations

The celebration of the Holy Eucharist may be according to Rite One or Rite Two. In either case, the rubrics of the service of ordination are followed. The Summary of the Law, the Gloria in excelsis, the Prayers of the People after the Creed, the General Confession, and the usual postcommunion prayer are not used.

At the Presentation of the Ordinand, the Declaration "I do believe the Holy Scriptures . . ." is to be provided as a separate document to be signed, as directed by Article VIII of the Constitution of this Church and by the rubrics in each of the ordination rites. (When there are more ordinands than one, each is to be presented with a separate copy for signature.)

The hymn to the Holy Spirit before the Prayer of Consecration may be sung responsively between a bishop and the congregation, or in some other convenient manner.

If vestments or other symbols of office are to be dedicated, such blessing is to take place at some convenient time prior to the service. The following form may be used

V. Our help is in the Name of the Lord;
R. The maker of heaven and earth.
V. The Lord be with you.
R. And also with you.

Let us pray.

Everliving God, whose power is limitless, we place before you, with our praise and thanks, *these tokens* of your servant's ministry and dignity. Grant that N., who has been called to leadership in your Church, and bears *these signs*, may faithfully serve you and share in the fullness of your life-giving Spirit; through the high priest and good shepherd of us all, Jesus Christ our Lord. *Amen.*

## At the Ordination of a Bishop

Following the Consecration Prayer, and while the new bishop is being clothed with the vesture of the episcopate, instrumental music may be played.

Following the presentation of the Bible, and the formula "Receive the Holy Scriptures . . ." a ring, staff, and mitre, or other suitable insignia of office may be presented.

During the Eucharistic Prayer, it is appropriate that some of the consecrating bishops, and representative presbyters of the diocese, stand with the new bishop at the Altar as fellow ministers of the Sacrament.

The newly ordained bishop, assisted by other ministers, distributes Holy Communion to the people. When necessary, the administration may take place at several conveniently separated places in the church.

After the pontifical blessing and the dismissal, a hymn of praise may be sung.

The bishops who are present are not to depart without signing the Letters of Consecration.

## At the Ordination of a Priest

Reasonable opportunity is to be given for the priests present to join in the laying on of hands.

The stole worn about the neck, or other insignia of the office of priest, is placed upon the new priest after the entire Prayer of Consecration is completed, and immediately before the Bible is presented. Afterwards, other instruments or symbols of office may be given.

If two or more are ordained together, each is to have *his* own presenters. The ordinands may be presented together, or in succession, as the bishop may direct. Thereafter, references to the ordinand in the singular are changed to the plural where necessary. The ordinands are examined together.

During the Prayer of Consecration, the bishop and priests lay their hands upon the head of each ordinand. During the laying on of hands, the bishop alone says over each ordinand "Father, through Jesus Christ your

Son, give your Holy Spirit to N.; fill *him* with grace and power, and make *him* a priest in your Church." When they have laid their hands upon all the ordinands, the bishop continues "May they exalt you, O Lord, in the midst . . ."

A Bible is to be given to each new priest, and the words "Receive this Bible . . ." are to be said to each one.

All the newly ordained take part in the exchange of the Peace, and join the bishop and other priests at the Altar for the Great Thanksgiving. Similarly, all the new priests break the consecrated Bread and receive Holy Communion.

## At the Ordination of a Deacon

The stole worn over the left shoulder, or other insignia of the office of deacon, is placed upon the new deacon after the entire Prayer of Consecration is completed, and immediately before the Bible is given.

If two or more are ordained together, each is to have *his* own presenters. The ordinands may be presented together, or in succession, as the bishop may direct. Thereafter, references to the ordinand in the singular are changed to the plural where necessary. The ordinands are examined together.

During the Prayer of Consecration the Bishop is to lay hands upon the head of each ordinand, and say over each one "Father, through Jesus Christ your Son, give your Holy Spirit to N.; fill *him* with grace and power, and make *him* a deacon in your Church." After laying hands upon all the ordinands, the bishop continues "Make them, O Lord, modest and humble. . ."

A Bible is to be given to each new deacon, and the words "Receive this Bible . . ." are also to be said to each one.

After participating in the Peace, the deacons go to the Altar for the Offertory. If there are many deacons, some assist in the Offertory and others administer Holy Communion. One, appointed by the bishop, is to say the dismissal.

When desired, deacons may be appointed to carry the Sacrament and minister Holy Communion to those communicants who, because of sickness or other grave cause, could not be present at the ordination.

If the remaining Elements are not required for the Communion of the absent, it is appropriate for the deacons to remove the vessels from the Altar, consume the remaining Elements, and cleanse the vessels in some convenient place.

# Letter of Institution of a Minister

N.N., Presbyter of the Church of God, you have been called to work together with your Bishop and fellow-Presbyters as a pastor, priest, and teacher, and to take your share in the councils of the Church.

Now, in accordance with the Canons, you have been selected to serve God in _____ Church [of] _____.

This letter is a sign that you are fully empowered and authorized to exercise this ministry, accepting its privileges and responsibilities as a priest of this Diocese, in communion with your Bishop.

Having committed yourself to this work, do not forget the trust of those who have chosen you. Care alike for young and old, strong and weak, rich and poor. By your words, and in your life, proclaim the Gospel. Love and serve Christ's people. Nourish them, and strengthen them to glorify God in this life and in the life to come.

May the Lord, who has given you the will to do these things, give you the grace and power to perform them.

Given under my hand and seal, in the city of _____,
on the _____ day of _____, 19_____, and in
the _____ year of my consecration.

(Signed) _____
Bishop of _____.

# Concerning the Service

This order is for use when a priest is being instituted and inducted as the rector of a parish. It may also be used for the installation of deans and canons of cathedrals, or the inauguration of other ministries, diocesan or parochial, including vicars of missions and assistant ministers. Alterations in the service are then made according to circumstances.

The chief minister is normally the bishop; but, if necessary, a deputy may be appointed. The bishop, when present, is the chief celebrant of the Eucharist. In the bishop's absence, a priest being inducted is the chief celebrant.

Other priests, if any, who serve in the same congregation also stand with the chief celebrant at the Altar, and deacons assist according to their order.

Lay persons from the congregation read the Old Testament Lesson and the Epistle, and perform other actions as indicated in the rubrics. A deacon or priest reads the Gospel. Other clergy of the diocese participate in this celebration as an expression of the collegiality of the ministry in which they share.

Ministers of other Churches may appropriately be invited to participate.

The new minister, if a deacon, should read the Gospel, prepare the elements at the Offertory, assist the celebrant at the Altar, and dismiss the congregation.

A lay person being instituted should read one of the Lessons and assist where appropriate.

Additional Directions are on page 564.

# Celebration of a
# New Ministry

*A hymn, psalm, or anthem may be sung.*

## The Institution

*The Wardens, standing before the bishop with the new minister, say these or similar words*

Bishop N., we have come together today to welcome N.N., who has been chosen to serve as *Rector* of (*name of church*). We believe that *he* is well qualified, and that *he* has been prayerfully and lawfully selected.

*The Bishop may read the Letter of Institution, or else may state the purpose of the new ministry.*

*The Bishop then says*

N., do you, in the presence of this congregation, commit yourself to this new trust and responsibility?

*New minister*    I do.

*The Bishop then addresses the congregation*

Will you who witness this new beginning support and uphold N. in this ministry?

*People*    We will.

*The Bishop, standing, says*

Let us then offer our prayers to God for all his people, for this congregation, and for N. their *Rector*.

*The Litany for Ordinations, or some other appropriate litany, is led by a person appointed. At the end of the litany, the Bishop, standing, says the following or some other Collect, first saying*

|        | The Lord be with you. |
|--------|----------------------|
| People | And also with you. |
| Bishop | Let us pray. |

Everliving God, strengthen and sustain N., that with patience and understanding *he* may love and care for your people; and grant that together they may follow Jesus Christ, offering to you their gifts and talents; through him who lives and reigns with you and the Holy Spirit, one God, for ever and ever. *Amen.*

## At the Liturgy of the Word

*The Readings are selected from the following list, or in accordance with the directions on page 565.*

*Old Testament*  Joshua 1:7-9,  *or* Numbers 11:16-17, 24-25a
*Psalm*  43,  *or* 132:1-9,  *or* 146,  *or* 133 and 134 (especially suitable for use in the evening)
*Epistle*  Romans 12:1-18,  *or* Ephesians 4:7, 11-16
*Gospel*  John 15:9-16,  *or* Luke 10:1-2,  *or* John 14:11-15

## The Sermon

*After the Sermon, and any responses to it, the congregation sings a hymn.*

# The Induction

*Representatives of the congregation and of the clergy of the diocese stand before the bishop with the new minister. Any of the presentations that follow may be added to, omitted, or adapted, as appropriate to the nature of the new ministry, and to the order of the minister. In the absence of the bishop, the deputy substitutes the words given in parentheses.*

*Representatives of the congregation present a Bible, saying*

N., accept this Bible, and be among us (*or* be in this place) as one who proclaims the Word.

People    Amen.

*The Bishop presents a vessel of water, saying*

N., take this water, and help me (help the bishop) baptize in obedience to our Lord.

People    Amen.

*Others present a stole or other symbol, saying*

N., receive this *stole,* and be among us as a pastor and priest.

People    Amen.

*Others present a book of prayers or other symbol, saying*

N., receive this *book,* and be among us as a *man* of prayer.

People    Amen.

*Others present olive oil or some other symbol, saying*

N., use this *oil,* and be among us as a healer and reconciler.

People    Amen.

*If the new minister is the rector or vicar of the parish, a Warden may now present the keys of the church, saying*

N., receive these keys, and let the doors of this place be open to all people.

*People*     Amen.

*Representative clergy of the diocese present the Constitution and Canons of this Church, saying*

N., obey these Canons, and be among us to share in the councils of this diocese.

*People*     Amen.

*Other Representatives of the congregation present bread and wine, saying*

N., take this bread and wine, and be among us to break the Bread and bless the Cup.

*People*     Amen.

*The Bishop then says*

N., let all these be signs of the ministry which is mine and yours (the Bishop's and yours) in this place.

*People*     Amen.

*The new Minister, if a priest, may then kneel in the midst of the church, and say*

O Lord my God, I am not worthy to have you come under my roof; yet you have called your servant to stand in your house, and to serve at your altar. To you and to your service I devote myself, body, soul, and spirit. Fill my memory with the record of your mighty works; enlighten my understanding with the light of your Holy Spirit; and may all the desires of my heart and will center in what you would have me do. Ma me an instrument of your salvation for the people entrusted to my care, and grant that I may faithfully administer your holy Sacraments, and by my life and teaching set forth your true and living Word. Be always with me in carrying out the duties of my ministry. In prayer, quicken my devotion; in praises, heighten my love and gratitude; in preaching, give me readiness of thought and expression; and grant that, by the clearness and brightness of your holy Word, all the world may be drawn into your blessed kingdom. All this I ask for the sake of your Son our Savior Jesus Christ. *Amen.*

*The Bishop then presents the new minister to the congregation, saying*

Greet your new *Rector.*

*When appropriate, the family of the new minister may also be presented at this time.*

*The Congregation expresses its approval. Applause is appropriate.*

*The Bishop greets the new minister.*

*The new Minister then says to the people*

The peace of the Lord be always with you.
*People*     And also with you.

*The new Minister then greets other members of the clergy, family members, and the congregation. The People greet one another.*


## At the Eucharist

*The service continues with the Offertory.*

*The Bishop, or in the Bishop's absence a Priest beginning a new ministry, standing at the Lord's Table as chief celebrant, and joined by the other clergy, proceeds with the Great Thanksgiving of the Eucharist.*

*Except on Major Feasts, the Preface may be that for Apostles and Ordinations.*

## After Communion

*At the Induction of a priest or deacon, in place of the usual post-communion prayer, the Bishop leads the people in the following prayer; but if the new minister is a lay person, the usual postcommunion prayer is used.*

Almighty Father, we thank you for feeding us with the holy food of the Body and Blood of your Son, and for uniting us through him in the fellowship of your Holy Spirit. We thank you for raising up among us faithful servants for the ministry of your Word and Sacraments. We pray that *N.* may be to us an effective example in word and action, in love and patience, and in holiness of life. Grant that we, with *him,* may serve you now, and always rejoice in your glory; through Jesus Christ your Son our Lord, who lives and reigns with you and the Holy Spirit, one God, now and for ever. Amen.

*A newly inducted Priest may, at the bishop's request, pronounce a blessing.*

*A Deacon, or a Priest if no deacon is present, dismisses the assembly.*

# Additional Directions

The Institution, the Ministry of the Word, and the Induction should occur at the entrance of the chancel, or in some other place where the bishop and other ministers may be clearly seen and heard by the people.

The Letter of Institution is appropriate for the induction of a rector of a parish, the dean of a cathedral, and others having similar tenure of office.

Its wording may be altered by the bishop when circumstances require. In other cases, the bishop may state briefly the nature of the person's office and the authority being conferred.

The new minister is normally presented to the bishop by the wardens of the parish, but additional, or other, persons may do this when desired.

The Litany may be sung or said standing or kneeling, but the bishop always stands for the salutation and Collect at the end of it. The Collect of the Day, or a Collect of the season, or another prayer suitable to the occasion, may be used instead.

Before the Gospel, there may be one or two Readings from Scripture. Any of the Readings, including the Gospel, may be selected from the Proper of the Day, or from the passages cited in the service. Other passages suitable to the circumstances may be substituted. Appropriate selections may be found in the service for the Ordination of a Deacon or in the Lectionary for Various Occasions.

The sermon may be preached by the bishop, the new minister, or some other person; or an address about the work of the congregation and of the new minister may be made. Representatives of the congregation or of the community, the bishop, or other persons present, may speak in response to the address or sermon.

The symbols presented should be large enough to be visible to all and should remain in the sight of the congregation during the Induction. The vestments and bread and wine may be used in the Eucharist which follows.

The priest's prayer on page 562 is appropriate only for rectors of parishes, vicars of missions, hospital chaplains, and other priests having similar canonical charge.

For the Great Thanksgiving, any of the authorized eucharistic prayers may be used.

# Concerning the Service

This service provides for the dedication and consecration of a church and its furnishings. Portions of the service may be used, or adapted when necessary, for dedicating parts of a building, or furnishings, that have been added, altered, or renovated. Likewise, suitable parts of this rite may be used for dedicating a chapel or an oratory within another building. Provisions for adapting the rite to special circumstances are given on page 576.

This service may be used to dedicate and consecrate a church at any time after the building is ready for regular use as a place of worship.

The service does not preclude the use of the building for educational or social purposes, or for other suitable activities.

The bishop presides. The rector or minister in charge takes part as indicated. Neighboring ministers should be invited to participate, and may be assigned appropriate parts in the service.

It is desirable that all members of the congregation, young and old, have some individual or collective part in the celebration, as well as the architect, builders, musicians, artists, benefactors, and friends.

For a church or chapel long in use, a special order is provided on page 57

Additional Directions are on page 575.

# The Dedication and Consecration of a Church

*On the day appointed, the clergy and people gather with the bishop in a place apart from the church or chapel.*

*When all are ready, the Bishop says the following or similar words*

Through the ages, Almighty God has moved his people to build houses of prayer and praise, and to set apart places for the ministry of his holy Word and Sacraments. With gratitude for the building (rebuilding, *or* adornment) of (*name of church*), we are now gathered to dedicate and consecrate it in God's Name.

Let us pray.

Almighty God, we thank you for making us in your image, to share in the ordering of your world. Receive the work of our hands in this place, now to be set apart for your worship, the building up of the living, and the remembrance of the dead, to the praise and glory of your Name; through Jesus Christ our Lord. *Amen.*

*Necessary announcements may now be made.*

*As the procession approaches the door of the church, singing and instrumental music are appropriate.*

*Standing at the door of the church, the Bishop says*

Let the door(s) be opened.

*The door is opened. With the pastoral staff the Bishop marks the threshold with the sign of the cross saying*

Peace be to this house, and to all who enter here: ✝ In the Name of the Father, and of the Son, and of the Holy Spirit. *Amen.*

*As the procession moves into the church, Psalm 122 or some other appropriate psalm is sung. Hymns and anthems may also be sung.*

*The congregation standing, the Bishop begins the Prayer for the Consecration of the Church*

|          | Our help is in the Name of the Lord; |
|----------|---------------------------------------|
| People   | The maker of heaven and earth.        |
| Bishop   | Let us pray.                          |

Everliving Father, watchful and caring, our source and our end: All that we are and all that we have is yours. Accept us now, as we dedicate this place to which we come to praise your Name, to ask your forgiveness, to know your healing power, to hear your Word, and to be nourished by the Body and Blood of your Son. Be present always to guide and to judge, to illumine and to bless your people.

*A Warden or other representative of the congregation continues*

Lord Jesus Christ, make this a temple of your presence and a house of prayer. Be always near us when we seek you in this place. Draw us to you, when we come alone and when we come with others, to find comfort and wisdom, to be support and strengthened, to rejoice and give thanks. May it be here, Lord Christ, that we are made one with you and with one

other, so that our lives are sustained and sanctified for
our service.

*The Rector or Minister in charge continues*

Holy Spirit, open our eyes, our ears, and our hearts, that we
may grow closer to you through joy and through suffering.
Be with us in the fullness of your power as new members are
added to your household, as we grow in grace through the
years, when we are joined in marriage, when we turn to you
in sickness or special need, and, at the last, when we are
committed into the Father's hands.

*The Bishop concludes*

> Now, O Father, Son, and Holy Spirit,
> sanctify this place;

*People*   For everything in heaven and on earth is yours.

*Bishop*   Yours, O Lord, is the kingdom;

*People*   And you are exalted as head over all. Amen.

*The Bishop moves to the Font, lays a hand upon it, and says*

Father, we thank you that through the waters of Baptism we
die to sin and are made new in Christ. Grant through your
Spirit that those baptized here may enjoy the liberty and
splendor of the children of God.

> There is one Lord, one Faith, one Baptism;
> One God and Father of all.

We dedicate this Font in the Name of the Father, and of the
Son, and of the Holy Spirit. *Amen.*

*If there are persons to be baptized, water is now poured into the Font,
and the service continues as directed on page 575.*

*If no Baptism is to take place [water may be poured into the Font, and] the Bishop says*

|  | The Lord be with you. |
| --- | --- |
| *People* | And also with you. |
| *Bishop* | Let us give thanks to the Lord our God. |
| *People* | It is right to give him thanks and praise. |

*Facing the Font, the Bishop says*

We thank you, Almighty God, for the gift of water. Over it the Holy Spirit moved in the beginning of creation. Through it you led the children of Israel out of their bondage in Egypt into the land of promise. In it your Son Jesus received the baptism of John and was anointed by the Holy Spirit as the Messiah, the Christ, to lead us, through his death and resurrection, from the bondage of sin into everlasting life.

We thank you, Father, for the water of Baptism. In it we are buried with Christ in his death. By it we share in his resurrection. Through it we are reborn by the Holy Spirit. Therefore in joyful obedience to your Son, we bring into his fellowship those who come to him in faith, baptizing them in the Name of the Father, and of the Son, and of the Holy Spirit.

Grant, by the power of your Holy Spirit, that those who here are cleansed from sin and born again may continue for ever in the risen life of Jesus Christ our Savior.

To him, to you, and to the Holy Spirit, be all honor and glory, now and for ever. *Amen.*

*The Bishop proceeds to the Lectern, lays a hand upon it, and says*

Father, your eternal Word speaks to us through the words of Holy Scripture. Here we read about your mighty acts and purposes in history, and about those whom you chose as the

gents of your will. Inspired by the revelation of your Son,
e seek your present purposes. Give us ears to hear and
earts to obey.

> May the words of our mouth, and the meditation
> of our heart,
> Be acceptable to you, O Lord our God.

e dedicate this Lectern in the Name of the Father, and of the
n, and of the Holy Spirit. *Amen.*

*e Bishop goes to the Pulpit, lays a hand upon it, and says*

ther, in every age you have spoken through the voices of
ophets, pastors, and teachers. Purify the lives and the lips
those who speak here, that your word only may be
oclaimed, and your word only may be heard.

> Your word is a lantern to our feet,
> And a light upon our path.

e dedicate this Pulpit in the Name of the Father, and of the
n, and of the Holy Spirit. *Amen.*

## the Liturgy of the Word

*ree Lessons are read. Lay persons read the Old Testament Lesson and
* Epistle. The Deacon (or a Priest) reads the Gospel. Selections are
dinarily made from the following list; but on a Major Feast, Sunday, or
tronal Feast, selections may be made from the Proper of the Day.*

d Testament   1 Kings 8:22-23, 27b-30,   *or* 2 Samuel 6:12-15, 17-19
slm   84,   *or* 48
istle   Revelation 21:2-7,   *or* 1 Corinthians 3:1-11, 16-17,
           *or* 1 Peter 2:1-9

*When an instrument of music is to be dedicated, after the Epistle the Bishop proceeds to an appropriate place, and says*

Father, your people worship you with many voices and sounds, in times of joy and sorrow. Move us to express the wonder, the power, and the glory of your creation in the music we make and in the songs we sing.

V. Praise him with the sound of the trumpet;
R. Praise him with strings and pipe.

We dedicate this (*name of instrument*) in the Name of the Father, and of the Son, and of the Holy Spirit. *Amen.*

*Instrumental music is now played, or a hymn or anthem sung.*

*All then stand for the Gospel, which may be the following*

Matthew 7:13-14, 24-25,   *or* Matthew 21:10-14

*Sermon or Address*

*Other Pastoral Offices may follow.*

*If the Apostles' Creed has not already been said, the Nicene Creed is no said or sung.*

*The Deacon or a member of the congregation leads the Prayers of the People.*

*After a period of silence, the Bishop concludes with the following praye*

Almighty God, all times are your seasons, and all occasions invite your tender mercies: Accept our prayers and intercessions offered in this place today and in the days to come; through Jesus Christ, our Mediator and Advocate. *Amen.*

We give you thanks, O God, for the gifts of your people, and for the work of many hands, which have beautified this place and furnished it for the celebration of your holy mysteries. Accept and bless all we have done, and grant that in these earthly things we may behold the order and beauty of things heavenly; through Jesus Christ our Lord. *Amen.*

*The Bishop then says*

Let us now pray for the setting apart of the Altar.

*The Bishop goes to the Table and, with arms extended, says*

We praise you, Almighty and eternal God, that for us and for our salvation, you sent your Son Jesus Christ to be born among us, that through him we might become your sons and daughters.
*Blessed be your Name, Lord God.*

We praise you for his life on earth, and for his death upon the cross, through which he offered himself as a perfect sacrifice.
*Blessed be your Name, Lord God.*

We praise you for raising him from the dead, and for exalting him to be our great High Priest.
*Blessed be your Name, Lord God.*

We praise you for sending your Holy Spirit to make us holy, and to unite us in your holy Church.
*Blessed be your Name, Lord God.*

*The Bishop lays a hand upon the Table, and continues*

Lord God, hear us. Sanctify this Table dedicated to you. Let it be to us a sign of the heavenly Altar where your saints and angels praise you for ever. Accept here the continual recalling of the sacrifice of your Son. Grant that all who eat and drink at this holy Table may be fed and refreshed by his flesh and blood, be forgiven for their sins, united with one another, and strengthened for your service.

*Blessed be your Name, Father, Son, and Holy Spirit; now and for endless ages. Amen.*

*Bells may now be rung and music played. Members of the congregation vest the Altar, place the vessels on it, and light the candles.*

## The Peace

*The Bishop says to the people*

The peace of the Lord be always with you.

*People*     And also with you.

*Then the bishop and other clergy and the people greet one another.*

## At the Eucharist

*The service continues with the Offertory.*

*The bishop, or a priest appointed, is the chief celebrant.*

*The Preface of the Dedication of a Church may be used.*

*After the postcommunion prayer, the Bishop blesses the people; and a Deacon or Priest dismisses them.*

# Additional Directions

The complete form of the service for the Dedication and Consecration of a Church is to be used at the opening of a church or chapel. This service does not require that the premises be debt-free or owned.

When the clergy and people assemble before the service, they may gather out of doors, in the parish house, in a former or neighboring place of worship, or in some other building. When convenient, the procession may go around the building(s) to be dedicated and then go to the principal door. Hymns or psalms may be used in procession. The use of portable musical instruments is suitable. If there is an organ, it is appropriate that it remain silent until dedicated. When the weather is inclement, or other circumstances make it necessary, the congregation may assemble inside the church; but the bishop, other clergy, and attendants will enter in procession through the principal door.

When a new church is being consecrated, it is desirable that sacred vessels, ornaments, and decorations be carried into the building in the procession. Such things as the deed for the property and the blueprint of the building(s), the keys, and tools used in its construction may also be carried by appropriate persons.

The cross signed on the threshold by the bishop may be marked in lasting form (incised, painted, inlaid). In place of a pastoral staff, the foot of a processional cross may be used for the signing.

At the dedication of the font, children or other lay persons are to be assigned the task of pouring the water. If Holy Baptism is not to be administered, in addition to saying the prayer over the font as given, the bishop may consecrate oil of Chrism, as in the service of Holy Baptism, for subsequent use in this church.

If Baptism is to be administered, the following order is used: the Gospel from "At Baptism," page 928; then the service of Holy Baptism, beginning with the Presentation of the Candidates, and concluding with the reception of the newly baptized.

As the furnishings in the church are dedicated, they may be decorated by members of the congregation with flowers, candles, hangings, or other ornaments.

Selected verses of psalms and hymns, or instrumental music may be used as the ministers move from one part of the church to another.

If one reading stand is to serve as both lectern and pulpit, only one of the prayers, and one of the versicles and responses, are used, followed by the words of dedication.

At the dedication of the lectern, the Bible is brought forward and put into place by a donor, or a lay reader, or another suitable person.

If there is an address instead of a sermon, it is suitable that a warden or other lay person outline the plans of the congregation for witness to the Gospel. The bishop may respond, indicating the place of this congregation within the life of the Diocese.

The sermon or address may be followed by an appropriate Pastoral Office, such as Thanksgiving for the Birth or Adoption of a Child, Commitment to Christian Service, or Blessing of Oil for the Sick.

Any of the usual forms of the Prayers of the People may be used; or some other form may be composed for the occasion, having due regard for the distinctive nature of the community, and with commemoration of benefactors, donors, artists, artisans, and others.

For the covering and decoration of the Altar, it is suitable that the donors of these furnishings, or other lay persons, bring them forward and put them in place. If incense is to be used, it is appropriate at this time.

Instead of the Proper Preface suggested, that of the season may be used, or one appropriate to the name of the church.

## For the Dedication of Churches and Chapels in Special Cases

If the place of public worship is also to serve as a school or parish hall, or for some other suitable purpose, the service may be adapted to the circumstances.

If the church is also to be used for regular worship by other Christian bodies, it is appropriate that their representatives take part in the service, and that the service be adapted.

Suitable portions of this service may be used by the bishop, or by a priest with the bishop's permission, for dedicating a private chapel or oratory.

## For the Dedication of Furnishings, or Parts of a Church or Chapel

Relevant portions of the service for the Dedication and Consecration of a Church may be used by the bishop or a priest for blessing alterations, additions, or new furnishings in a church or chapel. In each such case, the appropriate prayer may be said, or adapted to the circumstances; and prayers and Bible readings related to the particular occasion may be selected. When possible, the areas or furnishings should be put into use at this time.

The blessing of a new font or baptistry should always be done by a bishop, and should be followed, if possible, by the administration of Holy Baptism.

The blessing of an Altar is also reserved for a bishop, and is always to be followed by the celebration of the Holy Eucharist.

## For a Church or Chapel Long in Use

When buildings have been used for public worship for an extended period of time without having been consecrated, the following order may provide an opportunity for the congregation to reaffirm its commitment to its mission and ministry, and it will be particularly appropriate when a congregation attains recognition as a parish.

1. Procession
2. Signing of threshold
3. Litany of Thanksgiving for a Church, page 578
4. Te Deum

5. Liturgy of the Word, with sermon or address
6. Renewal of Baptismal Vows
7. Intercessions, including commemoration of benefactors
8. The Peace
9. The Eucharist, beginning with the Offertory

## A Litany of Thanksgiving for a Church

Let us thank God whom we worship here in the beauty of holiness.

Eternal God, the heaven of heavens cannot contain you, much less the walls of temples made with hands. Graciously receive our thanks for this place, and accept the work of our hands, offered to your honor and glory.

For the Church universal, of which these visible buildings are the symbol,
*We thank you, Lord.*

For your presence whenever two or three have gathered together in your Name,
*We thank you, Lord.*

For this place where we may be still and know that you are God,
*We thank you, Lord.*

For making us your children by adoption and grace, and refreshing us day by day with the bread of life.
*We thank you, Lord.*

For the knowledge of your will and the grace to perform it,
*We thank you, Lord.*

For the fulfilling of our desires and petitions as you see best for us,
*We thank you, Lord.*

For the pardon of our sins, which restores us to the company
of your faithful people,
*We thank you, Lord.*

For the blessing of our vows and the crowning of our years
with your goodness,
*We thank you, Lord.*

For the faith of those who have gone before us and for our
encouragement by their perseverance,
*We thank you, Lord.*

For the fellowship of [N., our patron, and of] all your
Saints,
*We thank you, Lord.*

*After a brief silence, the Celebrant concludes with the following Doxology*

Yours, O Lord, is the greatness, the power, the
glory, the victory, and the majesty;
*People*    For everything in heaven and on earth is yours.
*Celebrant* Yours, O Lord, is the kingdom;
*People*    And you are exalted as head over all. Amen.

*This Litany may also be used on the anniversary of the dedication or
consecration of a church, or on other suitable occasions.*

# The Psalter

# Concerning the Psalter

The Psalter is a body of liturgical poetry. It is designed for vocal, congregational use, whether by singing or reading. There are several traditional methods of psalmody. The exclusive use of a single method makes the recitation of the Psalter needlessly monotonous. The traditional methods, each of which can be elaborate or simple, are the following:

**Direct recitation** denotes the reading or chanting of a whole psalm, or portion of a psalm, in unison. It is particularly appropriate for the psalm verses suggested in the lectionary for use between the Lessons at the Eucharist, when the verses are recited rather than sung, and may often be found a satisfactory method of chanting them.

**Antiphonal recitation** is the verse-by-verse alternation between groups of singers or readers; *e.g.*, between choir and congregation, or between one side of the congregation and the other. The alternate recitation concludes either with the Gloria Patri, or with a refrain (called the antiphon) recited in unison. This is probably the most satisfying method for reciting the psalms in the Daily Office.

**Responsorial recitation** is the name given to a method of psalmody in which the verses of a psalm are sung by a solo voice, with the choir and congregation singing a refrain after each verse or group of verses. This was the traditional method of singing the Venite, and the restoration of Invitatory Antiphons for the Venite makes possible a recovery of this form of sacred song in the Daily Office. It was also a traditional manner of chanting the psalms between the Lessons at the Eucharist, and it is increasingly favored by modern composers.

**Responsive recitation** is the method which has been most frequently used in Episcopal churches, the minister alternating with the congregation, verse by verse.

The version of the Psalms which follows is set out in lines of poetry. The lines correspond to Hebrew versification, which is not based on meter or rhyme, but on parallelism of clauses, a symmetry of form and sense. The parallelism can take the form of similarity (The waters have lifted up, O Lord / the waters have lifted up their voice; / the waters have lifted up their pounding waves. *Psalm 93:4*), or of contrast (The Lord knows the ways of the righteous; / but the way of the wicked is doomed. *Psalm 1:6*), or of logical expansion (Our eyes look to the Lord our God, / until he show us his mercy. *Psalm 123:3*).

The most common verse is a couplet, but triplets are very frequent, and quatrains are not unknown; although quatrains are usually distributed over two verses.

An asterisk divides each verse into two parts for reading or chanting. In reading, a distinct pause should be made at the asterisk.

Three terms are used in the Psalms with reference to God: *Elohim* ("God"), *Adonai* ("Lord") and the personal name *YHWH*. The "Four-letter Name" (Tetragrammaton) is probably to be vocalized Yahweh; but this is by no means certain, because from very ancient times it has been considered too sacred to be pronounced; and, whenever it occurred, *Adonai* was substituted for it. In the oldest manuscripts, the Divine Name was written in antique and obsolete letters; in more recent manuscripts and in printed Bibles, after the invention of vowel points, the Name was provided with the vowels of the word *Adonai*. This produced a hybrid form which has been transliterated "Jehovah."

The Hebrew reverence and reticence with regard to the Name of God has been carried over into the classical English versions, the Prayer Book Psalter and the King James Old Testament, where it is regularly rendered "Lord". In order to distinguish it, however, from "Lord" as a translation of *Adonai*, *YHWH* is represented in capital and small capital letters: Lord.

From time to time, the Hebrew text has *Adonai* and *YHWH* in conjunction. Then, the Hebrew custom is to substitute *Elohim* for *YHWH*, and our English tradition follows suit, rendering the combined title as "Lord God."

In two passages *(Psalm 68:4* and *Psalm 83:18)*, the context requires that the Divine Name be spelled out, and it appears as YAHWEH. A similar construction occurs in the Canticle, "The Song of Moses."

The ancient praise-shout, "Hallelujah," has been restored, in place of its English equivalent, "Praise the Lord." The Hebrew form has been used, rather than the Latin form "Alleluia," as being more appropriate to this context; but also to regain for our liturgy a form of the word that is familiar from its use in many well-known anthems. The word may, if desired, be omitted during the season of Lent.

# The Psalter

**Book One**

*First Day: Morning Prayer*

I   *Beatus vir qui non abiit*

1   Happy are they who have not walked in the counsel of
the wicked, *
nor lingered in the way of sinners,
nor sat in the seats of the scornful!

2   Their delight is in the law of the LORD,*
and they meditate on his law day and night.

3   They are like trees planted by streams of water,
bearing fruit in due season, with leaves that do not wither; *
everything they do shall prosper.

4   It is not so with the wicked; *
they are like chaff which the wind blows away.

5   Therefore the wicked shall not stand upright when
judgment comes, *
nor the sinner in the council of the righteous.

6   For the LORD knows the way of the righteous, *
but the way of the wicked is doomed.

## 2 *Quare fremuerunt gentes?*

1 Why are the nations in an uproar? *
    Why do the peoples mutter empty threats?

2 Why do the kings of the earth rise up in revolt,
    and the princes plot together, *
        against the LORD and against his Anointed?

3 "Let us break their yoke," they say; *
    "let us cast off their bonds from us."

4 He whose throne is in heaven is laughing; *
    the Lord has them in derision.

5 Then he speaks to them in his wrath, *
    and his rage fills them with terror.

6 "I myself have set my king *
    upon my holy hill of Zion."

7 Let me announce the decree of the LORD: *
    he said to me, "You are my Son;
    this day have I begotten you.

8 Ask of me, and I will give you the nations for
            your inheritance *
    and the ends of the earth for your possession.

9 You shall crush them with an iron rod *
    and shatter them like a piece of pottery."

10 And now, you kings, be wise; *
    be warned, you rulers of the earth.

11 Submit to the LORD with fear, *
    and with trembling bow before him;

12 Lest he be angry and you perish; *
    for his wrath is quickly kindled.

13  Happy are they all *
        who take refuge in him!

3  *Domine, quid multiplicati*

1  LORD, how many adversaries I have! *
        how many there are who rise up against me!

2  How many there are who say of me, *
        "There is no help for him in his God."

3  But you, O LORD, are a shield about me; *
        you are my glory, the one who lifts up my head.

4  I call aloud upon the LORD, *
        and he answers me from his holy hill;

5  I lie down and go to sleep; *
        I wake again, because the LORD sustains me.

6  I do not fear the multitudes of people *
        who set themselves against me all around.

7  Rise up, O LORD; set me free, O my God; *
        surely, you will strike all my enemies across the face,
        you will break the teeth of the wicked.

8  Deliverance belongs to the LORD. *
        Your blessing be upon your people!

4  *Cum invocarem*

1  Answer me when I call, O God, defender of my cause; *
        you set me free when I am hard-pressed;
        have mercy on me and hear my prayer.

2    "You mortals, how long will you dishonor my glory; *
        how long will you worship dumb idols
        and run after false gods?"

3    Know that the LORD does wonders for the faithful; *
        when I call upon the LORD, he will hear me.

4    Tremble, then, and do not sin; *
        speak to your heart in silence upon your bed.

5    Offer the appointed sacrifices *
        and put your trust in the LORD.

6    Many are saying,
        "Oh, that we might see better times!" *
        Lift up the light of your countenance upon us, O LORD

7    You have put gladness in my heart, *
        more than when grain and wine and oil increase.

8    I lie down in peace; at once I fall asleep; *
        for only you, LORD, make me dwell in safety.


5    *Verba mea auribus*

1    Give ear to my words, O LORD; *
        consider my meditation.

2    Hearken to my cry for help, my King and my God, *
        for I make my prayer to you.

3    In the morning, LORD, you hear my voice; *
        early in the morning I make my appeal and watch for

4    For you are not a God who takes pleasure in wickednes
        and evil cannot dwell with you.

5    Braggarts cannot stand in your sight; *
        you hate all those who work wickedness.

You destroy those who speak lies; *
    the bloodthirsty and deceitful, O LORD, you abhor.

But as for me, through the greatness of your mercy I will
                  go into your house; *
    I will bow down toward your holy temple in awe of you.

Lead me, O LORD, in your righteousness,
because of those who lie in wait for me; *
    make your way straight before me.

For there is no truth in their mouth; *
    there is destruction in their heart;

Their throat is an open grave; *
    they flatter with their tongue.

Declare them guilty, O God; *
    let them fall, because of their schemes.

Because of their many transgressions cast them out, *
    for they have rebelled against you.

But all who take refuge in you will be glad; *
    they will sing out their joy for ever.

You will shelter them, *
    so that those who love your Name may exult in you.

For you, O LORD, will bless the righteous; *
    you will defend them with your favor as with a shield.


*First Day: Evening Prayer*

**6**   *Domine, ne in furore*

LORD, do not rebuke me in your anger; *
    do not punish me in your wrath.

2   Have pity on me, LORD, for I am weak; *
    heal me, LORD, for my bones are racked.

3   My spirit shakes with terror; *
    how long, O LORD, how long?

4   Turn, O LORD, and deliver me; *
    save me for your mercy's sake.

5   For in death no one remembers you; *
    and who will give you thanks in the grave?

6   I grow weary because of my groaning; *
    every night I drench my bed
    and flood my couch with tears.

7   My eyes are wasted with grief *
    and worn away because of all my enemies.

8   Depart from me, all evildoers, *
    for the LORD has heard the sound of my weeping.

9   The LORD has heard my supplication; *
    the LORD accepts my prayer.

10  All my enemies shall be confounded and quake with fear;
    they shall turn back and suddenly be put to shame.


## 7   *Domine, Deus meus*

1   O LORD my God, I take refuge in you; *
    save and deliver me from all who pursue me;

2   Lest like a lion they tear me in pieces *
    and snatch me away with none to deliver me.

3   O LORD my God, if I have done these things: *
    if there is any wickedness in my hands,

4    If I have repaid my friend with evil, *
         or plundered him who without cause is my enemy;

5    Then let my enemy pursue and overtake me, *
         trample my life into the ground,
         and lay my honor in the dust.

6    Stand up, O LORD, in your wrath; *
         rise up against the fury of my enemies.

7    Awake, O my God, decree justice; *
         let the assembly of the peoples gather round you.

8    Be seated on your lofty throne, O Most High; *
         O LORD, judge the nations.

9    Give judgment for me according to my
                              righteousness, O LORD, *
         and according to my innocence, O Most High.

10   Let the malice of the wicked come to an end,
     but establish the righteous; *
         for you test the mind and heart, O righteous God.

11   God is my shield and defense; *
         he is the savior of the true in heart.

12   God is a righteous judge; *
         God sits in judgment every day.

13   If they will not repent, God will whet his sword; *
         he will bend his bow and make it ready.

14   He has prepared his weapons of death; *
         he makes his arrows shafts of fire.

15   Look at those who are in labor with wickedness, *
         who conceive evil, and give birth to a lie.

16    They dig a pit and make it deep *
     and fall into the hole that they have made.

17    Their malice turns back upon their own head; *
     their violence falls on their own scalp.

18    I will bear witness that the LORD is righteous; *
     I will praise the Name of the LORD Most High.

# 8    *Domine, Dominus noster*

1    O LORD our Governor, *
     how exalted is your Name in all the world!

2    Out of the mouths of infants and children *
     your majesty is praised above the heavens.

3    You have set up a stronghold against your adversaries, *
     to quell the enemy and the avenger.

4    When I consider your heavens, the work of your fingers,
     the moon and the stars you have set in their courses,

5    What is man that you should be mindful of him? *
     the son of man that you should seek him out?

6    You have made him but little lower than the angels; *
     you adorn him with glory and honor;

7    You give him mastery over the works of your hands; *
     you put all things under his feet:

8    All sheep and oxen, *
     even the wild beasts of the field,

9    The birds of the air, the fish of the sea, *
     and whatsoever walks in the paths of the sea.

10    O LORD our Governor, *
     how exalted is your Name in all the world!

## 9 *Confitebor tibi*

1   I will give thanks to you, O LORD, with my whole heart; *
      I will tell of all your marvelous works.

2   I will be glad and rejoice in you; *
      I will sing to your Name, O Most High.

3   When my enemies are driven back, *
      they will stumble and perish at your presence.

4   For you have maintained my right and my cause; *
      you sit upon your throne judging right.

5   You have rebuked the ungodly and destroyed the wicked; *
      you have blotted out their name for ever and ever.

6   As for the enemy, they are finished, in perpetual ruin, *
      their cities plowed under, the memory of them perished;

7   But the LORD is enthroned for ever; *
      he has set up his throne for judgment.

8   It is he who rules the world with righteousness; *
      he judges the peoples with equity.

9   The LORD will be a refuge for the oppressed, *
      a refuge in time of trouble.

10   Those who know your Name will put their trust in you, *
      for you never forsake those who seek you, O LORD.

11   Sing praise to the LORD who dwells in Zion; *
      proclaim to the peoples the things he has done.

12   The Avenger of blood will remember them; *
      he will not forget the cry of the afflicted.

13    Have pity on me, O LORD; *
       see the misery I suffer from those who hate me,
        O you who lift me up from the gate of death;

14    So that I may tell of all your praises
    and rejoice in your salvation *
       in the gates of the city of Zion.

15    The ungodly have fallen into the pit they dug, *
       and in the snare they set is their own foot caught.

16    The LORD is known by his acts of justice; *
       the wicked are trapped in the works of their own hand

17    The wicked shall be given over to the grave, *
       and also all the peoples that forget God.

18    For the needy shall not always be forgotten, *
       and the hope of the poor shall not perish for ever.

19    Rise up, O LORD, let not the ungodly have the upper ha
       let them be judged before you.

20    Put fear upon them, O LORD; *
       let the ungodly know they are but mortal.

## 10   *Ut quid, Domine?*

1    Why do you stand so far off, O LORD, *
       and hide yourself in time of trouble?

2    The wicked arrogantly persecute the poor, *
       but they are trapped in the schemes they have devised

3    The wicked boast of their heart's desire; *
       the covetous curse and revile the LORD.

4    The wicked are so proud that they care not for God; *
       their only thought is, "God does not matter."

5 Their ways are devious at all times;
  your judgments are far above out of their sight; *
    they defy all their enemies.

6 They say in their heart," I shall not be shaken; *
    no harm shall happen to me ever."

7 Their mouth is full of cursing, deceit, and oppression; *
    under their tongue are mischief and wrong.

8 They lurk in ambush in public squares
  and in secret places they murder the innocent; *
    they spy out the helpless.

9 They lie in wait, like a lion in a covert;
  they lie in wait to seize upon the lowly; *
    they seize the lowly and drag them away in their net.

10 The innocent are broken and humbled before them; *
    the helpless fall before their power.

11 They say in their heart,"God has forgotten; *
    he hides his face; he will never notice."

12 Rise up, O LORD;
  lift up your hand, O God; *
    do not forget the afflicted.

13 Why should the wicked revile God? *
    why should they say in their heart,"You do not care"?

14 Surely, you behold trouble and misery; *
    you see it and take it into your own hand.

15 The helpless commit themselves to you, *
    for you are the helper of orphans.

16 Break the power of the wicked and evil; *
    search out their wickedness until you find none.

17 The LORD is King for ever and ever; *
    the ungodly shall perish from his land.

18 The LORD will hear the desire of the humble; *
    you will strengthen their heart and your ears shall hea

19 To give justice to the orphan and oppressed, *
    so that mere mortals may strike terror no more.

## II  *In Domino confido*

1 In the LORD have I taken refuge; *
    how then can you say to me,
    "Fly away like a bird to the hilltop;

2 For see how the wicked bend the bow
    and fit their arrows to the string, *
    to shoot from ambush at the true of heart.

3 When the foundations are being destroyed, *
    what can the righteous do?"

4 The LORD is in his holy temple; *
    the LORD's throne is in heaven.

5 His eyes behold the inhabited world; *
    his piercing eye weighs our worth.

6 The LORD weighs the righteous as well as the wicked, *
    but those who delight in violence he abhors.

7 Upon the wicked he shall rain coals of fire and
                            burning sulphur; *
    a scorching wind shall be their lot.

8 For the LORD is righteous;
    he delights in righteous deeds; *
    and the just shall see his face.

## 12 *Salvum me fac*

1   Help me, LORD, for there is no godly one left; *
    the faithful have vanished from among us.

2   Everyone speaks falsely with his neighbor; *
    with a smooth tongue they speak from a double heart.

3   Oh, that the LORD would cut off all smooth tongues, *
    and close the lips that utter proud boasts!

4   Those who say, "With our tongue will we prevail; *
    our lips are our own; who is lord over us?"

  "Because the needy are oppressed,
  and the poor cry out in misery, *
    I will rise up," says the LORD,
  "and give them the help they long for."

  The words of the LORD are pure words, *
    like silver refined from ore
    and purified seven times in the fire.

  O LORD, watch over us *
    and save us from this generation for ever.

  The wicked prowl on every side, *
    and that which is worthless is highly prized by everyone.

## 13 *Usquequo, Domine?*

How long, O LORD?
will you forget me for ever? *
  how long will you hide your face from me?

2 How long shall I have perplexity in my mind,
and grief in my heart, day after day? *
   how long shall my enemy triumph over me?

3 Look upon me and answer me, O LORD my God; *
   give light to my eyes, lest I sleep in death;

4 Lest my enemy say, "I have prevailed over him," *
   and my foes rejoice that I have fallen.

5 But I put my trust in your mercy; *
   my heart is joyful because of your saving help.

6 I will sing to the LORD, for he has dealt with me richly; *
   I will praise the Name of the Lord Most High.


## 14 *Dixit insipiens*

1 The fool has said in his heart, "There is no God." *
   All are corrupt and commit abominable acts;
   there is none who does any good.

2 The LORD looks down from heaven upon us all, *
   to see if there is any who is wise,
   if there is one who seeks after God.

3 Every one has proved faithless;
all alike have turned bad; *
   there is none who does good; no, not one.

4 Have they no knowledge, all those evildoers *
   who eat up my people like bread
   and do not call upon the LORD?

5 See how they tremble with fear, *
   because God is in the company of the righteous.

6 Their aim is to confound the plans of the afflicted, *
   but the LORD is their refuge.

7　Oh, that Israel's deliverance would come out of Zion! *
　　when the LORD restores the fortunes of his people,
　　Jacob will rejoice and Israel be glad.


*Third Day: Morning Prayer*

## 15　*Domine, quis habitabit?*

1　LORD, who may dwell in your tabernacle? *
　　who may abide upon your holy hill?

2　Whoever leads a blameless life and does what is right, *
　　who speaks the truth from his heart.

3　There is no guile upon his tongue;
　　he does no evil to his friend; *
　　he does not heap contempt upon his neighbor.

4　In his sight the wicked is rejected, *
　　but he honors those who fear the LORD.

5　He has sworn to do no wrong *
　　and does not take back his word.

6　He does not give his money in hope of gain, *
　　nor does he take a bribe against the innocent.

7　Whoever does these things *
　　shall never be overthrown.


## 16　*Conserva me, Domine*

1　Protect me, O God, for I take refuge in you; *
　　I have said to the LORD, "You are my Lord,
　　my good above all other."

2   All my delight is upon the godly that are in the land, *
        upon those who are noble among the people.

3   But those who run after other gods *
        shall have their troubles multiplied.

4   Their libations of blood I will not offer, *
        nor take the names of their gods upon my lips.

5   O Lord, you are my portion and my cup; *
        it is you who uphold my lot.

6   My boundaries enclose a pleasant land; *
        indeed, I have a goodly heritage.

7   I will bless the Lord who gives me counsel; *
        my heart teaches me, night after night.

8   I have set the Lord always before me; *
        because he is at my right hand I shall not fall.

9   My heart, therefore, is glad, and my spirit rejoices; *
        my body also shall rest in hope.

10  For you will not abandon me to the grave, *
        nor let your holy one see the Pit.

11  You will show me the path of life; *
        in your presence there is fullness of joy,
        and in your right hand are pleasures for evermore.

## 17   *Exaudi, Domine*

1   Hear my plea of innocence, O Lord;
        give heed to my cry; *
            listen to my prayer, which does not come from lying ▌

Let my vindication come forth from your presence; *
  let your eyes be fixed on justice.

Weigh my heart, summon me by night, *
  melt me down; you will find no impurity in me.

I give no offense with my mouth as others do; *
  I have heeded the words of your lips.

My footsteps hold fast to the ways of your law; *
  in your paths my feet shall not stumble.

I call upon you, O God, for you will answer me; *
  incline your ear to me and hear my words.

Show me your marvelous loving-kindness, *
  O Savior of those who take refuge at your right hand
  from those who rise up against them.

Keep me as the apple of your eye; *
  hide me under the shadow of your wings,

From the wicked who assault me, *
  from my deadly enemies who surround me.

They have closed their heart to pity, *
  and their mouth speaks proud things.

They press me hard,
now they surround me, *
  watching how they may cast me to the ground,

Like a lion, greedy for its prey, *
  and like a young lion lurking in secret places.

Arise, O LORD; confront them and bring them down; *
  deliver me from the wicked by your sword.

Deliver me, O LORD, by your hand *
  from those whose portion in life is this world;

15 Whose bellies you fill with your treasure, *
      who are well supplied with children
         and leave their wealth to their little ones.

16 But at my vindication I shall see your face; *
      when I awake, I shall be satisfied, beholding
         your likeness.


*Third Day: Evening Prayer*

# 18

**Part I**   *Diligam te, Domine.*

1 I love you, O LORD my strength, *
      O LORD my stronghold, my crag, and my haven.

2 My God, my rock in whom I put my trust, *
      my shield, the horn of my salvation, and my refuge;
         you are worthy of praise.

3 I will call upon the LORD, *
      and so shall I be saved from my enemies.

4 The breakers of death rolled over me, *
      and the torrents of oblivion made me afraid.

5 The cords of hell entangled me, *
      and the snares of death were set for me.

6 I called upon the LORD in my distress *
      and cried out to my God for help.

7 He heard my voice from his heavenly dwelling; *
      my cry of anguish came to his ears.

8   The earth reeled and rocked; *
        the roots of the mountains shook;
        they reeled because of his anger.

9   Smoke rose from his nostrils
    and a consuming fire out of his mouth; *
        hot burning coals blazed forth from him.

10  He parted the heavens and came down *
        with a storm cloud under his feet.

11  He mounted on cherubim and flew; *
        he swooped on the wings of the wind.

12  He wrapped darkness about him; *
        he made dark waters and thick clouds his pavilion.

13  From the brightness of his presence, through the clouds, *
        burst hailstones and coals of fire.

14  The LORD thundered out of heaven; *
        the Most High uttered his voice.

15  He loosed his arrows and scattered them; *
        he hurled thunderbolts and routed them.

16  The beds of the seas were uncovered,
    and the foundations of the world laid bare, *
        at your battle cry, O LORD,
        at the blast of the breath of your nostrils.

17  He reached down from on high and grasped me; *
        he drew me out of great waters.

18  He delivered me from my strong enemies
    and from those who hated me; *
        for they were too mighty for me.

19  They confronted me in the day of my disaster; *
        but the LORD was my support.

20    He brought me out into an open place; *
        he rescued me because he delighted in me.

### Psalm 18: Part II   *Et retribuet mihi*

21    The LORD rewarded me because of my righteous dealing
        because my hands were clean he rewarded me;

22    For I have kept the ways of the LORD *
        and have not offended against my God;

23    For all his judgments are before my eyes, *
        and his decrees I have not put away from me;

24    For I have been blameless with him *
        and have kept myself from iniquity;

25    Therefore the LORD rewarded me according to my
                righteous dealing, *
        because of the cleanness of my hands in his sight.

26    With the faithful you show yourself faithful, O God; *
        with the forthright you show yourself forthright.

27    With the pure you show yourself pure, *
        but with the crooked you are wily.

28    You will save a lowly people, *
        but you will humble the haughty eyes.

29    You, O LORD, are my lamp; *
        my God, you make my darkness bright.

30    With you I will break down an enclosure; *
        with the help of my God I will scale any wall.

31    As for God, his ways are perfect;
        the words of the LORD are tried in the fire; *
        he is a shield to all who trust in him.

32 For who is God, but the Lord? *
    who is the Rock, except our God?

33 It is God who girds me about with strength *
    and makes my way secure.

34 He makes me sure-footed like a deer *
    and lets me stand firm on the heights.

35 He trains my hands for battle *
    and my arms for bending even a bow of bronze.

36 You have given me your shield of victory; *
    your right hand also sustains me;
    your loving care makes me great.

37 You lengthen my stride beneath me, *
    and my ankles do not give way.

38 I pursue my enemies and overtake them; *
    I will not turn back till I have destroyed them.

39 I strike them down, and they cannot rise; *
    they fall defeated at my feet.

40 You have girded me with strength for the battle; *
    you have cast down my adversaries beneath me;
    you have put my enemies to flight.

41 I destroy those who hate me;
    they cry out, but there is none to help them; *
    they cry to the Lord, but he does not answer.

42 I beat them small like dust before the wind; *
    I trample them like mud in the streets.

43 You deliver me from the strife of the peoples; *
    you put me at the head of the nations.

44 A people I have not known shall serve me;
    no sooner shall they hear than they shall obey me; *
    strangers will cringe before me.

45 The foreign peoples will lose heart; *
    they shall come trembling out of their strongholds.

46 The LORD lives! Blessed is my Rock! *
    Exalted is the God of my salvation!

47 He is the God who gave me victory *
    and cast down the peoples beneath me.

48 You rescued me from the fury of my enemies;
    you exalted me above those who rose against me; *
    you saved me from my deadly foe.

49 Therefore will I extol you among the nations, O LORD,
    and sing praises to your Name.

50 He multiplies the victories of his king; *
    he shows loving-kindness to his anointed,
    to David and his descendants for ever.


*Fourth Day: Morning Prayer*

## 19 *Cæli enarrant*

1 The heavens declare the glory of God, *
    and the firmament shows his handiwork.

2 One day tells its tale to another, *
    and one night imparts knowledge to another.

3 Although they have no words or language, *
    and their voices are not heard,

4 Their sound has gone out into all lands, *
    and their message to the ends of the world.

5 In the deep has he set a pavilion for the sun; *
    it comes forth like a bridegroom out of his chamber;
    it rejoices like a champion to run its course.

6　It goes forth from the uttermost edge of the heavens
　　and runs about to the end of it again; *
　　　　nothing is hidden from its burning heat.

7　The law of the LORD is perfect
　　　　　　and revives the soul; *
　　the testimony of the LORD is sure
　　　　　　and gives wisdom to the innocent.

8　The statutes of the LORD are just
　　　　　　and rejoice the heart; *
　　the commandment of the LORD is clear
　　　　　　and gives light to the eyes.

9　The fear of the LORD is clean
　　　　　　and endures for ever; *
　　the judgments of the LORD are true
　　　　　　and righteous altogether.

10　More to be desired are they than gold,
　　　　　　more than much fine gold, *
　　sweeter far than honey,
　　　　　　than honey in the comb.

11　By them also is your servant enlightened, *
　　and in keeping them there is great reward.

12　Who can tell how often he offends? *
　　cleanse me from my secret faults.

13　Above all, keep your servant from presumptuous sins;
　　let them not get dominion over me; *
　　then shall I be whole and sound,
　　and innocent of a great offense.

14　Let the words of my mouth and the meditation of my
　　　　　　heart be acceptable in your sight, *
　　O LORD, my strength and my redeemer.

## 20  *Exaudiat te Dominus*

1   May the LORD answer you in the day of trouble, *
   the Name of the God of Jacob defend you;

2   Send you help from his holy place *
   and strengthen you out of Zion;

3   Remember all your offerings *
   and accept your burnt sacrifice;

4   Grant you your heart's desire *
   and prosper all your plans.

5   We will shout for joy at your victory
   and triumph in the Name of our God; *
     may the LORD grant all your requests.

6   Now I know that the LORD gives victory to his anointed;
   he will answer him out of his holy heaven,
     with the victorious strength of his right hand.

7   Some put their trust in chariots and some in horses, *
   but we will call upon the Name of the LORD our God.

8   They collapse and fall down, *
   but we will arise and stand upright.

9   O LORD, give victory to the king *
   and answer us when we call.


## 21  *Domine, in virtute tua*

1   The king rejoices in your strength, O LORD; *
   how greatly he exults in your victory!

2   You have given him his heart's desire; *
   you have not denied him the request of his lips.

3   For you meet him with blessings of prosperity, *
    and set a crown of fine gold upon his head.

4   He asked you for life, and you gave it to him: *
    length of days, for ever and ever.

5   His honor is great, because of your victory; *
    splendor and majesty have you bestowed upon him.

6   For you will give him everlasting felicity *
    and will make him glad with the joy of your presence.

7   For the king puts his trust in the LORD; *
    because of the loving-kindness of the Most High, he
        will not fall.


8   Your hand will lay hold upon all your enemies; *
    your right hand will seize all those who hate you.

9   You will make them like a fiery furnace *
    at the time of your appearing, O LORD;

10  You will swallow them up in your wrath, *
    and fire shall consume them.

11  You will destroy their offspring from the land *
    and their descendants from among the peoples of the earth.

12  Though they intend evil against you
    and devise wicked schemes, *
        yet they shall not prevail.

13  For you will put them to flight *
    and aim your arrows at them.

14  Be exalted, O LORD, in your might; *
    we will sing and praise your power.

## 22 *Deus, Deus meus*

1    My God, my God, why have you forsaken me? *
     and are so far from my cry
     and from the words of my distress?

2    O my God, I cry in the daytime, but you do not answer; *
     by night as well, but I find no rest.

3    Yet you are the Holy One, *
     enthroned upon the praises of Israel.

4    Our forefathers put their trust in you; *
     they trusted, and you delivered them.

5    They cried out to you and were delivered; *
     they trusted in you and were not put to shame.

6    But as for me, I am a worm and no man, *
     scorned by all and despised by the people.

7    All who see me laugh me to scorn; *
     they curl their lips and wag their heads, saying,

8    "He trusted in the LORD; let him deliver him; *
     let him rescue him, if he delights in him."

9    Yet you are he who took me out of the womb, *
     and kept me safe upon my mother's breast.

10    I have been entrusted to you ever since I was born; *
     you were my God when I was still in my
       mother's womb.

11    Be not far from me, for trouble is near, *
     and there is none to help.

12    Many young bulls encircle me; *
     strong bulls of Bashan surround me.

13    They open wide their jaws at me, *
     like a ravening and a roaring lion.

14    I am poured out like water;
   all my bones are out of joint; *
     my heart within my breast is melting wax.

15    My mouth is dried out like a pot-sherd;
   my tongue sticks to the roof of my mouth; *
     and you have laid me in the dust of the grave.

16    Packs of dogs close me in,
   and gangs of evildoers circle around me; *
     they pierce my hands and my feet;
     I can count all my bones.

17    They stare and gloat over me; *
     they divide my garments among them;
     they cast lots for my clothing.

18    Be not far away, O Lord; *
     you are my strength; hasten to help me.

19    Save me from the sword, *
     my life from the power of the dog.

20    Save me from the lion's mouth, *
     my wretched body from the horns of wild bulls.

21    I will declare your Name to my brethren; *
     in the midst of the congregation I will praise you.

22    Praise the Lord, you that fear him; *
     stand in awe of him, O offspring of Israel;
     all you of Jacob's line, give glory.

23     For he does not despise nor abhor the poor in their poverty,
       neither does he hide his face from them; *
          but when they cry to him he hears them.

24     My praise is of him in the great assembly; *
          I will perform my vows in the presence of those who
             worship him.

25     The poor shall eat and be satisfied,
       and those who seek the LORD shall praise him: *
          "May your heart live for ever!"

26     All the ends of the earth shall remember and turn to
             the LORD, *
          and all the families of the nations shall bow before him.

27     For kingship belongs to the LORD; *
          he rules over the nations.

28     To him alone all who sleep in the earth bow down
             in worship; *
          all who go down to the dust fall before him.

29     My soul shall live for him;
       my descendants shall serve him; *
          they shall be known as the LORD's for ever.

30     They shall come and make known to a people yet unborn
       the saving deeds that he has done.


## 23    *Dominus regit me*

1     The LORD is my shepherd; *
       I shall not be in want.

2     He makes me lie down in green pastures *
       and leads me beside still waters.

3   He revives my soul *
        and guides me along right pathways for his Name's sake.

4   Though I walk through the valley of the shadow of death,
        I shall fear no evil; *
        for you are with me;
        your rod and your staff, they comfort me.

5   You spread a table before me in the presence of those
                            who trouble me; *
        you have anointed my head with oil,
        and my cup is running over.

6   Surely your goodness and mercy shall follow me all the days
                            of my life, *
        and I will dwell in the house of the LORD for ever.


*Fifth Day: Morning Prayer*

## 24   *Domini est terra*

1   The earth is the LORD's and all that is in it, *
        the world and all who dwell therein.

2   For it is he who founded it upon the seas *
        and made it firm upon the rivers of the deep.

3   "Who can ascend the hill of the LORD? *
        and who can stand in his holy place?"

4   "Those who have clean hands and a pure heart, *
        who have not pledged themselves to falsehood,
        nor sworn by what is a fraud.

5   They shall receive a blessing from the LORD *
        and a just reward from the God of their salvation."

6   Such is the generation of those who seek him, *
        of those who seek your face, O God of Jacob.

7    Lift up your heads, O gates;
        lift them high, O everlasting doors; *
            and the King of glory shall come in.

8    "Who is this King of glory?" *
        "The LORD, strong and mighty,
            the LORD, mighty in battle."

9    Lift up your heads, O gates;
        lift them high, O everlasting doors; *
            and the King of glory shall come in.

10   "Who is he, this King of glory?" *
        "The LORD of hosts,
            he is the King of glory."


# 25    *Ad te, Domine, levavi*

1    To you, O LORD, I lift up my soul;
        my God, I put my trust in you; *
            let me not be humiliated,
            nor let my enemies triumph over me.

2    Let none who look to you be put to shame; *
        let the treacherous be disappointed in their schemes.

3    Show me your ways, O LORD, *
        and teach me your paths.

4    Lead me in your truth and teach me, *
        for you are the God of my salvation;
        in you have I trusted all the day long.

5    Remember, O LORD, your compassion and love, *
        for they are from everlasting.

6    Remember not the sins of my youth and my transgressions; *
     remember me according to your love
     and for the sake of your goodness, O LORD.

7    Gracious and upright is the LORD; *
     therefore he teaches sinners in his way.

8    He guides the humble in doing right *
     and teaches his way to the lowly.

9    All the paths of the LORD are love and faithfulness *
     to those who keep his covenant and his testimonies.

10    For your Name's sake, O LORD, *
     forgive my sin, for it is great.

11    Who are they who fear the LORD? *
     he will teach them the way that should choose.

12    They shall dwell in prosperity, *
     and their offspring shall inherit the land.

13    The LORD is a friend to those who fear him *
     and will show them his covenant.

14    My eyes are ever looking to the LORD, *
     for he shall pluck my feet out of the net.

15    Turn to me and have pity on me, *
     for I am left alone and in misery.

16    The sorrows of my heart have increased; *
     bring me out of my troubles.

17    Look upon my adversity and misery *
     and forgive me all my sin.

18    Look upon my enemies, for they are many, *
     and they bear a violent hatred against me.

19 Protect my life and deliver me; *
   let me not be put to shame, for I have trusted in you.

20 Let integrity and uprightness preserve me, *
   for my hope has been in you.

21 Deliver Israel, O God, *
   out of all his troubles.

## 26 *Judica me, Domine*

1 Give judgment for me, O LORD,
   for I have lived with integrity; *
      I have trusted in the Lord and have not faltered.

2 Test me, O LORD, and try me; *
   examine my heart and my mind.

3 For your love is before my eyes; *
   I have walked faithfully with you.

4 I have not sat with the worthless, *
   nor do I consort with the deceitful.

5 I have hated the company of evildoers; *
   I will not sit down with the wicked.

6 I will wash my hands in innocence, O LORD, *
   that I may go in procession round your altar,

7 Singing aloud a song of thanksgiving *
   and recounting all your wonderful deeds.

8 LORD, I love the house in which you dwell *
   and the place where your glory abides.

9 Do not sweep me away with sinners, *
   nor my life with those who thirst for blood,

10    Whose hands are full of evil plots, *
        and their right hand full of bribes.

11    As for me, I will live with integrity; *
        redeem me, O LORD, and have pity on me.

12    My foot stands on level ground; *
        in the full assembly I will bless the LORD.


*Fifth Day: Evening Prayer*

27   *Dominus illuminatio*

1    The LORD is my light and my salvation;
     whom then shall I fear? *
        the LORD is the strength of my life;
        of whom then shall I be afraid?

2    When evildoers came upon me to eat up my flesh, *
        it was they, my foes and my adversaries, who
            stumbled and fell.

3    Though an army should encamp against me, *
        yet my heart shall not be afraid;

4    And though war should rise up against me, *
        yet will I put my trust in him.

5    One thing have I asked of the LORD;
     one thing I seek; *
        that I may dwell in the house of the LORD all the days
            of my life;

6    To behold the fair beauty of the LORD *
        and to seek him in his temple.

7   For in the day of trouble he shall keep me safe
            in his shelter; *
        he shall hide me in the secrecy of his dwelling
        and set me high upon a rock.

8   Even now he lifts up my head *
        above my enemies round about me.

9   Therefore I will offer in his dwelling an oblation
    with sounds of great gladness; *
        I will sing and make music to the LORD.

10  Hearken to my voice, O LORD, when I call; *
        have mercy on me and answer me.

11  You speak in my heart and say, "Seek my face." *
        Your face, LORD, will I seek.

12  Hide not your face from me, *
        nor turn away your servant in displeasure.

13  You have been my helper;
    cast me not away; *
        do not forsake me, O God of my salvation.

14  Though my father and my mother forsake me, *
        the LORD will sustain me.

15  Show me your way, O LORD; *
        lead me on a level path, because of my enemies.

16  Deliver me not into the hand of my adversaries, *
        for false witnesses have risen up against me,
        and also those who speak malice.

17  What if I had not believed
    that I should see the goodness of the LORD *
        in the land of the living!

18    O tarry and await the LORD's pleasure;
be strong, and he shall comfort your heart; *
    wait patiently for the LORD.

## 28   *Ad te, Domine*

1    O LORD, I call to you;
my Rock, do not be deaf to my cry; *
    lest, if you do not hear me,
    I become like those who go down to the Pit.

2    Hear the voice of my prayer when I cry out to you, *
    when I lift up my hands to your holy of holies.

3    Do not snatch me away with the wicked or with the
             evildoers, *
    who speak peaceably with their neighbors,
    while strife is in their hearts.

4    Repay them according to their deeds, *
    and according to the wickedness of their actions.

5    According to the work of their hands repay them, *
    and give them their just deserts.

6    They have no understanding of the LORD's doings,
nor of the works of his hands; *
    therefore he will break them down and not
             build them up.

7    Blessed is the LORD! *
    for he has heard the voice of my prayer.

8    The LORD is my strength and my shield; *
    my heart trusts in him, and I have been helped;

9    Therefore my heart dances for joy, *
    and in my song will I praise him.

10    The LORD is the strength of his people, *
      a safe refuge for his anointed.

11    Save your people and bless your inheritance; *
      shepherd them and carry them for ever.


## 29 *Afferte Domino*

1    Ascribe to the LORD, you gods, *
      ascribe to the LORD glory and strength.

2    Ascribe to the LORD the glory due his Name; *
      worship the LORD in the beauty of holiness.

3    The voice of the LORD is upon the waters;
    the God of glory thunders; *
      the LORD is upon the mighty waters.

4    The voice of the LORD is a powerful voice; *
      the voice of the LORD is a voice of splendor.

5    The voice of the LORD breaks the cedar trees; *
      the LORD breaks the cedars of Lebanon;

6    He makes Lebanon skip like a calf, *
      and Mount Hermon like a young wild ox.

7    The voice of the LORD splits the flames of fire;
    the voice of the LORD shakes the wilderness; *
      the LORD shakes the wilderness of Kadesh.

8    The voice of the LORD makes the oak trees writhe *
      and strips the forests bare.

9    And in the temple of the LORD *
      all are crying, "Glory!"

10    The LORD sits enthroned above the flood; *
      the LORD sits enthroned as King for evermore.

1   The LORD shall give strength to his people; *
        the LORD shall give his people the blessing of peace.


*Sixth Day: Morning Prayer*

30   *Exaltabo te, Domine*

1   I will exalt you, O LORD,
    because you have lifted me up *
        and have not let my enemies triumph over me.

2   O LORD my God, I cried out to you, *
        and you restored me to health.

3   You brought me up, O LORD, from the dead; *
        you restored my life as I was going down to the grave.

4   Sing to the LORD, you servants of his; *
        give thanks for the remembrance of his holiness.

5   For his wrath endures but the twinkling of an eye, *
        his favor for a lifetime.

6   Weeping may spend the night, *
        but joy comes in the morning.

7   While I felt secure, I said,
    "I shall never be disturbed. *
        You, LORD, with your favor, made me as strong as
                the mountains."

8   Then you hid your face, *
        and I was filled with fear.

9   I cried to you, O LORD; *
        I pleaded with the Lord, saying,

0   "What profit is there in my blood, if I go down to the Pit? *
        will the dust praise you or declare your faithfulness?

11    Hear, O LORD, and have mercy upon me; *
      O LORD, be my helper."

12    You have turned my wailing into dancing; *
      you have put off my sack-cloth and clothed me with j

13    Therefore my heart sings to you without ceasing; *
      O LORD my God, I will give you thanks for ever.

## 31   *In te, Domine, speravi*

1    In you, O LORD, have I taken refuge;
   let me never be put to shame; *
      deliver me in your righteousness.

2    Incline your ear to me; *
      make haste to deliver me.

3    Be my strong rock, a castle to keep me safe,
   for you are my crag and my stronghold; *
      for the sake of your Name, lead me and guide me.

4    Take me out of the net that they have secretly set for me
      for you are my tower of strength.

5    Into your hands I commend my spirit, *
      for you have redeemed me,
      O LORD, O God of truth.

6    I hate those who cling to worthless idols, *
      and I put my trust in the LORD.

7    I will rejoice and be glad because of your mercy; *
      for you have seen my affliction;
      you know my distress.

8    You have not shut me up in the power of the enemy; *
     you have set my feet in an open place.

9    Have mercy on me, O LORD, for I am in trouble; *
     my eye is consumed with sorrow,
     and also my throat and my belly.

10    For my life is wasted with grief,
     and my years with sighing; *
     my strength fails me because of affliction,
     and my bones are consumed.

11    I have become a reproach to all my enemies and
                   even to my neighbors,
     a dismay to those of my acquaintance; *
     when they see me in the street they avoid me.

12    I am forgotten like a dead man, out of mind; *
     I am as useless as a broken pot.

13    For I have heard the whispering of the crowd;
     fear is all around; *
     they put their heads together against me;
     they plot to take my life.

14    But as for me, I have trusted in you, O LORD. *
     I have said, "You are my God.

15    My times are in your hand; *
     rescue me from the hand of my enemies,
     and from those who persecute me.

16    Make your face to shine upon your servant, *
     and in your loving-kindness save me."

17    LORD, let me not be ashamed for having called upon you; *
     rather, let the wicked be put to shame;
     let them be silent in the grave.

18  Let the lying lips be silenced which speak against
                    the righteous, *
     haughtily, disdainfully, and with contempt.

19  How great is your goodness, O LORD!
     which you have laid up for those who fear you; *
         which you have done in the sight of all
         for those who put their trust in you.

20  You hide them in the covert of your presence from those
                    who slander them; *
     you keep them in your shelter from the strife of tongue

21  Blessed be the LORD! *
     for he has shown me the wonders of his love in a
                    besieged city.

22  Yet I said in my alarm,
     "I have been cut off from the sight of your eyes." *
         Nevertheless, you heard the sound of my entreaty
         when I cried out to you.

23  Love the LORD, all you who worship him; *
     the LORD protects the faithful,
     but repays to the full those who act haughtily.

24  Be strong and let your heart take courage, *
     all you who wait for the LORD.


*Sixth Day: Evening Prayer*

# 32  *Beati quorum*

1  Happy are they whose transgressions are forgiven, *
     and whose sin is put away!

2 Happy are they to whom the LORD imputes no guilt, *
   and in whose spirit there is no guile!

3 While I held my tongue, my bones withered away, *
   because of my groaning all day long.

4 For your hand was heavy upon me day and night; *
   my moisture was dried up as in the heat of summer.

5 Then I acknowledged my sin to you, *
   and did not conceal my guilt.

6 I said, "I will confess my transgressions to the LORD." *
   Then you forgave me the guilt of my sin.

7 Therefore all the faithful will make their prayers to you in
      time of trouble; *
   when the great waters overflow, they shall not reach them.

8 You are my hiding-place;
   you preserve me from trouble; *
   you surround me with shouts of deliverance.

9 "I will instruct you and teach you in the way that you
      should go; *
   I will guide you with my eye.

10 Do not be like horse or mule, which have no understanding; *
   who must be fitted with bit and bridle,
      or else they will not stay near you."

11 Great are the tribulations of the wicked; *
   but mercy embraces those who trust in the LORD.

12 Be glad, you righteous, and rejoice in the LORD; *
   shout for joy, all who are true of heart.

## 33  *Exultate, justi*

1  Rejoice in the LORD, you righteous; *
    it is good for the just to sing praises.

2  Praise the LORD with the harp; *
    play to him upon the psaltery and lyre.

3  Sing for him a new song; *
    sound a fanfare with all your skill upon the trumpet.

4  For the word of the LORD is right, *
    and all his works are sure.

5  He loves righteousness and justice; *
    the loving-kindness of the LORD fills the whole earth.

6  By the word of the LORD were the heavens made, *
    by the breath of his mouth all the heavenly hosts.

7  He gathers up the waters of the ocean as in a water-skin
    and stores up the depths of the sea.

8  Let all the earth fear the LORD; *
    let all who dwell in the world stand in awe of him.

9  For he spoke, and it came to pass; *
    he commanded, and it stood fast.

10  The LORD brings the will of the nations to naught; *
    he thwarts the designs of the peoples.

11  But the LORD's will stands fast for ever, *
    and the designs of his heart from age to age.

12  Happy is the nation whose God is the LORD! *
    happy the people he has chosen to be his own!

13 The LORD looks down from heaven, *
   and beholds all the people in the world.

14 From where he sits enthroned he turns his gaze *
   on all who dwell on the earth.

15 He fashions all the hearts of them *
   and understands all their works.

16 There is no king that can be saved by a mighty army; *
   a strong man is not delivered by his great strength.

17 The horse is a vain hope for deliverance; *
   for all its strength it cannot save.

18 Behold, the eye of the LORD is upon those who fear him, *
   on those who wait upon his love,

19 To pluck their lives from death, *
   and to feed them in time of famine.

20 Our soul waits for the LORD; *
   he is our help and our shield.

21 Indeed, our heart rejoices in him, *
   for in his holy Name we put our trust.

22 Let your loving-kindness, O LORD, be upon us, *
   as we have put our trust in you.


# 34 *Benedicam Dominum*

1 I will bless the LORD at all times; *
   his praise shall ever be in my mouth.

2 I will glory in the LORD; *
   let the humble hear and rejoice.

3 Proclaim with me the greatness of the LORD; *
   let us exalt his Name together.

4    I sought the LORD, and he answered me *
        and delivered me out of all my terror.

5    Look upon him and be radiant, *
        and let not your faces be ashamed.

6    I called in my affliction and the LORD heard me *
        and saved me from all my troubles.

7    The angel of the LORD encompasses those who fear him,
        and he will deliver them.

8    Taste and see that the LORD is good; *
        happy are they who trust in him!

9    Fear the LORD, you that are his saints, *
        for those who fear him lack nothing.

10    The young lions lack and suffer hunger, *
        but those who seek the LORD lack nothing that is good.

11    Come, children, and listen to me; *
        I will teach you the fear of the LORD.

12    Who among you loves life *
        and desires long life to enjoy prosperity?

13    Keep your tongue from evil-speaking *
        and your lips from lying words.

14    Turn from evil and do good; *
        seek peace and pursue it.

15    The eyes of the LORD are upon the righteous, *
        and his ears are open to their cry.

16    The face of the LORD is against those who do evil, *
        to root out the remembrance of them from the earth.

17  The righteous cry, and the Lord hears them *
        and delivers them from all their troubles.

18  The Lord is near to the brokenhearted *
        and will save those whose spirits are crushed.

19  Many are the troubles of the righteous, *
        but the Lord will deliver him out of them all.

20  He will keep safe all his bones; *
        not one of them shall be broken.

21  Evil shall slay the wicked, *
        and those who hate the righteous will be punished.

22  The Lord ransoms the life of his servants, *
        and none will be punished who trust in him.


*Seventh Day: Morning Prayer*

## 35  *Judica, Domine*

1   Fight those who fight me, O Lord; *
        attack those who are attacking me.

2   Take up shield and armor *
        and rise up to help me.

3   Draw the sword and bar the way against those
                        who pursue me; *
        say to my soul, "I am your salvation."

4   Let those who seek after my life be shamed and humbled; *
        let those who plot my ruin fall back and be dismayed.

5   Let them be like chaff before the wind, *
        and let the angel of the Lord drive them away.

6    Let their way be dark and slippery, *
     and let the angel of the LORD pursue them.

7    For they have secretly spread a net for me without a caus
     without a cause they have dug a pit to take me alive.

8    Let ruin come upon them unawares; *
     let them be caught in the net they hid;
     let them fall into the pit they dug.

9    Then I will be joyful in the LORD; *
     I will glory in his victory.

10   My very bones will say, "LORD, who is like you? *
     You deliver the poor from those who are too strong fc
     the poor and needy from those who rob them."

11   Malicious witnesses rise up against me; *
     they charge me with matters I know nothing about.

12   They pay me evil in exchange for good; *
     my soul is full of despair.

13   But when they were sick I dressed in sack-cloth *
     and humbled myself by fasting;

14   I prayed with my whole heart,
     as one would for a friend or a brother; *
     I behaved like one who mourns for his mother,
     bowed down and grieving.

15   But when I stumbled, they were glad and gathered toge
     they gathered against me; *
     strangers whom I did not know tore me to pieces an
         would not stop.

16   They put me to the test and mocked me; *
     they gnashed at me with their teeth.

17    O Lord, how long will you look on? *
        rescue me from the roaring beasts,
        and my life from the young lions.

18    I will give you thanks in the great congregation; *
        I will praise you in the mighty throng.

19    Do not let my treacherous foes rejoice over me, *
        nor let those who hate me without a cause
            wink at each other.

20    For they do not plan for peace, *
        but invent deceitful schemes against the
            quiet in the land.

21    They opened their mouths at me and said, *
        "Aha! we saw it with our own eyes."

22    You saw it, O Lord; do not be silent; *
        O Lord, be not far from me.

23    Awake, arise, to my cause! *
        to my defense, my God and my Lord!

24    Give me justice, O Lord my God,
        according to your righteousness; *
        do not let them triumph over me.

25    Do not let them say in their hearts,
    "Aha! just what we want!" *
        Do not let them say, "We have swallowed him up."

26    Let all who rejoice at my ruin be ashamed and disgraced; *
        let those who boast against me be clothed with
            dismay and shame.

27    Let those who favor my cause sing out with joy and be glad; *
        let them say always, "Great is the Lord,
        who desires the prosperity of his servant."

28    And my tongue shall be talking of your righteousness *
       and of your praise all the day long.


## 36   *Dixit injustus*

1    There is a voice of rebellion deep in the heart of the wick
       there is no fear of God before his eyes.

2    He flatters himself in his own eyes *
       that his hateful sin will not be found out.

3    The words of his mouth are wicked and deceitful; *
       he has left off acting wisely and doing good.

4    He thinks up wickedness upon his bed
    and has set himself in no good way; *
       he does not abhor that which is evil.


5    Your love, O LORD, reaches to the heavens, *
       and your faithfulness to the clouds.

6    Your righteousness is like the strong mountains,
    your justice like the great deep; *
       you save both man and beast, O LORD.

7    How priceless is your love, O God! *
       your people take refuge under the
                  shadow of your wings.

8    They feast upon the abundance of your house; *
       you give them drink from the river of your delights.

9    For with you is the well of life, *
       and in your light we see light.

10    Continue your loving-kindness to those who know you
       and your favor to those who are true of heart.

11    Let not the foot of the proud come near me, *
        nor the hand of the wicked push me aside.

12    See how they are fallen, those who work wickedness! *
        they are cast down and shall not be able to rise.


*Seventh Day: Evening Prayer*

# 37

**Part I**   *Noli æmulari*

1    Do not fret yourself because of evildoers; *
        do not be jealous of those who do wrong.

2    For they shall soon wither like the grass, *
        and like the green grass fade away.

3    Put your trust in the LORD and do good; *
        dwell in the land and feed on its riches.

4    Take delight in the LORD, *
        and he shall give you your heart's desire.

5    Commit your way to the LORD and put your trust in him, *
        and he will bring it to pass.

6    He will make your righteousness as clear as the light *
        and your just dealing as the noonday.

7    Be still before the LORD *
        and wait patiently for him.

8    Do not fret yourself over the one who prospers, *
        the one who succeeds in evil schemes.

9    Refrain from anger, leave rage alone; *
        do not fret yourself; it leads only to evil.

10   For evildoers shall be cut off, *
        but those who wait upon the LORD shall possess the lan[d]

11   In a little while the wicked shall be no more; *
        you shall search out their place, but they will not be the[re]

12   But the lowly shall possess the land; *
        they will delight in abundance of peace.

13   The wicked plot against the righteous *
        and gnash at them with their teeth.

14   The Lord laughs at the wicked, *
        because he sees that their day will come.

15   The wicked draw their sword and bend their bow
     to strike down the poor and needy, *
        to slaughter those who are upright in their ways.

16   Their sword shall go through their own heart, *
        and their bow shall be broken.

17   The little that the righteous has *
        is better than great riches of the wicked.

18   For the power of the wicked shall be broken, *
        but the LORD upholds the righteous.


**Psalm 37: Part II**   *Novit Dominus*

19   The LORD cares for the lives of the godly, *
        and their inheritance shall last for ever.

20   They shall not be ashamed in bad times, *
        and in days of famine they shall have enough.

21   As for the wicked, they shall perish, *
        and the enemies of the LORD, like the glory of
                        the meadows, shall vanish;
        they shall vanish like smoke.

22 The wicked borrow and do not repay, *
    but the righteous are generous in giving.

23 Those who are blessed by God shall possess the land, *
    but those who are cursed by him shall be destroyed.

24 Our steps are directed by the LORD; *
    he strengthens those in whose way he delights.

25 If they stumble, they shall not fall headlong, *
    for the LORD holds them by the hand.

26 I have been young and now I am old, *
    but never have I seen the righteous forsaken,
    or their children begging bread.

27 The righteous are always generous in their lending, *
    and their children shall be a blessing.

28 Turn from evil, and do good, *
    and dwell in the land for ever.

29 For the LORD loves justice; *
    he does not forsake his faithful ones.

30 They shall be kept safe for ever, *
    but the offspring of the wicked shall be destroyed.

31 The righteous shall possess the land *
    and dwell in it for ever.

32 The mouth of the righteous utters wisdom, *
    and their tongue speaks what is right.

33 The law of their God is in their heart, *
    and their footsteps shall not falter.

34 The wicked spy on the righteous *
    and seek occasion to kill them.

35    The LORD will not abandon them to their hand, *
        nor let them be found guilty when brought to trial.

36    Wait upon the LORD and keep his way; *
        he will raise you up to possess the land,
        and when the wicked are cut off, you will see it.

37    I have seen the wicked in their arrogance, *
        flourishing like a tree in full leaf.

38    I went by, and behold, they were not there; *
        I searched for them, but they could not be found.

39    Mark those who are honest;
    observe the upright; *
        for there is a future for the peaceable.

40    Transgressors shall be destroyed, one and all; *
        the future of the wicked is cut off.

41    But the deliverance of the righteous comes from the LORD;
        he is their stronghold in time of trouble.

42    The LORD will help them and rescue them; *
        he will rescue them from the wicked and deliver them,
        because they seek refuge in him.


*Eighth Day: Morning Prayer*

# 38  *Domine, ne in furore*

1    O LORD, do not rebuke me in your anger; *
        do not punish me in your wrath.

2    For your arrows have already pierced me, *
        and your hand presses hard upon me.

3 There is no health in my flesh,
because of your indignation; *
  there is no soundness in my body, because of my sin.

4 For my iniquities overwhelm me; *
  like a heavy burden they are too much for me to bear.

5 My wounds stink and fester *
  by reason of my foolishness.

6 I am utterly bowed down and prostrate; *
  I go about in mourning all the day long.

7 My loins are filled with searing pain; *
  there is no health in my body.

8 I am utterly numb and crushed; *
  I wail, because of the groaning of my heart.

9 O Lord, you know all my desires, *
  and my sighing is not hidden from you.

10 My heart is pounding, my strength has failed me, *
  and the brightness of my eyes is gone from me.

11 My friends and companions draw back from my affliction; *
  my neighbors stand afar off.

12 Those who seek after my life lay snares for me; *
  those who strive to hurt me speak of my ruin
  and plot treachery all the day long.

13 But I am like the deaf who do not hear, *
  like those who are mute and do not open their mouth.

14 I have become like one who does not hear *
  and from whose mouth comes no defense.

15 For in you, O LORD, have I fixed my hope; *
  you will answer me, O Lord my God.

16    For I said,"Do not let them rejoice at my expense, *
         those who gloat over me when my foot slips."

17    Truly, I am on the verge of falling, *
         and my pain is always with me.

18    I will confess my iniquity *
         and be sorry for my sin.

19    Those who are my enemies without cause are mighty, *
         and many in number are those who wrongfully hate me

20    Those who repay evil for good slander me, *
         because I follow the course that is right.

21    O Lord, do not forsake me; *
         be not far from me, O my God.

22    Make haste to help me, *
         O Lord of my salvation.


## 39    Dixi, Custodiam

1    I said," I will keep watch upon my ways, *
         so that I do not offend with my tongue.

2    I will put a muzzle on my mouth *
         while the wicked are in my presence."

3    So I held my tongue and said nothing; *
         I refrained from rash words;
         but my pain became unbearable.

4    My heart was hot within me;
         while I pondered, the fire burst into flame; *
         I spoke out with my tongue:

5   LORD, let me know my end and the number of my days, *
       so that I may know how short my life is.

6   You have given me a mere handful of days,
       and my lifetime is as nothing in your sight; *
          truly, even those who stand erect are but a puff of wind.

7   We walk about like a shadow,
       and in vain we are in turmoil; *
          we heap up riches and cannot tell who will gather them.

8   And now, what is my hope? *
       O Lord, my hope is in you.

9   Deliver me from all my transgressions *
       and do not make me the taunt of the fool.

10  I fell silent and did not open my mouth, *
       for surely it was you that did it.

11  Take your affliction from me; *
       I am worn down by the blows of your hand.

12  With rebukes for sin you punish us;
       like a moth you eat away all that is dear to us; *
          truly, everyone is but a puff of wind.

13  Hear my prayer, O LORD,
       and give ear to my cry; *
          hold not your peace at my tears.

14  For I am but a sojourner with you, *
       a wayfarer, as all my forebears were.

15  Turn your gaze from me, that I may be glad again, *
       before I go my way and am no more.

## 40 *Expectans, expectavi*

1 I waited patiently upon the LORD; *
   he stooped to me and heard my cry.

2 He lifted me out of the desolate pit, out of the mire and cla
   he set my feet upon a high cliff and made my footing sur

3 He put a new song in my mouth,
   a song of praise to our God; *
      many shall see, and stand in awe,
      and put their trust in the LORD.

4 Happy are they who trust in the LORD! *
   they do not resort to evil spirits or turn to false gods.

5 Great things are they that you have done, O LORD my Go
   how great your wonders and your plans for us! *
      there is none who can be compared with you.

6 Oh, that I could make them known and tell them! *
   but they are more than I can count.

7 In sacrifice and offering you take no pleasure *
   (you have given me ears to hear you);

8 Burnt-offering and sin-offering you have not required, *
   and so I said, "Behold, I come.

9 In the roll of the book it is written concerning me: *
   'I love to do your will, O my God;
   your law is deep in my heart.'"

10 I proclaimed righteousness in the great congregation; *
   behold, I did not restrain my lips;
   and that, O LORD, you know.

11 Your righteousness have I not hidden in my heart;
   I have spoken of your faithfulness and your deliverance;
      I have not concealed your love and faithfulness from th
                           great congregation.

12 You are the LORD;
  do not withhold your compassion from me; *
   let your love and your faithfulness keep me safe for ever,

13 For innumerable troubles have crowded upon me;
  my sins have overtaken me, and I cannot see; *
   they are more in number than the hairs of my head,
   and my heart fails me.

14 Be pleased, O LORD, to deliver me; *
  O LORD, make haste to help me.


15 Let them be ashamed and altogether dismayed
  who seek after my life to destroy it; *
   let them draw back and be disgraced
   who take pleasure in my misfortune.

16 Let those who say "Aha!" and gloat over me be confounded, *
  because they are ashamed.

17 Let all who seek you rejoice in you and be glad; *
  let those who love your salvation continually say,
  "Great is the LORD!"

18 Though I am poor and afflicted, *
  the Lord will have regard for me.

19 You are my helper and my deliverer; *
  do not tarry, O my God.


*Eighth Day: Evening Prayer*

## 41 *Beatus qui intelligit*

1 Happy are they who consider the poor and needy! *
  the LORD will deliver them in the time of trouble.

2   The LORD preserves them and keeps them alive,
      so that they may be happy in the land; *
        he does not hand them over to the will of their enemies

3   The LORD sustains them on their sickbed *
      and ministers to them in their illness.

4   I said, "LORD, be merciful to me; *
      heal me, for I have sinned against you."

5   My enemies are saying wicked things about me: *
      "When will he die, and his name perish?"

6   Even if they come to see me, they speak empty words; *
      their heart collects false rumors;
      they go outside and spread them.

7   All my enemies whisper together about me *
      and devise evil against me.

8   "A deadly thing," they say, "has fastened on him; *
      he has taken to his bed and will never get up again."

9   Even my best friend, whom I trusted,
      who broke bread with me, *
        has lifted up his heel and turned against me.

10  But you, O LORD, be merciful to me and raise me up, *
      and I shall repay them.

11  By this I know you are pleased with me, *
      that my enemy does not triumph over me.

12  In my integrity you hold me fast, *
      and shall set me before your face for ever.


13  Blessed be the LORD God of Israel, *
      from age to age. Amen. Amen.

**Book Two**

## 42 *Quemadmodum*

1   As the deer longs for the water-brooks, *
    so longs my soul for you, O God.

2   My soul is athirst for God, athirst for the living God; *
    when shall I come to appear before the presence of God?

3   My tears have been my food day and night, *
    while all day long they say to me,
    "Where now is your God?"

4   I pour out my soul when I think on these things: *
    how I went with the multitude and led them into the
        house of God,

5   With the voice of praise and thanksgiving, *
    among those who keep holy-day.

6   Why are you so full of heaviness, O my soul? *
    and why are you so disquieted within me?

7   Put your trust in God; *
    for I will yet give thanks to him,
    who is the help of my countenance, and my God.


8   My soul is heavy within me; *
    therefore I will remember you from the land of Jordan,
    and from the peak of Mizar among the heights of Hermon.

9   One deep calls to another in the noise of your cataracts; *
    all your rapids and floods have gone over me.

10  The LORD grants his loving-kindness in the daytime; *
    in the night season his song is with me,
    a prayer to the God of my life.

11    I will say to the God of my strength,
        "Why have you forgotten me? *
           and why do I go so heavily while the enemy
                         oppresses me?"

12    While my bones are being broken, *
        my enemies mock me to my face;

13    All day long they mock me *
        and say to me, "Where now is your God?"

14    Why are you so full of heaviness, O my soul? *
        and why are you so disquieted within me?

15    Put your trust in God; *
        for I will yet give thanks to him,
        who is the help of my countenance, and my God.


## 43    *Judica me, Deus*

1    Give judgment for me, O God,
        and defend my cause against an ungodly people; *
        deliver me from the deceitful and the wicked.

2    For you are the God of my strength;
        why have you put me from you? *
           and why do I go so heavily while the enemy
                         oppresses me?

3    Send out your light and your truth, that they may lead m
        and bring me to your holy hill
        and to your dwelling;

4    That I may go to the altar of God,
        to the God of my joy and gladness; *
        and on the harp I will give thanks to you, O God my

5      Why are you so full of heaviness, O my soul? *
       and why are you so disquieted within me?

6      Put your trust in God; *
       for I will yet give thanks to him,
       who is the help of my countenance, and my God.


*Ninth Day: Morning Prayer*

## 44    *Deus, auribus*

1      We have heard with our ears, O God,
our forefathers have told us, *
       the deeds you did in their days,
       in the days of old.

2      How with your hand you drove the peoples out
and planted our forefathers in the land; *
       how you destroyed nations and made your people flourish.

3      For they did not take the land by their sword,
nor did their arm win the victory for them; *
       but your right hand, your arm, and the
                   light of your countenance,
       because you favored them.

4      You are my King and my God; *
       you command victories for Jacob.

5      Through you we pushed back our adversaries; *
       through your Name we trampled on those who
                   rose up against us.

6      For I do not rely on my bow, *
       and my sword does not give me the victory.

7      Surely, you gave us victory over our adversaries *
       and put those who hate us to shame.

8  Every day we gloried in God, *
      and we will praise your Name for ever.

9  Nevertheless, you have rejected and humbled us *
      and do not go forth with our armies.

10 You have made us fall back before our adversary, *
      and our enemies have plundered us.

11 You have made us like sheep to be eaten *
      and have scattered us among the nations.

12 You are selling your people for a trifle *
      and are making no profit on the sale of them.

13 You have made us the scorn of our neighbors, *
      a mockery and derision to those around us.

14 You have made us a byword among the nations, *
      a laughing-stock among the peoples.

15 My humiliation is daily before me, *
      and shame has covered my face;

16 Because of the taunts of the mockers and blasphemers, *
      because of the enemy and avenger.

17 All this has come upon us; *
      yet we have not forgotten you,
      nor have we betrayed your covenant.

18 Our heart never turned back, *
      nor did our footsteps stray from your path;

19 Though you thrust us down into a place of misery, *
      and covered us over with deep darkness.

20 If we have forgotten the Name of our God, *
      or stretched out our hands to some strange god,

21 Will not God find it out? *
      for he knows the secrets of the heart.

22  Indeed, for your sake we are killed all the day long; *
        we are accounted as sheep for the slaughter.

23  Awake, O Lord! why are you sleeping? *
        Arise! do not reject us for ever.

24  Why have you hidden your face *
        and forgotten our affliction and oppression?

25  We sink down into the dust; *
        our body cleaves to the ground.

26  Rise up, and help us, *
        and save us, for the sake of your steadfast love.


## 45 *Eructavit cor meum*

1   My heart is stirring with a noble song;
    let me recite what I have fashioned for the king; *
        my tongue shall be the pen of a skilled writer.

2   You are the fairest of men; *
        grace flows from your lips,
        because God has blessed you for ever.

3   Strap your sword upon your thigh, O mighty warrior, *
        in your pride and in your majesty.

4   Ride out and conquer in the cause of truth *
        and for the sake of justice.

5   Your right hand will show you marvelous things; *
        your arrows are very sharp, O mighty warrior.

6   The peoples are falling at your feet, *
        and the king's enemies are losing heart.

7    Your throne, O God, endures for ever and ever, *
      a scepter of righteousness is the scepter of your kingdo
      you love righteousness and hate iniquity.

8    Therefore God, your God, has anointed you *
      with the oil of gladness above your fellows.

9    All your garments are fragrant with myrrh, aloes, and ca
      and the music of strings from ivory palaces makes you

10    Kings' daughters stand among the ladies of the court; *
      on your right hand is the queen,
      adorned with the gold of Ophir.

11    "Hear, O daughter; consider and listen closely; *
      forget your people and your father's house.

12    The king will have pleasure in your beauty; *
      he is your master; therefore do him honor.

13    The people of Tyre are here with a gift; *
      the rich among the people seek your favor."

14    All glorious is the princess as she enters; *
      her gown is cloth-of-gold.

15    In embroidered apparel she is brought to the king; *
      after her the bridesmaids follow in procession.

16    With joy and gladness they are brought, *
      and enter into the palace of the king.

17    "In place of fathers, O king, you shall have sons; *
      you shall make them princes over all the earth.

18    I will make your name to be remembered
      from one generation to another; *
      therefore nations will praise you for ever and ever."

# 46 *Deus noster refugium*

1  God is our refuge and strength, *
    a very present help in trouble.

2  Therefore we will not fear, though the earth be moved, *
    and though the mountains be toppled into the
                        depths of the sea;

3  Though its waters rage and foam, *
    and though the mountains tremble at its tumult.

4  The LORD of hosts is with us; *
    the God of Jacob is our stronghold.


5  There is a river whose streams make glad the city of God, *
    the holy habitation of the Most High.

6  God is in the midst of her;
    she shall not be overthrown; *
    God shall help her at the break of day.

7  The nations make much ado, and the kingdoms are shaken; *
    God has spoken, and the earth shall melt away.

8  The LORD of hosts is with us; *
    the God of Jacob is our stronghold.


9  Come now and look upon the works of the LORD, *
    what awesome things he has done on earth.

10  It is he who makes war to cease in all the world; *
    he breaks the bow, and shatters the spear,
    and burns the shields with fire.

11 "Be still, then, and know that I am God; *
    I will be exalted among the nations;
    I will be exalted in the earth."

12 The LORD of hosts is with us; *
    the God of Jacob is our stronghold.


*Ninth Day: Evening Prayer*

# 47 *Omnes gentes, plaudite*

1 Clap your hands, all you peoples; *
    shout to God with a cry of joy.

2 For the LORD Most High is to be feared; *
    he is the great King over all the earth.

3 He subdues the peoples under us, *
    and the nations under our feet.

4 He chooses our inheritance for us, *
    the pride of Jacob whom he loves.

5 God has gone up with a shout, *
    the LORD with the sound of the ram's-horn.

6 Sing praises to God, sing praises; *
    sing praises to our King, sing praises.

7 For God is King of all the earth; *
    sing praises with all your skill.

8 God reigns over the nations; *
    God sits upon his holy throne.

9 The nobles of the peoples have gathered together *
    with the people of the God of Abraham.

10 The rulers of the earth belong to God, *
    and he is highly exalted.

*Magnus Dominus*

1   Great is the LORD, and highly to be praised; *
        in the city of our God is his holy hill.

2   Beautiful and lofty, the joy of all the earth, is the
                    hill of Zion, *
        the very center of the world and the city of the great King.

3   God is in her citadels; *
        he is known to be her sure refuge.

4   Behold, the kings of the earth assembled *
        and marched forward together.

5   They looked and were astounded; *
        they retreated and fled in terror.

6   Trembling seized them there; *
        they writhed like a woman in childbirth,
        like ships of the sea when the east wind shatters them.

7   As we have heard, so have we seen,
        in the city of the LORD of hosts, in the city of our God; *
        God has established her for ever.

8   We have waited in silence on your loving-kindness, O God, *
        in the midst of your temple.

9   Your praise, like your Name, O God, reaches to
                    the world's end; *
        your right hand is full of justice.

10  Let Mount Zion be glad
        and the cities of Judah rejoice, *
        because of your judgments.

11  Make the circuit of Zion;
        walk round about her; *
        count the number of her towers.

12     Consider well her bulwarks;
       examine her strongholds; *
         that you may tell those who come after.

13     This God is our God for ever and ever; *
       he shall be our guide for evermore.


## 49     *Audite hæc, omnes*

1     Hear this, all you peoples;
       hearken, all you who dwell in the world, *
         you of high degree and low, rich and poor together.

2     My mouth shall speak of wisdom, *
       and my heart shall meditate on understanding.

3     I will incline my ear to a proverb *
       and set forth my riddle upon the harp.

4     Why should I be afraid in evil days, *
       when the wickedness of those at my heels surrounds m

5     The wickedness of those who put their trust in their goo
       and boast of their great riches?

6     We can never ransom ourselves, *
       or deliver to God the price of our life;

7     For the ransom of our life is so great, *
       that we should never have enough to pay it,

8     In order to live for ever and ever, *
       and never see the grave.

9     For we see that the wise die also;
       like the dull and stupid they perish *
         and leave their wealth to those who come after them.

10 Their graves shall be their homes for ever,
   their dwelling places from generation to generation, *
      though they call the lands after their own names.

11 Even though honored, they cannot live for ever; *
      they are like the beasts that perish.

12 Such is the way of those who foolishly trust in themselves, *
      and the end of those who delight in their own words.

13 Like a flock of sheep they are destined to die;
   Death is their shepherd; *
      they go down straightway to the grave.

14 Their form shall waste away, *
      and the land of the dead shall be their home.

15 But God will ransom my life; *
      he will snatch me from the grasp of death.

16 Do not be envious when some become rich, *
      or when the grandeur of their house increases;

17 For they will carry nothing away at their death, *
      nor will their grandeur follow them.

18 Though they thought highly of themselves while they lived, *
      and were praised for their success,

19 They shall join the company of their forebears, *
      who will never see the light again.

20 Those who are honored, but have no understanding, *
      are like the beasts that perish.

## 50  *Deus deorum*

1   The LORD, the God of gods, has spoken; *
      he has called the earth from the rising of the sun to
            its setting.

2   Out of Zion, perfect in its beauty, *
      God reveals himself in glory.

3   Our God will come and will not keep silence; *
      before him there is a consuming flame,
      and round about him a raging storm.

4   He calls the heavens and the earth from above *
      to witness the judgment of his people.

5   "Gather before me my loyal followers, *
      those who have made a covenant with me
      and sealed it with sacrifice."

6   Let the heavens declare the rightness of his cause; *
      for God himself is judge.

7   Hear, O my people, and I will speak:
      "O Israel, I will bear witness against you; *
      for I am God, your God.

8   I do not accuse you because of your sacrifices; *
      your offerings are always before me.

9   I will take no bull-calf from your stalls, *
      nor he-goats out of your pens;

10  For all the beasts of the forest are mine, *
      the herds in their thousands upon the hills.

11 I know every bird in the sky, *
  and the creatures of the fields are in my sight.

12 If I were hungry, I would not tell you, *
  for the whole world is mine and all that is in it.

13 Do you think I eat the flesh of bulls, *
  or drink the blood of goats?

14 Offer to God a sacrifice of thanksgiving *
  and make good your vows to the Most High.

15 Call upon me in the day of trouble; *
  I will deliver you, and you shall honor me."

16 But to the wicked God says: *
  "Why do you recite my statutes,
  and take my covenant upon your lips;

17 Since you refuse discipline, *
  and toss my words behind your back?

18 When you see a thief, you make him your friend, *
  and you cast in your lot with adulterers.

19 You have loosed your lips for evil, *
  and harnessed your tongue to a lie.

20 You are always speaking evil of your brother *
  and slandering your own mother's son.

21 These things you have done, and I kept still, *
  and you thought that I am like you."

22 "I have made my accusation; *
  I have put my case in order before your eyes.

23 Consider this well, you who forget God, *
  lest I rend you and there be none to deliver you.

24 Whoever offers me the sacrifice of thanksgiving
honors me; *
but to those who keep in my way will I show
the salvation of God."


## 51 *Miserere mei, Deus*

1 Have mercy on me, O God, according to your
loving-kindness; *
in your great compassion blot out my offenses.

2 Wash me through and through from my wickedness *
and cleanse me from my sin.

3 For I know my transgressions, *
and my sin is ever before me.

4 Against you only have I sinned *
and done what is evil in your sight.

5 And so you are justified when you speak *
and upright in your judgment.

6 Indeed, I have been wicked from my birth, *
a sinner from my mother's womb.

7 For behold, you look for truth deep within me, *
and will make me understand wisdom secretly.

8 Purge me from my sin, and I shall be pure; *
wash me, and I shall be clean indeed.

9 Make me hear of joy and gladness, *
that the body you have broken may rejoice.

10 Hide your face from my sins *
and blot out all my iniquities.

1 Create in me a clean heart, O God, *
   and renew a right spirit within me.

2 Cast me not away from your presence *
   and take not your holy Spirit from me.

3 Give me the joy of your saving help again *
   and sustain me with your bountiful Spirit.

4 I shall teach your ways to the wicked, *
   and sinners shall return to you.

5 Deliver me from death, O God, *
   and my tongue shall sing of your righteousness,
   O God of my salvation.

6 Open my lips, O Lord, *
   and my mouth shall proclaim your praise.

7 Had you desired it, I would have offered sacrifice, *
   but you take no delight in burnt-offerings.

8 The sacrifice of God is a troubled spirit; *
   a broken and contrite heart, O God, you will not despise.

9 Be favorable and gracious to Zion, *
   and rebuild the walls of Jerusalem.

10 Then you will be pleased with the appointed sacrifices,
with burnt-offerings and oblations; *
   then shall they offer young bullocks upon your altar.

## 52 *Quid gloriaris?*

You tyrant, why do you boast of wickedness *
   against the godly all day long?

2     You plot ruin;
        your tongue is like a sharpened razor, *
           O worker of deception.

3     You love evil more than good *
        and lying more than speaking the truth.

4     You love all words that hurt, *
        O you deceitful tongue.

5     Oh, that God would demolish you utterly, *
        topple you, and snatch you from your dwelling,
        and root you out of the land of the living!

6     The righteous shall see and tremble, *
        and they shall laugh at him, saying,

7     "This is the one who did not take God for a refuge, *
        but trusted in great wealth
        and relied upon wickedness."

8     But I am like a green olive tree in the house of God; *
        I trust in the mercy of God for ever and ever.

9     I will give you thanks for what you have done *
        and declare the goodness of your Name in the presence
          of the godly.

*Tenth Day: Evening Prayer*

# 53    *Dixit insipiens*

1     The fool has said in his heart, "There is no God." *
        All are corrupt and commit abominable acts;
        there is none who does any good.

God looks down from heaven upon us all, *
    to see if there is any who is wise,
    if there is one who seeks after God.

Every one has proved faithless;
all alike have turned bad; *
    there is none who does good; no, not one.

Have they no knowledge, those evildoers *
    who eat up my people like bread
    and do not call upon God?

See how greatly they tremble,
such trembling as never was; *
    for God has scattered the bones of the enemy;
    they are put to shame, because God has rejected them.

Oh, that Israel's deliverance would come out of Zion! *
    when God restores the fortunes of his people
    Jacob will rejoice and Israel be glad.


## 54 *Deus, in nomine*

Save me, O God, by your Name; *
    in your might, defend my cause.

Hear my prayer, O God; *
    give ear to the words of my mouth.

For the arrogant have risen up against me,
and the ruthless have sought my life, *
    those who have no regard for God.

Behold, God is my helper; *
    it is the Lord who sustains my life.

Render evil to those who spy on me; *
    in your faithfulness, destroy them.

6    I will offer you a freewill sacrifice *
        and praise your Name, O LORD, for it is good.

7    For you have rescued me from every trouble, *
        and my eye has seen the ruin of my foes.


## 55    *Exaudi, Deus*

1    Hear my prayer, O God; *
        do not hide yourself from my petition.

2    Listen to me and answer me; *
        I have no peace, because of my cares.

3    I am shaken by the noise of the enemy *
        and by the pressure of the wicked;

4    For they have cast an evil spell upon me *
        and are set against me in fury.

5    My heart quakes within me, *
        and the terrors of death have fallen upon me.

6    Fear and trembling have come over me, *
        and horror overwhelms me.

7    And I said, "Oh, that I had wings like a dove! *
        I would fly away and be at rest.

8    I would flee to a far-off place *
        and make my lodging in the wilderness.

9    I would hasten to escape *
        from the stormy wind and tempest."

10   Swallow them up, O Lord;
     confound their speech; *
        for I have seen violence and strife in the city.

11 Day and night the watchmen make their rounds
             upon her walls, *
      but trouble and misery are in the midst of her.

12 There is corruption at her heart; *
      her streets are never free of oppression and deceit.

13 For had it been an adversary who taunted me,
   then I could have borne it; *
      or had it been an enemy who vaunted himself against me,
      then I could have hidden from him.

14 But it was you, a man after my own heart, *
      my companion, my own familiar friend.

15 We took sweet counsel together, *
      and walked with the throng in the house of God.

16 Let death come upon them suddenly;
   let them go down alive into the grave; *
      for wickedness is in their dwellings, in their very midst.

17 But I will call upon God, *
      and the LORD will deliver me.

18 In the evening, in the morning, and at noonday,
   I will complain and lament, *
      and he will hear my voice.

19 He will bring me safely back from the battle
             waged against me; *
      for there are many who fight me.

20 God, who is enthroned of old, will hear me and
             bring them down; *
      they never change; they do not fear God.

21 My companion stretched forth his hand against his comrade; *
      he has broken his covenant.

22     His speech is softer than butter, *
      but war is in his heart.

23     His words are smoother than oil, *
      but they are drawn swords.

24     Cast your burden upon the LORD,
      and he will sustain you; *
      he will never let the righteous stumble.

25     For you will bring the bloodthirsty and deceitful *
      down to the pit of destruction, O God.

26     They shall not live out half their days, *
      but I will put my trust in you.


*Eleventh Day: Morning Prayer*

# 56    *Miserere mei, Deus*

1     Have mercy on me, O God,
      for my enemies are hounding me; *
      all day long they assault and oppress me.

2     They hound me all the day long; *
      truly there are many who fight against me, O Most H

3     Whenever I am afraid, *
      I will put my trust in you.

4     In God, whose word I praise,
      in God I trust and will not be afraid, *
      for what can flesh do to me?

5     All day long they damage my cause; *
      their only thought is to do me evil.

They band together; they lie in wait; *
    they spy upon my footsteps;
    because they seek my life.

Shall they escape despite their wickedness? *
    O God, in your anger, cast down the peoples.

You have noted my lamentation;
put my tears into your bottle; *
    are they not recorded in your book?

Whenever I call upon you, my enemies will be put to flight; *
    this I know, for God is on my side.

In God the LORD, whose word I praise,
in God I trust and will not be afraid, *
    for what can mortals do to me?

I am bound by the vow I made to you, O God; *
    I will present to you thank-offerings;

For you have rescued my soul from death and my feet
                    from stumbling, *
    that I may walk before God in the light of the living.


# 57    *Miserere mei, Deus*

Be merciful to me, O God, be merciful,
for I have taken refuge in you; *
    in the shadow of your wings will I take refuge
    until this time of trouble has gone by.

I will call upon the Most High God, *
    the God who maintains my cause.

He will send from heaven and save me;
he will confound those who trample upon me; *
    God will send forth his love and his faithfulness.

4    I lie in the midst of lions that devour the people; *
         their teeth are spears and arrows,
         their tongue a sharp sword.

5    They have laid a net for my feet,
     and I am bowed low; *
         they have dug a pit before me,
         but have fallen into it themselves.

6    Exalt yourself above the heavens, O God, *
         and your glory over all the earth.

7    My heart is firmly fixed, O God, my heart is fixed; *
         I will sing and make melody.

8    Wake up, my spirit;
     awake, lute and harp; *
         I myself will waken the dawn.

9    I will confess you among the peoples, O LORD; *
         I will sing praise to you among the nations.

10   For your loving-kindness is greater than the heavens, *
         and your faithfulness reaches to the clouds.

11   Exalt yourself above the heavens, O God, *
         and your glory over all the earth.


## 58   *Si vere utique*

1    Do you indeed decree righteousness, you rulers? *
         do you judge the peoples with equity?

2    No; you devise evil in your hearts, *
         and your hands deal out violence in the land.

3    The wicked are perverse from the womb; *
         liars go astray from their birth.

4   They are as venomous as a serpent, *
      they are like the deaf adder which stops its ears,

5   Which does not heed the voice of the charmer, *
      no matter how skillful his charming.

6   O God, break their teeth in their mouths; *
      pull the fangs of the young lions, O LORD.

7   Let them vanish like water that runs off; *
      let them wither like trodden grass.

8   Let them be like the snail that melts away, *
      like a stillborn child that never sees the sun.

9   Before they bear fruit, let them be cut down like a brier; *
      like thorns and thistles let them be swept away.

10  The righteous will be glad when they see the vengeance; *
      they will bathe their feet in the blood of the wicked.

11  And they will say,
    "Surely, there is a reward for the righteous; *
      surely, there is a God who rules in the earth."


*Eleventh Day: Evening Prayer*

## 59   *Eripe me de inimicis*

1   Rescue me from my enemies, O God; *
      protect me from those who rise up against me.

2   Rescue me from evildoers *
      and save me from those who thirst for my blood.

3   See how they lie in wait for my life,
    how the mighty gather together against me; *
      not for any offense or fault of mine, O LORD.

4   Not because of any guilt of mine *
        they run and prepare themselves for battle.

5   Rouse yourself, come to my side, and see; *
        for you, LORD God of hosts, are Israel's God.

6   Awake, and punish all the ungodly; *
        show no mercy to those who are faithless and evil.

7   They go to and fro in the evening; *
        they snarl like dogs and run about the city.

8   Behold, they boast with their mouths,
        and taunts are on their lips; *
        "For who," they say, "will hear us?"

9   But you, O LORD, you laugh at them; *
        you laugh all the ungodly to scorn.

10  My eyes are fixed on you, O my Strength; *
        for you, O God, are my stronghold.

11  My merciful God comes to meet me; *
        God will let me look in triumph on my enemies.

12  Slay them, O God, lest my people forget; *
        send them reeling by your might
        and put them down, O Lord our shield.

13  For the sins of their mouths, for the words of their lips,
        for the cursing and lies that they utter, *
        let them be caught in their pride.

14  Make an end of them in your wrath; *
        make an end of them, and they shall be no more.

15  Let everyone know that God rules in Jacob, *
        and to the ends of the earth.

16  They go to and fro in the evening; *
        they snarl like dogs and run about the city.

17 They forage for food, *
    and if they are not filled, they howl.

18 For my part, I will sing of your strength; *
    I will celebrate your love in the morning;

19 For you have become my stronghold, *
    a refuge in the day of my trouble.

20 To you, O my Strength, will I sing; *
    for you, O God, are my stronghold and my merciful God.


## 60   Deus, repulisti nos

1  O God, you have cast us off and broken us; *
    you have been angry;
    oh, take us back to you again.

2  You have shaken the earth and split it open; *
    repair the cracks in it, for it totters.

3  You have made your people know hardship; *
    you have given us wine that makes us stagger.

4  You have set up a banner for those who fear you, *
    to be a refuge from the power of the bow.

5  Save us by your right hand and answer us, *
    that those who are dear to you may be delivered.

6  God spoke from his holy place and said: *
    "I will exult and parcel out Shechem;
    I will divide the valley of Succoth.

7  Gilead is mine and Manasseh is mine; *
    Ephraim is my helmet and Judah my scepter.

8   Moab is my wash-basin,
        on Edom I throw down my sandal to claim it, *
        and over Philistia will I shout in triumph."

9   Who will lead me into the strong city? *
        who will bring me into Edom?

10  Have you not cast us off, O God? *
        you no longer go out, O God, with our armies.

11  Grant us your help against the enemy, *
        for vain is the help of man.

12  With God we will do valiant deeds, *
        and he shall tread our enemies under foot.


## 61   *Exaudi, Deus*

1   Hear my cry, O God, *
        and listen to my prayer.

2   I call upon you from the ends of the earth
        with heaviness in my heart; *
        set me upon the rock that is higher than I.

3   For you have been my refuge, *
        a strong tower against the enemy.

4   I will dwell in your house for ever; *
        I will take refuge under the cover of your wings.

5   For you, O God, have heard my vows; *
        you have granted me the heritage of those
                        who fear your Name.

6   Add length of days to the king's life; *
        let his years extend over many generations.

7   Let him sit enthroned before God for ever; *
      bid love and faithfulness watch over him.

8   So will I always sing the praise of your Name, *
      and day by day I will fulfill my vows.


*Twelfth Day: Morning Prayer*

# 62 *Nonne Deo?*

1   For God alone my soul in silence waits; *
      from him comes my salvation.

2   He alone is my rock and my salvation, *
      my stronghold, so that I shall not be greatly shaken.

3   How long will you assail me to crush me,
    all of you together, *
      as if you were a leaning fence, a toppling wall?

4   They seek only to bring me down from my place of honor; *
      lies are their chief delight.

5   They bless with their lips, *
      but in their hearts they curse.

6   For God alone my soul in silence waits; *
      truly, my hope is in him.

7   He alone is my rock and my salvation, *
      my stronghold, so that I shall not be shaken.

8   In God is my safety and my honor; *
      God is my strong rock and my refuge.

9   Put your trust in him always, O people, *
      pour out your hearts before him, for God is our refuge.

10    Those of high degree are but a fleeting breath, *
      even those of low estate cannot be trusted.

11    On the scales they are lighter than a breath, *
      all of them together.

12    Put no trust in extortion;
      in robbery take no empty pride; *
      though wealth increase, set not your heart upon it.

13    God has spoken once, twice have I heard it, *
      that power belongs to God.

14    Steadfast love is yours, O Lord, *
      for you repay everyone according to his deeds.


## 63   *Deus, Deus meus*

1    O God, you are my God; eagerly I seek you; *
      my soul thirsts for you, my flesh faints for you,
      as in a barren and dry land where there is no water.

2    Therefore I have gazed upon you in your holy place, *
      that I might behold your power and your glory.

3    For your loving-kindness is better than life itself; *
      my lips shall give you praise.

4    So will I bless you as long as I live *
      and lift up my hands in your Name.

5    My soul is content, as with marrow and fatness, *
      and my mouth praises you with joyful lips,

6    When I remember you upon my bed, *
      and meditate on you in the night watches.

7    For you have been my helper, *
      and under the shadow of your wings I will rejoice.

8     My soul clings to you; *
        your right hand holds me fast.

9     May those who seek my life to destroy it *
        go down into the depths of the earth;

10    Let them fall upon the edge of the sword, *
        and let them be food for jackals.

11    But the king will rejoice in God;
        all those who swear by him will be glad; *
            for the mouth of those who speak lies shall be stopped.

# 64  *Exaudi, Deus*

1     Hear my voice, O God, when I complain; *
        protect my life from fear of the enemy.

2     Hide me from the conspiracy of the wicked, *
        from the mob of evildoers.

3     They sharpen their tongue like a sword, *
        and aim their bitter words like arrows,

4     That they may shoot down the blameless from ambush; *
        they shoot without warning and are not afraid.

5     They hold fast to their evil course; *
        they plan how they may hide their snares.

6     They say,"Who will see us?
        who will find out our crimes? *
        we have thought out a perfect plot."

7     The human mind and heart are a mystery; *
        but God will loose an arrow at them,
        and suddenly they will be wounded.

8    He will make them trip over their tongues, *
      and all who see them will shake their heads.

9    Everyone will stand in awe and declare God's deeds; *
      they will recognize his works.

10   The righteous will rejoice in the LORD and put their trust in hi
      and all who are true of heart will glory.

*Twelfth Day: Evening Prayer*

# 65 *Te decet hymnus*

1    You are to be praised, O God, in Zion; *
      to you shall vows be performed in Jerusalem.

2    To you that hear prayer shall all flesh come, *
      because of their transgressions.

3    Our sins are stronger than we are, *
      but you will blot them out.

4    Happy are they whom you choose
    and draw to your courts to dwell there! *
      they will be satisfied by the beauty of your house,
      by the holiness of your temple.

5    Awesome things will you show us in your righteousness,
    O God of our salvation, *
      O Hope of all the ends of the earth
      and of the seas that are far away.

6    You make fast the mountains by your power; *
      they are girded about with might.

7    You still the roaring of the seas, *
      the roaring of their waves,
      and the clamor of the peoples.

8     Those who dwell at the ends of the earth will tremble at your
marvelous signs; *
    you make the dawn and the dusk to sing for joy.

9     You visit the earth and water it abundantly;
you make it very plenteous; *
    the river of God is full of water.

10     You prepare the grain, *
    for so you provide for the earth.

11     You drench the furrows and smooth out the ridges; *
    with heavy rain you soften the ground and bless its increase.

12     You crown the year with your goodness, *
    and your paths overflow with plenty.

13     May the fields of the wilderness be rich for grazing, *
    and the hills be clothed with joy.

14     May the meadows cover themselves with flocks,
and the valleys cloak themselves with grain; *
    let them shout for joy and sing.

# 66  *Jubilate Deo*

1     Be joyful in God, all you lands; *
    sing the glory of his Name;
    sing the glory of his praise.

2     Say to God, "How awesome are your deeds! *
    because of your great strength your enemies
cringe before you.

3     All the earth bows down before you, *
    sings to you, sings out your Name."

4   Come now and see the works of God, *
        how wonderful he is in his doing toward all people.

5   He turned the sea into dry land,
        so that they went through the water on foot, *
        and there we rejoiced in him.

6   In his might he rules for ever;
        his eyes keep watch over the nations; *
        let no rebel rise up against him.

7   Bless our God, you peoples; *
        make the voice of his praise to be heard;

8   Who holds our souls in life, *
        and will not allow our feet to slip.

9   For you, O God, have proved us; *
        you have tried us just as silver is tried.

10  You brought us into the snare; *
        you laid heavy burdens upon our backs.

11  You let enemies ride over our heads;
        we went through fire and water; *
        but you brought us out into a place of refreshment.


12  I will enter your house with burnt-offerings
        and will pay you my vows, *
        which I promised with my lips
        and spoke with my mouth when I was in trouble.

13  I will offer you sacrifices of fat beasts
        with the smoke of rams; *
        I will give you oxen and goats.

14  Come and listen, all you who fear God, *
        and I will tell you what he has done for me.

15    I called out to him with my mouth, *
      and his praise was on my tongue.

16    If I had found evil in my heart, *
      the Lord would not have heard me;

17    But in truth God has heard me; *
      he has attended to the voice of my prayer.

18    Blessed be God, who has not rejected my prayer, *
      nor withheld his love from me.

## 67  *Deus misereatur*

1     May God be merciful to us and bless us, *
      show us the light of his countenance and come to us.

2     Let your ways be known upon earth, *
      your saving health among all nations.

3     Let the peoples praise you, O God; *
      let all the peoples praise you.

4     Let the nations be glad and sing for joy, *
      for you judge the peoples with equity
      and guide all the nations upon earth.

5     Let the peoples praise you, O God; *
      let all the peoples praise you.

6     The earth has brought forth her increase; *
      may God, our own God, give us his blessing.

7     May God give us his blessing, *
      and may all the ends of the earth stand in awe of him.

# 68   *Exsurgat Deus*

1   Let God arise, and let his enemies be scattered; *
       let those who hate him flee before him.

2   Let them vanish like smoke when the wind drives it away
       as the wax melts at the fire, so let the wicked perish at
                   the presence of God.

3   But let the righteous be glad and rejoice before God; *
       let them also be merry and joyful.

4   Sing to God, sing praises to his Name;
     exalt him who rides upon the heavens; *
       YAHWEH is his Name, rejoice before him!

5   Father of orphans, defender of widows, *
       God in his holy habitation!

6   God gives the solitary a home and brings forth prisoners
                   into freedom; *
       but the rebels shall live in dry places.

7   O God, when you went forth before your people, *
       when you marched through the wilderness,

8   The earth shook, and the skies poured down rain,
     at the presence of God, the God of Sinai, *
       at the presence of God, the God of Israel.

9   You sent a gracious rain, O God, upon your inheritance;
       you refreshed the land when it was weary.

10  Your people found their home in it; *
       in your goodness, O God, you have made provision
                   for the poor.

11    The Lord gave the word; *
          great was the company of women who bore the tidings:

12    "Kings with their armies are fleeing away; *
          the women at home are dividing the spoils."

13    Though you lingered among the sheepfolds, *
          you shall be like a dove whose wings are covered with silver,
          whose feathers are like green gold.

14    When the Almighty scattered kings, *
          it was like snow falling in Zalmon.

15    O mighty mountain, O hill of Bashan! *
          O rugged mountain, O hill of Bashan!

16    Why do you look with envy, O rugged mountain,
      at the hill which God chose for his resting place? *
          truly, the LORD will dwell there for ever.

17    The chariots of God are twenty thousand,
      even thousands of thousands; *
          the Lord comes in holiness from Sinai.

18    You have gone up on high and led captivity captive;
      you have received gifts even from your enemies, *
          that the LORD God might dwell among them.

19    Blessed be the Lord day by day, *
          the God of our salvation, who bears our burdens.

20    He is our God, the God of our salvation; *
          God is the LORD, by whom we escape death.


21    God shall crush the heads of his enemies, *
          and the hairy scalp of those who go on still in their
                              wickedness.


*Psalm 68*    677

22  The Lord has said," I will bring them back from Bashan;
        I will bring them back from the depths of the sea;

23  That your foot may be dipped in blood, *
        the tongues of your dogs in the blood of your enemies.


24  They see your procession, O God, *
        your procession into the sanctuary, my God and my K

25  The singers go before, musicians follow after, *
        in the midst of maidens playing upon the hand-drums.

26  Bless God in the congregation; *
        bless the LORD, you that are of the fountain of Israel.

27  There is Benjamin, least of the tribes, at the head;
        the princes of Judah in a company; *
        and the princes of Zebulon and Naphtali.

28  Send forth your strength, O God; *
        establish, O God, what you have wrought for us.

29  Kings shall bring gifts to you, *
        for your temple's sake at Jerusalem.

30  Rebuke the wild beast of the reeds, *
        and the peoples, a herd of wild bulls with its calves.

31  Trample down those who lust after silver; *
        scatter the peoples that delight in war.

32  Let tribute be brought out of Egypt; *
        let Ethiopia stretch out her hands to God.

33  Sing to God, O kingdoms of the earth; *
        sing praises to the Lord.

34  He rides in the heavens, the ancient heavens; *
        he sends forth his voice, his mighty voice.

35 Ascribe power to God; *
    his majesty is over Israel;
    his strength is in the skies.

36 How wonderful is God in his holy places! *
    the God of Israel giving strength and power to his people!
    Blessed be God!

*Thirteenth Day: Evening Prayer*

## 69 *Salvum me fac*

1 Save me, O God, *
    for the waters have risen up to my neck.

2 I am sinking in deep mire, *
    and there is no firm ground for my feet.

3 I have come into deep waters, *
    and the torrent washes over me.

4 I have grown weary with my crying;
    my throat is inflamed; *
    my eyes have failed from looking for my God.

5 Those who hate me without a cause are more than the hairs
                    of my head;
    my lying foes who would destroy me are mighty. *
    Must I then give back what I never stole?

6 O God, you know my foolishness, *
    and my faults are not hidden from you.

7 Let not those who hope in you be put to shame through me,
                    Lord GOD of hosts; *
    let not those who seek you be disgraced because of me,
                    O God of Israel.

8   Surely, for your sake have I suffered reproach, *
        and shame has covered my face.

9   I have become a stranger to my own kindred, *
        an alien to my mother's children.

10  Zeal for your house has eaten me up; *
        the scorn of those who scorn you has fallen upon me.

11  I humbled myself with fasting, *
        but that was turned to my reproach.

12  I put on sack-cloth also, *
        and became a byword among them.

13  Those who sit at the gate murmur against me, *
        and the drunkards make songs about me.

14  But as for me, this is my prayer to you, *
        at the time you have set, O LORD:

15  "In your great mercy, O God, *
        answer me with your unfailing help.

16  Save me from the mire; do not let me sink; *
        let me be rescued from those who hate me
        and out of the deep waters.

17  Let not the torrent of waters wash over me,
    neither let the deep swallow me up; *
        do not let the Pit shut its mouth upon me.

18  Answer me, O LORD, for your love is kind; *
        in your great compassion, turn to me."

19  "Hide not your face from your servant; *
        be swift and answer me, for I am in distress.

20  Draw near to me and redeem me; *
        because of my enemies deliver me.

21     You know my reproach, my shame, and my dishonor; *
       my adversaries are all in your sight."

22     Reproach has broken my heart, and it cannot be healed; *
       I looked for sympathy, but there was none,
       for comforters, but I could find no one.

23     They gave me gall to eat, *
       and when I was thirsty, they gave me vinegar to drink.

24     Let the table before them be a trap *
       and their sacred feasts a snare.

25     Let their eyes be darkened, that they may not see, *
       and give them continual trembling in their loins.

26     Pour out your indignation upon them, *
       and let the fierceness of your anger overtake them.

27     Let their camp be desolate, *
       and let there be none to dwell in their tents.

28     For they persecute him whom you have stricken *
       and add to the pain of those whom you have pierced.

29     Lay to their charge guilt upon guilt, *
       and let them not receive your vindication.

30     Let them be wiped out of the book of the living *
       and not be written among the righteous.

31     As for me, I am afflicted and in pain; *
       your help, O God, will lift me up on high.

32     I will praise the Name of God in song; *
       I will proclaim his greatness with thanksgiving.

33     This will please the LORD more than an offering of oxen, *
       more than bullocks with horns and hoofs.

34     The afflicted shall see and be glad; *
        you who seek God, your heart shall live.

35     For the LORD listens to the needy, *
        and his prisoners he does not despise.

36     Let the heavens and the earth praise him, *
        the seas and all that moves in them;

37     For God will save Zion and rebuild the cities of Judah; *
        they shall live there and have it in possession.

38     The children of his servants will inherit it, *
        and those who love his Name will dwell therein.


# 70    *Deus, in adjutorium*

1     Be pleased, O God, to deliver me; *
        O LORD, make haste to help me.

2     Let those who seek my life be ashamed
        and altogether dismayed; *
        let those who take pleasure in my misfortune
        draw back and be disgraced.

3     Let those who say to me "Aha!" and gloat over me turn b
        because they are ashamed.

4     Let all who seek you rejoice and be glad in you; *
        let those who love your salvation say for ever,
    "Great is the LORD!"

5     But as for me, I am poor and needy; *
        come to me speedily, O God.

6     You are my helper and my deliverer; *
        O LORD, do not tarry.

## 71 *In te, Domine, speravi*

1 In you, O LORD, have I taken refuge; *
   let me never be ashamed.

2 In your righteousness, deliver me and set me free; *
   incline your ear to me and save me.

3 Be my strong rock, a castle to keep me safe; *
   you are my crag and my stronghold.

4 Deliver me, my God, from the hand of the wicked, *
   from the clutches of the evildoer and the oppressor.

5 For you are my hope, O Lord GOD, *
   my confidence since I was young.

6 I have been sustained by you ever since I was born;
   from my mother's womb you have been my strength; *
   my praise shall be always of you.

7 I have become a portent to many; *
   but you are my refuge and my strength.

8 Let my mouth be full of your praise *
   and your glory all the day long.

9 Do not cast me off in my old age; *
   forsake me not when my strength fails.

10 For my enemies are talking against me, *
   and those who lie in wait for my life take counsel together.

11 They say, "God has forsaken him;
   go after him and seize him; *
   because there is none who will save."

12 O God, be not far from me; *
   come quickly to help me, O my God.

13 Let those who set themselves against me be put to shame
   be disgraced; *
   let those who seek to do me evil be covered with scorn
   and reproach.

14 But I shall always wait in patience, *
   and shall praise you more and more.

15 My mouth shall recount your mighty acts
   and saving deeds all day long; *
   though I cannot know the number of them.

16 I will begin with the mighty works of the Lord GOD; *
   I will recall your righteousness, yours alone.

17 O God, you have taught me since I was young, *
   and to this day I tell of your wonderful works.

18 And now that I am old and gray-headed, O God, do not
   forsake me, *
   till I make known your strength to this generation
   and your power to all who are to come.

19 Your righteousness, O God, reaches to the heavens; *
   you have done great things;
   who is like you, O God?

20 You have showed me great troubles and adversities, *
   but you will restore my life
   and bring me up again from the deep places of the earth.

21 You strengthen me more and more; *
   you enfold and comfort me,

2 Therefore I will praise you upon the lyre for your
      faithfulness, O my God; *
  I will sing to you with the harp, O Holy One of Israel.

3 My lips will sing with joy when I play to you, *
  and so will my soul, which you have redeemed.

4 My tongue will proclaim your righteousness all day long, *
  for they are ashamed and disgraced who sought
      to do me harm.

## 72  *Deus, judicium*

1 Give the King your justice, O God, *
  and your righteousness to the King's Son;

2 That he may rule your people righteously *
  and the poor with justice;

3 That the mountains may bring prosperity to the people, *
  and the little hills bring righteousness.

4 He shall defend the needy among the people; *
  he shall rescue the poor and crush the oppressor.

5 He shall live as long as the sun and moon endure, *
  from one generation to another.

6 He shall come down like rain upon the mown field, *
  like showers that water the earth.

7 In his time shall the righteous flourish; *
  there shall be abundance of peace till the moon shall
      be no more.

8 He shall rule from sea to sea, *
  and from the River to the ends of the earth.

9   His foes shall bow down before him, *
        and his enemies lick the dust.

10  The kings of Tarshish and of the isles shall pay tribute, *
        and the kings of Arabia and Saba offer gifts.

11  All kings shall bow down before him, *
        and all the nations do him service.

12  For he shall deliver the poor who cries out in distress, *
        and the oppressed who has no helper.

13  He shall have pity on the lowly and poor; *
        he shall preserve the lives of the needy.

14  He shall redeem their lives from oppression and violence,
        and dear shall their blood be in his sight.

15  Long may he live!
        and may there be given to him gold from Arabia; *
        may prayer be made for him always,
        and may they bless him all the day long.

16  May there be abundance of grain on the earth,
        growing thick even on the hilltops; *
        may its fruit flourish like Lebanon,
        and its grain like grass upon the earth.

17  May his Name remain for ever
        and be established as long as the sun endures; *
        may all the nations bless themselves in him and
                call him blessed.


18  Blessed be the Lord GOD, the God of Israel, *
        who alone does wondrous deeds!

19  And blessed be his glorious Name for ever! *
        and may all the earth be filled with his glory.
        Amen. Amen.

## Book Three

*Fourteenth Day: Evening Prayer*

**73**  *Quam bonus Israel!*

1  Truly, God is good to Israel, *
   to those who are pure in heart.

2  But as for me, my feet had nearly slipped; *
   I had almost tripped and fallen;

3  Because I envied the proud *
   and saw the prosperity of the wicked:

4  For they suffer no pain, *
   and their bodies are sleek and sound;

5  In the misfortunes of others they have no share; *
   they are not afflicted as others are;

6  Therefore they wear their pride like a necklace *
   and wrap their violence about them like a cloak.

7  Their iniquity comes from gross minds, *
   and their hearts overflow with wicked thoughts.

8  They scoff and speak maliciously; *
   out of their haughtiness they plan oppression.

9  They set their mouths against the heavens, *
   and their evil speech runs through the world.

10  And so the people turn to them *
    and find in them no fault.

11  They say, "How should God know? *
    is there knowledge in the Most High?"

12  So then, these are the wicked; *
        always at ease, they increase their wealth.

13  In vain have I kept my heart clean, *
        and washed my hands in innocence.

14  I have been afflicted all day long, *
        and punished every morning.

15  Had I gone on speaking this way, *
        I should have betrayed the generation of your children.

16  When I tried to understand these things, *
        it was too hard for me;

17  Until I entered the sanctuary of God *
        and discerned the end of the wicked.

18  Surely, you set them in slippery places; *
        you cast them down in ruin.

19  Oh, how suddenly do they come to destruction, *
        come to an end, and perish from terror!

20  Like a dream when one awakens, O Lord, *
        when you arise you will make their image vanish.

21  When my mind became embittered, *
        I was sorely wounded in my heart.

22  I was stupid and had no understanding; *
        I was like a brute beast in your presence.

23  Yet I am always with you; *
        you hold me by my right hand.

24  You will guide me by your counsel, *
        and afterwards receive me with glory.

25  Whom have I in heaven but you? *
        and having you I desire nothing upon earth.

Though my flesh and my heart should waste away, *
  God is the strength of my heart and my portion for ever.

7   Truly, those who forsake you will perish; *
  you destroy all who are unfaithful.

8   But it is good for me to be near God; *
  I have made the Lord GOD my refuge.

9   I will speak of all your works *
  in the gates of the city of Zion.


# 74   *Ut quid, Deus?*

1   O God, why have you utterly cast us off? *
  why is your wrath so hot against the sheep of your pasture?

2   Remember your congregation that you purchased long ago, *
  the tribe you redeemed to be your inheritance,
      and Mount Zion where you dwell.

3   Turn your steps toward the endless ruins; *
  the enemy has laid waste everything in your sanctuary.

4   Your adversaries roared in your holy place; *
  they set up their banners as tokens of victory.

5   They were like men coming up with axes to a grove of trees; *
  they broke down all your carved work with hatchets
      and hammers.

6   They set fire to your holy place; *
  they defiled the dwelling-place of your Name
      and razed it to the ground.

7   They said to themselves, "Let us destroy them altogether." *
  They burned down all the meeting-places of God
      in the land.

8    There are no signs for us to see;
     there is no prophet left; *
       there is not one among us who knows how long.

9    How long, O God, will the adversary scoff? *
     will the enemy blaspheme your Name for ever?

10    Why do you draw back your hand? *
     why is your right hand hidden in your bosom?

11    Yet God is my King from ancient times, *
     victorious in the midst of the earth.

12    You divided the sea by your might *
     and shattered the heads of the dragons upon the wate

13    You crushed the heads of Leviathan *
     and gave him to the people of the desert for food.

14    You split open spring and torrent; *
     you dried up ever-flowing rivers.

15    Yours is the day, yours also the night; *
     you established the moon and the sun.

16    You fixed all the boundaries of the earth; *
     you made both summer and winter.

17    Remember, O LORD, how the enemy scoffed, *
     how a foolish people despised your Name.

18    Do not hand over the life of your dove to wild beasts; *
     never forget the lives of your poor.

19    Look upon your covenant; *
     the dark places of the earth are haunts of violence.

20    Let not the oppressed turn away ashamed; *
     let the poor and needy praise your Name.

21    Arise, O God, maintain your cause; *
     remember how fools revile you all day long.

22    Forget not the clamor of your adversaries, *
         the unending tumult of those who rise up against you.

## 75    *Confitebimur tibi*

1    We give you thanks, O God, we give you thanks, *
         calling upon your Name and declaring all your
                 wonderful deeds.

2    "I will appoint a time," says God; *
         "I will judge with equity.

3    Though the earth and all its inhabitants are quaking, *
         I will make its pillars fast.

4    I will say to the boasters,'Boast no more,' *
         and to the wicked,'Do not toss your horns;

5    Do not toss your horns so high, *
         nor speak with a proud neck.' "

6    For judgment is neither from the east nor from the west, *
         nor yet from the wilderness or the mountains.

7    It is God who judges; *
         he puts down one and lifts up another.

8    For in the LORD's hand there is a cup,
     full of spiced and foaming wine, which he pours out, *
         and all the wicked of the earth shall drink and
                 drain the dregs.

9    But I will rejoice for ever; *
         I will sing praises to the God of Jacob.

10   He shall break off all the horns of the wicked; *
         but the horns of the righteous shall be exalted.

# 76 Notus in Judæa

1   In Judah is God known; *
        his Name is great in Israel.

2   At Salem is his tabernacle, *
        and his dwelling is in Zion.

3   There he broke the flashing arrows, *
        the shield, the sword, and the weapons of battle.

4   How glorious you are! *
        more splendid than the everlasting mountains!

5   The strong of heart have been despoiled;
        they sink into sleep; *
        none of the warriors can lift a hand.

6   At your rebuke, O God of Jacob, *
        both horse and rider lie stunned.

7   What terror you inspire! *
        who can stand before you when you are angry?

8   From heaven you pronounced judgment; *
        the earth was afraid and was still;

9   When God rose up to judgment *
        and to save all the oppressed of the earth.

10  Truly, wrathful Edom will give you thanks, *
        and the remnant of Hamath will keep your feasts.

11  Make a vow to the LORD your God and keep it; *
        let all around him bring gifts to him who is worthy
            to be feared.

12  He breaks the spirit of princes, *
        and strikes terror in the kings of the earth.

# 77 *Voce mea ad Dominum*

1   I will cry aloud to God; *
     I will cry aloud, and he will hear me.

2   In the day of my trouble I sought the Lord; *
     my hands were stretched out by night and did not tire;
     I refused to be comforted.

3   I think of God, I am restless, *
     I ponder, and my spirit faints.

4   You will not let my eyelids close; *
     I am troubled and I cannot speak.

5   I consider the days of old; *
     I remember the years long past;

6   I commune with my heart in the night; *
     I ponder and search my mind.

7   Will the Lord cast me off for ever? *
     will he no more show his favor?

8   Has his loving-kindness come to an end for ever? *
     has his promise failed for evermore?

9   Has God forgotten to be gracious? *
     has he, in his anger, withheld his compassion?

10   And I said, "My grief is this: *
     the right hand of the Most High has lost its power."

11   I will remember the works of the LORD, *
     and call to mind your wonders of old time.

12   I will meditate on all your acts *
     and ponder your mighty deeds.

13   Your way, O God, is holy; *
     who is so great a god as our God?

14     You are the God who works wonders *
       and have declared your power among the peoples.

15     By your strength you have redeemed your people, *
       the children of Jacob and Joseph.

16     The waters saw you, O God;
       the waters saw you and trembled; *
       the very depths were shaken.

17     The clouds poured out water;
       the skies thundered; *
       your arrows flashed to and fro;

18     The sound of your thunder was in the whirlwind;
       your lightnings lit up the world; *
       the earth trembled and shook.

19     Your way was in the sea,
       and your paths in the great waters, *
       yet your footsteps were not seen.

20     You led your people like a flock *
       by the hand of Moses and Aaron.

*Fifteenth Day: Evening Prayer*

# 78

**Part I**   *Attendite, popule*

1     Hear my teaching, O my people; *
       incline your ears to the words of my mouth.

2     I will open my mouth in a parable; *
       I will declare the mysteries of ancient times.

3   That which we have heard and known,
    and what our forefathers have told us, *
        we will not hide from their children.

4   We will recount to generations to come
    the praiseworthy deeds and the power of the LORD, *
        and the wonderful works he has done.

5   He gave his decrees to Jacob
    and established a law for Israel, *
        which he commanded them to teach their children;

6   That the generations to come might know,
    and the children yet unborn; *
        that they in their turn might tell it to their children;

7   So that they might put their trust in God, *
        and not forget the deeds of God,
        but keep his commandments;

8   And not be like their forefathers,
    a stubborn and rebellious generation, *
        a generation whose heart was not steadfast,
        and whose spirit was not faithful to God.

9   The people of Ephraim, armed with the bow, *
        turned back in the day of battle;

10  They did not keep the covenant of God, *
        and refused to walk in his law;

11  They forgot what he had done, *
        and the wonders he had shown them.

12  He worked marvels in the sight of their forefathers, *
        in the land of Egypt, in the field of Zoan.

13  He split open the sea and let them pass through; *
        he made the waters stand up like walls.

14 He led them with a cloud by day, *
    and all the night through with a glow of fire.

15 He split the hard rocks in the wilderness *
    and gave them drink as from the great deep.

16 He brought streams out of the cliff, *
    and the waters gushed out like rivers.

17 But they went on sinning against him, *
    rebelling in the desert against the Most High.

18 They tested God in their hearts, *
    demanding food for their craving.

19 They railed against God and said, *
    "Can God set a table in the wilderness?

20 True, he struck the rock, the waters gushed out, and the
                    gullies overflowed; *
    but is he able to give bread
    or to provide meat for his people?"

21 When the LORD heard this, he was full of wrath; *
    a fire was kindled against Jacob,
    and his anger mounted against Israel;

22 For they had no faith in God, *
    nor did they put their trust in his saving power.

23 So he commanded the clouds above *
    and opened the doors of heaven.

24 He rained down manna upon them to eat *
    and gave them grain from heaven.

25 So mortals ate the bread of angels; *
    he provided for them food enough.

26    He caused the east wind to blow in the heavens *
      and led out the south wind by his might.

27    He rained down flesh upon them like dust *
      and wingèd birds like the sand of the sea.

28    He let it fall in the midst of their camp *
      and round about their dwellings.

29    So they ate and were well filled, *
      for he gave them what they craved.

30    But they did not stop their craving, *
      though the food was still in their mouths.

31    So God's anger mounted against them; *
      he slew their strongest men
      and laid low the youth of Israel.

32    In spite of all this, they went on sinning *
      and had no faith in his wonderful works.

33    So he brought their days to an end like a breath *
      and their years in sudden terror.

34    Whenever he slew them, they would seek him, *
      and repent, and diligently search for God.

35    They would remember that God was their rock, *
      and the Most High God their redeemer.

36    But they flattered him with their mouths *
      and lied to him with their tongues.

37    Their heart was not steadfast toward him, *
      and they were not faithful to his covenant.

38   But he was so merciful that he forgave their sins
and did not destroy them; *
     many times he held back his anger
     and did not permit his wrath to be roused.

39   For he remembered that they were but flesh, *
     a breath that goes forth and does not return.

### Psalm 78: Part II   *Quoties exacerbaverunt*

40   How often the people disobeyed him in the wilderness *
     and offended him in the desert!

41   Again and again they tempted God *
     and provoked the Holy One of Israel.

42   They did not remember his power *
     in the day when he ransomed them from the enemy;

43   How he wrought his signs in Egypt *
     and his omens in the field of Zoan.

44   He turned their rivers into blood, *
     so that they could not drink of their streams.

45   He sent swarms of flies among them, which ate them up
and frogs, which destroyed them.

46   He gave their crops to the caterpillar, *
     the fruit of their toil to the locust.

47   He killed their vines with hail *
     and their sycamores with frost.

48   He delivered their cattle to hailstones *
     and their livestock to hot thunderbolts.

49  He poured out upon them his blazing anger: *
        fury, indignation, and distress,
        a troop of destroying angels.

50  He gave full rein to his anger;
        he did not spare their souls from death; *
        but delivered their lives to the plague.

51  He struck down all the firstborn of Egypt, *
        the flower of manhood in the dwellings of Ham.

52  He led out his people like sheep *
        and guided them in the wilderness like a flock.

53  He led them to safety, and they were not afraid; *
        but the sea overwhelmed their enemies.

54  He brought them to his holy land, *
        the mountain his right hand had won.

55  He drove out the Canaanites before them
        and apportioned an inheritance to them by lot; *
        he made the tribes of Israel to dwell in their tents.


56  But they tested the Most High God, and defied him, *
        and did not keep his commandments.

57  They turned away and were disloyal like their fathers; *
        they were undependable like a warped bow.

58  They grieved him with their hill-altars *
        and provoked his displeasure with their idols.

59  When God heard this, he was angry *
        and utterly rejected Israel.

60  He forsook the shrine at Shiloh, *
        the tabernacle where he had lived among his people.

61   He delivered the ark into captivity, *
     his glory into the adversary's hand.

62   He gave his people to the sword *
     and was angered against his inheritance.

63   The fire consumed their young men; *
     there were no wedding songs for their maidens.

64   Their priests fell by the sword, *
     and their widows made no lamentation.

65   Then the LORD woke as though from sleep, *
     like a warrior refreshed with wine.

66   He struck his enemies on the backside *
     and put them to perpetual shame.

67   He rejected the tent of Joseph *
     and did not choose the tribe of Ephraim;

68   He chose instead the tribe of Judah *
     and Mount Zion, which he loved.

69   He built his sanctuary like the heights of heaven, *
     like the earth which he founded for ever.

70   He chose David his servant, *
     and took him away from the sheepfolds.

71   He brought him from following the ewes, *
     to be a shepherd over Jacob his people
     and over Israel his inheritance.

72   So he shepherded them with a faithful and true heart *
     and guided them with the skillfulness of his hands.

## 79 *Deus, venerunt*

O God, the heathen have come into your inheritance;
they have profaned your holy temple; *
   they have made Jerusalem a heap of rubble.

They have given the bodies of your servants as food for the
         birds of the air, *
   and the flesh of your faithful ones to the beasts
         of the field.

They have shed their blood like water on every side
         of Jerusalem, *
   and there was no one to bury them.

We have become a reproach to our neighbors, *
   an object of scorn and derision to those around us.

How long will you be angry, O LORD? *
   will your fury blaze like fire for ever?

Pour out your wrath upon the heathen who have not
         known you *
   and upon the kingdoms that have not called upon
         your Name.

For they have devoured Jacob *
   and made his dwelling a ruin.

Remember not our past sins;
let your compassion be swift to meet us; *
   for we have been brought very low.

Help us, O God our Savior, for the glory of your Name; *
   deliver us and forgive us our sins, for your Name's sake.

10 Why should the heathen say, "Where is their God?" *
        Let it be known among the heathen and in our sight
            that you avenge the shedding of your servants' blood.

11 Let the sorrowful sighing of the prisoners come before y
        and by your great might spare those who are
                condemned to die.

12 May the revilings with which they reviled you, O Lord,
        return seven-fold into their bosoms.

13 For we are your people and the sheep of your pasture; *
        we will give you thanks for ever
            and show forth your praise from age to age.


# 80 *Qui regis Israel*

1 Hear, O Shepherd of Israel, leading Joseph like a flock.
        shine forth, you that are enthroned upon the cherubi

2 In the presence of Ephraim, Benjamin, and Manasseh,
        stir up your strength and come to help us.

3 Restore us, O God of hosts; *
        show the light of your countenance, and we shall be


4 O LORD God of hosts, *
        how long will you be angered
            despite the prayers of your people?

5 You have fed them with the bread of tears; *
        you have given them bowls of tears to drink.

6 You have made us the derision of our neighbors, *
        and our enemies laugh us to scorn.

7   Restore us, O God of hosts; *
        show the light of your countenance, and we shall be saved.

8   You have brought a vine out of Egypt; *
        you cast out the nations and planted it.

9   You prepared the ground for it; *
        it took root and filled the land.

10   The mountains were covered by its shadow *
        and the towering cedar trees by its boughs.

11   You stretched out its tendrils to the Sea *
        and its branches to the River.

12   Why have you broken down its wall, *
        so that all who pass by pluck off its grapes?

13   The wild boar of the forest has ravaged it, *
        and the beasts of the field have grazed upon it.

14   Turn now, O God of hosts, look down from heaven;
     behold and tend this vine; *
        preserve what your right hand has planted.

15   They burn it with fire like rubbish; *
        at the rebuke of your countenance let them perish.

16   Let your hand be upon the man of your right hand, *
        the son of man you have made so strong for yourself.

17   And so will we never turn away from you; *
        give us life, that we may call upon your Name.

18   Restore us, O LORD God of hosts; *
        show the light of your countenance, and we shall be saved.

# 81 *Exultate Deo*

1 Sing with joy to God our strength *
   and raise a loud shout to the God of Jacob.

2 Raise a song and sound the timbrel, *
   the merry harp, and the lyre.

3 Blow the ram's-horn at the new moon, *
   and at the full moon, the day of our feast.

4 For this is a statute for Israel, *
   a law of the God of Jacob.

5 He laid it as a solemn charge upon Joseph, *
   when he came out of the land of Egypt.

6 I heard an unfamiliar voice saying, *
   "I eased his shoulder from the burden;
   his hands were set free from bearing the load."

7 You called on me in trouble, and I saved you; *
   I answered you from the secret place of thunder
   and tested you at the waters of Meribah.

8 Hear, O my people, and I will admonish you: *
   O Israel, if you would but listen to me!

9 There shall be no strange god among you; *
   you shall not worship a foreign god.

10 I am the LORD your God,
   who brought you out of the land of Egypt and said, *
   "Open your mouth wide, and I will fill it."

11 And yet my people did not hear my voice, *
   and Israel would not obey me.

12 So I gave them over to the stubbornness of their hearts, *
   to follow their own devices.

13    Oh, that my people would listen to me! *
        that Israel would walk in my ways!

14    I should soon subdue their enemies *
        and turn my hand against their foes.

15    Those who hate the LORD would cringe before him, *
        and their punishment would last for ever.

16    But Israel would I feed with the finest wheat *
        and satisfy him with honey from the rock.

*Sixteenth Day: Evening Prayer*

# 82   *Deus stetit*

1    God takes his stand in the council of heaven; *
        he gives judgment in the midst of the gods:

2    "How long will you judge unjustly, *
        and show favor to the wicked?

3    Save the weak and the orphan; *
        defend the humble and needy;

4    Rescue the weak and the poor; *
        deliver them from the power of the wicked.

5    They do not know, neither do they understand;
    they go about in darkness; *
        all the foundations of the earth are shaken.

6    Now I say to you, 'You are gods, *
        and all of you children of the Most High;

7    Nevertheless, you shall die like mortals, *
        and fall like any prince.' "

8    Arise, O God, and rule the earth, *
      for you shall take all nations for your own.

## 83 *Deus, quis similis?*

1    O God, do not be silent; *
      do not keep still nor hold your peace, O God;

2    For your enemies are in tumult, *
      and those who hate you have lifted up their heads.

3    They take secret counsel against your people *
      and plot against those whom you protect.

4    They have said, "Come, let us wipe them out from among
           the nations; *
      let the name of Israel be remembered no more."

5    They have conspired together; *
      they have made an alliance against you:

6    The tents of Edom and the Ishmaelites; *
      the Moabites and the Hagarenes;

7    Gebal, and Ammon, and Amalek; *
      the Philistines and those who dwell in Tyre.

8    The Assyrians also have joined them, *
      and have come to help the people of Lot.

9    Do to them as you did to Midian, *
      to Sisera, and to Jabin at the river of Kishon:

10    They were destroyed at Endor; *
      they became like dung upon the ground.

11    Make their leaders like Oreb and Zeëb, *
      and all their commanders like Zebah and Zalmunna,

12   Who said,"Let us take for ourselves *
     the fields of God as our possession."

13   O my God, make them like whirling dust *
     and like chaff before the wind;

14   Like fire that burns down a forest, *
     like the flame that sets mountains ablaze.

15   Drive them with your tempest *
     and terrify them with your storm;

16   Cover their faces with shame, O LORD, *
     that they may seek your Name.

17   Let them be disgraced and terrified for ever; *
     let them be put to confusion and perish.

18   Let them know that you, whose Name is YAHWEH, *
     you alone are the Most High over all the earth.

# 84   *Quam dilecta!*

1   How dear to me is your dwelling, O LORD of hosts! *
     My soul has a desire and longing for the courts of
        the LORD;
     my heart and my flesh rejoice in the living God.

2   The sparrow has found her a house
   and the swallow a nest where she may lay her young; *
     by the side of your altars, O LORD of hosts,
     my King and my God.

3   Happy are they who dwell in your house! *
     they will always be praising you.

4   Happy are the people whose strength is in you! *
     whose hearts are set on the pilgrims' way.

5   Those who go through the desolate valley will find
                        it a place of springs, *
     for the early rains have covered it with pools of water.

6   They will climb from height to height, *
     and the God of gods will reveal himself in Zion.

7   Lord God of hosts, hear my prayer; *
     hearken, O God of Jacob.

8   Behold our defender, O God; *
     and look upon the face of your Anointed.

9   For one day in your courts is better than
                        a thousand in my own room, *
     and to stand at the threshold of the house of my God
     than to dwell in the tents of the wicked.

10  For the Lord God is both sun and shield; *
     he will give grace and glory;

11  No good thing will the Lord withhold *
     from those who walk with integrity.

12  O Lord of hosts, *
     happy are they who put their trust in you!

# 85   *Benedixisti, Domine*

1   You have been gracious to your land, O Lord, *
     you have restored the good fortune of Jacob.

2   You have forgiven the iniquity of your people *
     and blotted out all their sins.

3   You have withdrawn all your fury *
     and turned yourself from your wrathful indignation.

4 Restore us then, O God our Savior; *
   let your anger depart from us.

5 Will you be displeased with us for ever? *
   will you prolong your anger from age to age?

6 Will you not give us life again, *
   that your people may rejoice in you?

7 Show us your mercy, O LORD, *
   and grant us your salvation.

8 I will listen to what the LORD God is saying, *
   for he is speaking peace to his faithful people
   and to those who turn their hearts to him.

9 Truly, his salvation is very near to those who fear him, *
   that his glory may dwell in our land.

10 Mercy and truth have met together; *
   righteousness and peace have kissed each other.

11 Truth shall spring up from the earth, *
   and righteousness shall look down from heaven.

12 The LORD will indeed grant prosperity, *
   and our land will yield its increase.

13 Righteousness shall go before him, *
   and peace shall be a pathway for his feet.


*Seventeenth Day: Morning Prayer*

# 86  *Inclina, Domine*

1 Bow down your ear, O LORD, and answer me, *
   for I am poor and in misery.

2   Keep watch over my life, for I am faithful; *
        save your servant who puts his trust in you.

3   Be merciful to me, O LORD, for you are my God; *
        I call upon you all the day long.

4   Gladden the soul of your servant, *
        for to you, O LORD, I lift up my soul.

5   For you, O LORD, are good and forgiving, *
        and great is your love toward all who call upon you.

6   Give ear, O LORD, to my prayer, *
        and attend to the voice of my supplications.

7   In the time of my trouble I will call upon you, *
        for you will answer me.

8   Among the gods there is none like you, O LORD, *
        nor anything like your works.

9   All nations you have made will come and
                            worship you, O LORD, *
        and glorify your Name.

10  For you are great;
        you do wondrous things; *
            and you alone are God.

11  Teach me your way, O LORD,
        and I will walk in your truth; *
            knit my heart to you that I may fear your Name.

12  I will thank you, O LORD my God, with all my heart, *
        and glorify your Name for evermore.

13  For great is your love toward me; *
        you have delivered me from the nethermost Pit.

14 The arrogant rise up against me, O God,
and a band of violent men seeks my life; *
they have not set you before their eyes.

15 But you, O LORD, are gracious and full of compassion, *
slow to anger, and full of kindness and truth.

16 Turn to me and have mercy upon me; *
give your strength to your servant;
and save the child of your handmaid.

17 Show me a sign of your favor,
so that those who hate me may see it and be ashamed; *
because you, O LORD, have helped me and comforted me.

## 87 *Fundamenta ejus*

1 On the holy mountain stands the city he has founded; *
the LORD loves the gates of Zion
more than all the dwellings of Jacob.

2 Glorious things are spoken of you, *
O city of our God.

3 I count Egypt and Babylon among those who know me; *
behold Philistia, Tyre, and Ethiopia:
in Zion were they born.

4 Of Zion it shall be said, "Everyone was born in her, *
and the Most High himself shall sustain her."

5 The LORD will record as he enrolls the peoples, *
"These also were born there."

6 The singers and the dancers will say, *
"All my fresh springs are in you."

# 88 *Domine, Deus*

1 O LORD, my God, my Savior, *
   by day and night I cry to you.

2 Let my prayer enter into your presence; *
   incline your ear to my lamentation.

3 For I am full of trouble; *
   my life is at the brink of the grave.

4 I am counted among those who go down to the Pit; *
   I have become like one who has no strength;

5 Lost among the dead, *
   like the slain who lie in the grave,

6 Whom you remember no more, *
   for they are cut off from your hand.

7 You have laid me in the depths of the Pit, *
   in dark places, and in the abyss.

8 Your anger weighs upon me heavily, *
   and all your great waves overwhelm me.

9 You have put my friends far from me;
   you have made me to be abhorred by them; *
   I am in prison and cannot get free.

10 My sight has failed me because of trouble; *
   LORD, I have called upon you daily;
   I have stretched out my hands to you.

11 Do you work wonders for the dead? *
   will those who have died stand up and give you thank

12 Will your loving-kindness be declared in the grave? *
   your faithfulness in the land of destruction?

3   Will your wonders be known in the dark? *
        or your righteousness in the country where all
                                is forgotten?

4   But as for me, O LORD, I cry to you for help; *
        in the morning my prayer comes before you.

5   LORD, why have you rejected me? *
        why have you hidden your face from me?

6   Ever since my youth, I have been wretched and at the
                                point of death; *
        I have borne your terrors with a troubled mind.

7   Your blazing anger has swept over me; *
        your terrors have destroyed me;

8   They surround me all day long like a flood; *
        they encompass me on every side.

9   My friend and my neighbor you have put away from me, *
        and darkness is my only companion.


*Seventeenth Day: Evening Prayer*

# 89

**Part I**   *Misericordias Domini*

1   Your love, O LORD, for ever will I sing; *
        from age to age my mouth will proclaim your faithfulness.

2   For I am persuaded that your love is established for ever; *
        you have set your faithfulness firmly in the heavens.

3   "I have made a covenant with my chosen one; *
        I have sworn an oath to David my servant:

4   'I will establish your line for ever, *
        and preserve your throne for all generations.' "

5   The heavens bear witness to your wonders, O Lord, *
        and to your faithfulness in the assembly of the holy one

6   For who in the skies can be compared to the Lord? *
        who is like the Lord among the gods?

7   God is much to be feared in the council of the holy ones, *
        great and terrible to all those round about him.

8   Who is like you, Lord God of hosts? *
        O mighty Lord, your faithfulness is all around you.

9   You rule the raging of the sea *
        and still the surging of its waves.

10  You have crushed Rahab of the deep with a deadly wound
        you have scattered your enemies with your mighty arm

11  Yours are the heavens; the earth also is yours; *
        you laid the foundations of the world and all that is in

12  You have made the north and the south; *
        Tabor and Hermon rejoice in your Name.

13  You have a mighty arm; *
        strong is your hand and high is your right hand.

14  Righteousness and justice are the foundations of your th
        love and truth go before your face.

15  Happy are the people who know the festal shout! *
        they walk, O Lord, in the light of your presence.

16  They rejoice daily in your Name; *
        they are jubilant in your righteousness.

17  For you are the glory of their strength, *
        and by your favor our might is exalted.

18     Truly, the LORD is our ruler; *
      the Holy One of Israel is our King.


## Psalm 89: Part II   *Tunc locutus es*

19     You spoke once in a vision and said to your faithful people: *
      "I have set the crown upon a warrior
        and have exalted one chosen out of the people.

20     I have found David my servant; *
      with my holy oil have I anointed him.

21     My hand will hold him fast *
      and my arm will make him strong.

22     No enemy shall deceive him, *
      nor any wicked man bring him down.

23     I will crush his foes before him *
      and strike down those who hate him.

24     My faithfulness and love shall be with him, *
      and he shall be victorious through my Name.

25     I shall make his dominion extend *
      from the Great Sea to the River.

26     He will say to me, 'You are my Father, *
      my God, and the rock of my salvation.'

27     I will make him my firstborn *
      and higher than the kings of the earth.

28     I will keep my love for him for ever, *
      and my covenant will stand firm for him.

29     I will establish his line for ever *
      and his throne as the days of heaven."

30  "If his children forsake my law *
        and do not walk according to my judgments;

31  If they break my statutes *
        and do not keep my commandments;

32  I will punish their transgressions with a rod *
        and their iniquities with the lash;

33  But I will not take my love from him, *
        nor let my faithfulness prove false.

34  I will not break my covenant, *
        nor change what has gone out of my lips.

35  Once for all I have sworn by my holiness: *
        ' I will not lie to David.

36  His line shall endure for ever *
        and his throne as the sun before me;

37  It shall stand fast for evermore like the moon, *
        the abiding witness in the sky.' "

38  But you have cast off and rejected your anointed; *
        you have become enraged at him.

39  You have broken your covenant with your servant, *
        defiled his crown, and hurled it to the ground.

40  You have breached all his walls *
        and laid his strongholds in ruins.

41  All who pass by despoil him; *
        he has become the scorn of his neighbors.

42  You have exalted the right hand of his foes *
        and made all his enemies rejoice.

43  You have turned back the edge of his sword *
        and have not sustained him in battle.

44 You have put an end to his splendor *
      and cast his throne to the ground.

45 You have cut short the days of his youth *
      and have covered him with shame.

46 How long will you hide yourself, O LORD?
   will you hide yourself for ever? *
      how long will your anger burn like fire?

47 Remember, LORD, how short life is, *
      how frail you have made all flesh.

48 Who can live and not see death? *
      who can save himself from the power of the grave?

49 Where, Lord, are your loving-kindnesses of old, *
      which you promised David in your faithfulness?

50 Remember, Lord, how your servant is mocked, *
      how I carry in my bosom the taunts of many peoples,

51 The taunts your enemies have hurled, O LORD, *
      which they hurled at the heels of your anointed.

52 Blessed be the LORD for evermore! *
      Amen, I say, Amen.

## Book Four

*Eighteenth Day: Morning Prayer*

90 *Domine, refugium*

1 Lord, you have been our refuge *
      from one generation to another.

2 Before the mountains were brought forth,
  or the land and the earth were born, *
   from age to age you are God.

3 You turn us back to the dust and say, *
  "Go back, O child of earth."

4 For a thousand years in your sight are like yesterday
     when it is past *
  and like a watch in the night.

5 You sweep us away like a dream; *
  we fade away suddenly like the grass.

6 In the morning it is green and flourishes; *
  in the evening it is dried up and withered.

7 For we consume away in your displeasure; *
  we are afraid because of your wrathful indignation.

8 Our iniquities you have set before you, *
  and our secret sins in the light of your countenance.

9 When you are angry, all our days are gone; *
  we bring our years to an end like a sigh.

10 The span of our life is seventy years,
  perhaps in strength even eighty; *
   yet the sum of them is but labor and sorrow,
   for they pass away quickly and we are gone.

11 Who regards the power of your wrath? *
  who rightly fears your indignation?

12 So teach us to number our days *
  that we may apply our hearts to wisdom.

13 Return, O LORD; how long will you tarry? *
  be gracious to your servants.

14 Satisfy us by your loving-kindness in the morning; *
     so shall we rejoice and be glad all the days of our life.

15 Make us glad by the measure of the days that you afflicted us *
     and the years in which we suffered adversity.

16 Show your servants your works *
     and your splendor to their children.

17 May the graciousness of the LORD our God be upon us; *
     prosper the work of our hands;
     prosper our handiwork.


## 91 *Qui habitat*

1 He who dwells in the shelter of the Most High, *
     abides under the shadow of the Almighty.

2 He shall say to the LORD,
   "You are my refuge and my stronghold, *
     my God in whom I put my trust."

3 He shall deliver you from the snare of the hunter *
     and from the deadly pestilence.

4 He shall cover you with his pinions,
   and you shall find refuge under his wings; *
     his faithfulness shall be a shield and buckler.

5 You shall not be afraid of any terror by night, *
     nor of the arrow that flies by day;

6 Of the plague that stalks in the darkness, *
     nor of the sickness that lays waste at mid-day.

7 A thousand shall fall at your side
   and ten thousand at your right hand, *
     but it shall not come near you.

8  Your eyes have only to behold *
      to see the reward of the wicked.

9  Because you have made the LORD your refuge, *
      and the Most High your habitation,

10  There shall no evil happen to you, *
      neither shall any plague come near your dwelling.

11  For he shall give his angels charge over you, *
      to keep you in all your ways.

12  They shall bear you in their hands, *
      lest you dash your foot against a stone.

13  You shall tread upon the lion and adder; *
      you shall trample the young lion and the serpent
         under your feet.

14  Because he is bound to me in love,
      therefore will I deliver him; *
      I will protect him, because he knows my Name.

15  He shall call upon me, and I will answer him; *
      I am with him in trouble;
      I will rescue him and bring him to honor.

16  With long life will I satisfy him, *
      and show him my salvation.


## 92  *Bonum est confiteri*

1  It is a good thing to give thanks to the LORD, *
      and to sing praises to your Name, O Most High;

2  To tell of your loving-kindness early in the morning *
      and of your faithfulness in the night season;

3   On the psaltery, and on the lyre, *
        and to the melody of the harp.

4   For you have made me glad by your acts, O LORD; *
        and I shout for joy because of the works of your hands.

5   LORD, how great are your works! *
        your thoughts are very deep.

6   The dullard does not know,
        nor does the fool understand, *
        that though the wicked grow like weeds,
        and all the workers of iniquity flourish,

7   They flourish only to be destroyed for ever; *
        but you, O LORD, are exalted for evermore.

8   For lo, your enemies, O LORD,
        lo, your enemies shall perish, *
        and all the workers of iniquity shall be scattered.

9   But my horn you have exalted like the horns of wild bulls; *
        I am anointed with fresh oil.

10  My eyes also gloat over my enemies, *
        and my ears rejoice to hear the doom of the wicked who
            rise up against me.

11  The righteous shall flourish like a palm tree, *
        and shall spread abroad like a cedar of Lebanon.

12  Those who are planted in the house of the LORD *
        shall flourish in the courts of our God;

13  They shall still bear fruit in old age; *
        they shall be green and succulent;

14  That they may show how upright the LORD is, *
        my Rock, in whom there is no fault.

## 93 *Dominus regnavit*

1 The LORD is King;
    he has put on splendid apparel; *
        the LORD has put on his apparel
        and girded himself with strength.

2 He has made the whole world so sure *
        that it cannot be moved;

3 Ever since the world began, your throne has been establis
        you are from everlasting.

4 The waters have lifted up, O LORD,
    the waters have lifted up their voice; *
        the waters have lifted up their pounding waves.

5 Mightier than the sound of many waters,
    mightier than the breakers of the sea, *
        mightier is the LORD who dwells on high.

6 Your testimonies are very sure, *
        and holiness adorns your house, O LORD,
        for ever and for evermore.

## 94 *Deus ultionum*

1 O LORD God of vengeance, *
        O God of vengeance, show yourself.

2 Rise up, O Judge of the world; *
        give the arrogant their just deserts.

3 How long shall the wicked, O LORD, *
        how long shall the wicked triumph?

They bluster in their insolence; *
  all evildoers are full of boasting.

They crush your people, O LORD, *
  and afflict your chosen nation.

They murder the widow and the stranger *
  and put the orphans to death.

Yet they say,"The LORD does not see, *
  the God of Jacob takes no notice."

Consider well, you dullards among the people; *
  when will you fools understand?

He that planted the ear, does he not hear? *
  he that formed the eye, does he not see?

He who admonishes the nations, will he not punish? *
  he who teaches all the world, has he no knowledge?

The LORD knows our human thoughts; *
  how like a puff of wind they are.

Happy are they whom you instruct, O Lord! *
  whom you teach out of your law;

To give them rest in evil days, *
  until a pit is dug for the wicked.

For the LORD will not abandon his people, *
  nor will he forsake his own.

For judgment will again be just, *
  and all the true of heart will follow it.

Who rose up for me against the wicked? *
  who took my part against the evildoers?

If the LORD had not come to my help, *
  I should soon have dwelt in the land of silence.

18    As often as I said,"My foot has slipped," *
     your love, O LORD, upheld me.

19    When many cares fill my mind, *
     your consolations cheer my soul.

20    Can a corrupt tribunal have any part with you, *
     one which frames evil into law?

21    They conspire against the life of the just *
     and condemn the innocent to death.

22    But the LORD has become my stronghold, *
     and my God the rock of my trust.

23    He will turn their wickedness back upon them
     and destroy them in their own malice; *
     the LORD our God will destroy them.

*Nineteenth Day: Morning Prayer*

## 95   *Venite, exultemus*

1    Come, let us sing to the LORD; *
     let us shout for joy to the Rock of our salvation.

2    Let us come before his presence with thanksgiving *
     and raise a loud shout to him with psalms.

3    For the LORD is a great God, *
     and a great King above all gods.

4    In his hand are the caverns of the earth, *
     and the heights of the hills are his also.

5    The sea is his, for he made it, *
     and his hands have molded the dry land.

Come, let us bow down, and bend the knee, *
  and kneel before the LORD our Maker.

For he is our God,
and we are the people of his pasture and the sheep of his hand. *
  Oh, that today you would hearken to his voice!


Harden not your hearts,
as your forebears did in the wilderness, *
  at Meribah, and on that day at Massah,
  when they tempted me.

They put me to the test, *
  though they had seen my works.

Forty years long I detested that generation and said, *
  "This people are wayward in their hearts;
  they do not know my ways."

So I swore in my wrath, *
  "They shall not enter into my rest."


# 96  *Cantate Domino*

Sing to the LORD a new song; *
  sing to the LORD, all the whole earth.

Sing to the LORD and bless his Name; *
  proclaim the good news of his salvation from day to day.

Declare his glory among the nations *
  and his wonders among all peoples.

For great is the LORD and greatly to be praised; *
  he is more to be feared than all gods.

5    As for all the gods of the nations, they are but idols; *
         but it is the LORD who made the heavens.

6    Oh, the majesty and magnificence of his presence! *
         Oh, the power and the splendor of his sanctuary!

7    Ascribe to the LORD, you families of the peoples; *
         ascribe to the LORD honor and power.

8    Ascribe to the LORD the honor due his Name; *
         bring offerings and come into his courts.

9    Worship the LORD in the beauty of holiness; *
         let the whole earth tremble before him.

10   Tell it out among the nations: "The LORD is King! *
         he has made the world so firm that it cannot be mov
         he will judge the peoples with equity."

11   Let the heavens rejoice, and let the earth be glad;
         let the sea thunder and all that is in it; *
         let the field be joyful and all that is therein.

12   Then shall all the trees of the wood shout for joy
         before the LORD when he comes, *
         when he comes to judge the earth.

13   He will judge the world with righteousness *
         and the peoples with his truth.


# 97 *Dominus regnavit*

1    The LORD is King;
     let the earth rejoice; *
         let the multitude of the isles be glad.

2    Clouds and darkness are round about him, *
         righteousness and justice are the foundations of his

3  A fire goes before him *
      and burns up his enemies on every side.

4  His lightnings light up the world; *
      the earth sees it and is afraid.

5  The mountains melt like wax at the presence of the LORD, *
      at the presence of the Lord of the whole earth.

6  The heavens declare his righteousness, *
      and all the peoples see his glory.

7  Confounded be all who worship carved images
   and delight in false gods! *
      Bow down before him, all you gods.

8  Zion hears and is glad, and the cities of Judah rejoice, *
      because of your judgments, O LORD.

9  For you are the LORD,
   most high over all the earth; *
      you are exalted far above all gods.

0  The LORD loves those who hate evil; *
      he preserves the lives of his saints
      and delivers them from the hand of the wicked.

1  Light has sprung up for the righteous, *
      and joyful gladness for those who are truehearted.

2  Rejoice in the LORD, you righteous, *
      and give thanks to his holy Name.


*Nineteenth Day: Evening Prayer*

# 98  *Cantate Domino*

1  Sing to the LORD a new song, *
      for he has done marvelous things.

2   With his right hand and his holy arm *
       has he won for himself the victory.

3   The LORD has made known his victory; *
       his righteousness has he openly shown in
             the sight of the nations.

4   He remembers his mercy and faithfulness to
             the house of Israel, *
       and all the ends of the earth have seen the
             victory of our God.

5   Shout with joy to the LORD, all you lands; *
       lift up your voice, rejoice, and sing.

6   Sing to the LORD with the harp, *
       with the harp and the voice of song.

7   With trumpets and the sound of the horn *
       shout with joy before the King, the LORD.

8   Let the sea make a noise and all that is in it, *
       the lands and those who dwell therein.

9   Let the rivers clap their hands, *
       and let the hills ring out with joy before the LORD,
       when he comes to judge the earth.

10  In righteousness shall he judge the world *
       and the peoples with equity.


## 99  *Dominus regnavit*

1   The LORD is King;
       let the people tremble; *
          he is enthroned upon the cherubim;
          let the earth shake.

2    The LORD is great in Zion; *
        he is high above all peoples.

3    Let them confess his Name, which is great and awesome; *
        he is the Holy One.

4    "O mighty King, lover of justice,
     you have established equity; *
        you have executed justice and righteousness in Jacob."

5    Proclaim the greatness of the LORD our God
     and fall down before his footstool; *
        he is the Holy One.

6    Moses and Aaron among his priests,
     and Samuel among those who call upon his Name, *
        they called upon the LORD, and he answered them.

7    He spoke to them out of the pillar of cloud; *
        they kept his testimonies and the decree that he gave them.

8    "O LORD our God, you answered them indeed; *
     you were a God who forgave them,
        yet punished them for their evil deeds."

9    Proclaim the greatness of the LORD our God
     and worship him upon his holy hill; *
        for the LORD our God is the Holy One.


100    *Jubilate Deo*

1    Be joyful in the LORD, all you lands; *
        serve the LORD with gladness
        and come before his presence with a song.

2    Know this: The LORD himself is God; *
        he himself has made us, and we are his;
        we are his people and the sheep of his pasture.

3  Enter his gates with thanksgiving;
   go into his courts with praise; *
      give thanks to him and call upon his Name.

4  For the LORD is good;
   his mercy is everlasting; *
      and his faithfulness endures from age to age.


## 101 *Misericordiam et judicium*

1  I will sing of mercy and justice; *
      to you, O LORD, will I sing praises.

2  I will strive to follow a blameless course;
   oh, when will you come to me? *
      I will walk with sincerity of heart within my house.

3  I will set no worthless thing before my eyes; *
      I hate the doers of evil deeds;
      they shall not remain with me.

4  A crooked heart shall be far from me; *
      I will not know evil.

5  Those who in secret slander their neighbors I will destro
      those who have a haughty look and a proud
                     heart I cannot abide.

6  My eyes are upon the faithful in the land, that they may
                     dwell with me, *
      and only those who lead a blameless life shall
                     be my servants.

7  Those who act deceitfully shall not dwell in my house, *
      and those who tell lies shall not continue in my sight.

8  I will soon destroy all the wicked in the land, *
      that I may root out all evildoers from the city of the L

## 102 *Domine, exaudi*

1 LORD, hear my prayer, and let my cry come before you; *
   hide not your face from me in the day of my trouble.

2 Incline your ear to me; *
   when I call, make haste to answer me,

3 For my days drift away like smoke, *
   and my bones are hot as burning coals.

4 My heart is smitten like grass and withered, *
   so that I forget to eat my bread.

5 Because of the voice of my groaning *
   I am but skin and bones.

6 I have become like a vulture in the wilderness, *
   like an owl among the ruins.

7 I lie awake and groan; *
   I am like a sparrow, lonely on a house-top.

8 My enemies revile me all day long, *
   and those who scoff at me have taken an oath against me.

9 For I have eaten ashes for bread *
   and mingled my drink with weeping.

10 Because of your indignation and wrath *
   you have lifted me up and thrown me away.

11 My days pass away like a shadow, *
   and I wither like the grass.

12 But you, O LORD, endure for ever, *
   and your Name from age to age.

13 You will arise and have compassion on Zion,
for it is time to have mercy upon her; *
    indeed, the appointed time has come.

14 For your servants love her very rubble, *
    and are moved to pity even for her dust.

15 The nations shall fear your Name, O LORD, *
    and all the kings of the earth your glory.

16 For the LORD will build up Zion, *
    and his glory will appear.

17 He will look with favor on the prayer of the homeless; *
    he will not despise their plea.

18 Let this be written for a future generation, *
    so that a people yet unborn may praise the LORD.

19 For the LORD looked down from his holy place on high
    from the heavens he beheld the earth;

20 That he might hear the groan of the captive *
    and set free those condemned to die;

21 That they may declare in Zion the Name of the LORD, *
    and his praise in Jerusalem;

22 When the peoples are gathered together, *
    and the kingdoms also, to serve the LORD.

23 He has brought down my strength before my time; *
    he has shortened the number of my days;

24 And I said,"O my God,
do not take me away in the midst of my days; *
    your years endure throughout all generations.

25 In the beginning, O LORD, you laid the foundations
                of the earth, *
    and the heavens are the work of your hands;

26 They shall perish, but you will endure;
   they all shall wear out like a garment; *
      as clothing you will change them,
      and they shall be changed;

27 But you are always the same, *
      and your years will never end.

28 The children of your servants shall continue, *
      and their offspring shall stand fast in your sight."


## 103 *Benedic, anima mea*

1 Bless the LORD, O my soul, *
      and all that is within me, bless his holy Name.

2 Bless the LORD, O my soul, *
      and forget not all his benefits.

3 He forgives all your sins *
      and heals all your infirmities;

4 He redeems your life from the grave *
      and crowns you with mercy and loving-kindness;

5 He satisfies you with good things, *
      and your youth is renewed like an eagle's.

6 The LORD executes righteousness *
      and judgment for all who are oppressed.

7 He made his ways known to Moses *
      and his works to the children of Israel.

8 The LORD is full of compassion and mercy, *
      slow to anger and of great kindness.

9 He will not always accuse us, *
      nor will he keep his anger for ever.

10    He has not dealt with us according to our sins, *
       nor rewarded us according to our wickedness.

11    For as the heavens are high above the earth, *
       so is his mercy great upon those who fear him.

12    As far as the east is from the west, *
       so far has he removed our sins from us.

13    As a father cares for his children, *
       so does the LORD care for those who fear him.

14    For he himself knows whereof we are made; *
       he remembers that we are but dust.

15    Our days are like the grass; *
       we flourish like a flower of the field;

16    When the wind goes over it, it is gone, *
       and its place shall know it no more.

17    But the merciful goodness of the LORD endures for ever
       on those who fear him, *
       and his righteousness on children's children;

18    On those who keep his covenant *
       and remember his commandments and do them.

19    The LORD has set his throne in heaven, *
       and his kingship has dominion over all.

20    Bless the LORD, you angels of his,
       you mighty ones who do his bidding, *
       and hearken to the voice of his word.

21    Bless the LORD, all you his hosts, *
       you ministers of his who do his will.

22    Bless the LORD, all you works of his,
       in all places of his dominion; *
       bless the LORD, O my soul.

## 104 *Benedic, anima mea*

1   Bless the LORD, O my soul; *
    O LORD my God, how excellent is your greatness!
    you are clothed with majesty and splendor.

2   You wrap yourself with light as with a cloak *
    and spread out the heavens like a curtain.

3   You lay the beams of your chambers in the waters above; *
    you make the clouds your chariot;
    you ride on the wings of the wind.

4   You make the winds your messengers *
    and flames of fire your servants.

5   You have set the earth upon its foundations, *
    so that it never shall move at any time.

6   You covered it with the Deep as with a mantle; *
    the waters stood higher than the mountains.

7   At your rebuke they fled; *
    at the voice of your thunder they hastened away.

8   They went up into the hills and down to the valleys beneath, *
    to the places you had appointed for them.

9   You set the limits that they should not pass; *
    they shall not again cover the earth.

10  You send the springs into the valleys; *
    they flow between the mountains.

11  All the beasts of the field drink their fill from them, *
    and the wild asses quench their thirst.

12  Beside them the birds of the air make their nests *
    and sing among the branches.

13    You water the mountains from your dwelling on high; *
     the earth is fully satisfied by the fruit of your works.

14    You make grass grow for flocks and herds *
     and plants to serve mankind;

15    That they may bring forth food from the earth, *
     and wine to gladden our hearts,

16    Oil to make a cheerful countenance, *
     and bread to strengthen the heart.

17    The trees of the LORD are full of sap, *
     the cedars of Lebanon which he planted,

18    In which the birds build their nests, *
     and in whose tops the stork makes his dwelling.

19    The high hills are a refuge for the mountain goats, *
     and the stony cliffs for the rock badgers.

20    You appointed the moon to mark the seasons, *
     and the sun knows the time of its setting.

21    You make darkness that it may be night, *
     in which all the beasts of the forest prowl.

22    The lions roar after their prey *
     and seek their food from God.

23    The sun rises, and they slip away *
     and lay themselves down in their dens.

24    Man goes forth to his work *
     and to his labor until the evening.

25    O LORD, how manifold are your works! *
     in wisdom you have made them all;
     the earth is full of your creatures.

26  Yonder is the great and wide sea
    with its living things too many to number, *
        creatures both small and great.

27  There move the ships,
    and there is that Leviathan, *
        which you have made for the sport of it.

28  All of them look to you *
        to give them their food in due season.

29  You give it to them; they gather it; *
        you open your hand, and they are filled with good things.

30  You hide your face, and they are terrified; *
        you take away their breath,
        and they die and return to their dust.

31  You send forth your Spirit, and they are created; *
        and so you renew the face of the earth.

32  May the glory of the LORD endure for ever; *
        may the LORD rejoice in all his works.

33  He looks at the earth and it trembles; *
        he touches the mountains and they smoke.

34  I will sing to the LORD as long as I live; *
        I will praise my God while I have my being.

35  May these words of mine please him; *
        I will rejoice in the LORD.

36  Let sinners be consumed out of the earth, *
        and the wicked be no more.

37  Bless the LORD, O my soul. *
        Hallelujah!

# 105

**Part I**  *Confitemini Domino*

1 Give thanks to the LORD and call upon his Name; *
   make known his deeds among the peoples.

2 Sing to him, sing praises to him, *
   and speak of all his marvelous works.

3 Glory in his holy Name; *
   let the hearts of those who seek the LORD rejoice.

4 Search for the LORD and his strength; *
   continually seek his face.

5 Remember the marvels he has done, *
   his wonders and the judgments of his mouth,

6 O offspring of Abraham his servant, *
   O children of Jacob his chosen.

7 He is the LORD our God; *
   his judgments prevail in all the world.

8 He has always been mindful of his covenant, *
   the promise he made for a thousand generations:

9 The covenant he made with Abraham, *
   the oath that he swore to Isaac,

10 Which he established as a statute for Jacob, *
   an everlasting covenant for Israel,

11 Saying, "To you will I give the land of Canaan *
   to be your allotted inheritance."

12    When they were few in number, *
     of little account, and sojourners in the land,

13    Wandering from nation to nation *
     and from one kingdom to another,

14    He let no one oppress them *
     and rebuked kings for their sake,

15    Saying,"Do not touch my anointed *
     and do my prophets no harm."

16    Then he called for a famine in the land *
     and destroyed the supply of bread.

17    He sent a man before them, *
     Joseph, who was sold as a slave.

18    They bruised his feet in fetters; *
     his neck they put in an iron collar.

19    Until his prediction came to pass, *
     the word of the LORD tested him.

20    The king sent and released him; *
     the ruler of the peoples set him free.

21    He set him as a master over his household, *
     as a ruler over all his possessions,

22    To instruct his princes according to his will *
     and to teach his elders wisdom.

**Psalm 105: Part II**   *Et intravit Israel*

23    Israel came into Egypt, *
     and Jacob became a sojourner in the land of Ham.

24 The LORD made his people exceedingly fruitful; *
    he made them stronger than their enemies;

25 Whose heart he turned, so that they hated his people, *
    and dealt unjustly with his servants.

26 He sent Moses his servant, *
    and Aaron whom he had chosen.

27 They worked his signs among them, *
    and portents in the land of Ham.

28 He sent darkness, and it grew dark; *
    but the Egyptians rebelled against his words.

29 He turned their waters into blood *
    and caused their fish to die.

30 Their land was overrun by frogs, *
    in the very chambers of their kings.

31 He spoke, and there came swarms of insects *
    and gnats within all their borders.

32 He gave them hailstones instead of rain, *
    and flames of fire throughout their land.

33 He blasted their vines and their fig trees *
    and shattered every tree in their country.

34 He spoke, and the locust came, *
    and young locusts without number,

35 Which ate up all the green plants in their land *
    and devoured the fruit of their soil.

36 He struck down the firstborn of their land, *
    the firstfruits of all their strength.

37 He led out his people with silver and gold; *
    in all their tribes there was not one that stumbled.

8   Egypt was glad of their going, *
        because they were afraid of them.

9   He spread out a cloud for a covering *
        and a fire to give light in the night season.

10  They asked, and quails appeared, *
        and he satisfied them with bread from heaven.

11  He opened the rock, and water flowed, *
        so the river ran in the dry places.

12  For God remembered his holy word *
        and Abraham his servant.

13  So he led forth his people with gladness, *
        his chosen with shouts of joy.

14  He gave his people the lands of the nations, *
        and they took the fruit of others' toil,

15  That they might keep his statutes *
        and observe his laws.
        Hallelujah!

*Twenty-first Day: Evening Prayer*

# 106

**Part I**   *Confitemini Domino*

1   Hallelujah!
    Give thanks to the LORD, for he is good, *
        for his mercy endures for ever.

2   Who can declare the mighty acts of the LORD *
        or show forth all his praise?

3    Happy are those who act with justice *
      and always do what is right!

4    Remember me, O LORD, with the favor you have
                      for your people, *
      and visit me with your saving help;

5    That I may see the prosperity of your elect
      and be glad with the gladness of your people, *
      that I may glory with your inheritance.


6    We have sinned as our forebears did; *
      we have done wrong and dealt wickedly.

7    In Egypt they did not consider your marvelous works,
      nor remember the abundance of your love; *
      they defied the Most High at the Red Sea.

8    But he saved them for his Name's sake, *
      to make his power known.

9    He rebuked the Red Sea, and it dried up, *
      and he led them through the deep as through a desert.

10    He saved them from the hand of those who hated them
      and redeemed them from the hand of the enemy.

11    The waters covered their oppressors; *
      not one of them was left.

12    Then they believed his words *
      and sang him songs of praise.


13    But they soon forgot his deeds *
      and did not wait for his counsel.

14    A craving seized them in the wilderness, *
      and they put God to the test in the desert.

15  He gave them what they asked, *
        but sent leanness into their soul.

16  They envied Moses in the camp, *
        and Aaron, the holy one of the LORD.

17  The earth opened and swallowed Dathan *
        and covered the company of Abiram.

18  Fire blazed up against their company, *
        and flames devoured the wicked.


### Psalm 106: Part II  *Et fecerunt vitulum*

19  Israel made a bull-calf at Horeb *
        and worshiped a molten image;

20  And so they exchanged their Glory *
        for the image of an ox that feeds on grass.

21  They forgot God their Savior, *
        who had done great things in Egypt,

22  Wonderful deeds in the land of Ham, *
        and fearful things at the Red Sea.

23  So he would have destroyed them,
    had not Moses his chosen stood before him in the breach, *
        to turn away his wrath from consuming them.

24  They refused the pleasant land *
        and would not believe his promise.

25  They grumbled in their tents *
        and would not listen to the voice of the LORD.

26  So he lifted his hand against them, *
        to overthrow them in the wilderness,

27 To cast out their seed among the nations, *
      and to scatter them throughout the lands.

28 They joined themselves to Baal-Peor *
      and ate sacrifices offered to the dead.

29 They provoked him to anger with their actions, *
      and a plague broke out among them.

30 Then Phinehas stood up and interceded, *
      and the plague came to an end.

31 This was reckoned to him as righteousness *
      throughout all generations for ever.

32 Again they provoked his anger at the waters of Meribah,
      so that he punished Moses because of them;

33 For they so embittered his spirit *
      that he spoke rash words with his lips.


34 They did not destroy the peoples *
      as the LORD had commanded them.

35 They intermingled with the heathen *
      and learned their pagan ways,

36 So that they worshiped their idols, *
      which became a snare to them.

37 They sacrificed their sons *
      and their daughters to evil spirits.

38 They shed innocent blood,
      the blood of their sons and daughters, *
      which they offered to the idols of Canaan,
      and the land was defiled with blood.

39    Thus they were polluted by their actions *
      and went whoring in their evil deeds.

40    Therefore the wrath of the LORD was kindled against
             his people *
      and he abhorred his inheritance.

41    He gave them over to the hand of the heathen, *
      and those who hated them ruled over them.

42    Their enemies oppressed them, *
      and they were humbled under their hand.

43    Many a time did he deliver them,
      but they rebelled through their own devices, *
      and were brought down in their iniquity.

44    Nevertheless, he saw their distress, *
      when he heard their lamentation.

45    He remembered his covenant with them *
      and relented in accordance with his great mercy.

46    He caused them to be pitied *
      by those who held them captive.

47    Save us, O LORD our God,
      and gather us from among the nations, *
      that we may give thanks to your holy Name
      and glory in your praise.

48    Blessed be the LORD, the God of Israel,
      from everlasting and to everlasting; *
      and let all the people say, "Amen!"
      Hallelujah!

**Book Five**

*Twenty-second Day: Morning Prayer*

# 107

**Part I**  *Confitemini Domino*

1  Give thanks to the LORD, for he is good, *
     and his mercy endures for ever.

2  Let all those whom the LORD has redeemed proclaim *
     that he redeemed them from the hand of the foe.

3  He gathered them out of the lands; *
     from the east and from the west,
     from the north and from the south.

4  Some wandered in desert wastes; *
     they found no way to a city where they might dwell.

5  They were hungry and thirsty; *
     their spirits languished within them.

6  Then they cried to the LORD in their trouble, *
     and he delivered them from their distress.

7  He put their feet on a straight path *
     to go to a city where they might dwell.

8  Let them give thanks to the LORD for his mercy *
     and the wonders he does for his children.

9  For he satisfies the thirsty *
     and fills the hungry with good things.

10    Some sat in darkness and deep gloom, *
      bound fast in misery and iron;

11    Because they rebelled against the words of God *
      and despised the counsel of the Most High.

12    So he humbled their spirits with hard labor; *
      they stumbled, and there was none to help.

13    Then they cried to the LORD in their trouble, *
      and he delivered them from their distress.

14    He led them out of darkness and deep gloom *
      and broke their bonds asunder.

15    Let them give thanks to the LORD for his mercy *
      and the wonders he does for his children.

16    For he shatters the doors of bronze *
      and breaks in two the iron bars.


17    Some were fools and took to rebellious ways; *
      they were afflicted because of their sins.

18    They abhorred all manner of food *
      and drew near to death's door.

19    Then they cried to the LORD in their trouble, *
      and he delivered them from their distress.

20    He sent forth his word and healed them *
      and saved them from the grave.

21    Let them give thanks to the LORD for his mercy *
      and the wonders he does for his children.

22    Let them offer a sacrifice of thanksgiving *
      and tell of his acts with shouts of joy.

23    Some went down to the sea in ships *
       and plied their trade in deep waters;

24    They beheld the works of the LORD *
       and his wonders in the deep.

25    Then he spoke, and a stormy wind arose, *
       which tossed high the waves of the sea.

26    They mounted up to the heavens and fell back to the depth
       their hearts melted because of their peril.

27    They reeled and staggered like drunkards *
       and were at their wits' end.

28    Then they cried to the LORD in their trouble, *
       and he delivered them from their distress.

29    He stilled the storm to a whisper *
       and quieted the waves of the sea.

30    Then were they glad because of the calm, *
       and he brought them to the harbor they were bound fo

31    Let them give thanks to the LORD for his mercy *
       and the wonders he does for his children.

32    Let them exalt him in the congregation of the people *
       and praise him in the council of the elders.

**Psalm 107: Part II**   *Posuit flumina*

33    The LORD changed rivers into deserts, *
       and water-springs into thirsty ground,

34    A fruitful land into salt flats, *
       because of the wickedness of those who dwell there.

35    He changed deserts into pools of water *
       and dry land into water-springs.

36    He settled the hungry there, *
     and they founded a city to dwell in.

37    They sowed fields, and planted vineyards, *
     and brought in a fruitful harvest.

38    He blessed them, so that they increased greatly; *
     he did not let their herds decrease.

39    Yet when they were diminished and brought low, *
     through stress of adversity and sorrow,

40    (He pours contempt on princes *
     and makes them wander in trackless wastes)

41    He lifted up the poor out of misery *
     and multiplied their families like flocks of sheep.

42    The upright will see this and rejoice, *
     but all wickedness will shut its mouth.

43    Whoever is wise will ponder these things, *
     and consider well the mercies of the LORD.

*Twenty-second Day: Evening Prayer*

## 108   *Paratum cor meum*

1    My heart is firmly fixed, O God, my heart is fixed; *
     I will sing and make melody.

2    Wake up, my spirit;
awake, lute and harp; *
     I myself will waken the dawn.

3    I will confess you among the peoples, O LORD; *
     I will sing praises to you among the nations.

4   For your loving-kindness is greater than the heavens, *
        and your faithfulness reaches to the clouds.

5   Exalt yourself above the heavens, O God, *
        and your glory over all the earth.

6   So that those who are dear to you may be delivered, *
        save with your right hand and answer me.


7   God spoke from his holy place and said, *
        "I will exult and parcel out Shechem;
        I will divide the valley of Succoth.

8   Gilead is mine and Manasseh is mine; *
        Ephraim is my helmet and Judah my scepter.

9   Moab is my washbasin,
        on Edom I throw down my sandal to claim it, *
        and over Philistia will I shout in triumph."

10  Who will lead me into the strong city? *
        who will bring me into Edom?

11  Have you not cast us off, O God? *
        you no longer go out, O God, with our armies.

12  Grant us your help against the enemy, *
        for vain is the help of man.

13  With God we will do valiant deeds, *
        and he shall tread our enemies under foot.


## 109  *Deus, laudem*

1   Hold not your tongue, O God of my praise; *
        for the mouth of the wicked,
        the mouth of the deceitful, is opened against me.

2   They speak to me with a lying tongue; *
        they encompass me with hateful words
        and fight against me without a cause.

3   Despite my love, they accuse me; *
        but as for me, I pray for them.

4   They repay evil for good, *
        and hatred for my love.


5   Set a wicked man against him, *
        and let an accuser stand at his right hand.

6   When he is judged, let him be found guilty, *
        and let his appeal be in vain.

7   Let his days be few, *
        and let another take his office.

8   Let his children be fatherless, *
        and his wife become a widow.

9   Let his children be waifs and beggars; *
        let them be driven from the ruins of their homes.

10  Let the creditor seize everything he has; *
        let strangers plunder his gains.

11  Let there be no one to show him kindness, *
        and none to pity his fatherless children.

12  Let his descendants be destroyed, *
        and his name be blotted out in the next generation.

13  Let the wickedness of his fathers be remembered before
                    the LORD, *
        and his mother's sin not be blotted out;

14  Let their sin be always before the LORD; *
        but let him root out their names from the earth;

15    Because he did not remember to show mercy, *
         but persecuted the poor and needy
         and sought to kill the brokenhearted.

16    He loved cursing,
      let it come upon him; *
         he took no delight in blessing,
         let it depart from him.

17    He put on cursing like a garment, *
         let it soak into his body like water
         and into his bones like oil;

18    Let it be to him like the cloak which he
                     wraps around himself, *
         and like the belt that he wears continually.

19    Let this be the recompense from the LORD to my accuser
         and to those who speak evil against me.


20    But you, O Lord my GOD,
      oh, deal with me according to your Name; *
         for your tender mercy's sake, deliver me.

21    For I am poor and needy, *
         and my heart is wounded within me.

22    I have faded away like a shadow when it lengthens; *
         I am shaken off like a locust.

23    My knees are weak through fasting, *
         and my flesh is wasted and gaunt.

24    I have become a reproach to them; *
         they see and shake their heads.

25    Help me, O LORD my God; *
         save me for your mercy's sake.

26     Let them know that this is your hand, *
       that you, O LORD, have done it.

27     They may curse, but you will bless; *
       let those who rise up against me be put to shame,
       and your servant will rejoice.

28     Let my accusers be clothed with disgrace *
       and wrap themselves in their shame as in a cloak.

29     I will give great thanks to the LORD with my mouth; *
       in the midst of the multitude will I praise him;

30     Because he stands at the right hand of the needy, *
       to save his life from those who would condemn him.

*Twenty-third Day: Morning Prayer*

# 110   *Dixit Dominus*

1     The LORD said to my Lord, "Sit at my right hand, *
       until I make your enemies your footstool."

2     The LORD will send the scepter of your power out of Zion, *
       saying, "Rule over your enemies round about you.

3     Princely state has been yours from the day of your birth; *
       in the beauty of holiness have I begotten you,
       like dew from the womb of the morning."

4     The LORD has sworn and he will not recant: *
       "You are a priest for ever after the order of Melchizedek."

5     The Lord who is at your right hand
    will smite kings in the day of his wrath; *
       he will rule over the nations.

6   He will heap high the corpses; *
        he will smash heads over the wide earth.

7   He will drink from the brook beside the road; *
        therefore he will lift high his head.


# III   *Confitebor tibi*

1   Hallelujah!
    I will give thanks to the LORD with my whole heart, *
        in the assembly of the upright, in the congregation.

2   Great are the deeds of the LORD! *
        they are studied by all who delight in them.

3   His work is full of majesty and splendor, *
        and his righteousness endures for ever.

4   He makes his marvelous works to be remembered; *
        the LORD is gracious and full of compassion.

5   He gives food to those who fear him; *
        he is ever mindful of his covenant.

6   He has shown his people the power of his works *
        in giving them the lands of the nations.

7   The works of his hands are faithfulness and justice; *
        all his commandments are sure.

8   They stand fast for ever and ever, *
        because they are done in truth and equity.

9   He sent redemption to his people;
    he commanded his covenant for ever; *
        holy and awesome is his Name.

10    The fear of the LORD is the beginning of wisdom; *
          those who act accordingly have a good understanding;
          his praise endures for ever.


## 112 *Beatus vir*

1     Hallelujah!
      Happy are they who fear the Lord *
          and have great delight in his commandments!

2     Their descendants will be mighty in the land; *
          the generation of the upright will be blessed.

3     Wealth and riches will be in their house, *
          and their righteousness will last for ever.

4     Light shines in the darkness for the upright; *
          the righteous are merciful and full of compassion.

5     It is good for them to be generous in lending *
          and to manage their affairs with justice.

6     For they will never be shaken; *
          the righteous will be kept in everlasting remembrance.

7     They will not be afraid of any evil rumors; *
          their heart is right;
          they put their trust in the Lord.

8     Their heart is established and will not shrink, *
          until they see their desire upon their enemies.

9     They have given freely to the poor, *
          and their righteousness stands fast for ever;
          they will hold up their head with honor.

10    The wicked will see it and be angry;
      they will gnash their teeth and pine away; *
          the desires of the wicked will perish.

## 113 *Laudate, pueri*

1 Hallelujah!
Give praise, you servants of the LORD; *
    praise the Name of the LORD.

2 Let the Name of the LORD be blessed, *
    from this time forth for evermore.

3 From the rising of the sun to its going down *
    let the Name of the LORD be praised.

4 The LORD is high above all nations, *
    and his glory above the heavens.

5 Who is like the LORD our God, who sits enthroned on hi
    but stoops to behold the heavens and the earth?

6 He takes up the weak out of the dust *
    and lifts up the poor from the ashes.

7 He sets them with the princes, *
    with the princes of his people.

8 He makes the woman of a childless house *
    to be a joyful mother of children.


*Twenty-third Day: Evening Prayer*

## 114 *In exitu Israel*

1 Hallelujah!
When Israel came out of Egypt, *
    the house of Jacob from a people of strange speech,

2 Judah became God's sanctuary *
    and Israel his dominion.

3  The sea beheld it and fled; *
      Jordan turned and went back.

4  The mountains skipped like rams, *
      and the little hills like young sheep.

5  What ailed you, O sea, that you fled? *
      O Jordan, that you turned back?

6  You mountains, that you skipped like rams? *
      you little hills like young sheep?

7  Tremble, O earth, at the presence of the Lord, *
      at the presence of the God of Jacob,

8  Who turned the hard rock into a pool of water *
      and flint-stone into a flowing spring.


# 115   *Non nobis, Domine*

1  Not to us, O LORD, not to us,
   but to your Name give glory; *
      because of your love and because of your faithfulness.

2  Why should the heathen say, *
      "Where then is their God?"

3  Our God is in heaven; *
      whatever he wills to do he does.

4  Their idols are silver and gold, *
      the work of human hands.

5  They have mouths, but they cannot speak; *
      eyes have they, but they cannot see;

6  They have ears, but they cannot hear; *
      noses, but they cannot smell;

7    They have hands, but they cannot feel;
     feet, but they cannot walk; *
       they make no sound with their throat.

8    Those who make them are like them, *
       and so are all who put their trust in them.

9    O Israel, trust in the LORD; *
       he is their help and their shield.

10   O house of Aaron, trust in the LORD; *
       he is their help and their shield.

11   You who fear the LORD, trust in the LORD; *
       he is their help and their shield.

12   The LORD has been mindful of us, and he will bless us; *
       he will bless the house of Israel;
       he will bless the house of Aaron;

13   He will bless those who fear the LORD, *
       both small and great together.

14   May the LORD increase you more and more, *
       you and your children after you.

15   May you be blessed by the LORD, *
       the maker of heaven and earth.

16   The heaven of heavens is the LORD's, *
       but he entrusted the earth to its peoples.

17   The dead do not praise the LORD, *
       nor all those who go down into silence;

18   But we will bless the LORD, *
       from this time forth for evermore.
       Hallelujah!

# 116 *Dilexi, quoniam*

1    I love the LORD, because he has heard the voice of
              my supplication, *
      because he has inclined his ear to me whenever
              I called upon him.

2    The cords of death entangled me;
      the grip of the grave took hold of me; *
        I came to grief and sorrow.

3    Then I called upon the Name of the LORD: *
      "O LORD, I pray you, save my life."

4    Gracious is the LORD and righteous; *
      our God is full of compassion.

5    The LORD watches over the innocent; *
      I was brought very low, and he helped me.

6    Turn again to your rest, O my soul, *
      for the LORD has treated you well.

7    For you have rescued my life from death, *
      my eyes from tears, and my feet from stumbling.

8    I will walk in the presence of the LORD *
      in the land of the living.

9    I believed, even when I said,
    "I have been brought very low." *
      In my distress I said, "No one can be trusted."

10    How shall I repay the LORD *
      for all the good things he has done for me?

11    I will lift up the cup of salvation *
      and call upon the Name of the LORD.

12  I will fulfill my vows to the LORD *
    in the presence of all his people.

13  Precious in the sight of the LORD *
    is the death of his servants.

14  O LORD, I am your servant; *
    I am your servant and the child of your handmaid;
    you have freed me from my bonds.

15  I will offer you the sacrifice of thanksgiving *
    and call upon the Name of the LORD.

16  I will fulfill my vows to the LORD *
    in the presence of all his people,

17  In the courts of the LORD's house, *
    in the midst of you, O Jerusalem.
    Hallelujah!

## 117 *Laudate Dominum*

1  Praise the LORD, all you nations; *
    laud him, all you peoples.

2  For his loving-kindness toward us is great, *
    and the faithfulness of the LORD endures for ever.
    Hallelujah!

## 118 *Confitemini Domino*

1  Give thanks to the LORD, for he is good; *
    his mercy endures for ever.

2  Let Israel now proclaim, *
    "His mercy endures for ever."

3   Let the house of Aaron now proclaim, *
        "His mercy endures for ever."

4   Let those who fear the LORD now proclaim, *
        "His mercy endures for ever."

5   I called to the LORD in my distress; *
        the LORD answered by setting me free.

6   The LORD is at my side, therefore I will not fear; *
        what can anyone do to me?

7   The LORD is at my side to help me; *
        I will triumph over those who hate me.

8   It is better to rely on the LORD *
        than to put any trust in flesh.

9   It is better to rely on the LORD *
        than to put any trust in rulers.

10  All the ungodly encompass me; *
        in the name of the LORD I will repel them.

11  They hem me in, they hem me in on every side; *
        in the name of the LORD I will repel them.

12  They swarm about me like bees;
        they blaze like a fire of thorns; *
        in the name of the LORD I will repel them.

13  I was pressed so hard that I almost fell, *
        but the LORD came to my help.


14  The LORD is my strength and my song, *
        and he has become my salvation.

15  There is a sound of exultation and victory *
        in the tents of the righteous:

16   "The right hand of the LORD has triumphed! *
      the right hand of the LORD is exalted!
      the right hand of the LORD has triumphed!"

17   I shall not die, but live, *
      and declare the works of the LORD.

18   The LORD has punished me sorely, *
      but he did not hand me over to death.

19   Open for me the gates of righteousness; *
      I will enter them;
      I will offer thanks to the LORD.

20   "This is the gate of the LORD; *
      he who is righteous may enter."

21   I will give thanks to you, for you answered me *
      and have become my salvation.

22   The same stone which the builders rejected *
      has become the chief cornerstone.

23   This is the LORD's doing, *
      and it is marvelous in our eyes.

24   On this day the LORD has acted; *
      we will rejoice and be glad in it.

25   Hosanna, LORD, hosanna! *
      LORD, send us now success.

26   Blessed is he who comes in the name of the Lord; *
      we bless you from the house of the LORD.

27   God is the LORD; he has shined upon us; *
      form a procession with branches up to the horns of th

28 "You are my God, and I will thank you; *
        you are my God, and I will exalt you."

29 Give thanks to the LORD, for he is good; *
        his mercy endures for ever.


*Twenty-fourth Day: Evening Prayer*

# 119

**Aleph** *Beati immaculati*

1 Happy are they whose way is blameless, *
        who walk in the law of the LORD!

2 Happy are they who observe his decrees *
        and seek him with all their hearts!

3 Who never do any wrong, *
        but always walk in his ways.

4 You laid down your commandments, *
        that we should fully keep them.

5 Oh, that my ways were made so direct *
        that I might keep your statutes!

6 Then I should not be put to shame, *
        when I regard all your commandments.

7 I will thank you with an unfeigned heart, *
        when I have learned your righteous judgments.

8 I will keep your statutes; *
        do not utterly forsake me.

**Beth**  *In quo corrigit?*

9    How shall a young man cleanse his way? *
      By keeping to your words.

10   With my whole heart I seek you; *
      let me not stray from your commandments.

11   I treasure your promise in my heart, *
      that I may not sin against you.

12   Blessed are you, O LORD; *
      instruct me in your statutes.

13   With my lips will I recite *
      all the judgments of your mouth.

14   I have taken greater delight in the way of your decrees *
      than in all manner of riches.

15   I will meditate on your commandments *
      and give attention to your ways.

16   My delight is in your statutes; *
      I will not forget your word.

**Gimel**  *Retribue servo tuo*

17   Deal bountifully with your servant, *
      that I may live and keep your word.

18   Open my eyes, that I may see *
      the wonders of your law.

19   I am a stranger here on earth; *
      do not hide your commandments from me.

20   My soul is consumed at all times *
      with longing for your judgments.

21  You have rebuked the insolent; *
    cursed are they who stray from your commandments!

22  Turn from me shame and rebuke, *
    for I have kept your decrees.

23  Even though rulers sit and plot against me, *
    I will meditate on your statutes.

24  For your decrees are my delight, *
    and they are my counselors.

Daleth  *Adhæsit pavimento*

25  My soul cleaves to the dust; *
    give me life according to your word.

26  I have confessed my ways, and you answered me; *
    instruct me in your statutes.

27  Make me understand the way of your commandments, *
    that I may meditate on your marvelous works.

28  My soul melts away for sorrow; *
    strengthen me according to your word.

29  Take from me the way of lying; *
    let me find grace through your law.

30  I have chosen the way of faithfulness; *
    I have set your judgments before me.

31  I hold fast to your decrees; *
    O LORD, let me not be put to shame.

32  I will run the way of your commandments, *
    for you have set my heart at liberty.

**He**   *Legem pone*

33   Teach me, O LORD, the way of your statutes, *
     and I shall keep it to the end.

34   Give me understanding, and I shall keep your law; *
     I shall keep it with all my heart.

35   Make me go in the path of your commandments, *
     for that is my desire.

36   Incline my heart to your decrees *
     and not to unjust gain.

37   Turn my eyes from watching what is worthless; *
     give me life in your ways.

38   Fulfill your promise to your servant, *
     which you make to those who fear you.

39   Turn away the reproach which I dread, *
     because your judgments are good.

40   Behold, I long for your commandments; *
     in your righteousness preserve my life.

**Waw**   *Et veniat super me*

41   Let your loving-kindness come to me, O LORD, *
     and your salvation, according to your promise.

42   Then shall I have a word for those who taunt me, *
     because I trust in your words.

43   Do not take the word of truth out of my mouth, *
     for my hope is in your judgments.

44    I shall continue to keep your law; *
      I shall keep it for ever and ever.

45    I will walk at liberty, *
      because I study your commandments.

46    I will tell of your decrees before kings *
      and will not be ashamed.

47    I delight in your commandments, *
      which I have always loved.

48    I will lift up my hands to your commandments, *
      and I will meditate on your statutes.

### Zayin   *Memor esto verbi tui*

49    Remember your word to your servant, *
      because you have given me hope.

50    This is my comfort in my trouble, *
      that your promise gives me life.

51    The proud have derided me cruelly, *
      but I have not turned from your law.

52    When I remember your judgments of old, *
      O Lord, I take great comfort.

53    I am filled with a burning rage, *
      because of the wicked who forsake your law.

54    Your statutes have been like songs to me *
      wherever I have lived as a stranger.

55    I remember your Name in the night, O Lord, *
      and dwell upon your law.

56    This is how it has been with me, *
      because I have kept your commandments.

### Heth  *Portio mea, Domine*

57 You only are my portion, O LORD; *
 I have promised to keep your words.

58 I entreat you with all my heart, *
 be merciful to me according to your promise.

59 I have considered my ways *
 and turned my feet toward your decrees.

60 I hasten and do not tarry *
 to keep your commandments.

61 Though the cords of the wicked entangle me, *
 I do not forget your law.

62 At midnight I will rise to give you thanks, *
 because of your righteous judgments.

63 I am a companion of all who fear you *
 and of those who keep your commandments.

64 The earth, O LORD, is full of your love; *
 instruct me in your statutes.

### Teth  *Bonitatem fecisti*

65 O LORD, you have dealt graciously with your servant, *
 according to your word.

66 Teach me discernment and knowledge, *
 for I have believed in your commandments.

67 Before I was afflicted I went astray, *
 but now I keep your word.

68 You are good and you bring forth good; *
 instruct me in your statutes.

The proud have smeared me with lies, *
  but I will keep your commandments with my whole heart.

Their heart is gross and fat, *
  but my delight is in your law.

It is good for me that I have been afflicted, *
  that I might learn your statutes.

The law of your mouth is dearer to me *
  than thousands in gold and silver.

*Twenty-fifth Day: Evening Prayer*

**Yodh**  *Manus tuæ fecerunt me*

Your hands have made me and fashioned me; *
  give me understanding, that I may learn your
                  commandments.

Those who fear you will be glad when they see me, *
  because I trust in your word.

I know, O LORD, that your judgments are right *
  and that in faithfulness you have afflicted me.

Let your loving-kindness be my comfort, *
  as you have promised to your servant.

Let your compassion come to me, that I may live, *
  for your law is my delight.

Let the arrogant be put to shame, for they wrong me
                  with lies; *
  but I will meditate on your commandments.

Let those who fear you turn to me, *
  and also those who know your decrees.

80    Let my heart be sound in your statutes, *
         that I may not be put to shame.


      **Kaph**   *Defecit in salutare*

81    My soul has longed for your salvation; *
         I have put my hope in your word.

82    My eyes have failed from watching for your promise,
         and I say, "When will you comfort me?"

83    I have become like a leather flask in the smoke, *
         but I have not forgotten your statutes.

84    How much longer must I wait? *
         when will you give judgment against those who
                                             persecute me?

85    The proud have dug pits for me; *
         they do not keep your law.

86    All your commandments are true; *
         help me, for they persecute me with lies.

87    They had almost made an end of me on earth, *
         but I have not forsaken your commandments.

88    In your loving-kindness, revive me, *
         that I may keep the decrees of your mouth.


      **Lamedh**   *In æternum, Domine*

89    O LORD, your word is everlasting; *
         it stands firm in the heavens.

90    Your faithfulness remains from one generation to ano
         you established the earth, and it abides.

91  By your decree these continue to this day, *
       for all things are your servants.

92  If my delight had not been in your law, *
       I should have perished in my affliction.

93  I will never forget your commandments, *
       because by them you give me life.

94  I am yours; oh, that you would save me! *
       for I study your commandments.

95  Though the wicked lie in wait for me to destroy me, *
       I will apply my mind to your decrees.

96  I see that all things come to an end, *
       but your commandment has no bounds.


**Mem**  *Quomodo dilexi!*

97  Oh, how I love your law! *
       all the day long it is in my mind.

98  Your commandment has made me wiser than my enemies, *
       and it is always with me.

99  I have more understanding than all my teachers, *
       for your decrees are my study.

00  I am wiser than the elders, *
       because I observe your commandments.

01  I restrain my feet from every evil way, *
       that I may keep your word.

02  I do not shrink from your judgments, *
       because you yourself have taught me.

03  How sweet are your words to my taste! *
       they are sweeter than honey to my mouth.

104 Through your commandments I gain understanding; *
   therefore I hate every lying way.


*Twenty-sixth Day: Morning Prayer*

**Nun** *Lucerna pedibus meis*

105 Your word is a lantern to my feet *
   and a light upon my path.

106 I have sworn and am determined *
   to keep your righteous judgments.

107 I am deeply troubled; *
   preserve my life, O LORD, according to your word.

108 Accept, O LORD, the willing tribute of my lips, *
   and teach me your judgments.

109 My life is always in my hand, *
   yet I do not forget your law.

110 The wicked have set a trap for me, *
   but I have not strayed from your commandments.

111 Your decrees are my inheritance for ever; *
   truly, they are the joy of my heart.

112 I have applied my heart to fulfill your statutes *
   for ever and to the end.


**Samekh** *Iniquos odio habui*

113 I hate those who have a divided heart, *
   but your law do I love.

14    You are my refuge and shield; *
        my hope is in your word.

15    Away from me, you wicked! *
        I will keep the commandments of my God.

16    Sustain me according to your promise, that I may live, *
        and let me not be disappointed in my hope.

17    Hold me up, and I shall be safe, *
        and my delight shall be ever in your statutes.

18    You spurn all who stray from your statutes; *
        their deceitfulness is in vain.

19    In your sight all the wicked of the earth are but dross; *
        therefore I love your decrees.

20    My flesh trembles with dread of you; *
        I am afraid of your judgments.


      **Ayin**  *Feci judicium*

21    I have done what is just and right; *
        do not deliver me to my oppressors.

22    Be surety for your servant's good; *
        let not the proud oppress me.

23    My eyes have failed from watching for your salvation *
        and for your righteous promise.

24    Deal with your servant according to your loving-kindness *
        and teach me your statutes.

25    I am your servant; grant me understanding, *
        that I may know your decrees.

26    It is time for you to act, O LORD, *
        for they have broken your law.

127 Truly, I love your commandments *
    more than gold and precious stones.

128 I hold all your commandments to be right for me; *
    all paths of falsehood I abhor.

**Pe** *Mirabilia*

129 Your decrees are wonderful; *
    therefore I obey them with all my heart.

130 When your word goes forth it gives light; *
    it gives understanding to the simple.

131 I open my mouth and pant; *
    I long for your commandments.

132 Turn to me in mercy, *
    as you always do to those who love your Name.

133 Steady my footsteps in your word; *
    let no iniquity have dominion over me.

134 Rescue me from those who oppress me, *
    and I will keep your commandments.

135 Let your countenance shine upon your servant *
    and teach me your statutes.

136 My eyes shed streams of tears, *
    because people do not keep your law.

**Sadhe** *Justus es, Domine*

137 You are righteous, O LORD, *
    and upright are your judgments.

8   You have issued your decrees *
        with justice and in perfect faithfulness.

9   My indignation has consumed me, *
        because my enemies forget your words.

10  Your word has been tested to the uttermost, *
        and your servant holds it dear.

11  I am small and of little account, *
        yet I do not forget your commandments.

12  Your justice is an everlasting justice *
        and your law is the truth.

13  Trouble and distress have come upon me, *
        yet your commandments are my delight.

14  The righteousness of your decrees is everlasting; *
        grant me understanding, that I may live.


*Twenty-sixth Day: Evening Prayer*

**Qoph** *Clamavi in toto corde meo*

15  I call with my whole heart; *
        answer me, O LORD, that I may keep your statutes.

16  I call to you;
    oh, that you would save me! *
        I will keep your decrees.

17  Early in the morning I cry out to you, *
        for in your word is my trust.

18  My eyes are open in the night watches, *
        that I may meditate upon your promise.

149    Hear my voice, O LORD, according to your loving-kind⟩
       according to your judgments, give me life.

150    They draw near who in malice persecute me; *
       they are very far from your law.

151    You, O LORD, are near at hand, *
       and all your commandments are true.

152    Long have I known from your decrees *
       that you have established them for ever.


**Resh**   *Vide humilitatem*

153    Behold my affliction and deliver me, *
       for I do not forget your law.

154    Plead my cause and redeem me; *
       according to your promise, give me life.

155    Deliverance is far from the wicked, *
       for they do not study your statutes.

156    Great is your compassion, O LORD; *
       preserve my life, according to your judgments.

157    There are many who persecute and oppress me, *
       yet I have not swerved from your decrees.

158    I look with loathing at the faithless, *
       for they have not kept your word.

159    See how I love your commandments! *
       O LORD, in your mercy, preserve me.

160    The heart of your word is truth; *
       all your righteous judgments endure for evermore.

### Shin *Principes persecuti sunt*

161    Rulers have persecuted me without a cause, *
      but my heart stands in awe of your word.

162    I am as glad because of your promise *
      as one who finds great spoils.

163    As for lies, I hate and abhor them, *
      but your law is my love.

164    Seven times a day do I praise you, *
      because of your righteous judgments.

165    Great peace have they who love your law; *
      for them there is no stumbling block.

166    I have hoped for your salvation, O LORD, *
      and I have fulfilled your commandments.

167    I have kept your decrees *
      and I have loved them deeply.

168    I have kept your commandments and decrees, *
      for all my ways are before you.

### Taw *Appropinquet deprecatio*

169    Let my cry come before you, O LORD; *
      give me understanding, according to your word.

170    Let my supplication come before you; *
      deliver me, according to your promise.

171    My lips shall pour forth your praise, *
      when you teach me your statutes.

172    My tongue shall sing of your promise, *
      for all your commandments are righteous.

173   Let your hand be ready to help me, *
      for I have chosen your commandments.

174   I long for your salvation, O LORD, *
      and your law is my delight.

175   Let me live, and I will praise you, *
      and let your judgments help me.

176   I have gone astray like a sheep that is lost; *
      search for your servant,
      for I do not forget your commandments.


*Twenty-seventh Day: Morning Prayer*

## 120   *Ad Dominum*

1   When I was in trouble, I called to the LORD; *
      I called to the LORD, and he answered me.

2   Deliver me, O LORD, from lying lips *
      and from the deceitful tongue.

3   What shall be done to you, and what more besides, *
      O you deceitful tongue?

4   The sharpened arrows of a warrior, *
      along with hot glowing coals.

5   How hateful it is that I must lodge in Meshech *
      and dwell among the tents of Kedar!

6   Too long have I had to live *
      among the enemies of peace.

7   I am on the side of peace, *
      but when I speak of it, they are for war.

## 121 *Levavi oculos*

1  I lift up my eyes to the hills; *
    from where is my help to come?

2  My help comes from the LORD, *
    the maker of heaven and earth.

3  He will not let your foot be moved *
    and he who watches over you will not fall asleep.

4  Behold, he who keeps watch over Israel *
    shall neither slumber nor sleep;

5  The LORD himself watches over you; *
    the LORD is your shade at your right hand,

6  So that the sun shall not strike you by day, *
    nor the moon by night.

7  The LORD shall preserve you from all evil; *
    it is he who shall keep you safe.

8  The LORD shall watch over your going out and
                     your coming in, *
    from this time forth for evermore.

## 122 *Lætatus sum*

1  I was glad when they said to me, *
    "Let us go to the house of the LORD."

2  Now our feet are standing *
    within your gates, O Jerusalem.

3  Jerusalem is built as a city *
    that is at unity with itself;

4   To which the tribes go up,
        the tribes of the LORD, *
            the assembly of Israel,
                to praise the Name of the LORD.

5   For there are the thrones of judgment, *
        the thrones of the house of David.

6   Pray for the peace of Jerusalem: *
        "May they prosper who love you.

7   Peace be within your walls *
        and quietness within your towers.

8   For my brethren and companions' sake, *
        I pray for your prosperity.

9   Because of the house of the LORD our God, *
        I will seek to do you good."


## 123   *Ad te levavi oculos meos*

1   To you I lift up my eyes, *
        to you enthroned in the heavens.

2   As the eyes of servants look to the hand of their masters,
        and the eyes of a maid to the hand of her mistress,

3   So our eyes look to the LORD our God, *
        until he show us his mercy.

4   Have mercy upon us, O LORD, have mercy, *
        for we have had more than enough of contempt,

5   Too much of the scorn of the indolent rich, *
        and of the derision of the proud.

# 124 *Nisi quia Dominus*

If the LORD had not been on our side, *
 let Israel now say;

If the LORD had not been on our side, *
 when enemies rose up against us;

Then would they have swallowed us up alive *
 in their fierce anger toward us;

Then would the waters have overwhelmed us *
 and the torrent gone over us;

Then would the raging waters *
 have gone right over us.

Blessed be the LORD! *
 he has not given us over to be a prey for their teeth.

We have escaped like a bird from the snare of the fowler; *
 the snare is broken, and we have escaped.

Our help is in the Name of the LORD, *
 the maker of heaven and earth.


# 125 *Qui confidunt*

Those who trust in the LORD are like Mount Zion, *
 which cannot be moved, but stands fast for ever.

The hills stand about Jerusalem; *
 so does the LORD stand round about his people,
 from this time forth for evermore.

The scepter of the wicked shall not hold sway over the
   land allotted to the just, *
 so that the just shall not put their hands to evil.

4   Show your goodness, O LORD, to those who are good *
       and to those who are true of heart.

5   As for those who turn aside to crooked ways,
       the LORD will lead them away with the evildoers; *
       but peace be upon Israel.

*Twenty-seventh Day: Evening Prayer*

## 126  *In convertendo*

1   When the LORD restored the fortunes of Zion, *
       then were we like those who dream.

2   Then was our mouth filled with laughter, *
       and our tongue with shouts of joy.

3   Then they said among the nations, *
       "The LORD has done great things for them."

4   The LORD has done great things for us, *
       and we are glad indeed.

5   Restore our fortunes, O LORD, *
       like the watercourses of the Negev.

6   Those who sowed with tears *
       will reap with songs of joy.

7   Those who go out weeping, carrying the seed, *
       will come again with joy, shouldering their sheaves.

## 127  *Nisi Dominus*

1   Unless the LORD builds the house, *
       their labor is in vain who build it.

2   Unless the LORD watches over the city, *
     in vain the watchman keeps his vigil.

3   It is in vain that you rise so early and go to bed so late; *
     vain, too, to eat the bread of toil,
     for he gives to his beloved sleep.

4   Children are a heritage from the LORD, *
     and the fruit of the womb is a gift.

5   Like arrows in the hand of a warrior *
     are the children of one's youth.

6   Happy is the man who has his quiver full of them! *
     he shall not be put to shame
     when he contends with his enemies in the gate.

# 128 *Beati omnes*

1   Happy are they all who fear the LORD, *
     and who follow in his ways!

2   You shall eat the fruit of your labor; *
     happiness and prosperity shall be yours.

3   Your wife shall be like a fruitful vine within your house, *
     your children like olive shoots round about your table.

4   The man who fears the LORD *
     shall thus indeed be blessed.

5   The LORD bless you from Zion, *
     and may you see the prosperity of Jerusalem all the days
        of your life.

6   May you live to see your children's children; *
     may peace be upon Israel.

## 129 *Sæpe expugnaverunt*

1  "Greatly have they oppressed me since my youth," *
   let Israel now say;

2  "Greatly have they oppressed me since my youth, *
   but they have not prevailed against me."

3  The plowmen plowed upon my back *
   and made their furrows long.

4  The LORD, the Righteous One, *
   has cut the cords of the wicked.

5  Let them be put to shame and thrown back, *
   all those who are enemies of Zion.

6  Let them be like grass upon the housetops, *
   which withers before it can be plucked;

7  Which does not fill the hand of the reaper, *
   nor the bosom of him who binds the sheaves;

8  So that those who go by say not so much as,
   "The LORD prosper you. *
   We wish you well in the Name of the LORD."


## 130 *De profundis*

1  Out of the depths have I called to you, O LORD;
   LORD, hear my voice; *
   let your ears consider well the voice of my supplication

2  If you, LORD, were to note what is done amiss, *
   O Lord, who could stand?

3  For there is forgiveness with you; *
   therefore you shall be feared.

I wait for the LORD; my soul waits for him; *
  in his word is my hope.

My soul waits for the LORD,
more than watchmen for the morning, *
  more than watchmen for the morning.

O Israel, wait for the LORD, *
  for with the LORD there is mercy;

With him there is plenteous redemption, *
  and he shall redeem Israel from all their sins.


## 131   *Domine, non est*

O LORD, I am not proud; *
  I have no haughty looks.

I do not occupy myself with great matters, *
  or with things that are too hard for me.

But I still my soul and make it quiet,
like a child upon its mother's breast; *
  my soul is quieted within me.

O Israel, wait upon the LORD, *
  from this time forth for evermore.


*Twenty-eighth Day: Morning Prayer*

## 132   *Memento, Domine*

LORD, remember David, *
  and all the hardships he endured;

2  How he swore an oath to the LORD *
   and vowed a vow to the Mighty One of Jacob:

3  "I will not come under the roof of my house, *
   nor climb up into my bed;

4  I will not allow my eyes to sleep, *
   nor let my eyelids slumber;

5  Until I find a place for the LORD, *
   a dwelling for the Mighty One of Jacob."

6  "The ark! We heard it was in Ephratah; *
   we found it in the fields of Jearim.

7  Let us go to God's dwelling place; *
   let us fall upon our knees before his footstool."

8  Arise, O LORD, into your resting-place, *
   you and the ark of your strength.

9  Let your priests be clothed with righteousness; *
   let your faithful people sing with joy.

10 For your servant David's sake, *
   do not turn away the face of your Anointed.

11 The LORD has sworn an oath to David; *
   in truth, he will not break it:

12 "A son, the fruit of your body *
   will I set upon your throne.

13 If your children keep my covenant
   and my testimonies that I shall teach them, *
   their children will sit upon your throne for evermore."

14 For the LORD has chosen Zion; *
   he has desired her for his habitation:

15 "This shall be my resting-place for ever; *
   here will I dwell, for I delight in her.

16  I will surely bless her provisions, *
    and satisfy her poor with bread.

17  I will clothe her priests with salvation, *
    and her faithful people will rejoice and sing.

18  There will I make the horn of David flourish; *
    I have prepared a lamp for my Anointed.

19  As for his enemies, I will clothe them with shame; *
    but as for him, his crown will shine."


## 133  *Ecce, quam bonum!*

1  Oh, how good and pleasant it is, *
   when brethren live together in unity!

2  It is like fine oil upon the head *
   that runs down upon the beard,

3  Upon the beard of Aaron, *
   and runs down upon the collar of his robe.

4  It is like the dew of Hermon *
   that falls upon the hills of Zion.

5  For there the LORD has ordained the blessing: *
   life for evermore.


## 134  *Ecce nunc*

1  Behold now, bless the LORD, all you servants of the LORD, *
   you that stand by night in the house of the LORD.

2  Lift up your hands in the holy place and bless the LORD; *
   the LORD who made heaven and earth bless
                   you out of Zion.

1   Hallelujah!
Praise the Name of the LORD; *
   give praise, you servants of the LORD,

2   You who stand in the house of the LORD, *
   in the courts of the house of our God.

3   Praise the LORD, for the LORD is good; *
   sing praises to his Name, for it is lovely.

4   For the LORD has chosen Jacob for himself *
   and Israel for his own possession.

5   For I know that the LORD is great, *
   and that our Lord is above all gods.

6   The LORD does whatever pleases him, in heaven and on e
   in the seas and all the deeps.

7   He brings up rain clouds from the ends of the earth; *
   he sends out lightning with the rain,
   and brings the winds out of his storehouse.

8   It was he who struck down the firstborn of Egypt, *
   the firstborn both of man and beast.

9   He sent signs and wonders into the midst of you, O Egyp
   against Pharaoh and all his servants.

10   He overthrew many nations *
   and put mighty kings to death:

11   Sihon, king of the Amorites,
   and Og, the king of Bashan, *
   and all the kingdoms of Canaan.

12   He gave their land to be an inheritance, *
   an inheritance for Israel his people.

13     O LORD, your Name is everlasting; *
       your renown, O LORD, endures from age to age.

14     For the LORD gives his people justice *
       and shows compassion to his servants.

15     The idols of the heathen are silver and gold, *
       the work of human hands.

16     They have mouths, but they cannot speak; *
       eyes have they, but they cannot see.

17     They have ears, but they cannot hear; *
       neither is there any breath in their mouth.

18     Those who make them are like them, *
       and so are all who put their trust in them.

19     Bless the LORD, O house of Israel; *
       O house of Aaron, bless the LORD.

20     Bless the LORD, O house of Levi; *
       you who fear the LORD, bless the LORD.

21     Blessed be the LORD out of Zion, *
       who dwells in Jerusalem.
       Hallelujah!

*Twenty-eighth Day: Evening Prayer*

# 136   *Confitemini*

1     Give thanks to the LORD, for he is good, *
       for his mercy endures for ever.

2     Give thanks to the God of gods, *
       for his mercy endures for ever.

3   Give thanks to the Lord of lords, *
        for his mercy endures for ever.


4   Who only does great wonders, *
        for his mercy endures for ever;

5   Who by wisdom made the heavens, *
        for his mercy endures for ever;

6   Who spread out the earth upon the waters, *
        for his mercy endures for ever;

7   Who created great lights, *
        for his mercy endures for ever;

8   The sun to rule the day, *
        for his mercy endures for ever;

9   The moon and the stars to govern the night, *
        for his mercy endures for ever.


10  Who struck down the firstborn of Egypt, *
        for his mercy endures for ever;

11  And brought out Israel from among them, *
        for his mercy endures for ever;

12  With a mighty hand and a stretched-out arm, *
        for his mercy endures for ever;

13  Who divided the Red Sea in two, *
        for his mercy endures for ever;

14  And made Israel to pass through the midst of it, *
        for his mercy endures for ever;

15  But swept Pharaoh and his army into the Red Sea, *
        for his mercy endures for ever;

16    Who led his people through the wilderness, *
       for his mercy endures for ever.

17    Who struck down great kings, *
       for his mercy endures for ever;

18    And slew mighty kings, *
       for his mercy endures for ever;

19    Sihon, king of the Amorites, *
       for his mercy endures for ever;

20    And Og, the king of Bashan, *
       for his mercy endures for ever;

21    And gave away their lands for an inheritance, *
       for his mercy endures for ever;

22    An inheritance for Israel his servant, *
       for his mercy endures for ever.

23    Who remembered us in our low estate, *
       for his mercy endures for ever;

24    And delivered us from our enemies, *
       for his mercy endures for ever;

25    Who gives food to all creatures, *
       for his mercy endures for ever.

26    Give thanks to the God of heaven, *
       for his mercy endures for ever.

# 137 *Super flumina*

1   By the waters of Babylon we sat down and wept, *
        when we remembered you, O Zion.

2   As for our harps, we hung them up *
        on the trees in the midst of that land.

3   For those who led us away captive asked us for a song,
    and our oppressors called for mirth: *
        "Sing us one of the songs of Zion."

4   How shall we sing the LORD's song *
        upon an alien soil?

5   If I forget you, O Jerusalem, *
        let my right hand forget its skill.

6   Let my tongue cleave to the roof of my mouth
    if I do not remember you, *
        if I do not set Jerusalem above my highest joy.

7   Remember the day of Jerusalem, O LORD,
    against the people of Edom, *
        who said,"Down with it! down with it!
        even to the ground!"

8   O Daughter of Babylon, doomed to destruction, *
        happy the one who pays you back
        for what you have done to us!

9   Happy shall he be who takes your little ones, *
        and dashes them against the rock!

# 138 *Confitebor tibi*

I will give thanks to you, O LORD, with my whole heart; *
    before the gods I will sing your praise.

I will bow down toward your holy temple
and praise your Name, *
    because of your love and faithfulness;

For you have glorified your Name *
    and your word above all things.

When I called, you answered me; *
    you increased my strength within me.

All the kings of the earth will praise you, O LORD, *
    when they have heard the words of your mouth.

They will sing of the ways of the LORD, *
    that great is the glory of the LORD.

Though the LORD be high, he cares for the lowly; *
    he perceives the haughty from afar.

Though I walk in the midst of trouble, you keep me safe; *
    you stretch forth your hand against the fury of my enemies;
    your right hand shall save me.

The LORD will make good his purpose for me; *
    O LORD, your love endures for ever;
    do not abandon the works of your hands.

## 139   *Domine, probasti*

1  LORD, you have searched me out and known me; *
     you know my sitting down and my rising up;
     you discern my thoughts from afar.

2  You trace my journeys and my resting-places *
     and are acquainted with all my ways.

3  Indeed, there is not a word on my lips, *
     but you, O LORD, know it altogether.

4  You press upon me behind and before *
     and lay your hand upon me.

5  Such knowledge is too wonderful for me; *
     it is so high that I cannot attain to it.

6  Where can I go then from your Spirit? *
     where can I flee from your presence?

7  If I climb up to heaven, you are there; *
     if I make the grave my bed, you are there also.

8  If I take the wings of the morning *
     and dwell in the uttermost parts of the sea,

9  Even there your hand will lead me *
     and your right hand hold me fast.

10  If I say, "Surely the darkness will cover me, *
     and the light around me turn to night,"

11  Darkness is not dark to you;
     the night is as bright as the day; *
     darkness and light to you are both alike.

12  For you yourself created my inmost parts; *
     you knit me together in my mother's womb.

13  I will thank you because I am marvelously made; *
        your works are wonderful, and I know it well.

14  My body was not hidden from you, *
        while I was being made in secret
        and woven in the depths of the earth.

15  Your eyes beheld my limbs, yet unfinished in the womb;
        all of them were written in your book; *
        they were fashioned day by day,
        when as yet there was none of them.

16  How deep I find your thoughts, O God! *
        how great is the sum of them!

17  If I were to count them, they would be more in number
                                than the sand; *
        to count them all, my life span would need to
                                be like yours.

18  Oh, that you would slay the wicked, O God! *
        You that thirst for blood, depart from me.

19  They speak despitefully against you; *
        your enemies take your Name in vain.

20  Do I not hate those, O LORD, who hate you? *
        and do I not loathe those who rise up against you?

21  I hate them with a perfect hatred; *
        they have become my own enemies.

22  Search me out, O God, and know my heart; *
        try me and know my restless thoughts.

23  Look well whether there be any wickedness in me *
        and lead me in the way that is everlasting.

# 140 *Eripe me, Domine*

1 Deliver me, O LORD, from evildoers; *
  protect me from the violent,

2 Who devise evil in their hearts *
  and stir up strife all day long.

3 They have sharpened their tongues like a serpent; *
  adder's poison is under their lips.

4 Keep me, O LORD, from the hands of the wicked; *
  protect me from the violent,
  who are determined to trip me up.

5 The proud have hidden a snare for me
  and stretched out a net of cords; *
  they have set traps for me along the path.

6 I have said to the LORD, "You are my God; *
  listen, O LORD, to my supplication.

7 O Lord GOD, the strength of my salvation, *
  you have covered my head in the day of battle.

8 Do not grant the desires of the wicked, O LORD, *
  nor let their evil plans prosper.

9 Let not those who surround me lift up their heads; *
  let the evil of their lips overwhelm them.

10 Let hot burning coals fall upon them; *
  let them be cast into the mire, never to rise up again."

11 A slanderer shall not be established on the earth, *
  and evil shall hunt down the lawless.

12 I know that the LORD will maintain the cause of the poor
  and render justice to the needy.

13  Surely, the righteous will give thanks to your Name, *
       and the upright shall continue in your sight.

## 141  *Domine, clamavi*

1  O LORD, I call to you; come to me quickly; *
      hear my voice when I cry to you.

2  Let my prayer be set forth in your sight as incense, *
      the lifting up of my hands as the evening sacrifice.

3  Set a watch before my mouth, O LORD,
      and guard the door of my lips; *
      let not my heart incline to any evil thing.

4  Let me not be occupied in wickedness with evildoers, *
      nor eat of their choice foods.

5  Let the righteous smite me in friendly rebuke;
      let not the oil of the unrighteous anoint my head; *
      for my prayer is continually against their wicked deeds.

6  Let their rulers be overthrown in stony places, *
      that they may know my words are true.

7  As when a plowman turns over the earth in furrows, *
      let their bones be scattered at the mouth of the grave.

8  But my eyes are turned to you, Lord GOD; *
      in you I take refuge;
      do not strip me of my life.

9  Protect me from the snare which they have laid for me *
      and from the traps of the evildoers.

10 Let the wicked fall into their own nets, *
      while I myself escape.

## 142 *Voce mea ad Dominum*

1 I cry to the LORD with my voice; *
   to the LORD I make loud supplication.

2 I pour out my complaint before him *
   and tell him all my trouble.

3 When my spirit languishes within me, you know my path;
   in the way wherein I walk they have hidden a trap for m

4 I look to my right hand and find no one who knows me; *
   I have no place to flee to, and no one cares for me.

5 I cry out to you, O LORD; *
   I say,"You are my refuge,
       my portion in the land of the living."

6 Listen to my cry for help, for I have been brought very lov
   save me from those who pursue me,
       for they are too strong for me.

7 Bring me out of prison, that I may give thanks to your Na
   when you have dealt bountifully with me,
       the righteous will gather around me.

## 143 *Domine, exaudi*

1 LORD, hear my prayer,
   and in your faithfulness heed my supplications; *
       answer me in your righteousness.

2 Enter not into judgment with your servant, *
   for in your sight shall no one living be justified.

3   For my enemy has sought my life;
    he has crushed me to the ground; *
        he has made me live in dark places like those who
                                    are long dead.

4   My spirit faints within me; *
        my heart within me is desolate.

5   I remember the time past;
    I muse upon all your deeds; *
        I consider the works of your hands.

6   I spread out my hands to you; *
        my soul gasps to you like a thirsty land.

7   O LORD, make haste to answer me; my spirit fails me; *
        do not hide your face from me
        or I shall be like those who go down to the Pit.

8   Let me hear of your loving-kindness in the morning,
    for I put my trust in you; *
        show me the road that I must walk,
        for I lift up my soul to you.

9   Deliver me from my enemies, O LORD, *
        for I flee to you for refuge.

10  Teach me to do what pleases you, for you are my God; *
        let your good Spirit lead me on level ground.

11  Revive me, O LORD, for your Name's sake; *
        for your righteousness' sake, bring me out of trouble.


12  Of your goodness, destroy my enemies
    and bring all my foes to naught, *
        for truly I am your servant.

# 144 *Benedictus Dominus*

1 Blessed be the LORD my rock! *
   who trains my hands to fight and my fingers to battle;

2 My help and my fortress, my stronghold and my deliverer,
   my shield in whom I trust,
   who subdues the peoples under me.

3 O LORD, what are we that you should care for us? *
   mere mortals that you should think of us?

4 We are like a puff of wind; *
   our days are like a passing shadow.

5 Bow your heavens, O LORD, and come down; *
   touch the mountains, and they shall smoke.

6 Hurl the lightning and scatter them; *
   shoot out your arrows and rout them.

7 Stretch out your hand from on high; *
   rescue me and deliver me from the great waters,
   from the hand of foreign peoples,

8 Whose mouths speak deceitfully *
   and whose right hand is raised in falsehood.

9 O God, I will sing to you a new song; *
   I will play to you on a ten-stringed lyre.

10 You give victory to kings *
   and have rescued David your servant.

11 Rescue me from the hurtful sword *
   and deliver me from the hand of foreign peoples,

12 Whose mouths speak deceitfully *
   and whose right hand is raised in falsehood.

13    May our sons be like plants well nurtured from their youth, *
      and our daughters like sculptured corners of a palace.

14    May our barns be filled to overflowing with all manner
                                              of crops; *
      may the flocks in our pastures increase by thousands
                                    and tens of thousands;
      may our cattle be fat and sleek.

15    May there be no breaching of the walls, no going into exile, *
      no wailing in the public squares.

16    Happy are the people of whom this is so! *
      happy are the people whose God is the LORD!


## 145    *Exaltabo te, Deus*

1     I will exalt you, O God my King, *
      and bless your Name for ever and ever.

2     Every day will I bless you *
      and praise your Name for ever and ever.

3     Great is the LORD and greatly to be praised; *
      there is no end to his greatness.

4     One generation shall praise your works to another *
      and shall declare your power.

5     I will ponder the glorious splendor of your majesty *
      and all your marvelous works.

6     They shall speak of the might of your wondrous acts, *
      and I will tell of your greatness.

7     They shall publish the remembrance of your great goodness; *
      they shall sing of your righteous deeds.

8 The LORD is gracious and full of compassion, *
    slow to anger and of great kindness.

9 The LORD is loving to everyone *
    and his compassion is over all his works.

10 All your works praise you, O LORD, *
    and your faithful servants bless you.

11 They make known the glory of your kingdom *
    and speak of your power;

12 That the peoples may know of your power *
    and the glorious splendor of your kingdom.

13 Your kingdom is an everlasting kingdom; *
    your dominion endures throughout all ages.

14 The LORD is faithful in all his words *
    and merciful in all his deeds.

15 The LORD upholds all those who fall; *
    he lifts up those who are bowed down.

16 The eyes of all wait upon you, O LORD, *
    and you give them their food in due season.

17 You open wide your hand *
    and satisfy the needs of every living creature.

18 The LORD is righteous in all his ways *
    and loving in all his works.

19 The LORD is near to those who call upon him, *
    to all who call upon him faithfully.

20 He fulfills the desire of those who fear him; *
    he hears their cry and helps them.

21 The LORD preserves all those who love him, *
    but he destroys all the wicked.

22   My mouth shall speak the praise of the LORD; *
    let all flesh bless his holy Name for ever and ever.


## 146   *Lauda, anima mea*

1   Hallelujah!
Praise the LORD, O my soul! *
    I will praise the LORD as long as I live;
    I will sing praises to my God while I have my being.

2   Put not your trust in rulers, nor in any child of earth, *
    for there is no help in them.

3   When they breathe their last, they return to earth, *
    and in that day their thoughts perish.

4   Happy are they who have the God of Jacob for their help! *
    whose hope is in the LORD their God;

5   Who made heaven and earth, the seas, and all that is in them; *
    who keeps his promise for ever;

6   Who gives justice to those who are oppressed, *
    and food to those who hunger.

7   The LORD sets the prisoners free;
the LORD opens the eyes of the blind; *
    the LORD lifts up those who are bowed down;

8   The LORD loves the righteous;
the LORD cares for the stranger; *
    he sustains the orphan and widow,
    but frustrates the way of the wicked.

9   The LORD shall reign for ever, *
    your God, O Zion, throughout all generations.
    Hallelujah!

# 147 *Laudate Dominum*

1 Hallelujah!
  How good it is to sing praises to our God! *
     how pleasant it is to honor him with praise!

2 The LORD rebuilds Jerusalem; *
     he gathers the exiles of Israel.

3 He heals the brokenhearted *
     and binds up their wounds.

4 He counts the number of the stars *
     and calls them all by their names.

5 Great is our LORD and mighty in power; *
     there is no limit to his wisdom.

6 The LORD lifts up the lowly, *
     but casts the wicked to the ground.

7 Sing to the LORD with thanksgiving; *
     make music to our God upon the harp.

8 He covers the heavens with clouds *
     and prepares rain for the earth;

9 He makes grass to grow upon the mountains *
     and green plants to serve mankind.

10 He provides food for flocks and herds *
     and for the young ravens when they cry.

11 He is not impressed by the might of a horse; *
     he has no pleasure in the strength of a man;

12 But the LORD has pleasure in those who fear him, *
     in those who await his gracious favor.

13  Worship the LORD, O Jerusalem; *
        praise your God, O Zion;

14  For he has strengthened the bars of your gates; *
        he has blessed your children within you.

15  He has established peace on your borders; *
        he satisfies you with the finest wheat.

16  He sends out his command to the earth, *
        and his word runs very swiftly.

17  He gives snow like wool; *
        he scatters hoarfrost like ashes.

18  He scatters his hail like bread crumbs; *
        who can stand against his cold?

19  He sends forth his word and melts them; *
        he blows with his wind, and the waters flow.

20  He declares his word to Jacob, *
        his statutes and his judgments to Israel.

21  He has not done so to any other nation; *
        to them he has not revealed his judgments.
        Hallelujah!

# 148  *Laudate Dominum*

1   Hallelujah!
    Praise the LORD from the heavens; *
        praise him in the heights.

2   Praise him, all you angels of his; *
        praise him, all his host.

3   Praise him, sun and moon; *
        praise him, all you shining stars.

4   Praise him, heaven of heavens, *
     and you waters above the heavens.

5   Let them praise the Name of the LORD; *
     for he commanded, and they were created.

6   He made them stand fast for ever and ever; *
     he gave them a law which shall not pass away.


7   Praise the LORD from the earth, *
     you sea-monsters and all deeps;

8   Fire and hail, snow and fog, *
     tempestuous wind, doing his will;

9   Mountains and all hills, *
     fruit trees and all cedars;

10   Wild beasts and all cattle, *
     creeping things and wingèd birds;

11   Kings of the earth and all peoples, *
     princes and all rulers of the world;

12   Young men and maidens, *
     old and young together.

13   Let them praise the Name of the LORD, *
     for his Name only is exalted,
     his splendor is over earth and heaven.

14   He has raised up strength for his people
     and praise for all his loyal servants, *
     the children of Israel, a people who are near him.
     Hallelujah!

# 149 *Cantate Domino*

1   Hallelujah!
    Sing to the LORD a new song; *
      sing his praise in the congregation of the faithful.

2   Let Israel rejoice in his Maker; *
      let the children of Zion be joyful in their King.

3   Let them praise his Name in the dance; *
      let them sing praise to him with timbrel and harp.

4   For the LORD takes pleasure in his people *
      and adorns the poor with victory.

5   Let the faithful rejoice in triumph; *
      let them be joyful on their beds.

6   Let the praises of God be in their throat *
      and a two-edged sword in their hand;

7   To wreak vengeance on the nations *
      and punishment on the peoples;

8   To bind their kings in chains *
      and their nobles with links of iron;

9   To inflict on them the judgment decreed; *
      this is glory for all his faithful people.
      Hallelujah!

# 150 *Laudate Dominum*

1   Hallelujah!
    Praise God in his holy temple; *
      praise him in the firmament of his power.

2   Praise him for his mighty acts; *
      praise him for his excellent greatness.

3   Praise him with the blast of the ram's-horn; *
      praise him with lyre and harp.

4   Praise him with timbrel and dance; *
      praise him with strings and pipe.

5   Praise him with resounding cymbals; *
      praise him with loud-clanging cymbals.

6   Let everything that has breath *
      praise the LORD.
      Hallelujah!

# Prayers and
# Thanksgivings

# Prayers and Thanksgivings

## Prayers

### Prayers for the World

### Prayers for the Church

*Prayers for the Ordained Ministry are on pages 205 and 256.*

### Prayers for National Life

## Other Prayers

## Thanksgivings

### General Thanksgivings

*The General Thanksgiving is on pages 58 and 101.*

## Thanksgivings for the Church

3. For the Mission of the Church
4. For the Saints and Faithful Departed

## Thanksgivings for National Life

5. For the Nation
6. For Heroic Service

## Thanksgiving for the Social Order

7. For the Diversity of Races and Cultures

## Thanksgivings for the Natural Order

8. For the Beauty of the Earth
9. For the Harvest

## Thanksgivings for Family and Personal Life

10. For the Gift of a Child
11. For the Restoration of Health

*Thanksgivings for the departed are on pages 487-489 and 503-504.*

*The term "Various Occasions" in the following pages refers to the numbered Collects beginning on pages 199 and 251.*

# Prayers and Thanksgivings

## Prayers

*For use after the Collects of Morning or Evening Prayer or separately.*

*Prayers originally composed in traditional idiom have not been modernized; but, except in certain classical prayers which do not lend themselves to modernization, pronouns and verbs have been put in italics to assist in rendering them into contemporary speech.*

### Prayers for the World

#### 1. For Joy in God's Creation

O heavenly Father, *who hast* filled the world with beauty: Open our eyes to behold *thy* gracious hand in all *thy* works; that, rejoicing in *thy* whole creation, we may learn to serve *thee* with gladness; for the sake of him through whom all things were made, *thy* Son Jesus Christ our Lord. *Amen.*

#### 2. For All Sorts and Conditions of Men

O God, the creator and preserver of all mankind, we humbly beseech thee for all sorts and conditions of men; that thou wouldest be pleased to make thy ways known unto them, thy saving health unto all nations. More especially we pray for thy holy Church universal; that it may be so guided and governed by thy good Spirit, that all who profess and call themselves Christians may be led into the way of truth, and hold the faith in unity of spirit, in the bond of peace, and in righteousness of life. Finally, we commend to thy fatherly goodness all those who are in any ways afflicted or distressed, in mind, body, or estate; [especially those for whom our prayers are desired]; that it may please thee to comfort and relieve them according to their several necessities, giving them patience under their sufferings, and a happy issue out of all their afflictions. And this we beg for Jesus Christ's sake. *Amen.*

## 3. For the Human Family

O God, you made us in your own image and redeemed us through Jesus your Son: Look with compassion on the whole human family; take away the arrogance and hatred which infect our hearts; break down the walls that separate us; unite us in bonds of love; and work through our struggle and confusion to accomplish your purposes on earth; that, in your good time, all nations and races may serve you in harmony around your heavenly throne; through Jesus Christ our Lord. *Amen.*

## 4. For Peace

*See also Various Occasions no. 18.*

Eternal God, in whose perfect kingdom no sword is drawn but the sword of righteousness, no strength known but the strength of love: So mightily spread abroad your Spirit, that all peoples may be gathered under the banner of the Prince of Peace, as children of one Father; to whom be dominion and glory, now and for ever. *Amen.*

### 5. For Peace Among the Nations

Almighty God our heavenly Father, guide the nations of the world into the way of justice and truth, and establish among them that peace which is the fruit of righteousness, that they may become the kingdom of our Lord and Savior Jesus Christ. *Amen.*

### 6. For our Enemies

O God, the Father of all, whose Son commanded us to love our enemies: Lead them and us from prejudice to truth; deliver them and us from hatred, cruelty, and revenge; and in your good time enable us all to stand reconciled before you; through Jesus Christ our Lord. *Amen.*

## Prayers for the Church

### 7. For the Church

Gracious Father, we pray for thy holy Catholic Church. Fill it with all truth, in all truth with all peace. Where it is corrupt, purify it; where it is in error, direct it; where in any thing it is amiss, reform it. Where it is right, strengthen it; where it is in want, provide for it; where it is divided, reunite it; for the sake of Jesus Christ thy Son our Savior. *Amen.*

### 8. For the Mission of the Church

*See also the prayers for the Mission of the Church on pages 58, 100 and 101, and Various Occasions no. 16.*

Everliving God, whose will it is that all should come to you through your Son Jesus Christ: Inspire our witness to him, that all may know the power of his forgiveness and the hope of his resurrection; who lives and reigns with you and the Holy Spirit, one God, now and for ever. *Amen.*

9. *For Clergy and People*

Almighty and everlasting God, from whom cometh every good and perfect gift: Send down upon our bishops, and other clergy, and upon the congregations committed to their charge, the healthful Spirit of thy grace; and, that they may truly please thee, pour upon them the continual dew of thy blessing. Grant this, O Lord, for the honor of our Advocate and Mediator, Jesus Christ. *Amen.*

10. *For the Diocese*

O God, by your grace you have called us in this Diocese to a goodly fellowship of faith. Bless our Bishop(s) N. [and N.], and other clergy, and all our people. Grant that your Word may be truly preached and truly heard, your Sacraments faithfully administered and faithfully received. By your Spirit, fashion our lives according to the example of your Son, and grant that we may show the power of your love to all among whom we live; through Jesus Christ our Lord. *Amen.*

11. *For the Parish*

Almighty and everliving God, ruler of all things in heaven and earth, hear our prayers for this parish family. Strengthen the faithful, arouse the careless, and restore the penitent. Grant us all things necessary for our common life, and bring us all to be of one heart and mind within your holy Church; through Jesus Christ our Lord. *Amen.*

## 12. For a Church Convention or Meeting

*See also Various Occasions no. 13.*

Almighty and everliving God, source of all wisdom and understanding, be present with those who take counsel [in _____] for the renewal and mission of your Church. Teach us in all things to seek first your honor and glory. Guide us to perceive what is right, and grant us both the courage to pursue it and the grace to accomplish it; through Jesus Christ our Lord. *Amen.*

## 13. For the Election of a Bishop or other Minister

Almighty God, giver of every good gift: Look graciously on your Church, and so guide the minds of those who shall choose a bishop for this Diocese (*or*, rector for this parish), that we may receive a faithful pastor, who will care for your people and equip us for our ministries; through Jesus Christ our Lord. *Amen.*

## 14. For the Unity of the Church

*See also Various Occasions no. 14, and Collect no. 6 (page 395).*

O God the Father of our Lord Jesus Christ, our only Savior, the Prince of Peace: Give us grace seriously to lay to heart the great dangers we are in by our unhappy divisions; take away all hatred and prejudice, and whatever else may hinder us from godly union and concord; that, as there is but one Body and one Spirit, one hope of our calling, one Lord, one Faith, one Baptism, one God and Father of us all, so we may be all of one heart and of one soul, united in one holy bond of truth and peace, of faith and charity, and may with one mind and one mouth glorify *thee*; through Jesus Christ our Lord. *Amen.*

5. *For those about to be Baptized or to renew their Baptismal Covenant*

O God, you prepared your disciples for the coming of the Spirit through the teaching of your Son Jesus Christ: Make the hearts and minds of your servants ready to receive the blessing of the Holy Spirit, that they may be filled with the strength of his presence; through Jesus Christ our Lord. Amen.

*For those to be ordained, see Various Occasions no. 15.*

6. *For Monastic Orders and Vocations*

O Lord Jesus Christ, you became poor for our sake, that we might be made rich through your poverty: Guide and sanctify, we pray, those whom you call to follow you under the vows of poverty, chastity, and obedience, that by their prayer and service they may enrich your Church, and by their life and worship may glorify your Name; for you reign with the Father and the Holy Spirit, one God, now and for ever. Amen.

7. *For Church Musicians and Artists*

O God, whom saints and angels delight to worship in heaven: Be ever present with your servants who seek through art and music to perfect the praises offered by your people on earth; and grant to them even now glimpses of your beauty, and make them worthy at length to behold it unveiled for evermore; through Jesus Christ our Lord. Amen.

## Prayers for National Life

### 18. For our Country

*See also Various Occasions no. 17.*

Almighty God, who hast given us this good land for our heritage: We humbly beseech thee that we may always prove ourselves a people mindful of thy favor and glad to do thy will Bless our land with honorable industry, sound learning, and pure manners. Save us from violence, discord, and confusion; from pride and arrogance, and from every evil way. Defend our liberties, and fashion into one united people the multitude brought hither out of many kindreds and tongues. Endue with the spirit of wisdom those to whom in thy Name we entru the authority of government, that there may be justice and peace at home, and that, through obedience to thy law, we may show forth thy praise among the nations of the earth. In the time of prosperity, fill our hearts with thankfulness, and in the day of trouble, suffer not our trust in thee to fail; all which we ask through Jesus Christ our Lord. *Amen.*

### 19. For the President of the United States and all in Civil Authority

O Lord our Governor, whose glory is in all the world: We commend this nation to *thy* merciful care, that, being guided by *thy* Providence, we may dwell secure in *thy* peace. Grant to the President of the United States, the Governor of this State (*or* Commonwealth), and to all in authority, wisdom and strength to know and to do *thy* will. Fill them with the love of truth and righteousness, and make them ever mindful of their calling to serve this people in *thy* fear; through Jesus Christ our Lord, who *liveth* and *reigneth* with *thee* and the Holy Spirit, one God, world without end. *Amen.*

## 20. For Congress or a State Legislature

O God, the fountain of wisdom, whose will is good and
gracious, and whose law is truth: We beseech *thee* so to guide
and bless our Senators and Representatives in Congress
assembled (*or* in the Legislature of this State, *or* Commonwealth), that they may enact such laws as shall please *thee*,
to the glory of *thy* Name and the welfare of this people;
through Jesus Christ our Lord. *Amen.*

## 21. For Courts of Justice

Almighty God, *who sittest* in the throne judging right: We
humbly beseech *thee* to bless the courts of justice and the
magistrates in all this land; and give *unto* them the spirit of
wisdom and understanding, that they may discern the truth,
and impartially administer the law in the fear of *thee* alone;
through him who shall come to be our Judge, *thy* Son our
Savior Jesus Christ. *Amen.*

## 22. For Sound Government

*The responses in italics may be omitted.*

O Lord our Governor, bless the leaders of our land, that we
may be a people at peace among ourselves and a blessing to
other nations of the earth.
*Lord, keep this nation under your care.*

To the President and members of the Cabinet, to Governors
of States, Mayors of Cities, and to all in administrative
authority, grant wisdom and grace in the exercise of their
duties.
*Give grace to your servants, O Lord.*

To Senators and Representatives, and those who make our laws in States, Cities, and Towns, give courage, wisdom, and foresight to provide for the needs of all our people, and to fulfill our obligations in the community of nations.
*Give grace to your servants, O Lord.*

To the Judges and officers of our Courts give understanding and integrity, that human rights may be safeguarded and justice served.
*Give grace to your servants, O Lord.*

And finally, teach our people to rely on your strength and to accept their responsibilities to their fellow citizens, that they may elect trustworthy leaders and make wise decisions for the well-being of our society; that we may serve you faithfully in our generation and honor your holy Name.
*For yours is the kingdom, O Lord, and you are exalted as head above all. Amen.*

### 23. For Local Government

Almighty God our heavenly Father, send down upon those who hold office in this State (Commonwealth, City, County, Town, _____ ) the spirit of wisdom, charity, and justice; that with steadfast purpose they may faithfully serve in their offices to promote the well-being of all people; through Jesus Christ our Lord. *Amen.*

### 24. For an Election

Almighty God, to whom we must account for all our powers and privileges: Guide the people of the United States (*or of this community*) in the election of officials and representatives, that, by faithful administration and wise laws, the rights of all may be protected and our nation be enabled to fulfill your purposes; through Jesus Christ our Lord. *Amen.*

## 25. For those in the Armed Forces of our Country

Almighty God, we commend to your gracious care and keeping all the men and women of our armed forces at home and abroad. Defend them day by day with your heavenly grace; strengthen them in their trials and temptations; give them courage to face the perils which beset them; and grant them a sense of your abiding presence wherever they may be; through Jesus Christ our Lord. *Amen.*

## 26. For those who suffer for the sake of Conscience

O God our Father, whose Son forgave his enemies while he was suffering shame and death: Strengthen those who suffer for the sake of conscience; when they are accused, save them from speaking in hate; when they are rejected, save them from bitterness; when they are imprisoned, save them from despair; and to us your servants, give grace to respect their witness and to discern the truth, that our society may be cleansed and strengthened. This we ask for the sake of Jesus Christ, our merciful and righteous Judge. *Amen.*

## Prayers for the Social Order

## 27. For Social Justice

*See also Various Occasions no. 21.*

Grant, O God, that your holy and life-giving Spirit may so move every human heart [and especially the hearts of the people of this land], that barriers which divide us may crumble, suspicions disappear, and hatreds cease; that our divisions being healed, we may live in justice and peace; through Jesus Christ our Lord. *Amen.*

## 28. In Times of Conflict

O God, you have bound us together in a common life. Help us, in the midst of our struggles for justice and truth, to confront one another without hatred or bitterness, and to work together with mutual forbearance and respect; through Jesus Christ our Lord. *Amen.*

## 29. For Agriculture

*See also Various Occasions no. 19.*

Almighty God, we thank you for making the earth fruitful, so that it might produce what is needed for life: Bless those who work in the fields; give us seasonable weather; and grant that we may all share the fruits of the earth, rejoicing in your goodness; through Jesus Christ our Lord. *Amen.*

*For prayers for Industry and Labor, see Various Occasions no. 19, no. 24, and no. 25.*

## 30. For the Unemployed

Heavenly Father, we remember before you those who suffer want and anxiety from lack of work. Guide the people of this land so to use our public and private wealth that all may find suitable and fulfilling employment, and receive just payment for their labor; through Jesus Christ our Lord. *Amen.*

## 31. For Schools and Colleges

O Eternal God, bless all schools, colleges, and universities [and especially _____], that they may be lively centers fo sound learning, new discovery, and the pursuit of wisdom; and grant that those who teach and those who learn may find you to be the source of all truth; through Jesus Christ our Lord. *Amen.*

*For Education, see Various Occasions no. 23.*

## 32. For the Good Use of Leisure

O God, in the course of this busy life, give us times of refreshment and peace; and grant that we may so use our leisure to rebuild our bodies and renew our minds, that our spirits may be opened to the goodness of your creation; through Jesus Christ our Lord. *Amen.*

## 33. For Cities

Heavenly Father, in your Word you have given us a vision of that holy City to which the nations of the world bring their glory: Behold and visit, we pray, the cities of the earth. Renew the ties of mutual regard which form our civic life. Send us honest and able leaders. Enable us to eliminate poverty, prejudice, and oppression, that peace may prevail with righteousness, and justice with order, and that men and women from different cultures and with differing talents may find with one another the fulfillment of their humanity; through Jesus Christ our Lord. *Amen.*

## 34. For Towns and Rural Areas

Lord Christ, when you came among us, you proclaimed the kingdom of God in villages, towns, and lonely places: Grant that your presence and power may be known throughout this land. Have mercy upon all of us who live and work in rural areas [especially _____]; and grant that all the people of our nation may give thanks to you for food and drink and all other bodily necessities of life, respect those who labor to produce them, and honor the land and the water from which these good things come. All this we ask in your holy Name. *Amen.*

### 35. For the Poor and the Neglected

Almighty and most merciful God, we remember before you all poor and neglected persons whom it would be easy for us to forget: the homeless and the destitute, the old and the sick, and all who have none to care for them. Help us to heal those who are broken in body or spirit, and to turn their sorrow into joy. Grant this, Father, for the love of your Son, who for our sake became poor, Jesus Christ our Lord. *Amen.*

### 36. For the Oppressed

Look with pity, O heavenly Father, upon the people in this land who live with injustice, terror, disease, and death as their constant companions. Have mercy upon us. Help us to eliminate our cruelty to these our neighbors. Strengthen those who spend their lives establishing equal protection of the law and equal opportunities for all. And grant that every one of us may enjoy a fair portion of the riches of this land; through Jesus Christ our Lord. *Amen.*

### 37. For Prisons and Correctional Institutions

Lord Jesus, for our sake you were condemned as a criminal: Visit our jails and prisons with your pity and judgment. Remember all prisoners, and bring the guilty to repentance and amendment of life according to your will, and give them hope for their future. When any are held unjustly, bring them release; forgive us, and teach us to improve our justice. Remember those who work in these institutions; keep them humane and compassionate; and save them from becoming brutal or callous. And since what we do for those in prison, O Lord, we do for you, constrain us to improve their lot. All this we ask for your mercy's sake. *Amen.*

### 38. *For the Right Use of God's Gifts*

Almighty God, whose loving hand *hath* given us all that we possess: Grant us grace that we may honor *thee* with our substance, and, remembering the account which we must one day give, may be faithful stewards of *thy* bounty, through Jesus Christ our Lord. *Amen.*

### 39. *For those who Influence Public Opinion*

Almighty God, you proclaim your truth in every age by many voices: Direct, in our time, we pray, those who speak where many listen and write what many read; that they may do their part in making the heart of this people wise, its mind sound, and its will righteous; to the honor of Jesus Christ our Lord. *Amen.*

*For Social Service, see Various Occasions no.22.*

## Prayers for the Natural Order

### 40. *For Knowledge of God's Creation*

Almighty and everlasting God, you made the universe with all its marvelous order, its atoms, worlds, and galaxies, and the infinite complexity of living creatures: Grant that, as we probe the mysteries of your creation, we may come to know you more truly, and more surely fulfill our role in your eternal purpose; in the name of Jesus Christ our Lord. *Amen.*

### 41. *For the Conservation of Natural Resources*

*See also Various Occasions no. 19.*

Almighty God, in giving us dominion over things on earth, you made us fellow workers in your creation: Give us wisdom and reverence so to use the resources of nature, that no one may suffer from our abuse of them, and that generations yet to come may continue to praise you for your bounty; through Jesus Christ our Lord. *Amen.*

### 42. *For the Harvest of Lands and Waters*

O gracious Father, *who openest thine* hand and *fillest* all
things living with plenteousness: Bless the lands and waters,
and multiply the harvests of the world; let *thy* Spirit go
forth, that it may renew the face of the earth; show *thy*
loving-kindness, that our land may give her increase; and
save us from selfish use of what *thou givest*, that men and
women everywhere may give *thee* thanks; through Christ
our Lord. *Amen.*

### 43. *For Rain*

O God, heavenly Father, who by *thy* Son Jesus Christ
*hast* promised to all those who seek *thy* kingdom and its
righteousness all things necessary to sustain their life: Send
us, we entreat *thee*, in this time of need, such moderate rain
and showers, that we may receive the fruits of the earth, to
our comfort and to *thy* honor; through Jesus Christ our
Lord. *Amen.*

### 44. *For the Future of the Human Race*

O God our heavenly Father, you have blessed us and given us
dominion over all the earth: Increase our reverence before
the mystery of life; and give us new insight into your purposes
for the human race, and new wisdom and determination in
making provision for its future in accordance with your will;
through Jesus Christ our Lord. *Amen.*

### Prayers for Family and Personal Life

### 45. *For Families*

Almighty God, our heavenly Father, who settest the solitary
in families: We commend to thy continual care the homes in
which thy people dwell. Put far from them, we beseech thee,

every root of bitterness, the desire of vainglory, and the pride of life. Fill them with faith, virtue, knowledge, temperance, patience, godliness. Knit together in constant affection those who, in holy wedlock, have been made one flesh. Turn the hearts of the parents to the children, and the hearts of the children to the parents; and so enkindle fervent charity among us all, that we may evermore be kindly affectioned one to another; through Jesus Christ our Lord. *Amen.*

*A prayer for parents is on page 444.*

## 46. *For the Care of Children*

Almighty God, heavenly Father, you have blessed us with the joy and care of children: Give us calm strength and patient wisdom as we bring them up, that we may teach them to love whatever is just and true and good, following the example of our Savior Jesus Christ. *Amen.*

## 47. *For Young Persons*

God our Father, you see your children growing up in an unsteady and confusing world: Show them that your ways give more life than the ways of the world, and that following you is better than chasing after selfish goals. Help them to take failure, not as a measure of their worth, but as a chance for a new start. Give them strength to hold their faith in you, and to keep alive their joy in your creation; through Jesus Christ our Lord. *Amen.*

## 48. *For Those Who Live Alone*

Almighty God, whose Son had nowhere to lay his head: Grant that those who live alone may not be lonely in their solitude, but that, following in his steps, they may find fulfillment in loving you and their neighbors; through Jesus Christ our Lord. *Amen.*

### 49. *For the Aged*

Look with mercy, O God our Father, on all whose increasing years bring them weakness, distress, or isolation. Provide for them homes of dignity and peace; give them understanding helpers, and the willingness to accept help; and, as their strength diminishes, increase their faith and their assurance of your love. This we ask in the name of Jesus Christ our Lord. *Amen.*

### 50. *For a Birthday*

O God, our times are in your hand: Look with favor, we pray, on your servant N. as *he* begins another year. Grant that *he* may grow in wisdom and grace, and strengthen *his* trust in your goodness all the days of *his* life; through Jesus Christ our Lord. *Amen.*

### 51. *For a Birthday*

Watch over thy child, O Lord, as *his* days increase; bless and guide *him* wherever *he* may be. Strengthen *him* when *he* stands; comfort *him* when discouraged or sorrowful; raise *him* up if *he* fall; and in *his* heart may thy peace which passeth understanding abide all the days of *his* life; through Jesus Christ our Lord. *Amen.*

### 52. *For the Absent*

O God, whose fatherly care *reacheth* to the uttermost parts of the earth: We humbly beseech *thee* graciously to behold and bless those whom we love, now absent from us. Defend them from all dangers of soul and body; and grant that both they and we, drawing nearer to *thee*, may be bound together by *thy* love in the communion of *thy* Holy Spirit, and in the fellowship of *thy* saints; through Jesus Christ our Lord. *Amen.*

### 53. For Travelers

O God, our heavenly Father, whose glory fills the whole creation, and whose presence we find wherever we go: Preserve those who travel [in particular _____]; surround them with your loving care; protect them from every danger; and bring them in safety to their journey's end; through Jesus Christ our Lord. *Amen.*

### 54. For those we Love

Almighty God, we entrust all who are dear to us to *thy* never-failing care and love, for this life and the life to come, knowing that *thou art* doing for them better things than we can desire or pray for; through Jesus Christ our Lord. *Amen.*

### 55. For a Person in Trouble or Bereavement

O merciful Father, who hast taught us in thy holy Word that thou dost not willingly afflict or grieve the children of men: Look with pity upon the sorrows of thy servant for whom our prayers are offered. Remember *him*, O Lord, in mercy, nourish *his* soul with patience, comfort *him* with a sense of thy goodness, lift up thy countenance upon *him*, and give *him* peace; through Jesus Christ our Lord. *Amen.*

*Prayers for the sick are on pages 458-461. See also Various Occasions no. 20.*

### 56. For the Victims of Addiction

O blessed Lord, you ministered to all who came to you: Look with compassion upon all who through addiction have lost their health and freedom. Restore to them the assurance of your unfailing mercy; remove from them the fears that beset them; strengthen them in the work of their recovery; and to those who care for them, give patient understanding and persevering love. *Amen.*

### 57. For Guidance

Direct us, O Lord, in all our doings with *thy* most gracious favor, and further us with *thy* continual help; that in all our works begun, continued, and ended in *thee*, we may glorify *thy* holy Name, and finally, by *thy* mercy, obtain everlasting life; through Jesus Christ our Lord. *Amen.*

### 58. For Guidance

O God, by whom the meek are guided in judgment, and light *riseth* up in darkness for the godly: Grant us, in all our doubts and uncertainties, the grace to ask what *thou wouldest* have us to do, that the Spirit of wisdom may save us from all false choices, and that in *thy* light we may see light, and in *thy* straight path may not stumble; through Jesus Christ our Lord. *Amen.*

### 59. For Quiet Confidence

O God of peace, *who hast* taught us that in returning and rest we shall be saved, in quietness and in confidence shall be our strength: By the might of *thy* Spirit lift us, we pray *thee*, to *thy* presence, where we may be still and know that *thou art* God; through Jesus Christ our Lord. *Amen.*

### 60. For Protection

Assist us mercifully, O Lord, in these our supplications and prayers, and dispose the way of *thy* servants towards the attainment of everlasting salvation; that, among all the changes and chances of this mortal life, they may ever be defended by *thy* gracious and ready help; through Jesus Christ our Lord. *Amen.*

### 61. A Prayer of Self-Dedication

Almighty and eternal God, so draw our hearts to *thee*, so guide our minds, so fill our imaginations, so control our wills, that we may be wholly *thine*, utterly dedicated *unto thee*; and then use us, we pray *thee*, as *thou wilt*, and always to *thy* glory and the welfare of *thy* people; through our Lord and Savior Jesus Christ. *Amen.*

## 62. A Prayer attributed to St. Francis

Lord, make us instruments of your peace. Where there is hatred, let us sow love; where there is injury, pardon; where there is discord, union; where there is doubt, faith; where there is despair, hope; where there is darkness, light; where there is sadness, joy. Grant that we may not so much seek to be consoled as to console; to be understood as to understand; to be loved as to love. For it is in giving that we receive; it is in pardoning that we are pardoned; and it is in dying that we are born to eternal life. *Amen.*

## Other Prayers

*Prayers for Friday, Saturday, and Sunday, and for morning and evening, are on pages 56, 69, 98, and 123.*

## 63. In the Evening

O Lord, support us all the day long, until the shadows lengthen, and the evening comes, and the busy world is hushed, and the fever of life is over, and our work is done. Then in *thy* mercy, grant us a safe lodging, and a holy rest, and peace at the last. *Amen.*

## 64. Before Worship

O Almighty God, *who pourest* out on all who desire it the spirit of grace and of supplication: Deliver us, when we draw near to *thee*, from coldness of heart and wanderings of mind, that with steadfast thoughts and kindled affections we may worship *thee* in spirit and in truth; through Jesus Christ our Lord. *Amen.*

### 65. *For the Answering of Prayer*

Almighty God, who hast promised to hear the petitions of
those who ask in thy Son's Name: We beseech thee mercifully
to incline thine ear to us who have now made our prayers and
supplications unto thee; and grant that those things which we
have faithfully asked according to thy will, may effectually be
obtained, to the relief of our necessity, and to the setting forth
of thy glory; through Jesus Christ our Lord. *Amen.*

### 66. *Before Receiving Communion*

*See also the Prayer of Humble Access on page 337.*

Be present, be present, O Jesus, our great High Priest, as you
were present with your disciples, and be known to us in the
breaking of bread; who live and reign with the Father and
the Holy Spirit, now and for ever. *Amen.*

### 67. *After Receiving Communion*

O Lord Jesus Christ, who in a wonderful Sacrament hast left
unto us a memorial of thy passion: Grant us, we beseech
thee, so to venerate the sacred mysteries of thy Body and
Blood, that we may ever perceive within ourselves the fruit of
thy redemption; who livest and reignest with the Father and
the Holy Spirit, one God, for ever and ever. *Amen.*

### 68. *After Worship*

Grant, we beseech *thee*, Almighty God, that the words which
we have heard this day with our outward ears, may, through
*thy* grace, be so grafted inwardly in our hearts, that they may
bring forth in us the fruit of good living, to the honor and
praise of *thy* Name; through Jesus Christ our Lord. *Amen.*

### 9.  On Sunday

O God our King, by the resurrection of your Son Jesus Christ
on the first day of the week, you conquered sin, put death to
flight, and gave us the hope of everlasting life: Redeem all
our days by this victory; forgive our sins, banish our fears,
make us bold to praise you and to do your will; and steel us
to wait for the consummation of your kingdom on the last
great Day; through the same Jesus Christ our Lord. *Amen.*

### 10.  Grace at Meals

Give us grateful hearts, our Father, for all *thy* mercies, and
make us mindful of the needs of others; through Jesus Christ
our Lord. *Amen.*

*or this*

Bless, O Lord, *thy* gifts to our use and us to *thy* service; for
Christ's sake. *Amen.*

*or this*

Blessed are you, O Lord God, King of the Universe, for you
give us food to sustain our lives and make our hearts glad;
through Jesus Christ our Lord. *Amen.*

*or this*

For these and all his mercies, God's holy Name be blessed
and praised; through Jesus Christ our Lord. *Amen.*

# Thanksgivings

## General Thanksgivings

### 1. A General Thanksgiving

Accept, O Lord, our thanks and praise for all that you have done for us. We thank you for the splendor of the whole creation, for the beauty of this world, for the wonder of life, and for the mystery of love.

We thank you for the blessing of family and friends, and for the loving care which surrounds us on every side.

We thank you for setting us at tasks which demand our best efforts, and for leading us to accomplishments which satisfy and delight us.

We thank you also for those disappointments and failures that lead us to acknowledge our dependence on you alone.

Above all, we thank you for your Son Jesus Christ; for the truth of his Word and the example of his life; for his steadfast obedience, by which he overcame temptation; for his dying, through which he overcame death; and for his rising to life again, in which we are raised to the life of your kingdom.

Grant us the gift of your Spirit, that we may know Christ and make him known; and through him, at all times and in all places, may give thanks to you in all things. *Amen.*

### 2. A Litany of Thanksgiving

*For optional use on Thanksgiving Day, in place of the Prayers of the People at the Eucharist, or at any time after the Collects at Morning or Evening Prayer, or separately.*

Let us give thanks to God our Father for all his gifts so freely bestowed upon us.

For the beauty and wonder of your creation, in earth and sky and sea,
*We thank you, Lord.*

For all that is gracious in the lives of men and women, revealing the image of Christ,
*We thank you, Lord.*

For our daily food and drink, our homes and families, and our friends,
*We thank you, Lord.*

For minds to think, and hearts to love, and hands to serve,
*We thank you, Lord.*

For health and strength to work, and leisure to rest and play,
*We thank you, Lord.*

For the brave and courageous, who are patient in suffering and faithful in adversity,
*We thank you, Lord.*

For all valiant seekers after truth, liberty, and justice,
*We thank you, Lord.*

For the communion of saints, in all times and places,
*We thank you, Lord.*

Above all, we give you thanks for the great mercies and promises given to us in Christ Jesus our Lord;
*to him be praise and glory, with you, O Father, and the Holy Spirit, now and for ever. Amen.*

See also The General Thanksgiving on pages 58 and 101.

## Thanksgivings for the Church

### 3. For the Mission of the Church

Almighty God, you sent your Son Jesus Christ to reconcile
the world to yourself: We praise and bless you for those
whom you have sent in the power of the Spirit to preach the
Gospel to all nations. We thank you that in all parts of the
earth a community of love has been gathered together by
their prayers and labors, and that in every place your servant
call upon your Name; for the kingdom and the power and
the glory are yours for ever. *Amen.*

### 4. For the Saints and Faithful Departed

*See also the prayer "O God, the King of Saints," page 489 and 504.*

We give thanks to you, O Lord our God, for all your servants
and witnesses of time past: for Abraham, the father of believ
and Sarah his wife; for Moses, the lawgiver, and Aaron, the
priest; for Miriam and Joshua, Deborah and Gideon, and
Samuel with Hannah his mother; for Isaiah and all the prop
for Mary, the mother of our Lord; for Peter and Paul and all
the apostles; for Mary and Martha, and Mary Magdalene;
Stephen, the first martyr, and all the martyrs and saints in
every age and in every land. In your mercy, O Lord our God
give us, as you gave to them, the hope of salvation and the
promise of eternal life; through Jesus Christ our Lord, the
first-born of many from the dead. *Amen.*

## Thanksgivings for National Life

### 5. For the Nation

Almighty God, giver of all good things:
We thank you for the natural majesty and beauty of this lan
They restore us, though we often destroy them.
*Heal us.*

We thank you for the great resources of this nation. They make us rich, though we often exploit them.
*Forgive us.*

We thank you for the men and women who have made this country strong. They are models for us, though we often fall short of them.
*Inspire us.*

We thank you for the torch of liberty which has been lit in this land. It has drawn people from every nation, though we have often hidden from its light.
*Enlighten us.*

We thank you for the faith we have inherited in all its rich variety. It sustains our life, though we have been faithless again and again.
*Renew us.*

Help us, O Lord, to finish the good work here begun. Strengthen our efforts to blot out ignorance and prejudice, and to abolish poverty and crime. And hasten the day when all our people, with many voices in one united chorus, will glorify your holy Name. *Amen.*

### For Heroic Service

O Judge of the nations, we remember before you with grateful hearts the men and women of our country who in the day of decision ventured much for the liberties we now enjoy. Grant that we may not rest until all the people of this land share the benefits of true freedom and gladly accept its disciplines. This we ask in the Name of Jesus Christ our Lord. *Amen.*

## Thanksgiving for the Social Order

### 7. For the Diversity of Races and Cultures

O God, who created all peoples in your image, we thank you
for the wonderful diversity of races and cultures in this world.
Enrich our lives by ever-widening circles of fellowship, and
show us your presence in those who differ most from us, until
our knowledge of your love is made perfect in our love for all
your children; through Jesus Christ our Lord. *Amen.*

## Thanksgivings for the Natural Order

### 8. For the Beauty of the Earth

We give you thanks, most gracious God, for the beauty of
earth and sky and sea; for the richness of mountains, plains,
and rivers; for the songs of birds and the loveliness of flowers.
We praise you for these good gifts, and pray that we may
safeguard them for our posterity. Grant that we may continue
to grow in our grateful enjoyment of your abundant creation,
to the honor and glory of your Name, now and for ever. *Amen.*

### 9. For the Harvest

Most gracious God, by whose knowledge the depths are
broken up and the clouds drop down the dew: We yield thee
hearty thanks and praise for the return of seedtime and harvest,
for the increase of the ground and the gathering in of its fruits,
and for all the other blessings of thy merciful providence
bestowed upon this nation and people. And, we beseech thee,
give us a just sense of these great mercies, such as may appear
in our lives by a humble, holy, and obedient walking before
thee all our days; through Jesus Christ our Lord, to whom,
with thee and the Holy Ghost be all glory and honor, world
without end. *Amen.*

# Thanksgivings for Family and Personal Life

## 10. *For the Gift of a Child*

*See also the Thanksgiving for a Child on page 439.*

Heavenly Father, you sent your own Son into this world. We
thank you for the life of this child, *N.,* entrusted to our care.
Help us to remember that we are all your children, and so to
love and nurture *him,* that *he* may attain to that full stature
intended for *him* in your eternal kingdom; for the sake of
your dear Son, Jesus Christ our Lord. *Amen.*

## 11. *For the Restoration of Health*

Almighty God and heavenly Father, we give *thee* humble
thanks because *thou hast* been graciously pleased to deliver
from *his* sickness *thy* servant *N.,* in whose behalf we bless
and praise *thy* Name. Grant, O gracious Father, that *he,*
through *thy* help, may live in this world according to *thy* will,
and also be partaker of everlasting glory in the life to come;
through Jesus Christ our Lord. *Amen.*

*Thanksgivings for the departed are on pages 487-489 and 503-504.*

# An Outline
of the Faith

# Concerning the Catechism

This catechism is primarily intended for use by parish priests, deacons, and lay catechists, to give an outline for instruction. It is a commentary on the creeds, but is not meant to be a complete statement of belief and practice; rather, it is a point of departure for the teacher, and it is cast in the traditional question and answer form for ease of reference.

The second use of this catechism is to provide a brief summary of the Church's teaching for an inquiring stranger who picks up a Prayer Book.

It may also be used to form a simple service; since the matter is arranged under headings, it is suitable for selective use, and the leader may introduce prayers and hymns as needed.

# An Outline of the Faith

## commonly called the Catechism

### Human Nature

Q. What are we by nature?
A. We are part of God's creation, made in the image of God.

Q. What does it mean to be created in the image of God?
A. It means that we are free to make choices: to love, to create, to reason, and to live in harmony with creation and with God.

Q. Why then do we live apart from God and out of harmony with creation?
. From the beginning, human beings have misused their freedom and made wrong choices.

. Why do we not use our freedom as we should?
. Because we rebel against God, and we put ourselves in the place of God.

. What help is there for us?
. Our help is in God.

. How did God first help us?
. God first helped us by revealing himself and his will, through nature and history, through many seers and saints, and especially through the prophets of Israel.

## God the Father

Q. What do we learn about God as creator from the revelation to Israel?

A. We learn that there is one God, the Father Almighty, creator of heaven and earth, of all that is, seen and unseen.

Q. What does this mean?

A. This means that the universe is good, that it is the work of a single loving God who creates, sustains, and directs it.

Q. What does this mean about our place in the universe?

A. It means that the world belongs to its creator; and that we are called to enjoy it and to care for it in accordance with God's purposes.

Q. What does this mean about human life?

A. It means that all people are worthy of respect and honor, because all are created in the image of God, and all can respond to the love of God.

Q. How was this revelation handed down to us?

A. This revelation was handed down to us through a community created by a covenant with God.

## The Old Covenant

Q. What is meant by a covenant with God?

A. A covenant is a relationship initiated by God, to which a body of people responds in faith.

Q. What is the Old Covenant?

A. The Old Covenant is the one given by God to the Hebrew people.

Q. What did God promise them?

God promised that they would be his people to bring all the nations of the world to him.

What response did God require from the chosen people?
God required the chosen people to be faithful; to love justice, to do mercy, and to walk humbly with their God.

Where is this Old Covenant to be found?
The covenant with the Hebrew people is to be found in the books which we call the Old Testament.

Where in the Old Testament is God's will for us shown most clearly?
God's will for us is shown most clearly in the Ten Commandments.

## The Ten Commandments

*pages 317 and 350.*

What are the Ten Commandments?
The Ten Commandments are the laws given to Moses and the people of Israel.

What do we learn from these commandments?
We learn two things: our duty to God, and our duty to our neighbors.

What is our duty to God?
Our duty is to believe and trust in God;
  I    To love and obey God and to bring others to
       know him;
  II   To put nothing in the place of God;
  III  To show God respect in thought, word, and
       deed;
  IV   And to set aside regular times for worship,
       prayer, and the study of God's ways.

Q. What is our duty to our neighbors?
A. Our duty to our neighbors is to love them as ourselves, and to do to other people as we wish them to do to us;

  V   To love, honor, and help our parents and family; to honor those in authority, and to meet their just demands;

  VI  To show respect for the life God has given us; to work and pray for peace; to bear no malice, prejudice, or hatred in our hearts; and to be kind to all the creatures of God;

  VII To use all our bodily desires as God intended;

  VIII To be honest and fair in our dealings; to seek justice, freedom, and the necessities of life for all people; and to use our talents and possessions as ones who must answer for them to God;

  IX  To speak the truth, and not to mislead others by our silence;

  X   To resist temptations to envy, greed, and jealousy; to rejoice in other people's gifts and graces; and to do our duty for the love of God, who has called us into fellowship with him.

Q. What is the purpose of the Ten Commandments?
A. The Ten Commandments were given to define our relationship with God and our neighbors.

Q. Since we do not fully obey them, are they useful at all?
A. Since we do not fully obey them, we see more clearly our sin and our need for redemption.


## Sin and Redemption

Q. What is sin?
A. Sin is the seeking of our own will instead of the will of God, thus distorting our relationship with God, with other people, and with all creation.

Q. How does sin have power over us?
A. Sin has power over us because we lose our liberty when our relationship with God is distorted.

Q. What is redemption?
A. Redemption is the act of God which sets us free from the power of evil, sin, and death.

Q. How did God prepare us for redemption?
A. God sent the prophets to call us back to himself, to show us our need for redemption, and to announce the coming of the Messiah.

Q. What is meant by the Messiah?
A. The Messiah is one sent by God to free us from the power of sin, so that with the help of God we may live in harmony with God, within ourselves, with our neighbors, and with all creation.

Q. Who do we believe is the Messiah?
A. The Messiah, or Christ, is Jesus of Nazareth, the only Son of God.

## God the Son

Q. What do we mean when we say that Jesus is the only Son of God?
A. We mean that Jesus is the only perfect image of the Father, and shows us the nature of God.

Q. What is the nature of God revealed in Jesus?
A. God is love.

Q. What do we mean when we say that Jesus was conceived by the power of the Holy Spirit and became incarnate from the Virgin Mary?
A. We mean that by God's own act, his divine Son received our human nature from the Virgin Mary, his mother.

Q. Why did he take our human nature?
A. The divine Son became human, so that in him human beings might be adopted as children of God, and be made heirs of God's kingdom.

Q. What is the great importance of Jesus' suffering and death?
A. By his obedience, even to suffering and death, Jesus made the offering which we could not make; in him we are freed from the power of sin and reconciled to God.

Q. What is the significance of Jesus' resurrection?
A. By his resurrection, Jesus overcame death and opened for us the way of eternal life.

Q. What do we mean when we say that he descended to the dead?
A. We mean that he went to the departed and offered them also the benefits of redemption.

Q. What do we mean when we say that he ascended into heaven and is seated at the right hand of the Father?
A. We mean that Jesus took our human nature into heaven where he now reigns with the Father and intercedes for us.

Q. How can we share in his victory over sin, suffering, and death?
A. We share in his victory when we are baptized into the New Covenant and become living members of Christ.


The New Covenant

Q. What is the New Covenant?
A. The New Covenant is the new relationship with God given by Jesus Christ, the Messiah, to the apostles; and. through them, to all who believe in him.

Q. What did the Messiah promise in the New Covenant?
A. Christ promised to bring us into the kingdom of God and give us life in all its fullness.

Q. What response did Christ require?
A. Christ commanded us to believe in him and to keep his commandments.

Q. What are the commandments taught by Christ?
A. Christ taught us the Summary of the Law and gave us the New Commandment.

Q. What is the Summary of the Law?
A. You shall love the Lord your God with all your heart, with all your soul, and with all your mind. This is the first and the great commandment. And the second is like it: You shall love your neighbor as yourself.

Q. What is the New Commandment?
A. The New Commandment is that we love one another as Christ loved us.

Q. Where may we find what Christians believe about Christ?
A. What Christians believe about Christ is found in the Scriptures and summed up in the creeds.

## The Creeds

See pages 53, 96, 326, 327, and 864.

Q. What are the creeds?
A. The creeds are statements of our basic beliefs about God.

Q. How many creeds does this Church use in its worship?
A. This Church uses two creeds: The Apostles' Creed and the Nicene Creed.

Q. What is the Apostles' Creed?
A. The Apostles' Creed is the ancient creed of Baptism; it is used in the Church's daily worship to recall our Baptismal Covenant.

Q. What is the Nicene Creed?
A. The Nicene Creed is the creed of the universal Church and is used at the Eucharist.

Q. What, then, is the Athanasian Creed?
A. The Athanasian Creed is an ancient document proclaiming the nature of the Incarnation and of God as Trinity.

Q. What is the Trinity?
A. The Trinity is one God: Father, Son, and Holy Spirit.

## The Holy Spirit

Q. Who is the Holy Spirit?
A. The Holy Spirit is the Third Person of the Trinity, God at work in the world and in the Church even now.

Q. How is the Holy Spirit revealed in the Old Covenant?
A. The Holy Spirit is revealed in the Old Covenant as the giver of life, the One who spoke through the prophets.

Q. How is the Holy Spirit revealed in the New Covenant?
A. The Holy Spirit is revealed as the Lord who leads us into all truth and enables us to grow in the likeness of Christ.

Q. How do we recognize the presence of the Holy Spirit in our lives?
A. We recognize the presence of the Holy Spirit when we confess Jesus Christ as Lord and are brought into love and harmony with God, with ourselves, with our neighbors, and with all creation.

Q. How do we recognize the truths taught by the Holy Spirit?
A. We recognize truths to be taught by the Holy Spirit when they are in accord with the Scriptures.

## The Holy Scriptures

Q. What are the Holy Scriptures?
A. The Holy Scriptures, commonly called the Bible, are the books of the Old and New Testaments; other books, called the Apocrypha, are often included in the Bible.

Q. What is the Old Testament?
A. The Old Testament consists of books written by the people of the Old Covenant, under the inspiration of the Holy Spirit, to show God at work in nature and history.

Q. What is the New Testament?
A. The New Testament consists of books written by the people of the New Covenant, under the inspiration of the Holy Spirit, to set forth the life and teachings of Jesus and to proclaim the Good News of the Kingdom for all people.

Q. What is the Apocrypha?
A. The Apocrypha is a collection of additional books written by people of the Old Covenant, and used in the Christian Church.

Q. Why do we call the Holy Scriptures the Word of God?
A. We call them the Word of God because God inspired their human authors and because God still speaks to us through the Bible.

Q. How do we understand the meaning of the Bible?
A. We understand the meaning of the Bible by the help of

the Holy Spirit, who guides the Church in the true
interpretation of the Scriptures.


## The Church

Q. What is the Church?
A. The Church is the community of the New Covenant.

Q. How is the Church described in the Bible?
A. The Church is described as the Body of which Jesus
Christ is the Head and of which all baptized persons are
members. It is called the People of God, the New Israel,
a holy nation, a royal priesthood, and the pillar and
ground of truth.

Q. How is the Church described in the creeds?
A. The Church is described as one, holy, catholic, and
apostolic.

Q. Why is the Church described as one?
A. The Church is one, because it is one Body, under one
Head, our Lord Jesus Christ.

Q. Why is the Church described as holy?
A. The Church is holy, because the Holy Spirit dwells in it,
consecrates its members, and guides them to do God's
work.

Q. Why is the Church described as catholic?
A. The Church is catholic, because it proclaims the whole
Faith to all people, to the end of time.

Q. Why is the Church described as apostolic?
A. The Church is apostolic, because it continues in the
teaching and fellowship of the apostles and is sent
to carry out Christ's mission to all people.

Q. What is the mission of the Church?
A. The mission of the Church is to restore all people to unity with God and each other in Christ.

Q. How does the Church pursue its mission?
A. The Church pursues its mission as it prays and worships, proclaims the Gospel, and promotes justice, peace, and love.

Q. Through whom does the Church carry out its mission?
A. The Church carries out its mission through the ministry of all its members.

## The Ministry

Q. Who are the ministers of the Church?
A. The ministers of the Church are lay persons, bishops, priests, and deacons.

Q. What is the ministry of the laity?
A. The ministry of lay persons is to represent Christ and his Church; to bear witness to him wherever they may be; and, according to the gifts given them, to carry on Christ's work of reconciliation in the world; and to take their place in the life, worship, and governance of the Church.

Q. What is the ministry of a bishop?
A. The ministry of a bishop is to represent Christ and his Church, particularly as apostle, chief priest, and pastor of a diocese; to guard the faith, unity, and discipline of the whole Church; to proclaim the Word of God; to act in Christ's name for the reconciliation of the world and the building up of the Church; and to ordain others to continue Christ's ministry.

Q. What is the ministry of a priest or presbyter?
A. The ministry of a priest is to represent Christ and his Church, particularly as pastor to the people; to share with the bishop in the overseeing of the Church; to proclaim the Gospel; to administer the sacraments; and to bless and declare pardon in the name of God.

Q. What is the ministry of a deacon?
A. The ministry of a deacon is to represent Christ and his Church, particularly as a servant of those in need; and to assist bishops and priests in the proclamation of the Gospel and the administration of the sacraments.

Q. What is the duty of all Christians?
A. The duty of all Christians is to follow Christ; to come together week by week for corporate worship; and to work, pray, and give for the spread of the kingdom of God.

**Prayer and Worship**

Q. What is prayer?
A. Prayer is responding to God, by thought and by deeds, with or without words.

Q. What is Christian Prayer?
A. Christian prayer is response to God the Father, through Jesus Christ, in the power of the Holy Spirit.

Q. What prayer did Christ teach us?
A. Our Lord gave us the example of prayer known as the Lord's Prayer. *See page 364.*

Q. What are the principal kinds of prayer?
A. The principal kinds of prayer are adoration, praise, thanksgiving, penitence, oblation, intercession, and petition.

Q. What is adoration?
A. Adoration is the lifting up of the heart and mind to God, asking nothing but to enjoy God's presence.

Q. Why do we praise God?
A. We praise God, not to obtain anything, but because God's Being draws praise from us.

Q. For what do we offer thanksgiving?
A. Thanksgiving is offered to God for all the blessings of this life, for our redemption, and for whatever draws us closer to God.

Q. What is penitence?
A. In penitence, we confess our sins and make restitution where possible, with the intention to amend our lives.

Q. What is prayer of oblation?
A. Oblation is an offering of ourselves, our lives and labors, in union with Christ, for the purposes of God.

Q. What are intercession and petition?
A. Intercession brings before God the needs of others; in petition, we present our own needs, that God's will may be done.

Q. What is corporate worship?
A. In corporate worship, we unite ourselves with others to acknowledge the holiness of God, to hear God's Word, to offer prayer, and to celebrate the sacraments.

## The Sacraments

Q. What are the sacraments?
A. The sacraments are outward and visible signs of inward and spiritual grace, given by Christ as sure and certain means by which we receive that grace.

Q. What is grace?
A. Grace is God's favor towards us, unearned and undeserved; by grace God forgives our sins, enlightens our minds, stirs our hearts, and strengthens our wills.

Q. What are the two great sacraments of the Gospel?
A. The two great sacraments given by Christ to his Church are Holy Baptism and the Holy Eucharist.

## Holy Baptism

Q. What is Holy Baptism?
A. Holy Baptism is the sacrament by which God adopts us as his children and makes us members of Christ's Body, the Church, and inheritors of the kingdom of God.

Q. What is the outward and visible sign in Baptism?
A. The outward and visible sign in Baptism is water, in which the person is baptized in the Name of the Father, and of the Son, and of the Holy Spirit.

Q. What is the inward and spiritual grace in Baptism?
A. The inward and spiritual grace in Baptism is union with Christ in his death and resurrection, birth into God's family the Church, forgiveness of sins, and new life in the Holy Spirit.

Q. What is required of us at Baptism?
A. It is required that we renounce Satan, repent of our sins, and accept Jesus as our Lord and Savior.

Q. Why then are infants baptized?
A. Infants are baptized so that they can share citizenship in the Covenant, membership in Christ, and redemption by God.

Q. How are the promises for infants made and carried out?

A. Promises are made for them by their parents and sponsors, who guarantee that the infants will be brought up within the Church, to know Christ and be able to follow him.

## The Holy Eucharist

Q. What is the Holy Eucharist?
A. The Holy Eucharist is the sacrament commanded by Christ for the continual remembrance of his life, death, and resurrection, until his coming again.

Q. Why is the Eucharist called a sacrifice?
A. Because the Eucharist, the Church's sacrifice of praise and thanksgiving, is the way by which the sacrifice of Christ is made present, and in which he unites us to his one offering of himself.

Q. By what other names is this service known?
A. The Holy Eucharist is called the Lord's Supper, and Holy Communion; it is also known as the Divine Liturgy, the Mass, and the Great Offering.

Q. What is the outward and visible sign in the Eucharist?
A. The outward and visible sign in the Eucharist is bread and wine, given and received according to Christ's command.

Q. What is the inward and spiritual grace given in the Eucharist?
A. The inward and spiritual grace in the Holy Communion is the Body and Blood of Christ given to his people, and received by faith.

Q. What are the benefits which we receive in the Lord's Supper?
A. The benefits we receive are the forgiveness of our sins,

the strengthening of our union with Christ and one another, and the foretaste of the heavenly banquet which is our nourishment in eternal life.

Q. What is required of us when we come to the Eucharist?
A. It is required that we should examine our lives, repent of our sins, and be in love and charity with all people.

## Other Sacramental Rites

Q. What other sacramental rites evolved in the Church under the guidance of the Holy Spirit?
A. Other sacramental rites which evolved in the Church include confirmation, ordination, holy matrimony, reconciliation of a penitent, and unction.

Q. How do they differ from the two sacraments of the Gospel?
A. Although they are means of grace, they are not necessary for all persons in the same way that Baptism and the Eucharist are.

Q. What is Confirmation?
A. Confirmation is the rite in which we express a mature commitment to Christ, and receive strength from the Holy Spirit through prayer and the laying on of hands by a bishop.

Q. What is required of those to be confirmed?
A. It is required of those to be confirmed that they have been baptized, are sufficiently instructed in the Christian Faith, are penitent for their sins, and are ready to affirm their confession of Jesus Christ as Savior and Lord.

Q. What is Ordination?
A. Ordination is the rite in which God gives authority and the grace of the Holy Spirit to those being made bishops,

priests, and deacons, through prayer and the laying on of hands by bishops.

Q. What is Holy Matrimony?
A. Holy Matrimony is Christian marriage, in which the woman and man enter into a life-long union, make their vows before God and the Church, and receive the grace and blessing of God to help them fulfill their vows.

Q. What is Reconciliation of a Penitent?
A. Reconciliation of a Penitent, or Penance, is the rite in which those who repent of their sins may confess them to God in the presence of a priest, and receive the assurance of pardon and the grace of absolution.

Q. What is Unction of the Sick?
A. Unction is the rite of anointing the sick with oil, or the laying on of hands, by which God's grace is given for the healing of spirit, mind, and body.

Q. Is God's activity limited to these rites?
A. God does not limit himself to these rites; they are patterns of countless ways by which God uses material things to reach out to us.

Q. How are the sacraments related to our Christian hope?
A. Sacraments sustain our present hope and anticipate its future fulfillment.

## The Christian Hope

Q. What is the Christian hope?
A. The Christian hope is to live with confidence in newness and fullness of life, and to await the coming of Christ in glory, and the completion of God's purpose for the world.

Q. What do we mean by the coming of Christ in glory?

A. By the coming of Christ in glory, we mean that Christ will come, not in weakness but in power, and will make all things new.

Q. What do we mean by heaven and hell?

A. By heaven, we mean eternal life in our enjoyment of God; by hell, we mean eternal death in our rejection of God.

Q. Why do we pray for the dead?

A. We pray for them, because we still hold them in our love, and because we trust that in God's presence those who have chosen to serve him will grow in his love, until they see him as he is.

Q. What do we mean by the last judgment?

A. We believe that Christ will come in glory and judge the living and the dead.

Q. What do we mean by the resurrection of the body?

A. We mean that God will raise us from death in the fullness of our being, that we may live with Christ in the communion of the saints.

Q. What is the communion of saints?

A. The communion of saints is the whole family of God, the living and the dead, those whom we love and those whom we hurt, bound together in Christ by sacrament, prayer, and praise.

Q. What do we mean by everlasting life?

A. By everlasting life, we mean a new existence, in which we are united with all the people of God, in the joy of fully knowing and loving God and each other.

Q. What, then, is our assurance as Christians?

A. Our assurance as Christians is that nothing, not even death, shall separate us from the love of God which is in Christ Jesus our Lord. Amen.

# Historical
# Documents
# of the Church

# Definition of the Union of the Divine and Human Natures in the Person of Christ

*Council of Chalcedon, 451 A.D., Act V*

Therefore, following the holy fathers, we all with one accord teach men to acknowledge one and the same Son, our Lord Jesus Christ, at once complete in Godhead and complete in manhood, truly God and truly man, consisting also of a reasonable soul and body; of one substance (homoousios) with the Father as regards his Godhead, and at the same time of one substance with us as regards his manhood; like us in all respects, apart from sin; as regards his Godhead, begotten of the Father before the ages, but yet as regards his manhood begotten, for us men and for our salvation, of Mary the Virgin, the God-bearer (Theotokos); one and the same Christ, Son, Lord, Only-begotten, recognized in two natures, without confusion, without change, without division, without separation; the distinction of natures being in no way annulled by the union, but rather the characteristics of each nature being preserved and coming together to form one person and subsistence, not as parted or separated into two persons, but one and the same Son and Only-begotten God the Word, Lord Jesus Christ; even as the prophets from earliest times spoke of him, and our Lord Jesus Christ himself taught us, and the creed of the Fathers has handed down to us.

# Quicunque Vult

*commonly called*

# The Creed of Saint Athanasius

Whosoever will be saved, before all things it is necessary that he hold the Catholic Faith.
Which Faith except everyone do keep whole and undefiled, without doubt he shall perish everlastingly.
And the Catholic Faith is this: That we worship one God in Trinity, and Trinity in Unity, neither confounding the Persons, nor dividing the Substance.
For there is one Person of the Father, another of the Son, and another of the Holy Ghost.
But the Godhead of the Father, of the Son, and of the Holy Ghost, is all one, the Glory equal, the Majesty co-eternal.
Such as the Father is, such is the Son, and such is the Holy Ghost.
The Father uncreate, the Son uncreate, and the Holy Ghost uncreate.
The Father incomprehensible, the Son incomprehensible, and the Holy Ghost incomprehensible.
The Father eternal, the Son eternal, and the Holy Ghost eternal.
And yet they are not three eternals, but one eternal.
As also there are not three incomprehensibles, nor three uncreated, but one uncreated, and one incomprehensible.
So likewise the Father is Almighty, the Son Almighty, and the Holy Ghost Almighty.
And yet they are not three Almighties, but one Almighty.

he Father is God, the Son is God, and the Holy Ghost is God.

d yet they are not three Gods, but one God.

ikewise the Father is Lord, the Son Lord, and the Holy Ghost Lord.

d yet not three Lords, but one Lord.

like as we are compelled by the Christian verity to acknowledge every Person by himself to be both God and Lord,

are we forbidden by the Catholic Religion, to say, There be three Gods, or three Lords.

e Father is made of none, neither created, nor begotten.

e Son is of the Father alone, not made, nor created, but begotten.

e Holy Ghost is of the Father and of the Son, neither made, nor created, nor begotten, but proceeding.

there is one Father, not three Fathers; one Son, not three Sons; one Holy Ghost, not three Holy Ghosts.

d in this Trinity none is afore, or after other; none is greater, or less than another;

t the whole three Persons are co-eternal together and co-equal.

that in all things, as is aforesaid, the Unity in Trinity and the Trinity in Unity is to be worshipped.

therefore that will be saved must thus think of the Trinity.

rthermore, it is necessary to everlasting salvation that he also believe rightly the Incarnation of our Lord Jesus Christ.

r the right Faith is, that we believe and confess, that our Lord Jesus Christ, the Son of God, is God and Man;

d, of the Substance of the Father, begotten before the worlds; and Man, of the Substance of his Mother, born in the world;

fect God and perfect Man, of a reasonable soul and human flesh subsisting;

ual to the Father, as touching his Godhead; and inferior to the Father, as touching his Manhood.

10 although he be God and Man, yet he is not two, but one Christ;

e, not by conversion of the Godhead into flesh, but by taking of the Manhood into God;

1e altogether; not by confusion of Substance, but by unity of Person.

r as the reasonable soul and flesh is one man, so God and Man is one Christ;

10 suffered for our salvation, descended into hell, rose again the third day from the dead.

ascended into heaven, he sitteth on the right hand of the Father, God Almighty, from whence he shall come to judge the quick and the dead.

whose coming all men shall rise again with their bodies and shall give account for their own works.

d they that have done good shall go into life everlasting; and they that have done evil into everlasting fire.

is is the Catholic Faith, which except a man believe faithfully, he cannot be saved.

# Preface

# The First Book of Common Prayer (1549)

There was never any thing by the wit of man so well devised, or so sure established, which in continuance of time hath not been corrupted: as, among other things, it may plainly appear by the common prayers in the Church, commonly called Divine Service: the first original and ground whereof, if a man would search out by the ancient fathers, he shall find, that the same was not ordained, but of a good purpose, and for a great advancement of godliness: For they so ordered the matter, that all the whole Bible (or the greatest part thereof) should be read over once in the year, intending thereby, that the Clergy, and especially such as were Ministers of the congregation, should (by often reading, and meditation of God's word) be stirred up to godliness themselves, and be more able to exhort others by wholesome doctrine, and to confute them that were adversaries to the truth. And further, that the people (by daily hearing of holy Scripture read in the Church) should continually profit more and more in the knowledge of God, and be the more inflamed with the love of his true religion.

But these many years passed, this godly and decent order of the ancient fathers hath been so altered, broken, and neglected, by planting in uncertain stories, Legends, Responds, Verses, vain repetitions, Commemorations, and Synodals, that commonly when any book of the Bible was begun, before three or four Chapters were read out, all the rest were unread. And in this sort the book of Isaiah was begun in Advent, and the book of Genesis in Septuagesima; but they were only begun, and never read through. After a like sort were other books of holy Scripture used. And moreover, whereas St. Paul would have such language spoken to the people in the Church, as they might understand, and have profit by hearing the same, the Service in the Church of England (these many years) hath been read in Latin to the people, which they understood not; so that they have heard with their ears only; and their hearts, spirit, and mind, have not been edified thereby. And furthermore, notwithstanding that the ancient fathers had divided the Psalms into seven portions, whereof every one was called a nocturn, now of late time a few of them have been daily said (and oft repeated), and the rest utterly omitted. Moreover, the number and hardness of the Rules called the Pie, and the manifold changings of the service, was the cause, that to turn the Book only, was so hard and intricate a matter, that many times, there was more business to find out what should be read, than to read it when it was found out.

These inconveniences therefore considered, here is set forth such an order, whereby the same shall be redressed. And for a readiness in this matter, here is drawn out a Kalendar for that purpose, which is plain and easy to be understood, wherein (so much as may be) the reading of holy Scripture is so set forth, that all things shall be done in order, without breaking one piece thereof from another. For this cause be cut off Anthems, Responds, Invitatories, and such like things, as did break the continual course of the reading of the Scripture.

Yet because there is no remedy, but that of necessity there must be some rules: therefore certain rules are here set forth, which, as they be few in number; so they be plain and easy to be understood. So that here you have an order for prayer (as touching the reading of the holy Scripture), much agreeable to the mind and purpose of the old fathers, and a great deal more profitable and commodious, than that which of late was used. It is more profitable, because here are left out many things, whereof some be untrue, some uncertain, some vain and superstitious: and is ordained nothing to be read, but the very pure word of God, the holy Scriptures, or that which is evidently grounded upon the same; and that in such a language and order as is most easy and plain for the understanding, both of the readers and hearers. It is also more commodious, both for the shortness thereof, and for the plainness of the order, and for that the rules be few and easy. Furthermore, by this order the curates shall need none other books for their public service, but this book and the Bible: by the means whereof, the people shall not be at so great charge for books, as in time past they have been.

And where heretofore, there hath been great diversity in saying and singing in churches within this realm: some following Salisbury use, some Hereford use, some the use of Bangor, some of York, and some of Lincoln: now from henceforth, all the whole realm shall have but one use. And if any would judge this way more painful, because that all things must be read upon the book, whereas before, by reason of so often repetition, they could say many things by heart: if those men will weigh their labor with the profit in knowledge, which daily they shall obtain by reading upon the book, they will not refuse the pain, in consideration of the great profit that shall ensue thereof.

And forasmuch as nothing can, almost, be so plainly set forth, but doubts may arise in the use and practicing of the same: to appease all such diversity (if any arise), and for the resolution of all doubts, concerning the manner how to understand, do, and execute, the things contained in this book: the parties that so doubt, or diversely take any thing, shall always resort to the Bishop of the Diocese, who by his discretion shall take order for the quieting and appeasing of the same; so that the same order be not contrary to any thing contained in this book.

Though it be appointed in the afore written preface, that all things shall be read and sung in the church in the English tongue, to the end that the congregation may be thereby edified: yet it is not meant, but when men say Matins and Evensong privately, they may say the same in any language that they themselves do understand. Neither that any man shall be bound to the saying of them, but such as from time to time, in Cathedral and Collegiate churches, parish Churches, and Chapels to the same annexed, shall serve the congregation.

# Articles of Religion

*as established by the Bishops, the Clergy, and the Laity
of the Protestant Episcopal Church in the United States
of America, in Convention, on the twelfth
day of September, in the Year of our Lord, 1801.*

### I. Of Faith in the Holy Trinity.

There is but one living and true God, everlasting, without body, parts, or passions; of infinite power, wisdom, and goodness; the Maker, and Preserver of all things both visible and invisible. And in unity of this Godhead there be three Persons, of one substance, power, and eternity; the Father, the Son, and the Holy Ghost.

## II. Of the Word or Son of God, which was made very Man.

The Son, which is the Word of the Father, begotten from everlasting of the Father, the very and eternal God, and of one substance with the Father, took Man's nature in the womb of the blessed Virgin, of her substance: so that two whole and perfect Natures, that is to say, the Godhead and Manhood, were joined together in one Person, never to be divided, whereof is one Christ, very God, and very Man; who truly suffered, was crucified, dead, and buried, to reconcile his Father to us, and to be a sacrifice, not only for original guilt, but also for actual sins of men.

## III. Of the going down of Christ into Hell.

As Christ died for us, and was buried; so also is it to be believed, that he went down into Hell.

## IV. Of the Resurrection of Christ.

Christ did truly rise again from death, and took again his body, with flesh, bones, and all things appertaining to the perfection of Man's nature; wherewith he ascended into Heaven, and there sitteth, until he return to judge all Men at the last day.

## V. Of the Holy Ghost.

The Holy Ghost, proceeding from the Father and the Son, is of one substance, majesty, and glory, with the Father and the Son, very and eternal God.

## VI. Of the Sufficiency of the Holy Scriptures for Salvation.

Holy Scripture containeth all things necessary to salvation: so that whatsoever is not read therein, nor may be proved thereby, is not to be required of any man, that it should be believed as an article of the Faith, or be thought requisite or necessary to salvation. In the name of the Holy Scripture we do understand those canonical Books of the Old and New Testament, of whose authority was never any doubt in the Church.

### Of the Names and Number of the Canonical Books.

| | | |
|---|---|---|
| Genesis, | The First Book of Samuel, | The Book of Esther, |
| Exodus, | The Second Book of Samuel, | The Book of Job, |
| Leviticus, | The First Book of Kings, | The Psalms, |
| Numbers, | The Second Book of Kings, | The Proverbs, |
| Deuteronomy, | The First Book of Chronicles, | Ecclesiastes or Preacher, |
| Joshua, | The Second Book of Chronicles, | Cantica, or Songs of Solomon, |
| Judges, | The First Book of Esdras, | Four Prophets the greater, |
| Ruth, | The Second Book of Esdras, | Twelve Prophets the less. |

And the other Books (as Hierome saith) the Church doth read for example of life and instruction of manners; but yet doth it not apply them to establish any doctrine; such are these following:

| | |
|---|---|
| The Third Book of Esdras, | The rest of the Book of Esther, |
| The Fourth Book of Esdras, | The Book of Wisdom, |
| The Book of Tobias, | Jesus the Son of Sirach, |
| The Book of Judith, | Baruch the Prophet, |

The Song of the Three Children,    The Prayer of Manasses,
The Story of Susanna,              The First Book of Maccabees,
Of Bel and the Dragon,            The Second Book of Maccabees.

All the Books of the New Testament, as they are commonly received, we do receive, and account them Canonical.

## II. Of the Old Testament.

The Old Testament is not contrary to the New: for both in the Old and New Testament everlasting life is offered to Mankind by Christ, who is the only Mediator between God and Man, being both God and Man. Wherefore they are not to be heard, which feign that the old Fathers did look only for transitory promises. Although the Law given from God by Moses, as touching Ceremonies and Rites, do not bind Christian men, nor the Civil precepts thereof ought of necessity to be received in any commonwealth; yet notwithstanding, no Christian man whatsoever is free from the obedience of the Commandments which are called Moral.

## III. Of the Creeds.

The Nicene Creed, and that which is commonly called the Apostles' Creed, ought thoroughly to be received and believed: for they may be proved by most certain warrants of Holy Scripture.

*The original Article given Royal assent in 1571 and reaffirmed in 1662, was entitled "Of the Three Creeds; and began as follows,"The Three Creeds, Nicene Creed, Athanasius's Creed, and that which is commonly called the Apostles' Creed . . ."*

## IV. Of Original or Birth-Sin.

Original sin standeth not in the following of Adam, (as the Pelagians do vainly talk;) but it is the fault and corruption of the Nature of every man, that naturally is engendered of the offspring of Adam; whereby man is very far gone from original righteousness, and is of his own nature inclined to evil, so that the flesh lusteth always contrary to the Spirit; and therefore in every person born into this world, it deserveth God's wrath and damnation. And this infection of nature doth remain, yea in them that are regenerated; whereby the lust of the flesh, called in Greek, φρόνημα σαρκός, (which some do expound the wisdom, some sensuality, some the affection, some the desire, of the flesh), is not subject to the Law of God. And although there is no condemnation for them that believe and are baptized; yet the Apostle doth confess, that concupiscence and lust hath of itself the nature of sin.

## Of Free-Will.

The condition of Man after the fall of Adam is such, that he cannot turn and prepare himself, by his own natural strength and good works, to faith; and calling upon God. Therefore we have no power to do good works pleasant and acceptable to God, without the grace of God by Christ preventing us, that we may have a good will, and working with us when we have that good will.

### XI. Of the Justification of Man.

We are accounted righteous before God, only for the merit of our Lord and Saviour Jesus Christ by Faith, and not for our own works or deservings. Wherefore, that we are justified by Faith only, is a most wholesome Doctrine, and very full of comfort, as more largely is expressed in the Homily of Justification.

### XII. Of Good Works.

Albeit that Good Works, which are the fruits of Faith, and follow after Justification, cannot put away our sins, and endure the severity of God's judgment; yet are they pleasing and acceptable to God in Christ, and do spring out necessarily of a true and lively Faith; insomuch that by them a lively Faith may be as evidently known as a tree discerned by the fruit.

### XIII. Of Works before Justification.

Works done before the grace of Christ, and the Inspiration of his Spirit, are not pleasant to God, forasmuch as they spring not of faith in Jesus Christ; neither do they make men meet to receive grace, or (as the School-authors say) deserve grace of congruity: yea rather, for that they are not done as God hath willed and commanded them to be done, we doubt not but they have the nature of sin.

### XIV. Of Works of Supererogation.

Voluntary Works besides, over and above, God's Commandments, which they call Works of Supererogation, cannot be taught without arrogancy and impiety: for by them men do declare, that they do not only render unto God as much as they are bound to do, but that they do more for his sake, than of bounden duty is required: whereas Christ saith plainly, When ye have done all that are commanded to you, say, We are unprofitable servants.

### XV. Of Christ alone without Sin.

Christ in the truth of our nature was made like unto us in all things, sin only except, from which he was clearly void, both in his flesh, and in his spirit. He came to be the Lamb without spot, who, by sacrifice of himself once made, should take away the sins of the world; and sin (as Saint John saith) was not in him. But all we the rest, although baptized, and born again in Christ, yet offend in many things; and if we say we have no sin, we deceive ourselves, and the truth is not in us.

### XVI. Of Sin after Baptism.

Not every deadly sin willingly committed after Baptism is sin against the Holy Ghost, and unpardonable. Wherefore the grant of repentance is not to be denied to such as fall into sin after Baptism. After we have received the Holy Ghost, we may depart from grace given, and fall into sin, and by the grace of God we may arise again, and amend our lives. And therefore they are to be condemned, which say, they can no more sin as long as they live here, or deny the place of forgiveness to such as truly repent.

# XVII. Of Predestination and Election.

Predestination to Life is the everlasting purpose of God, whereby (before the foundations of the world were laid) he hath constantly decreed by his counsel secret to us, to deliver from curse and damnation those whom he hath chosen in Christ out of mankind, and to bring them by Christ to everlasting salvation, as vessels made to honour. Wherefore, they which be endued with so excellent a benefit of God, be called according to God's purpose by his Spirit working in due season: they through Grace obey the calling: they be justified freely: they be made sons of God by adoption: they be made like the image of his only-begotten Son Jesus Christ: they walk religiously in good works, and at length, by God's mercy, they attain to everlasting felicity.

As the godly consideration of Predestination, and our Election in Christ, is full of sweet, pleasant, and unspeakable comfort to godly persons, and such as feel in themselves the working of the Spirit of Christ, mortifying the works of the flesh, and their earthly members, and drawing up their mind to high and heavenly things, as well because it doth greatly stablish and confirm their faith of eternal Salvation to be enjoyed through Christ, as because it doth fervently kindle their love towards God: So, for curious and carnal persons, lacking the Spirit of Christ, to have continually before their eyes the sentence of God's Predestination, is a most dangerous downfall, whereby the Devil doth thrust them either into desperation, or into wretchlessness of most unclean living, no less perilous than desperation.

Furthermore, we must receive God's promises in such wise, as they be generally set forth to us in Holy Scripture: and, in our doings, that Will of God is to be followed, which we have expressly declared unto us in the Word of God.

# XVIII. Of obtaining eternal Salvation only by the Name of Christ.

They also are to be had accursed that presume to say, That every man shall be saved by the Law or Sect which he professeth, so that he be diligent to frame his life according to that Law, and the light of Nature. For Holy Scripture doth set out unto us only the Name of Jesus Christ, whereby men must be saved.

# XIX. Of the Church.

The visible Church of Christ is a congregation of faithful men, in which the pure Word of God is preached, and the Sacraments be duly ministered according to Christ's ordinance, in all those things that of necessity are requisite to the same.

As the Church of Jerusalem, Alexandria, and Antioch, have erred; so also the Church of Rome hath erred, not only in their living and manner of Ceremonies, but also in matters of Faith.

# XX. Of the Authority of the Church.

The Church hath power to decree Rites or Ceremonies, and authority in Controversies of Faith: and yet it is not lawful for the Church to ordain any thing that is contrary to God's Word written, neither may it so expound one place of Scripture, that it be repugnant to another. Wherefore, although the Church be a witness and a keeper of Holy Writ, yet, as it ought not to decree any thing against the same, so besides the same ought it not to enforce any thing to be believed for necessity of Salvation.

### XXI. Of the Authority of General Councils.

[The Twenty-first of the former Articles is omitted; because it is partly of a local and civil nature, and is provided for, as to the remaining parts of it, in other Articles.]

*The original 1571, 1662 text of this Article, omitted in the version of 1801, reads as follows:"General Councils may not be gathered together without the commandment and will of Princes. And when they be gathered together, (forasmuch as they be an assembly of men, whereof all be not governed with the Spirit and Word of God,) they may err, and sometimes have erred, even in things pertaining unto God. Wherefore things ordained by them as necessary to salvation have neither strength nor authority, unless it may be declared that they be taken out of holy Scripture."*

### XXII. Of Purgatory.

The Romish Doctrine concerning Purgatory, Pardons, Worshipping and Adoration, as well of Images as of Relics, and also Invocation of Saints, is a fond thing, vainly invented, and grounded upon no warranty of Scripture, but rather repugnant to the Word of God.

### XXIII. Of Ministering in the Congregation.

It is not lawful for any man to take upon him the office of public preaching, or ministering the Sacraments in the Congregation, before he be lawfully called, and sent to execute the same. And those we ought to judge lawfully called and sent, which be chosen and called to this work by men who have public authority given unto them in the Congregation, to call and send Ministers into the Lord's vineyard.

### XXIV. Of Speaking in the Congregation in such a Tongue as the people understandeth.

It is a thing plainly repugnant to the Word of God, and the custom of the Primitive Church, to have public Prayer in the Church, or to minister the Sacraments, in a tongue not understanded of the people.

### XXV. Of the Sacraments.

Sacraments ordained of Christ be not only badges or tokens of Christian men's profession, but rather they be certain sure witnesses, and effectual signs of grace, and God's good will towards us, by the which he doth work invisibly in us, and doth not only quicken, but also strengthen and confirm our Faith in him.

There are two Sacraments ordained of Christ our Lord in the Gospel, that is to say, Baptism, and the Supper of the Lord.

Those five commonly called Sacraments, that is to say, Confirmation, Penance, Orders, Matrimony, and Extreme Unction, are not to be counted for Sacraments of the Gospel, being such as have grown partly of the corrupt following of the Apostles, partly are states of life allowed in the Scriptures; but yet have not like nature of Sacraments with Baptism, and the Lord's Supper, for that they have not any visible sign or ceremony ordained of God.

The Sacraments were not ordained of Christ to be gazed upon, or to be carried about, but that we should duly use them. And in such only as worthily receive the same, they have a wholesome effect or operation: but they that receive them unworthily, purchase to themselves damnation, as Saint Paul saith.

## XXVI. Of the Unworthiness of the Ministers, which hinders not the effect of the Sacraments.

Although in the visible Church the evil be ever mingled with the good, and sometimes the evil have chief authority in the Ministration of the Word and Sacraments, yet forasmuch as they do not the same in their own name, but in Christ's, and do minister by his commission and authority, we may use their Ministry, both in hearing the Word of God, and in receiving the Sacraments. Neither is the effect of Christ's ordinance taken away by their wickedness, nor the grace of God's gifts diminished from such as by faith, and rightly, do receive the Sacraments ministered unto them; which be effectual, because of Christ's institution and promise, although they be ministered by evil men.

Nevertheless, it appertaineth to the discipline of the Church, that inquiry be made of evil Ministers, and that they be accused by those that have knowledge of their offences; and finally, being found guilty, by just judgment be deposed.

## XXVII. Of Baptism.

Baptism is not only a sign of profession, and mark of difference, whereby Christian men are discerned from others that be not christened, but it is also a sign of Regeneration or New-Birth, whereby, as by an instrument, they that receive Baptism rightly are grafted into the Church; the promises of the forgiveness of sin, and of our adoption to be the sons of God by the Holy Ghost, are visibly signed and sealed; Faith is confirmed, and Grace increased by virtue of prayer unto God.

The Baptism of young Children is in any wise to be retained in the Church, as most agreeable with the institution of Christ.

## XXVIII. Of the Lord's Supper.

The Supper of the Lord is not only a sign of the love that Christians ought to have among themselves one to another; but rather it is a Sacrament of our Redemption by Christ's death: insomuch that to such as rightly, worthily, and with faith, receive the same, the Bread which we break is a partaking of the Body of Christ; and likewise the Cup of Blessing is a partaking of the Blood of Christ.

Transubstantiation (or the change of the substance of Bread and Wine) in the Supper of the Lord, cannot be proved by Holy Writ; but is repugnant to the plain words of Scripture, overthroweth the nature of a Sacrament, and hath given occasion to many superstitions.

The Body of Christ is given, taken, and eaten, in the Supper, only after an heavenly and spiritual manner. And the mean whereby the Body of Christ is received and eaten in the Supper, is Faith.

The Sacrament of the Lord's Supper was not by Christ's ordinance reserved, carried about, lifted up, or worshipped.

## XXIX. Of the Wicked, which eat not the Body of Christ in the use of the Lord's Supper.

The Wicked, and such as be void of a lively faith, although they do carnally and visibly press with their teeth (as Saint Augustine saith) the Sacrament of the Body and Blood of Christ; yet in no wise are they partakers of Christ: but rather, to their condemnation, do eat and drink the sign or Sacrament of so great a thing.

### XXX. Of both Kinds.

The Cup of the Lord is not to be denied to the Lay-people: for both the parts of the Lord's Sacrament, by Christ's ordinance and commandment, ought to be ministered to all Christian men alike.

### XXXI. Of the one Oblation of Christ finished upon the Cross.

The Offering of Christ once made is that perfect redemption, propitiation, and satisfaction, for all the sins of the whole world, both original and actual; and there is none other satisfaction for sin, but that alone. Wherefore the sacrifices of Masses, in the which it was commonly said, that the Priest did offer Christ for the quick and the dead, to have remission of pain or guilt, were blasphemous fables, and dangerous deceits.

### XXXII. Of the Marriage of Priests.

Bishops, Priests, and Deacons, are not commanded by God's Law, either to vow the estate of single life, or to abstain from marriage: therefore it is lawful for them, as for all other Christian men, to marry at their own discretion, as they shall judge the same to serve better to godliness.

### XXXIII. Of excommunicate Persons, how they are to be avoided.

That person which by open denunciation of the Church is rightly cut off from the unity of the Church, and excommunicated, ought to be taken of the whole multitude of the faithful, as an Heathen and Publican, until he be openly reconciled by penance, and received into the Church by a Judge that hath authority thereunto.

### XXXIV. Of the Traditions of the Church.

It is not necessary that Traditions and Ceremonies be in all places one, or utterly like; for at all times they have been divers, and may be changed according to the diversity of countries, times, and men's manners, so that nothing be ordained against God's Word. Whosoever through his private judgment, willingly and purposely, doth openly break the Traditions and Ceremonies of the Church, which be not repugnant to the Word of God, and be ordained and approved by common authority, ought to be rebuked openly, (that others may fear to do the like,) as he that offendeth against the common order of the Church, and hurteth the authority of the Magistrate, and woundeth the consciences of the weak brethren.

Every particular or national Church hath authority to ordain, change, and abolish, Ceremonies or Rites of the Church ordained only by man's authority, so that all things be done to edifying.

### XXXV. Of the Homilies.

The Second Book of Homilies, the several titles whereof we have joined under this Article, doth contain a godly and wholesome Doctrine, and necessary for these times, as doth the former Book of Homilies, which were set forth in the time of Edward the Sixth; and therefore we judge them to be read in Churches by the Ministers, diligently and distinctly, that they may be understanded of the people.

### Of the Names of the Homilies.

[This Article is received in this Church, so far as it declares the Books of Homilies to be an explication of Christian doctrine, and instructive in piety and morals. But all references to the constitution and laws of England are considered as inapplicable to the circumstances of this Church; which also suspends the order for the reading of said Homilies in churches, until a revision of them may be conveniently made, for the clearing of them, as well from obsolete words and phrases, as from the local references.]

## XXXVI. Of Consecration of Bishops and Ministers.

The Book of Consecration of Bishops, and Ordering of Priests and Deacons, as set forth by the General Convention of this Church in 1792, doth contain all things necessary to such Consecration and Ordering; neither hath it any thing that, of itself, is superstitious and ungodly. And, therefore, whosoever are consecrated or ordered according to said Form, we decree all such to be rightly, orderly, and lawfully consecrated and ordered.

*The original 1571, 1662 text of this Article reads as follows: "The Book of Consecration of Archbishops and Bishops, and Ordering of Priests and Deacons, lately set forth in the time of Edward the Sixth, and confirmed at the same time by authority of Parliament, doth contain all things necessary to such Consecration and Ordering; neither hath it any thing, that of itself is superstitious and ungodly. And therefore whosoever are consecrated or ordered according to the Rites of that Book, since the second year of the forenamed King Edward unto this time, or hereafter shall be consecrated or ordered according to the same Rites; we decree all such to be rightly, orderly, and lawfully consecrated and ordered."*

## XXXVII. Of the Power of the Civil Magistrates.

The Power of the Civil Magistrate extendeth to all men, as well Clergy as Laity, in all things temporal; but hath no authority in things purely spiritual. And we hold it to be the duty of all men who are professors of the Gospel, to pay respectful obedience to the Civil Authority, regularly and legitimately constituted.

*The original 1571, 1662 text of this Article reads as follows: "The King's Majesty hath the chief power in this Realm of England, and other his Dominions, unto whom the chief Government of all Estates of this Realm, whether they be Ecclesiastical or Civil, in all causes doth appertain, and is not, nor ought to be, subject to any foreign Jurisdiction. Where we attribute to the King's Majesty the chief government, by which Titles we understand the minds of some slanderous folks to be offended; we give not our Princes the ministering either of God's Word, or of the Sacraments, the which thing the Injunctions also lately set forth by Elizabeth our Queen do most plainly testify; but that only prerogative, which we see to have been given always to all godly Princes in holy Scriptures by God himself; that is, that they should rule all estates and degrees committed to their charge by God, whether they be Ecclesiastical or Temporal, and restrain with the civil sword the stubborn and evil-doers.*

*The Bishop of Rome hath no jurisdiction in this Realm of England.*

*The Laws of the Realm may punish Christian men with death, for heinous and grievous offences.*

*It is lawful for Christian men, at the commandment of the Magistrate, to wear weapons, and serve in the wars."*

### XXXVIII. Of Christian Men's Goods, which are not common.

The Riches and Goods of Christians are not common, as touching the right, title, and possession of the same; as certain Anabaptists do falsely boast. Notwithstanding, every man ought, of such things as he possesseth, liberally to give alms to the poor, according to his ability.

### XXXIX. Of a Christian Man's Oath.

As we confess that vain and rash Swearing is forbidden Christian men by our Lord Jesus Christ, and James his Apostle, so we judge, that Christian Religion doth not prohibit, but that a man may swear when the Magistrate requireth, in a cause of faith and charity, so it be done according to the Prophet's teaching in justice, judgment, and truth.


# The Chicago-Lambeth Quadrilateral 1886, 1888

## Adopted by the House of Bishops
## Chicago, 1886

We, Bishops of the Protestant Episcopal Church in the United States of America, in Council assembled as Bishops in the Church of God, do hereby solemnly declare to all whom it may concern, and especially to our fellow-Christians of the different Communions in this land, who, in their several spheres, have contended for the religion of Christ:

1.   Our earnest desire that the Saviour's prayer, "That we all may be one," may, in its deepest and truest sense, be speedily fulfilled;

2.   That we believe that all who have been duly baptized with water, in the name of the Father, and of the Son, and of the Holy Ghost, are members of the Holy Catholic Church;

3.   That in all things of human ordering or human choice, relating to modes of worship and discipline, or to traditional customs, this Church is ready in the spirit of love and humility to forego all preferences of her own;

.. That this Church does not seek to absorb other Communions, but rather, co-operating with them on the basis of a common Faith and Order, to discountenance schism, to heal the wounds of the Body of Christ, and to promote the charity which is the chief of Christian graces and the visible manifestation of Christ to the world;

but furthermore, we do hereby affirm that the Christian unity . . . can be restored only by the return of all Christian communions to the principles of unity exemplified by the undivided Catholic Church during the first ages of its existence; which principles we believe to be the substantial deposit of Christian Faith and Order committed by Christ and his apostles to the Church unto the end of the world, and therefore incapable of compromise or surrender by those who have been ordained to be its stewards and trustees for the common and equal benefit of all men.

s inherent parts of this sacred deposit, and therefore as essential to the restoration of unity among the divided branches of Christendom, we account the following, to wit:

The Holy Scriptures of the Old and New Testament as the revealed Word of God.

The Nicene Creed as the sufficient statement of the Christian Faith.

The two Sacraments, — Baptism and the Supper of the Lord, — ministered with unfailing use of Christ's words of institution and of the elements ordained by Him.

The Historic Episcopate, locally adapted in the methods of its administration to the varying needs of the nations and peoples called of God into the unity of His Church.

Furthermore, Deeply grieved by the sad divisions which affect the Christian Church in our own land, we hereby declare our desire and readiness, so soon as there shall be any authorized response to this Declaration, to enter into brotherly conference with all or any Christian Bodies seeking the restoration of the organic unity of the Church, with a view to the earnest study of the conditions under which so priceless a blessing might happily be brought to pass.

Note: While the above form of the Quadrilateral was adopted by the House of Bishops, it was not enacted by the House of Deputies, but rather incorporated in a general plan referred for study and action to a newly created Joint Commission on Christian Reunion.

## Lambeth Conference of 1888
### Resolution 11

That, in the opinion of this Conference, the following Articles supply a basis on which approach may be by God's blessing made towards Home Reunion:

The Holy Scriptures of the Old and New Testaments, as "containing all things necessary to salvation," and as being the rule and ultimate standard of faith.

The Apostles' Creed, as the Baptismal Symbol; and the Nicene Creed, as the sufficient statement of the Christian faith.

(c) The two Sacraments ordained by Christ Himself — Baptism and the Supper of the Lord — ministered with unfailing use of Christ's words of Institution, and of the elements ordained by Him.

(d) The Historic Episcopate, locally adapted in the methods of its administration to the varying needs of the nations and peoples called of God into the Unity of His Church.

# Tables for Finding Holy Days

# Tables and Rules for Finding the Date of Easter Day

## Rules for Finding the Date of Easter Day

Easter Day is always the Sunday after the full moon that occurs on or after the spring equinox on March 21, a date which is fixed in accordance with an ancient ecclesiastical computation, and which does not always correspond to the astronomical equinox. This full moon may happen on any date between March 21 and April 18 inclusive. If the full moon falls on a Sunday, Easter Day is the Sunday following. But Easter Day cannot be earlier than March 22 or later than April 25.

To find the date of Easter Day in any particular year, it is necessary to have two points of reference—the Golden Number and the Sunday Letter for that year.

**1. The Golden Number** indicates the date of the full moon on or after the spring equinox of March 21, according to a nineteen-year cycle. These Numbers are prefixed in the Calendar to the days of the month from March 22 to April 18 inclusive. In the present Calendar they are applicable from A.D. 1900 to A.D. 2099, after which they will change.

**2. The Sunday Letter** identifies the days of the year when Sundays occur. After every date in the Calendar a letter appears—from A to g. Thus, if January 1 is a Sunday, the Sunday Letter for the year is A, and every date in the Calendar marked by A is a Sunday. If January 2 is a Sunday, then every date marked with b is a Sunday, and so on through the seven letters.

In Leap Years, however, the Sunday Letter changes on the first day of March. In such years, when A is the Sunday Letter, this applies only to Sundays in January and February, and g is the Sunday Letter for the rest of the year. Or if d is the Sunday Letter, then c is the Sunday Letter on and after March 1.

### To Find the Golden Number

The Golden Number of any year is calculated as follows: Take the number of the year, add 1, and then divide the sum by 19. The remainder, if any, is the Golden Number. If nothing remains, then 19 is the Golden Number.

### To Find the Sunday Letter

The following Table provides ready reference to the Sunday Letter of any year between A.D. 1900 and A.D. 2099. It will be found on the line of the hundredth year above the column that contains the remaining digits of the year. But in Leap Years the Letter above the number marked with an asterisk is the Sunday Letter for January and February, and the Letter over the number not so marked is the Sunday Letter for the rest of the year.

| Hundred Years: | 1900 | | g | f | e | d | c | b | A |
|---|---|---|---|---|---|---|---|---|---|
| | 2000 | b | A | g | f | e | d | c | b |
| Years in Excess of Hundreds | 00* | 00 | 01 | 02 | 03 | 04* | 04 | 05 |
| | | 06 | 07 | 08* | 08 | 09 | 10 | 11 |
| | | 12* | 12 | 13 | 14 | 15 | 16* | 16 |
| | | 17 | 18 | 19 | 20* | 20 | 21 | 22 |
| | | 23 | 24* | 24 | 25 | 26 | 27 | 28* |
| | | 28 | 29 | 30 | 31 | 32* | 32 | 33 |
| | | 34 | 35 | 36* | 36 | 37 | 38 | 39 |
| | | 40* | 40 | 41 | 42 | 43 | 44* | 44 |
| | | 45 | 46 | 47 | 48* | 48 | 49 | 50 |
| | | 51 | 52* | 52 | 53 | 54 | 55 | 56* |
| | | 56 | 57 | 58 | 59 | 60* | 60 | 61 |
| | | 62 | 63 | 64* | 64 | 65 | 66 | 67 |
| | | 68* | 68 | 69 | 70 | 71 | 72* | 72 |
| | | 73 | 74 | 75 | 76* | 76 | 77 | 78 |
| | | 79 | 80* | 80 | 81 | 82 | 83 | 84* |
| | | 84 | 85 | 86 | 87 | 88* | 88 | 89 |
| | | 90 | 91 | 92* | 92 | 93 | 94 | 95 |
| | 96* | 96 | 97 | 98 | 99 | | | |

## To Find Easter Day

When one has both the Golden Number and the Sunday Letter for any particular year, then the date of Easter Day may be found in the Calendar, pages 21 and 22, as follows:

. The Golden Number prefixed to a day in the month of March or of April in the Calendar marks the date of the full moon in that year.

. Easter Day will be the next date bearing the Sunday Letter of that year. But when the Golden Number of a given year and the Sunday Letter of that year occur on the same date, hen Easter day is one week later. (For example, if the Golden Number is 19—which appears in the Calendar prefixed to March 27—and the Sunday Letter is d, then Easter Day that year will fall on March 29. If the Golden Number is 10 and the Sunday Letter is A, hen Easter Day will fall on April 9. But if the Golden Number is 19 and the Sunday Letter b, then Easter Day will be one week later, namely April 3.)

# A Table to Find Easter Day

| Golden Number | Year | Easter Day | Year | Easter Day | Year | Easter Day |
|---|---|---|---|---|---|---|
| 1 | 1900 | April 15 | 1938 | April 17 | 1976* | April 18 |
| 2 | 1901 | April 7 | 1939 | April 9 | 1977 | April 10 |
| 3 | 1902 | March 30 | 1940* | March 24 | 1978 | March 26 |
| 4 | 1903 | April 12 | 1941 | April 13 | 1979 | April 15 |
| 5 | 1904* | April 3 | 1942 | April 5 | 1980* | April 6 |
| 6 | 1905 | April 23 | 1943 | April 25 | 1981 | April 19 |
| 7 | 1906 | April 15 | 1944* | April 9 | 1982 | April 11 |
| 8 | 1907 | March 31 | 1945 | April 1 | 1983 | April 3 |
| 9 | 1908* | April 19 | 1946 | April 21 | 1984* | April 22 |
| 10 | 1909 | April 11 | 1947 | April 6 | 1985 | April 7 |
| 11 | 1910 | March 27 | 1948* | March 28 | 1986 | March 30 |
| 12 | 1911 | April 16 | 1949 | April 17 | 1987 | April 19 |
| 13 | 1912* | April 7 | 1950 | April 9 | 1988* | April 3 |
| 14 | 1913 | March 23 | 1951 | March 25 | 1989 | March 26 |
| 15 | 1914 | April 12 | 1952* | April 13 | 1990 | April 15 |
| 16 | 1915 | April 4 | 1953 | April 5 | 1991 | March 31 |
| 17 | 1916* | April 23 | 1954 | April 18 | 1992* | April 19 |
| 18 | 1917 | April 8 | 1955 | April 10 | 1993 | April 11 |
| 19 | 1918 | March 31 | 1956* | April 1 | 1994 | April 3 |
| | | | | | | |
| 1 | 1919 | April 20 | 1957 | April 21 | 1995 | April 16 |
| 2 | 1920* | April 4 | 1958 | April 6 | 1996* | April 7 |
| 3 | 1921 | March 27 | 1959 | March 29 | 1997 | March 30 |
| 4 | 1922 | April 16 | 1960* | April 17 | 1998 | April 12 |
| 5 | 1923 | April 1 | 1961 | April 2 | 1999 | April 4 |
| 6 | 1924* | April 20 | 1962 | April 22 | 2000* | April 23 |
| 7 | 1925 | April 12 | 1963 | April 14 | 2001 | April 15 |
| 8 | 1926 | April 4 | 1964* | March 29 | 2002 | March 31 |
| 9 | 1927 | April 17 | 1965 | April 18 | 2003 | April 20 |
| 10 | 1928* | April 8 | 1966 | April 10 | 2004* | April 11 |
| 11 | 1929 | March 31 | 1967 | March 26 | 2005 | March 27 |
| 12 | 1930 | April 20 | 1968* | April 14 | 2006 | April 16 |
| 13 | 1931 | April 5 | 1969 | April 6 | 2007 | April 8 |
| 14 | 1932* | March 27 | 1970 | March 29 | 2008* | March 23 |
| 15 | 1933 | April 16 | 1971 | April 11 | 2009 | April 12 |
| 16 | 1934 | April 1 | 1972* | April 2 | 2010 | April 4 |
| 17 | 1935 | April 21 | 1973 | April 22 | 2011 | April 24 |
| 18 | 1936* | April 12 | 1974 | April 14 | 2012* | April 8 |
| 19 | 1937 | March 28 | 1975 | March 30 | 2013 | March 31 |

# A Table to Find Easter Day

| Golden Number | Year | Easter Day | Year | Easter Day |
|---|---|---|---|---|
| 1 | 2014 | April 20 | 2052* | April 21 |
| 2 | 2015 | April 5 | 2053 | April 6 |
| 3 | 2016* | March 27 | 2054 | March 29 |
| 4 | 2017 | April 16 | 2055 | April 18 |
| 5 | 2018 | April 1 | 2056* | April 2 |
| 6 | 2019 | April 21 | 2057 | April 22 |
| 7 | 2020* | April 12 | 2058 | April 14 |
| 8 | 2021 | April 4 | 2059 | March 30 |
| 9 | 2022 | April 17 | 2060* | April 18 |
| 10 | 2023 | April 9 | 2061 | April 10 |
| 11 | 2024* | March 31 | 2062 | March 26 |
| 12 | 2025 | April 20 | 2063 | April 15 |
| 13 | 2026 | April 5 | 2064* | April 6 |
| 14 | 2027 | March 28 | 2065 | March 29 |
| 15 | 2028* | April 16 | 2066 | April 11 |
| 16 | 2029 | April 1 | 2067 | April 3 |
| 17 | 2030 | April 21 | 2068* | April 22 |
| 18 | 2031 | April 13 | 2069 | April 14 |
| 19 | 2032* | March 28 | 2070 | March 30 |
| 1 | 2033 | April 17 | 2071 | April 19 |
| 2 | 2034 | April 9 | 2072* | April 10 |
| 3 | 2035 | March 25 | 2073 | March 26 |
| 4 | 2036* | April 13 | 2074 | April 15 |
| 5 | 2037 | April 5 | 2075 | April 7 |
| 6 | 2038 | April 25 | 2076* | April 19 |
| 7 | 2039 | April 10 | 2077 | April 11 |
| 8 | 2040* | April 1 | 2078 | April 3 |
| 9 | 2041 | April 21 | 2079 | April 23 |
| 10 | 2042 | April 6 | 2080* | April 7 |
| 11 | 2043 | March 29 | 2081 | March 30 |
| 12 | 2044* | April 17 | 2082 | April 19 |
| 13 | 2045 | April 9 | 2083 | April 4 |
| 14 | 2046 | March 25 | 2084* | March 26 |
| 15 | 2047 | April 14 | 2085 | April 15 |
| 16 | 2048* | April 5 | 2086 | March 31 |
| 17 | 2049 | April 18 | 2087 | April 20 |
| 18 | 2050 | April 10 | 2088* | April 11 |
| 19 | 2051 | April 2 | 2089 | April 3 |

*The years marked with an asterisk are Leap Years.

# A Table to Find Movable Feasts and Holy Days

| Easter Day | Sundays after Epiphany* | Ash Wednesday† | Ascension Day | Pentecost | Numbered Proper of 2 Pentecost‡ | Advent Sunday |
|---|---|---|---|---|---|---|
| March 22 | 4 | Feb. 4 | April 30 | May 10 | #3 | November 29 |
| March 23 | 4 | Feb. 5 | May 1 | May 11 | #3 | November 30 |
| March 24 | 4 | Feb. 6 | May 2 | May 12 | #3 | December 1 |
| March 25 | 5 | Feb. 7 | May 3 | May 13 | #3 | December 2 |
| March 26 | 5 | Feb. 8 | May 4 | May 14 | #3 | December 3 |
| March 27 | 5 | Feb. 9 | May 5 | May 15 | #4 | November 27 |
| March 28 | 5 | Feb. 10 | May 6 | May 16 | #4 | November 28 |
| March 29 | 5 | Feb. 11 | May 7 | May 17 | #4 | November 29 |
| March 30 | 5 | Feb. 12 | May 8 | May 18 | #4 | November 30 |
| March 31 | 5 | Feb. 13 | May 9 | May 19 | #4 | December 1 |
| April 1 | 6 | Feb. 14 | May 10 | May 20 | #4 | December 2 |
| April 2 | 6 | Feb. 15 | May 11 | May 21 | #4 | December 3 |
| April 3 | 6 | Feb. 16 | May 12 | May 22 | #5 | November 27 |
| April 4 | 6 | Feb. 17 | May 13 | May 23 | #5 | November 28 |
| April 5 | 6 | Feb. 18 | May 14 | May 24 | #5 | November 29 |
| April 6 | 6 | Feb. 19 | May 15 | May 25 | #5 | November 30 |
| April 7 | 6 | Feb. 20 | May 16 | May 26 | #5 | December 1 |

* In Leap Years, the number of Sundays after the Epiphany will be the same as if Easter Day were one day later than in the above Table.

† In Leap Years, the date of Ash Wednesday will be one day later in the month of February than in the above Table.

‡ Indicates the numbered Proper to be used on the Sunday after Trinity Sunday. Subsequently, the Propers are used consecutively.

| Easter Day | Sundays after Epiphany* | Ash Wednesday† | Ascension Day | Pentecost | Numbered Proper of 2 Pentecost‡ | Advent Sunday |
|---|---|---|---|---|---|---|
| April 8 | 7 | Feb. 21 | May 17 | May 27 | #5 | December 2 |
| April 9 | 7 | Feb. 22 | May 18 | May 28 | #5 | December 3 |
| April 10 | 7 | Feb. 23 | May 19 | May 29 | #6 | November 27 |
| April 11 | 7 | Feb. 24 | May 20 | May 30 | #6 | November 28 |
| April 12 | 7 | Feb. 25 | May 21 | May 31 | #6 | November 29 |
| April 13 | 7 | Feb. 26 | May 22 | June 1 | #6 | November 30 |
| April 14 | 7 | Feb. 27 | May 23 | June 2 | #6 | December 1 |
| April 15 | 8 | Feb. 28 | May 24 | June 3 | #6 | December 2 |
| April 16 | 8 | March 1 | May 25 | June 4 | #6 | December 3 |
| April 17 | 8 | March 2 | May 26 | June 5 | #7 | November 27 |
| April 18 | 8 | March 3 | May 27 | June 6 | #7 | November 28 |
| April 19 | 8 | March 4 | May 28 | June 7 | #7 | November 29 |
| April 20 | 8 | March 5 | May 29 | June 8 | #7 | November 30 |
| April 21 | 8 | March 6 | May 30 | June 9 | #7 | December 1 |
| April 22 | 9 | March 7 | May 31 | June 10 | #7 | December 2 |
| April 23 | 9 | March 8 | June 1 | June 11 | #7 | December 3 |
| April 24 | 9 | March 9 | June 2 | June 12 | #8 | November 27 |
| April 25 | 9 | March 10 | June 3 | June 13 | #8 | November 28 |

*In Leap Years, the number of Sundays after the Epiphany will be the same as if Easter Day were one day later than in the above Table.

†In Leap Years, the date of Ash Wednesday will be one day later in the month of February than in the above Table.

‡Indicates the numbered Proper to be used on the Sunday after Trinity Sunday. Subsequently, the Propers are used consecutively.

# The Lectionary

# Concerning the Lectionary

The Lectionary for Sundays is arranged in a three-year cycle, in which Year A always begins on the First Sunday of Advent in years evenly divisible by three. (For example, 1977 divided by 3 is 659 with no remainder. Year A, therefore, begins on Advent Sunday of that year.)

The Psalms and Lessons appointed for the Sundays and for other major Holy Days are intended for use at all public services on such days, except when the same congregation attends two or more services. Thus, the same Lessons are to be read at the principal morning service, whether the Liturgy of the Word takes the form given in the Holy Eucharist, or that of the Daily Office.

When the same congregation is present for Morning or Evening Prayer, in addition to the Eucharist, the Lessons at the Office may be selected from one of the other years of the three-year Sunday cycle, or from the Lectionary for the Daily Office. The Psalms at such Offices are normally those appointed in the Office Lectionary; but, when desired, the Psalm cited in the selected Sunday Proper may be used instead.

In this Lectionary, the selections from the Psalter are frequently cited in a longer and shorter version, usually from the same Psalm. The longer version is particularly appropriate for use at the Office, the shorter version when the Psalm is sung between the Lessons at the Eucharist. The selection may be further lengthened or shortened at discretion.

When an alternative Lesson is cited, it is sometimes identical with a Lesson appointed for the same day in the Daily Office Lectionary.

In the opening verses of Lessons, the Reader should omit initial conjunctions which refer only to what has preceded, substitute nouns for pronouns when the referent is not otherwise clear, or else prefix to the Reading some such introduction as, "N. said (to N.)."

Any Reading may be lengthened at discretion. Suggested lengthenings are shown in parentheses.

# The Lectionary

## Year A

| | Psalm | Lessons |
|---|---|---|
| **First Sunday of Advent** | 122 | Isaiah 2:1-5<br>Romans 13:8-14<br>Matthew 24:37-44 |
| **Second Sunday of Advent** | 72<br>or 72:1-8 | Isaiah 11:1-10<br>Romans 15:4-13<br>Matthew 3:1-12 |
| **Third Sunday of Advent** | 146<br>or 146:4-9 | Isaiah 35:1-10<br>James 5:7-10<br>Matthew 11:2-11 |
| **Fourth Sunday of Advent** | 24<br>or 24:1-7 | Isaiah 7:10-17<br>Romans 1:1-7<br>Matthew 1:18-25 |
| **Christmas Day I** | 96<br>or 96:1-4,11-12 | Isaiah 9:2-4,6-7<br>Titus 2:11-14<br>Luke 2:1-14(15-20) |
| **Christmas Day II** | 97<br>or 97:1-4,11-12 | Isaiah 62:6-7,10-12<br>Titus 3:4-7<br>Luke 2:(1-14)15-20 |

|  | Psalm | Lessons |
|---|---|---|
| **Christmas Day III** | 98<br>*or* 98:1-6 | Isaiah 52:7-10<br>Hebrews 1:1-12<br>John 1:1-14 |
| **First Sunday**<br>**after Christmas** | 147<br>*or* 147:13-21 | Isaiah 61:10—62:3<br>Galatians 3:23-25;  4:4-7<br>John 1:1-18 |
| **Holy Name**<br>*January 1* | 8 | Exodus 34:1-8<br>Romans 1:1-7<br>*or* Philippians 2:9-13<br>Luke 2:15-21 |
| **Second Sunday**<br>**after Christmas** | 84<br>*or* 84:1-8 | Jeremiah 31:7-14<br>Ephesians 1:3-6,15-19a<br>Matthew 2:13-15,19-23<br>*or* Luke 2:41-52<br>*or* Matthew 2:1-12 |
| **The Epiphany**<br>*January 6* | 72<br>*or* 72:1-2,10-17 | Isaiah 60:1-6,9<br>Ephesians 3:1-12<br>Matthew 2:1-12 |
| **First Sunday**<br>**after Epiphany** | 89:1-29<br>*or* 89:20-29 | Isaiah 42:1-9<br>Acts 10:34-38<br>Matthew 3:13-17 |
| **Second Sunday**<br>**after Epiphany** | 40:1-10 | Isaiah 49:1-7<br>1 Corinthians 1:1-9<br>John 1:29-41 |
| **Third Sunday**<br>**after Epiphany** | 139:1-17<br>*or* 139:1-11 | Amos 3:1-8<br>1 Corinthians 1:10-17<br>Matthew 4:12-23 |

|  | Psalm | Lessons |
|---|---|---|
| Fourth Sunday after Epiphany | 37:1-18 *or* 37:1-6 | Micah 6:1-8<br>1 Corinthians 1:(18-25)26-31<br>Matthew 5:1-12 |
| Fifth Sunday after Epiphany | 27 *or* 27:1-7 | Habakkuk 3:2-6,17-19<br>1 Corinthians 2:1-11<br>Matthew 5:13-20 |
| Sixth Sunday after Epiphany | 119:1-16 *or* 119:9-16 | Ecclesiasticus 15:11-20<br>1 Corinthians 3:1-9<br>Matthew 5:21-24,27-30,33-37 |
| Seventh Sunday after Epiphany | 71 *or* 71:16-24 | Leviticus 19:1-2,9-18<br>1 Corinthians 3:10-11,16-23<br>Matthew 5:38-48 |
| Eighth Sunday after Epiphany | 62 *or* 62:6-14 | Isaiah 49:8-18<br>1 Corinthians 4:1-5(6-7)8-13<br>Matthew 6:24-34 |
| Last Sunday after Epiphany | 99 | Exodus 24:12(13-14)15-18<br>Philippians 3:7-14<br>Matthew 17:1-9 |
| Ash Wednesday | 103 *or* 103:8-14 | Joel 2:1-2,12-17<br>*or* Isaiah 58:1-12<br>2 Corinthians 5:20b—6:10<br>Matthew 6:1-6,16-21 |
| First Sunday in Lent | 51 *or* 51:1-13 | Genesis 2:4b-9,15-17,25—3:7<br>Romans 5:12-19(20-21)<br>Matthew 4:1-11 |
| Second Sunday in Lent | 33:12-22 | Genesis 12:1-8<br>Romans 4:1-5(6-12)13-17<br>John 3:1-17 |

|                            | Psalm            | Lessons                                             |
|----------------------------|------------------|-----------------------------------------------------|
| **Third Sunday in Lent**   | 95 *or* 95:6-11  | Exodus 17:1-7 Romans 5:1-11 John 4:5-26(27-38)39-42 |
| **Fourth Sunday in Lent**  | 23               | 1 Samuel 16:1-13 Ephesians 5:(1-7)8-14 John 9:1-13(14-27)28-38 |
| **Fifth Sunday in Lent**   | 130              | Ezekiel 37:1-3(4-10)11-14 Romans 6:16-23 **John 11:(1-16)17-44** |

**Palm Sunday**

| Liturgy of the Palms | 118:19-29 | Matthew 21:1-11 |
|---|---|---|
| Liturgy of the Word | 22:1-21 *or* 22:1-11 | Isaiah 45:21-25 *or* Isaiah 52:13—53:12 Philippians 2:5-11 Matthew (26:36-75) 27:1-54(55-66) |

| **Monday in Holy Week** | 36:5-10 | Isaiah 42:1-9 Hebrews 11:39—12:3 John 12:1-11 *or* Mark 14:3-9 |
|---|---|---|
| **Tuesday in Holy Week** | 71:1-12 | Isaiah 49:1-6 1 Corinthians 1:18-31 John 12:37-38,42-50 *or* Mark 11:15-19 |
| **Wednesday in Holy Week** | 69:7-15, 22-23 | Isaiah 50:4-9a Hebrews 9:11-15,24-28 John 13:21-35 *or* Matthew 26:1-5,14-25 |

|  | Psalm | Lessons |
|---|---|---|
| **Maundy Thursday** | 78:14-20,23-25 | Exodus 12:1-14a<br>1 Corinthians 11:23-26(27-32)<br>John 13:1-15<br>or Luke 22:14-30 |
| **Good Friday** | 22:1-21<br>or 22:1-11<br>or 40:1-14<br>or 69:1-23 | Isaiah 52:13—53:12<br>or Genesis 22:1-18<br>or Wisdom 2:1,12-24<br>Hebrews 10:1-25<br>John (18:1-40)<br>    19:1-37 |
| **Holy Saturday** | 130<br>or 31:1-5 | Job 14:1-14<br>1 Peter 4:1-8<br>Matthew 27:57-66<br>or John 19:38-42 |
| **Easter Day** | | |
| The Great Vigil | *See pages 288-291.* | |
| Early Service | *Use one of the Old Testament Lessons<br>from the Vigil with* | |
|  | 114 | Romans 6:3-11<br>Matthew 28:1-10 |
| Principal Service | 118:14-29<br>or 118:14-17,22-24 | Acts 10:34-43<br>or Exodus 14:10-14,21-25;<br>    15:20-21<br>Colossians 3:1-4<br>or Acts 10:34-43<br>John 20:1-10(11-18)<br>or Matthew 28:1-10 |
| Evening Service | 114<br>or 136<br>or 118:14-17,22-24 | Acts 5:29a,30-32<br>or Daniel 12:1-3<br>1 Corinthians 5:6b-8<br>or Acts 5:29a,30-32<br>Luke 24:13-35 |

|                            | Psalm                    | Lessons                                                                                    |
|----------------------------|--------------------------|--------------------------------------------------------------------------------------------|
| Monday in<br>Easter Week   | 16:8-11<br>*or* 118:19-24  | Acts 2:14,22b-32<br>Matthew 28:9-15                                                        |
| Tuesday in<br>Easter Week  | 33:18-22<br>*or* 118:19-24 | Acts 2:36-41<br>John 20:11-18                                                              |
| Wednesday in<br>Easter Week | 105:1-8<br>*or* 118:19-24 | Acts 3:1-10<br>Luke 24:13-35                                                               |
| Thursday in<br>Easter Week | 8 *or* 114<br>*or* 118:19-24 | Acts 3:11-26<br>Luke 24:36b-48                                                           |
| Friday in<br>Easter Week   | 116:1-8<br>*or* 118:19-24 | Acts 4:1-12<br>John 21:1-14                                                                |
| Saturday in<br>Easter Week | 118:14-18<br>*or* 118:19-24 | Acts 4:13-21<br>Mark 16:9-15,20                                                          |
| Second Sunday<br>of Easter | 111<br>*or* 118:19-24     | Acts 2:14a,22-32<br>*or* Genesis 8:6-16;  9:8-16<br>1 Peter 1:3-9<br>*or* Acts 2:14a,22-32<br>John 20:19-31 |
| Third Sunday<br>of Easter  | 116<br>*or* 116:10-17     | Acts 2:14a,36-47<br>*or* Isaiah 43:1-12<br>1 Peter 1:17-23<br>*or* Acts 2:14a,36-47<br>Luke 24:13-35 |

|  | Psalm | Lessons |
|---|---|---|
| Fourth Sunday of Easter | 23 | Acts 6:1-9; 7:2a,51-60 *or* Nehemiah 9:6-15 1 Peter 2:19-25 *or* Acts 6:1-9; 7:2a,51-60 John 10:1-10 |
| Fifth Sunday of Easter | 66:1-11 *or* 66:1-8 | Acts 17:1-15 *or* Deuteronomy 6:20-25 1 Peter 2:1-10 *or* Acts 17:1-15 John 14:1-14 |
| Sixth Sunday of Easter | 148 *or* 148:7-14 | Acts 17:22-31 *or* Isaiah 41:17-20 1 Peter 3:8-18 *or* Acts 17:22-31 John 15:1-8 |
| Ascension Day | 47 *or* 110:1-5 | Acts 1:1-11 *or* Daniel 7:9-14 Ephesians 1:15-23 *or* Acts 1:1-11 Luke 24:49-53 *or* Mark 16:9-15,19-20 |
| Seventh Sunday of Easter | 68:1-20 *or* 47 | Acts 1:(1-7)8-14 *or* Ezekiel 39:21-29 1 Peter 4:12-19 *or* Acts 1:(1-7)8-14 John 17:1-11 |

|  | Psalm | Lessons |
|---|---|---|

**Day of Pentecost**

| Early or | 33:12-22 | Genesis 11:1-9 |
|---|---|---|
| Vigil Service | Canticle 2 or 13 | *or Exodus 19:1-9a,16-20a;*<br>20:18-20 |
|  | 130 | *or Ezekiel 37:1-14* |
|  | Canticle 9 | *or Joel 2:28-32* |
|  | 104:25-32 | Acts 2:1-11 |
|  |  | *or Romans 8:14-17,22-27* |
|  |  | John 7:37-39a |

| Principal Service | 104:25-37 | Acts 2:1-11 |
|---|---|---|
|  | *or 104:25-32* | *or Ezekiel 11:17-20* |
|  | *or 33:12-15,18-22* | 1 Corinthians 12:4-13 |
|  |  | *or Acts 2:1-11* |
|  |  | John 20:19-23 |
|  |  | *or John 14:8-17* |

*On the weekdays which follow, the numbered Proper which corresponds most closely to the date of Pentecost in that year is used. See page 158.*

| Trinity Sunday | 150 | Genesis 1:1—2:3 |
|---|---|---|
|  | *or Canticle 2* | 2 Corinthians 13:(5-10)11-14 |
|  | or 13 | Matthew 28:16-20 |

*On the weekdays which follow, the numbered Proper which corresponds most closely to the date of Trinity Sunday in that year is used.*

## The Season after Pentecost

*Directions for the use of the Propers which follow are on page 158.*

| **Proper 1** | 119:1-16 | Ecclesiasticus 15:11-20 |
|---|---|---|
| *Closest to* | *or 119:9-16* | 1 Corinthians 3:1-9 |
| *May 11* |  | Matthew 5:21-24,27-30,33-37 |

|  | Psalm | Lessons |
|---|---|---|
| **Proper 2**<br>*Closest to*<br>*May 18* | 71<br>or 71:16-24 | Leviticus 19:1-2,9-18<br>1 Corinthians 3:10-11,16-23<br>Matthew 5:38-48 |
| **Proper 3**<br>*Closest to*<br>*May 25* | 62<br>or 62:6-14 | Isaiah 49:8-18<br>1 Corinthians 4:1-5(6-7)8-13<br>Matthew 6:24-34 |
| **Proper 4**<br>*Closest to*<br>*June 1* | 31<br>or 31:1-5,19-24 | Deuteronomy 11:18-21,26-28<br>Romans 3:21-25a,28<br>Matthew 7:21-27 |
| **Proper 5**<br>*Closest to*<br>*June 8* | 50<br>or 50:7-15 | Hosea 5:15—6:6<br>Romans 4:13-18<br>Matthew 9:9-13 |
| **Proper 6**<br>*Closest to*<br>*June 15* | 100 | Exodus 19:2-8a<br>Romans 5:6-11<br>Matthew 9:35—10:8(9-15) |
| **Proper 7**<br>*Closest to*<br>*June 22* | 69:1-18<br>or 69:7-10,16-18 | Jeremiah 20:7-13<br>Romans 5:15b-19<br>Matthew 10:(16-23)24-33 |
| **Proper 8**<br>*Closest to*<br>*June 29* | 89:1-18<br>or 89:1-4,15-18 | Isaiah 2:10-17<br>Romans 6:3-11<br>Matthew 10:34-42 |
| **Proper 9**<br>*Closest to*<br>*July 6* | 145<br>or 145:8-14 | Zechariah 9:9-12<br>Romans 7:21—8:6<br>Matthew 11:25-30 |
| **Proper 10**<br>*Closest to*<br>*July 13* | 65<br>or 65:9-14 | Isaiah 55:1-5,10-13<br>Romans 8:9-17<br>Matthew 13:1-9,18-23 |

|  | **Psalm** | **Lessons** |
|---|---|---|
| **Proper 11** *Closest to July 20* | 86 or 86:11-17 | Wisdom 12:13,16-19 Romans 8:18-25 Matthew 13:24-30,36-43 |
| **Proper 12** *Closest to July 27* | 119:121-136 or 119:129-136 | 1 Kings 3:5-12 Romans 8:26-34 Matthew 13:31-33,44-49a |
| **Proper 13** *Closest to August 3* | 78:1-29 or 78:14-20,23-25 | Nehemiah 9:16-20 Romans 8:35-39 Matthew 14:13-21 |
| **Proper 14** *Closest to August 10* | 29 | Jonah 2:1-9 Romans 9:1-5 Matthew 14:22-33 |
| **Proper 15** *Closest to August 17* | 67 | Isaiah 56:1(2-5)6-7 Romans 11:13-15,29-32 Matthew 15:21-28 |
| **Proper 16** *Closest to August 24* | 138 | Isaiah 51:1-6 Romans 11:33-36 Matthew 16:13-20 |
| **Proper 17** *Closest to August 31* | 26 or 26:1-8 | Jeremiah 15:15-21 Romans 12:1-8 Matthew 16:21-27 |
| **Proper 18** *Closest to September 7* | 119:33-48 or 119:33-40 | Ezekiel 33:(1-6)7-11 Romans 12:9-21 Matthew 18:15-20 |
| **Proper 19** *Closest to September 14* | 103 or 103:8-13 | Ecclesiasticus 27:30—28:7 Romans 14:5-12 Matthew 18:21-35 |

|  | Psalm | Lessons |
|---|---|---|
| **Proper 20**<br>*Closest to*<br>*September 21* | 145<br>or 145:1-8 | Jonah 3:10—4:11<br>Philippians 1:21-27<br>Matthew 20:1-16 |
| **Proper 21**<br>*Closest to*<br>*September 28* | 25:1-14<br>or 25:3-9 | Ezekiel 18:1-4,25-32<br>Philippians 2:1-13<br>Matthew 21:28-32 |
| **Proper 22**<br>*Closest to*<br>*October 5* | 80<br>or 80:7-14 | Isaiah 5:1-7<br>Philippians 3:14-21<br>Matthew 21:33-43 |
| **Proper 23**<br>*Closest to*<br>*October 12* | 23 | Isaiah 25:1-9<br>Philippians 4:4-13<br>Matthew 22:1-14 |
| **Proper 24**<br>*Closest to*<br>*October 19* | 96<br>or 96:1-9 | Isaiah 45:1-7<br>1 Thessalonians 1:1-10<br>Matthew 22:15-22 |
| **Proper 25**<br>*Closest to*<br>*October 26* | 1 | Exodus 22:21-27<br>1 Thessalonians 2:1-8<br>Matthew 22:34-46 |
| **Proper 26**<br>*Closest to*<br>*November 2* | 43 | Micah 3:5-12<br>1 Thessalonians 2:9-13,17-20<br>Matthew 23:1-12 |
| **Proper 27**<br>*Closest to*<br>*November 9* | 70 | Amos 5:18-24<br>1 Thessalonians 4:13-18<br>Matthew 25:1-13 |
| **Proper 28**<br>*Closest to*<br>*November 16* | 90<br>or 90:1-8,12 | Zephaniah 1:7,12-18<br>1 Thessalonians 5:1-10<br>Matthew 25:14-15,19-29 |

|  | Psalm | Lessons |
|---|---|---|
| **Proper 29** | 95:1-7 | Ezekiel 34:11-17 |
| *Closest to* | | 1 Corinthians 15:20-28 |
| *November 23* | | Matthew 25:31-46 |

# Year B

| | Psalm | Lessons |
|---|---|---|
| **First Sunday** | 80 | Isaiah 64:1-9a |
| **of Advent** | *or* 80:1-7 | 1 Corinthians 1:1-9 |
| | | Mark 13:(24-32)33-37 |
| **Second Sunday** | 85 | Isaiah 40:1-11 |
| **of Advent** | *or* 85:7-13 | 2 Peter 3:8-15a,18 |
| | | Mark 1:1-8 |
| **Third Sunday** | 126 | Isaiah 65:17-25 |
| **of Advent** | *or* Canticle 3 | 1 Thessalonians 5:(12-15)16-28 |
| | *or* 15 | John 1:6-8,19-28 |
| | | *or* John 3:23-30 |
| **Fourth Sunday** | 132 | 2 Samuel 7:4,8-16 |
| **of Advent** | *or* 132:8-15 | Romans 16:25-27 |
| | | Luke 1:26-38 |
| **Christmas Day I** | 96 | Isaiah 9:2-4,6-7 |
| | *or* 96:1-4,11-12 | Titus 2:11-14 |
| | | Luke 2:1-14(15-20) |

|  | Psalm | Lessons |
|---|---|---|
| Christmas Day II | 97<br>or 97:1-4,11-12 | Isaiah 62:6-7,10-12<br>Titus 3:4-7<br>Luke 2:(1-14)15-20 |
| Christmas Day III | 98<br>or 98:1-6 | Isaiah 52:7-10<br>Hebrews 1:1-12<br>John 1:1-14 |
| First Sunday<br>after Christmas | 147<br>or 147:13-21 | Isaiah 61:10—62:3<br>Galatians 3:23-25; 4:4-7<br>John 1:1-18 |
| Holy Name<br>*January 1* | 8 | Exodus 34:1-8<br>Romans 1:1-7<br>Luke 2:15-21 |
| Second Sunday<br>after Christmas | 84<br>or 84:1-8 | Jeremiah 31:7-14<br>Ephesians 1:3-6,15-19a<br>Matthew 2:13-15,19-23<br>*or* Luke 2:41-52<br>*or* Matthew 2:1-12 |
| The Epiphany<br>*January 6* | 72<br>or 72:1-2,10-17 | Isaiah 60:1-6,9<br>Ephesians 3:1-12<br>Matthew 2:1-12 |
| First Sunday<br>after Epiphany | 89:1-29<br>or 89:20-29 | Isaiah 42:1-9<br>Acts 10:34-38<br>Mark 1:7-11 |
| Second Sunday<br>after Epiphany | 63:1-8 | 1 Samuel 3:1-10(11-20)<br>1 Corinthians 6:11b-20<br>John 1:43-51 |
| Third Sunday<br>after Epiphany | 130 | Jeremiah 3:21—4:2<br>1 Corinthians 7:17-23<br>Mark 1:14-20 |

|                             | Psalm              | Lessons                                              |
|-----------------------------|--------------------|------------------------------------------------------|
| Fourth Sunday after Epiphany | 111                | Deuteronomy 18:15-20<br>1 Corinthians 8:1b-13<br>Mark 1:21-28 |
| Fifth Sunday after Epiphany | 142                | 2 Kings 4:(8-17)18-21(22-31) 32-37<br>1 Corinthians 9:16-23<br>Mark 1:29-39 |
| Sixth Sunday after Epiphany | 42<br>or 42:1-7    | 2 Kings 5:1-15b<br>1 Corinthians 9:24-27<br>Mark 1:40-45 |
| Seventh Sunday after Epiphany | 32<br>or 32:1-8  | Isaiah 43:18-25<br>2 Corinthians 1:18-22<br>Mark 2:1-12 |
| Eighth Sunday after Epiphany | 103<br>or 103:1-6 | Hosea 2:14-23<br>2 Corinthians 3:(4-11)17—4:2<br>Mark 2:18-22 |
| Last Sunday after Epiphany  | 27<br>or 27:5-11   | 1 Kings 19:9-18<br>2 Peter 1:16-19(20-21)<br>Mark 9:2-9 |
| Ash Wednesday               | 103<br>or 103:8-14 | Joel 2:1-2,12-17<br>or Isaiah 58:1-12<br>2 Corinthians 5:20b—6:10<br>Matthew 6:1-6,16-21 |
| First Sunday in Lent        | 25<br>or 25:3-9    | Genesis 9:8-17<br>1 Peter 3:18-22<br>Mark 1:9-13 |
| Second Sunday in Lent       | 16<br>or 16:5-11   | Genesis 22:1-14<br>Romans 8:31-39<br>Mark 8:31-38 |

|  | Psalm | Lessons |
|---|---|---|
| Third Sunday in Lent | 19:7-14 | Exodus 20:1-17<br>Romans 7:13-25<br>John 2:13-22 |
| Fourth Sunday in Lent | 122 | 2 Chronicles 36:14-23<br>Ephesians 2:4-10<br>John 6:4-15 |
| Fifth Sunday in Lent | 51<br>or 51:11-16 | Jeremiah 31:31-34<br>Hebrews 5:(1-4)5-10<br>John 12:20-33 |
| Palm Sunday |  |  |
| Liturgy of the Palms | 118:19-29 | Mark 11:1-11a |
| Liturgy of the Word | 22:1-21<br>or 22:1-11 | Isaiah 45:21-25<br>or Isaiah 52:13—53:12<br>Philippians 2:5-11<br>Mark (14:32-72)<br>15:1-39(40-47) |
| Monday in Holy Week | 36:5-10 | Isaiah 42:1-9<br>Hebrews 11:39—12:3<br>John 12:1-11<br>or Mark 14:3-9 |
| Tuesday in Holy Week | 71:1-12 | Isaiah 49:1-6<br>1 Corinthians 1:18-31<br>John 12:37-38,42-50<br>or Mark 11:15-19 |
| Wednesday in Holy Week | 69:7-15,22-23 | Isaiah 50:4-9a<br>Hebrews 9:11-15,24-28<br>John 13:21-35<br>or Matthew 26:1-5,14-25 |

|                    | Psalm                    | Lessons                       |
|--------------------|--------------------------|-------------------------------|
| **Maundy Thursday** | 78:14-20,23-25          | Exodus 12:1-14a               |
|                    |                          | 1 Corinthians 11:23-26(27-32) |
|                    |                          | John 13:1-15                  |
|                    |                          | *or* Luke 22:14-30            |
| **Good Friday**    | 22:1-21                  | Isaiah 52:13—53:12            |
|                    | *or* 22:1-11             | *or* Genesis 22:1-18          |
|                    | *or* 40:1-14             | *or* Wisdom 2:1,12-24         |
|                    | *or* 69:1-23             | Hebrews 10:1-25               |
|                    |                          | John (18:1-40)                |
|                    |                          |       19:1-37                 |
| **Holy Saturday**  | 130                      | Job 14:1-14                   |
|                    | *or* 31:1-5              | 1 Peter 4:1-8                 |
|                    |                          | Matthew 27:57-66              |
|                    |                          | *or* John 19:38-42            |

**Easter Day**

| The Great Vigil | *See pages 288-291.* |  |
|-----------------|----------------------|--|
| Early Service   | *Use one of the Old Testament Lessons from the Vigil with* | |
|                 | 114                  | Romans 6:3-11 |
|                 |                      | Matthew 28:1-10 |
| Principal Service | 118:14-29          | Acts 10:34-43 |
|                 | *or* 118:14-17,22-24 | *or* Isaiah 25:6-9 |
|                 |                      | Colossians 3:1-4 |
|                 |                      | *or* Acts 10:34-43 |
|                 |                      | Mark 16:1-8 |
| Evening Service | 114                  | Acts 5:29a,30-32 |
|                 | *or* 136             | *or* Daniel 12:1-3 |
|                 | *or* 118:14-17,22-24 | 1 Corinthians 5:6b-8 |
|                 |                      | *or* Acts 5:29a,30-32 |
|                 |                      | Luke 24:13-35 |

|  | Psalm | Lessons |
|---|---|---|
| Monday in<br>Easter Week | 16:8-11<br>or 118:19-24 | Acts 2:14,22b-32<br>Matthew 28:9-15 |
| Tuesday in<br>Easter Week | 33:18-22<br>or 118:19-24 | Acts 2:36-41<br>John 20:11-18 |
| Wednesday in<br>Easter Week | 105:1-8<br>or 118:19-24 | Acts 3:1-10<br>Luke 24:13-35 |
| Thursday in<br>Easter Week | 8 or 114<br>or 118:19-24 | Acts 3:11-26<br>Luke 24:36b-48 |
| Friday in<br>Easter Week | 116:1-8<br>or 118:19-24 | Acts 4:1-12<br>John 21:1-14 |
| Saturday in<br>Easter Week | 118:14-18<br>or 118:19-24 | Acts 4:13-21<br>Mark 16:9-15,20 |
| Second Sunday<br>of Easter | 111<br>or 118:19-24 | Acts 3:12a,13-15,17-26<br>or Isaiah 26:2-9,19<br>1 John 5:1-6<br>or Acts 3:12a,13-15,17-26<br>John 20:19-31 |
| Third Sunday<br>of Easter | 98<br>or 98:1-5 | Acts 4:5-12<br>or Micah 4:1-5<br>1 John 1:1—2:2<br>or Acts 4:5-12<br>Luke 24:36b-48 |
| Fourth Sunday<br>of Easter | 23<br>or 100 | Acts 4:(23-31)32-37<br>or Ezekiel 34:1-10<br>1 John 3:1-8<br>or Acts 4:(23-31)32-37<br>John 10:11-16 |

|  | Psalm | Lessons |
|---|---|---|
| **Fifth Sunday of Easter** | 66:1-11 *or* 66:1-8 | Acts 8:26-40 *or* Deuteronomy 4:32-40 1 John 3:(14-17)18-24 *or* Acts 8:26-40 John 14:15-21 |
| **Sixth Sunday of Easter** | 33 *or* 33:1-8,18-22 | Acts 11:19-30 *or* Isaiah 45:11-13,18-19 1 John 4:7-21 *or* Acts 11:19-30 John 15:9-17 |
| **Ascension Day** | 47 *or* 110:1-5 | Acts 1:1-11 *or* Ezekiel 1:3-5a,15-22,26-28 Ephesians 1:15-23 *or* Acts 1:1-11 Luke 24:49-53 *or* Mark 16:9-15,19-20 |
| **Seventh Sunday of Easter** | 68:1-20 *or* 47 | Acts 1:15-26 *or* Exodus 28:1-4,9-10,29-30 1 John 5:9-15 *or* Acts 1:15-26 John 17:11b-19 |
| **Day of Pentecost** | | |
| Early or Vigil Service | 33:12-22 Canticle 2 or 13  130 Canticle 9 104:25-32 | Genesis 11:1-9 *or* Exodus 19:1-9a,16-20a; 20:18-20 *or* Ezekiel 37:1-14 *or* Joel 2:28-32 Acts 2:1-11 *or* Romans 8:14-17,22-27 John 7:37-39a |

|                   | Psalm            | Lessons                |
|-------------------|------------------|------------------------|
| Principal Service | 104:25-37        | Acts 2:1-11            |
|                   | or 104:25-32     | or Isaiah 44:1-8       |
|                   | or 33:12-15,18-22| 1 Corinthians 12:4-13  |
|                   |                  | or Acts 2:1-11         |
|                   |                  | John 20:19-23          |
|                   |                  | or John 14:8-17        |

*On the weekdays which follow, the numbered Proper which corresponds most closely to the date of Pentecost in that year is used. See page 158.*

| Trinity Sunday | 93             | Exodus 3:1-6    |
|----------------|----------------|-----------------|
|                | or Canticle 2  | Romans 8:12-17  |
|                | or 13          | John 3:1-16     |

*On the weekdays which follow, the numbered Proper which corresponds most closely to the date of Trinity Sunday in that year is used.*

# The Season after Pentecost

*Directions for the use of the Propers which follow are on page 158.*

| Proper 1<br>closest to<br>May 11 | 42<br>or 42:1-7   | 2 Kings 5:1-15ab<br>1 Corinthians 9:24-27<br>Mark 1:40-45 |
|---|---|---|
| Proper 2<br>closest to<br>May 18 | 32<br>or 32:1-8   | Isaiah 43:18-25<br>2 Corinthians 1:18-22<br>Mark 2:1-12 |
| Proper 3<br>closest to<br>May 25 | 103<br>or 103:1-6 | Hosea 2:14-23<br>2 Corinthians 3:(4-11)17—4:2<br>Mark 2:18-22 |

|  | Psalm | Lessons |
|---|---|---|
| **Proper 4**<br>*Closest to*<br>*June 1* | 81<br>or 81:1-10 | Deuteronomy 5:6-21<br>2 Corinthians 4:5-12<br>Mark 2:23-28 |
| **Proper 5**<br>*Closest to*<br>*June 8* | 130 | Genesis 3:(1-7)8-21<br>2 Corinthians 4:13-18<br>Mark 3:20-35 |
| **Proper 6**<br>*Closest to*<br>*June 15* | 92<br>or 92:1-4,11-14 | Ezekiel 31:1-6,10-14<br>2 Corinthians 5:1-10<br>Mark 4:26-34 |
| **Proper 7**<br>*Closest to*<br>*June 22* | 107:1-32<br>or 107:1-3,23-32 | Job 38:1-11,16-18<br>2 Corinthians 5:14-21<br>**Mark 4:35-41(5:1-20)** |
| **Proper 8**<br>*Closest to*<br>*June 29* | 112 | Deuteronomy 15:7-11<br>2 Corinthians 8:1-9,13-15<br>Mark 5:22-24,35b-43 |
| **Proper 9**<br>*Closest to*<br>*July 6* | 123 | Ezekiel 2:1-7<br>2 Corinthians 12:2-10<br>Mark 6:1-6 |
| **Proper 10**<br>*Closest to*<br>*July 13* | 85<br>or 85:7-13 | Amos 7:7-15<br>Ephesians 1:1-14<br>Mark 6:7-13 |
| **Proper 11**<br>*Closest to*<br>*July 20* | 22:22-30 | Isaiah 57:14b-21<br>Ephesians 2:11-22<br>Mark 6:30-44 |
| **Proper 12**<br>*Closest to*<br>*July 27* | 114 | 2 Kings 2:1-15<br>Ephesians 4:1-7,11-16<br>Mark 6:45-52 |

|  | Psalm | Lessons |
|---|---|---|
| **Proper 13**<br>*Closest to*<br>*August 3* | 78:1-25<br>or 78:14-20,23-25 | Exodus 16:2-4,9-15<br>Ephesians 4:17-25<br>John 6:24-35 |
| **Proper 14**<br>*Closest to*<br>*August 10* | 34<br>or 34:1-8 | Deuteronomy 8:1-10<br>Ephesians 4:(25-29)30—5:2<br>John 6:37-51 |
| **Proper 15**<br>*Closest to*<br>*August 17* | 147<br>or 34:9-14 | Proverbs 9:1-6<br>Ephesians 5:15-20<br>John 6:53-59 |
| **Proper 16**<br>*Closest to*<br>*August 24* | 16<br>or 34:15-22 | Joshua 24:1-2a,14-25<br>Ephesians 5:21-33<br>John 6:60-69 |
| **Proper 17**<br>*Closest to*<br>*August 31* | 15 | Deuteronomy 4:1-9<br>Ephesians 6:10-20<br>Mark 7:1-8,14-15,21-23 |
| **Proper 18**<br>*Closest to*<br>*September 7* | 146<br>or 146:4-9 | Isaiah 35:4-7a<br>James 1:17-27<br>Mark 7:31-37 |
| **Proper 19**<br>*Closest to*<br>*September 14* | 116<br>or 116:1-8 | Isaiah 50:4-9<br>James 2:1-5,8-10,14-18<br>Mark 8:27-38<br>or Mark 9:14-29 |
| **Proper 20**<br>*Closest to*<br>*September 21* | 54 | Wisdom 1:16—2:1(6-11)12-22<br>James 3:16—4:6<br>Mark 9:30-37 |
| **Proper 21**<br>*Closest to*<br>*September 28* | 19<br>or 19:7-14 | Numbers 11:4-6,10-16,24-29<br>James 4:7-12(13—5:6)<br>Mark 9:38-43,45,47-48 |

*Lectionary B*   909

|  | Psalm | Lessons |
|---|---|---|
| **Proper 22**<br>*Closest to*<br>*October 5* | 8<br>*or* 128 | Genesis 2:18-24<br>Hebrews 2:(1-8)9-18<br>Mark 10:2-9 |
| **Proper 23**<br>*Closest to*<br>*October 12* | 90<br>*or* 90:1-8,12 | Amos 5:6-7,10-15<br>Hebrews 3:1-6<br>Mark 10:17-27(28-31) |
| **Proper 24**<br>*Closest to*<br>*October 19* | 91<br>*or* 91:9-16 | Isaiah 53:4-12<br>Hebrews 4:12-16<br>Mark 10:35-45 |
| **Proper 25**<br>*Closest to*<br>*October 26* | 13 | Isaiah 59:(1-4)9-19<br>Hebrews 5:12—6:1,9-12<br>Mark 10:46-52 |
| **Proper 26**<br>*Closest to*<br>*November 2* | 119:1-16<br>*or* 119:1-8 | Deuteronomy 6:1-9<br>Hebrews 7:23-28<br>Mark 12:28-34 |
| **Proper 27**<br>*Closest to*<br>*November 9* | 146<br>*or* 146:4-9 | 1 Kings 17:8-16<br>Hebrews 9:24-28<br>Mark 12:38-44 |
| **Proper 28**<br>*Closest to*<br>*November 16* | 16<br>*or* 16:5-11 | Daniel 12:1-4a(5-13)<br>Hebrews 10:31-39<br>Mark 13:14-23 |
| **Proper 29**<br>*Closest to*<br>*November 23* | 93 | Daniel 7:9-14<br>Revelation 1:1-8<br>John 18:33-37<br>*or* Mark 11:1-11 |

# Year C

| | Psalm | Lessons |
|---|---|---|
| **First Sunday of Advent** | 50<br>*or* 50:1-6 | Zechariah 14:4-9<br>1 Thessalonians 3:9-13<br>Luke 21:25-31 |
| **Second Sunday of Advent** | 126 | Baruch 5:1-9<br>Philippians 1:1-11<br>Luke 3:1-6 |
| **Third Sunday of Advent** | 85<br>*or* 85:7-13<br>*or* Canticle 9 | Zephaniah 3:14-20<br>Philippians 4:4-7(8-9)<br>Luke 3:7-18 |
| **Fourth Sunday of Advent** | 80<br>*or* 80:1-7 | Micah 5:2-4<br>Hebrews 10:5-10<br>Luke 1:39-49(50-56) |
| **Christmas Day I** | 96<br>*or* 96:1-4,11-12 | Isaiah 9:2-4,6-7<br>Titus 2:11-14<br>Luke 2:1-14(15-20) |
| **Christmas Day II** | 97<br>*or* 97:1-4,11-12 | Isaiah 62:6-7,10-12<br>Titus 3:4-7<br>Luke 2:(1-14)15-20 |
| **Christmas Day III** | 98<br>*or* 98:1-6 | Isaiah 52:7-10<br>Hebrews 1:1-12<br>John 1:1-14 |
| **First Sunday after Christmas** | 147<br>*or* 147:13-21 | Isaiah 61:10—62:3<br>Galatians 3:23-25; 4:4-7<br>John 1:1-18 |

|  | Psalm | Lessons |
|---|---|---|
| **Holy Name**<br>*January 1* | 8 | Exodus 34:1-8<br>Romans 1:1-7<br>Luke 2:15-21 |
| **Second Sunday**<br>**after Christmas** | 84<br>*or* 84:1-8 | Jeremiah 31:7-14<br>Ephesians 1:3-6,15-19a<br>Matthew 2:13-15,19-23<br>*or* Luke 2:41-52<br>*or* Matthew 2:1-12 |
| **The Epiphany**<br>*January 6* | 72<br>*or* 72:1-2,10-17 | Isaiah 60:1-6,9<br>Ephesians 3:1-12<br>Matthew 2:1-12 |
| **First Sunday**<br>**after Epiphany** | 89:1-29<br>*or* 89:20-29 | Isaiah 42:1-9<br>Acts 10:34-38<br>Luke 3:15-16,21-22 |
| **Second Sunday**<br>**after Epiphany** | 96<br>*or* 96:1-10 | Isaiah 62:1-5<br>1 Corinthians 12:1-11<br>John 2:1-11 |
| **Third Sunday**<br>**after Epiphany** | 113 | Nehemiah 8:2-10<br>1 Corinthians 12:12-27<br>Luke 4:14-21 |
| **Fourth Sunday**<br>**after Epiphany** | 71:1-17<br>*or* 71:1-6,15-17 | Jeremiah 1:4-10<br>1 Corinthians 14:12b-20<br>Luke 4:21-32 |
| **Fifth Sunday**<br>**after Epiphany** | 85<br>*or* 85:7-13 | Judges 6:11-24a<br>1 Corinthians 15:1-11<br>Luke 5:1-11 |
| **Sixth Sunday**<br>**after Epiphany** | 1 | Jeremiah 17:5-10<br>1 Corinthians 15:12-20<br>Luke 6:17-26 |

|  | Psalm | Lessons |
|---|---|---|
| eventh Sunday<br>fter Epiphany | 37:1-18<br>or 37:3-10 | Genesis 45:3-11,21-28<br>1 Corinthians 15:35-38,42-50<br>Luke 6:27-38 |
| ighth Sunday<br>fter Epiphany | 92<br>or 92:1-5,11-14 | Jeremiah 7:1-7(8-15)<br>1 Corinthians 15:50-58<br>Luke 6:39-49 |
| ast Sunday<br>fter Epiphany | 99 | Exodus 34:29-35<br>1 Corinthians 12:27—13:13<br>Luke 9:28-36 |
| sh Wednesday | 103<br>or 103:8-14 | Joel 2:1-2,12-17<br>or Isaiah 58:1-12<br>2 Corinthians 5:20b—6:10<br>Matthew 6:1-6,16-21 |
| irst Sunday<br>Lent | 91<br>or 91:9-15 | Deuteronomy 26:(1-4)5-11<br>Romans 10:(5-8a)8b-13<br>Luke 4:1-13 |
| econd Sunday<br>Lent | 27<br>or 27:10-18 | Genesis 15:1-12,17-18<br>Philippians 3:17—4:1<br>Luke 13:(22-30)31-35 |
| hird Sunday<br>Lent | 103<br>or 103:1-11 | Exodus 3:1-15<br>1 Corinthians 10:1-13<br>Luke 13:1-9 |
| ourth Sunday<br>Lent | 34<br>or 34:1-8 | Joshua (4:19-24); 5:9-12<br>2 Corinthians 5:17-21<br>Luke 15:11-32 |
| ifth Sunday<br>Lent | 126 | Isaiah 43:16-21<br>Philippians 3:8-14<br>Luke 20:9-19 |

|  | Psalm | Lessons |
|---|---|---|
| **Palm Sunday** | | |
| Liturgy of the Palms | 118:19-29 | Luke 19:29-40 |
| Liturgy of the Word | 22:1-21 *or* 22:1-11 | Isaiah 45:21-25 *or* Isaiah 52:13—53:12 Philippians 2:5-11 Luke (22:39-71) 23:1-49(50-56) |
| **Monday in Holy Week** | 36:5-10 | Isaiah 42:1-9 Hebrews 11:39—12:3 John 12:1-11 *or* Mark 14:3-9 |
| **Tuesday in Holy Week** | 71:1-12 | Isaiah 49:1-6 1 Corinthians 1:18-31 John 12:37-38,42-50 *or* Mark 11:15-19 |
| **Wednesday in Holy Week** | 69:7-15,22-23 | Isaiah 50:4-9a Hebrews 9:11-15,24-28 John 13:21-35 *or* Matthew 26:1-5,14-25 |
| **Maundy Thursday** | 78:14-20,23-25 | Exodus 12:1-14a 1 Corinthians 11:23-26(27-32) John 13:1-15 *or* Luke 22:14-30 |
| **Good Friday** | 22:1-21 *or* 22:1-11 *or* 40:1-14 *or* 69:1-23 | Isaiah 52:13—53:12 *or* Genesis 22:1-18 *or* Wisdom 2:1,12-24 Hebrews 10:1-25 John (18:1-40) 19:1-37 |

|  | Psalm | Lessons |
|---|---|---|
| Holy Saturday | 130<br>or 31:1-5 | Job 14:1-14<br>1 Peter 4:1-8<br>Matthew 27:57-66<br>or John 19:38-42 |
| **Easter Day** | | |
| The Great Vigil | *See pages 288-291.* | |
| Early Service | *Use one of the Old Testament Lessons from the Vigil with* | |
|  | 114 | Romans 6:3-11<br>Matthew 28:1-10 |
| Principal Service | 118:14-29<br>or 118:14-17,22-24 | Acts 10:34-43<br>or Isaiah 51:9-11<br>Colossians 3:1-4<br>or Acts 10:34-43<br>Luke 24:1-10 |
| Evening Service | 114<br>or 136<br>or 118:14-17,22-24 | Acts 5:29a,30-32<br>or Daniel 12:1-3<br>1 Corinthians 5:6b-8<br>or Acts 5:29a,30-32<br>Luke 24:13-35 |
| Monday in<br>Easter Week | 16:8-11<br>or 118:19-24 | Acts 2:14,22b-32<br>Matthew 28:9-15 |
| Tuesday in<br>Easter Week | 33:18-22<br>or 118:19-24 | Acts 2:36-41<br>John 20:11-18 |
| Wednesday in<br>Easter Week | 105:1-8<br>or 118:19-24 | Acts 3:1-10<br>Luke 24:13-35 |
| Thursday in<br>Easter Week | 8 or 114<br>or 118:19-24 | Acts 3:11-26<br>Luke 24:36b-48 |

|  | Psalm | Lessons |
|---|---|---|
| **Friday in Easter Week** | 116:1-8 *or* 118:19-24 | Acts 4:1-12 John 21:1-14 |
| **Saturday in Easter Week** | 118:14-18 *or* 118:19-24 | Acts 4:13-21 Mark 16:9-15,20 |
| **Second Sunday of Easter** | 111 *or* 118:19-24 | Acts 5:12a,17-22,25-29 *or* Job 42:1-6 Revelation 1:(1-8)9-19 *or* Acts 5:12a,17-22,25-29 John 20:19-31 |
| **Third Sunday of Easter** | 33 *or* 33:1-11 | Acts 9:1-19a *or* Jeremiah 32:36-41 Revelation 5:6-14 *or* Acts 9:1-19a John 21:1-14 |
| **Fourth Sunday of Easter** | 100 | Acts 13:15-16,26-33(34-39) *or* Numbers 27:12-23 Revelation 7:9-17 *or* Acts 13:15-16,26-33(34-39) John 10:22-30 |
| **Fifth Sunday of Easter** | 145 *or* 145:1-9 | Acts 13:44-52 *or* Leviticus 19:1-2,9-18 Revelation 19:1,4-9 *or* Acts 13:44-52 John 13:31-35 |
| **Sixth Sunday of Easter** | 67 | Acts 14:8-18 *or* Joel 2:21-27 Revelation 21:1—22:5 *or* Acts 14:8-18 John 14:23-29 |

|  | Psalm | Lessons |
|---|---|---|
| **Ascension Day** | 47<br>*or* 110:1-5 | Acts 1:1-11<br>*or* 2 Kings 2:1-15<br>Ephesians 1:15-23<br>*or* Acts 1:1-11<br>Luke 24:49-53<br>*or* Mark 16:9-15,19-20 |
| **Seventh Sunday<br>of Easter** | 68:1-20<br>*or* 47 | Acts 16:16-34<br>*or* 1 Samuel 12:19-24<br>Revelation 22:12-14,16-17,20<br>*or* Acts 16:16-34<br>John 17:20-26 |
| **Day of Pentecost** | | |
| **Early or<br>Vigil Service** | 33:12-22<br>Canticle 2 or 13<br><br>130<br>Canticle 9<br>104:25-32 | Genesis 11:1-9<br>*or* Exodus 19:1-9a,16-20a;<br>        20:18-20<br>*or* Ezekiel 37:1-14<br>*or* Joel 2:28-32<br>Acts 2:1-11<br>*or* Romans 8:14-17,22-27<br>John 7:37-39a |
| **Principal Service** | 104:25-37<br>*or* 104:25-32<br>*or* 33:12-15,18-22 | Acts 2:1-11<br>*or* Joel 2:28-32<br>1 Corinthians 12:4-13<br>*or* Acts 2:1-11<br>John 20:19-23<br>*or* John 14:8-17 |

*On the weekdays which follow, the numbered Proper which corresponds most closely to the date of Pentecost in that year is used. See page 158.*

|  | Psalms | Lessons |
|---|---|---|
| Trinity Sunday | 29<br>or Canticle 2<br>or 13 | Isaiah 6:1-8<br>Revelation 4:1-11<br>John 16:(5-11)12-15 |

*On the weekdays which follow, the numbered Proper which corresponds most closely to the date of Trinity Sunday in that year is used.*

## The Season after Pentecost

*Directions for the use of the Propers which follow are on page 158.*

| | | |
|---|---|---|
| **Proper 1**<br>*Closest to*<br>*May 11* | 1 | Jeremiah 17:5-10<br>1 Corinthians 15:12-20<br>Luke 6:17-26 |
| **Proper 2**<br>*Closest to*<br>*May 18* | 37:1-18<br>or 37:3-10 | Genesis 45:3-11,21-28<br>1 Corinthians 15:35-38,42-50<br>Luke 6:27-38 |
| **Proper 3**<br>*Closest to*<br>*May 25* | 92<br>or 92:1-5,11-14 | Jeremiah 7:1-7(8-15)<br>1 Corinthians 15:50-58<br>Luke 6:39-49 |
| **Proper 4**<br>*Closest to*<br>*June 1* | 96<br>or 96:1-9 | 1 Kings 8:22-23,27-30,41-43<br>Galatians 1:1-10<br>Luke 7:1-10 |
| **Proper 5**<br>*Closest to*<br>*June 8* | 30<br>or 30:1-6,12-13 | 1 Kings 17:17-24<br>Galatians 1:11-24<br>Luke 7:11-17 |
| **Proper 6**<br>*Closest to*<br>*June 15* | 32<br>or 32:1-8 | 2 Samuel 11:26—12:10,13-15<br>Galatians 2:11-21<br>Luke 7:36-50 |

|  | Psalm | Lessons |
|---|---|---|
| **Proper 7**<br>*Closest to*<br>*June 22* | 63:1-8 | Zechariah 12:8-10; 13:1<br>Galatians 3:23-29<br>Luke 9:18-24 |
| **Proper 8**<br>*Closest to*<br>*June 29* | 16<br>*or* 16:5-11 | 1 Kings 19:15-16,19-21<br>Galatians 5:1,13-25<br>Luke 9:51-62 |
| **Proper 9**<br>*Closest to*<br>*July 6* | 66<br>*or* 66:1-8 | Isaiah 66:10-16<br>Galatians 6:(1-10)14-18<br>Luke 10:1-12,16-20 |
| **Proper 10**<br>*Closest to*<br>*July 13* | 25<br>*or* 25:3-9 | Deuteronomy 30:9-14<br>Colossians 1:1-14<br>Luke 10:25-37 |
| **Proper 11**<br>*Closest to*<br>*July 20* | 15 | Genesis 18:1-10a(10b-14)<br>Colossians 1:21-29<br>Luke 10:38-42 |
| **Proper 12**<br>*Closest to*<br>*July 27* | 138 | Genesis 18:20-33<br>Colossians 2:6-15<br>Luke 11:1-13 |
| **Proper 13**<br>*Closest to*<br>*August 3* | 49<br>*or* 49:1-11 | Ecclesiastes 1:12-14;<br>2:(1-7,11)18-23<br>Colossians 3:(5-11)12-17<br>Luke 12:13-21 |
| **Proper 14**<br>*Closest to*<br>*August 10* | 33<br>*or* 33:12-15,18-22 | Genesis 15:1-6<br>Hebrews 11:1-3(4-7)8-16<br>Luke 12:32-40 |
| **Proper 15**<br>*Closest to*<br>*August 17* | 82 | Jeremiah 23:23-29<br>Hebrews 12:1-7(8-10)11-14<br>Luke 12:49-56 |

|  | Psalm | Lessons |
|---|---|---|
| **Proper 16**<br>*Closest to*<br>*August 24* | 46 | Isaiah 28:14-22<br>Hebrews 12:18-19,22-29<br>Luke 13:22-30 |
| **Proper 17**<br>*Closest to*<br>*August 31* | 112 | Ecclesiasticus 10:(7-11)12-18<br>Hebrews 13:1-8<br>Luke 14:1,7-14 |
| **Proper 18**<br>*Closest to*<br>*September 7* | 1 | Deuteronomy 30:15-20<br>Philemon 1-20<br>Luke 14:25-33 |
| **Proper 19**<br>*Closest to*<br>*September 14* | 51:1-18<br>or 51:1-11 | Exodus 32:1,7-14<br>1 Timothy 1:12-17<br>Luke 15:1-10 |
| **Proper 20**<br>*Closest to*<br>*September 21* | 138 | Amos 8:4-7(8-12)<br>1 Timothy 2:1-8<br>Luke 16:1-13 |
| **Proper 21**<br>*Closest to*<br>*September 28* | 146<br>or 146:4-9 | Amos 6:1-7<br>1 Timothy 6:11-19<br>Luke 16:19-31 |
| **Proper 22**<br>*Closest to*<br>*October 5* | 37:1-18<br>or 37:3-10 | Habakkuk 1:1-6(7-11)12-13;<br>2:1-4<br>2 Timothy 1:(1-5)6-14<br>Luke 17:5-10 |
| **Proper 23**<br>*Closest to*<br>*October 12* | 113 | Ruth 1:(1-7)8-19a<br>2 Timothy 2:(3-7)8-15<br>Luke 17:11-19 |
| **Proper 24**<br>*Closest to*<br>*October 19* | 121 | Genesis 32:3-8,22-30<br>2 Timothy 3:14—4:5<br>Luke 18:1-8a |

| | Psalm | Lessons |
|---|---|---|
| Proper 25<br>closest to<br>October 26 | 84<br>or 84:1-6 | Jeremiah 14:(1-6)7-10,19-22<br>2 Timothy 4:6-8,16-18<br>Luke 18:9-14 |
| Proper 26<br>closest to<br>November 2 | 32<br>or 32:1-8 | Isaiah 1:10-20<br>2 Thessalonians 1:1-5(6-10)11-12<br>Luke 19:1-10 |
| Proper 27<br>closest to<br>November 9 | 17<br>or 17:1-8 | Job 19:23-27a<br>2 Thessalonians 2:13—3:5<br>Luke 20:27(28-33)34-38 |
| Proper 28<br>closest to<br>November 16 | 98<br>or 98:5-10 | Malachi 3:13—4:2a,5-6<br>2 Thessalonians 3:6-13<br>Luke 21:5-19 |
| Proper 29<br>closest to<br>November 23 | 46 | Jeremiah 23:1-6<br>Colossians 1:11-20<br>Luke 23:35-43<br>or Luke 19:29-38 |

# Holy Days

| | | |
|---|---|---|
| St. Andrew<br>November 30 | 19<br>or 19:1-6 | Deuteronomy 30:11-14<br>Romans 10:8b-18<br>Matthew 4:18-22 |
| St. Thomas<br>December 21 | 126 | Habakkuk 2:1-4<br>Hebrews 10:35—11:1<br>John 20:24-29 |

|  | Psalm | Lessons |
|---|---|---|
| **St. Stephen**<br>*December 26* | 31<br>*or* 31:1-5 | Jeremiah 26:1-9,12-15<br>Acts 6:8—7:2a,51c-60<br>Matthew 23:34-39 |
| **St. John**<br>*December 27* | 92<br>*or* 92:1-4,11-14 | Exodus 33:18-23<br>1 John 1:1-9<br>John 21:19b-24 |
| **Holy Innocents**<br>*December 28* | 124 | Jeremiah 31:15-17<br>Revelation 21:1-7<br>Matthew 2:13-18 |
| **Confession of St. Peter**<br>*January 18* | 23 | Acts 4:8-13<br>1 Peter 5:1-4<br>Matthew 16:13-19 |
| **Conversion of St. Paul**<br>*January 25* | 67 | Acts 26:9-21<br>Galatians 1:11-24<br>Matthew 10:16-22 |
| **The Presentation**<br>*February 2* | 84<br>*or* 84:1-6 | Malachi 3:1-4<br>Hebrews 2:14-18<br>Luke 2:22-40 |
| **St. Matthias**<br>*February 24* | 15 | Acts 1:15-26<br>Philippians 3:13b-21<br>John 15:1,6-16 |
| **St. Joseph**<br>*March 19* | 89:1-29<br>*or* 89:1-4,26-29 | 2 Samuel 7:4,8-16<br>Romans 4:13-18<br>Luke 2:41-52 |
| **The Annunciation**<br>*March 25* | 40:1-11<br>*or* 40:5-10<br>*or* Canticle 3<br>*or* 15 | Isaiah 7:10-14<br>Hebrews 10:5-10<br>Luke 1:26-38 |

|  | Psalm | Lessons |
|---|---|---|
| **St. Mark**<br>*April 25* | 2<br>or 2:7-10 | Isaiah 52:7-10<br>Ephesians 4:7-8,11-16<br>Mark 1:1-15<br>or Mark 16:15-20 |
| **St. Philip &**<br>**St. James**<br>*May 1* | 119:33-40 | Isaiah 30:18-21<br>2 Corinthians 4:1-6<br>John 14:6-14 |
| **The Visitation**<br>*May 31* | 113<br>or Canticle 9 | Zephaniah 3:14-18a<br>Colossians 3:12-17<br>Luke 1:39-49 |
| **St. Barnabas**<br>*June 11* | 112 | Isaiah 42:5-12<br>Acts 11:19-30; 13:1-3<br>Matthew 10:7-16 |
| **Nativity of**<br>**St. John**<br>**the Baptist**<br>*June 24* | 85<br>or 85:7-13 | Isaiah 40:1-11<br>Acts 13:14b-26<br>Luke 1:57-80 |
| **St. Peter &**<br>**St. Paul**<br>*June 29* | 87 | Ezekiel 34:11-16<br>2 Timothy 4:1-8<br>John 21:15-19 |
| **Independence Day**<br>July 4 | 145<br>or 145:1-9 | Deuteronomy 10:17-21<br>Hebrews 11:8-16<br>Matthew 5:43-48 |

*The Psalm and Lessons "For the Nation," page 930, may be used instead.*

|  | Psalm | Lessons |
|---|---|---|
| **St. Mary**<br>**Magdalene**<br>*July 22* | 42:1-7 | Judith 9:1,11-14<br>2 Corinthians 5:14-18<br>John 20:11-18 |

| | Psalm | Lessons |
|---|---|---|
| **St. James**<br>*July 25* | 7:1-10 | Jeremiah 45:1-5<br>Acts 11:27—12:3<br>Matthew 20:20-28 |
| **The Transfiguration**<br>*August 6* | 99<br>*or* 99:5-9 | Exodus 34:29-35<br>2 Peter 1:13-21<br>Luke 9:28-36 |
| **St. Mary**<br>**the Virgin**<br>*August 15* | 34<br>*or* 34:1-9 | Isaiah 61:10-11<br>Galatians 4:4-7<br>Luke 1:46-55 |
| **St. Bartholomew**<br>*August 24* | 91<br>*or* 91:1-4 | Deuteronomy 18:15-18<br>1 Corinthians 4:9-15<br>Luke 22:24-30 |
| **Holy Cross Day**<br>*September 14* | 98<br>*or* 98:1-4 | Isaiah 45:21-25<br>Philippians 2:5-11<br>*or* Galatians 6:14-18<br>John 12:31-36a |
| **St. Matthew**<br>*September 21* | 119:33-40 | Proverbs 3:1-6<br>2 Timothy 3:14-17<br>Matthew 9:9-13 |
| **St. Michael &**<br>**All Angels**<br>*September 29* | 103<br>*or* 103:19-22 | Genesis 28:10-17<br>Revelation 12:7-12<br>John 1:47-51 |
| **St. Luke**<br>*October 18* | 147<br>*or* 147:1-7 | Ecclesiasticus 38:1-4,6-10,12-14<br>2 Timothy 4:5-13<br>Luke 4:14-21 |
| **St. James**<br>**of Jerusalem**<br>*October 23* | 1 | Acts 15:12-22a<br>1 Corinthians 15:1-11<br>Matthew 13:54-58 |

| | Psalm | Lessons |
|---|---|---|
| **St. Simon &**<br>**St. Jude**<br>*October 28* | 119:89-96 | Deuteronomy 32:1-4<br>Ephesians 2:13-22<br>John 15:17-27 |
| **All Saints' Day**<br>*November 1* | 149 | Ecclesiasticus 44:1-10,13-14<br>Revelation 7:2-4,9-17<br>Matthew 5:1-12 |
| *or this* | 149 | Ecclesiasticus 2:(1-6)7-11<br>Ephesians 1:(11-14)15-23<br>Luke 6:20-26(27-36) |
| **Thanksgiving Day** | 65<br>*or* 65:9-14 | Deuteronomy 8:1-3,6-10(17-20)<br>James 1:17-18,21-27<br>Matthew 6:25-33 |

# The Common of Saints

| | | |
|---|---|---|
| **Of a Martyr I** | 126<br>*or* 121 | 2 Esdras 2:42-48<br>1 Peter 3:14-18,22<br>Matthew 10:16-22 |
| **Of a Martyr II** | 116<br>*or* 116:1-8 | Ecclesiasticus 51:1-12<br>Revelation 7:13-17<br>Luke 12:2-12 |
| **Of a Martyr III** | 124<br>*or* 31:1-5 | Jeremiah 15:15-21<br>1 Peter 4:12-19<br>Mark 8:34-38 |
| **Of a Missionary I** | 96<br>*or* 96:1-7 | Isaiah 52:7-10<br>Acts 1:1-9<br>Luke 10:1-9 |

|  | Psalm | Lessons |
|---|---|---|
| Of a Missionary II | 98<br>or 98:1-4 | Isaiah 49:1-6<br>Acts 17:22-31<br>Matthew 28:16-20 |
| Of a Pastor I | 23 | Ezekiel 34:11-16<br>1 Peter 5:1-4<br>John 21:15-17 |
| Of a Pastor II | 84<br>or 84:7-12 | Acts 20:17-35<br>Ephesians 3:14-21<br>Matthew 24:42-47 |
| Of a Theologian<br>and Teacher I | 119:97-104 | Wisdom 7:7-14<br>1 Corinthians 2:6-10,13-16<br>John 17:18-23 |
| Of a Theologian<br>and Teacher II | 119:89-96 | Proverbs 3:1-7<br>1 Corinthians 3:5-11<br>Matthew 13:47-52 |
| Of a Monastic I | 34<br>or 34:1-8 | Song of Songs 8:6-7<br>Philippians 3:7-15<br>Luke 12:33-37<br>or Luke 9:57-62 |
| Of a Monastic II | 133<br>or 119:161-168 | Acts 2:42-47a<br>2 Corinthians 6:1-10<br>Matthew 6:24-33 |
| Of a Saint I | 15 | Micah 6:6-8<br>Hebrews 12:1-2<br>Matthew 25:31-40 |
| Of a Saint II | 34<br>or 34:15-22 | Wisdom 3:1-9<br>Philippians 4:4-9<br>Luke 6:17-23 |

|                        | Psalm | Lessons |
|------------------------|-------|---------|
| Of a Saint III         | 1     | Ecclesiasticus 2:7-11<br>1 Corinthians 1:26-31<br>Matthew 25:1-13 |

# Various Occasions

| | Psalm | Lessons |
|---|---|---|
| 1. Of the<br>Holy Trinity | 29 | Exodus 3:11-15<br>Romans 11:33-36<br>Matthew 28:18-20 |
| 2. Of the<br>Holy Spirit | 139:1-17<br>or 139:1-9 | Isaiah 61:1-3<br>1 Corinthians 12:4-14<br>Luke 11:9-13 |
| 3. Of the<br>Holy Angels | 148<br>or 103:19-22 | Daniel 7:9-10a<br>or 2 Kings 6:8-17<br>Revelation 5:11-14<br>John 1:47-51 |
| 4. Of the<br>Incarnation | 111<br>or 132:11-19 | Isaiah 11:1-10<br>or Genesis 17:1-8<br>1 John 4:1-11<br>or 1 Timothy 3:14-16<br>Luke 1:26-33(34-38)<br>or Luke 11:27-28 |
| 5. Of the<br>Holy Eucharist | 34<br>or 116:10-17 | Deuteronomy 8:2-3<br>Revelation 19:1-2a,4-9<br>or 1 Corinthians 10:1-4,16-17<br>or 1 Corinthians 11:23-29<br>John 6:47-58 |

|   | Psalm | Lessons |
|---|-------|---------|
| 6. Of the Holy Cross | 40:1-11 *or* 40:5-11 | Isaiah 52:13-15;  53:10-12<br>1 Corinthians 1:18-24<br>John 12:23-33 |
| 7. For All Baptized Christians | 16:5-11 | Jeremiah 17:7-8<br>*or* Ezekiel 36:24-28<br>Romans 6:3-11<br>Mark 10:35-45 |
| 8. For the Departed | 116 *or* 103:13-22 *or* 130 | Isaiah 25:6-9<br>*or* Wisdom 3:1-9<br>1 Corinthians 15:50-58<br>John 5:24-27<br>*or* John 6:37-40<br>*or* John 11:21-27 |

*Any of the Psalms and Lessons appointed at the Burial of the Dead may be used instead.*

|   | Psalm | Lessons |
|---|-------|---------|
| 9. Of the Reign of Christ | 93 *or* Canticle 18 | Daniel 7:9-14<br>Colossians 1:11-20<br>John 18:33-37 |

*Any of the Psalms and Lessons appointed in Proper 29 may be used instead.*

|   | Psalm | Lessons |
|---|-------|---------|
| 10. At Baptism | 15 *or* 23 *or* 27 *or* 42:1-7 *or* 84 *or* Canticle 9 | Ezekiel 36:24-28*<br>Romans 6:3-5<br>*or* Romans 8:14-17<br>*or* 2 Corinthians 5:17-20<br>Mark 1:9-11<br>*or* Mark 10:13-16<br>*or* John 3:1-6 |

*\* Any of the other Old Testament Lessons for the Easter Vigil may be substituted.*

|  | Psalm | Lessons |
|---|---|---|
| 11. At Confirmation | 1<br>*or* 139:1-9 | Isaiah 61:1-9<br>*or* Jeremiah 31:31-34<br>*or* Ezekiel 37:1-10<br>Romans 8:18-27<br>*or* Romans 12:1-8<br>*or* Galatians 5:16-25<br>*or* Ephesians 4:7,11-16<br>Matthew 5:1-12<br>*or* Matthew 16:24-27<br>*or* Luke 4:16-21<br>*or* John 14:15-21 |
| 12. Anniversary<br>of the<br>Dedication<br>of a Church | 84<br>*or* 84:1-6 | 1 Kings 8:22-30<br>*or* Genesis 28:10-17<br>1 Peter 2:1-5,9-10<br>Matthew 21:12-16 |
| 13. For a Church<br>Convention | 19:7-14 | Isaiah 55:1-13<br>2 Corinthians 4:1-10<br>John 15:1-11 |
| 14. For the Unity<br>of the Church | 122 | Isaiah 35:1-10<br>Ephesians 4:1-6<br>John 17:6a,15-23 |
| 15. For the<br>Ministry I | 99<br>*or* 27:1-9 | Numbers 11:16-17,24-29<br>1 Corinthians 3:5-11<br>John 4:31-38 |
| 15. For the<br>Ministry II | 63:1-8 | 1 Samuel 3:1-10<br>Ephesians 4:11-16<br>Matthew 9:35-38 |
| 15. For the<br>Ministry III | 15 | Exodus 19:3-8<br>1 Peter 4:7-11<br>Matthew 16:24-27 |

| | Psalm | Lessons |
|---|---|---|
| 16. For the Mission of the Church I | 96 *or* 96:1-7 | Isaiah 2:2-4 Ephesians 2:13-22 Luke 10:1-9 |
| 16. For the Mission of the Church II | 67 | Isaiah 49:5-13 Ephesians 3:1-12 Matthew 28:16-20 |
| 17. For the Nation | 47 | Isaiah 26:1-8 Romans 13:1-10 Mark 12:13-17 |

*The Psalm and any of the Lessons appointed for Independence Day may be used instead.*

| | | |
|---|---|---|
| 18. For Peace | 85:7-13 | Micah 4:1-5 Ephesians 2:13-18 *or* Colossians 3:12-15 John 16:23-33 *or* Matthew 5:43-48 |
| 19. For Rogation Days I | 147 *or* 147:1-13 | Deuteronomy 11:10-15 *or* Ezekiel 47:6-12 *or* Jeremiah 14:1-9 Romans 8:18-25 Mark 4:26-32 |
| 19. For Rogation Days II | 107:1-9 | Ecclesiasticus 38:27-32 1 Corinthians 3:10-14 Matthew 6:19-24 |
| 19. For Rogation Days III | 104:25-37 *or* 104:1,13-15, 25-32 | Job 38:1-11,16-18 1 Timothy 6:7-10,17-19 Luke 12:13-21 |

|  | Psalm | Lessons |
|---|---|---|
| 20. For the Sick | 13 <br> or 86:1-7 | 2 Kings 20:1-5 <br> James 5:13-16 <br> Mark 2:1-12 |

*Any of the Psalms and Lessons appointed at the Ministration to the Sick may be used instead.*

|  | Psalm | Lessons |
|---|---|---|
| 21. For Social Justice | 72 <br> or 72:1-4,12-14 | Isaiah 42:1-7 <br> James 2:5-9,12-17 <br> Matthew 10:32-42 |
| 22. For Social Service | 146 <br> or 22:22-27 | Zechariah 8:3-12,16-17 <br> 1 Peter 4:7-11 <br> Mark 10:42-52 |
| 23. For Education | 78:1-7 | Deuteronomy 6:4-9,20-25 <br> 2 Timothy 3:14—4:5 <br> Matthew 11:25-30 |
| 24. For Vocation in Daily Work | 8 | Ecclesiastes 3:1,9-13 <br> 1 Peter 2:11-17 <br> Matthew 6:19-24 |
| 25. For Labor Day | 107:1-9 <br> or 90:1-2,16-17 | Ecclesiasticus 38:27-32 <br> 1 Corinthians 3:10-14 <br> Matthew 6:19-24 |

# Daily Office
# Lectionary

# Concerning the Daily Office Lectionary

The Daily Office Lectionary is arranged in a two-year cycle. Year One begins on the First Sunday of Advent preceding odd-numbered years, and Year Two begins on the First Sunday of Advent preceding even-numbered years. (Thus, on the First Sunday of Advent, 1976, the Lectionary for Year One is begun.)

Three Readings are provided for each Sunday and weekday in each of the two years. Two of the Readings may be used in the morning and one in the evening; or, if the Office is read only once in the day, all three Readings may be used. When the Office is read twice in the day, it is suggested that the Gospel Reading be used in the evening in Year One, and in the morning in Year Two. If two Readings are desired at both Offices, the Old Testament Reading for the alternate year is used as the First Reading at Evening Prayer.

When more than one Reading is used at an Office, the first is always from the Old Testament (or the Apocrypha).

When a Major Feast interrupts the sequence of Readings, they may be re-ordered by lengthening, combining, or omitting some of them, to secure continuity or avoid repetition.

Any Reading may be lengthened at discretion. Suggested lengthenings are shown in parentheses.

In this Lectionary (except in the weeks from 4 Advent to 1 Epiphany, and Palm Sunday to 2 Easter), the Psalms are arranged in a seven-week pattern which recurs throughout the year, except for appropriate variations in Lent and Easter Season.

In the citation of the Psalms, those for the morning are given first, and then those for the evening. At the discretion of the officiant, however, any of the Psalms appointed for a given day may be used in the morning or in the evening. Likewise, Psalms appointed for any day may be used on any other day in the same week, except on major Holy Days.

Brackets and parentheses are used (brackets in the case of whole Psalms, parentheses in the case of verses) to indicate Psalms and verses of Psalms which may be omitted. In some instances, the entire portion of the Psalter assigned to a given Office has been bracketed, and alternative Psalmody provided. Those who desire to recite the Psalter in its entirety should, in each instance, use the bracketed Psalms rather than the alternatives.

Antiphons drawn from the Psalms themselves, or from the opening sentences given in the Offices, or from other passages of Scripture, may be used with the Psalms and biblical Canticles. The antiphons may be sung or said at the beginning and end of each Psalm or Canticle, or may be used as refrains after each verse or group of verses.

On Special Occasions, the officiant may select suitable Psalms and Readings.

### Week of 1 Advent

| | | |
|---|---|---|
| *Sunday* | 146, 147 ❖ 111, 112, 113 | |
| | Isa. 1:1-9    2 Pet. 3:1-10    Matt. 25:1-13 | |

*Monday*  1, 2, 3 ❖ 4, 7
Isa. 1:10-20    1 Thess. 1:1-10    Luke 20:1-8

*Tuesday*  5, 6 ❖ 10, 11
Isa. 1:21-31    1 Thess. 2:1-12    Luke 20:9-18

*Wednesday*  119:1-24 ❖ 12, 13, 14
Isa. 2:1-11    1 Thess. 2:13-20    Luke 20:19-26

*Thursday*  18:1-20 ❖ 18:21-50
Isa. 2:12-22    1 Thess. 3:1-13    Luke 20:27-40

*Friday*  16, 17 ❖ 22
Isa. 3:8-15    1 Thess. 4:1-12    Luke 20:41—21:4

*Saturday*  20, 21:1-7(8-14) ❖ 110:1-5(6-7), 116, 117
Isa. 4:2-6    1 Thess. 4:13-18    Luke 21:5-19

### Week of 2 Advent

*Sunday*  148, 149, 150 ❖ 114, 115
Isa. 5:1-7    2 Pet. 3:11-18    Luke 7:28-35

*Monday*  25 ❖ 9, 15
Isa. 5:8-12, 18-23    1 Thess. 5:1-11    Luke 21:20-28

*Tuesday*  26, 28 ❖ 36, 39
Isa. 5:13-17, 24-25    1 Thess. 5:12-28    Luke 21:29-38

*Wednesday*  38 ❖ 119:25-48
Isa. 6:1-13    2 Thess. 1:1-12    John 7:53—8:11

*Thursday*  37:1-18 ❖ 37:19-42
Isa. 7:1-9    2 Thess. 2:1-12    Luke 22:1-13

*Friday*  31 ❖ 35
Isa. 7:10-25    2 Thess. 2:13—3:5    Luke 22:14-30

*Saturday*  30, 32 ❖ 42, 43
Isa. 8:1-15    2 Thess. 3:6-18    Luke 22:31-38

## Week of 1 Advent

| | | |
|---|---|---|
| Sunday | 146, 147  ∴  111, 112, 113 | |
| | Amos 1:1-5, 13—2:8  1 Thess. 5:1-11  Luke 21:5-19 | |
| Monday | 1, 2, 3  ∴  4, 7 | |
| | Amos 2:6-16  2 Pet. 1:1-11  Matt. 21:1-11 | |
| Tuesday | 5, 6  ∴  10, 11 | |
| | Amos 3:1-11  2 Pet. 1:12-21  Matt. 21:12-22 | |
| Wednesday | 119:1-24  ∴  12, 13, 14 | |
| | Amos 3:12—4:5  2 Pet. 3:1-10  Matt. 21:23-32 | |
| Thursday | 18:1-20  ∴  18:21-50 | |
| | Amos 4:6-13  2 Pet. 3:11-18  Matt. 21:33-46 | |
| Friday | 16, 17  ∴  22 | |
| | Amos 5:1-17  Jude 1-16  Matt. 22:1-14 | |
| Saturday | 20, 21:1-7(8-14)  ∴  110:1-5(6-7), 116, 117 | |
| | Amos 5:18-27  Jude 17-25  Matt. 22:15-22 | |

## Week of 2 Advent

| | | |
|---|---|---|
| Sunday | 148, 149, 150  ∴  114, 115 | |
| | Amos 6:1-14  2 Thess. 1:5-12  Luke 1:57-68 | |
| Monday | 25  ∴  9, 15 | |
| | Amos 7:1-9  Rev. 1:1-8  Matt. 22:23-33 | |
| Tuesday | 26, 28  ∴  36, 39 | |
| | Amos 7:10-17  Rev. 1:9-16  Matt. 22:34-46 | |
| Wednesday | 38  ∴  119:25-48 | |
| | Amos 8:1-14  Rev. 1:17—2:7  Matt. 23:1-12 | |
| Thursday | 37:1-18  ∴  37:19-42 | |
| | Amos 9:1-10  Rev. 2:8-17  Matt. 23:13-26 | |
| Friday | 31  ∴  35 | |
| | Haggai 1:1-15  Rev. 2:18-29  Matt. 23:27-39 | |
| Saturday | 30, 32  ∴  42, 43 | |
| | Haggai 2:1-9  Rev. 3:1-6  Matt. 24:1-14 | |

### Week of 3 Advent

| | | | |
|---|---|---|---|
| *Sunday* | 63:1-8(9-11), 98 ❖ 103 | | |
| | Isa. 13:6-13 | Heb. 12:18-29 | John 3:22-30 |
| *Monday* | 41, 52 ❖ 44 | | |
| | Isa. 8:16—9:1 | 2 Pet. 1:1-11 | Luke 22:39-53 |
| *Tuesday* | 45 ❖ 47, 48 | | |
| | Isa. 9:1-7 | 2 Pet. 1:12-21 | Luke 22:54-69 |
| *Wednesday* | 119:49-72 ❖ 49, [53] | | |
| | Isa. 9:8-17 | 2 Pet. 2:1-10a | Mark 1:1-8 |
| *Thursday* | 50 ❖ [59, 60] or 33 | | |
| | Isa. 9:18—10:4 | 2 Pet. 2:10b-16 | Matt. 3:1-12 |
| *Friday* | 40, 54 ❖ 51 | | |
| | Isa. 10:5-19 | 2 Pet. 2:17-22 | Matt. 11:2-15 |
| *Saturday* | 55 ❖ 138, 139:1-17(18-23) | | |
| | Isa. 10:20-27 | Jude 17-25 | Luke 3:1-9 |

### Week of 4 Advent

| | | | |
|---|---|---|---|
| *Sunday* | 24, 29 ❖ 8, 84 | | |
| | Isa. 42:1-12 | Eph. 6:10-20 | John 3:16-21 |
| *Monday* | 61, 62 ❖ 112, 115 | | |
| | Isa. 11:1-9 | Rev. 20:1-10 | John 5:30-47 |
| *Tuesday* | 66, 67 ❖ 116, 117 | | |
| | Isa. 11:10-16 | Rev. 20:11—21:8 | Luke 1:5-25 |
| *Wednesday* | 72 ❖ 111, 113 | | |
| | Isa. 28:9-22 | Rev. 21:9-21 | Luke 1:26-38 |
| *Thursday* | 80 ❖ 146, 147 | | |
| | Isa. 29:13-24 | Rev. 21:22—22:5 | Luke 1:39-48a(48b-56) |
| *Friday* | 93, 96 ❖ 148, 150 | | |
| | Isa. 33:17-22 | Rev. 22:6-11, 18-20 | Luke 1:57-66 |
| *Dec. 24* | 45, 46 ❖ —— | | |
| | Isa. 35:1-10 | Rev. 22:12-17, 21 | Luke 1:67-80 |
| *Christmas Eve* | —— ❖ 89:1-29 | | |
| | Isa. 59:15b-21 | Phil. 2:5-11 | |

## Week of 3 Advent

| Sunday | 63:1-8(9-11), 98 ∻ 103 |
| | Amos 9:11-15    2 Thess. 2:1-3, 13-17    John 5:30-47 |

| Monday | 41, 52 ∻ 44 |
| | Zech. 1:7-17    Rev. 3:7-13    Matt. 24:15-31 |

| Tuesday | 45 ∻ 47, 48 |
| | Zech. 2:1-13    Rev. 3:14-22    Matt. 24:32-44 |

| Wednesday | 119:49-72 ∻ 49, [53] |
| | Zech. 3:1-10    Rev. 4:1-8    Matt. 24:45-51 |

| Thursday | 50 ∻ [59, 60] or 33 |
| | Zech. 4:1-14    Rev. 4:9—5:5    Matt. 25:1-13 |

| Friday | 40, 54 ∻ 51 |
| | Zech. 7:8—8:8    Rev. 5:6-14    Matt. 25:14-30 |

| Saturday | 55 ∻ 138, 139:1-17(18-23) |
| | Zech. 8:9-17    Rev. 6:1-17    Matt. 25:31-46 |

## Week of 4 Advent

| Sunday | 24, 29 ∻ 8, 84 |
| | Gen. 3:8-15    Rev. 12:1-10    John 3:16-21 |

| Monday | 61, 62 ∻ 112, 115 |
| | Zeph. 3:14-20    Titus 1:1-16    Luke 1:1-25 |

| Tuesday | 66, 67 ∻ 116, 117 |
| | 1 Samuel 2:1b-10    Titus 2:1-10    Luke 1:26-38 |

| Wednesday | 72 ∻ 111, 113 |
| | 2 Samuel 7:1-17    Titus 2:11—3:8a    Luke 1:39-48a(48b-56) |

| Thursday | 80 ∻ 146, 147 |
| | 2 Samuel 7:18-29    Gal. 3:1-14    Luke 1:57-66 |

| Friday | 93, 96 ∻ 148, 150 |
| | Baruch 4:21-29    Gal. 3:15-22    Luke 1:67-80 or Matt. 1:1-17 |

| Dec. 24 | 45, 46 ∻ —— |
| | Baruch 4:36—5:9    Gal. 3:23—4:7    Matt. 1:18-25 |

| Christmas Eve | —— ∻ 89:1-29 |
| | Isa. 59:15b-21    Phil. 2:5-11 |

**Christmas Day and Following**

*Christmas Day*    2, 85    ❖    110:1-5(6-7), 132
     Zech. 2:10-13    1 John 4:7-16    John 3:31-36

*First Sunday after Christmas*    93, 96    ❖    34
     Isa. 62:6-7, 10-12    Heb. 2:10-18    Matt. 1:18-25

*Dec. 29*    18:1-20    ❖    18:21-50*
     Isa. 12:1-6    Rev. 1:1-8    John 7:37-52

*Dec. 30*    20, 21:1-7(8-14)    ❖    23, 27
     Isa. 25:1-9    Rev. 1:9-20    John 7:53—8:11

*Dec. 31*    46, 48    ❖    ——
     Isa. 26:1-9    2 Cor. 5:16—6:2    John 8:12-19

*Eve of Holy Name*    ——    ❖    90
     Isa. 65:15b-25    Rev. 21:1-6

*Holy Name*    103    ❖    148
     Gen. 17:1-12a, 15-16    Col. 2:6-12    John 16:23b-30

*Second Sunday after Christmas*    66, 67    ❖    145
     Ecclus. 3:3-9, 14-17    1 John 2:12-17    John 6:41-47

*Jan. 2*    34    ❖    33
     Gen. 12:1-7    Heb. 11:1-12    John 6:35-42, 48-51

*Jan. 3*    68    ❖    72**
     Gen. 28:10-22    Heb. 11:13-22    John 10:7-17

*Jan. 4*    85, 87    ❖    89:1-29**
     Exod. 3:1-12    Heb. 11:23-31    John 14:6-14

*Jan. 5*    2, 110:1-5(6-7)    ❖
     Joshua 1:1-9    Heb. 11:32—12:2    John 15:1-16

*Eve of Epiphany*    ——    ❖    29, 98
     Isa. 66:18-23    Rom. 15:7-13

*\*If today is Saturday, use Psalms 23 and 27 at Evening Prayer.*
*\*\*If today is Saturday, use Psalm 136 at Evening Prayer.*

## Christmas Day and Following

*Christmas Day*  2, 85  ❖  110:1-5(6-7), 132
     Micah 4:1-5; 5:2-4  1 John 4:7-16  John 3:31-36

*First Sunday after Christmas*  93, 96  ❖  34
     1 Samuel 1:1-2, 7b-28  Col. 1:9-20  Luke 2:22-40

*Dec. 29*  18:1-20  ❖  18:21-50*
     2 Samuel 23:13-17b  2 John 1-13  John 2:1-11

*Dec. 30*  20, 21:1-7(8-14)  ❖  23, 27
     1 Kings 17:17-24  3 John 1-15  John 4:46-54

*Dec. 31*  46, 48  ❖  ———
     1 Kings 3:5-14  James 4:13-17; 5:7-11  John 5:1-15

*Eve of Holy Name*  ———  ❖  90
     Isa. 65:15b-25  Rev. 21:1-6

*Holy Name*  103  ❖  148
     Isa. 62:1-5, 10-12  Rev. 19:11-16  Matt. 1:18-25

*Second Sunday after Christmas*  66, 67  ❖  145
     Wisdom 7:3-14  Col. 3:12-17  John 6:41-47

*Jan. 2*  34  ❖  33
     1 Kings 19:1-8  Eph. 4:1-16  John 6:1-14

*Jan. 3*  68  ❖  72**
     1 Kings 19:9-18  Eph. 4:17-32  John 6:15-27

*Jan. 4*  85, 87  ❖  89:1-29**
     Joshua 3:14—4:7  Eph. 5:1-20  John 9:1-12, 35-38

*Jan. 5*  2, 110:1-5(6-7)  ❖  ———
     Jonah 2:2-9  Eph. 6:10-20  John 11:17-27, 38-44

*Eve of Epiphany*  ———  ❖  29, 98
     Isa. 66:18-23  Rom. 15:7-13

*If today is Saturday, use Psalms 23 and 27 at Evening Prayer.*
**If today is Saturday, use Psalm 136 at Evening Prayer.*

### The Epiphany and Following

| *Epiphany* | 46, 97 ∻ 96, 100 |
| | Isa. 52:7-10    Rev. 21:22-27    Matt. 12:14-21 |

| *Jan. 7\** | 103 ∻ 114, 115 |
| | Isa. 52:3-6    Rev. 2:1-7    John 2:1-11 |

| *Jan. 8* | 117, 118 ∻ 112, 113 |
| | Isa. 59:15-21    Rev. 2:8-17    John 4:46-54 |

| *Jan. 9* | 121, 122, 123 ∻ 131, 132 |
| | Isa. 63:1-5    Rev. 2:18-29    John 5:1-15 |

| *Jan. 10* | 138, 139:1-17(18-23) ∻ 147 |
| | Isa. 65:1-9    Rev. 3:1-6    John 6:1-14 |

| *Jan. 11* | 148, 150 ∻ 91, 92 |
| | Isa. 65:13-16    Rev. 3:7-13    John 6:15-27 |

| *Jan. 12* | 98, 99, [100] ∻ —— |
| | Isa. 66:1-2, 22-23    Rev. 3:14-22    John 9:1-12, 35-38 |

| *Eve of 1 Epiphany* | —— ∻ 104 |
| | Isa. 61:1-9    Gal. 3:23-29; 4:4-7 |

### Week of 1 Epiphany

| *Sunday* | 146, 147 ∻ 111, 112, 113 |
| | Isa. 40:1-11    Heb. 1:1-12    John 1:1-7, 19-20, 29-34 |

| *Monday* | 1, 2, 3 ∻ 4, 7 |
| | Isa. 40:12-23    Eph. 1:1-14    Mark 1:1-13 |

| *Tuesday* | 5, 6 ∻ 10, 11 |
| | Isa. 40:25-31    Eph. 1:15-23    Mark 1:14-28 |

| *Wednesday* | 119:1-24 ∻ 12, 13, 14 |
| | Isa. 41:1-16    Eph. 2:1-10    Mark 1:29-45 |

| *Thursday* | 18:1-20 ∻ 18:21-50 |
| | Isa. 41:17-29    Eph. 2:11-22    Mark 2:1-12 |

| *Friday* | 16, 17 ∻ 22 |
| | Isa. 42:(1-9)10-17    Eph. 3:1-13    Mark 2:13-22 |

| *Saturday* | 20, 21:1-7(8-14) ∻ 110:1-5(6-7), 116, 117 |
| | Isa. 43:1-13    Eph. 3:14-21    Mark 2:23—3:6 |

*\*The Psalms and Readings for the dated days after the Epiphany
are used only until the following Saturday evening.*

## The Epiphany and Following

**Epiphany**
46, 97 ❖ 96, 100
Isa. 49:1-7    Rev. 21:22-27    Matt. 12:14-21

**Jan. 7***
103 ❖ 114, 115
Deut. 8:1-3    Col. 1:1-14    John 6:30-33, 48-51

**Jan. 8**
117, 118 ❖ 112, 113
Exod. 17:1-7    Col. 1:15-23    John 7:37-52

**Jan. 9**
121, 122, 123 ❖ 131, 132
Isa. 45:14-19    Col. 1:24—2:7    John 8:12-19

**Jan. 10**
138, 139:1-17(18-23) ❖ 147
Jer. 23:1-8    Col. 2:8-23    John 10:7-17

**Jan. 11**
148, 150 ❖ 91, 92
Isa. 55:3-9    Col. 3:1-17    John 14:6-14

**Jan. 12**
98, 99, [100] ❖ ——
Gen. 49:1-2, 8-12    Col. 3:18—4:6    John 15:1-16

**Eve of 1 Epiphany**
—— ❖ 104
Isa. 61:1-9    Gal. 3:23-29; 4:4-7

## Week of 1 Epiphany

**Sunday**
146, 147 ❖ 111, 112, 113
Gen. 1:1—2:3    Eph. 1:3-14    John 1:29-34

**Monday**
1, 2, 3 ❖ 4, 7
Gen. 2:4-9(10-15)16-25    Heb. 1:1-14    John 1:1-18

**Tuesday**
5, 6 ❖ 10, 11
Gen. 3:1-24    Heb. 2:1-10    John 1:19-28

**Wednesday**
119:1-24 ❖ 12, 13, 14
Gen. 4:1-16    Heb. 2:11-18    John 1:(29-34)35-42

**Thursday**
18:1-20 ❖ 18:21-50
Gen. 4:17-26    Heb. 3:1-11    John 1:43-51

**Friday**
16, 17 ❖ 22
Gen. 6:1-8    Heb. 3:12-19    John 2:1-12

**Saturday**
20, 21:1-7(8-14) ❖ 110:1-5(6-7), 116, 117
Gen. 6:9-22    Heb. 4:1-13    John 2:13-22

*The Psalms and Readings for the dated days after the Epiphany are used only until the following Saturday evening.

*Daily Office Year Two* 943

**Week of 2 Epiphany**

Sunday        148, 149, 150   ∴   114, 115
              Isa. 43:14—44:5   Heb. 6:17—7:10   John 4:27-42

Monday        25   ∴   9, 15
              Isa. 44:6-8, 21-23   Eph. 4:1-16   Mark 3:7-19a

Tuesday       26, 28   ∴   36, 39
              Isa. 44:9-20   Eph. 4:17-32   Mark 3:19b-35

Wednesday     38   ∴   119:25-48
              Isa. 44:24—45:7   Eph. 5:1-14   Mark 4:1-20

Thursday      37:1-18   ∴   37:19-42
              Isa. 45:5-17   Eph. 5:15-33   Mark 4:21-34

Friday        31   ∴   35
              Isa. 45:18-25   Eph. 6:1-9   Mark 4:35-41

Saturday      30, 32   ∴   42, 43
              Isa. 46:1-13   Eph. 6:10-24   Mark 5:1-20

**Week of 3 Epiphany**

Sunday        63:1-8(9-11), 98   ∴   103
              Isa. 47:1-15   Heb. 10:19-31   John 5:2-18

Monday        41, 52   ∴   44
              Isa. 48:1-11   Gal. 1:1-17   Mark 5:21-43

Tuesday       45   ∴   47, 48
              Isa. 48:12-21   Gal. 1:18—2:10   Mark 6:1-13

Wednesday     119:49-72   ∴   49, [53]
              Isa. 49:1-12   Gal. 2:11-21   Mark 6:13-29

Thursday      50   ∴   [59, 60] or 118
              Isa. 49:13-23   Gal. 3:1-14   Mark 6:30-46

Friday        40, 54   ∴   51
              Isa. 50:1-11   Gal. 3:15-22   Mark 6:47-56

Saturday      55   ∴   138, 139:1-17(18-23)
              Isa. 51:1-8   Gal. 3:23-29   Mark 7:1-23

## Week of 2 Epiphany

| | | | |
|---|---|---|---|
| *Sunday* | 148, 149, 150 ❖ 114, 115 | | |
| | Gen. 7:1-10, 17-23 | Eph. 4:1-16 | Mark 3:7-19 |
| *Monday* | 25 ❖ 9, 15 | | |
| | Gen. 8:6-22 | Heb. 4:14—5:6 | John 2:23—3:15 |
| *Tuesday* | 26, 28 ❖ 36, 39 | | |
| | Gen. 9:1-17 | Heb. 5:7-14 | John 3:16-21 |
| *Wednesday* | 38 ❖ 119:25-48 | | |
| | Gen. 9:18-29 | Heb. 6:1-12 | John 3:22-36 |
| *Thursday* | 37:1-18 ❖ 37:19-42 | | |
| | Gen. 11:1-9 | Heb. 6:13-20 | John 4:1-15 |
| *Friday* | 31 ❖ 35 | | |
| | Gen. 11:27—12:8 | Heb. 7:1-17 | John 4:16-26 |
| *Saturday* | 30, 32 ❖ 42, 43 | | |
| | Gen. 12:9—13:1 | Heb. 7:18-28 | John 4:27-42 |

## Week of 3 Epiphany

| | | | |
|---|---|---|---|
| *Sunday* | 63:1-8(9-11), 98 ❖ 103 | | |
| | Gen. 13:2-18 | Gal. 2:1-10 | Mark 7:31-37 |
| *Monday* | 41, 52 ❖ 44 | | |
| | Gen. 14:(1-7)8-24 | Heb. 8:1-13 | John 4:43-54 |
| *Tuesday* | 45 ❖ 47, 48 | | |
| | Gen. 15:1-11, 17-21 | Heb. 9:1-14 | John 5:1-18 |
| *Wednesday* | 119:49-72 ❖ 49, [53] | | |
| | Gen. 16:1-14 | Heb. 9:15-28 | John 5:19-29 |
| *Thursday* | 50 ❖ [59, 60] *or* 118 | | |
| | Gen. 16:15—17:14 | Heb. 10:1-10 | John 5:30-47 |
| *Friday* | 40, 54 ❖ 51 | | |
| | Gen. 17:15-27 | Heb. 10:11-25 | John 6:1-15 |
| *Saturday* | 55 ❖ 138, 139:1-17(18-23) | | |
| | Gen. 18:1-16 | Heb. 10:26-39 | John 6:16-27 |

### Week of 4 Epiphany

| | | | |
|---|---|---|---|
| *Sunday* | 24, 29 ❖ 8, 84 | | |
| | Isa. 51:9-16 | Heb. 11:8-16 | John 7:14-31 |
| *Monday* | 56, 57, [58] ❖ 64, 65 | | |
| | Isa. 51:17-23 | Gal. 4:1-11 | Mark 7:24-37 |
| *Tuesday* | 61, 62 ❖ 68:1-20(21-23)24-36 | | |
| | Isa. 52:1-12 | Gal. 4:12-20 | Mark 8:1-10 |
| *Wednesday* | 72 ❖ 119:73-96 | | |
| | Isa. 54:1-10(11-17) | Gal. 4:21-31 | Mark 8:11-26 |
| *Thursday* | [70], 71 ❖ 74 | | |
| | Isa. 55:1-13 | Gal. 5:1-15 | Mark 8:27—9:1 |
| *Friday* | 69:1-23(24-30)31-38 ❖ 73 | | |
| | Isa. 56:1-8 | Gal. 5:16-24 | Mark 9:2-13 |
| *Saturday* | 75, 76 ❖ 23, 27 | | |
| | Isa. 57:3-13 | Gal. 5:25—6:10 | Mark 9:14-29 |

### Week of 5 Epiphany

| | | | |
|---|---|---|---|
| *Sunday* | 93, 96 ❖ 34 | | |
| | Isa. 57:14-21 | Heb. 12:1-6 | John 7:37-46 |
| *Monday* | 80 ❖ 77, [79] | | |
| | Isa. 58:1-12 | Gal. 6:11-18 | Mark 9:30-41 |
| *Tuesday* | 78:1-39 ❖ 78:40-72 | | |
| | Isa. 59:1-15a | 2 Tim. 1:1-14 | Mark 9:42-50 |
| *Wednesday* | 119:97-120 ❖ 81, 82 | | |
| | Isa. 59:15b-21 | 2 Tim. 1:15—2:13 | Mark 10:1-16 |
| *Thursday* | [83] or 146, 147 ❖ 85, 86 | | |
| | Isa. 60:1-17 | 2 Tim. 2:14-26 | Mark 10:17-31 |
| *Friday* | 88 ❖ 91, 92 | | |
| | Isa. 61:1-9 | 2 Tim. 3:1-17 | Mark 10:32-45 |
| *Saturday* | 87, 90 ❖ 136 | | |
| | Isa. 61:10—62:5 | 2 Tim. 4:1-8 | Mark 10:46-52 |

## Week of 4 Epiphany

*Sunday*     24, 29   ❖   8, 84
Gen. 18:16-33    Gal. 5:13-25    Mark 8:22-30

*Monday*    56, 57, [58]   ❖   64, 65
Gen. 19:1-17(18-23)24-29    Heb. 11:1-12    John 6:27-40

*Tuesday*    61, 62   ❖   68:1-20(21-23)24-36
Gen. 21:1-21    Heb. 11:13-22    John 6:41-51

*Wednesday*    72   ❖   119:73-96
Gen. 22:1-18    Heb. 11:23-31    John 6:52-59

*Thursday*    [70], 71   ❖   74
Gen. 23:1-20    Heb. 11:32—12:2    John 6:60-71

*Friday*    69:1-23(24-30)31-38   ❖   73
Gen. 24:1-27    Heb. 12:3-11    John 7:1-13

*Saturday*    75, 76   ❖   23, 27
Gen. 24:28-38, 49-51    Heb. 12:12-29    John 7:14-36

## Week of 5 Epiphany

*Sunday*    93, 96   ❖   34
Gen. 24:50-67    2 Tim. 2:14-21    Mark 10:13-22

*Monday*    80   ❖   77, [79]
Gen. 25:19-34    Heb. 13:1-16    John 7:37-52

*Tuesday*    78:1-39   ❖   78:40-72
Gen. 26:1-6, 12-33    Heb. 13:17-25    John 7:53—8:11

*Wednesday*    119:97-120   ❖   81, 82
Gen. 27:1-29    Rom. 12:1-8    John 8:12-20

*Thursday*    [83] *or* 146, 147   ❖   85, 86
Gen. 27:30-45    Rom. 12:9-21    John 8:21-32

*Friday*    88   ❖   91, 92
Gen. 27:46—28:4, 10-22    Rom. 13:1-14    John 8:33-47

*Saturday*    87, 90   ❖   136
Gen. 29:1-20    Rom. 14:1-23    John 8:47-59

**Week of 6 Epiphany**

| | | | |
|---|---|---|---|
| Sunday | 66, 67 ❖ 19, 46 | | |
| | Isa. 62:6-12 | 1 John 2:3-11 | John 8:12-19 |
| Monday | 89:1-18 ❖ 89:19-52 | | |
| | Isa. 63:1-6 | 1 Tim. 1:1-17 | Mark 11:1-11 |
| Tuesday | 97, 99, [100] ❖ 94, [95] | | |
| | Isa. 63:7-14 | 1 Tim. 1:18—2:8 | Mark 11:12-26 |
| Wednesday | 101, 109:1-4(5-19)20-30 ❖ 119:121-144 | | |
| | Isa. 63:15—64:9 | 1 Tim. 3:1-16 | Mark 11:27—12:12 |
| Thursday | 105:1-22 ❖ 105:23-45 | | |
| | Isa. 65:1-12 | 1 Tim. 4:1-16 | Mark 12:13-27 |
| Friday | 102 ❖ 107:1-32 | | |
| | Isa. 65:17-25 | 1 Tim 5:17-22(23-25) | Mark 12:28-34 |
| Saturday | 107:33-43, 108:1-6(7-13) ❖ 33 | | |
| | Isa. 66:1-6 | 1 Tim. 6:6-21 | Mark 12:35-44 |

**Week of 7 Epiphany**

| | | | |
|---|---|---|---|
| Sunday | 118 ❖ 145 | | |
| | Isa. 66:7-14 | 1 John 3:4-10 | John 10:7-16 |
| Monday | 106:1-18 ❖ 106:19-48 | | |
| | Ruth 1:1-14 | 2 Cor. 1:1-11 | Matt. 5:1-12 |
| Tuesday | [120], 121, 122, 123 ❖ 124, 125, 126, [127] | | |
| | Ruth 1:15-22 | 2 Cor. 1:12-22 | Matt. 5:13-20 |
| Wednesday | 119:145-176 ❖ 128, 129, 130 | | |
| | Ruth 2:1-13 | 2 Cor. 1:23—2:17 | Matt. 5:21-26 |
| Thursday | 131, 132, [133] ❖ 134, 135 | | |
| | Ruth 2:14-23 | 2 Cor. 3:1-18 | Matt. 5:27-37 |
| Friday | 140, 142 ❖ 141, 143:1-11(12) | | |
| | Ruth 3:1-18 | 2 Cor. 4:1-12 | Matt. 5:38-48 |
| Saturday | 137:1-6(7-9), 144 ❖ 104 | | |
| | Ruth 4:1-17 | 2 Cor. 4:13—5:10 | Matt. 6:1-6 |

|          |                                                                              |
|----------|------------------------------------------------------------------------------|
|          | **Week of 6 Epiphany**                                                        |
| *Sunday* | 66, 67 ❖ 19, 46                                                               |
|          | Gen. 29:20-35    1 Tim. 3:14—4:10    Mark 10:23-31                            |
| *Monday* | 89:1-18 ❖ 89:19-52                                                            |
|          | Gen. 30:1-24    1 John 1:1-10    John 9:1-17                                  |
| *Tuesday* | 97, 99, [100] ❖ 94, [95]                                                     |
|          | Gen. 31:1-24    1 John 2:1-11    John 9:18-41                                 |
| *Wednesday* | 101, 109:1-4(5-19)20-30 ❖ 119:121-144                                      |
|          | Gen. 31:25-50    1 John 2:12-17    John 10:1-18                              |
| *Thursday* | 105:1-22 ❖ 105:23-45                                                        |
|          | Gen. 32:3-21    1 John 2:18-29    John 10:19-30                             |
| *Friday* | 102 ❖ 107:1-32                                                               |
|          | Gen. 32:22—33:17    1 John 3:1-10    John 10:31-42                           |
| *Saturday* | 107:33-43, 108:1-6(7-13) ❖ 33                                              |
|          | Gen. 35:1-20    1 John 3:11-18    John 11:1-16                              |

**Week of 7 Epiphany**

| *Sunday* | 118 ❖ 145 |
|----------|-----------|
|          | Prov. 1:20-33    2 Cor. 5:11-21    Mark 10:35-45 |
| *Monday* | 106:1-18 ❖ 106:19-48 |
|          | Prov. 3:11-20    1 John 3:18—4:6    John 11:17-29 |
| *Tuesday* | [120], 121, 122, 123 ❖ 124, 125, 126, [127] |
|          | Prov. 4:1-27    1 John 4:7-21    John 11:30-44 |
| *Wednesday* | 119:145-176 ❖ 128, 129, 130 |
|          | Prov. 6:1-19    1 John 5:1-12    John 11:45-54 |
| *Thursday* | 131, 132, [133] ❖ 134, 135 |
|          | Prov. 7:1-27    1 John 5:13-21    John 11:55—12:8 |
| *Friday* | 140, 142 ❖ 141, 143:1-11(12) |
|          | Prov. 8:1-21    Philemon 1-25    John 12:9-19 |
| *Saturday* | 137:1-6(7-9), 144 ❖ 104 |
|          | Prov. 8:22-36    2 Tim. 1:1-14    John 12:20-26 |

### Week of 8 Epiphany

| | | |
|---|---|---|
| *Sunday* | 146, 147  ❖  111, 112, 113 | |
| | Deut. 4:1-9    2 Tim. 4:1-8    John 12:1-8 | |
| *Monday* | 1, 2, 3  ❖  4, 7 | |
| | Deut. 4:9-14    2 Cor. 10:1-18    Matt. 6:7-15 | |
| *Tuesday* | 5, 6  ❖  10, 11 | |
| | Deut. 4:15-24    2 Cor. 11:1-21a    Matt. 6:16-23 | |
| *Wednesday* | 119:1-24  ❖  12, 13, 14 | |
| | Deut. 4:25-31    2 Cor. 11:21b-33    Matt. 6:24-34 | |
| *Thursday* | 18:1-20  ❖  18:21-50 | |
| | Deut. 4:32-40    2 Cor. 12:1-10    Matt. 7:1-12 | |
| *Friday* | 16, 17  ❖  22 | |
| | Deut. 5:1-22    2 Cor. 12:11-21    Matt. 7:13-21 | |
| *Saturday* | 20, 21:1-7(8-14)  ❖  110:1-5(6-7), 116, 117 | |
| | Deut. 5:22-33    2 Cor. 13:1-14    Matt. 7:22-29 | |

### Week of Last Epiphany

| | | |
|---|---|---|
| *Sunday* | 148, 149, 150  ❖  114, 115 | |
| | Deut. 6:1-9    Heb. 12:18-29    John 12:24-32 | |
| *Monday* | 25  ❖  9, 15 | |
| | Deut. 6:10-15    Heb. 1:1-14    John 1:1-18 | |
| *Tuesday* | 26, 28  ❖  36, 39 | |
| | Deut. 6:16-25    Heb. 2:1-10    John 1:19-28 | |
| *Ash Wednesday* | 95* & 32, 143  ❖  102, 130 | |
| | Jonah 3:1—4:11    Heb. 12:1-14    Luke 18:9-14 | |
| *Thursday* | 37:1-18  ❖  37:19-42 | |
| | Deut. 7:6-11    Titus 1:1-16    John 1:29-34 | |
| *Friday* | 95* & 31  ❖  35 | |
| | Deut. 7:12-16    Titus 2:1-15    John 1:35-42 | |
| *Saturday* | 30, 32  ❖  42, 43 | |
| | Deut. 7:17-26    Titus 3:1-15    John 1:43-51 | |

*For the Invitatory

### Week of 8 Epiphany

| | | |
|---|---|---|
| *Sunday* | 146, 147 ❖ 111, 112, 113 | |
| | Prov. 9:1-12 2 Cor. 9:6b-15 Mark 10:46-52 | |
| *Monday* | 1, 2, 3 ❖ 4, 7 | |
| | Prov. 10:1-12 2 Tim. 1:15—2:13 John 12:27-36a | |
| *Tuesday* | 5, 6 ❖ 10, 11 | |
| | Prov. 15:16-33 2 Tim. 2:14-26 John 12:36b-50 | |
| *Wednesday* | 119:1-24 ❖ 12, 13, 14 | |
| | Prov. 17:1-20 2 Tim 3:1-17 John 13:1-20 | |
| *Thursday* | 18:1-20 ❖ 18:21-50 | |
| | Prov. 21:30—22:6 2 Tim. 4:1-8 John 13:21-30 | |
| *Friday* | 16, 17 ❖ 22 | |
| | Prov. 23:19-21, 29—24:2 2 Tim. 4:9-22 John 13:31-38 | |
| *Saturday* | 20, 21:1-7(8-14) ❖ 110:1-5(6-7), 116, 117 | |
| | Prov. 25:15-28 Phil. 1:1-11 John 18:1-14 | |

### Week of Last Epiphany

| | | |
|---|---|---|
| *Sunday* | 148, 149, 150 ❖ 114, 115 | |
| | Ecclus. 48:1-11 2 Cor. 3:7-18 Luke 9:18-27 | |
| *Monday* | 25 ❖ 9, 15 | |
| | Prov. 27:1-6, 10-12 Phil. 2:1-13 John 18:15-18, 25-27 | |
| *Tuesday* | 26, 28 ❖ 36, 39 | |
| | Prov. 30:1-4, 24-33 Phil. 3:1-11 John 18:28-38 | |
| *Ash Wednesday* | 95* & 32, 143 ❖ 102, 130 | |
| | Amos 5:6-15 Heb. 12:1-14 Luke 18:9-14 | |
| *Thursday* | 37:1-18 ❖ 37:19-42 | |
| | Hab. 3:1-10(11-15)16-18 Phil. 3:12-21 John 17:1-8 | |
| *Friday* | 95* & 31 ❖ 35 | |
| | Ezek. 18:1-4, 25-32 Phil. 4:1-9 John 17:9-19 | |
| *Saturday* | 30, 32 ❖ 42, 43 | |
| | Ezek. 39:21-29 Phil. 4:10-20 John 17:20-26 | |

*For the Invitatory

### Week of 1 Lent

| | | | |
|---|---|---|---|
| *Sunday* | 63:1-8(9-11), 98 ∻ 103 | | |
| | Deut. 8:1-10 | 1 Cor. 1:17-31 | Mark 2:18-22 |
| *Monday* | 41, 52 ∻ 44 | | |
| | Deut. 8:11-20 | Heb. 2:11-18 | John 2:1-12 |
| *Tuesday* | 45 ∻ 47, 48 | | |
| | Deut. 9:4-12 | Heb. 3:1-11 | John 2:13-22 |
| *Wednesday* | 119:49-72 ∻ 49, [53] | | |
| | Deut. 9:13-21 | Heb. 3:12-19 | John 2:23—3:15 |
| *Thursday* | 50 ∻ [59, 60] *or* 19, 46 | | |
| | Deut. 9:23—10:5 | Heb. 4:1-10 | John 3:16-21 |
| *Friday* | 95* & 40, 54 ∻ 51 | | |
| | Deut. 10:12-22 | Heb. 4:11-16 | John 3:22-36 |
| *Saturday* | 55 ∻ 138, 139:1-17(18-23) | | |
| | Deut. 11:18-28 | Heb. 5:1-10 | John 4:1-26 |

### Week of 2 Lent

| | | | |
|---|---|---|---|
| *Sunday* | 24, 29 ∻ 8, 84 | | |
| | Jer. 1:1-10 | 1 Cor. 3:11-23 | Mark 3:31—4:9 |
| *Monday* | 56, 57, [58] ∻ 64, 65 | | |
| | Jer. 1:11-19 | Rom. 1:1-15 | John 4:27-42 |
| *Tuesday* | 61, 62 ∻ 68:1-20(21-23)24-36 | | |
| | Jer. 2:1-13 | Rom. 1:16-25 | John 4:43-54 |
| *Wednesday* | 72 ∻ 119:73-96 | | |
| | Jer. 3:6-18 | Rom. 1:28—2:11 | John 5:1-18 |
| *Thursday* | [70], 71 ∻ 74 | | |
| | Jer. 4:9-10, 19-28 | Rom. 2:12-24 | John 5:19-29 |
| *Friday* | 95* & 69:1-23(24-30)31-38 ∻ 73 | | |
| | Jer. 5:1-9 | Rom. 2:25—3:18 | John 5:30-47 |
| *Saturday* | 75, 76 ∻ 23, 27 | | |
| | Jer. 5:20-31 | Rom. 3:19-31 | John 7:1-13 |

*For the Invitatory

### Week of 1 Lent

| | | | |
|---|---|---|---|
| *Sunday* | 63:1-8(9-11), 98 | ∴ | 103 |
| | Dan. 9:3-10 | Heb. 2:10-18 | John 12:44-50 |
| *Monday* | 41, 52 | ∴ | 44 |
| | Gen. 37:1-11 | 1 Cor. 1:1-19 | Mark 1:1-13 |
| *Tuesday* | 45 | ∴ | 47, 48 |
| | Gen. 37:12-24 | 1 Cor. 1:20-31 | Mark 1:14-28 |
| *Wednesday* | 119:49-72 | ∴ | 49, [53] |
| | Gen. 37:25-36 | 1 Cor. 2:1-13 | Mark 1:29-45 |
| *Thursday* | 50 | ∴ | [59, 60] *or* 19, 46 |
| | Gen. 39:1-23 | 1 Cor. 2:14—3:15 | Mark 2:1-12 |
| *Friday* | 95* & 40, 54 | ∴ | 51 |
| | Gen. 40:1-23 | 1 Cor. 3:16-23 | Mark 2:13-22 |
| *Saturday* | 55 | ∴ | 138, 139:1-17(18-23) |
| | Gen. 41:1-13 | 1 Cor. 4:1-7 | Mark 2:23—3:6 |

### Week of 2 Lent

| | | | |
|---|---|---|---|
| *Sunday* | 24, 29 | ∴ | 8, 84 |
| | Gen. 41:14-45 | Rom. 6:3-14 | John 5:19-24 |
| *Monday* | 56, 57, [58] | ∴ | 64, 65 |
| | Gen. 41:46-57 | 1 Cor. 4:8-20(21) | Mark 3:7-19a |
| *Tuesday* | 61, 62 | ∴ | 68:1-20(21-23)24-36 |
| | Gen. 42:1-17 | 1 Cor. 5:1-8 | Mark 3:19b-35 |
| *Wednesday* | 72 | ∴ | 119:73-96 |
| | Gen. 42:18-28 | 1 Cor. 5:9—6:8 | Mark 4:1-20 |
| *Thursday* | [70], 71 | ∴ | 74 |
| | Gen. 42:29-38 | 1 Cor. 6:12-20 | Mark 4:21-34 |
| *Friday* | 95* & 69:1-23(24-30)31-38 | ∴ | 73 |
| | Gen. 43:1-15 | 1 Cor. 7:1-9 | Mark 4:35-41 |
| *Saturday* | 75, 76 | ∴ | 23, 27 |
| | Gen. 43:16-34 | 1 Cor. 7:10-24 | Mark 5:1-20 |

*For the Invitatory

**Week of 3 Lent**

| Sunday | 93, 96 | ÷ | 34 | |
|---|---|---|---|---|
| | Jer. 6:9-15 | 1 Cor. 6:12-20 | Mark 5:1-20 | |

| Monday | 80 | ÷ | 77, [79] | |
|---|---|---|---|---|
| | Jer. 7:1-15 | Rom. 4:1-12 | John 7:14-36 | |

| Tuesday | 78:1-39 | ÷ | 78:40-72 | |
|---|---|---|---|---|
| | Jer. 7:21-34 | Rom. 4:13-25 | John 7:37-52 | |

| Wednesday | 119:97-120 | ÷ | 81, 82 | |
|---|---|---|---|---|
| | Jer. 8:18—9:6 | Rom. 5:1-11 | John 8:12-20 | |

| Thursday | [83] or 42, 43 | ÷ | 85, 86 | |
|---|---|---|---|---|
| | Jer. 10:11-24 | Rom. 5:12-21 | John 8:21-32 | |

| Friday | 95* & 88 | ÷ | 91, 92 | |
|---|---|---|---|---|
| | Jer. 11:1-8, 14-20 | Rom. 6:1-11 | John 8:33-47 | |

| Saturday | 87, 90 | ÷ | 136 | |
|---|---|---|---|---|
| | Jer. 13:1-11 | Rom. 6:12-23 | John 8:47-59 | |

**Week of 4 Lent**

| Sunday | 66, 67 | ÷ | 19, 46 | |
|---|---|---|---|---|
| | Jer. 14:1-9, 17-22 | Gal. 4:21—5:1 | Mark 8:11-21 | |

| Monday | 89:1-18 | ÷ | 89:19-52 | |
|---|---|---|---|---|
| | Jer. 16:10-21 | Rom. 7:1-12 | John 6:1-15 | |

| Tuesday | 97, 99, [100] | ÷ | 94, [95] | |
|---|---|---|---|---|
| | Jer. 17:19-27 | Rom. 7:13-25 | John 6:16-27 | |

| Wednesday | 101, 109:1-4(5-19)20-30 | ÷ | 119:121-144 | |
|---|---|---|---|---|
| | Jer. 18:1-11 | Rom. 8:1-11 | John 6:27-40 | |

| Thursday | 69:1-23(24-30)31-38 | ÷ | 73 | |
|---|---|---|---|---|
| | Jer. 22:13-23 | Rom. 8:12-27 | John 6:41-51 | |

| Friday | 95* & 102 | ÷ | 107:1-32 | |
|---|---|---|---|---|
| | Jer. 23:1-8 | Rom. 8:28-39 | John 6:52-59 | |

| Saturday | 107:33-43, 108:1-6(7-13) | ÷ | 33 | |
|---|---|---|---|---|
| | Jer. 23:9-15 | Rom. 9:1-18 | John 6:60-71 | |

*For the Invitatory*

## Week of 3 Lent

| | | | |
|---|---|---|---|
| *Sunday* | 93, 96 ❖ 34 | | |
| | Gen. 44:1-17 | Rom. 8:1-10 | John 5:25-29 |
| *Monday* | 80 ❖ 77, [79] | | |
| | Gen. 44:18-34 | 1 Cor. 7:25-31 | Mark 5:21-43 |
| *Tuesday* | 78:1-39 ❖ 78:40-72 | | |
| | Gen. 45:1-15 | 1 Cor. 7:32-40 | Mark 6:1-13 |
| *Wednesday* | 119:97-120 ❖ 81, 82 | | |
| | Gen. 45:16-28 | 1 Cor. 8:1-13 | Mark 6:13-29 |
| *Thursday* | [83] *or* 42, 43 ❖ 85, 86 | | |
| | Gen. 46:1-7, 28-34 | 1 Cor. 9:1-15 | Mark 6:30-46 |
| *Friday* | 95* & 88 ❖ 91, 92 | | |
| | Gen. 47:1-26 | 1 Cor. 9:16-27 | Mark 6:47-56 |
| *Saturday* | 87, 90 ❖ 136 | | |
| | Gen. 47:27—48:7 | 1 Cor. 10:1-13 | Mark 7:1-23 |

## Week of 4 Lent

| | | | |
|---|---|---|---|
| *Sunday* | 66, 67 ❖ 19, 46 | | |
| | Gen. 48:8-22 | Rom. 8:11-25 | John 6:27-40 |
| *Monday* | 89:1-18 ❖ 89:19-52 | | |
| | Gen. 49:1-28 | 1 Cor. 10:14—11:1 | Mark 7:24-37 |
| *Tuesday* | 97, 99, [100] ❖ 94, [95] | | |
| | Gen. 49:29—50:14 | 1 Cor. 11:17-34 | Mark 8:1-10 |
| *Wednesday* | 101, 109:1-4(5-19)20-30 ❖ 119:121-144 | | |
| | Gen. 50:15-26 | 1 Cor. 12:1-11 | Mark 8:11-26 |
| *Thursday* | 69:1-23(24-30)31-38 ❖ 73 | | |
| | Exod. 1:6-22 | 1 Cor. 12:12-26 | Mark 8:27—9:1 |
| *Friday* | 95* & 102 ❖ 107:1-32 | | |
| | Exod. 2:1-22 | 1 Cor. 12:27—13:3 | Mark 9:2-13 |
| *Saturday* | 107:33-43, 108:1-6(7-13) ❖ 33 | | |
| | Exod. 2:23—3:15 | 1 Cor. 13:1-13 | Mark 9:14-29 |

*For the Invitatory

### Week of 5 Lent

*Sunday*    118   ❖   145
Jer. 23:16-32   1 Cor. 9:19-27   Mark 8:31—9:1

*Monday*    31   ❖   35
Jer. 24:1-10   Rom. 9:19-33   John 9:1-17

*Tuesday*    [120], 121, 122, 123   ❖   124, 125, 126, [127]
Jer. 25:8-17   Rom. 10:1-13   John 9:18-41

*Wednesday*    119:145-176   ❖   128, 129, 130
Jer. 25:30-38   Rom. 10:14-21   John 10:1-18

*Thursday*    131, 132, [133]   ❖   140, 142
Jer. 26:1-16   Rom. 11:1-12   John 10:19-42

*Friday*    95* & 22   ❖   141, 143:1-11(12)
Jer. 29:1, 4-13   Rom. 11:13-24   John 11:1-27, or 12:1-10

*Saturday*    137:1-6(7-9), 144   ❖   42, 43
Jer. 31:27-34   Rom. 11:25-36   John 11:28-44, or 12:37-50

### Holy Week

*Palm Sunday*    24, 29   ❖   103
Zech. 9:9-12**   1 Tim. 6:12-16**
Zech. 12:9-11; 13:1, 7-9***   Matt. 21:12-17***

*Monday*    51:1-18(19-20)   ❖   69:1-23
Jer. 12:1-16   Phil. 3:1-14   John 12:9-19

*Tuesday*    6, 12   ❖   94
Jer. 15:10-21   Phil. 3:15-21   John 12:20-26

*Wednesday*    55   ❖   74
Jer. 17:5-10, 14-17   Phil. 4:1-13   John 12:27-36

*Maundy Thursday*    102   ❖   142, 143
Jer. 20:7-11   1 Cor. 10:14-17; 11:27-32   John 17:1-11(12-26

*Good Friday*    95* & 22   ❖   40:1-14(15-19), 54
Wisdom 1:16—2:1, 12-22   1 Peter 1:10-20   John 13:36-38**
or Gen. 22:1-14      John 19:38-42**

*Holy Saturday*    95* & 88   ❖   27
Job 19:21-27a   Heb. 4:1-16**   Rom. 8:1-11***

---

*For the Invitatory   ** Intended for use in the morning   ***Intended for use in the evening*

## Week of 5 Lent

**Sunday**
118 ❖ 145
Exod. 3:16—4:12    Rom. 12:1-21    John 8:46-59

**Monday**
31 ❖ 35
Exod. 4:10-20(21-26)27-31    1 Cor. 14:1-19    Mark 9:30-41

**Tuesday**
[120], 121, 122, 123 ❖ 124, 125, 126, [127]
Exod. 5:1—6:1    1 Cor. 14:20-33a, 39-40    Mark 9:42-50

**Wednesday**
119:145-176 ❖ 128, 129, 130
Exod. 7:8-24    2 Cor. 2:14—3:6    Mark 10:1-16

**Thursday**
131, 132, [133] ❖ 140, 142
Exod. 7:25—8:19    2 Cor. 3:7-18    Mark 10:17-31

**Friday**
95* & 22 ❖ 141, 143:1-11(12)
Exod. 9:13-35    2 Cor. 4:1-12    Mark 10:32-45

**Saturday**
137:1-6(7-9), 144 ❖ 42, 43
Exod. 10:21—11:8    2 Cor. 4:13-18    Mark 10:46-52

## Holy Week

**Palm Sunday** 24, 29 ❖ 103
Zech. 9:9-12**    1 Tim. 6:12-16**
Zech. 12:9-11; 13:1, 7-9***    Luke 19:41-48***

**Monday** 51:1-18(19-20) ❖ 69:1-23
Lam. 1:1-2, 6-12    2 Cor. 1:1-7    Mark 11:12-25

**Tuesday** 6, 12 ❖ 94
Lam. 1:17-22    2 Cor. 1:8-22    Mark 11:27-33

**Wednesday** 55 ❖ 74
Lam. 2:1-9    2 Cor. 1:23—2:11    Mark 12:1-11

**Maundy Thursday** 102 ❖ 142, 143
Lam. 2:10-18    1 Cor. 10:14-17; 11:27-32    Mark 14:12-25

**Good Friday** 95* & 22 ❖ 40:1-14(15-19), 54
Lam. 3:1-9, 19-33    1 Pet. 1:10-20    John 13:36-38**
John 19:38-42***

**Holy Saturday** 95* & 88 ❖ 27
Lam. 3:37-58    Heb. 4:1-16**    Rom. 8:1-11***

*For the Invitatory    **Intended for use in the morning    ***Intended for use in the evening*

**Easter Week**

| | | | |
|---|---|---|---|
| *Easter Day* | 148, 149, 150 | ∴ | 113, 114, *or* 118 |
| | Exod. 12:1-14** | —— | John 1:1-18** |
| | Isa. 51:9-11*** | | Luke 24:13-35, *or* John 20:19-23*** |

| *Monday* | 93, 98 | ∴ | 66 | |
|---|---|---|---|---|
| | Jonah 2:1-9 | Acts 2:14, 22-32* | John 14:1-14 |

| *Tuesday* | 103 | ∴ | 111, 114 | |
|---|---|---|---|---|
| | Isa. 30:18-21 | Acts 2:36-41(42-47)* | John 14:15-31 |

| *Wednesday* | 97, 99 | ∴ | 115 | |
|---|---|---|---|---|
| | Micah 7:7-15 | Acts 3:1-10* | John 15:1-11 |

| *Thursday* | 146, 147 | ∴ | 148, 149 | |
|---|---|---|---|---|
| | Ezek. 37:1-14 | Acts 3:11-26* | John 15:12-27 |

| *Friday* | 136 | ∴ | 118 | |
|---|---|---|---|---|
| | Dan. 12:1-4, 13 | Acts 4:1-12* | John 16:1-15 |

| *Saturday* | 145 | ∴ | 104 | |
|---|---|---|---|---|
| | Isa. 25:1-9 | Acts 4:13-21(22-31)* | John 16:16-33 |

**Week of 2 Easter**

| *Sunday* | 146, 147 | ∴ | 111, 112, 113 | |
|---|---|---|---|---|
| | Isa. 43:8-13 | 1 Pet. 2:2-10 | John 14:1-7· |

| *Monday* | 1, 2, 3 | ∴ | 4, 7 | |
|---|---|---|---|---|
| | Dan. 1:1-21 | 1 John 1:1-10 | John 17:1-11 |

| *Tuesday* | 5, 6 | ∴ | 10, 11 | |
|---|---|---|---|---|
| | Dan. 2:1-16 | 1 John 2:1-11 | John 17:12-19 |

| *Wednesday* | 119:1-24 | ∴ | 12, 13, 14 | |
|---|---|---|---|---|
| | Dan. 2:17-30 | 1 John 2:12-17 | John 17:20-26 |

| *Thursday* | 18:1-20 | ∴ | 18:21-50 | |
|---|---|---|---|---|
| | Dan. 2:31-49 | 1 John 2:18-29 | Luke 3:1-14 |

| *Friday* | 16, 17 | ∴ | 134, 135 | |
|---|---|---|---|---|
| | Dan. 3:1-18 | 1 John 3:1-10 | Luke 3:15-22 |

| *Saturday* | 20, 21:1-7(8-14) | ∴ | 110:1-5(6-7), 116, 117 | |
|---|---|---|---|---|
| | Dan. 3:19-30 | 1 John 3:11-18 | Luke 4:1-13 |

---

**Intended for use in the morning    *Duplicates the First Lesson at the Eucharist.
***Intended for use in the evening    Readings from Year Two may be substituted.

### Easter Week

| | | | |
|---|---|---|---|
| *Easter Day* | 148, 149, 150 ∴ 113, 114, *or* 118 | | |
| | Exod. 12:1-14** —— John 1:1-18** | | |
| | Isa. 51:9-11*** Luke 24:13-35, *or* John 20:19-23*** | | |
| *Monday* | 93, 98 ∴ 66 | | |
| | Exod. 12:14-27 1 Cor. 15:1-11 Mark 16:1-8 | | |
| *Tuesday* | 103 ∴ 111, 114 | | |
| | Exod. 12:28-39 1 Cor. 15:12-28 Mark 16:9-20 | | |
| *Wednesday* | 97, 99 ∴ 115 | | |
| | Exod. 12:40-51 1 Cor. 15:(29)30-41 Matt. 28:1-16 | | |
| *Thursday* | 146, 147 ∴ 148, 149 | | |
| | Exod. 13:3-10 1 Cor. 15:41-50 Matt. 28:16-20 | | |
| *Friday* | 136 ∴ 118 | | |
| | Exod. 13:1-2, 11-16 1 Cor. 15:51-58 Luke 24:1-12 | | |
| *Saturday* | 145 ∴ 104 | | |
| | Exod. 13:17—14:4 2 Cor. 4:16—5:10 Mark 12:18-27 | | |

### Week of 2 Easter

| | | | |
|---|---|---|---|
| *Sunday* | 146, 147 ∴ 111, 112, 113 | | |
| | Exod. 14:5-22 1 John 1:1-7 John 14:1-7 | | |
| *Monday* | 1, 2, 3 ∴ 4, 7 | | |
| | Exod. 14:21-31 1 Pet. 1:1-12 John 14:(1-7)8-17 | | |
| *Tuesday* | 5, 6 ∴ 10, 11 | | |
| | Exod. 15:1-21 1 Pet. 1:13-25 John 14:18-31 | | |
| *Wednesday* | 119:1-24 ∴ 12, 13, 14 | | |
| | Exod. 15:22—16:10 1 Pet. 2:1-10 John 15:1-11 | | |
| *Thursday* | 18:1-20 ∴ 18:21-50 | | |
| | Exod. 16:10-21 1 Pet. 2:11-25 John 15:12-27 | | |
| *Friday* | 16, 17 ∴ 134, 135 | | |
| | Exod. 16:22-36 1 Pet. 3:13—4:6 John 16:1-15 | | |
| *Saturday* | 20, 21:1-7(8-14) ∴ 110:1-5(6-7), 116, 117 | | |
| | Exod. 17:1-16 1 Pet. 4:7-19 John 16:16-33 | | |

*Intended for use in the morning     ***Intended for use in the evening

## Week of 3 Easter

| | | | |
|---|---|---|---|
| *Sunday* | 148, 149, 150 | ❖ 114, 115 | |
| | Dan. 4:1-18 | 1 Pet. 4:7-11 | John 21:15-25 |
| *Monday* | 25 | ❖ 9, 15 | |
| | Dan. 4:19-27 | 1 John 3:19—4:6 | Luke 4:14-30 |
| *Tuesday* | 26, 28 | ❖ 36, 39 | |
| | Dan. 4:28-37 | 1 John 4:7-21 | Luke 4:31-37 |
| *Wednesday* | 38 | ❖ 119:25-48 | |
| | Dan. 5:1-12 | 1 John 5:1-12 | Luke 4:38-44 |
| *Thursday* | 37:1-18 | ❖ 37:19-42 | |
| | Dan. 5:13-30 | 1 John 5:13-20(21) | Luke 5:1-11 |
| *Friday* | 105:1-22 | ❖ 105:23-45 | |
| | Dan. 6:1-15 | 2 John 1-13 | Luke 5:12-26 |
| *Saturday* | 30, 32 | ❖ 42, 43 | |
| | Dan. 6:16-28 | 3 John 1-15 | Luke 5:27-39 |

## Week of 4 Easter

| | | | |
|---|---|---|---|
| *Sunday* | 63:1-8(9-11), 98 | ❖ 103 | |
| | Wisdom 1:1-15 | 1 Pet. 5:1-11 | Matt. 7:15-29 |
| *Monday* | 41, 52 | ❖ 44 | |
| | Wisdom 1:16—2:11, 21-24 | Col. 1:1-14 | Luke 6:1-11 |
| *Tuesday* | 45 | ❖ 47, 48 | |
| | Wisdom 3:1-9 | Col. 1:15-23 | Luke 6:12-26 |
| *Wednesday* | 119:49-72 | ❖ 49, [53] | |
| | Wisdom 4:16—5:8 | Col. 1:24—2:7 | Luke 6:27-38 |
| *Thursday* | 50 | ❖ [59, 60] *or* 114, 115 | |
| | Wisdom 5:9-23 | Col. 2:8-23 | Luke 6:39-49 |
| *Friday* | 40, 54 | ❖ 51 | |
| | Wisdom 6:12-23 | Col. 3:1-11 | Luke 7:1-17 |
| *Saturday* | 55 | ❖ 138, 139:1-17(18-23) | |
| | Wisdom 7:1-14 | Col. 3:12-17 | Luke 7:18-28(29-30)31-35 |

### Week of 3 Easter

| | | | |
|---|---|---|---|
| *Sunday* | 148, 149, 150 ∴ 114, 115 | | |
| | Exod. 18:1-12 | 1 John 2:7-17 | Mark 16:9-20 |
| *Monday* | 25 ∴ 9, 15 | | |
| | Exod. 18:13-27 | 1 Pet. 5:1-14 | Matt. (1:1-17); 3:1-6 |
| *Tuesday* | 26, 28 ∴ 36, 39 | | |
| | Exod. 19:1-16 | Col. 1:1-14 | Matt. 3:7-12 |
| *Wednesday* | 38 ∴ 119:25-48 | | |
| | Exod. 19:16-25 | Col. 1:15-23 | Matt. 3:13-17 |
| *Thursday* | 37:1-18 ∴ 37:19-42 | | |
| | Exod. 20:1-21 | Col. 1:24—2:7 | Matt. 4:1-11 |
| *Friday* | 105:1-22 ∴ 105:23-45 | | |
| | Exod. 24:1-18 | Col. 2:8-23 | Matt. 4:12-17 |
| *Saturday* | 30, 32 ∴ 42, 43 | | |
| | Exod. 25:1-22 | Col. 3:1-17 | Matt. 4:18-25 |

### Week of 4 Easter

| | | | |
|---|---|---|---|
| *Sunday* | 63:1-8(9-11), 98 ∴ 103 | | |
| | Exod. 28:1-4, 30-38 | 1 John 2:18-29 | Mark 6:30-44 |
| *Monday* | 41, 52 ∴ 44 | | |
| | Exod. 32:1-20 | Col. 3:18—4:6(7-18) | Matt. 5:1-10 |
| *Tuesday* | 45 ∴ 47, 48 | | |
| | Exod. 32:21-34 | 1 Thess. 1:1-10 | Matt. 5:11-16 |
| *Wednesday* | 119:49-72 ∴ 49, [53] | | |
| | Exod. 33:1-23 | 1 Thess. 2:1-12 | Matt. 5:17-20 |
| *Thursday* | 50 ∴ [59, 60] or 114, 115 | | |
| | Exod. 34:1-17 | 1 Thess. 2:13-20 | Matt. 5:21-26 |
| *Friday* | 40, 54 ∴ 51 | | |
| | Exod. 34:18-35 | 1 Thess. 3:1-13 | Matt. 5:27-37 |
| *Saturday* | 55 ∴ 138, 139:1-17(18-23) | | |
| | Exod. 40:18-38 | 1 Thess. 4:1-12 | Matt. 5:38-48 |

**Week of 5 Easter**

| | | | |
|---|---|---|---|
| *Sunday* | 24, 29 ❖ 8, 84 | | |
| | Wisdom 7:22—8:1 | 2 Thess. 2:13-17 | Matt. 7:7-14 |
| *Monday* | 56, 57, [58] ❖ 64, 65 | | |
| | Wisdom 9:1, 7-18 | Col. (3:18—4:1)2-18 | Luke 7:36-50 |
| *Tuesday* | 61, 62 ❖ 68:1-20(21-23)24-36 | | |
| | Wisdom 10:1-4(5-12)13-21 | Rom. 12:1-21 | Luke 8:1-15 |
| *Wednesday* | 72 ❖ 119:73-96 | | |
| | Wisdom 13:1-9 | Rom. 13:1-14 | Luke 8:16-25 |
| *Thursday* | [70], 71 ❖ 74 | | |
| | Wisdom 14:27—15:3 | Rom. 14:1-12 | Luke 8:26-39 |
| *Friday* | 106:1-18 ❖ 106:19-48 | | |
| | Wisdom 16:15—17:1 | Rom. 14:13-23 | Luke 8:40-56 |
| *Saturday* | 75, 76 ❖ 23, 27 | | |
| | Wisdom 19:1-8, 18-22 | Rom. 15:1-13 | Luke 9:1-17 |

**Week of 6 Easter**

| | | | |
|---|---|---|---|
| *Sunday* | 93, 96 ❖ 34 | | |
| | Ecclus. 43:1-12, 27-32 | 1 Tim. 3:14—4:5 | Matt. 13:24-34a |
| *Monday* | 80 ❖ 77, [79] | | |
| | Deut. 8:1-10 | James 1:1-15 | Luke 9:18-27 |
| *Tuesday* | 78:1-39 ❖ 78:40-72 | | |
| | Deut. 8:11-20 | James 1:16-27 | Luke 11:1-13 |
| *Wednesday* | 119:97-120 ❖ —— | | |
| | Baruch 3:24-37 | James 5:13-18 | Luke 12:22-31 |
| *Eve of Ascension* | —— ❖ 68:1-20 | | |
| | 2 Kings 2:1-15 | Rev. 5:1-14 | |
| *Ascension Day* | 8, 47 ❖ 24, 96 | | |
| | Ezek. 1:1-14, 24-28b | Heb. 2:5-18 | Matt. 28:16-20 |
| *Friday* | 85, 86 ❖ 91, 92 | | |
| | Ezek. 1:28—3:3 | Heb. 4:14—5:6 | Luke 9:28-36 |
| *Saturday* | 87, 90 ❖ 136 | | |
| | Ezek. 3:4-17 | Heb. 5:7-14 | Luke 9:37-50 |

## Week of 5 Easter

| Sunday | 24, 29 ❖ 8, 84 |
| | Lev. 8:1-13, 30-36    Heb. 12:1-14    Luke 4:16-30 |

| Monday | 56, 57, [58] ❖ 64, 65 |
| | Lev. 16:1-19    1 Thess. 4:13-18    Matt. 6:1-6, 16-18 |

| Tuesday | 61, 62 ❖ 68:1-20(21-23)24-36 |
| | Lev. 16:20-34    1 Thess. 5:1-11    Matt. 6:7-15 |

| Wednesday | 72 ❖ 119:73-96 |
| | Lev. 19:1-18    1 Thess. 5:12-28    Matt. 6:19-24 |

| Thursday | [70], 71 ❖ 74 |
| | Lev. 19:26-37    2 Thess. 1:1-12    Matt. 6:25-34 |

| Friday | 106:1-18 ❖ 106:19-48 |
| | Lev. 23:1-22    2 Thess. 2:1-17    Matt. 7:1-12 |

| Saturday | 75, 76 ❖ 23, 27 |
| | Lev. 23:23-44    2 Thess. 3:1-18    Matt. 7:13-21 |

## Week of 6 Easter

| Sunday | 93, 96 ❖ 34 |
| | Lev. 25:1-17    James 1:2-8, 16-18    Luke 12:13-21 |

| Monday | 80 ❖ 77, [79] |
| | Lev. 25:35-55    Col. 1:9-14    Matt. 13:1-16 |

| Tuesday | 78:1-39 ❖ 78:40-72 |
| | Lev. 26:1-20    1 Tim. 2:1-6    Matt. 13:18-23 |

| Wednesday | 119:97-120 ❖ —— |
| | Lev. 26:27-42    Eph. 1:1-10    Matt. 22:41-46 |

| Eve of Ascension | —— ❖ 68:1-20 |
| | 2 Kings 2:1-15    Rev. 5:1-14 |

| Ascension Day | 8, 47 ❖ 24, 96 |
| | Dan. 7:9-14    Heb. 2:5-18    Matt. 28:16-20 |

| Friday | 85, 86 ❖ 91, 92 |
| | 1 Sam. 2:1-10    Eph. 2:1-10    Matt. 7:22-27 |

| Saturday | 87, 90 ❖ 136 |
| | Num. 11:16-17, 24-29    Eph. 2:11-22    Matt. 7:28—8:4 |

**Week of 7 Easter**

| | | | |
|---|---|---|---|
| *Sunday* | 66, 67 ∴ 19, 46 | | |
| | Ezek. 3:16-27 | Eph. 2:1-10 | Matt. 10:24-33, 40-42 |
| *Monday* | 89:1-18 ∴ 89:19-52 | | |
| | Ezek. 4:1-17 | Heb. 6:1-12 | Luke 9:51-62 |
| *Tuesday* | 97, 99, [100] ∴ 94, [95] | | |
| | Ezek. 7:10-15, 23b-27 | Heb. 6:13-20 | Luke 10:1-17 |
| *Wednesday* | 101, 109:1-4(5-19)20-30 ∴ 119:121-144 | | |
| | Ezek. 11:14-25 | Heb. 7:1-17 | Luke 10:17-24 |
| *Thursday* | 105:1-22 ∴ 105:23-45 | | |
| | Ezek. 18:1-4, 19-32 | Heb. 7:18-28 | Luke 10:25-37 |
| *Friday* | 102 ∴ 107:1-32 | | |
| | Ezek. 34:17-31 | Heb. 8:1-13 | Luke 10:38-42 |
| *Saturday* | 107:33-43, 108:1-6(7-13) ∴ —— | | |
| | Ezek. 43:1-12 | Heb. 9:1-14 | Luke 11:14-23 |
| *Eve of Pentecost* | —— ∴ 33 | | |
| | Exod. 19:3-8a, 16-20 | 1 Pet. 2:4-10 | |
| *The Day of Pentecost* | 118 ∴ 145 | | |
| | Isa. 11:1-9 | 1 Cor. 2:1-13 | John 14:21-29 |

> *On the weekdays which follow, the Readings are taken from the numbered Proper (one through six) which corresponds most closely to the date of Pentecost.*

| | | | |
|---|---|---|---|
| *Eve of Trinity Sunday* | —— ∴ 104 | | |
| | Ecclus. 42:15-25 | Eph. 3:14-21 | |
| *Trinity Sunday* | 146, 147 ∴ 111, 112, 113 | | |
| | Ecclus. 43:1-12(27-33) | Eph. 4:1-16 | John 1:1-18 |

> *On the weekdays which follow, the Readings are taken from the numbered Proper (two through seven) which corresponds most closely to the date of Trinity Sunday.*

**Week of 7 Easter**

| | | | |
|---|---|---|---|
| *Sunday* | 66, 67 ❖ | 19, 46 | |
| | Exod. 3:1-12 | Heb. 12:18-29 | Luke 10:17-24 |
| *Monday* | 89:1-18 ❖ | 89:19-52 | |
| | Joshua 1:1-9 | Eph. 3:1-13 | Matt. 8:5-17 |
| *Tuesday* | 97, 99, [100] ❖ | 94, [95] | |
| | 1 Sam. 16:1-13a | Eph. 3:14-21 | Matt. 8:18-27 |
| *Wednesday* | 101, 109:1-4(5-19)20-30 ❖ | 119:121-144 | |
| | Isa. 4:2-6 | Eph. 4:1-16 | Matt. 8:28-34 |
| *Thursday* | 105:1-22 ❖ | 105:23-45 | |
| | Zech. 4:1-14 | Eph. 4:17-32 | Matt. 9:1-8 |
| *Friday* | 102 ❖ | 107:1-32 | |
| | Jer. 31:27-34 | Eph. 5:1-20 | Matt. 9:9-17 |
| *Saturday* | 107:33-43, 108:1-6(7-13) ❖ | —— | |
| | Ezek. 36:22-27 | Eph. 6:10-24 | Matt. 9:18-26 |

| | | | |
|---|---|---|---|
| *Eve of Pentecost* | —— ❖ | 33 | |
| | Exod. 19:3-8a, 16-20 | 1 Pet. 2:4-10 | |
| *The Day of Pentecost* | 118 ❖ | 145 | |
| | Deut. 16:9-12 | Acts 4:18-21, 23-33 | John 4:19-26 |

*On the weekdays which follow, the Readings are taken from the numbered Proper (one through six) which corresponds most closely to the date of Pentecost.*

| | | | |
|---|---|---|---|
| *Eve of Trinity Sunday* | —— ❖ | 104 | |
| | Ecclus. 42:15-25 | Eph. 3:14-21 | |
| *Trinity Sunday* | 146, 147 ❖ | 111, 112, 113 | |
| | Job 38:1-11; 42:1-5 | Rev. 19:4-16 | John 1:29-34 |

*On the weekdays which follow, the Readings are taken from the numbered Proper (two through seven) which corresponds most closely to the date of Trinity Sunday.*

# The Season after Pentecost

*Directions for the use of the Propers which follow are on page 158.*

**Proper 1**  *Week of the Sunday closest to May 11*

Monday  106:1-18  ∴  106:19-48
Isa. 63:7-14  2 Tim. 1:1-14  Luke 11:24-36

Tuesday  [120], 121, 122, 123  ∴  124, 125, 126, [127]
Isa. 63:15—64:9  2 Tim. 1:15—2:13  Luke 11:37-52

Wednesday  119:145-176  ∴  128, 129, 130
Isa. 65:1-12  2 Tim. 2:14-26  Luke 11:53—12:12

Thursday  131, 132, [133]  ∴  134, 135
Isa. 65:17-25  2 Tim. 3:1-17  Luke 12:13-31

Friday  140, 142  ∴  141, 143:1-11(12)
Isa. 66:1-6  2 Tim. 4:1-8  Luke 12:32-48

Saturday  137:1-6(7-9), 144  ∴  104
Isa. 66:7-14  2 Tim. 4:9-22  Luke 12:49-59

**Proper 2**  *Week of the Sunday closest to May 18*

Monday  1, 2, 3  ∴  4, 7
Ruth 1:1-18  1 Tim. 1:1-17  Luke 13:1-9

Tuesday  5, 6  ∴  10, 11
Ruth 1:19—2:13  1 Tim. 1:18—2:8  Luke 13:10-17

Wednesday  119:1-24  ∴  12, 13, 14
Ruth 2:14-23  1 Tim. 3:1-16  Luke 13:18-30

Thursday  18:1-20  ∴  18:21-50
Ruth 3:1-18  1 Tim. 4:1-16  Luke 13:31-35

Friday  16, 17  ∴  22
Ruth 4:1-17  1 Tim. 5:17-22(23-25)  Luke 14:1-11

Saturday  20, 21:1-7(8-14)  ∴  110:1-5(6-7), 116, 117
Deut. 1:1-8  1 Tim. 6:6-21  Luke 14:12-24

## The Season after Pentecost

*Directions for the use of the Propers which follow are on page 158.*

**Proper 1**   *Week of the Sunday closest to May 11*

Monday
106:1-18   ❖   106:19-48
Ezek. 33:1-11      1 John 1:1-10      Matt. 9:27-34

Tuesday
[120], 121, 122, 123   ❖   124, 125, 126, [127]
Ezek. 33:21-33      1 John 2:1-11      Matt. 9:35—10:4

Wednesday
119:145-176   ❖   128, 129, 130
Ezek. 34:1-16      1 John 2:12-17      Matt. 10:5-15

Thursday
131, 132, [133]   ❖   134, 135
Ezek. 37:21b-28      1 John 2:18-29      Matt. 10:16-23

Friday
140, 142   ❖   141, 143:1-11(12)
Ezek. 39:21-29      1 John 3:1-10      Matt. 10:24-33

Saturday
137:1-6(7-9), 144   ❖   104
Ezek. 47:1-12      1 John 3:11-18      Matt. 10:34-42

**Proper 2**   *Week of the Sunday closest to May 18*

Monday
1, 2, 3   ❖   4, 7
Prov. 3:11-20      1 John 3:18—4:6      Matt. 11:1-6

Tuesday
5, 6   ❖   10, 11
Prov. 4:1-27      1 John 4:7-21      Matt. 11:7-15

Wednesday
119:1-24   ❖   12, 13, 14
Prov. 6:1-19      1 John 5:1-12      Matt. 11:16-24

Thursday
18:1-20   ❖   18:21-50
Prov. 7:1-27      1 John 5:13-21      Matt. 11:25-30

Friday
16, 17   ❖   22
Prov. 8:1-21      2 John 1-13      Matt. 12:1-14

Saturday
20, 21:1-7(8-14)   ❖   110:1-5(6-7), 116, 117
Prov. 8:22-36      3 John 1-15      Matt. 12:15-21

**Proper 3**    *Week of the Sunday closest to May 25*

*Sunday*      148, 149, 150    ∴    114, 115
              Deut. 4:1-9      Rev. 7:1-4, 9-17      Matt. 12:33-45

*Monday*      25    ∴    9, 15
              Deut. 4:9-14     2 Cor. 1:1-11      Luke 14:25-35

*Tuesday*     26, 28    ∴    36, 39
              Deut. 4:15-24    2 Cor. 1:12-22     Luke 15:1-10

*Wednesday*   38    ∴    119:25-48
              Deut. 4:25-31    2 Cor. 1:23—2:17     Luke 15:1-2, 11-32

*Thursday*    37:1-18    ∴    37:19-42
              Deut. 4:32-40    2 Cor. 3:1-18      Luke 16:1-9

*Friday*      31    ∴    35
              Deut. 5:1-22     2 Cor. 4:1-12      Luke 16:10-17(18)

*Saturday*    30, 32    ∴    42, 43
              Deut. 5:22-33    2 Cor. 4:13—5:10     Luke 16:19-31

**Proper 4**    *Week of the Sunday closest to June 1*

*Sunday*      63:1-8(9-11), 98    ∴    103
              Deut. 11:1-12    Rev. 10:1-11     Matt. 13:44-58

*Monday*      41, 52    ∴    44
              Deut. 11:13-19   2 Cor. 5:11—6:2     Luke 17:1-10

*Tuesday*     45    ∴    47, 48
              Deut. 12:1-12    2 Cor. 6:3-13 (14—7:1)     Luke 17:11-19

*Wednesday*   119:49-72    ∴    49, [53]
              Deut. 13:1-11    2 Cor. 7:2-16      Luke 17:20-37

*Thursday*    50    ∴    [59, 60] or 8, 84
              Deut. 16:18-20; 17:14-20    2 Cor. 8:1-16     Luke 18:1-8

*Friday*      40, 54    ∴    51
              Deut. 26:1-11    2 Cor. 8:16-24     Luke 18:9-14

*Saturday*    55    ∴    138, 139:1-17(18-23)
              Deut. 29:2-15    2 Cor. 9:1-15      Luke 18:15-30

**Proper 3**    *Week of the Sunday closest to May 25*

*Sunday*        148, 149, 150    ∻    114, 115
                Prov. 9:1-12        Acts 8:14-25      Luke 10:25-28, 38-42

*Monday*        25    ∻    9, 15
                Prov. 10:1-12      1 Tim. 1:1-17       Matt. 12:22-32

*Tuesday*       26, 28    ∻    36, 39
                Prov. 15:16-33     1 Tim. 1:18—2:8       Matt. 12:33-42

*Wednesday*     38    ∻    119:25-48
                Prov. 17:1-20      1 Tim. 3:1-16       Matt. 12:43-50

*Thursday*      37:1-18    ∻    37:19-42
                Prov. 21:30—22:6     1 Tim. 4:1-16       Matt. 13:24-30

*Friday*        31    ∻    35
                Prov. 23:19-21, 29—24:2     1 Tim. 5:17-22(23-25)     Matt. 13:31-35

*Saturday*      30, 32    ∻    42, 43
                Prov. 25:15-28     1 Tim. 6:6-21       Matt. 13:36-43

**Proper 4**    *Week of the Sunday closest to June 1*

*Sunday*        63:1-8(9-11), 98    ∻    103
                Eccles. 1:1-11     Acts 8:26-40       Luke 11:1-13

*Monday*        41, 52    ∻    44
                Eccles. 2:1-15     Gal. 1:1-17       Matt. 13:44-52

*Tuesday*       45    ∻    47, 48
                Eccles. 2:16-26    Gal. 1:18—2:10       Matt. 13:53-58

*Wednesday*     119:49-72    ∻    49, [53]
                Eccles. 3:1-15     Gal. 2:11-21       Matt. 14:1-12

*Thursday*      50    ∻    [59, 60] *or* 8, 84
                Eccles. 3:16—4:3     Gal. 3:1-14       Matt. 14:13-21

*Friday*        40, 54    ∻    51
                Eccles. 5:1-7      Gal. 3:15-22       Matt. 14:22-36

*Saturday*      55    ∻    138, 139:1-17(18-23)
                Eccles. 5:8-20     Gal. 3:23—4:11       Matt. 15:1-20

**Proper 5**   *Week of the Sunday closest to June 8*

| | | | |
|---|---|---|---|
| *Sunday* | 24, 29 ❖ 8, 84 | | |
| | Deut. 29:16-29 | Rev. 12:1-12 | Matt. 15:29-39 |
| *Monday* | 56, 57, [58] ❖ 64, 65 | | |
| | Deut. 30:1-10 | 2 Cor. 10:1-18 | Luke 18:31-43 |
| *Tuesday* | 61, 62 ❖ 68:1-20(21-23)24-36 | | |
| | Deut. 30:11-20 | 2 Cor. 11:1-21a | Luke 19:1-10 |
| *Wednesday* | 72 ❖ 119:73-96 | | |
| | Deut. 31:30—32:14 | 2 Cor. 11:21b-33 | Luke 19:11-27 |
| *Thursday* | [70], 71 ❖ 74 | | |
| | Ecclus. 44:19—45:5 | 2 Cor. 12:1-10 | Luke 19:28-40 |
| *Friday* | 69:1-23(24-30)31-38 ❖ 73 | | |
| | Ecclus. 45:6-16 | 2 Cor. 12:11-21 | Luke 19:41-48 |
| *Saturday* | 75, 76 ❖ 23, 27 | | |
| | Ecclus. 46:1-10 | 2 Cor. 13:1-14 | Luke 20:1-8 |

**Proper 6**   *Week of the Sunday closest to June 15*

| | | | |
|---|---|---|---|
| *Sunday* | 93, 96 ❖ 34 | | |
| | Ecclus. 46:11-20 | Rev. 15:1-8 | Matt. 18:1-14 |
| *Monday* | 80 ❖ 77, [79] | | |
| | 1 Samuel 1:1-20 | Acts 1:1-14 | Luke 20:9-19 |
| *Tuesday* | 78:1-39 ❖ 78:40-72 | | |
| | 1 Samuel 1:21—2:11 | Acts 1:15-26 | Luke 20:19-26 |
| *Wednesday* | 119:97-120 ❖ 81, 82 | | |
| | 1 Samuel 2:12-26 | Acts 2:1-21 | Luke 20:27-40 |
| *Thursday* | [83] *or* 34 ❖ 85, 86 | | |
| | 1 Samuel 2:27-36 | Acts 2:22-36 | Luke 20:41—21:4 |
| *Friday* | 88 ❖ 91, 92 | | |
| | 1 Samuel 3:1-21 | Acts 2:37-47 | Luke 21:5-19 |
| *Saturday* | 87, 90 ❖ 136 | | |
| | 1 Samuel 4:1b-11 | Acts 4:32—5:11 | Luke 21:20-28 |

**Proper 5**    *Week of the Sunday closest to June 8*

| | | | |
|---|---|---|---|
| Sunday | 24, 29 ∻ 8, 84 | | |
| | Eccles. 6:1-12 | Acts 10:9-23 | Luke 12:32-40 |
| Monday | 56, 57, [58] ∻ 64, 65 | | |
| | Eccles. 7:1-14 | Gal. 4:12-20 | Matt. 15:21-28 |
| Tuesday | 61, 62 ∻ 68:1-20(21-23)24-36 | | |
| | Eccles. 8:14—9:10 | Gal. 4:21-31 | Matt. 15:29-39 |
| Wednesday | 72 ∻ 119:73-96 | | |
| | Eccles. 9:11-18 | Gal. 5:1-15 | Matt. 16:1-12 |
| Thursday | [70], 71 ∻ 74 | | |
| | Eccles. 11:1-8 | Gal. 5:16-24 | Matt. 16:13-20 |
| Friday | 69:1-23(24-30)31-38 ∻ 73 | | |
| | Eccles. 11:9—12:14 | Gal. 5:25—6:10 | Matt. 16:21-28 |
| Saturday | 75, 76 ∻ 23, 27 | | |
| | Num. 3:1-13 | Gal. 6:11-18 | Matt. 17:1-13 |

**Proper 6**    *Week of the Sunday closest to June 15*

| | | | |
|---|---|---|---|
| Sunday | 93, 96 ∻ 34 | | |
| | Num. 6:22-27 | Acts 13:1-12 | Luke 12:41-48 |
| Monday | 80 ∻ 77, [79] | | |
| | Num. 9:15-23; 10:29-36 | Rom. 1:1-15 | Matt. 17:14-21 |
| Tuesday | 78:1-39 ∻ 78:40-72 | | |
| | Num. 11:1-23 | Rom. 1:16-25 | Matt. 17:22-27 |
| Wednesday | 119:97-120 ∻ 81, 82 | | |
| | Num. 11:24-33(34-35) | Rom. 1:28—2:11 | Matt. 18:1-9 |
| Thursday | [83] or 34 ∻ 85, 86 | | |
| | Num. 12:1-16 | Rom. 2:12-24 | Matt. 18:10-20 |
| Friday | 88 ∻ 91, 92 | | |
| | Num. 13:1-3, 21-30 | Rom. 2:25—3:8 | Matt. 18:21-35 |
| Saturday | 87, 90 ∻ 136 | | |
| | Num. 13:31—14:25 | Rom. 3:9-20 | Matt. 19:1-12 |

**Proper 7**  *Week of the Sunday closest to June 22*

| | | | |
|---|---|---|---|
| *Sunday* | 66, 67 ❖ 19, 46 | | |
| | 1 Samuel 4:12-22 | James 1:1-18 | Matt. 19:23-30 |
| *Monday* | 89:1-18 ❖ 89:19-52 | | |
| | 1 Samuel 5:1-12 | Acts 5:12-26 | Luke 21:29-36 |
| *Tuesday* | 97, 99, [100] ❖ 94, [95] | | |
| | 1 Samuel 6:1-16 | Acts 5:27-42 | Luke 21:37—22:13 |
| *Wednesday* | 101, 109:1-4(5-19) 20-30 ❖ 119:121-144 | | |
| | 1 Samuel 7:2-17 | Acts 6:1-15 | Luke 22:14-23 |
| *Thursday* | 105:1-22 ❖ 105:23-45 | | |
| | 1 Samuel 8:1-22 | Acts 6:15—7:16 | Luke 22:24-30 |
| *Friday* | 102 ❖ 107:1-32 | | |
| | 1 Samuel 9:1-14 | Acts 7:17-29 | Luke 22:31-38 |
| *Saturday* | 107:33-43, 108:1-6(7-13) ❖ 33 | | |
| | 1 Samuel 9:15—10:1 | Acts 7:30-43 | Luke 22:39-51 |

**Proper 8**  *Week of the Sunday closest to June 29*

| | | | |
|---|---|---|---|
| *Sunday* | 118 ❖ 145 | | |
| | 1 Samuel 10:1-16 | Rom. 4:13-25 | Matt. 21:23-32 |
| *Monday* | 106:1-18 ❖ 106:19-48 | | |
| | 1 Samuel 10:17-27 | Acts 7:44—8:1a | Luke 22:52-62 |
| *Tuesday* | [120], 121, 122, 123 ❖ 124, 125, 126, [127] | | |
| | 1 Samuel 11:1-15 | Acts 8:1-13 | Luke 22:63-71 |
| *Wednesday* | 119:145-176 ❖ 128, 129, 130 | | |
| | 1 Samuel 12:1-6, 16-25 | Acts 8:14-25 | Luke 23:1-12 |
| *Thursday* | 131, 132, [133] ❖ 134, 135 | | |
| | 1 Samuel 13:5-18 | Acts 8:26-40 | Luke 23:13-25 |
| *Friday* | 140, 142 ❖ 141, 143:1-11(12) | | |
| | 1 Samuel 13:19—14:15 | Acts 9:1-9 | Luke 23:26-31 |
| *Saturday* | 137:1-6(7-9), 144 ❖ 104 | | |
| | 1 Samuel 14:16-30 | Acts 9:10-19a | Luke 23:32-43 |

**Proper 7**  *Week of the Sunday closest to June 22*

| | | | |
|---|---|---|---|
| Sunday | 66, 67  ÷  19, 46 | | |
| | Num. 14:26-45 | Acts 15:1-12 | Luke 12:49-56 |
| Monday | 89:1-18  ÷  89:19-52 | | |
| | Num. 16:1-19 | Rom. 3:21-31 | Matt. 19:13-22 |
| Tuesday | 97, 99, [100]  ÷  94, [95] | | |
| | Num. 16:20-35 | Rom. 4:1-12 | Matt. 19:23-30 |
| Wednesday | 101, 109:1-4(5-19)20-30  ÷  119:121-144 | | |
| | Num. 16:36-50 | Rom. 4:13-25 | Matt. 20:1-16 |
| Thursday | 105:1-22  ÷  105:23-45 | | |
| | Num. 17:1-11 | Rom. 5:1-11 | Matt. 20:17-28 |
| Friday | 102  ÷  107:1-32 | | |
| | Num. 20:1-13 | Rom. 5:12-21 | Matt. 20:29-34 |
| Saturday | 107:33-43, 108:1-6(7-13)  ÷  33 | | |
| | Num. 20:14-29 | Rom. 6:1-11 | Matt. 21:1-11 |

**Proper 8**  *Week of the Sunday closest to June 29*

| | | | |
|---|---|---|---|
| Sunday | 118  ÷  145 | | |
| | Num. 21:4-9, 21-35 | Acts 17:(12-21)22-34 | Luke 13:10-17 |
| Monday | 106:1-18  ÷  106:19-48 | | |
| | Num. 22:1-21 | Rom. 6:12-23 | Matt. 21:12-22 |
| Tuesday | [120], 121, 122, 123  ÷  124, 125, 126, [127] | | |
| | Num. 22:21-38 | Rom. 7:1-12 | Matt. 21:23-32 |
| Wednesday | 119:145-176  ÷  128, 129, 130 | | |
| | Num. 22:41—23:12  ÷  Rom. 7:13-25 | | Matt. 21:33-46 |
| Thursday | 131, 132, [133]  ÷  134, 135 | | |
| | Num. 23:11-26 | Rom. 8:1-11 | Matt. 22:1-14 |
| Friday | 140, 142  ÷  141, 143:1-11(12) | | |
| | Num. 24:1-13 | Rom. 8:12-17 | Matt. 22:15-22 |
| Saturday | 137:1-6(7-9), 144  ÷  104 | | |
| | Num. 24:12-25 | Rom. 8:18-25 | Matt. 22:23-40 |

**Proper 9**     *Week of the Sunday closest to July 6*

*Sunday*      146, 147    ∴    111, 112, 113
1 Samuel 14:36-45      Rom. 5:1-11      Matt. 22:1-14

*Monday*      1, 2, 3    ∴    4, 7
1 Samuel 15:1-3, 7-23      Acts 9:19b-31      Luke 23:44-56a

*Tuesday*      5, 6    ∴    10, 11
1 Samuel 15:24-35      Acts 9:32-43      Luke 23:56b—24:11

*Wednesday*      119:1-24    ∴    12, 13, 14
1 Samuel 16:1-13      Acts 10:1-16      Luke 24:13-35

*Thursday*      18:1-20    ∴    18:21-50
1 Samuel 16:14—17:11      Acts 10:17-33      Luke 24:36-53

*Friday*      16, 17    ∴    22
1 Samuel 17:17-30      Acts 10:34-48      Mark 1:1-13

*Saturday*      20, 21:1-7(8-14)    ∴    110:1-5(6-7), 116, 117
1 Samuel 17:31-49      Acts 11:1-18      Mark 1:14-28

**Proper 10**     *Week of the Sunday closest to July 13*

*Sunday*      148, 149, 150    ∴    114, 115
1 Samuel 17:50—18:4      Rom. 10:4-17      Matt. 23:29-39

*Monday*      25    ∴    9, 15
1 Samuel 18:5-16, 27b-30      Acts 11:19-30      Mark 1:29-45

*Tuesday*      26, 28    ∴    36, 39
1 Samuel 19:1-18      Acts 12:1-17      Mark 2:1-12

*Wednesday*      38    ∴    119:25-48
1 Samuel 20:1-23      Acts 12:18-25      Mark 2:13-22

*Thursday*      37:1-18    ∴    37:19-42
1 Samuel 20:24-42      Acts 13:1-12      Mark 2:23—3:6

*Friday*      31    ∴    35
1 Samuel 21:1-15      Acts 13:13-25      Mark 3:7-19a

*Saturday*      30, 32    ∴    42, 43
1 Samuel 22:1-23      Acts 13:26-43      Mark 3:19b-35

**Proper 9**  *Week of the Sunday closest to July 6*

| | | | |
|---|---|---|---|
| *Sunday* | 146, 147 ❖ 111, 112, 113 | | |
| | Num. 27:12-23 | Acts 19:11-20 | Mark 1:14-20 |
| *Monday* | 1, 2, 3 ❖ 4, 7 | | |
| | Num. 32:1-6, 16-27 | Rom. 8:26-30 | Matt. 23:1-12 |
| *Tuesday* | 5, 6 ❖ 10, 11 | | |
| | Num. 35:1-3, 9-15, 30-34 | Rom. 8:31-39 | Matt. 23:13-26 |
| *Wednesday* | 119:1-24 ❖ 12, 13, 14 | | |
| | Deut. 1:1-18 | Rom. 9:1-18 | Matt. 23:27-39 |
| *Thursday* | 18:1-20 ❖ 18:21-50 | | |
| | Deut. 3:18-28 | Rom. 9:19-33 | Matt. 24:1-14 |
| *Friday* | 16, 17 ❖ 22 | | |
| | Deut. 31:7-13, 24—32:4 | Rom. 10:1-13 | Matt. 24:15-31 |
| *Saturday* | 20, 21:1-7(8-14) ❖ 110:1-5(6-7), 116, 117 | | |
| | Deut. 34:1-12 | Rom. 10:14-21 | Matt. 24:32-51 |

**Proper 10**  *Week of the Sunday closest to July 13*

| | | | |
|---|---|---|---|
| *Sunday* | 148, 149, 150 ❖ 114, 115 | | |
| | Joshua 1:1-18 | Acts 21:3-15 | Mark 1:21-27 |
| *Monday* | 25 ❖ 9, 15 | | |
| | Joshua 2:1-14 | Rom. 11:1-12 | Matt. 25:1-13 |
| *Tuesday* | 26, 28 ❖ 36, 39 | | |
| | Joshua 2:15-24 | Rom. 11:13-24 | Matt. 25:14-30 |
| *Wednesday* | 38 ❖ 119:25-48 | | |
| | Joshua 3:1-13 | Rom. 11:25-36 | Matt. 25:31-46 |
| *Thursday* | 37:1-18 ❖ 37:19-42 | | |
| | Joshua 3:14—4:7 | Rom. 12:1-8 | Matt. 26:1-16 |
| *Friday* | 31 ❖ 35 | | |
| | Joshua 4:19—5:1, 10-15 | Rom. 12:9-21 | Matt. 26:17-25 |
| *Saturday* | 30, 32 ❖ 42, 43 | | |
| | Joshua 6:1-14 | Rom. 13:1-7 | Matt. 26:26-35 |

**Proper 11**    *Week of the Sunday closest to July 20*

| | | | |
|---|---|---|---|
| *Sunday* | 63:1-8(9-11), 98    ∻    103 | | |
| | 1 Samuel 23:7-18 | Rom. 11:33—12:2 | Matt. 25:14-30 |
| *Monday* | 41, 52    ∻    44 | | |
| | 1 Samuel 24:1-22 | Acts 13:44-52 | Mark 4:1-20 |
| *Tuesday* | 45    ∻    47, 48 | | |
| | 1 Samuel 25:1-22 | Acts 14:1-18 | Mark 4:21-34 |
| *Wednesday* | 119:49-72    ∻    49, [53] | | |
| | 1 Samuel 25:23-44 | Acts 14:19-28 | Mark 4:35-41 |
| *Thursday* | 50    ∻    [59, 60] or 66, 67 | | |
| | 1 Samuel 28:3-20 | Acts 15:1-11 | Mark 5:1-20 |
| *Friday* | 40, 54    ∻    51 | | |
| | 1 Samuel 31:1-13 | Acts 15:12-21 | Mark 5:21-43 |
| *Saturday* | 55    ∻    138, 139:1-17(18-23) | | |
| | 2 Samuel 1:1-16 | Acts 15:22-35 | Mark 6:1-13 |

**Proper 12**    *Week of the Sunday closest to July 27*

| | | | |
|---|---|---|---|
| *Sunday* | 24, 29    ∻    8, 84 | | |
| | 2 Samuel 1:17-27 | Rom. 12:9-21 | Matt. 25:31-46 |
| *Monday* | 56, 57, [58]    ∻    64, 65 | | |
| | 2 Samuel 2:1-11 | Acts 15:36—16:5 | Mark 6:14-29 |
| *Tuesday* | 61, 62    ∻    68:1-20(21-23)24-36 | | |
| | 2 Samuel 3:6-21 | Acts 16:6-15 | Mark 6:30-46 |
| *Wednesday* | 72    ∻    119:73-96 | | |
| | 2 Samuel 3:22-39 | Acts 16:16-24 | Mark 6:47-56 |
| *Thursday* | [70], 71    ∻    74 | | |
| | 2 Samuel 4:1-12 | Acts 16:25-40 | Mark 7:1-23 |
| *Friday* | 69:1-23(24-30)31-38    ∻    73 | | |
| | 2 Samuel 5:1-12 | Acts 17:1-15 | Mark 7:24-37 |
| *Saturday* | 75, 76    ∻    23, 27 | | |
| | 2 Samuel 5:22—6:11 | Acts 17:16-34 | Mark 8:1-10 |

**Proper 11**    *Week of the Sunday closest to July 20*

|            |                              |     |                             |                |
|------------|------------------------------|-----|-----------------------------|----------------|
| *Sunday*   | 63:1-8(9-11), 98             | ❖   | 103                         |                |
|            | Joshua 6:15-27               |     | Acts 22:30—23:11            | Mark 2:1-12    |
| *Monday*   | 41, 52                       | ❖   | 44                          |                |
|            | Joshua 7:1-13                |     | Rom. 13:8-14                | Matt. 26:36-46 |
| *Tuesday*  | 45                           | ❖   | 47, 48                      |                |
|            | Joshua 8:1-22                |     | Rom. 14:1-12                | Matt. 26:47-56 |
| *Wednesday*| 119:49-72                    | ❖   | 49, [53]                    |                |
|            | Joshua 8:30-35               |     | Rom. 14:13-23               | Matt. 26:57-68 |
| *Thursday* | 50                           | ❖   | [59, 60] or 66, 67          |                |
|            | Joshua 9:3-21                |     | Rom. 15:1-13                | Matt. 26:69-75 |
| *Friday*   | 40, 54                       | ❖   | 51                          |                |
|            | Joshua 9:22—10:15            |     | Rom. 15:14-24               | Matt. 27:1-10  |
| *Saturday* | 55                           | ❖   | 138, 139:1-17(18-23)        |                |
|            | Joshua 23:1-16               |     | Rom. 15:25-33               | Matt. 27:11-23 |

**Proper 12**    *Week of the Sunday closest to July 27*

|            |                              |     |                             |                |
|------------|------------------------------|-----|-----------------------------|----------------|
| *Sunday*   | 24, 29                       | ❖   | 8, 84                       |                |
|            | Joshua 24:1-15               |     | Acts 28:23-31               | Mark 2:23-28   |
| *Monday*   | 56, 57, [58]                 | ❖   | 64, 65                      |                |
|            | Joshua 24:16-33              |     | Rom. 16:1-16                | Matt. 27:24-31 |
| *Tuesday*  | 61, 62                       | ❖   | 68:1-20(21-23)24-36         |                |
|            | Judges 2:1-5, 11-23          |     | Rom. 16:17-27               | Matt. 27:32-44 |
| *Wednesday*| 72                           | ❖   | 119:73-96                   |                |
|            | Judges 3:12-30               |     | Acts 1:1-14                 | Matt. 27:45-54 |
| *Thursday* | [70], 71                     | ❖   | 74                          |                |
|            | Judges 4:4-23                |     | Acts 1:15-26                | Matt. 27:55-66 |
| *Friday*   | 69:1-23(24-30)31-38          | ❖   | 73                          |                |
|            | Judges 5:1-18                |     | Acts 2:1-21                 | Matt. 28:1-10  |
| *Saturday* | 75, 76                       | ❖   | 23, 27                      |                |
|            | Judges 5:19-31               |     | Acts 2:22-36                | Matt. 28:11-20 |

| | Proper 13 | *Week of the Sunday closest to August 3* | |
|---|---|---|---|
| Sunday | 93, 96 | ❖ 34 | |
| | 2 Samuel 6:12-23 | Rom. 14:7-12 | John 1:43-51 |
| Monday | 80 | ❖ 77, [79] | |
| | 2 Samuel 7:1-17 | Acts 18:1-11 | Mark 8:11-21 |
| Tuesday | 78:1-39 | ❖ 78:40-72 | |
| | 2 Samuel 7:18-29 | Acts 18:12-28 | Mark. 8:22-33 |
| Wednesday | 119:97-120 | ❖ 81, 82 | |
| | 2 Samuel 9:1-13 | Acts 19:1-10 | Mark 8:34—9:1 |
| Thursday | [83] or 145 | ❖ 85, 86 | |
| | 2 Samuel 11:1-27 | Acts 19:11-20 | Mark 9:2-13 |
| Friday | 88 | ❖ 91, 92 | |
| | 2 Samuel 12:1-14 | Acts 19:21-41 | Mark 9:14-29 |
| Saturday | 87, 90 | ❖ 136 | |
| | 2 Samuel 12:15-31 | Acts 20:1-16 | Mark 9:30-41 |

| | Proper 14 | *Week of the Sunday closest to August 10* | |
|---|---|---|---|
| Sunday | 66, 67 | ❖ 19, 46 | |
| | 2 Samuel 13:1-22 | Rom. 15:1-13 | John 3:22-36 |
| Monday | 89:1-18 | ❖ 89:19-52 | |
| | 2 Samuel 13:23-39 | Acts 20:17-38 | Mark 9:42-50 |
| Tuesday | 97, 99, [100] | ❖ 94, [95] | |
| | 2 Samuel 14:1-20 | Acts 21:1-14 | Mark 10:1-16 |
| Wednesday | 101, 109:1-4(5-19)20-30 | ❖ 119:121-144 | |
| | 2 Samuel 14:21-33 | Acts 21:15-26 | Mark 10:17-31 |
| Thursday | 105:1-22 | ❖ 105:23-45 | |
| | 2 Samuel 15:1-18 | Acts 21:27-36 | Mark 10:32-45 |
| Friday | 102 | ❖ 107:1-32 | |
| | 2 Samuel 15:19-37 | Acts 21:37—22:16 | Mark 10:46-52 |
| Saturday | 107:33-43, 108:1-6(7-13) | ❖ 33 | |
| | 2 Samuel 16:1-23 | Acts 22:17-29 | Mark 11:1-11 |

**Proper 13**    *Week of the Sunday closest to August 3*

| | | |
|---|---|---|
| *Sunday* | 93, 96   ∻   34 | |
| | Judges 6:1-24    2 Cor. 9:6-15      Mark 3:20-30 | |
| *Monday* | 80   ∻   77, [79] | |
| | Judges 6:25-40    Acts 2:37-47     John 1:1-18 | |
| *Tuesday* | 78:1-39   ∻   78:40-72 | |
| | Judges 7:1-18    Acts 3:1-11     John 1:19-28 | |
| *Wednesday* | 119:97-120   ∻   81, 82 | |
| | Judges 7:19—8:12    Acts 3:12-26     John 1:29-42 | |
| *Thursday* | [83] *or* 145   ∻   85, 86 | |
| | Judges 8:22-35    Acts 4:1-12     John 1:43-51 | |
| *Friday* | 88   ∻   91, 92 | |
| | Judges 9:1-16, 19-21    Acts 4:13-31     John 2:1-12 | |
| *Saturday* | 87, 90   ∻   136 | |
| | Judges 9:22-25, 50-57    Acts 4:32—5:11     John 2:13-25 | |

**Proper 14**    *Week of the Sunday closest to August 10*

| | | |
|---|---|---|
| *Sunday* | 66, 67   ∻   19, 46 | |
| | Judges 11:1-11, 29-40    2 Cor. 11:21b-31      Mark 4:35-41 | |
| *Monday* | 89:1-18   ∻   89:19-52 | |
| | Judges 12:1-7    Acts 5:12-26     John 3:1-21 | |
| *Tuesday* | 97, 99, [100]   ∻   94, [95] | |
| | Judges 13:1-15    Acts 5:27-42     John 3:22-36 | |
| *Wednesday* | 101, 109:1-4(5-19)20-30   ∻   119:121-144 | |
| | Judges 13:15-24    Acts 6:1-15     John 4:1-26 | |
| *Thursday* | 105:1-22   ∻   105:23-45 | |
| | Judges 14:1-19    Acts 6:15—7:16     John 4:27-42 | |
| *Friday* | 102   ∻   107:1-32 | |
| | Judges 14:20—15:20    Acts 7:17-29     John 4:43-54 | |
| *Saturday* | 107:33-43, 108:1-6(7-13)   ∻   33 | |
| | Judges 16:1-14    Acts 7:30-43     John 5:1-18 | |

| | Proper 15 | *Week of the Sunday closest to August 17* |
|---|---|---|

| Sunday | 118 ∻ 145 |
|---|---|
| | 2 Samuel 17:1-23     Gal. 3:6-14     John 5:30-47 |

| Monday | 106:1-18 ∻ 106:19-48 |
|---|---|
| | 2 Samuel 17:24—18:8     Acts 22:30—23:11     Mark 11:12-26 |

| Tuesday | [120], 121, 122, 123 ∻ 124, 125, 126, [127] |
|---|---|
| | 2 Samuel 18:9-18     Acts 23:12-24     Mark 11:27—12:12 |

| Wednesday | 119:145-176 ∻ 128, 129, 130 |
|---|---|
| | 2 Samuel 18:19-33     Acts 23:23-35     Mark 12:13-27 |

| Thursday | 131, 132, [133] ∻ 134, 135 |
|---|---|
| | 2 Samuel 19:1-23     Acts 24:1-23     Mark 12:28-34 |

| Friday | 140, 142 ∻ 141, 143:1-11(12) |
|---|---|
| | 2 Samuel 19:24-43     Acts 24:24—25:12     Mark 12:35-44 |

| Saturday | 137:1-6(7-9), 144 ∻ 104 |
|---|---|
| | 2 Samuel 23:1-7, 13-17     Acts 25:13-27     Mark 13:1-13 |

| | Proper 16 | *Week of the Sunday closest to August 24* |
|---|---|---|

| Sunday | 146, 147 ∻ 111, 112, 113 |
|---|---|
| | 2 Samuel 24:1-2, 10-25     Gal. 3:23—4:7     John 8:12-20 |

| Monday | 1, 2, 3 ∻ 4, 7 |
|---|---|
| | 1 Kings 1:5-31     Acts 26:1-23     Mark 13:14-27 |

| Tuesday | 5, 6 ∻ 10, 11 |
|---|---|
| | 1 Kings 1:38—2:4     Acts 26:24—27:8     Mark 13:28-37 |

| Wednesday | 119:1-24 ∻ 12, 13, 14 |
|---|---|
| | 1 Kings 3:1-15     Acts 27:9-26     Mark 14:1-11 |

| Thursday | 18:1-20 ∻ 18:21-50 |
|---|---|
| | 1 Kings 3:16-28     Acts 27:27-44     Mark 14:12-26 |

| Friday | 16, 17 ∻ 22 |
|---|---|
| | 1 Kings 5:1—6:1, 7     Acts 28:1-16     Mark 14:27-42 |

| Saturday | 20, 21:1-7(8-14) ∻ 110:1-5(6-7), 116, 117 |
|---|---|
| | 1 Kings 7:51—8:21     Acts 28:17-31     Mark 14:43-52 |

**Proper 15**    *Week of the Sunday closest to August 17*

| | | |
|---|---|---|
| *Sunday* | 118   ∴   145 | |
| | Judges 16:15-31    2 Cor. 13:1-11    Mark 5:25-34 | |
| *Monday* | 106:1-18   ∴   106:19-48 | |
| | Judges 17:1-13    Acts 7:44—8:1a    John 5:19-29 | |
| *Tuesday* | [120], 121, 122, 123   ∴   124, 125, 126, [127] | |
| | Judges 18:1-15    Acts 8:1-13    John 5:30-47 | |
| *Wednesday* | 119:145-176   ∴   128, 129, 130 | |
| | Judges 18:16-31    Acts 8:14-25    John 6:1-15 | |
| *Thursday* | 131, 132, [133]   ∴   134, 135 | |
| | Job 1:1-22    Acts 8:26-40    John 6:16-27 | |
| *Friday* | 140, 142   ∴   141, 143:1-11(12) | |
| | Job 2:1-13    Acts 9:1-9    John 6:27-40 | |
| *Saturday* | 137:1-6(7-9), 144   ∴   104 | |
| | Job 3:1-26    Acts 9:10-19a    John 6:41-51 | |

**Proper 16**    *Week of the Sunday closest to August 24*

| | | |
|---|---|---|
| *Sunday* | 146, 147   ∴   111, 112, 113 | |
| | Job 4:1-6, 12-21    Rev. 4:1-11    Mark 6:1-6a | |
| *Monday* | 1, 2, 3   ∴   4, 7 | |
| | Job 4:1; 5:1-11, 17-21, 26-27    Acts 9:19b-31    John 6:52-59 | |
| *Tuesday* | 5, 6   ∴   10, 11 | |
| | Job 6:1-4, 8-15, 21    Acts 9:32-43    John 6:60-71 | |
| *Wednesday* | 119:1-24   ∴   12, 13, 14 | |
| | Job 6:1; 7:1-21    Acts 10:1-16    John 7:1-13 | |
| *Thursday* | 18:1-20   ∴   18:21-50 | |
| | Job 8:1-10, 20-22    Acts 10:17-33    John 7:14-36 | |
| *Friday* | 16, 17   ∴   22 | |
| | Job 9:1-15, 32-35    Acts 10:34-48    John 7:37-52 | |
| *Saturday* | 20, 21:1-7(8-14)   ∴   110:1-5(6-7), 116, 117 | |
| | Job 9:1; 10:1-9, 16-22    Acts 11:1-18    John 8:12-20 | |

**Proper 17**    *Week of the Sunday closest to August 31*

| *Sunday* | 148, 149, 150 | ÷ | 114, 115 | | |
|---|---|---|---|---|---|
| | 1 Kings 8:22-30(31-40) | 1 Tim. 4:7b-16 | | John 8:47-59 |

*Monday*    25    ÷    9, 15
2 Chron. 6:32—7:7    James 2:1-13    Mark 14:53-65

*Tuesday*    26, 28    ÷    36, 39
1 Kings 8:65—9:9    James 2:14-26    Mark 14:66-72

*Wednesday*    38    ÷    119:25-48
1 Kings 9:24—10:13    James 3:1-12    Mark 15:1-11

*Thursday*    37:1-18    ÷    37:19-42
1 Kings 11:1-13    James 3:13—4:12    Mark 15:12-21

*Friday*    31    ÷    35
1 Kings 11:26-43    James 4:13—5:6    Mark 15:22-32

*Saturday*    30, 32    ÷    42, 43
1 Kings 12:1-20    James 5:7-12, 19-20    Mark 15:33-39

**Proper 18**    *Week of the Sunday closest to September 7*

*Sunday*    63:1-8(9-11), 98    ÷    103
1 Kings 12:21-33    Acts 4:18-31    John 10:31-42

*Monday*    41, 52    ÷    44
1 Kings 13:1-10    Phil. 1:1-11    Mark 15:40-47

*Tuesday*    45    ÷    47, 48
1 Kings 16:23-34    Phil. 1:12-30    Mark 16:1-8(9-20)

*Wednesday*    119:49-72    ÷    49, [53]
1 Kings 17:1-24    Phil. 2:1-11    Matt. 2:1-12

*Thursday*    50    ÷    [59, 60] *or* 93, 96
1 Kings 18:1-19    Phil. 2:12-30    Matt. 2:13-23

*Friday*    40, 54    ÷    51
1 Kings 18:20-40    Phil. 3:1-16    Matt. 3:1-12

*Saturday*    55    ÷    138, 139:1-17(18-23)
1 Kings 18:41—19:8    Phil. 3:17—4:7    Matt. 3:13-17

| | | | | |
|---|---|---|---|---|
| | **Proper 17** | *Week of the Sunday closest to August 31* | | |
| *Sunday* | 148, 149, 150 | ❖ 114, 115 | | |
| | Job 11:1-9, 13-20 | Rev. 5:1-14 | Matt. 5:1-12 | |
| *Monday* | 25 | ❖ 9, 15 | | |
| | Job 12:1-6, 13-25 | Acts 11:19-30 | John 8:21-32 | |
| *Tuesday* | 26, 28 | ❖ 36, 39 | | |
| | Job 12:1; 13:3-17, 21-27 | Acts 12:1-17 | John 8:33-47 | |
| *Wednesday* | 38 | ❖ 119:25-48 | | |
| | Job 12:1; 14:1-22 | Acts 12:18-25 | John 8:47-59 | |
| *Thursday* | 37:1-18 | ❖ 37:19-42 | | |
| | Job 16:16-22; 17:1, 13-16 | Acts 13:1-12 | John 9:1-17 | |
| *Friday* | 31 | ❖ 35 | | |
| | Job 19:1-7, 14-27 | Acts 13:13-25 | John 9:18-41 | |
| *Saturday* | 30, 32 | ❖ 42, 43 | | |
| | Job 22:1-4, 21—23:7 | Acts 13:26-43 | John 10:1-18 | |

| | | | | |
|---|---|---|---|---|
| | **Proper 18** | *Week of the Sunday closest to September 7* | | |
| *Sunday* | 63:1-8(9-11), 98 | ❖ 103 | | |
| | Job 25:1-6; 27:1-6 | Rev. 14:1-7, 13 | Matt. 5:13-20 | |
| *Monday* | 41, 52 | ❖ 44 | | |
| | Job 32:1-10, 19—33:1, 19-28 | Acts 13:44-52 | John 10:19-30 | |
| *Tuesday* | 45 | ❖ 47, 48 | | |
| | Job 29:1-20 | Acts 14:1-18 | John 10:31-42 | |
| *Wednesday* | 119:49-72 | ❖ 49, [53] | | |
| | Job 29:1; 30:1-2, 16-31 | Acts 14:19-28 | John 11:1-16 | |
| *Thursday* | 50 | ❖ [59, 60] or 93, 96 | | |
| | Job 29:1; 31:1-23 | Acts 15:1-11 | John 11:17-29 | |
| *Friday* | 40, 54 | ❖ 51 | | |
| | Job 29:1; 31:24-40 | Acts 15:12-21 | John 11:30-44 | |
| *Saturday* | 55 | ❖ 138, 139:1-17(18-23) | | |
| | Job 38:1-17 | Acts 15:22-35 | John 11:45-54 | |

**Proper 19**    *Week of the Sunday closest to September 14*

| *Sunday* | 24, 29 ∻ 8, 84 | | |
| | 1 Kings 19:8-21 | Acts 5:34-42 | John 11:45-57 |

| *Monday* | 56, 57, [58] ∻ 64, 65 | | |
| | 1 Kings 21:1-16 | 1 Cor. 1:1-19 | Matt. 4:1-11 |

| *Tuesday* | 61, 62 ∻ 68:1-20(21-23)24-36 | | |
| | 1 Kings 21:17-29 | 1 Cor. 1:20-31 | Matt. 4:12-17 |

| *Wednesday* | 72 ∻ 119:73-96 | | |
| | 1 Kings 22:1-28 | 1 Cor. 2:1-13 | Matt. 4:18-25 |

| *Thursday* | [70], 71 ∻ 74 | | |
| | 1 Kings 22:29-45 | 1 Cor. 2:14—3:15 | Matt. 5:1-10 |

| *Friday* | 69:1-23(24-30)31-38 ∻ 73 | | |
| | 2 Kings 1:2-17 | 1 Cor. 3:16-23 | Matt. 5:11-16 |

| *Saturday* | 75, 76 ∻ 23, 27 | | |
| | 2 Kings 2:1-18 | 1 Cor. 4:1-7 | Matt. 5:17-20 |

**Proper 20**    *Week of the Sunday closest to September 21*

| *Sunday* | 93, 96 ∻ 34 | | |
| | 2 Kings 4:8-37 | Acts 9:10-31 | Luke 3:7-18 |

| *Monday* | 80 ∻ 77, [79] | | |
| | 2 Kings 5:1-19 | 1 Cor. 4:8-21 | Matt. 5:21-26 |

| *Tuesday* | 78:1-39 ∻ 78:40-72 | | |
| | 2 Kings 5:19-27 | 1 Cor. 5:1-8 | Matt. 5:27-37 |

| *Wednesday* | 119:97-120 ∻ 81, 82 | | |
| | 2 Kings 6:1-23 | 1 Cor. 5:9—6:8 | Matt. 5:38-48 |

| *Thursday* | [83] or 116, 117 ∻ 85, 86 | | |
| | 2 Kings 9:1-16 | 1 Cor. 6:12-20 | Matt. 6:1-6, 16-18 |

| *Friday* | 88 ∻ 91, 92 | | |
| | 2 Kings 9:17-37 | 1 Cor. 7.1-9 | Matt. 6:7-15 |

| *Saturday* | 87, 90 ∻ 136 | | |
| | 2 Kings 11:1-20a | 1 Cor. 7:10-24 | Matt. 6:19-24 |

**Proper 19**    *Week of the Sunday closest to September 14*

| | | | |
|---|---|---|---|
| Sunday | 24, 29 ❖ 8, 84 | | |
| | Job 38:1, 18-41 | Rev. 18:1-8 | Matt. 5:21-26 |
| Monday | 56, 57, [58] ❖ 64, 65 | | |
| | Job 40:1-24 | Acts 15:36—16:5 | John 11:55—12:8 |
| Tuesday | 61, 62 ❖ 68:1-20(21-23)24-36 | | |
| | Job 40:1; 41:1-11 | Acts 16:6-15 | John 12:9-19 |
| Wednesday | 72 ❖ 119:73-96 | | |
| | Job 42:1-17 | Acts 16:16-24 | John 12:20-26 |
| Thursday | [70], 71 ❖ 74 | | |
| | Job 28:1-28 | Acts 16:25-40 | John 12:27-36a |
| Friday | 69:1-23(24-30)31-38 ❖ 73 | | |
| | Esther 1:1-4, 10-19* | Acts 17:1-15 | John 12:36b-43 |
| Saturday | 75, 76 ❖ 23, 27 | | |
| | Esther 2:5-8, 15-23* | Acts 17:16-34 | John 12:44-50 |

**Proper 20**    *Week of the Sunday closest to September 21*

| | | | |
|---|---|---|---|
| Sunday | 93, 96 ❖ 34 | | |
| | Esther 3:1—4:3* | James 1:19-27 | Matt. 6:1-6, 16-18 |
| Monday | 80 ❖ 77, [79] | | |
| | Esther 4:4-17* | Acts 18:1-11 | Luke (1:1-4); 3:1-14 |
| Tuesday | 78:1-39 ❖ 78:40-72 | | |
| | Esther 5:1-14* | Acts 18:12-28 | Luke 3:15-22 |
| Wednesday | 119:97-120 ❖ 81, 82 | | |
| | Esther 6:1-14* | Acts 19:1-10 | Luke 4:1-13 |
| Thursday | [83] or 116, 117 ❖ 85, 86 | | |
| | Esther 7:1-10* | Acts 19:11-20 | Luke 4:14-30 |
| Friday | 88 ❖ 91, 92 | | |
| | Esther 8:1-8, 15-17* | Acts 19:21-41 | Luke 4:31-37 |
| Saturday | 87, 90 ❖ 136 | | |
| | Hosea 1:1—2:1 | Acts 20:1-16 | Luke 4:38-44 |

*1 place of Esther may be read Judith:*

| | | | |
|---|---|---|---|
| 4:1-15 | Su 5:22—6:4, 10-21 | Tu 8:9-17; 9:1, 7-10 | Th 12:1-20 |
| 1 5:1-21 | M 7:1-7, 19-32 | W 10:1-23 | F 13:1-20 |

| | | | | |
|---|---|---|---|---|
| | **Proper 21** | *Week of the Sunday closest to September 28* | | |
| *Sunday* | 66, 67 | ❖ | 19, 46 | |
| | 2 Kings 17:1-18 | Acts 9:36-43 | Luke 5:1-11 | |
| *Monday* | 89:1-18 | ❖ | 89:19-52 | |
| | 2 Kings 17:24-41 | 1 Cor. 7:25-31 | Matt. 6:25-34 | |
| *Tuesday* | 97, 99, [100] | ❖ | 94, [95] | |
| | 2 Chron. 29: 1-3; | 1 Cor. 7:32-40 | Matt. 7:1-12 | |
| | 30:1(2-9) 10-27 | | | |
| *Wednesday* | 101, 109:1-4(5-19)20-30 | ❖ | 119:121-144 | |
| | 2 Kings 18:9-25 | 1 Cor. 8:1-13 | Matt. 7:13-21 | |
| *Thursday* | 105:1-22 | ❖ | 105:23-45 | |
| | 2 Kings 18:28-37 | 1 Cor. 9:1-15 | Matt. 7:22-29 | |
| *Friday* | 102 | ❖ | 107:1-32 | |
| | 2 Kings 19:1-20 | 1 Cor. 9:16-27 | Matt. 8:1-17 | |
| *Saturday* | 107:33-43, 108:1-6(7-13) | ❖ | 33 | |
| | 2 Kings 19:21-36 | 1 Cor. 10:1-13 | Matt. 8:18-27 | |
| | **Proper 22** | *Week of the Sunday closest to October 5* | | |
| *Sunday* | 118 | ❖ | 145 | |
| | 2 Kings 20:1-21 | Acts 12:1-17 | Luke 7:11-17 | |
| *Monday* | 106:1-18 | ❖ | 106:19-48 | |
| | 2 Kings 21:1-18 | 1 Cor. 10:14—11:1 | Matt. 8:28-34 | |
| *Tuesday* | [120], 121, 122, 123 | ❖ | 124, 125, 126, [127] | |
| | 2 Kings 22:1-13 | 1 Cor. 11:2, 17-22 | Matt. 9:1-8 | |
| *Wednesday* | 119:145-176 | ❖ | 128, 129, 130 | |
| | 2 Kings 22:14—23:3 | 1 Cor. 11:23-34 | Matt. 9:9-17 | |
| *Thursday* | 131, 132, [133] | ❖ | 134, 135 | |
| | 2 Kings 23:4-25 | 1 Cor. 12:1-11 | Matt. 9:18-26 | |
| *Friday* | 140, 142 | ❖ | 141, 143:1-11(12) | |
| | 2 Kings 23:36—24:17 | 1 Cor. 12:12-26 | Matt. 9:27-34 | |
| *Saturday* | 137:1-6(7-9), 144 | ❖ | 104 | |
| | Jer. 35:1-19 | 1 Cor. 12:27—13:3 | Matt. 9:35—10:4 | |

**Proper 21**     *Week of the Sunday closest to September 28*

| | | | |
|---|---|---|---|
| *Sunday* | 66, 67   ∻   19, 46 | | |
| | Hosea 2:2-14 | James 3:1-13 | Matt. 13:44-52 |
| *Monday* | 89:1-18   ∻   89:19-52 | | |
| | Hosea 2:14-23 | Acts 20:17-38 | Luke 5:1-11 |
| *Tuesday* | 97, 99, [100]   ∻   94, [95] | | |
| | Hosea 4:1-10 | Acts 21:1-14 | Luke 5:12-26 |
| *Wednesday* | 101, 109:1-4(5-19)20-30   ∻   119:121-144 | | |
| | Hosea 4:11-19 | Acts 21:15-26 | Luke 5:27-39 |
| *Thursday* | 105:1-22   ∻   105:23-45 | | |
| | Hosea 5:8—6:6 | Acts 21:27-36 | Luke 6:1-11 |
| *Friday* | 102   ∻   107:1-32 | | |
| | Hosea 10:1-15 | Acts 21:37—22:16 | Luke 6:12-26 |
| *Saturday* | 107:33-43, 108:1-6(7-13)   ∻   33 | | |
| | Hosea 11:1-9 | Acts 22:17-29 | Luke 6:27-38 |

**Proper 22**     *Week of the Sunday closest to October 5*

| | | | |
|---|---|---|---|
| *Sunday* | 118   ∻   145 | | |
| | Hosea 13:4-14 | 1 Cor. 2:6-16 | Matt. 14:1-12 |
| *Monday* | 106:1-18   ∻   106:19-48 | | |
| | Hosea 14:1-9 | Acts 22:30—23:11 | Luke 6:39-49 |
| *Tuesday* | [120], 121, 122, 123   ∻   124, 125, 126, [127] | | |
| | Micah 1:1-9 | Acts 23:12-24 | Luke 7:1-17 |
| *Wednesday* | 119:145-176   ∻   128, 129, 130 | | |
| | Micah 2:1-13 | Acts 23:23-35 | Luke 7:18-35 |
| *Thursday* | 131, 132, [133]   ∻   134, 135 | | |
| | Micah 3:1-8 | Acts 24:1-23 | Luke 7:36-50 |
| *Friday* | 140, 142   ∻   141, 143:1-11(12) | | |
| | Micah 3:9—4:5 | Acts 24:24—25:12 | Luke 8:1-15 |
| *Saturday* | 137:1-6(7-9), 144   ∻   104 | | |
| | Micah 5:1-4, 10-15 | Acts 25:13-27 | Luke 8:16-25 |

**Proper 23**  *Week of the Sunday closest to October 12*

| | | |
|---|---|---|
| *Sunday* | 146, 147  ❖  111, 112, 113 | |
| | Jer. 36:1-10   Acts 14:8-18 | Luke 7:36-50 |
| *Monday* | 1, 2, 3  ❖  4, 7 | |
| | Jer. 36:11-26   1 Cor. 13:(1-3)4-13 | Matt. 10:5-15 |
| *Tuesday* | 5, 6  ❖  10, 11 | |
| | Jer. 36:27—37:2   1 Cor. 14:1-12 | Matt. 10:16-23 |
| *Wednesday* | 119:1-24  ❖  12, 13, 14 | |
| | Jer. 37:3-21   1 Cor. 14:13-25 | Matt. 10:24-33 |
| *Thursday* | 18:1-20  ❖  18:21-50 | |
| | Jer. 38:1-13   1 Cor. 14:26-33a, 37-40 | Matt. 10:34-42 |
| *Friday* | 16, 17  ❖  22 | |
| | Jer. 38:14-28   1 Cor. 15:1-11 | Matt. 11:1-6 |
| *Saturday* | 20, 21:1-7(8-14)  ❖  110:1-5(6-7), 116, 117 | |
| | 2 Kings 25:8-12, 22-26   1 Cor. 15:12-29 | Matt. 11:7-15 |

**Proper 24**  *Week of the Sunday closest to October 19*

| | | |
|---|---|---|
| *Sunday* | 148, 149, 150  ❖  114, 115 | |
| | Jer. 29:1, 4-14   Acts 16:6-15 | Luke 10:1-12, 17-20 |
| *Monday* | 25  ❖  9, 15 | |
| | Jer. 44:1-14   1 Cor. 15:30-41 | Matt. 11:16-24 |
| *Tuesday* | 26, 28  ❖  36, 39 | |
| | Lam. 1:1-5(6-9)10-12   1 Cor. 15:41-50 | Matt. 11:25-30 |
| *Wednesday* | 38  ❖  119:25-48 | |
| | Lam. 2:8-15   1 Cor. 15:51-58 | Matt. 12:1-14 |
| *Thursday* | 37:1-18  ❖  37:19-42 | |
| | Ezra 1:1-11   1 Cor. 16:1-9 | Matt. 12:15-21 |
| *Friday* | 31  ❖  35 | |
| | Ezra 3:1-13   1 Cor. 16:10-24 | Matt. 12:22-32 |
| *Saturday* | 30, 32  ❖  42, 43 | |
| | Ezra 4:7, 11-24   Philemon 1-25 | Matt. 12:33-42 |

| | | | |
|---|---|---|---|
| | **Proper 23** | *Week of the Sunday closest to October 12* | |
| Sunday | 146, 147 | ÷ 111, 112, 113 | |
| | Micah 6:1-8 | 1 Cor. 4:9-16 | Matt. 15:21-28 |
| Monday | 1, 2, 3 | ÷ 4, 7 | |
| | Micah 7:1-7 | Acts 26:1-23 | Luke 8:26-39 |
| Tuesday | 5, 6 | ÷ 10, 11 | |
| | Jonah 1:1-17a | Acts 26:24—27:8 | Luke 8:40-56 |
| Wednesday | 119:1-24 | ÷ 12, 13, 14 | |
| | Jonah 1:17—2:10 | Acts 27:9-26 | Luke 9:1-17 |
| Thursday | 18:1-20 | ÷ 18:21-50 | |
| | Jonah 3:1—4:11 | Acts 27:27-44 | Luke 9:18-27 |
| Friday | 16, 17 | ÷ 22 | |
| | Ecclus. 1:1-10, 18-27 | Acts 28:1-16 | Luke 9:28-36 |
| Saturday | 20, 21:1-7(8-14) | ÷ 110:1-5(6-7), 116, 117 | |
| | Ecclus. 3:17-31 | Acts 28:17-31 | Luke 9:37-50 |

| | | | |
|---|---|---|---|
| | **Proper 24** | *Week of the Sunday closest to October 19* | |
| Sunday | 148, 149, 150 | ÷ 114, 115 | |
| | Ecclus. 4:1-10 | 1 Cor. 10:1-13 | Matt. 16:13-20 |
| Monday | 25 | ÷ 9, 15 | |
| | Ecclus. 4:20—5:7 | Rev. 7:1-8 | Luke 9:51-62 |
| Tuesday | 26, 28 | ÷ 36, 39 | |
| | Ecclus. 6:5-17 | Rev. 7:9-17 | Luke 10:1-16 |
| Wednesday | 38 | ÷ 119:25-48 | |
| | Ecclus. 7:4-14 | Rev. 8:1-13 | Luke 10:17-24 |
| Thursday | 37:1-18 | ÷ 37:19-42 | |
| | Ecclus. 10:1-18 | Rev. 9:1-12 | Luke 10:25-37 |
| Friday | 31 | ÷ 35 | |
| | Ecclus. 11:2-20 | Rev. 9:13-21 | Luke 10:38-42 |
| Saturday | 30, 32 | ÷ 42, 43 | |
| | Ecclus. 15:9-20 | Rev. 10:1-11 | Luke 11:1-13 |

**Proper 25**     *Week of the Sunday closest to October 26*

| | | | |
|---|---|---|---|
| *Sunday* | 63:1-8(9-11), 98 ❖ 103 | | |
| | Haggai 1:1—2:9 | Acts 18:24—19:7 | Luke 10:25-37 |
| *Monday* | 41, 52 ❖ 44 | | |
| | Zech. 1:7-17 | Rev. 1:4-20 | Matt. 12:43-50 |
| *Tuesday* | 45 ❖ 47, 48 | | |
| | Ezra 5:1-17 | Rev. 4:1-11 | Matt. 13:1-9 |
| *Wednesday* | 119:49-72 ❖ 49, [53] | | |
| | Ezra 6:1-22 | Rev. 5:1-10 | Matt. 13:10-17 |
| *Thursday* | 50 ❖ [59, 60] or 103 | | |
| | Neh. 1:1-11 | Rev. 5:11—6:11 | Matt. 13:18-23 |
| *Friday* | 40, 54 ❖ 51 | | |
| | Neh. 2:1-20 | Rev. 6:12—7:4 | Matt. 13:24-30 |
| *Saturday* | 55 ❖ 138, 139:1-17(18-23) | | |
| | Neh. 4:1-23 | Rev. 7:(4-8)9-17 | Matt. 13:31-35 |

**Proper 26**     *Week of the Sunday closest to November 2*

| | | | |
|---|---|---|---|
| *Sunday* | 24, 29 ❖ 8, 84 | | |
| | Neh. 5:1-19 | Acts 20:7-12 | Luke 12:22-31 |
| *Monday* | 56, 57, [58] ❖ 64, 65 | | |
| | Neh. 6:1-19 | Rev. 10:1-11 | Matt. 13:36-43 |
| *Tuesday* | 61, 62 ❖ 68:1-20(21-23)24-36 | | |
| | Neh. 12:27-31a, 42b-47 | Rev. 11:1-19 | Matt. 13:44-52 |
| *Wednesday* | 72 ❖ 119:73-96 | | |
| | Neh. 13:4-22 | Rev. 12:1-12 | Matt. 13:53-58 |
| *Thursday* | [70], 71 ❖ 74 | | |
| | Ezra 7:(1-10)11-26 | Rev. 14:1-13 | Matt. 14:1-12 |
| *Friday* | 69:1-23(24-30)31-38 ❖ 73 | | |
| | Ezra 7:27-28; 8:21-36 | Rev. 15:1-8 | Matt. 14:13-21 |
| *Saturday* | 75, 76 ❖ 23, 27 | | |
| | Ezra 9:1-15 | Rev. 17:1-14 | Matt. 14:22-36 |

**Proper 25**    *Week of the Sunday closest to October 26*

| | | |
|---|---|---|
| *Sunday* | 63:1-8(9-11), 98   ∻   103 | |
| | Ecclus. 18:19-33    1 Cor. 10:15-24     Matt. 18:15-20 | |

*Monday*    41, 52   ∻   44
Ecclus. 19:4-17    Rev. 11:1-14     Luke 11:14-26

*Tuesday*    45   ∻   47, 48
Ecclus. 24:1-12    Rev. 11:14-19     Luke 11:27-36

*Wednesday*    119:49-72   ∻   49, [53]
Ecclus. 28:14-26    Rev. 12:1-6     Luke 11:37-52

*Thursday*    50   ∻   [59, 60] *or* 103
Ecclus. 31:12-18, 25—32:2    Rev. 12:7-17     Luke 11:53—12:12

*Friday*    40, 54   ∻   51
Ecclus. 34:1-8, 18-22    Rev. 13:1-10     Luke 12:13-31

*Saturday*    55   ∻   138, 139:1-17(18-23)
Ecclus. 35:1-17    Rev. 13:11-18     Luke 12:32-48

**Proper 26**    *Week of the Sunday closest to November 2*

*Sunday*    24, 29   ∻   8, 84
Ecclus. 36:1-17    1 Cor. 12:27—13:13     Matt. 18:21-35

*Monday*    56, 57, [58]   ∻   64, 65
Ecclus. 38:24-34    Rev. 14:1-13     Luke 12:49-59

*Tuesday*    61, 62   ∻   68:1-20(21-23)24-36
Ecclus. 43:1-22    Rev. 14:14—15:8     Luke 13:1-9

*Wednesday*    72   ∻   119:73-96
Ecclus. 43:23-33    Rev. 16:1-11     Luke 13:10-17

*Thursday*    [70], 71   ∻   74
Ecclus. 44:1-15    Rev. 16:12-21     Luke 13:18-30

*Friday*    69:1-23(24-30)31-38   ∻   73
Ecclus. 50:1, 11-24    Rev. 17:1-18     Luke 13:31-35

*Saturday*    75, 76   ∻   23, 27
Ecclus. 51:1-12    Rev. 18:1-14     Luke 14:1-11

**Proper 27**     *Week of the Sunday closest to November 9*

| | | | |
|---|---|---|---|
| *Sunday* | 93, 96 ∴ 34 | | |
| | Ezra 10:1-17 | Acts 24:10-21 | Luke 14:12-24 |
| *Monday* | 80 ∴ 77, [79] | | |
| | Neh. 9:1-15(16-25) | Rev. 18:1-8 | Matt. 15:1-20 |
| *Tuesday* | 78:1-39 ∴ 78:40-72 | | |
| | Neh. 9:26-38 | Rev. 18:9-20 | Matt. 15:21-28 |
| *Wednesday* | 119:97-120 ∴ 81, 82 | | |
| | Neh. 7:73b—8:3, 5-18 | Rev. 18:21-24 | Matt. 15:29-39 |
| *Thursday* | [83] or 23, 27 ∴ 85, 86 | | |
| | 1 Macc. 1:1-28 | Rev. 19:1-10 | Matt. 16:1-12 |
| *Friday* | 88 ∴ 91, 92 | | |
| | 1 Macc. 1:41-63 | Rev. 19:11-16 | Matt. 16:13-20 |
| *Saturday* | 87, 90 ∴ 136 | | |
| | 1 Macc. 2:1-28 | Rev. 20:1-6 | Matt. 16:21-28 |

**Proper 28**     *Week of the Sunday closest to November 16*

| | | | |
|---|---|---|---|
| *Sunday* | 66, 67 ∴ 19, 46 | | |
| | 1 Macc. 2:29-43, 49-50 | Acts 28:14b-23 | Luke 16:1-13 |
| *Monday* | 89:1-18 ∴ 89:19-52 | | |
| | 1 Macc. 3:1-24 | Rev. 20:7-15 | Matt. 17:1-13 |
| *Tuesday* | 97, 99, [100] ∴ 94, [95] | | |
| | 1 Macc. 3:25-41 | Rev. 21:1-8 | Matt. 17:14-21 |
| *Wednesday* | 101, 109:1-4(5-19)20-30 ∴ 119:121-144 | | |
| | 1 Macc. 3:42-60 | Rev. 21:9-21 | Matt. 17:22-27 |
| *Thursday* | 105:1-22 ∴ 105:23-45 | | |
| | 1 Macc. 4:1-25 | Rev. 21:22—22:5 | Matt. 18:1-9 |
| *Friday* | 102 ∴ 107:1-32 | | |
| | 1 Macc. 4:36-59 | Rev. 22:6-13 | Matt. 18:10-20 |
| *Saturday* | 107:33-43, 108:1-6(7-13) ∴ 33 | | |
| | Isa. 65:17-25 | Rev. 22:14-21 | Matt. 18:21-35 |

| | **Proper 27** | *Week of the Sunday closest to November 9* |
|---|---|---|
| Sunday | 93, 96   ∻   34 | |
| | Ecclus. 51:13-22    1 Cor. 14:1-12    Matt. 20:1-16 | |
| Monday | 80   ∻   77, [79] | |
| | Joel 1:1-13    Rev. 18:15-24    Luke 14:12-24 | |
| Tuesday | 78:1-39   ∻   78:40-72 | |
| | Joel 1:15—2:2(3-11)    Rev. 19:1-10    Luke 14:25-35 | |
| Wednesday | 119:97-120   ∻   81, 82 | |
| | Joel 2:12-19    Rev. 19:11-21    Luke 15:1-10 | |
| Thursday | [83] *or* 23, 27   ∻   85, 86 | |
| | Joel 2:21-27    James 1:1-15    Luke 15:1-2, 11-32 | |
| Friday | 88   ∻   91, 92 | |
| | Joel 2:28—3:8    James 1:16-27    Luke 16:1-9 | |
| Saturday | 87, 90   ∻   136 | |
| | Joel 3:9-17    James 2:1-13    Luke 16:10-17(18) | |

| | **Proper 28** | *Week of the Sunday closest to November 16* |
|---|---|---|
| Sunday | 66, 67   ∻   19, 46 | |
| | Hab. 1:1-4(5-11)12—2:1    Phil. 3:13—4:1    Matt. 23:13-24 | |
| Monday | 89:1-18   ∻   89:19-52 | |
| | Hab. 2:1-4, 9-20    James 2:14-26    Luke 16:19-31 | |
| Tuesday | 97, 99, [100]   ∻   94, [95] | |
| | Hab. 3:1-10(11-15)16-18    James 3:1-12    Luke 17:1-10 | |
| Wednesday | 101, 109:1-4(5-19)20-30   ∻   119:121-144 | |
| | Mal. 1:1, 6-14    James 3:13—4:12    Luke 17:11-19 | |
| Thursday | 105:1-22   ∻   105:23-45 | |
| | Mal. 2:1-16    James 4:13—5:6    Luke 17:20-37 | |
| Friday | 102   ∻   107:1-32 | |
| | Mal. 3:1-12    James 5:7-12    Luke 18:1-8 | |
| Saturday | 107:33-43, 108:1-6(7-13)   ∻   33 | |
| | Mal. 3:13—4:6    James 5:13-20    Luke 18:9-14 | |

| | | | |
|---|---|---|---|
| *Sunday* | 118    ❖    145 | | |
| | Isa. 19:19-25 | Rom. 15:5-13 | Luke 19:11-27 |
| *Monday* | 106:1-18    ❖    106:19-48 | | |
| | Joel 3:1-2, 9-17 | 1 Pet. 1:1-12 | Matt. 19:1-12 |
| *Tuesday* | [120], 121, 122, 123    ❖    124, 125, 126, [127] | | |
| | Nahum 1:1-13 | 1 Pet. 1:13-25 | Matt. 19:13-22 |
| *Wednesday* | 119:145-176    ❖    128, 129, 130 | | |
| | Obadiah 15-21 | 1 Pet. 2:1-10 | Matt. 19:23-30 |
| *Thursday* | 131, 132, [133]    ❖    134, 135 | | |
| | Zeph. 3:1-13 | 1 Pet. 2:11-25 | Matt. 20:1-16 |
| *Friday* | 140, 142    ❖    141, 143:1-11(12) | | |
| | Isa. 24:14-23 | 1 Pet. 3:13—4:6 | Matt. 20:17-28 |
| *Saturday* | 137:1-6(7-9), 144    ❖    104 | | |
| | Micah 7:11-20 | 1 Pet. 4:7-19 | Matt. 20:29-34 |

**Proper 29**     *Week of the Sunday closest to November 23*

*Sunday*       118     ÷     145
               Zech. 9:9-16     1 Pet. 3:13-22     Matt. 21:1-13

*Monday*       106:1-18     ÷     106:19-48
               Zech. 10:1-12     Gal. 6:1-10     Luke 18:15-30

*Tuesday*      [120], 121, 122, 123     ÷     124, 125, 126, [127]
               Zech. 11:4-17     1 Cor. 3:10-23     Luke 18:31-43

*Wednesday*    119:145-176     ÷     128, 129, 130
               Zech. 12:1-10     Eph. 1:3-14     Luke 19:1-10

*Thursday*     131, 132, [133]     ÷     134, 135
               Zech. 13:1-9     Eph. 1:15-23     Luke 19:11-27

*Friday*       140, 142     ÷     141, 143:1-11(12)
               Zech. 14:1-11     Rom. 15:7-13     Luke 19:28-40

*Saturday*     137:1-6(7-9), 144     ÷     104
               Zech. 14:12-21     Phil. 2:1-11     Luke 19:41-48

# Holy Days

|  | Morning Prayer | Evening Prayer |
|---|---|---|
| **St. Andrew**<br>*November 30* | 34<br>Isaiah 49:1-6<br>1 Corinthians 4:1-16 | 96,100<br>Isaiah 55:1-5<br>John 1:35-42 |
| **St. Thomas**<br>*December 21* | 23,121<br>Job 42:1-6<br>1 Peter 1:3-9 | 27<br>Isaiah 43:8-13<br>John 14:1-7 |
| **St. Stephen**<br>*December 26* | 28,30<br>2 Chronicles 24:17-22<br>Acts 6:1-7 | 118<br>Wisdom 4:7-15<br>Acts 7:59—8:8 |
| **St. John**<br>*December 27* | 97,98<br>Proverbs 8:22-30<br>John 13:20-35 | 145<br>Isaiah 44:1-8<br>1 John 5:1-12 |
| **Holy Innocents**<br>*December 28* | 2,26<br>Isaiah 49:13-23<br>Matthew 18:1-14 | 19,126<br>Isaiah 54:1-13<br>Mark 10:13-16 |
| **Confession of<br>St. Peter**<br>*January 18* | 66,67<br>Ezekiel 3:4-11<br>Acts 10:34-44 | 118<br>Ezekiel 34:11-16<br>John 21:15-22 |
| **Conversion of<br>St. Paul**<br>*January 25* | 19<br>Isaiah 45:18-25<br>Philippians 3:4b-11 | 119:89-112<br>Ecclesiasticus 39:1-10<br>Acts 9:1-22 |
| **Eve of the<br>Presentation** |  | 113,122<br>1 Samuel 1:20-28a<br>Romans 8:14-21 |

|  | Morning Prayer | Evening Prayer |
|---|---|---|
| The Presentation<br>February 2 | 42,43<br>1 Samuel 2:1-10<br>John 8:31-36 | 48,87<br>Haggai 2:1-9<br>1 John 3:1-8 |
| St. Matthias<br>February 24 | 80<br>1 Samuel 16:1-13<br>1 John 2:18-25 | 33<br>1 Samuel 12:1-5<br>Acts 20:17-35 |
| St. Joseph<br>March 19 | 132<br>Isaiah 63:7-16<br>Matthew 1:18-25 | 34<br>2 Chronicles 6:12-17<br>Ephesians 3:14-21 |
| Eve of the<br>Annunciation | | 8,138<br>Genesis 3:1-15<br>Romans 5:12-21<br>    or Galatians 4:1-7 |
| Annunciation<br>March 25 | 85,87<br>Isaiah 52:7-12<br>Hebrews 2:5-10 | 110:1-5(6-7),132<br>Wisdom 9:1-12<br>John 1:9-14 |
| St. Mark<br>April 25 | 145<br>Ecclesiasticus 2:1-11<br>Acts 12:25—13:3 | 67,96<br>Isaiah 62:6-12<br>2 Timothy 4:1-11 |
| SS. Philip & James<br>May 1 | 119:137-160<br>Job 23:1-12<br>John 1:43-51 | 139<br>Proverbs 4:7-18<br>John 12:20-26 |
| Eve of the<br>Visitation | | 132<br>Isaiah 11:1-10<br>Hebrews 2:11-18 |
| The Visitation<br>May 31 | 72<br>1 Samuel 1:1-20<br>Hebrews 3:1-6 | 146,147<br>Zechariah 2:10-13<br>John 3:25-30 |

|  | Morning Prayer | Evening Prayer |
|---|---|---|
| **St. Barnabas**<br>*June 11* | 15,67<br>Ecclesiasticus 31:3-11<br>Acts 4:32-37 | 19,146<br>Job 29:1-16<br>Acts 9:26-31 |
| **Eve of St. John<br>the Baptist** | | 103<br>Ecclesiasticus 48:1-11<br>Luke 1:5-23 |
| **Nativity of<br>St. John<br>the Baptist**<br>*June 24* | 82,98<br>Malachi 3:1-5<br>John 3:22-30 | 80<br>Malachi 4:1-6<br>Matthew 11:2-19 |
| **SS. Peter & Paul**<br>*June 29* | 66<br>Ezekiel 2:1-7<br>Acts 11:1-18 | 97,138<br>Isaiah 49:1-6<br>Galatians 2:1-9 |
| **Independence Day**<br>*July 4* | 33<br>Ecclesiasticus 10:1-8,12-18<br>James 5:7-10 | 107:1-32<br>Micah 4:1-5<br>Revelation 21:1-7 |
| **St. Mary Magdalene**<br>*July 22* | 116·<br>Zephaniah 3:14-20<br>**Mark 15:47—16:7** | 30,149<br>Exodus 15:19-21<br>2 Corinthians 1:3-7 |
| **St. James**<br>*July 25* | 34<br>Jeremiah 16:14-21<br>Mark 1:14-20 | 33<br>Jeremiah 26:1-15<br>Matthew 10:16-32 |
| **Eve of the<br>Transfiguration** | | 84<br>1 Kings 19:1-12<br>2 Corinthians 3:1-9,18 |
| **The Transfiguration**<br>*August 6* | 2,24<br>Exodus 24:12-18<br>2 Corinthians 4:1-6 | 72<br>Daniel 7:9-10,13-14<br>John 12:27-36a |

|  | Morning Prayer | Evening Prayer |
|---|---|---|
| **St. Mary the Virgin** *August 15* | 113,115<br>1 Samuel 2:1-10<br>John 2:1-12 | 45, *or* 138, 149<br>Jeremiah 31:1-14<br>*or* Zechariah 2:10-13<br>John 19:23-27<br>*or* Acts 1:6-14 |
| **St. Bartholomew** *August 24* | 86<br>Genesis 28:10-17<br>John 1:43-51 | 15,67<br>Isaiah 66:1-2,18-23<br>1 Peter 5:1-11 |
| **Eve of Holy Cross** | | 46,87<br>1 Kings 8:22-30<br>Ephesians 2:11-22 |
| **Holy Cross Day** *September 14* | 66<br>Numbers 21:4-9<br>John 3:11-17 | 118<br>Genesis 3:1-15<br>1 Peter 3:17-22 |
| **St. Matthew** *September 21* | 119:41-64<br>Isaiah 8:11-20<br>Romans 10:1-15 | 19,112<br>Job 28:12-28<br>Matthew 13:44-52 |
| **St. Michael & All Angels** *September 29* | 8,148<br>Job 38:1-7<br>Hebrews 1:1-14 | 34, 150, *or* 104<br>Daniel 12:1-3<br>*or* 2 Kings 6:8-17<br>Mark 13:21-27<br>*or* Revelation 5:1-14 |
| **St. Luke** *October 18* | 103<br>Ezekiel 47:1-12<br>Luke 1:1-4 | 67,96<br>Isaiah 52:7-10<br>Acts 1:1-8 |
| **St. James of Jerusalem** *October 23* | 119:145-168<br>Jeremiah 11:18-23<br>Matthew 10:16-22 | 122,125<br>Isaiah 65:17-25<br>Hebrews 12:12-24 |

|  | Morning Prayer | Evening Prayer |
|---|---|---|
| **SS. Simon & Jude**<br>*October 28* | 66<br>Isaiah 28:9-16<br>Ephesians 4:1-16 | 116,117<br>Isaiah 4:2-6<br>John 14:15-31 |
| **Eve of All Saints** | | 34<br>Wisdom 3:1-9<br>Revelation 19:1,4-10 |
| **All Saints' Day**<br>*November 1* | 111,112<br>2 Esdras 2:42-47<br>Hebrews 11:32—12:2 | 148,150<br>Wisdom 5:1-5,14-16<br>Revelation 21:1-4,22—22:5 |
| **Thanksgiving Day** | 147<br>Deuteronomy 26:1-11<br>John 6:26-35 | 145<br>Joel 2:21-27<br>1 Thessalonians 5:12-24 |

# Special Occasions

|  | Morning Prayer | Evening Prayer |
|---|---|---|
| **Eve of the Dedication** | | 48,122<br>Haggai 2:1-9<br>1 Corinthians 3:9-17 |
| **Anniversary of the Dedication of a Church** | 132<br>1 Kings 8:1-13<br>John 10:22-30 | 29,46<br>1 Kings 8:54-62<br>Hebrews 10:19-25 |
| **Eve of the Patronal Feast** | | 27, *or* 116,117<br>Isaiah 49:1-13<br>*or* Ecclesiasticus 51:6b-12<br>Ephesians 4:1-13<br>*or* Revelation 7:9-17<br>*or* Luke 10:38-42 |

|  | Morning Prayer | Evening Prayer |
|---|---|---|
| The Patronal Feast | 92,93, *or* 148,149<br>Isaiah 52:7-10<br>*or* Job 5:8-21<br>Acts 4:5-13<br>*or* Luke 12:1-12 | 96,97, *or* 111,112<br>Jeremiah 31:10-14<br>*or* Ecclesiasticus 2:7-18<br>Romans 12:1-21<br>*or* Luke 21:10-19 |
| Eves of Apostles and Evangelists | | 48, 122, *or* 84, 150<br>Isaiah 43:10-15*<br>*or* Isaiah 52:7-10**<br>Revelation 21:1-4,9-14<br>*or* Matthew 9:35—10:4 |

Except on the Eve of St. Thomas
Except on the Eves of St. Mark and St. Luke

ISBN: 0-89869-179-6

9 780898 691795